Minako Ishii Kent

Robert Perkinson is a professor of American studies at
the University of Hawai'i at Mānoa. He lives in Honolulu, Hawai'i.

www.texastough.com

## Additional Praise for *Texas Tough*

"Ambitious . . . Perkinson makes a convincing case that mass incarceration is the most pressing civil rights issue today."

—*The Boston Globe*

"Perkinson . . . takes readers on an eminently horrifying journey into America's own heart of darkness." —*Columbia Journalism Review*

"A sweeping and troubling account of the Lone Star State's penal system from the days of slavery to the present . . . In graphic and often disturbing detail, Perkinson chronicles the many ways punishment has been repeatedly used 'to assert supremacy and debase prisoners' since the state began to build its first penitentiary in 1848." —*The New Republic*

"Sprawling, ambitious . . . A rich narrative . . . Perkinson directs the clear light of reason onto the Lone Star State."

—*The Dallas Morning News*

"An intensively researched, disturbing history of American penology . . . A convincing and discouraging argument that the Texas model of a profit-making, retributive prison system has become the national template." —*Kirkus Reviews*

"Sheds light on the evolution of penal systems across the country . . . A fascinating and often deeply troubling book." —*Booklist*

"*Texas Tough* shows that the politics of race has always governed the politics of punishment and explains why our criminal justice system is the frontline of America's human rights struggle in the twenty-first century. This book is a must-read for anyone who wants to build a stronger America and put these decades of over-incarceration (and under-education) of Americans behind us."

—Benjamin Todd Jealous, President, NAACP

# TEXAS TOUGH

## THE RISE OF AMERICA'S
## PRISON EMPIRE

## ROBERT PERKINSON

PICADOR

A METROPOLITAN BOOK
HENRY HOLT AND COMPANY
NEW YORK

www.picadorusa.com

Picador® is a U.S. registered trademark and is used by Henry Holt and Company under license from Pan Books Limited.

For information on Picador Reading Group Guides, please contact Picador.
E-mail: readinggroupguides@picadorusa.com

The research contained in this document was coordinated in part by the Texas Department of Criminal Justice Project #217-R02. The contents of this report reflect the views of the author and do not necessarily reflect the views or policies of the Texas Department of Criminal Justice.

*Designed by Kelly Too*

The Library of Congress has cataloged the Henry Holt edition as follows:

Perkinson, Robert.
    Texas tough : the rise of America's prison empire / Robert Perkinson.—1st ed.
        p. cm.
    Includes bibliographical references.
    ISBN 978-0-8050-8069-8
    1. Prisons—Texas—History. 2. Prison administration—Texas—History. 3. Prisoners—Texas—History. I. Title.
    HV9475.T4P47   2009
    365'.9764—dc22

                                                                        2009014670

Picador ISBN 978-0-312-68047-3

First published in the United States by Henry Holt and Company

10   9   8   7   6   5   4   3

*To my friends behind bars
and their dreams of freedom*

# CONTENTS

# INTRODUCTION

Distrust all in whom the impulse to punish is strong.[1]
——FRIEDRICH NIETZSCHE

Freedom is the United States' founding creed. "Every spot of the old world is overrun with oppression," cried Thomas Paine, but America promises "asylum for the persecuted lovers of civil and religious liberty." Andrew Jackson later told his countrymen, "Providence has showered on this favored land blessings without number, and has chosen you as the guardians of freedom, to preserve it for the benefit of the human race." Subsequent presidents, in wartime and peace, have renewed this sacred charge, proclaiming freedom as America's supranational mission, its unifying cause. In his inaugural address, Barack Obama cast the tradition forward. "Let it be said by our children's children," he said, that "we carried forth that great gift of freedom and delivered it safely to future generations."[2]

America is "the land of the free," yet by one vital measure, it is less free than any other country on earth: it incarcerates a greater portion of its citizenry than any other, about 1 out of every 100 adults. With some 2.4 million persons under lock and key, the United States manages the largest penal system in the world, the grandest ever conceived by a democratic government.[3] Just as slavery once stood as a glaring exception to the American promise, so does imprisonment more than two centuries after the birth of the republic.

The stated purpose of the U.S. prison colossus, which now outstrips the combined populations of Boston, Washington, and San Francisco, is to keep the public safe. Yet the majority of criminologists agree that the phenomenal expansion of incarceration has only modestly reduced crime, accounting for perhaps a quarter of the crime drop since the early 1990s.[4] Even as the experts increasingly doubt the utility of incarceration, however, our society has come to rely on it as never before.

Imprisonment in the United States has achieved unprecedented scale. Combining law enforcement, courts, and prisons, the U.S. criminal justice system consumes $212 billion a year and employs 2.4 million people, more than Wal-Mart and McDonald's combined, the nation's two largest private employers. There are more than eighteen hundred separate prisons in operation across the country—not counting local jails, juvenile lockups, and immigration facilities. Concrete and concertina wire have become integral features of the American landscape.[5]

Even as the use of incarceration has expanded exponentially, however, many Americans still don't know anyone who has been to prison. In middle- and upper-income, predominantly white neighborhoods, imprisonment remains a rare and shocking experience. According to the federal Bureau of Justice Statistics, only one in thirty-nine white men has ever been to prison, with the odds plummeting in the higher income brackets. Along the margins of American society, however—in poverty-blighted rural areas and struggling urban cores—imprisonment has become commonplace. One out of every six African American men has spent time in prison, one out of every thirteen Hispanics. If one takes a snapshot of those currently incarcerated, the socioeconomic indicators read more like a fact sheet from Afghanistan than the first world. Roughly half of today's prison inmates are functionally illiterate. Four out of five criminal defendants qualify as indigent before the courts.[6]

That prisons concentrate poverty and ignorance—in addition to rough and shady personalities—is nothing new. "It is well known that most of these individuals on whom the criminal law inflicts punishments, have been unfortunate before they became guilty," noted Gustave de Beaumont and Alexis de Tocqueville in 1833. More surprising is that measurable inequities in criminal justice have widened over the past few decades, particularly across the barrier that has always divided Americans most intractably—race. A half century ago—before the Montgomery bus boycott, before the War on Poverty, and before the conservative reaction against the social experimentation of the 1960s—blacks in the United States were imprisoned at roughly four times the rate of whites. Today, a generation after the triumphs of the civil rights movement, African Americans are incarcerated at seven times the rate of whites, nearly double the disparity measured before desegregation.[7] Although two generations have passed since *Brown v. Board of Education*, African American men today go to prison at twice the rate they go to college.[8]

Almost no one would have predicted this dire state of affairs two generations ago. Had you proposed in 1965 to increase the U.S. prison expenditures forty-four-fold and widen racial disparities over the next forty years, even the hardest hard-liners would have scoffed. Toward the end of the civil rights era, in fact, most observers believed the country was moving in the opposite direction. Although "there is a long way to go," concluded the authors of a 1969 primer on constitutional rights, we are making "orderly progress" toward the day when "the poor man, the Negro, the suspect, and the defender of unpopular causes truly enjoy . . . equal protection under the law." Conventional prisons, many experts believed, were destined for obsolescence. As counseling and community corrections came to the fore, one of the country's leading criminologists, Norval Morris, advised criminal justice professions to begin "conscious planning" for "the decline and likely fall of the 'prison' as that term is now understood."[9]

We now know that Professor Morris and his colleagues were not just off the mark but off the map. But why? What, indeed, propelled a resurgence of the prison precisely at the moment of its predicted demise? When I began researching criminal justice in the 1990s, analysts of all stripes were struggling with this question. Law-and-order conservatives had the simplest answers. They argued that cultural hedonism and welfare dependency had gradually eroded family values, unleashing a frightful crime wave in the 1960s that was finally brought under control only by decisive government action.[10] Critics of the crackdown, by contrast, have floated a raft of alternate explanations, from media-driven panic to a reduced tolerance for risk in late modernity.[11] Some have suggested that America's titanic penal system has reached the point of self-sustaining profitability, that a "prison-industrial complex" has emerged as a rival to the military-industrial complex first assailed by President Dwight Eisenhower in 1961.[12]

In graduate school at Yale, I learned a great deal from this growing body of literature, but I felt increasingly dissatisfied. Many commentators agreed that race plays an important role in the justice system, but relatively few were making the entwined histories of criminal punishment and racial subjugation a central category of analysis.[13] Fewer still carried the story further back than Barry Goldwater's 1964 presidential campaign, one of the first to make law and order a polarizing partisan issue.[14] Almost no one was grappling seriously with the role of the American South, despite the region's leadership in extending sentences, building new prisons, and resurrecting bygone punishments like chain gangs and striped uniforms.[15]

I suspected that vital insights lay buried in these neglected areas, so I focused my research on the history of crime and punishment in the South. I traveled to Florida, where venerable traditions like electrocution survived into the twenty-first century, then to Georgia, where I studied the rise and fall of the chain gang. In my mother's home state of Mississippi, I surveyed the legendary penal farm at Parchman. Next door in Louisiana, I conducted a round of interviews with inmates and guards at the Angola prison plantation. The more I read and the more people I spoke with, however, the more I realized that in the realm of punishment, all roads lead to Texas.

Why Texas? Because just as New York dominates finance and California the film industry, Texas reigns supreme in the punishment business. With 173,000 inmates and more than twice as many paid employees as Google, Texas's prison system is the largest in the United States, outstripping even California, which has an overall population 50 percent larger.[16] By almost any measure, Texas stands out. The state's per capita imprisonment rate (691 per 100,000 residents) is second only to Louisiana's and three times higher than the Islamic Republic of Iran's.[17] Although Texas ranks fiftieth among states in the amount of money it spends on indigent criminal defense, it ranks first in prison growth, first in for-profit imprisonment, first in supermax lockdown, first in total number of adults under criminal justice supervision, and a resounding first in executions. When it comes to imprisonment, writes Joseph Hallinan, a reporter for the *Wall Street Journal,* Texas is "where it's happening."[18]

Texas casts a long shadow in politics as well. Since World War II, the state has produced more presidents than any other, with the differences among them providing a measure of the nation's postwar journey. Born in Denison, Eisenhower embodied the cold war consensus. In the 1960s, Lyndon Johnson championed civil rights, social democracy, and preventative criminal justice, even as he shipwrecked his Great Society in Vietnam. LBJ's two Texas successors then led the country rightward: George H. W. Bush, who rode the specter of Willie Horton, a black rapist, to the White House and widened the war on drugs when he got there, and his son George W. Bush, who funneled more money into law enforcement and incarceration, both foreign and domestic, than any chief executive before him. By the early twenty-first century, Texas had come to exercise unrivaled leadership in the political arena, especially in criminal justice, where it pioneered all manner of punitive policies, from lethal injection to prison privatization. With political conservatism ascendant, Texas became the country's new bellwether state.[19]

To a large extent, Texas stands for the country as a whole. With its mythic history, multiracial population, and immense territory that stretches from the South to the Southwest, Texas, brings together vital threads of the American fabric. Its hardscrabble folk and wide-open spaces symbolize individual liberty. Yet this freedom has always traveled with a wrathful twin. Torn by social divisions and wracked by violent conflict—dramatized by the lynching of James Bird in 1998—Texas also signifies for many Americans intolerance, bigotry, and sanguinary justice.[20] In the film *Thelma and Louise,* when Susan Sarandon makes Geena Davis drive hundreds of miles out of the way to avoid the state, audiences are meant to understand that Texas is no place for free spirits on the run.

For both its punitive singularity and historical contradictions, Texas is a fruitful site to study criminal justice over the *longue durée,* from one period of pervasive unfreedom to another, from the age of slavery to the age of incarceration. From its inception, the state has served as a contentious testing ground for rival styles of penal discipline: corporal punishment versus Christian charity, exploitative field labor versus penitentiary-based confinement, retribution versus rehabilitation. A populist strain in Texas politics has inspired the most spirited penal reform movements in the South, from agrarian radicals who railed against forced labor to civil rights activists who assailed prison segregation. But an even stronger tradition of racial demagoguery and penny-pinching conservatism, combined with the intransigence of the state's prison guard establishment, has managed to beat back each of these challenges. In Texas justice, as in politics, left has always battled right, but the right has usually won. "It was one of the clichés . . . that we were dragging our state, kicking and screaming, into the twentieth century," recalls Ronnie Dugger, the founding editor of the *Texas Observer*, the state's liberal standard-bearer. "But lo and behold . . . Texas has dragged the United States back into the nineteenth."[21]

The product of this mismatched historical struggle is a uniquely harsh model of criminal justice, a regime of state-sanctioned punishment based on roughshod legal proceedings, racial subjugation, corporal punishment, and unpaid field labor that has persevered into the twenty-first century. Texas's plantations are "probably the best example of slavery remaining in the country," reported a national corrections expert in 1978.[22] Twenty years later, when I first started visiting southern prisons, I reached the same conclusion. Nowhere else in turn-of-the-millennium America could one witness gangs of African American men filling cotton sacks under the watchful eyes of armed whites on horseback. Plantation prisons at Sugar Land, Huntsville, and elsewhere have preserved the lifeways of slavery in carceral amber.

For most of American history, Texas's implacable punishment traditions relegated it to the margins of penology, a field devoted—in theory if not practice—to the "moral regeneration . . . of criminals." In the late civil rights era, however, as rehabilitation programs faltered, crime rates soared, and a new breed of politician discovered that crime, especially black crime, galvanized white voters, Texas's Lone Star became a guiding light. State after state began copying elements of what prison experts called the "Texas control model," while politicians looked with new fondness on the state's severe sentencing statutes. Once dismissed as a "disgrace of Christian civilization," Texas became the template for a more fearful and vengeful society.[23]

Nationwide, tough new crime policies—far more than rising crime rates—fueled prodigious prison growth. Between 1965 and 2000, the U.S. prison population swelled by 600 percent, in Texas by 1,200 percent. Over the same period, sentences grew longer and early releases rarer. Prison education and counseling programs withered, while supermaxes and death rows sprang up from coast to coast. "We were building prisons so fast we couldn't find wardens to run them," a criminal justice professor at Sam Houston State University told me. "It was like mobilizing for world war."[24] By the end of the century, the United States had embarked on an unprecedented experiment in mass incarceration, one that not only is changing the country's approach to crime and punishment but is reworking the fabric of American society.

This book tells the story of this punitive revolution with Texas at its epicenter. Examining the interplay of race, crime, and politics over almost two centuries, it explains how a proud frontier republic forged in democratic revolt came to build one of the roughest penal regimes in American history. It shows how a uniquely calloused, racialized, and profit-driven style of punishment that developed on slavery's frontier became a model for the nation in the post–civil rights era.

By analyzing the life and times of America's harshest, largest penal system, *Texas Tough* proposes fresh ways of thinking about imprisonment and society. First it argues that the history of punishment in the United States is more of a southern story than has generally been realized. By the numbers, the South has long been the dominant player in criminal justice.[25] Open almost any book on the subject, however, and the states of the former Confederacy are scarcely mentioned—except perhaps to underline their particularity.[26] In the historiography of imprisonment scholars have hued to a remarkably unitary story line, with the first northeastern penitentiaries—foreboding public institutions that were meant to restore wayward citizens to virtue through penitent solitude—imperfectly evolving into modern correctional bureaucracies, complete with psychological counseling and parole. Although historians vary widely in their approaches and viewpoints, they have overwhelmingly replicated narratives of halting progress in pursuit of the rehabilitative ideal.[27]

Until recently, this progressive, regionally restrictive version of history possessed a certain logic. Because prison managers, whatever their shortcomings, steadfastly claimed reformation as their goal, and because most rehabilitative innovations originated in the North, it seemed only logical for historians to thus focus their efforts.[28] Alas, now that the country's prison establishment has largely abandoned the cause of "moral regeneration," it is easier for us to detect southern roots. Over the last few decades, prisons have not become more humane, less racially divisive, less authoritarian, or even more supple in their exercise of power, as the dominant literature had led us to expect. Rather, American lockups have become harsher, more regimented, more racially divisive, and markedly less rehabilitative. They no longer aim to repair and redeem but to warehouse, avenge, and permanently differentiate convicted criminals from law-abiding citizens. Today's prisons operate less in the tradition of what the founding penologist Enoch Wines called "the reformatory idea" than in a retributive mode that has long been practiced and promoted in the South.[29]

To piece together a more complete genealogy of the modern prison, therefore, this book redirects the spotlight from the North, the birthplace of rehabilitative penology, to the South, the fountainhead of subjugationist discipline. In addition to tracing the evolution of social welfare and the gospel of redemption, it examines the development of labor control, racial division, and corporal debasement. The result is that two ancestral lines come into view: one reformatory, one retributive; one integrative, one exclusionary; one conceived in northern churches and the other on southern work farms. Over the course of American history, these rival traditions have contended for influence, and in the closing decades of the twentieth century, exclusion and revenge gained the upper hand. In short, this book posits that most historians have studied only half of the family tree. American prisons trace their lineage not only back to Pennsylvania penitentiaries but to Texas slave plantations.

This historical reorientation leads to the book's second principal argument: the evolution of the prison has had surprisingly little to do with crime and a great deal to do with America's troubled history of racial conflict and social stratification. Decoupling punishment from crime defies conventional wisdom; most citizens like to think that prisons keep predatory villains off the streets—and to a certain extent they do. Yet an examination of the historical record, as well as present-day statistics, reveals that state punishment has consistently served purposes beyond crime control. Indeed, the strong arm of the law has been regularly deployed not only to protect public safety but to preserve privilege, bolster political fortunes, and, most of all, to discipline those on the social margins, especially African Americans.

The notion that the law serves the powerful is probably as old as the law itself. A character in Plato's *Republic* asserted, "In every case the laws are made by the ruling party in its own interest."[30] Yet in the United States, where the highest court bears the inscription "Equal Justice Under

Law," this basic critique is too often ignored. We tend to see justice even where dominion resides.

The history of Texas brings dominion into sharp focus. Although the Lone Star Republic was founded on the lofty principles of liberty and independence, its 1836 constitution codified an inviolable hierarchy of rights, barring all "Africans, the descendants of Africans, and Indians" from citizenship.[31] After abolition, these rigid distinctions blurred, but a two-tiered legal framework persisted. During the protracted epoch of formal segregation, a variety of de jure and de facto controls ensured that African Americans, and to a significant extent Mexican Americans, rarely interacted with the legal system in any capacity other than defendant. For more than two-thirds of Texas history, the state's criminal justice institutions—from the Texas Rangers to the jury box to the prison farms—remained legally and rigidly stratified, guided more by the exigencies of white supremacy than equal justice.

Despite the historic victories of the civil rights movement—culminating with the election of the country's first black president in 2008—the criminal justice patterns set during slavery and segregation have not faded away. Rather, according to key statistical indicators on crime, arrest, conviction, imprisonment, and release, the United States is dispensing less equitable justice today than it was a generation ago. Even as segregationist barriers to equal opportunity and achievement have crumbled in the free world, we have fortified the racial divide in criminal justice. Denied a place in society at large, Jim Crow has moved behind bars.

This paradoxical resurgence of racial injustice in the face of racial progress has a troubling precedent. In the aftermath of the Civil War and Reconstruction, white conservatives regrouped and regained power in the states of the former Confederacy, largely through violence and intimidation. The result was a restoration of white supremacy, combined with peonage, convict leasing, and lynching, practices that delayed emancipation's promise of equal rights for a century. In the wake of the modern civil rights movement—or the "Second Reconstruction"—an analogous historic turn took place.[32] In reaction against court-ordered integration, rising crime rates, and urban unrest, white conservatives, most effectively in the South, again regrouped and returned to power, often by campaigning on the issue of law and order. The consequence, this book contends, was an explosion of racialized imprisonment and a retreat, once again, from liberty.

• • •

In addition to reexamining the dynamic between imprisonment and society, *Texas Tough* examines the prison itself as a peculiar species of "total institution."[33] The book wrestles with a question that has long puzzled students of the law and public policy: Why has the penitentiary failed so spectacularly to fulfill its founding objectives—to rehabilitate criminals and prevent crime—yet persisted so tenaciously as our primary sanction for serious lawbreaking? Why have prisons resisted every effort at reformation? After analyzing the trials and tribulations of northern and especially southern penal institutions over two centuries, I believe the answer resides both inside and outside the prison walls.

In the first place, it is important to recognize that the rehabilitative prison has failed, in part, because it was never allowed to succeed. Although politicians and prison managers have perennially trumpeted the cause of inmate reclamation, in practice they have more often prioritized cost savings, control, and political maneuvering. This is particularly true in Texas. Just as promising reform efforts got under way in the 1880s, 1910s, and 1920s, state leaders slashed the prison budget and demanded that convicts return to the fields, thus squashing innovations in their infancy. Prison reforms have repeatedly disappointed, therefore—in Texas and to a substantial extent in other states—largely because they haven't really been tried. Or even desired. Prisons have persisted, conversely, despite their putative failures, not because they effectively protect the public but because they excel in other, generally unspoken ways, at dispensing patronage, fortifying social hierarchies, enacting public vengeance, and symbolizing government resolve.

But this is only part of the story. By stepping into the shrouded world of the prison itself, this book will also show how convicts and staff—not just policy makers—have sabotaged efforts at reform and reconciliation, and how, in the process, they have extended penitential discipline. On the prisoner side, even cooperative inmates determined to "do their own time" find the daily deprivations and petty humiliations of prison life maddening. Many turn to scamming, smuggling, and, when opportunities arise, escaping and rioting—acts of defiance that occasionally jump-start reforms but more often infuriate prison managers and lawmakers.[34] In this way, insurgent convict politics has often undermined inmate welfare, inspiring not innovation but backlash. More subtly, by chafing against the depersonalizing regimentation of prison life—as almost all convicts do—prisoners inadvertently validate the justice of their convictions. By breaking rules and lashing out, they mark themselves as criminal and further legitimate their incarceration.

The flip side of this corrosive dynamic plays out among the guards. Over time, even the most high-minded officers find the daily grind of prison work hardening. Charged to manage inmates who always seem to be working an angle, they come to think of their wards as untrustworthy and treacherous, as generic criminals rather than troubled individuals. Vested with near absolute authority over inmates, they come to wield power with confidence and sometimes capriciousness. Just as the kept inexorably slip into the role of contumacious convict, the keepers morph into hardhearted screws. "It gets to where there's not a whole lot of difference between the prisoners and the bosses," recalls an officer at the Ramsey farm, one of the state's oldest plantations. "See, [the Texas Department of Corrections] alters your mind. You live TDC. You work TDC. Your friends work at TDC. You were a bad ass and that's all there was to it."[35]

Over time, this guard-prisoner dialectic has played a critical role in destabilizing prison environments and discrediting reform efforts. By herding together edgy individuals against their will and enacting daily rituals of subjection, even the best prisons tend to foster more conflict than cooperation. They tend to drive forward cycles of reform, rebellion, and retrenchment that have characterized prison history in Texas and beyond. Conceived to enforce the law and impose order on chaos, prisons, by their very nature, tend to become bastions of lawlessness. This is not to say that no prisons are better than others. Yet by assessing the wreckage of prison reform movements, we may conclude that the prison itself is more irredeemable than most of its inmates.

These arguments—and the tortured history of Texas justice upon which they are based—invite grim conclusions: that prisons not only waste money but waste lives; that they're doing more to resegregate American society than to safeguard America's streets; that they helped transform the Great Society into a mean society.

While the purpose of *Texas Tough* is to diagnose, however, it is not to dishearten. Rather, my hope is that readers will turn from this story of mistreatment and mismanagement toward glimmerings of hope that are starting to appear. Although the Texas tough ethos still reigns supreme in the Lone Star State and most of the South, there are signs that twilight may be upon it. In recent years, New York, California, Michigan, and other states have started scaling back mandatory drug sentences. After Illinois's Republican governor George Ryan evacuated the state's death row in 2003, a national conversation broke out about innocence in capital cases. [36] Even devout law-and-order politicians in Louisiana, the only state that incarcerates at a higher rate than Texas, are starting to wonder how many more prison cells they can afford.

If these scattered developments coalesce—if, indeed, the United States is about to embark on another era of humanitarian criminal justice experimentation—then this book holds important lessons. By demonstrating how unequal societies produce inequitable justice, how penal regimes rise and fall, and how reforms can generate unwanted consequences, it highlights both the pitfalls and overlooked alternatives of the past. By recounting our troubled journey to the present, it can help point the way toward a more egalitarian, tolerant, and genuinely democratic future. Imprisonment, I believe, has grown pervasive enough to threaten American democracy, but only democracy can throw open the prison's door.

This book is the product of a decade of archival and ethnographic research, but the road to its writing stretches back further. In important ways, the questions I grapple with here originated on my grandparents' front porch in Bay St. Louis, Mississippi. When I was growing up, my siblings and I spent every summer at their salt-washed home on the Gulf Coast, sailing and baiting crab traps by day and soaking up family stories over gumbo by night.

Lu and Henry Fly, my mother's folks, were products of rural Mississippi, the descendants of slaveholders. They came of age at the height of Jim Crow, a social structure that took hold, ironically, in what we call the Progressive Era, and many of the remembrances they shared around the supper table involved the racial poison that shaped their earliest sensibilities. Speaking regretfully in a quavering drawl, Lu voiced suspicions that her father, a Methodist minister, had helped "run the blacks out of Amite County." Her brother-in-law, she added, later joined the Citizens' Council, a racist businessmen's association that helped turn Mississippi into a veritable police state in the fifties and sixties. [37]

Henry, born in tiny Durant, recounted hiding behind a service station one day when a rough bunch of men came around recruiting for a "nigger hunt." His mother's idea of racial benevolence, he noted, was letting itinerant blacks sleep in the barn—but she drew the line at providing them with blankets. "No," she explained to Henry when he went to fetch one. "They don't feel the cold like we do."

Lu and Henry might well have grown up with the same narrow outlook but for a stint as young adults in Washington, D.C., where my great-grandfather had gone to work for a New Dealer on Capitol Hill. After World War II, the couple moved back to Mississippi to raise a family, but already they had become outsiders. When "Massive Resistance" to *Brown v. Board of Education* broke out, they took to arguing with friends. Henry went a step further, writing caustic letters to the editor in favor of integration. This provoked the Citizens' Council to blackball his fledgling law practice, and when ostracism and death threats followed, Lu and Henry decided to sell their home in Jackson and relocate to the comparably tolerant coast.[38]

Modest protests cost my grandparents friends and fortune, but they related these events without bitterness. Acts of conscience might be punished in the short term, they believed, but history and righteousness were on their side. Too often, their home state of Mississippi had surrendered to hate, but they had faith that, in the end, reason would triumph over ignorance and tolerance over bigotry.

I believed that, too, but as a child of the conservative counterrevolution (I was born in 1969, five months after the inauguration of Richard Nixon), I had to grapple in my adulthood with the fact that reality veered from my grandparents' sanguine expectations. Jim Crow was laid to rest, to be sure, but racial inequality persisted. Bilbo-style demagoguery no longer got candidates elected to office, but harangues against crime, welfare queens, and affirmative action did. Schools were no longer segregated by law, but they remained mostly separate and unequal. In Lu and Henry's prime, African Americans had braved bullets to "March Against Fear," but by the 1980s, young African American men were more likely to be marched off to prison. Although my grandparents always believed the South would become more like the rest of America, in welfare, tax, military, and especially criminal justice policy, America became more like the South.[39]

This book grew out of my many conversations with Lu and Henry over the years and the disillusionment I felt as the country turned away from their ideals. In their long lifetimes, my grandparents have witnessed their world change shape around them. During the presidential primaries, Lu pushed her walker into Hancock County's Democratic Party headquarters to make phone calls for Barack Obama, a candidate whose trajectory, until recently, defied imagination. Yet in other ways, the South of my grandparents' generation lives on. Mississippi's electorate remains fiercely polarized by race. Economic disparities have widened.[40] In the aftermath of Hurricane Katrina, the world was reminded how much two Souths—one black, one white—still occupy common soil.

My grandparents lost everything in the storm. The normally placid waters of the Gulf rose up with biblical fury and swept their home from the earth, leaving behind only a debris-strewn concrete slab and the bronzed shoes of their firstborn. In a sense, this book is an elegy for the inundated dreams that Lu and Henry cultivated in their Mississippi home—as well as an effort to reanimate them. By journeying deep into the past, the following pages chart how the United States has arrived at an astonishingly punitive juncture in its history, so that we might, in turn, depart from it. By examining southern injustices that have persisted far beyond the demise of segregation, this book yearns for the alternate America my grandparents thought they were bringing into existence half a century ago. May they see it emerge now.

# 1

## PRISON HEARTLAND

There's tough. And then there's Texas tough.
—LIEUTENANT GOVERNOR DAVID DEWHURST[1]

If we are to fully understand the causes and consequences of America's prison buildup, a good place to start is Huntsville, Texas. Although dozens of prison-dominated communities now dot the American landscape from Florence, Arizona, to Wallens Ridge, Virginia, Huntsville stands above the rest: it is the most locked-down town in the most imprisoned state in the most incarcerated country in the world. Although America's sprawling penal system—a collection of some five thousand jails and prisons—is highly decentralized, Huntsville, perhaps even more than Washington, D.C., could stake a claim to serve as its capital city.[2] For 160 years, it has coordinated criminal punishment for the Lone Star State and, in the last half century, it has stood at the forefront of a carceral revolution that has remade American society and governance.

A sleepy town surrounded by pine forests and tumbledown farms, seventy miles north of Houston, Huntsville was selected in 1848 to build the state's first residential institution, a penitentiary. Ever since, the community's fortunes have depended on crime and punishment; as Texas's prison system grew, so did Huntsville. "We sort of live within the shadows of the Walls," comments Jim Willett, a longtime resident and former warden. "Three times a day we hear the 'all clear' count whistle. When you think about it, it marks the passing of our days."[3]

Today more than ever, imprisonment is Huntsville's lifeblood. Nearly half of the town's residents (16,227 out of 35,567) live behind bars.[4] Some 7,500 adults earn their paychecks keeping them there. Each morning, thousands of guards in ill-fitting gray uniforms pile into pickups and head to one of the area's nine prisons, while starched administrators drive to one of the offices that make up the Texas Department of Criminal Justice (TDCJ) headquarters. From their cubicles they oversee the largest state prison system in the United States, one that incarcerates more people than Germany, France, Belgium, and the Netherlands combined. "We've grown so massive, we need a building like the Pentagon," remarks a harried TDCJ bureaucrat.[5]

At first glance, Huntsville looks like any other small southern city. National chains dominate the two main highway exits. In prosperous neighborhoods, spacious homes line up behind tidy lawns along wide, oak-draped streets. In the poorest sections, weather-worn shotgun houses share overgrown lots with rusting trailers. Although Huntsville has a college, Sam Houston State University, churches outnumber bars and hunting shops outnumber cinemas. A well-kept central plaza features a new limestone courthouse, but downtown merchants have fallen on hard times since Wal-Mart began siphoning retail dollars to the outskirts. Rogers Shoes and Ernst Jewelers cling to life behind historic storefronts, but out of habit more than profit. Like most American towns, Huntsville is increasingly governed by the economics of scale and the geography of parking.

What sets Huntsville apart is the prison business. Just a stone's throw from the plaza rises the town's most impressive and imposing building, a redbrick fortress known as "the Walls," Texas's flagship penitentiary. Surrounded by twenty-five-foot fortifications, the Walls complex contains a small town in its own right: office space, kitchen facilities, an auto shop, massive classrooms, a chapel, an infirmary, and, most famously, the busiest death house in the nation. Some of the structures are twenty-first-century vintage, others nineteenth. "Working at the Walls you have a special sense of history," says Willett, a heavyset man with droopy eyes who served as warden for four years. Some longtime residents claim the prison has been locking up and executing offenders for so long that restless ghosts prowl its dusty tiers.[6]

The Walls is Huntsville's icon, but rival landmarks abound. Just beyond the prison's eastern gun towers, a crumbling stadium recalls the "world's toughest rodeo," a gladiatorial convict spectacular that served as one of Texas's main tourist attractions between 1931 and 1986. A short walk down the road sits an army surplus store, formerly named Bustin' Loose Mens Wear, the first stop for roughly sixty prisoners released daily. Adjacent to the Greyhound station, where ex-cons exchange vouchers for one-way tickets to Dallas or Houston, the shop buys used prison-issue boots for two dollars and proudly announces, "TDCJ discharge checks cashed for free." Many prisoners spend their entire hundred-dollar allotment before they leave town.[7]

For less fortunate inmates who discharge in boxes rather than boots, the final destination is often a somber expanse of lawn spread out behind the prison's back gate: Captain Joe Byrd cemetery. With spare concrete crosses forming gridlines across the grass—like Arlington without honor—the graveyard has marked the end of the line for forsaken convicts for as long as anyone can remember. In the older sections, weather-beaten headstones are sinking into the soil, many of them identified only by a prison number, some marked with an X for execution. Along the edge, a row of fresh pits covered by metal plates await another round of indigents. Resting against one headstone, a faded display of blue plastic flowers spells out "DAD."

Drive in any direction from the Walls and you will soon run into other TDCJ institutions: a massive transfer facility that brings new inmates into the system, a gleaming supermax that points toward Texas's high-tech future, or an expansive prison plantation that gestures toward its past.

Residents of Huntsville are conscious, even proud, of their carceral history. In 1989, a local foundation opened the Texas Prison Museum, a squat redbrick building made to resemble a prison, wedged between two real prisons on the north side of town.[8] Jim Willett, whose gentle manner and nasal voice are hard to reconcile with his long career as a prison boss, serves as the museum's director. Four days a week, he works the front desk, hawking bobble-head convict dolls and sharing escape and riot stories with old-timers who drop by in the afternoons. Although the museum's exhibit room features humdrum poster-board displays, visitors take their time. They inspect faded striped uniforms, rusted cane knives, and a thick leather strap known as "the Bat." Clyde Barrow of Bonnie and Clyde fame, the state's most notorious escapee, and Fred Carrasco, its most infamous hostage taker, have special prominence, as does the prison system's epic civil rights lawsuit, *Ruiz v. Estelle*, in which Texas prisons were declared "cruel and unusual" by a federal judge in 1980. What holds visitors' gaze the longest, however, is a sturdy, stiff-backed, generously proportioned oak armchair with leather restraints and a metal headband. This is Ol' Sparky, the electric chair that Texas officials used to cut short 361 lives between 1924 and 1964.[9]

Most visitors don't realize that Willett himself supervised eighty-nine executions—albeit standing over a gurney rather than a chair—more than any other living American. If they stop to ask, he'll say that executions were the most unpleasant part of his job. "I guess I haven't fully made up my mind about the death penalty," he said shortly after we first met, an honest but jarring remark from a man who used to carry it out, sometimes two or three times a week. Having read through grisly case briefings prepared by the Texas attorney general, Willett is convinced that most of the men and women he watched die earned their fate. But as a Christian he isn't sure it was his due to seal it.[10]

Huntsville packs its prison memories, both flattering and unsettling, into this modest, sun-baked museum, but history spills beyond it. To outsiders, the town can feel like a living theme park, a grittier version of Colonial Williamsburg. The stately homes of top TDCJ administrators are tended by convict "yard boys" with outdoor trusty status. When I stopped to ask for directions on one of my first visits, a portly African American trusty quickly reminded me that deferential etiquette still rules. Dropping his rake, he hoofed it over to my rental, hat in hand, and asked, "Yes sir, what can I do for you, boss?" Up the road at the gate to the Wynne Farm, Texas's oldest prison plantation, I watched as a squad of convict cotton pickers, almost all of them black, marched out to the fields, their duck-cloth coveralls gleaming in the early morning light. Trailing them on horseback was a white overseer, a .30-.30 jostling in his scabbard.

Southern justice brings southern history close to the surface in Huntsville, lending credence to William Faulkner's oft-cited observation that in the South "the past is never dead, it's not even past." Yet Huntsville isn't trapped looking backward. Thanks overwhelmingly to the state's breakneck prison buildup, it's racing into the future. Since 1980, the local prison workforce has more than quadrupled, and although prison jobs are low paying, new strip malls, highway interchanges, and prefab apartment complexes all attest to economic growth. As *Forbes* magazine observes, Huntsville is a "town where crime pays."[11]

To a remarkable extent, this unassuming backwoods community has become a crossroads. Thousands of law enforcement and corrections officers cycle through each year for training, while inmates, by the tens of thousands, arrive for intake or discharge. From TDCJ's headquarters across the street from the Walls, administrators manage a $3 billion annual corrections budget. They supervise a free-world workforce of almost 50,000 and manage 114 separate prison facilities. Most significantly, they govern the lives of 705,000 prisoners, parolees, and probationers, equivalent to the population of Texas's booming capital, Austin.[13]

With the command of a punishment colossus that stretches from the Gulf Coast to the Llano Estacado, from the Rio Grande to the Panhandle, Huntsville, Texas, is unique but also emblematic. It represents the ultimate product of the country's punitive political turn, the distillation of a punishment paroxysm that has redefined American exceptionalism for a new century. Standing, as it does, at the center of a prison empire, Huntsville is not just a prison town but a new sort of American everytown.

## "WHAT THE HELL HAPPENED?"

Most Texans believe that their state's vast network of prisons was constructed to corral dangerous men, to keep "baby killers and murderers" off the streets. A bloody kernel of truth underlies this sentiment: Texas is dangerous terrain. Although the state's crime rate has fallen sharply since the late 1980s, it remains about 24 percent higher than the national average. When it comes to murder—regarded by criminologists as the most accurate index of lawbreaking since almost all homicides come to the attention of police—Texas fares somewhat better, exceeding the national average by just 5 percent.[14] But in Texas's largest cities killing proceeds with dismaying regularity. In Dallas, which in 2003 had a higher overall crime rate than any other major U.S. city, the murder rate hovers 167 percent above the national average. Despite the fact that Dallas annually ships off nearly nine thousand young felons to prison, its roughest neighborhoods remain so dangerous that building contractors have written them off as no-go zones.[15]

Violence is hardly new to Texas. The state's most exalted heroes are martyrs or killers, usually both. Although the state missed out on the worst carnage of the Civil War, it has been playing catch-up ever since. Over the decades, Texas has witnessed terror attacks by the Ku

Klux Klan, unrelenting campaigns against Indians, raids and counter-raids along the Mexican border, as well as individual violence aplenty. During Reconstruction, one of the state's first serial killers, John Wesley Hardin, reportedly murdered more than twenty men—most of them "impudent negroes" and "Yankee soldiers"—before being locked up at the Walls.[16]

Over the course of the twentieth century, tempers mellowed but only just. While many Americans remember the 1960s for the Summer of Love, Texans have to look back to John F. Kennedy's assassination in Dallas and Charles Whitman's shooting spree from the University of Texas clock tower, a stunt that inaugurated the all-American tradition of the mass school shooting. "Homicide in Texas has a long history," begins a chronology of notable murders published in the *Texas Monthly*'s special crime issue. "From the slaying of La Salle [1687] to the killing of Madalyn Murray O'Hair [2001], we present a crash course in murder and mayhem."[17]

Even now, Texas atrocities make the news with dismaying regularity. Since 1990, the state has played host to a mass killing at Luby's cafeteria in Killeen, an eyeball-excising serial killer in Dallas, the Branch Davidian conflagration in Waco, a shooting rampage at the Wedgwood Baptist Church in Fort Worth, and a multiple-baby drowning in Houston. There was the case of John King, an ex-con and white-supremacist gang member, who together with two pals abducted an African American man, chained him to the back of a truck, and dragged him to death along country roads, as well as that of Karla Faye Tucker, who murdered a young couple with a pickax and then became an international cause célèbre after her jailhouse conversion to Christianity.

Most of the prisoners I have come to know are serving long sentences for relatively pedestrian offenses—drug dealing, assault, and robbery—but a few of their rap sheets make even a jaded researcher wince. One fellow, a self-described "white country boy" who used to work as a hospital clerk, reportedly gunned down his father, stepmother, and stepbrother and then scattered hair and cigarette butts he had collected from black patients so as to pin the crime on "drug-crazed niggers." One faithful correspondent told me he had killed a 7-Eleven clerk back in 1971. It wasn't until I rifled through old newspaper clippings that I learned he had also shot two schoolchildren and an eighty-six-year-old woman. Every state has its heinous criminals, of course, but Texas and other southern states—for a variety of historical, social, and cultural reasons—have more. Due largely to the legacy of slavery and its violent "code of honor," argues Roger Lane, who has written extensively on the history of murder, "the South has led all sectors in violent behavior." For "generations after the Civil War," the states of the former Confederacy, sometimes joined by the frontier West, have served as "well-springs of American homicide."[18]

When lawmakers extend sentences or cut services for prisoners, they tend to think of criminals like these, "monsters" like Kenneth McDuff, who abducted and murdered women across Central Texas. Such "predators" have a pronounced effect on public policy, but they do not accurately stand for the whole. They stalk our imaginations, but they don't fill many of our prison beds. Of the roughly 170,000 persons confined in Texas prisons, some 90,000 of them are classified as nonviolent. This means that a majority have been sentenced for crimes that neither threatened nor caused bodily harm. Counterintuitively, it is this group, mainly due to the war on drugs, that has contributed most to the growth of imprisonment in Texas and the United States generally. Between 1985 and 1995, the incarceration rate for violent offenders increased by 86 percent, but the nonviolent rate soared by 478 percent.[19]

Ironically, imprisonment rates have grown most aggressively among the groups we traditionally think of as most redeemable: low-level substance abusers, women, and juveniles. In Texas, 81 percent of all new inmates are sent to prison for nonviolent property or drug offenses. Almost half "catch the chain," as inmates call the trip to TDCJ, not after being convicted of a new crime but for parole and probation violations—infractions that might include failing a marijuana test or changing jobs without notifying a parole officer. "I saw probably more than ten thousand inmates a year who didn't belong in prison," says Richard Watkins, one of Texas's first African American wardens and former chief of a large intake unit in Huntsville. "Most of the inmates we got had been convicted of drug crimes or property crimes to support a habit. What they needed was treatment."[20]

Texas still locks up plenty of violent offenders, of course, some 85,000 of them. But even this cohort is, in aggregate, less scary than most people think. This is partly because a wide variety of crimes qualify as violent. The classification includes homicide and pedophilia, to be sure, but also fighting, resisting arrest, or even illegal possession of pepper spray. In 2000, a Chicano teenager in Amarillo was convicted of assault and sentenced to five years in prison for throwing a nasty elbow during a high-school basketball game.[21]

Moreover, because violent offenders tend to receive long sentences, many of them are serving time well beyond their predatory prime. Criminologists agree that the danger posed by violent felons peaks in the early twenties, declines through middle age, and bottoms out in the early fifties. In the age of "life without parole," however, prison sentences stretch into the autumn years and beyond.[22]

One prisoner I know, a dimple-faced lifer named Michael Jewell, admits that he was a thug when he went to prison for capital murder in 1970. But that was almost forty years ago. As a twenty-two-year-old, Jewell shot and killed a store clerk. As an aging baby boomer, he works full time as an inventory clerk and spends long hours in his cell reading psychology books and practicing Buddhist meditation. He is a different man than the one jurors sent to prison, yet his fate is defined by a single act.[23]

Even in 1970, Jewell was a more complicated individual than the killer sketched by prosecutors. Like so many defendants, his life had been shaped by violence. "One of my first memories is fear," he explained in a letter. When he was a child, he came home from a movie with his sister one day to find his mother curled up on the floor against the bed. Towering over her was Michael's father, gripping her hair with one fist and pummeling her with the other. Another time, he proudly presented his father with a baby sparrow his brother had found. Drinking heavily with neighbors in the backyard, his father took the bird in his hand, stroked its back, and then popped its head off with his thumb. "I watched my own innocence thrashing around and dying in the bloody dirt," Jewell said, looking back.[24]

By the time Michael was eight, he was turning the violence he experienced at home outward. He remembered capturing and killing birds himself, whacking them with sticks. Soon he graduated to fistfights with other kids, then knife fights, then glue sniffing, and finally armed robbery. He went to reform school at the age of twelve and landed his first prison sentence at eighteen. It was after an escape that he murdered the store clerk. Jewell and his partner thought the man was going for a gun, but after they searched his slumped body, they realized he was just reaching down to hand them the night deposit bag.[25]

Only in middle age did Jewell have the wherewithal to ask, "What the hell happened?" He does not know what turned him "from an innocent little kid into a young man who fired a bullet into another man's chest," he says. "But it wasn't that I was naturally cold-blooded."[26]

Prisoners in Texas, as elsewhere, share a great many characteristics. They tend to be poor, poorly educated, and nonwhite. They also tend to be young, heedless, and angry, at least for the first few years behind bars. When you sit down and talk to inmates about their lives, however, you soon discover that what unites them most of all is pain: pain that they have soaked up as victims and pain they have inflicted on others.

Kimberly Leavelle, a recent parolee, epitomizes this dynamic, though like most women offenders she has suffered more than harmed. A middle-aged white woman with a corny sense of humor, Leavelle is tirelessly optimistic but with little cause. After serving twelve years for armed robbery, she made parole on her fourth attempt in May 2005. With serious health problems, few marketable skills, and $100 in discharge money, she moved into a trailer with her mother outside of Dallas. Kim's mother, Linda, has served time for bad checks, drugs, and prostitution. Her three siblings have also been to jail—one brother is still in prison—and one of her teenage daughters, whose childhood she largely missed just as her mother missed much of hers, was recently arrested for marijuana possession. When I talked to her shortly after her release, Leavelle was exuberant. "Freedom is strangely beautiful, new, and exciting," she said. Still, the challenges of making ends meet and paying for medical treatment, all while tethered to an ankle bracelet, was already wearing her down. In December, she lost her first job.[27]

Like many ex-prisoners, Leavelle has made a lifetime's worth of bad decisions. She fell in love in junior high school and had a baby at the age of fifteen. Like her mother, she got into alcohol and drugs. In 1985, she shot a man she said was trying to rape her; she left him for dead and got ten years for attempted murder. Not long after she got out of prison in 1988, she and a girlfriend concocted "a Thelma and Louise scheme" to get Christmas presents for their kids. Borrowing a BB gun, Leavelle and her partner robbed eight stores in the Dallas–Fort Worth area before getting nabbed. Although the weapon was relatively harmless, the charge was armed robbery. After accepting a guilty plea suggested by her court-appointed attorney, Leavelle received eight concurrent sentences, six of them for fifty years.[28]

Leavelle's recklessness led her straight to prison, but given the arc of her life, I found it hard to imagine how she could have ended up anyplace else. Born in Dallas in 1964, Kimberly Leavelle spent her early years with her mother and her mother's second husband, a middleclass developer named Lloyd Wallace. "During the first four years of my life I had everything a child needs," she writes. "I had my own room, nice clothes, a bike, and we even had a maid. . . . She was sweet as pie." Kimberly is fond of such sentimental sayings, almost as if to make up for a life devoid of tender sentiment. We were "the family that looks perfect from the outside," she says, "but on the inside my mom was a caged human being."

As the oldest of two half brothers and a sister, Kim remembers the terrors of her suburban household more clearly than her siblings. Wallace was a tyrant. He became obsessive about Kim's mother, Linda, checking and rechecking her odometer and timing her excursions. Returning late from the grocery store one evening, Kim remembers that when her mother, who was pregnant with her baby brother at the time, made it up to the porch, Wallace "stepped out and punched her so hard in the face that the groceries went flying, along with my mom." Then he locked them out. Another time, Leavelle was awakened by banging and scratching in a closet. When she mustered up the courage to investigate, she found her mother "naked, tied up with cords from the blinds. Wallace had stomped her eye glasses, cut up all her clothes, cut her hair off."

Linda finally escaped with her children, but the family fled from abuse into the abyss. Kim remembers teetering over her brother's crib to give him a nighttime bottle because her mother was working late. She remembers standing in relief lines and going hungry. "We all looked dirty," she recalls, "not clean and pretty like we used to. . . . My mom always had to work. She cried a lot."

One day, a distant aunt, "a fat, sweaty, huffy-voiced" woman named Gladys, with a no-account husband, L.D., in tow, came to fetch Kimberly. She didn't know it at the time, but she was being sent away because her mother was going to prison.

Gladys and L.D. restored Kimberly to middle-class comforts but at a price. She was too young to go to school when she first moved in, so L.D. used to watch her when Aunt Gladys went to work. He also used to take off her clothes "for washing" with unusual regularity. Kimberly was only four years old when it started, but she has searing flashes of memory. Sweating and reeking of beer, L.D. would have Kim sit on his lap and put her hand on his penis. Before long, as she disengaged from the world, Kimberly says that she forged a desperate friendship with a "glorious set of green and gold curtains with tassels" that hung by the living room window. L.D. perched her on a stool in front of the curtains. "[I was wearing] nothing but my black patent leather shoes and my white frilly socks," she recalls. He peeked out through the drapes from time to time and told "his special little girl not to cry." Then he raped her. "I clung to those curtains with little white knuckles," she says. "I looked down and I remember that blood was on my legs and my pretty white socks and on my shoes." Afterward, she explains, she became just like those curtains: "ugly, no feeling, just hanging there."

When Gladys found out that her husband could no better control himself with Kim than he had with their own daughter—who has been in and out of mental hospitals as an adult—she passed the little girl on to different relatives. But deliverance from L.D. didn't spare Kim further trauma. Two other men molested her as she bounced from house to house. After her mother's release from prison, the family got a second chance. Linda signed up for welfare and started nursing school, but when the bills exceeded her income she started selling prescription diet pills on the side. Chaos ensued. Over the next few years, they moved frequently. At a party one night, Kimberly witnessed her uncle, Ray Jr., shoot himself in the head. Not long after, when she was twelve, she found out that her biological father had been murdered.

Kimberly became a survivor. She got into some trouble at school but made drill team and the cheerleading squad (other parents chipped in to buy the uniforms). She stayed with friends as often as she could. As soon as she was able, she moved in with her first boyfriend, Rudy, and his mother, a cleaning lady with eight kids of her own. The winter before she turned sixteen, Kim got pregnant.[29]

"I was just overwhelmed when they brought my baby to me," she recalls of her daughter's birth. "I took everything off to make sure all of the parts were there." She and Rudy both worked minimum-wage jobs and made a go of it as parents. They stayed with Linda, then with Rudy's mom. They struggled to make ends meet, but fraud, petty theft, and drugs beckoned—familiar ways to boost lousy paychecks. Just after her toddler turned three, Kimberly first went to jail for forgery and credit card abuse. Little Kambry was one year younger than Kimberly had been when her own mother had been sent away.[30]

Leavelle's journey into lawbreaking followed the same road map as tens of thousands of other women living behind bars. "There is nothing spectacular about my life," Kim wrote from the Mountain View Unit in Gatesville about a year before her release. "My life reads like any other female in an institution. Physical and sexual abuse, trauma, poverty. We're products of our environments."[31]

Indeed, repeated studies have shown that women prisoners, even more than men, follow grueling pathways into prison. Although women are six times less likely than men to have committed crimes of violence, they are more than three times as likely to have been violently victimized as children or adults (57 percent of women versus 16 percent of men).[32] According to researchers at Sam Houston State, roughly a fourth of female offenders in Texas report that as children they lacked basic shelter, food, or physical safety. As in Leavelle's case, most female prisoners in Texas have wrestled with poverty and substance abuse. Forty percent report that they were unemployed at the time of their arrest. Less than a third graduated from high school. More than half of women inmates report abusing alcohol or other drugs, with 40 percent admitting that they were using at the time they committed their offense.[33]

For most of American history, relatively few women went to prison, but that has changed dramatically with the escalation of the drug war, which now accounts for nearly 40 percent of all female felony convictions. Largely because the likelihood of imprisonment has increased most intensively among defendants convicted of low-level, nonviolent crimes (seriously violent felons were already being locked up under the old rules), the incarceration rate for women has increased more dramatically than for men. Since 1980, the male imprisonment rate has tripled, but it has sextupled for women. The result is that the United States now incarcerates more than 215,000 women, which is greater than the total U.S. prison population, including both women and men, before 1961. Nearly two-thirds of these women are African American or Latina, and more than 90 percent have been convicted of nonviolent offenses.[34]

Although women tend to draw shorter sentences than men, the rapid expansion of female imprisonment has had a disproportionate impact on the "free world," as prisoners sometimes call the rest of society. More than 11,000 female offenders go to prison in Texas each year, with a somewhat smaller number being discharged. As with Kim Leavelle and her mother, most of these women, 64 percent, leave at least one dependent child behind. At least 10 percent of these children end up in foster care. "Children of incarcerated women are among society's most vulnerable citizens and are the hidden victims of the expansion of the penal state," asserts Beth E. Richie, a criminal justice and women's studies professor at the University of Illinois. "Their lives are destabilized . . . [and] their material needs go unmet."[35]

Discharged women prisoners who manage to reunite with their children face another set of challenges. According to a 2004 study released by the Urban Institute, the vast majority of released prisoners in Texas make their way back to the roughest neighborhoods, places like Cadillac Heights in Dallas or the Third Ward in Houston, where poverty, joblessness, broken households, drugs, and crime make up the fabric of everyday life. Most of these women are single mothers who had difficulty maintaining stable households, and their prospects only diminish after being released from prison; they have accrued stigma but not skills. Because so many released offenders have been convicted of drug crimes, they are subject to federal bans on public housing, welfare, and other social services. During the 1990s alone, 4,700 women in Texas were barred for life from food stamps, thus making it even more difficult for ex-offenders to provide basic sustenance for their families. Unsurprisingly, many of their children, like Kim and her siblings, start getting into trouble themselves once they hit adolescence. "Incarceration today is a family matter," says a researcher at the National Council on Crime and Delinquency. "There is an entire kinship system that is now moving through jail, prison, probation, and parole."[36]

Corrosive cycles of poverty, child neglect, crime, and imprisonment are defining features of correctional populations. Women prisoners tend to be more open about the connections between their childhoods and criminal careers, but most male inmates have tragic stories as well. Justice Department surveys show that one in three men in jail grew up with a parent or guardian who abused alcohol or other drugs; one in two has a family member who has been incarcerated; and one in nine had been taken away from his parents by the state.[37] As with women prisoners, male inmates tend to come from as much trouble as they have caused.

Kenneth Broussard has seen a good deal of trouble. A skinny African American man with a bulky head, mural-sized tattoos, and a youthful smile, he is serving thirty-one years for armed robbery. In and out of institutions since he was a teenager, Broussard is proud of his tough convict reputation and makes a point never to display weakness. "I'm a very strong-willed person," he writes in a letter. "I'm not a trouble maker, I just don't take shit off no one, not even the guards."[38] Young, intelligent, and angry, with a long list of criminal convictions, Broussard is the type of offender corrections officers worry about. Held at the Michael Unit, one of the meanest lockups in the Texas system, he has regularly clashed with white guards on his cell block. Yet Broussard not only creates mayhem on occasion; he is its product.

Born in the port city of Beaumont in 1972, Ken started out his life in a downwardly mobile neighborhood defined by white flight and concentrated poverty. In a florid autobiographical essay he penned for a prison writing class, he explains that he was "raised among prostitutes who stank with the odors of their trade, among pimps with big hats, flashy jewelry, and cheap cologne, and on cracked streets littered with broken bottles, trash, winos, and the occasional overdosed junkie." Ken's mother, Brenda—a "simple country girl" with "jet black wavy hair and olive skin"—had Ken when she was sixteen. She was hooked on heroin and cocaine at the time and already had a two-year-old at home. Ken describes his father, Jesse, as "a very abusive man, a drunk, dope fiend, and a pimp." Each of his parents have spent more than a decade in prison. Between them, they have twelve children, but only Ken and his little brother Jerry share the same mother and father.[39]

Not long after Jerry was born, Ken's mother left Jesse for a new man who turned out to be even meaner than the boys' father. Echoing a familiar prison story, Ken says that one of his earliest memories is of his mother being hit. "Paul used to beat my mother senseless when he was drunk," he remembers. "I once tried hitting him with a broomstick, but he just backhanded me across the room."[40]

When Ken was about nine years old, his mother snuck away and made for California. With her five kids crammed into an Oldsmobile Delta 88, she set off on Interstate #10 with high hopes of a better life. "From the stories Momma told, we thought California was the promised land," Ken chuckles. As for so many California dreamers, however, the road proved bumpier than expected. The family ran out of money before making it across the arid expanse of West Texas. "Momma wrote bad checks for gas," he says, "and when she ran out of checks we hit truck stops so she could sell her body for gas and food money." It was wintertime, so the kids froze while their mother hustled. "That was the first time I got drunk," Ken remembers. "Momma gave us some vodka to cut the chill."[41]

Brenda had a sister in Los Angeles, but South Central during the crack wars turned out to be as unforgiving as Beaumont. The Delta 88 was stolen on the family's first day in the city, and Ken's mother got raped walking home from her new job at a store. "Momma went into a funk after that," he says. "She would sit staring blankly into space." Soon she was "hanging out with a shady bunch and shooting dope." To support her drug habit, she started turning tricks in the apartment, making the kids wait in the living room while she shot up and conducted her business. "Every week we had a new 'step dad,'" Ken remarks acidly. Even with the extra income, the kids went hungry. "Momma was gone for days at a time," he says, "so I would mix flour and water and make 'pancakes.'"

Ken's aunt finally scraped together enough money to ship the whole crew back to Texas, but geography wasn't the problem. Brenda was soon back on the streets. Ken and his four siblings lived with her parents, but before long Ken and Jerry got turned out. "We were bad," he admits. With nowhere else to go, Brenda finally drove the two boys to their paternal grandparents' house on the Louisiana border. She dragged them up to the entrance, pounded on the door, and, when no one answered, gave them five dollars apiece. "Momma said she was going to make a quick trip to the store, but she never came back."[42]

A few hours later, the grandmother they hardly knew came home. "She saw two dirty kids on her front porch and actually tried to shoo us away," he writes. Once they told her their story, she took them in and tried to reconcile herself to raising the two wild, wounded boys. Never much of a parent herself, the woman didn't do much better as a grandparent. She was an alcoholic, like the boys' father, and mean with a switch. Her man, Matthew Hawkins, hung around the house and tried to have his way with the boys. "He would wait until my grandmother was in a drunken stupor," Ken reports, and then "creep into our bedroom and fondle our genitals and try to penetrate our rectums with his finger while holding his hand over our mouths to keep us from screaming." The boys fought back, once adding rat poison to his coffee, but their grandmother never believed their pleas. "Every time we told, we got our asses beat."[43]

Looking back on his life from his concrete two-bunk cell at the Michael Unit, Ken hardly remembers when he first started stealing. "I was around eight or nine," he says. "My values were so twisted as a kid that I actually thought it was okay to steal despite what the crazy preacher on the street corner used to say. Everybody around me was stealing."[44]

Ken has few fond memories but the most exhilarating involve thieving and troublemaking. He laughs about nailing a police car while playing stickball and marvels about how easy it was to filch cakes and pies from a neighborhood bakery owned by a bigoted white man. "When I first started stealing it was to survive," he says. "Later on in life it was because I was tired of being teased for not having the latest in fashion items other kids my age had, and finally it was to support a drug habit."[45]

The state of Texas never did much for Ken when he was hungry, neglected, beaten, or sexually abused, but once he started breaking the law the government took notice. He managed to avoid long-term confinement as a juvenile, but he landed a prison sentence when he was seventeen. "So many men in my family had been to prison that I just assumed it was my ticket into manhood," he says. Ken has been to prison four times since then—"a year here, two there, four here, etc."— and has been continually locked up since 1998 on an aggravated robbery conviction. "Man, sometimes it feel like I have been in prison my whole life," he writes. "The only time I felt any sense of freedom was when I was high."[46]

## "THE LONGEST AND LONELIEST RIDE OF YOUR LIFE"

Prisoners like Ken Broussard, Michael Jewell, and Kimberly Leavelle carry their stories with them to prison, but once inside they find few opportunities to share them. Exchanging raw childhood memories has little place among convicts, especially in male prisons. "Predatory types sniff out signs of weakness," says Michael Jewell. "You have to develop a glare, a Billy Badass 'fuck it' attitude."[47] Observers from the free world don't show much interest either. When I take undergraduates on prison tours, they often ask what a particular convict did, but only rarely do they probe what makes the person tick as an individual.

"Offenders," as TDCJ officially labels people in prison, are defined above all by their crimes.

Convicts themselves resist this narrow conception of themselves, but the prison experience is so harsh that they invariably end up contorting their public personae to survive. They keep feelings locked up and over time come to silently carry their stories as burdens. "Exhuming repressed trauma is a painful process," explains Jewell, and "the average con in the population seeks pleasure not pain." In prison, you survive by "posturing and suppressing sensitivity. Eventually the conscience sort of goes to sleep."[48]

When rehabilitation was in vogue, prison social workers used to coax life stories out of inmates, developing detailed case files that were used to customize treatment plans. In California, where rehabilitative programming reached its zenith in the 1950s and 1960s, prison social workers not only conducted in-depth psychological and background interviews with each new prisoner but sought out spouses and even high-school principals for additional insights. "The treatment program for the inmate in the prison [is] planned in terms of understanding him as a person," explained Dr. Norman Fenton, California's deputy director of corrections.[49]

These days, there is little time for individual attention. Across the country, 749,798 persons go to prison each year, 71,927 of them in Texas.[50] With budgets tight and personnel limited, this means that intake and classification departments have to operate quickly and efficiently. They tend to rely on questionnaires, screening tests, and computerized "risk assessment instruments," rather than exhaustive individual interviews.

In Texas, a ten-person State Classification Committee is charged with evaluating each new inmate and making decisions on unit placement, job assignment, and treatment or educational programming, if any. But with more than thirteen hundred files to process a week, committee members eschew face-to-face meetings. Instead, they classify inmates based on law-enforcement dossiers, standardized test results, and any available information from previous incarcerations. TDCJ calls the committee's recommendations Individuated Treatment Plans, but inmates have little say in defining themselves as individuals. "The classification committee has access to a great deal of information," explains Becky Price, manager for classification operations in Huntsville. "But they usually go by the inmate's file or our computer system's recommendation."[51]

After conviction and sentencing, incoming prisoners, or "drive ups," are sent first to a TDCJ "transfer facility." One of the largest is located just across the street from the Texas Prison Museum in Huntsville. A hastily constructed industrial-scale complex with sheet metal siding and low sloping roofs, the Holliday Unit looks like an assemblage of discount tire outlets. Only the guard towers and shimmering coils of razor wire suggest its business is processing people rather than products. Jim Willett describes it as "a giant tin barn that serves as Texas's prison purgatory, the place you go between jail and the real thing."[52]

Prisoners arrive here on a stuffy prison transport vehicle known as "the chain bus." These days inmates are generally "deuced up," or shackled to a partner, but through the 1950s all convicts made the trip chained together at the neck. Whatever the restraints, inmates arrive tired, uncomfortable, and afraid. "I can tell you it is the longest and loneliest ride of your life," comments Broussard.[53]

After piling off the bus into holding pens, drive ups spend their first hours in prison vacillating between anxiety and boredom. "Inmates sit around in shorts and socks for hours at a time," explains Jorge Renaud, who has made three trips into the system. Inmates may practice their "big yard stare" and try to glean as much information as they can from veterans. But the distinguishing feature of intake is what the sociologist Erving Goffman calls "loss and mortification," or "the personal defacement that comes from being stripped of one's identity kit."[54]

During their first two days in prison, newcomers are numbered, photographed, tested, fingerprinted, cavity searched, disinfected, and shaved. Although few show up with significant property, much of what they do have, they lose. Arriving prisoners are allowed one religious text, one pair of shower shoes, seven white bras (women only), select legal documents, approved photographs, a wedding ring, and a wristwatch (no bling). Everything else gets shipped home or destroyed.[55]

Stripped back to nature, inmates will eventually be allowed to accumulate—provided someone in the free world sends them commissary money—as much authorized property as can fit in a 1.75-square-foot box. To get started, they receive a mini bar of soap, a package of tooth powder, and a short-handled toothbrush (the full-sized version can be filed into a shank). For clothing, they get clunky black leather shoes, a T-shirt, three pairs of underwear and socks, pajama pants, and a pullover smock—the outer layers all made of white duck cloth. Once they're suited up, the prisoners look like shapeless hospital orderlies. "The state prison does not want inmates to be individuals," postulates Renaud, and "the quickest way to depersonalization is to have them all look the same."[56]

Powerlessness and despair are what Kimberly Leavelle remembers most about intake. Arriving in winter, she recalls shivering naked in "a fenced-in kennel" while each woman stepped up to a taped line on the floor for an exhaustive cavity search—"behind the ears, in the mouth, vagina, and rectum, even between your toes." Everything came as a shock, she remembers: the "degrading strip show," the "officers screaming obscenities at you," the "delousing of your head and private areas. . . . Everyone was too humiliated and emotionally exhausted to look anyone in the eye. You realize that you are no longer a human but a number."[57]

After initial processing, TDCJ officers outline basic procedures and expectations in a formal orientation. They also provide prisoners with an all-important bureaucratic manual, the TDCJ *Offender Orientation Handbook,* which consists mainly of rules—numbered and subnumbered, sweeping and tedious rules that carry on for 111 pages and that are supposed to govern all aspects of prison society.

Modeled on the free-world penal code but without rights or judicial review, prison rules have expanded over time in response to countless incidents, managerial initiative, and court orders. They cover a bewildering range of restrictions and obligations: from the sensible ("no fighting") to the well meaning ("offenders will brush their teeth daily") to the catchall ("horseplay is prohibited").[58]

The *Offender Orientation Handbook* encapsulates the weary institutional dream of imposing perfect discipline on potential chaos. In practice, however, totalitarian order is never achieved. Churlish convicts have neither the inclination nor, often, the reading ability to follow the finer dictates, and their warders—moderately trained, high-turnover stiffs earning Waffle House wages—have neither time nor energy to enforce them to the letter. Nowhere is the *Handbook* fully or consistently enforced, yet, as daily conflicts arise it is constantly invoked. When disputes escalate, officers write "a case" and inmates appear before a make-shift court. As a vestige of lapsed federal court orders, these institutional tribunals have all the trappings of adversarial justice—witnesses, physical evidence, and even defense counsel of sorts (a corrections officer appointed by the presiding major). Even so, the house rarely loses. "Once an inmate has been charged with an offense in a Texas prison," asserts Renaud, "the only question . . . is the severity of the punishment." Renaud knows this first hand. He once got a parole setoff and spent an extra year in prison for smuggling two tablespoons of peanut butter out of the chow hall.[59]

After classification and once long-term space opens up (a process that can take months), prisoners again board a chain bus and are transported to a new institutional home. The lucky ones carry a low-security designation. They might get sent to a dormitory-style housing unit with education, counseling, and job training, though the number of such facilities has dwindled. Some inmates might even end up in familiar surroundings not far from friends and family, although this is not a high priority for TDCJ. Most prisoners, however, will land at a work-oriented, relatively high-security unit located in rural East Texas or the Gulf Coastal plain—far from home, far from loved ones, far from familiar radio stations, far from the free world.

Most women prisoners end up in the tiny town of Gatesville. Surrounded by squat scrubby hills twenty miles west of George W. Bush's ranch in Crawford, Gatesville started off as a frontier military post and prospered briefly during the blackland cotton boom of the late nineteenth century. In 1897, the town's fathers erected an ornate Beaux Arts courthouse, complete with Romanesque arches and cupolas, but there hasn't been much excitement since.[60] Today, most of the town-square storefronts are shuttered, with only the sheriff's department and the bail bondsman showing signs of life. Gatesville looks as worn out as the dusty farmland surrounding it.

Despite a century of hard times, the town's doyens remain undaunted. Gatesville is "the sort of 'Home Town' everyone dreams of," boasts a spiffy municipal Web site, "full of friendly people, fond memories, . . . low taxes and lower crime!" Hoping to morph into an exurb, the "spur capital of Texas" promotes tax abatements for businesses and touts a doubling of the population since 1980. What the Web site doesn't mention is that almost all of that population growth has resulted from increased incarceration. More than 9,000 of Gatesville's 15,591 official residents live behind bars.[61]

Just north of town on State School Road, prisons pop up in every direction—six in all, five of them for women. The most famous, situated on a grassy bluff next to a peach orchard, is the Gatesville Unit. Established as the State School for Boys in 1887, the facility originally represented a humanitarian triumph; it was the first state reform school anywhere in the South. Victorian reformers believed that schooling and farmwork in a dry climate would rescue boys from vice, but over the decades the institution developed a reputation for ruthlessness. Stoop labor, gang fights, sexual assault, beatings by staff, and long stints in solitary—these were all facts of life at the Gatesville school, says Jewell, who went there in 1961. In 1974, a federal judge ordered it shut down, condemning "widespread physical and psychological brutality."[62] Six years later, the facility reopened as a women's prison.

Until the last few years, the unit was still known as a work farm. With twelve hundred acres of sandy cropland, prison officials used to start all new prisoners in the fields. "It was terribly grueling work," recalls Leavelle, who went out on a grass-clearing detail shortly after she arrived. In response to staff cuts and stricter security mandates, however, the prison has been scaling back agricultural operations. "There's lots of idleness," complains Lieutenant J. W. Campbell, who took me on a tour.[63]

Idleness wasn't much tolerated when Campbell started with the prison system a quarter of a century ago. In those days, Texas prisons emphasized labor above all, most of it on "hoe squads" or "on the line." Campbell believes the system was better back then, but he is too weary of prison life for nostalgia. "They call me 'the grinch' because I canceled commissary on Christmas," he says with some satisfaction as we drive between buildings in his silver pickup. "I suppose I am, but the prison system has made me what I am now."

Campbell is a sturdy, straight-backed man with a soldier's buzz cut, but he seems hollowed out by prison work. "I've seen more than thirty dead convicts," he says in a low smoker's voice more often used for command than self-reflection. "When I was twenty years old, I had a boy die in my arms. I've seen an inmate get beat up and thrown in an industrial dryer until his lungs collapsed. I know what the blood of my own officers smells like." Like many veterans, Campbell has spent most of his adult life in and around prisons; for many years, he lived on prison grounds in the bachelors' quarters. He takes pride in hard-earned experience, but he also recognizes that a life of intermittent violence, combined with long hours, stagnant wages, and grinding everyday stress, has made him disconnect from himself and the world. "I'm cold; I'm hard. I don't care," he says flatly. "I'm institutionalized."[64]

Compared to most Texas prisons, the Gatesville Unit offers a rich assortment of programming. Campbell thinks most of it is junk, but he waits patiently, propped up on a desk and looking out the window, as I talk to treatment staffers, sometimes for an hour or more. After spending a few days inside a prison, you come to realize that corrections officers spend as much time waiting around as convicts. Not so differently from those they guard, most of them are passing time, waiting for shift change, waiting for payday, waiting for something better to come along.

Unlike the guards, treatment personnel are generally enthusiastic about their work, even if the programs they manage reflect the whims of politicians more than outcome-oriented research. At Gatesville's boot camp, young women with short sentences and starched uniforms march in formation, eat in regimented silence, and answer my every question by leaping up and shouting "Sir, yes, sir!" or less frequently, "Sir, no, sir!" In the Substance Abuse Felony Prevention program, by contrast, another set of short-timers attend group counseling sessions, where they share stories about their lives, exchange hugs and tears, and work through a twelve-step program.

It's unclear how well these programs reduce recidivism (the findings for boot camp are especially weak), but the reality is that most women are not assigned to any sort of rehabilitative initiative. "I had a drug problem, but I don't think my judge was aware of SAFP," says Leavelle, who did twelve years at Gatesville and Mountain View next door but never received drug or incest counseling. "He thought I could just go to prison and get help."[65]

More than many inmates, Leavelle struggled to take advantage of whatever opportunities she could find in prison. She completed every education series and filed a lawsuit so that she could change units and continue with college classes. "Whatever rehabilitation I received I had to fight for," she says. By keeping her record clear, Kimberly also landed one of the better prison jobs, refurbishing old computers for financially strapped schools. Even so, she speaks of her prison experience with bitterness. In a letter she wrote while still incarcerated, she complained, "I provide forty hours of free labor a week. Texas inmates are slaves of the state."[66]

Gatesville's security staff doesn't present a much rosier picture. Lieutenant Campbell appreciates that officers are less likely to get severely assaulted at a women's unit, but he complains of daily annoyances. While I was there, a heavily armored extraction squad was preparing to take down a naked woman in the Mentally Retarded Offender Program who had barricaded herself in the shower for the second time that week. Every officer griped about "cubicle crawling," illicit liaisons made possible by slinking between dormitory partitions at night. By all accounts, most inmates on the unit—and not infrequently staff—get mixed up in sexual encounters at some point during their stay, sometimes consensual, sometimes not.[67]

This is one of the reasons that prison employees claim that female units are more emotionally draining than male prisons. "The system treats them better, but female offenders are harder to manage," contends Pamela Baggett, a former warden at Mountain View who now runs a male unit in Huntsville. "A male inmate won't come in and start crying."[68]

## SILENT NIGHT

Gatesville is not the hardest place to do time in Texas. That distinction probably belongs to the Polunsky Unit, a supermaximum-security outpost sixty miles east of Huntsville. It's not that the location is gloomy. Situated alongside the Big Thicket outside Livingston, the surrounding area provides all manner of recreational opportunities: fishing, hunting, even Civil War reenactments. Nor is the unit itself dangerously dilapidated. Recently constructed of reinforced white concrete with blue steel supports, the unit is functionally designed and pleasantly asymmetrical; if not for the three-inch window slits, one might mistake it for a community college. The problem with Polunsky is existential: the prison houses Texas's main death row.[69]

California has a larger death row, but Texas's is indisputably the most lethal, not just in the United States but anywhere in the democratic world. Since the Supreme Court allowed executions to resume in 1976, the Lone Star State has taken the lives of three women and 439 men, more than a third of the national total. During the final year of George W. Bush's governorship, the state administered lethal injections forty times, an American record.[70]

Lethal injections themselves take place in an antiseptic brick room at the Walls in Huntsville, but until the day of execution, condemned male inmates live at Polunsky. On average, condemned inmates wait ten years to be executed, so they have plenty of time to make the prison a peculiar type of home.[71] Their anxious wait—punctuated by nail-biting stays and setbacks—makes Polunsky an usually stressful prison: stressful for everyone who works there; for the children, wives, and parents who cram into noncontact visiting booths on weekends; and most of all for the men who count down their days under conditions of extraordinary isolation and security.

Jonathan Reed, a willowy man with hollow cheeks and pale skin that fades into his white uniform, knows this waiting as well as anyone. He has been on death row since 1978, which means that he has been anticipating execution for most of his life. Convicted of raping and strangling a flight attendant in Dallas, Reed has waged an uphill battle to save himself based on an innocence claim. In the process, as his case has crawled from court to court, he has grown into middle age. He has bid farewell to 170 friends before they were removed from the row and shipped off to the death chamber, and he suspects that his own time is approaching. "I will probably get a 'date' within two years and be executed for a crime I did not commit," he predicts dryly. "I won't be the first."[72]

Despite this grim prognosis, Reed struggles to remain upbeat. He corresponds regularly with death penalty opponents and makes decorative cards by hand. It used to be easier, he says. Until 1999 death row was housed at the Ellis Unit, where the "attitude was, 'We can afford you some sort of reasonable life—within security confines.'" On the old death row, inmates worked in a garment factory, helped each other with legal work, played basketball, and worshipped together. "We broke the prison rules at times," he admits. "We smoked, tattooed, had sex (with inmates and officers), made wine, whatever." Most important, Jon says he was able to develop close friendships and make peace before they ended: officers used to let prisoners gather for good-byes the night before an execution. "We lived as humans," he remembers. "We were a community."[73]

Privileges dried up over the years, and in 1999, after a failed escape attempt and as Governor Bush ramped up his presidential campaign, death row was moved to the new set of supermax pods at Polunsky. Prisoners recall the journey vividly because it afforded their last glimpses of the outside world. "The first thing I noticed was how much the cars had changed," one inmate wrote shortly before his execution in 2004. Although he was hobbled, cuffed, and belly chained for the forty-five-minute van ride that he called "a caravan of death," he struggled to take in everything he saw. "We all got quiet when we finally came to Lake Livingston," he remembered. "You never realize how much the simple things in life like splashing in cool water mean until they are taken away."[74]

Since that day, Texas's death row inmates have lived under some of the most restrictive prison conditions anywhere. They spend all but one hour a day in six-by-nine-foot cells. A solid steel door blocks any meaningful communication between prisoners. The only human contact occurs when an inmate backs up to the door and sticks his hands through a slot for cuffing. Recreation, too, is solitary; prisoners take turns pacing or playing handball in an outdoor or indoor cage about twice as large as their cells. Visits take place through thick Plexiglas and a tinny phone connection. There is no air-conditioning, no programming, no work, and no televisions. "This unit's mentality is, 'we keep you kenneled until your date,'" observes Reed.[75]

What he and many psychologists call sensory deprivation has taken a toll.[76] Reed has lost weight, not just fat but muscle, and under the fluorescent lights in the visiting room his skeleton is visible through sallow skin. His speech is slowed and hesitant, atrophied from lack of use. "We are deprived of so many of the things that make a human being stable and sane," comments a fellow resident; Jon admits that he sometimes asks where his humanity went. Other prisoners break. In the winter of 2004 and 2005, there were two successful suicides and several attempts, this in addition to prisoners who gave up their appeals and requested the earliest possible execution date.[77]

When a condemned man's time expires, he gets one last look at the world. On the afternoon of his scheduled death, he travels in a three-vehicle convoy from Livingston to Huntsville, from death row to the death house. (Women leave from the Mountain View Unit.) At the Walls, the person enters through a back gate, goes through one more cavity search, and is deposited in a cool, windowless holding cell, where he will spend his last hours. The Walls chaplain or an outside spiritual advisor is on hand to talk. For some men, this is the first real conversation they have had in months, but they are often too keyed up to effectively communicate.[78]

According to tradition, the damned is allowed a last meal, and most prisoners order standard American fare in heaping portions, the sorts of meals that recall a childhood Sunday. "Eight soft fried eggs, bacon, sausage, one T-bone steak (well-done), six slices of buttered toast with strawberry jelly, and a pitcher of cold milk" reads one request. Another: "four pieces of fried chicken, mashed potatoes, two pints of ice cream, one bacon cheeseburger, and two vanilla cokes."[79] Many request a pack of cigarettes, though TDCJ no longer allows smoking.[80] Women prisoners often fast.[81]

A little before six p.m., after conferring with the attorney general and the governor's office, the warden arrives at the holding cell to tell the prisoner that time is up. That used to be Jim Willett's job, and he has managed so many executions that he recites the sequence of events by rote. If there is no expected trouble, the tie-down team lets the condemned man walk unrestrained to the chamber, a nine-by-twelve-foot room with bright lights, turquoise walls, and a dominant centerpiece, a bolted-down silver gurney with brown leather straps, white sheets, and a pillow (an accommodation added by Willett). The prisoner steps up to the bed, reclines, and is quickly strapped down. A medical team then starts two IVs, while the chaplain places his hand on the person's leg. "It never crossed my mind that some of these people are just like the rest of us and are scared to death of a needle," recalls Willett of his first time. The chaplain says that most of the prisoners are trembling.[82]

Once the machinery is primed and double-checked, reporters, family members, and other observers are escorted into two adjacent rooms separated from the death chamber by glass windows; one is for the crime victim's family, and one for the inmate's. "When they're on the gurney, they're stretched out," comments Mike Graczyk, an AP reporter who has witnessed more than two hundred executions. The "arms are extended. I've often compared it to almost a crucifixion."[83] With an audience assembled, a boom mike drops from the ceiling and hangs in front of the inmate's face for a final statement.

What prisoners choose to say varies. Many decline to say anything. Others confess or apologize. Others send love to family members and fellow inmates. "To everyone at the Polunsky Unit, just keep your heads up and stay strong," urged Richard Cartwright on May 19, 2005. Some prisoners remain defiant until the end. Cameron Todd Willingham, a man who used to write me long letters, declared, "I am an innocent man convicted of a crime I did not commit." (A subsequent investigation by the *Chicago Tribune* and the Innocence Project determined he was telling the truth.)[84] Some inmates assail the death penalty, politicians, and their trial lawyers, while others turn to their maker. "I am going to be face to face with Jesus now," proclaimed Karla Faye Tucker. "I will see you all when you get there." Whatever they say, "the voice is emotional, nervous, cracks a little bit," says a regular witness. On one occasion, recalls Willett, an inmate just wanted to sing. "He made his final statement and then . . . he started singing 'Silent Night.'" "Mother and child" were his last words.[85]

Once the prisoner has finished a statement, the warden gives a signal—Willett used to remove his glasses—and the executioner, an anonymous TDCJ employee behind a one-way mirror, pumps fatal doses of three separate medications into the IV line. The prisoner immediately detects the change; "I can taste it," gasped one man as the first drug, a general anesthetic, sodium thiopental, first started to flow. The second drug, a muscle relaxant called pancuronium bromide, collapses the lungs. Through the boom mike, observers say they hear a final sputter, "kind of like . . . squishing the air out of . . . a balloon," as the prisoner releases a last breath. The final drug, potassium chloride, stops the heart.[86]

Working executions adds special stresses to an already stressful job, say corrections officers who volunteer for the death team and receive no extra pay. "Just from a Christian standpoint, you can't see one of these and not consider that maybe it's not right," admits Willett. Officers find their own ways to carry the burden. "I take my mind off things when I go fishing," explains a supervisor in a radio interview. Toward the end of Willett's tenure, one of his most experienced team members broke. "I was just working in the shop and all of a sudden something just triggered in me and I started shaking," says Fred Allen, who had taken part in more than one hundred executions. "I walked back into the house and my wife asked, 'What's the matter?' and I said, 'I don't feel good.' And tears—uncontrollable tears—was coming out of my eyes. . . . Something triggered within, and it just—everybody—all of these executions all of a sudden all sprung forward." Other officers worry that they don't feel enough. "You expect to feel a certain way, then you think, 'Is there something wrong with me if I don't?' . . . 'Why isn't this bothering me?'"[87]

Since 1996, Texas has allowed family members of crime victims to witness the procedure. Some observers say the scene provides closure. "I'm very glad I came," said the mother of a seven-year-old who was raped and murdered in 1989. "I had to see him gone." Others complain that the process is too clinical. "He's getting off too easy," remarked the sister of a stabbing victim. "No pain or suffering like he caused." Some witnesses find less release than they had hoped. Their loss remains just as powerful, their wounds reopened. "Him dying now or dying of old age, it's not going to change anything," said one survivor after watching the killer of his daughter die. "And it's not going to bring me any satisfaction or happiness."[88]

Willett regrets that while executions may bring peace to some victims, they also create more victims. "Can you imagine watching your son die?" he wonders. Journalists on the execution beat get separated into either the victim's or the inmate's viewing room, and they dread the latter. "I've had a mother collapse right in front of me," says Graczyk. She "hit the floor, went into hyperventilation, almost convulsions." "I've seen them scream and wail. I've seen them beat the glass," adds another. "You'll never hear another sound like a mother wailing when she is watching her son be executed. There's no other sound like it."[89]

## "HOUSE OF PAIN"

A chasm of experience lies between the singular stresses of death row and the comparative comforts of the Substance Abuse Program at Gatesville. Like most states, Texas manages a dizzying array of carceral facilities: halfway houses, short-term state jails, special lockups for parole violators, and all sorts of privately run prisons. There are prisons for juveniles, women, and men; for the mentally retarded, the physically disabled, the elderly, and the terminally ill. Substance-abuse units, sex-offender units, prerelease units, even a fundamentalist Christian unit. There are outside trusty camps, high-security dormitories, single-bunk cell blocks, double-bunk cell blocks, protective custody areas, special gang units, administrative segregation wings, and high-tech supermaxes. "The system is so big that no person, no twenty people, can run it anymore," says Bill Habern, a Huntsville attorney who has represented inmates since the 1970s.[90]

Out of this hodgepodge, it is difficult to pinpoint an emblematic Texas prison. But if any unit stands for the rest, it's an old East Texas penal farm one-third of the way between Polunsky and Gatesville—a place that typifies the rural isolation of most Texas lockups, that houses all classification types but tilts toward maximum security, and that binds present-day prisons to their unburied past. Eastham.

A thirteen-thousand-acre cotton plantation forty miles up the Trinity River from death row, the Eastham Unit is one of Texas's oldest and roughest institutions. Known as "the Ham," the prison was historically a dreaded assignment for convicts: arduous, dangerous, and hard to escape. Spread out beyond the dead end of FM 230, a narrow farm-to-market road, "Eastham [was a] God-forsaken hole," remarked a sheriff in 1937; it's a "burning hell" echoed a convict forty years later.[91]

Among convicts and guards alike, Eastham's history is legendary: the site of a bloody breakout by the Bonnie and Clyde gang, starting point of the Texas Prison Rodeo, incubator of the famous *Ruiz v. Estelle* case, and staging ground for countless work strikes and club-wielding crackdowns. Its fields were cleared before the Civil War by slaves, and from those days forward free labor rarely brought in a crop. After emancipation, sharecroppers took over the work, but they were later replaced by convicts. In 1896, for example, Mrs. D. Eastham agreed to pay the state "$14.50 per month per head" for 119 men, "consisting in large measure of negroes," who themselves were paid nothing.[92]

As evidenced by ruins scattered about its extensive grounds—a crumbled textile mill here, an ancient whitewashed cell block there—Eastham has gone through numerous permutations over the years. In the early twentieth century, it served briefly as a women's farm until a sexual-abuse scandal compelled administrators to move female inmates closer to Huntsville. Later, the prison specialized in young male offenders, first for whites and then, once the facilities wore out, blacks.[93] For most of its long history, however, Eastham has corralled maximum-security male convicts and worked them relentlessly in the fields. In their annual reports, successive wardens recorded the size and value of the annual cotton harvest before anything else.

Eastham's institutional goals were to profit and punish, and its labor and disciplinary practices developed accordingly. Walter Siros, a middle-class kid from Houston who wound up at Eastham in 1960 for car theft, described the farm regime as "murderous." "Those field bosses were the deadliest humans I've ever known," he recalled in an interview from his mobile home in Huntsville. "They didn't care about anything but how much cotton you picked. We worked sun to sun. I didn't think I was going to make it." In 1986, amidst an outbreak of stabbings, *Newsweek* titled its cover story on Eastham, "America's Toughest Prison."[94]

The Ham's reputation has mellowed a bit since those days—largely because new units like Polunsky impose even stricter discipline—but some of its old-time employers are doing their best to stay in the game. One of them, John Massingill, the farm manager and number-two man at the prison, showed me around on a scorching July day. A towering man with ice-blue eyes and a Marine Corps haircut, Massingill would rather be supervising hoe squads, but due to budget cuts he lacks sufficient staff for outside security. Instead, this season, he's focusing on livestock operations worked by minimum-security trusties, which leaves him spare time for a tour.[95]

Outside the main redbrick complex that was originally built by convicts, Massingill explains why Eastham's "telephone-pole" layout—with dead-end cell blocks extending out from central pickets—makes guarding the prison difficult, so difficult in fact that, for decades, the guarding was left to convict enforcers known as "building tenders." If maintaining order is challenging, preventing escapes is not. "We get a runner every now and again," Massingill says, gesturing to an infinity of crop and grassland, "but the dogs usually have them treed within forty-five minutes. You've got to be faster than a rabbit to make it off this farm."[96]

Massingill, who comes to work in jeans, a western shirt, and a Stetson, has little patience for the bureaucratic headaches that lurk inside the main building, so before long we're hurtling along Eastham's dusty back roads in his one-ton Chevy. He checks in on a pungent pig complex, wooden longhouses stuffed with mangy chickens, and a cattle burial pit mobbed with buzzards. The whole operation is tended by convicts, who trade blistering labor for light supervision. "Best job in the system," one of the trusties tells me as he takes a break from digging a hole. "Out here you do your work and you got no trouble."[97]

With no trouble in sight, Massingill drives me around to his favorite spots. A ditch where Clyde Barrow hid a pistol to help break out his comrades in 1932. A Caddo campsite dating to the days before the profits of slavery attracted outsiders to East Texas. The rusted carcass of a cotton gin that the state kept operational until 1992 when the last spare parts ran out. "We did 496 bales in '92," he says.[98]

Today Massingill runs a massive agricultural operation (4,000 head of free-range cattle, 5,000 hogs, 52,000 laying hens, and 1,400 acres of field crops) with only eleven paid employees. Nonetheless, he complains, "These convicts today, they don't know the first thing about work." Since the 1980s, he laments, the prison system has lost its focus on labor and discipline, as well as its moral compass. "The place is a nightmare of paperwork," he grumbles. "We can't discipline 'em. We can't work 'em. We operate under a microscope."[99]

If Massingill is disappointed with the quality of modern-day inmates—most of them are dopeheads who "should be executed on sight," he says—he is equally contemptuous of the guards. When he was a young man, corrections officers made prison work a life, he explains. Most of them lived in state-issued housing on the units, as he still does. They ate what the prison produced, employed favorite trusties as house boys, socialized with other guards at barbeques, and often raised their sons to work in the system. "They're just in it for the paycheck" now, he regrets. "They turn over faster than convicts and aren't much better." He rejects the charge that low pay generates low morale. "The problem is the degradation of society's rules," he counters. "These employees don't know right from wrong. We catch them having sex with inmates, bringing in cell phones, guns, you name it." Most bitterly of all, the farm manager rails against lawyers and "weak liberals," who, in his opinion, "just bend over and take it in the ass whenever an inmate whines." "Used to be we were self-sufficient," he claims. "But the *Ruiz* thing ruined it."[100]

Although Massingill has observed deep changes at Eastham over the course of his career, the prison's continuities are striking. Its daily rhythms were set in the nineteenth century and have scarcely changed. As on other TDCJ units, the routine is designed to facilitate farmwork—lights on at 3:00 a.m., and breakfast shortly thereafter. Work turnout before dawn. Lunch at 10:00 a.m., often a "johnny sack" in the fields. Turn in, showers, and supper starting at 4:00 in the afternoon. Lights out at 10:00. Like their bonded forebears stretching back to the 1850s, convicts put in long days of unpaid physical labor. "We work 'em from can till can't," Massingill says. Inside the main building, some twenty-four hundred convicts, the majority African Americans and Chicanos from the cities, populate the tiers. This is generally their first trip to a farm and the journey seems to carry them back in time. "This here is a slave plantation," claims one convict.[101]

Places like Eastham complicate the way criminal justice analysts think about prisons. Because correctional institutions have proliferated so wildly over the past thirty years, commentators tend to focus on what makes America's prison system new: privatization, supermax isolation units, the decline of treatment, the war on drugs, and, most of all, growth. What the irrepressible history at Eastham suggests, however, is that the harshest elements of modern-day imprisonment are hardly unprecedented. Long before the most ambitious efforts at prisoner rehabilitation rose and then fell in states like California, southern prisons like Eastham were dishing out rough justice of the sort that is now back in vogue. For six generations going back to the antebellum period, Eastham has been extracting hard labor and dispensing punishment, almost always along traditional racial lines: white bosses lording over black workers. While the scale and technologies of Texas justice have certainly changed, its essential character has not.

Picking up a clump of Eastham's rich, red soil—soil that has been turned and tilled by unpaid hands for a century and a half—one comes to realize that we can never fully understand America's most recent experiment in restricted liberty, mass imprisonment, without tracing the story back to the first—slavery.

# 2

## PLANTATION AND PENITENTIARY

> While society in the United States gives the example of the most extended liberty, the prisons of the same country offer the spectacle of the most complete despotism.
>
> —GUSTAVE DE BEAUMONT AND ALEXIS DE TOCQUEVILLE[1]

Although it is seldom recognized, Texas's most famous prisoner was also its "founding father," Stephen F. Austin. Memorialized as a gallant colonizer whose "great work consisted in the making of Anglo-American Texas," Austin was arrested for advocating independence from Mexico in 1833. His subsequent imprisonment helped make that independence a reality.[2]

Detained at a time of momentous upheaval, with Mexico on the verge of civil war, Austin endured a year and a half of "very rigid" confinement. For three months, he was held *"incomunicado"* in conditions not unlike today's supermaxes. "[I] was shut up in one of the dungeons of the inquisition," he wrote to his brother-in-law shortly after his release, "locked up day and night with very little light except candles and not allowed to speak or communicate with anyone, not to have books, pen, ink, or paper." In Texas, the "empresario," as Austin was known by his legal title, governed a land-grant colony larger than many countries, but in prison his world shrank to a sixteen-by-thirteen-foot stone cell with solid bolted doors and a tiny skylight. He received his meals through "an oblong hole large enough to admit a plate" and was permitted only two hours of fresh air a day, "alone and locked in . . . one of the *solederos* or sunning places." Occasionally he saw other prisoners—mostly political detainees like himself—but he "could not salute or speak."[3]

Although Austin endeavored to "bear . . . [his] misfortunes . . . firmly," solitary confinement and his uncertain future took a toll. After being released from isolation, he was moved from prison to prison while his case worked its way through the courts. By the fall of 1834, he was paranoid and depressed. "My situation is desolate," he wrote, "almost destitute of friends and money, in a prison, amidst foes who are active to destroy me, and forgotten at home by those I have faithfully labored to serve." Wounded by rumors that rivals were plotting against him and dejected by legal delays, he spoke forebodingly of his fate. "My friends . . . may look on me as dead for a long time to come and probably forever."[4]

When he was finally released in June 1835, Austin was a changed man. Since taking over Texas's first Anglo settlement from his domineering father in 1821, he had long counseled moderation in Mexican politics, advocating immigration and provincial autonomy but forswearing rebellion. "My own principles . . . always have been *peace, quietness, patience and submission to the laws and no revolutions,*" he insisted. After "suffer[ing] a long persecution and imprisonment," however, he veered from accommodation to anger, as would so many prisoners after him. Upon his return, Austin endorsed a Declaration for Taking Up Arms, asserting that Texas citizens would fight to defend "their rights and Liberties" against a "reign of despotism."[5] The Texas Revolution had begun.

As a tireless advocate for white settlers, Austin became a hero to the fledgling Texas Republic and to the United States, which later absorbed it. "Few men have accomplished so much in so little time as did Stephen F. Austin," wrote one biographer. "He explored the Texan wilderness, led in the first settlers, built a new free country, and on his deathbed handed the world a new nation." What gets lost in this hagiography is precisely what Austin and his brave compatriots were fighting for. Over the course of their revolt, Anglo immigrants to Texas, or "Texians," as they styled themselves, nursed a variety of grievances against Mexico's central government. They railed against corrupt courts and Catholic favoritism; one historian labeled the war "a contest of civilizations."[6] But the issue that most animated leading Texians was the legal status of their most valuable investments: slaves.

From the 1810s forward, Mexican politicians moved repeatedly against slavery, even as Anglo immigrants increasingly regarded the institution as indispensable, so indispensable that they were willing to fight two wars of secession, the first against Mexico and the second against the United States, to preserve it. Although Stephen Austin's dreams of freedom were incubated in a prison cell and the War for Independence fought in the name of "natural rights," his revolution embodied Texas's founding contradiction, its original sin.[7] "To believe them, they have no motive but to establish 'free institutions, civil and religious,'" inveighed the British geographer George Featherstonehaugh, who visited Texas just before the rebellion. "Yet in defiance of human freedom, just laws, and true religion, they proceed to consummate their real purpose, which is to people the country with slaves in order to cover it with cotton crops."[8] The liberty that rebellious Texians most cherished was the right to deny liberty to others.

Devotion to slavery touched every corner of the short-lived Texas Republic and later the state, forging a legacy that extends into the present. All of Texas's principal institutions—its political and legal systems, its economy and cultural mores—rested on a bedrock fracture: exalted liberty secured through systematic debasement. So, too, did its first prison at Huntsville. As in other southern polities that later coalesced into the Confederacy, Texas developed criminal justice traditions uniquely suited to the political economy of human bondage. Slavery itself was ultimately swept away by the American Civil War, but its criminal justice institutions endured. As Alexis de Tocqueville once remarked, "the law may abolish slavery, [but] God alone can obliterate the traces of its existence."[9]

## "TEXAS MUST BE A SLAVE COUNTRY"

Although most historians have minimized the connection, slavery and the "peopling of the wilderness of Texas," as Austin called it, were bound together like sinew and bone. An African slave, Estevanico, accompanied the first European explorer to traverse the territory, and although the institution gained only a foothold under Spanish rule, Stephen Austin's father, Moses, changed that forever. In 1820, he traveled from Missouri to San Antonio along with an enslaved manservant and convinced authorities to open the border with the American South. Because the expansion of slavery was being restricted in the United States, Texas soon became a "land of refuge for the American slaveholders."[10]

Moses himself did not lead Africans into bondage. He fell deathly ill on his trek homeward and had to pass the dream of creating an American colony on to his twenty-eight-year-old son Stephen, a slight but determined young man with almond eyes and lush brown hair. Somewhat reluctantly, the younger Austin retraced his father's footsteps to Texas and finalized a settlement contract on terms exceedingly favorable to slaveholders. To attract settlers, the agreement stipulated that each head of household would receive generous land allotments for himself and his family and would get an additional fifty acres for every imported slave. Although Stephen harbored some doubts about slavery, he recognized its profitability. Only by encouraging "emigrants to bring in their Slaves and Servants," he reasoned, could Mexico attract the best class of settlers. Without bonded labor, "these fertile lands, instead of being occupied by wealthy planters, will remain for many years, in the hands of mere shepherds or poor people."[11]

Anglo immigrants, overwhelmingly from the American South, wasted no time in taking advantage of Austin's promise of cheap and abundant land. Almost as soon as planters began rolling across the Mexican border, however, they had to contend with a rising threat to their peculiar form of proprietorship. Mexico had just won its independence from Spain, and the new country's politicians spoke out forcefully against slavery, which they said "dishonors the human race." From 1823 on, the central government and the state of Coahuila and Texas took steps to circumscribe or even abolish slavery. Most categorically, on Mexico's Independence Day in 1829, President Vicente Guerrero decreed "by an act of Justice and Beneficence . . . that slavery be exterminated in the Republic."[12]

Each restriction enflamed Anglo settlers. "In the name of God what shall we do? We are ruined," one Texian wailed. In response, Austin devoted his considerable diplomatic skills to rolling back or circumventing Mexico's successive efforts at abolition. When the state constitution banned slavery, he helped enact a slippery indentured servant law that enabled white settlers to bond black laborers for ninety-nine years so they could learn "the art and mystery of planting." Even after President Guerrero's emancipation decree, Austin's allies managed to carve out an exemption for Texas. Yet shortly thereafter, another presidential order shut off all immigration from the United States, whether free or slave.[13] This inspired Austin to embark on his ill-fated mission to Mexico City, during which he was imprisoned.

The empresario himself equivocated on the slavery question. In some letters, he called slavery the "worst of evils." In others, he insisted that it "serves the cause of humanity [by] accelerating the epoch of civilization." Whatever his personal views, however, he invariably deferred to "the wishes of [his] colonists." By 1825, sixty-nine of his colony's families owned 443 slaves, and as their economic dependence on the institution deepened, so did their ideological commitment. "I have been averse to the principle of slavery in Texas," Austin admitted. But after much back and forth, he concluded: "Texas *must be* a slave country. Circumstances and unavoidable necessity compel it. It is the wish of the people there, and it is my duty to do all I can, prudently, in favor of it."[14]

When full-scale warfare broke out between Texians and the Mexican army in 1836, slavery loomed, as one contemporary put it, as "the immediate cause and leading object of this contest." President Santa Anna promised to liberate "those wretches [who] moan in chains," while Texians vowed to protect their property interests at all costs. Like their forebears in the American Revolution, Texians paradoxically vowed to resist "ambitious tyrants, whose chains are forged to manacle our citizens," even as they insisted on forging chains to manacle their slaves.[15]

Even before the Battle of San Jacinto made the Republic of Texas a reality, prominent white Texians had started codifying what type of republic it would be. In a quickly drafted constitution, they declared that "all political power is inherent in the people" and that "all men . . . have equal rights." So wary of state power were the revolutionaries that they adopted an expansive Declaration of Rights. Citizens of Texas would not only enjoy the freedoms of speech and the press, as well as habeas corpus and jury trials, but would be constitutionally protected from debtor prison and monopolies. The framers also instructed Congress to draft a new penal code, one based on "principles of reformation, and not vindictive justice."[16]

When it came to race, however, the Texas constitution was as unyielding as its counterparts in the American South. "Africans, the descendants of Africans, and Indians" were excluded from citizenship, and "all persons of color who were slaves for life . . . [would] remain in the like state of servitude." Lest there be any doubt about the permanency of slavery in the new republic, the framers forbid even masters from emancipating their slaves without the "express consent of congress."[17] From its legal foundation, then, independent Texas distributed rights by race, a tradition that would prove enormously difficult to overcome.

Early efforts to enforce order were similarly bound up with slavery and white supremacy. Historians generally trace the rise of modern law enforcement to mid-nineteenth-century cities like Philadelphia, Boston, and New York. In the American South and independent Texas, however, government policing developed less to impose order on polyglot urbanites than to reinforce the barricades between citizen and subject, settler and dispossessed. The purpose, as one Texas governor later phrased it, was to protect "the fairest portion of Texas" from "unruly Negroes, wild Indians," and "Mexican marauders."[18]

Anglo settlers maintained that they themselves needed little supervision. "The character of [our] inhabitants is . . . peaceful and easy to govern," insisted a group of Austin's colonists in 1828. "From the beginning, [the empresario] has governed . . . without appointing a single soldier, without any necessity of force, and without a single jail or house of correction." When it came to slaves and Indians, however, Austin's compatriots favored a sterner hand.[19]

Like masters everywhere, prominent Texians fretted most of all about their servants and field workers, whom they accused of laziness, insolence, and thievery. "They do behave so bad, some of 'em," complained one slaveholder. "They steal just like hogs." Given the proximity to Native American communities and emancipated Mexico, Texas slaveholders were especially concerned about escape, always a tempting proposition along the frontier. Accordingly, white settlers organized patrols and issued bounties for "Nigger-hunting," the first systematic attempt at policing in Texas.[20] On most nights, these prototypical guardians of property and public order engaged in low-level law enforcement: patrolling, whipping, and chasing down runaways. But at crisis points they could unleash breathtaking violence. When rumors of a slave revolt swept through plantations along the Brazos in October 1835, for instance, white Texians responded just as they would years later on the eve of the American Civil War—by rounding up scores of suspects and dispensing grisly punishments without trial. "Near 100 [have] been taken up many whipd nearly to death some hung etc.," read a terse dispatch from the town of Goliad.[21] In Texas, as elsewhere, slavery was a labor system managed by terror.

A contemporaneous conflict that shaped the emergence of law enforcement in Texas involved the original occupants of the very lands that white colonists hoped to "people . . . [with] industrious agricultural settlers." By 1821, when Austin first beckoned U.S. immigrants across the Sabine, indigenous peoples in the region had interacted with Europeans for centuries. Occasional skirmishes and scourges like smallpox had nearly obliterated some groups, but outside of colonial outposts like San Antonio and Nacogdoches, Native societies maintained effective control of Texas's 268,581 square miles well into the nineteenth century. Once Anglos and their bonded workers started pouring across the border, however, Native Americans faced a new kind of threat, not just to their lifeways but to their very existence.[22]

"The father of Texas" styled himself a moderate on slavery and in politics, but when it came to Natives he was hard tempered. "The Indians . . . may be called universal enemies to man," Austin wrote on his first journey to Texas. "There will be no way of subduing them but extermination." True to promise, Austin's colonists reacted to an early cattle dispute with the Karankawa by wiping out an entire camp on Skull Creek near present-day Columbus. The settlers reported killing nineteen people and returning home with scalps as "troph[ies] from battle." In 1825, the empresario gave orders to "pursue and kill all those Indians wherever they are found." Shortly thereafter, an Anglo force trapped a Karankawa band along the Colorado, gunning down women, men, and children as they desperately tried to swim across the river and climb the opposite bank to safety. Settlers later named the crossing Dressing Point, because they believed the Indians got the dressing they deserved.[23]

Although small by comparison to the pogroms that would come later, the Skull Creek and Dressing Point atrocities set the tone for the conquest of Texas, a bloody contest even by frontier standards. One historian has called it an "angry and brutal" campaign of "ethnic cleansing." For more than fifty years after Austin's colonists first set out to "chastise" their Karankawa neighbors, Texas remained in a state of almost constant warfare, the most protracted struggle of its kind in North American history.[24]

In the early years, most of the killing was carried out by loosely organized gangs of white fighters known as "rangers." Austin himself was the first to use the term when he commissioned settlers to fight the Karankawa, but the "rangers" designation soon came to stand for any volunteer militia dispatched to expand and protect Anglo settlements. The Texas Rangers, formally established in 1835, were the territory's first border guard and police force. To this day, they remain the most elite law enforcement corps in the state.

With their "wild life and exciting combats, [the Rangers] were as romantic and attractive to adventurous young men as any crusade of old," wrote Frederick Law Olmsted, the famous naturalist who journeyed through Texas in the mid-1850s. Over decades of violent racial conflict, they became Texas's most iconic heroes—the personification of hardscrabble, honor-bound masculinity. The ranger was a "flame of courage," waxed Walter Prescott Webb, their preeminent chronicler. "Intelligent, cool, calculating, and capable of sustained endurance and suffering," he was "a fighting man . . . standing alone between a society and its enemies."[25]

Those enemies changed over time. Rangers fought in the Texas Revolution, the Mexican-American War, and the Civil War. They chased outlaws of any stripe and were "ready at any time to make a couple of hundred dollars" bringing in runaway slaves, reported Olmsted. Until the final defeat of Native Americans in the southern plains, however, the Texas Rangers' "principal occupation [was] Indian fighting."[26]

It was in this arena that the Texas Rangers built their legend. As depicted in countless westerns, the hardy frontiersmen reluctantly left their homes and rode from feat to fantastic feat, especially against the fearsome Comanches. In truth, we know that ranger companies were distinguished by brutality as much as bravery.[27] Since Indian war parties were difficult to track down, the rangers routinely attacked poorly defended villages, often striking in winter or at dawn. "[They] charged and fired a volley into the tents and wigwams, killing indiscriminately a number of all ages and sexes," read one early report. Gary Anderson, the leading historian of Texas-Indian relations, concludes that rangers displayed pluck and fighting ability but that they also engaged in plunder, rape, enslavement, and massacre. "Their goal was to spread terror so that neighboring Native groups would leave."[28]

Texas Rangers were "always ready for the chase of the red skin," according to Olmsted, but they also trained their sights on another population in possession of coveted lands, Mexicans. Early colonists like Austin had accommodated themselves to Mexican culture. They learned Spanish, intermarried with Mexican families, and at least nominally converted to Catholicism. As more headstrong and culturally insular Anglos gained sway, however, Mexican farmers and ranchers, known as Tejanos, found themselves increasingly under siege. After the revolution and again after the Mexican-American War, Tejano families were driven out of Nacogdoches, Goliad, Austin, Seguin, and elsewhere under force of arms. "The Mexicans were treated . . . like a conquered people," noted Olmsted. "Newcomers . . . seized their lands and property without a shadow of claim, and drove hundreds of them homeless across the Rio Grande." Accused of harboring runaway slaves and denigrated by racial stereotypes ("They're most as black as niggers . . . and ten times as treacherous," grumbled a ranger), Tejanos steadily lost ground through the nineteenth and early twentieth centuries.[29] When they fought back, most notably under the leadership of Juan Cortina, who led a series of border rebellions between 1859 and 1875, Texas Rangers responded with indiscriminate killing and forced depopulation. Anglo officials dismissed irredentism as "bandit activity" and justified race war as law enforcement.

Such is the historical foundation of policing in Texas. From the beginning, the territory's pioneering lawmen did less to suppress crime in any conventional sense than to force open lands for Anglo American settlement. Acting on behalf of a constitutional order that defined slavery as an inviolable property right and excluded Native Americans, African Americans, and many Tejanos from citizenship, the Texas Rangers, according to historian David Montejano, "represented the armed force of the Anglo-Texas order."[30] The result was not domestic tranquility but white hegemony, structured by law and reinforced by violence—what would become the defining characteristic of Texas criminal justice for most of its history.

By clearing the land for slavery-based agriculture, the Texas Rangers set the stage for rapid population and economic growth. After Texas's independence, and even more furiously after annexation by the United States, American immigrants flooded into the territory. Between the revolution and 1860, Texas grew by an astonishing 1,100 percent, from fifty-three thousand to more than six hundred thousand. So common were the overland migrations that travelers reported seeing ubiquitous "Gone to Texas" shingles hanging from abandoned homesteads across the South.[31]

Fueling this prodigious growth was a single precious commodity—cotton, a crop that grew so thick in Texas, according to Featherstone-haugh, that "dazzling white [fields] create rather a painful sensation in the eyes." Between 1849 and 1859, total production soared from 58,072 to 431,463 bales. So lucrative was the cash crop that investors devoted every dollar of available capital to land and forced labor. "Many a planter . . . allowed his corn to go to waste in order to apply the time of his hands to picking cotton," observed Olmsted. Whatever proceeds accumulated, Texans used to "buy *more negroes* and *enlarge* their plantations."[32]

Stephen Austin had worried early on that his beloved colony would become "San Domingonized"—that is, that slavery would overwhelm free labor and undermine social stability as it had in the Caribbean—and this is precisely the direction in which Texas moved after he led it to independence. Although whites flocked to the territory, bonded blacks arrived at an even faster rate. In 1836, there were about five thousand slaves in Texas, roughly 10 percent of the total population. By 1860, the slave population had multiplied thirty-six-fold to constitute a third of the total. In its soil and slaves lie "the germ of Texas's future greatness," asserted a French traveler, Frederic Gaillardet, in 1839. And if ever the "issue of slavery . . . shall at last erupt . . . [and] . . . that great association, the American Union, should be one day torn apart," he prophesied, "Texas unquestionably would be in the forefront of the new confederacy."[33]

Despite Texas's vastness, slave agriculture developed within a comparably narrow swath of territory. It stretched from the piney woods of the upper Sabine in the north to the hill country in the west and to the Nueces in the south. This cotton-slavery belt made up only two-fifths of the state's landmass, yet it constituted the core of Texas settler society. Before the Civil War, more than 90 percent of the state's population lived within this plantation zone. Although the majority of Texans were subsistence-oriented family farmers, nine of every ten bales of cotton—the mainstay of the cash economy—were produced by slaves.[34] Most Americans think of the Lone Star State as western, but in reality the heart of Texas lies in the Deep South.

Around Austin's original colony, where shallow-draft steamboats on the Colorado, Brazos, and Trinity rivers facilitated transport to market, slavery developed with special intensity. In counties like Brazoria, Fort Bend, Walker, and Polk, slaves made up a majority of the population by

1860. These same counties would later host the state's largest penal plantations, institutions like Wynne, Goree, Harlem, Ramsey, and Polunsky. To this day, Texas prison units remain clustered within the boundaries of the old cotton-slavery belt. Not until the 1980s did the state locate a prison beyond it.[35]

Slavery dominated Texas's political economy for less than two generations, yet it left a deep and lasting imprint on the state's social relations. Because the largest plantations worked by the most slaves tended to generate the highest returns, slavery not only institutionalized the racial divide but widened class inequities among whites. By 1860, slaveholders made up 27 percent of Texas households but controlled 73 percent of all wealth. Concentration of capital, in turn, brokered disproportionate political influence. In 1850, slave owners held 58 percent of all local, state, and federal offices in Texas; by 1860, their share had climbed to 68 percent. Just as Stephen Austin had feared, Texas was becoming not just a society with slaves but a slave society.[36]

In the realm of culture, too, slavery had a profound impact—one with abiding implications for the evolution of crime and punishment. Among African Americans, the institution of slavery, along with draconian restrictions on free blacks, ruled out economic or educational advancement except in the rarest cases. Although slaves produced the lion's share of wealth in Texas, they were consigned to a legally structured underclass from which their descendants would have great difficulty escaping.

Slavery's violence also left its mark. Although not every slave was physically brutalized, they all lived within brutality's shadow. "If [the master's slaves] act like they his work hosses they git along all right," recalled Allen Manning, a former slave from the Gatesville area. "But if they don't—Oh, oh!" With only the weakest protections under law, slaves could be whipped, beaten, burned, crippled, or killed for any real or perceived infraction.[37] A slave named Ida Henry recounted that her mistress had once grabbed a fork and gouged out a cook's eye for undercooking the potatoes. Outside the big house, slaves had it bad, too, she said. If the overseer didn't like the quality of the slaves' work, "he would lock 'em in jail some nights without food and kept 'em dere all night, and after whipping 'em de next morning would only give 'em bread and water to work on till noon."[38]

Slave discipline not only left physical and psychological scars but fostered a cynical view of law and the master class. "I wouldn't trust a white man no more than a rattler," pronounced Millie Manuel. Although the risks were great, some slaves took to mitigating their wretched lot through theft. Shortly after his arrival in Texas, Frederick Olmsted was warned "never to leave anything portable within sight of a negro," advice he took to heart after losing a favorite rope. From the perspective of many slaves, pinching represented illicit compensation rather than crime. "Them that was in the white folks' house had pretty good meals, but them that was in the field they would feed just about like they would the hogs," recalled John Williams, who was born a slave in Dallas. To supplement, "they'd go out and steal ol' master's sweet potatoes and roast them in the fire. They'd go out and steal a hog and kill it. All of it was theirn; they raised it. They wasn't to say stealin' it; they just went out and got it."[39] Such reasoning persisted into the twentieth century. As W. E. B. DuBois observed in *The Souls of Black Folk,* "Negroes . . . look upon the courts as instruments of injustice and oppression, and upon those convicted in them as martyrs and victims."[40]

Among whites, Texas's preeminent socioeconomic institution had enduring effects as well. Just as Austin feared, the proliferation of slavery, which he once called "the unanswerable inconsistency of *free* and liberal republicans," had a corrosive influence on Texas's political culture. Fearful of rebellion and antagonistic to humanitarian reform, slaveholders embraced anti-intellectualism in the public sphere and hostility to regulation and taxation in government—ideological traditions that characterize southern conservatism into the present. Although Texas's various constitutions safeguarded the civil liberties of white citizens, in practice dissent or even debate on the slavery question was barely tolerated. During the buildup to the Civil War, churches and newspapers suspected of disloyalty were closed. In 1862, forty suspected abolitionists were rounded up and hung in Gainesville, some of them convicted in irregular, military-style tribunals. "Those who are not for us, must be against us," admonished the *Galveston Weekly News,* summing up the spirit of the times. "There can be no middle ground. Those who denounce slavery as an evil, in any sense, are the enemies of the South."[41]

The coercive habits of slavery also crept into everyday life. Masters and overseers most frequently enacted slavery's violence, but according to law, all able-bodied white men were expected to serve on patrols, which administered whippings and beatings for pass-law violations and other infractions. Because so many whites took part in the physical brutalization of blacks, Olmsted argued that slavery blunted their sensibilities. Not only did Anglo Texans curse at and abuse their slaves, he reported, but they mistreated each other as well. "Slavery . . . draws out and strengthens, by example and exercise, . . . the natural lust of authority." Many slaves agreed. "I can tell you the life of a slave was not rosy," explained Martin Jackson, but "slavery, I believe, had a more degrading influence upon slave owners than it had upon the slaves."[42]

Raised in a culture of dominion, white men in Texas and other southern states came to place an unusually high premium on personal valor and patriarchal respect. Whereas the merchant-friendly value of restraint held sway in the North, a chivalric code prevailed in the South. A "cult of honor" took hold, argues the cultural historian Bertram Wyatt-Brown. Honor became "a people's theology, a set of prescriptions endowed with an almost sacred symbolism."[43]

According to honor's strictures, manly self-assurance and martial daring earned community esteem, whereas any public slight invited violent retaliation. "At the slightest quarrel, knife or pistol comes to hand," reported Tocqueville. The result was an extraordinary prevalence of male violence, not only between master and slave but among whites themselves. Dueling, feuds, lynching, and public executions all developed with greater intensity in the South, as did everyday homicides, which have occurred with more frequency for as long as records have been kept. "Violence was inextricably woven into the most fundamental aspects of life in the South," observed historian John Hope Franklin. Even today, despite the desectionalizing effects of migration and mass communication, southerners kill one another at twice the national rate.[44]

A fractious culture of honor combined with the routine brutality of slavery—not to mention near-constant warfare and liberal consumption of alcohol—fostered vice and viciousness in Texas. Although too few statistics exist for us to measure antebellum crime rates with any precision, court records and newspapers, as well as accounts by visitors and residents, suggest that lawlessness ran rampant. So prevalent were reports of drunkenness, banditry, and murder that Olmsted concluded Texas must have been settled disproportionately by ruffians. "Probably a more reckless and vicious crew was seldom gathered," he remarked.[45]

Much of the violence took place in rural areas, but Texas's growing towns held their own. According to Jeff Hamilton, a former slave, the new city of Houston was already a "wild and wooly place" by the middle of the nineteenth century, "a paradise for saloon-keepers, dance-hall men, and knights of the green cloth." "Nobody will ever know how many men were drugged, robbed, and knocked on the head, and their bodies thrown into the Buffalo Bayou."[46]

Leading citizens fretted that an inconsistent and poorly designed legal system only exacerbated Texas's crime problems. Although the Republic's 1836 penal code itemized a long list of torments—the gallows for "entic[ing] away any slave," and branding with a "T" for theft—prosecutors complained that they were too seldom applied.[47] Anglos, in particular, cleared up most convictions with a fine. Even in homicide cases, defendants simply asserted that they had acted in defense of person or honor and thereby escaped punishment altogether. "Killing of a fellow was looked upon with greater lenience than theft," grumbled a physician.

Critics assailed juries for "seizing upon the slightest points . . . to rescue a victim of punishment." Yet from the 1840s forward, a growing number of town-dwelling politicians began to argue that Texas's bloody code was itself the problem. "[Our criminal law is] vindictive in its character, impolitic in its consequences . . . and revolting to the finer feelings of the heart," asserted one lawmaker. Nothing had ever come of the 1836 constitution's call for the law to be based on "the principles of reformation" rather than "vindictive justice." But by the middle of the nineteenth century, with war brewing and the promise of American annexation growing nearer, Texans looked with renewed interest to reforms being implemented in the United States. To replace the republic's "sanguinary laws," they began advocating the construction of a new sort of institution, one that had been conceived shortly after the American Revolution and had already planted itself across the Atlantic and throughout the Americas: the penitentiary.[48]

## "HOUSE OF REPENTANCE"

Most of us take prisons for granted. Every American state has prisons, as do the vast majority of countries. Likewise, most of us accept imprisonment as the normal penalty for serious lawbreaking. We say casually, "If you do the crime, you do the time." Prisons attract their share of policy debates, of course. Politicians disagree about how prisons ought to be managed or how long inmates ought to stay in them. Rarely, however, do they question whether prisons ought to exist in the first place, whether imprisonment ought to be our felony punishment of first resort.[49]

The prevalence of prisons and their formidable architecture suggest permanence not change. Yet the prison as we know it—an institution that houses convicted lawbreakers for protracted, precisely measured periods of time—is a product only of the modern age. It was "discovered," in the words of historian David Rothman, toward the end of the eighteenth century. Although we tend to associate prisons with grim deprivation, at their founding they were promoted as citadels of the Enlightenment. They were expected not only to regenerate the wicked but ultimately to rid society of crime altogether, thus making orderly societies safe for democracy.

Originally called "penitentiaries," because they promised to induce holy penitence among their wards, these novel disciplinary institutions took shape in the United States soon after the birth of the republic. The rise of the penitentiary was thus bound up with the rise of American democracy, a paradox not lost on Tocqueville and Beaumont, who toured the young nation's prisons on behalf of the French government. "While society in the United States gives the example of the most extended liberty," they observed, "the prisons of the same country offer the spectacle of the most complete despotism."[50]

Prisons, the archaeological record suggests, are as old as civilization. Yet until modern times, they were rarely used for prolonged confinement of common criminals, much less for rehabilitation. In medieval Europe, the Catholic Church assembled an early network of monastic detention chambers, but they typically confined refractory clergy and targets of the Inquisition rather than lay offenders. A more prevalent precursor to the modern prison was the workhouse, which took hold in northern Europe from the sixteenth century, an era of widespread economic dislocation and hardening bourgeois attitudes toward the poor. Known in England as "houses of correction" because they aspired to inculcate idlers with "the habits of industry," these garrisons of forced labor sometimes held convicted felons, but overwhelmingly they disciplined debtors, vagabonds, and unruly servants.[51]

With respect to crime—a legally defined category of conduct that has demonstrated considerable elasticity over time—early modern leaders favored corporal over carceral sanctions. Throughout Europe, whipping, fines, and banishment were the most common penalties, followed by every type of mutilation, from branding to amputation. For crimes defined as especially grievous—murder and arson, to be sure, but also, in England, rioting, beast stealing, and even illegal fruit picking—the standard punishment was death, which European powers inflicted with both regularity and theatricality. There were "merciful," presumably quick deaths: beheading, hanging, garroting, and burying alive. But there were also nastier ways to go: boiling or burning alive, as well as breaking on the wheel, in which the executioner fractured bones one by one with an iron bar before delivering the coup de grâce to the heart.[52]

Europe's most horrific execution techniques declined from the seventeenth century. Merchant elites—their own bodies increasingly insulated from physical violence—began to fear that such spectacles incited rather than intimidated the rabble.[53] Instead, European powers, especially England, turned to a sanction that bolstered their growing empires: transportation. Tens of thousands of miscreants were captured on the streets and shipped across the high seas, sometimes to labor unto death, other times to found new societies. In Colonial America, as many as a quarter of eighteenth-century British immigrants were convicts, and an even greater number were slaves. The future "land of the free" began as a land of the bound.[54]

In the New World, too, legal authorities primarily relied on punishments of pain and shame: branding, stocks, and, above all, the whip. The purpose, according to clergymen at the time, was not so much to cure crime, which seemed beyond reach, but to control it, to check humankind's natural inclination toward sin. "By These [laws], Sinners are often awed and restrained, and kept from many Villanies which otherwise their Lusts and Passions would hurry them on unto," proferred Reverend Samuel Checkley in 1733. A range of penalties also reinforced the reigning social hierarchy. Free and propertied whites could escape all but the most serious convictions with a fine. Outsiders generally faced banishment. Slaves, free blacks, Indians, and white servants, by contrast, most often felt the lash.[55]

Lurking beyond all of these punishments was the gallows, the ultimate threat to serious offenders and recidivists of all sorts, even pickpockets. Although America's penal codes were never so bloody as England's, executions proliferated over the course of the eighteenth century. This was especially true in the southern colonies with the largest slave populations. Even in the Northeast, however, race added intensity to capital cases. After a Massachusetts slave named Mark was hanged in 1755 for poisoning his master, for example, his body was hung in chains for years afterward so that "servants [would remember] their own Place, the Masters serve with Fear."

In such cases, the visible infliction of court-ordered death was meant not only to extirpate enemies but to instruct the public on the dangers of crime and the potency of the law. They were pedagogical as well as punitive affairs, and they reached a great many pupils. Although executions were relatively rare outside of the largest cities, they drew great crowds, among the largest in Colonial America. When Katherine Garrett, a Native American convicted of infanticide, was hung in New London, Connecticut, in 1738, she "was surrounded with a Vast Circle of people . . . more Numerous, perhaps, than Ever was gathered together before, on any Occasion, in this Colony." Ministers vied to deliver sermons from the scaffold. As he prepared to preach before "one of the greatest Assemblies, ever known in these parts of the World," Cotton Mather noted in his diary that a hanging could be "a very *miserable*, but . . . also a *very profitable* Spectacle."[56]

Terrible punishments accompanied by edifying sermons made for effective theater in small, stable communities, but their meanings were hard to control in the colonies' burgeoning cities. As towns like Boston, New York, and Philadelphia swelled with multihued immigrants, the Anglo-American elite began to worry that public punishments were doing more harm than good. "Far from preventing crimes by the terror they excite in . . . spectators, [public punishments] are directly calculated to produce them," admonished the renowned physician Benjamin Rush. "How often do we find pockets picked under a gallows, and highway robberies committed in sight of the gibbet?"[57]

Leading colonists also worried that gruesome penalties discouraged juries from delivering guilty verdicts, with more crime the result. "Scarce a morning arrives, but we hear of some house or store having been broken open the past night," exclaimed one Massachusetts resident. "It must give every man of feeling the most sensible pain, when he observes how insufficient our penal laws are to answer."[58] Like their counterparts across the Atlantic, prominent Americans feared that sanguinary sanctions were inadequate for an emerging age of the market, that the gallows was too harsh an instrument of discipline and the whip insufficiently severe.

As Americans broke from the mother country, they devoted special attention to moderating the "Bloody Code." "Capital punishments are the natural offspring of monarchical governments," Rush contended. "Kings consider their subjects as property; no wonder, therefore, they shed their blood with as little emotion as men shed the blood of their sheep." But criminal justice innovation did not tilt entirely toward mercy. Propertied men at the helm of the new government spoke proudly of creating a "land of liberty," but they also worried about every man, particularly among the rabble, doing "just as he pleases." Democratic governance—predicated as it was on "the public good"—could only survive if "natural liberty [were] restrained in such a manner as to render society one large family; where every one must consult his neighbor's happiness as well as his own."[59] To the nation's framers, this contradiction lay at the heart of republicanism. They desired to safeguard individual rights but also to impose order, to expand liberty but also constrict it.

In the interest of a stable democracy, early American elites came to believe that the franchise would have to be closely guarded and that some persons' liberty would have to be curtailed. But how? With respect to slaves and other subject persons, private or military discipline prevailed. When it came time to design court-ordered sanctions for transgressive citizens, however, no immediate consensus emerged. Selling lawbreakers into servitude remained an option, but by the late eighteenth century there were few buyers (African slaves were regarded as better investments). In Pennsylvania, officials organized chained work gangs, known as "wheelbarrow men," but when the wretches rioted and ran off, policy makers went back to the drawing board. Each alternative presented its own difficulties, and a growing assortment of reformers convinced themselves that the time had come to invest in houses of long-term confinement and criminal reformation. What they needed was a new type of institution "suited to the genius of a republic."[60]

Benjamin Rush was one of the most outspoken and influential of these reform advocates. A signer of the Declaration of Independence and an eloquent, energetic man with aquiline features and penetrating eyes, Rush was the most acclaimed medical doctor in early America. When yellow fever broke out in 1793, he famously stayed in Philadelphia to treat the afflicted (though his relentless bloodletting may well have led some victims to wish he had left). A decade later, when Thomas Jefferson asked Rush to prepare a medical kit for the Lewis and Clark expedition, the doctor included six hundred "Thunderclapper" pills, all-purpose purgatives that consisted largely of toxic mercury.[61]

In the treatment of mental illness, Rush is regarded as such a forerunner that his visage graces the seal of the American Psychiatric Association, yet here, too, his efforts may have caused more harm than healing. As treatments for insanity, Rush ordered solitary confinement, dietary restrictions, and bleeding, as well as prolonged spins on a rotating board meant to force blood to the head. All these cures were available to his own son, who suffered from mental infirmity, but still the young man descended into madness. He spent the remainder of his life in another of his father's favored institutions, the insane asylum.[62]

While most noted for his contributions to science, Rush also weighed in on politics and society. As a child of the Great Awakening and student of the Enlightenment, he embraced all manner of causes: abolitionism, medical care for the indigent, and public education for boys and girls. While Rush devoted much of his career to aiding the ill and unfortunate, however, he was motivated as much by fear as sympathy. Like other bourgeois reformers, he desired not only to succor the suffering but to stabilize the social order.

Rush's writings on education reveal this repressive strain of reformism as clearly as his later pronouncements on punishment. His classic essay "Thoughts Upon the Mode of Education Proper in a Republic," for example, proposed that "the authority of our masters be as absolute as possible," so that "we prepare our youth for the subordination of laws and thereby qualify them for becoming good citizens." The ultimate objective of education, he contended, was "to convert men into republican machines."[63]

The study of crime, Rush believed, was a natural complement to his work on education and mental illness, and once he formulated his views, he presented them with characteristic zeal. The occasion was a March 1787 gathering of merchants, ministers, and physicians at the town house of Benjamin Franklin, who had recently returned from Paris. The assembled gentlemen shared an acute concern for social stability. Only a month before, the Massachusetts militia had crushed Shays's Rebellion, sentencing fourteen radical farmers to death. In Pennsylvania, the legislature had recently mandated sanctions that "reclaim rather than destroy," but the first attempts with the wheelbarrow men were going badly.[64] As Rush stood in Franklin's salon to speak, therefore, he had the rapt attention of his audience.

Rush began his address with a cocksure assault on public and physical punishments. Sanguinary sanctions were injurious for a flotilla of reasons, he argued. They humiliated and hardened offenders, and, by arbitrary application, they created "a hatred of all law and government." More philosophically, Rush asserted that punishment dramas blunted sensibility—"the vicegerent of the divine benevolence of our world"— and thus tattered the moral fabric of civilization. In short, Rush insisted, "all *public* punishments tend to make bad men worse, and to increase crimes, by their influence upon society."[65]

To replace "the gallows, the pillory, the stocks, the whipping-post, and the wheel-barrow," Rush proposed that "a large house be erected" capable of "reforming criminals and preventing crimes." Bringing together ideas from the pioneering Italian criminologist Cesare Beccaria, the English penal reformer John Howard, as well as Christian Universalism and medical science, this new type of institution would represent a revolutionary advance over its forebears. Since public punishments corrupt, it would administer secret penalties behind foreboding walls. Since idleness and carousing breed crime, it would hold delinquents in solitary silence and make them work. And since "personal liberty is so dear to all men," this "receptacle for criminals" would inflict, by denying individuals their freedom, a "punishment so severe that death has often been preferred to it." With its cells and warders, Rush recognized that his creation would resemble jails and workhouses, which were already commonplace in the early republic, but he insisted that it "by no means be called a prison." By contrast, Rush envisioned a "benevolent and salutary" institution, more akin to a hospital than a dungeon. He called it a "house of repentance."[66]

As with all of Rush's projects, he invested this one with grand ambition. Just as public punishments had undermined civilization, this house of repentance would be its salvation. In the image of the messiah who "opened the gates of paradise to a dying thief," it would reclaim the offender from fiendish habits and return him to society, where "friends and family [will] bathe his cheeks with tears of joy." Because prolonged solitude and loss of liberty would "diffuse terror through a community," Rush also believed his "abode of misery" would deter crime.

The end result, he concluded grandiloquently, would be a scientific marvel that would earn him and his collaborators universal gratitude. Just as Americans had devised a superior form of government, he proclaimed, they would now "invent the most speedy and effectual method . . . of restoring the vicious part of mankind to virtue and happiness, and of extirpating a portion of vice from the world."[67]

Rush's address electrified his audience. The text was distributed as a pamphlet, and prominent citizens, many of them Quakers, soon convinced the legislature to reorganize Philadelphia's Walnut Street Jail into the world's first "penitentiary," the word borrowed from ecclesiastical law. Disappointments followed. As the inmate population grew, drunkenness, sex, escapes, arson, and riots flowered, such that the first penitentiary ended up concentrating the same ills it was supposed to extinguish.[68]

Undeterred, Rush's allies insisted that the problem lay not with the penitentiary ideal but its imperfect realization. They proposed the construction of an entirely new and expanded penitentiary, one designed for solitary confinement rather than adapted to it. After a particularly bloody melee on Walnut Street in 1820, the legislature agreed, and construction began three years later. Dr. Rush himself would not live to see the result—he died in 1813—but the new structure represented the culmination of his vision. Built atop a cleared cherry orchard northwest of downtown, the penitentiary was the most expensive building in America when it opened in 1829, and the most philosophically ambitious prison ever conceived.[69]

With its thirty-foot walls, castellated guard towers, and gothic facade, the Eastern State Penitentiary, or Cherry Hill, became an instant sensation, attracting thousands of visitors from around the world. It represented the architectural union of coercion and Christian charity, a monument to both the idealism and determination of the early republic. From the outside, the fortress was meant to inspire "wholesome dread" and deter transgression. Behind the walls, it had an even grander purpose: to so completely isolate some 450 inmates that they would fall "prey to remorses of [the] soul and the terrors of . . . imagination" and finally turn to their only remaining companion, God.

By the standards of the time, the architects went to extraordinary lengths toward this end. They built cell blocks in an expensive wheel-and-spoke design, such that every tier could be constantly watched from a central rotunda. In theory, though, there was little need for surveillance because each cell constituted a universe in itself. Enclosed by thick stone walls and double doors, with vaulted ceilings and indoor plumbing, each housing compartment contained a meal slot, a skylight, a peephole for guards, and a tiny individual exercise yard. New prisoners arrived hooded, so they had no sense of their surroundings, and once a heavy oak door shut behind them they were expected to labor and live in their cell "without interruption until the expiration of [their] punishment." Tocqueville and Beaumont reported that Cherry Hill achieved "perfect isolation." Each "convict . . . is separated from the whole world."[70]

Although Pennsylvania's "silent system" represented the purest embodiment of the penitentiary ideal, it was not without rivals. New York was building prisons of its own, and by the 1820s its two most notable institutions—Auburn, located near the Erie Canal, and Sing Sing, up the Hudson from New York City—had settled into a regimen that many observers regarded as equally reformatory but more pragmatic. Whereas Pennsylvania focused on reclaiming the soul, New York emphasized disciplining the body. It constructed prisons that resembled factories more than monasteries and that aimed for obedience before redemption. As in Philadelphia, the New York penitentiaries maintained solitary cells and prohibited inmate interaction. "The silence within these vast walls . . . is that of death," attested Beaumont and Tocqueville. By day, however, New York inmates marched in lockstep from their cells and set to toil in communal workshops. Labor rather than solitude reigned, without "a single instant given to recreation." The ultimate purpose, explained the principal keeper at Auburn, was to make man into "a silent and insulated working machine."[71]

Although the Pennsylvania and New York systems seem similar in retrospect—both promised criminal reformation through silence, labor, and solitary confinement—their differences ignited a furious debate in Jacksonian America. Friends of Cherry Hill denounced the New York lockups as fatally compromised. Congregate workshops would allow "mutual contagion" or would require "barbarous discipline" to maintain silence, they warned. New York advocates countered that Pennsylvania's regime was unworkable, needlessly expensive, and "at variance with the human constitution." If every inmate ultimately returns to his community, they reasoned, better to "give him the habits of society and first teach him to obey" than to seal him in stone.[72]

Both camps attracted followers. The silent system appealed to ministers and philosophers, but New York had the edge with policy makers. Cheaper to build and more profitable to operate, Auburn and Sing Sing served as prototypes for all but a handful of the penitentiaries that sprang up in the 1830s and 1840s. In the end, economy trumped moral absolutism.[73]

Whatever their differences, the New York and Pennsylvania systems proved foundational not only as blueprints of penitential discipline but for the failures they produced. With their strict prohibitions undermined by congregate temptations, New York's prisons were especially prone to disorder. Silence, the managers discovered, could only be maintained by force. Whipping is "very frequent; and the least fault is punished with its application," noted Beaumont and Tocqueville.[74]

Practice diverged most sharply from idealism with respect to women prisoners. Shut up in a third-floor attic at Auburn, women were spared the isolation and regimentation of men, but they were also neglected and left vulnerable to assault. "To be a *male* convict in this prison would be quite tolerable," opined the chaplain, "but to be a *female* convict, for any protracted period, would be worse than death." A major scandal erupted in 1826 when an inmate became pregnant at Auburn and then died after being flogged by guards.[75] Although the penitentiary had been proposed as a replacement for corporal punishment, in practice, it only subsumed it.

The Pennsylvania system, its champions maintained, allowed fewer opportunities for conflict and abuse. "Each cell is a prison in itself," reported Beaumont and Tocqueville, "and the convicts who are detained there cannot render themselves guilty of offenses. . . . There is no punishment, because there is no infraction." In truth, isolated prisoners found myriad ways to communicate with each other and provoke their keepers. They tapped out messages on pipes and dug tunnels in search of deliverance. In response, officials developed an arsenal of supposedly nonviolent sanctions: food deprivation, cold water ducking, and an "iron gag" designed to render speech impossible.[76]

Even in the absence of such disciplinary techniques, long-term isolation could be devastating. It was for this reason that Charles Dickens, who visited the prison in 1842, concluded that the silent system was "cruel and wrong." "In its intention . . . it is kind, humane, and meant for reformation," he acknowledged, but "I believe that very few men are capable of estimating the immense amount of torture and agony which this dreadful punishment, prolonged for years, inflicts upon the sufferers." Although the author of *Oliver Twist* was familiar with bleak institutions, he wrote that he had never seen "more dejected, heart-broken, wretched creature[s]" anywhere. Even the bloody code was preferable, he remarked, for the "daily tampering with the mysteries of the brain [is] immeasurably worse than any torture of the body."[77]

In light of their propensity to abuse and in the absence of any sign that they reformed criminals or prevented crime, we might expect this grand institutional experiment to have been abandoned. Yet even as the penitentiary proved itself a practical failure, it coincided so neatly with the nation's emerging political economy and reigning ideas about disorder and discipline that it flourished rather than fading away. Precisely measured penalties predicated on the denial of cherished liberty; spiritual discipline in private instead of gory displays before unruly crowds; profitable labor wrested from previously idle miscreants; deterrence wrapped in Christian benevolence—the penitentiary promised so much that it was embraced even as it delivered so little. Propelled by widening class fissures and widespread unease about social stability, all but a handful of northern and border states erected penitentiaries. Latin America and Europe built them, too, and by the middle of the nineteenth century they had come to seem as natural as schools and hospitals. Even as the first versions degenerated, subsequent institution builders would become so convinced of their righteousness that they would hold up the penitentiary as a model for all of society. "Could we all be put on prison fare, for the span of two or three generations," proposed Ohio's prison chaplain in 1851, "the world would ultimately be better for it."[78]

## THE WALLS

In the slave states, noted Beaumont and Tocqueville, the utopian "*monomanie* of the penitentiary system" never caught fire.[79] Southerners built local jails, but they came to the state penitentiary movement haltingly and with anemic budgets. In contrast to their northern counterparts, southern prisons faced withering criticism and were subject to protracted debate; in many cases, the institutions were abandoned during Reconstruction. Ironically, the states that would become the nation's most avid jailers in the twentieth century gave the penitentiary the cold shoulder in the nineteenth.

Historians have proposed various reasons for the South's go-slow approach. In the early 1800s, most southern states were sparsely populated and overwhelmingly rural. The electorate tended to be parochial rather than cosmopolitan, skeptical of expensive schemes cooked up by distant central governments. Accustomed to settling disputes themselves, often violently, white southerners only reluctantly embraced formal legal institutions. As Andrew Jackson's mother once famously admonished, "the law affords no remedy . . . that can satisfy the feelings of a true man."[80]

At the heart of southern ambivalence toward penitentiaries was slavery, "upon which the very existence of the [South] depended," according to John Calhoun. Out of the cauldron of slavery, with its endemic violence and dehumanization, emerged a political culture that favored honor-bound eye-for-an-eye retaliation over legalistic restraint, sanguinary over spiritual sanctions. Because of slavery, leading southerners fought vigorously against intrusive government and all types of humanitarian initiatives, which they feared led inexorably to abolitionism—a fear only confirmed by the abolitionist pronouncements of Benjamin Rush and other penitentiary *philosophes*.[81]

To white southerners, the "republican edifice" rested on the ideal of individual sovereignty free from any external interference. A stable democracy, they believed, required that no white man entrusted with the vote be dependent on another and that degradation be concentrated exclusively among utterly dependent slaves. For southern critics, then, the notion of locking up white men and making them toil amounted to an intolerable inversion of a divinely ordained social hierarchy. "Under the Penitentiary system, the free-born citizen is made to labor directly under the lash as a slave," fulminated a North Carolina commentator in 1846. "Is not this worse than death?"[82]

These criticisms notwithstanding, southern states did build prisons, though reluctantly. In the few instances that penitentiaries were put up to a popular vote—in Alabama in 1834 and North Carolina in 1846—they were soundly rejected. Nonetheless, southern governors, who stood to augment their executive powers, and legislators, who tended to be more swayed by transatlantic currents in legal thought than their constituents, by and large came to support prison building. They worried about the institutions' "encroachment on individual rights," but they also came to see the penitentiary as the embodiment of progress, the intellectual progeny of "the wisest and best of men that have lived."

The South's integration into the global market also factored in. Border states and those with thriving commercial cities—Virginia, Kentucky, Georgia, Maryland, and Tennessee—built prisons first, followed in the late 1830s and 1840s by Louisiana, Missouri, Arkansas, Mississippi, Alabama, and Texas. Only Florida and the Carolinas held out beyond the Civil War.[83]

As the region's early flagship state, Virginia provides an illustrative case study. An avid reader of Beccaria, Thomas Jefferson was among the first to advocate replacing the state's corporal sanctions with reform-oriented alternatives. "The experience of all ages and countries hath shewn that cruel and sanguinary laws defeat their own purpose," he averred. While chairing a 1776 committee to revise Virginia's laws, he proposed a "gradation of punishments" oriented toward "the reformation of offenders" and their "useful [deployment] in various labors for the public." Virginia's House of Delegates—in a "rage against Horse Stealers," according to James Madison—ignored the recommendations. But when the state finally curtailed capital punishment in 1796, lawmakers authorized the construction of "a gaol and penitentiary house."

Jefferson himself sketched an early plan, an ambitious panoptical design that he borrowed from an architect in France. The institution that Virginia actually built, however, was considerably more modest, an elegant but impractical four-story horseshoe without plumbing or adequate ventilation. Although dedicated nominally to mercy, it delivered misery. Moisture oozed from its cold walls. The stench from an open sewer pit filled the air. Cholera crept from cell to cell. After six years, the first keeper, a brick contractor with no prison experience, admitted that his institution was a "truly disagreeable and dangerous place."[84]

As in Philadelphia's Walnut Street Jail, Virginia's prison ended up congregating rather than replacing corporal punishments. Officials came to regard their wards as "obstinate, irritable, and often desperate," and they reached regularly for the whip. Keepers developed special animus toward slaves and free blacks, who made up a larger portion of the prison population than in other southern states, where master discipline prevailed. "Although the free white persons usually confined in this institution, are, for the most part, of the lowest order of society," commented the superintendent in 1823, "the free negroes and mulattos are certainly a grade or so below them, and should not be associated with them."[85]

Although they got off to a slow start, other southern states followed Virginia's degenerative example. Penitentiaries were everywhere introduced as beacons of civilization but invariably became blots on it. Even more so than in the North, finances were always tight. Politicians complained that prisons were "vampire[s] upon the public treasury" and demanded profits rather than appropriations requests. The result was a bevy of moneymaking schemes, from railroad contracts to cotton milling, some of which proved remunerative but rarely reformatory. In every state, disorder and scandal reigned. Escapes, beatings, killings, fires, revolts, pardon-selling imbroglios, and outbreaks of disease were perennial events. Almost no effort was made at reclamation. "With the exception of 170 copies of small, badly printed Bibles," Alabama's inspectors bitterly reported in 1852, "not a dime has ever been expended by . . . the legislature in furnishing the miserable inmates of the Penitentiary with Knowledge or the means of reformation of any kind."[86]

Northern penitentiaries were plagued by similar troubles but, according to Beaumont and Tocqueville, a spirit of millennial idealism mitigated their torments. The "zeal of religious instructors" infused northern penitentiaries with a higher purpose, they argued. "It is because their aim is great" that "the penitentiary establishment [reaches] a much higher morality."[87] Antebellum southern states by contrast, even though the majority of their prisoners were white, made few serious, systematic efforts at prisoner reformation. After emancipation upturned convict demographics, such efforts, meager as they were, generally ceased.

Texas was the last southern state to introduce the penitentiary before the Civil War. For nearly two decades before construction began, authorities had debated and periodically endorsed plans to build a central prison, partly to reduce pressure on local jails. In 1829, the same year that Cherry Hill opened in Pennsylvania, the Mexican state of Coahuila and Texas approved the establishment of a "panoptic prison" in San Antonio.[88] After independence, Texians took up their own prison proposals, though they never managed to erect more than a temporary log barracks. Only in 1848, three years after joining the United States, did Texas finally enact a penitentiary statute that resulted in brick and iron.[89]

Despite the delays, prominent Texans generally supported the establishment of a state penitentiary. Proponents argued that a new prison would "reform the criminal by habits and industry" and put Texas on the map. A penitentiary will "afford the most satisfactory demonstration to the world of our onward march in improvement and civilization," claimed one lawmaker. Profit and production also figured in. Penitentiary builders promised that counties would save money by unloading their felons on the state and that "productive labor" would defray the expenses of confinement. "If a profit of several thousand dollars can be made on the labor of twenty slaves," posited the *Telegraph and Texas Register*, "why may not a similar profit be made on the labor of twenty convicts?"[90]

Before felons could produce profits, however, they first had to be sentenced to forced labor. As the dust of war settled in 1848, therefore, lawmakers not only appropriated funds for a penitentiary but overhauled the state's sanguinary penal code. Henceforth, "the savage practice of the whipping posts" would be abandoned and "confinement to hard labor in the penitentiary" would become the standard penalty for most serious crimes. Such was "the spirit of the age."[91]

Although juries were to set sentences under the new code, the limits defined by legislators reflected a high regard for property and a comparatively permissive attitude toward interpersonal violence. For putting out an eye, cutting off someone's nose, or severing a limb, the term of incarceration ranged from one to ten years. Counterfeiting banknotes, by contrast, earned a sentence of five to ten years. Similarly, nighttime home burglary carried a minimum sentence five times more severe than for rape. Ironically, despite Beaumont and Tocqueville's faith that "every day, punishments which wound humanity become supplanted by milder ones," almost all of Texas's penalties set in 1848 were more lenient than they are today.[92]

If Texas's new penal code was supposed to "elevate the moral character of the whole community," its virtues were never intended for free blacks and slaves. For these subject groups, Texas developed an entirely separate body of law. It defined, on the one hand, generous protections for slaveholders and, on the other, a unique set of crimes that could be committed only by persons of African descent—the use of "insulting or abusive language to . . . any free white person," for instance. For the most part, owners, overseers, and patrollers were free to punish these infractions as they saw fit. When it came to slave crimes defined as serious, however, including insurrection, poisoning, rape, arson, murder, and burglary—whether actually committed or merely attempted—the state prescribed execution, for which masters were duly compensated. Overall, Texas's antebellum statutes "for slaves and free persons of color" included whipping and death but not incarceration or fines. As one expert of southern race law explained, the slave "can be reached only through his body."[93]

Confinement in the penitentiary, dubious honor though it was, would be reserved almost exclusively for nonblacks in the antebellum period. As a consequence, Texas's early penal system enjoyed more generous government support than it would after emancipation. To start operations, the legislature approved expenses totaling nearly fourteen thousand dollars in the first year, 17 percent of the state budget.[94] The penitentiary was to be Texas's premier public institution, "the first public work of any importance in this state."[95]

After selecting Huntsville over competing communities, the governor's first commissioners purchased a "beautiful eminence" just off the town square and began construction in August 1848.[96] While less elaborate than some northern penitentiaries, the plans called for a substantial complex of one hundred thousand square feet. Borrowing from New York more than Pennsylvania, they proposed solitary nighttime cells and communal workshops. The cells themselves would be cramped (five by seven feet), poorly ventilated, without plumbing, and difficult to guard, but in certain areas the prison plans included advances over contemporaries. There would be a hospital, for example, and an entirely separate building for women inmates, who would have their own work area.[97] Surrounding the complex would be an impenetrable brick wall, fifteen feet tall and three feet thick.

An institution designed for forced labor, the prison was built by free and unfree hands alike. Directors hired brick makers, carpenters, and a blacksmith, but they also contracted for slaves, some of them owned by the architect and first superintendent Abner Cook. Once convicts started to arrive at the unsecured site, they were fitted with balls and chains and put to work.[98]

At the time, Huntsville seemed like an odd choice for the state prison. A tiny community cut from the pine forest only a decade earlier, Huntsville had no navigable waterway, no railway, no industry, and a negligible population. What it lacked in amenities, however, it made up in ambition. Sam Houston, the hero of San Jacinto, relocated to the area in 1845, and with his boosting, civic leaders hoped to land not just the prison but a university and the state capitol. Although just five hundred people called Huntsville home, the future "political metropolis of the state," as one newspaper called it, was fast growing.[99] Only a shout away from the prison site, a new courthouse was going up, with storefronts and houses taking positions around the square. Across the street, in front of T. & S. Gibb's general store, traders and gawkers gathered for slave auctions, which took place almost every day.[100]

Although the prison remained unfinished for several years, the first inmate—William Sansom, a farmer sentenced to three years for cattle theft—arrived in October 1849. Fifteen other men took up residence by the end of 1850. Within a decade, the inmate population reached 186.[101] These first prisoners left no record of their experiences, but their statistical profile, painstakingly assembled by the superintendent, bears resemblance to the present. A typical convict in the 1850s was a young, unmarried man carrying a sentence of one to four years. He had been convicted of a property offense—anything from larceny to "Negro stealing"—but had already stumbled before his fateful day in court. Three-fifths of those arriving at the penitentiary admitted that they had no stable trade. Only 7 percent reported that they had received a "good education." Roughly a third were classified as drunkards. Because Texas's penal code was so rigidly partitioned by race, only a handful of African Americans saw the inside of the prison. Among the tatterdemalions deemed worthy of incarceration, however, were a disproportionate number with Mexican roots.[102] Although Texas had only recently broken from Mexico, penitentiary records suggest that the ethnic group we now call Hispanic was already coalescing into an underclass.

If prisoner abjection has shown remarkable continuity over time, so, too, have the problems of prison management. Although the penitentiary in its infancy contained only a modest population and received regular appropriations, it demonstrated precociousness in scandal. In December 1849, only two months after Huntsville began accepting convicts, the state launched its first official investigation into mismanagement and contracting fraud, inaugurating a tradition that would engage nearly every legislature for a century and a half.[103]

As more prisoners arrived, greater difficulties arose. Lawmakers in 1857 heard reports of unauthorized punishments, including whipping, hanging by the thumbs, even branding. As female prisoners joined the mix, beginning with Elizabeth Hofman, a servant convicted of infanticide, the first superintendent faced criticism for making women work as domestics in his private residence. Because managers never followed through on the original plan to house women in a partitioned barracks, allegations of sexual mischief soon followed.[104]

Known as "the Walls" for its impressive fortifications, the new prison quickly proved its ability to concentrate misery and disorder. Yet little of Huntsville's unseemliness made it into the institution's annual reviews. Like bureaucratic hallelujahs everywhere, official documents prepared by the board of directors tended to portray prison management in the best possible light. They highlighted problems only to disparage predecessors or to show how they were being overcome. Typical were surveys drafted for Governor Elisha Pease for the 1855 biennium. Despite seven escapes and five deaths, an outbreak of scurvy, and building delays so serious that the penitentiary still lacked a complete exterior wall seven years after its founding, the directors reported that prison operations were proceeding "harmoniously and satisfactorily." Not only was the "sanitary condition of the institution . . . remarkable" and the construction work progressing "beyond our most sanguine expectations," they announced, but the prisoners themselves "almost without exception [were] orderly and industrious. Indeed, a spirit of rivalry appears to exist, in the amounts of labor, and quality of work done."[105] These roseate reports, like so many that came after them, represented the aspirations of prison managers rather than the reality they governed, a distinction that has too often eluded historians.

Texas's early prison reviews are also instructive for their relentless focus on labor. From the very beginning, directors assured governors that the Walls would be "a source of revenue to the state." They wrote regularly of plans to "make the convicts' labor more profitable" but rarely found space to mention reformation. In the start-up years, convicts were put to work as bricklayers, wagon builders, cabinetmakers, and blacksmiths. But because these trades never generated sizable returns, an enterprising board under the leadership of John Besser, the former keeper of the Walker County jail, seized on the idea of pressing prisoners into a vital but undeveloped sector of the economy. "Situated as we are in the South, with southern principles and views, in as fine a cotton growing region of the country as in the world, would it not be the true policy of our legislature . . . [to] enable our 'State Penitentiary' to be converted into a manufactory of cotton fabrics?" Playing on sectional resentments against "over-grown monopolies" in the North, Besser proposed forging the prison into an instrument of southern industrialization and economic independence.[106]

Although the costs were considerable, construction began on a massive cotton mill within the still unfinished walls at Huntsville in 1853. It was a momentous undertaking. Not only were unskilled convicts required to erect a two-story 13,500-square-foot factory, but some $32,000 worth of spindles, looms, shafting, hangers, pulleys, boilers, and an eighty-horsepower engine had to be imported from Boston to Galveston, then floated up the shallow Trinity (where it got stuck for months), and finally transported overland on a rutty wagon road to Huntsville, where everything was to be reassembled. Two years later, the state had spent $70,000, roughly $20 million in today's dollars.[107]

When completed in 1856, the mill was by far the largest factory in Texas. Although Besser complained that half-grown children could do more work than three-fourths of the convicts, the facility soon proved its worth. Its forty looms could crank out two thousand yards of cotton and wool fabric a day, much of it coarse material favored for slave clothing. Texas's "factory system" thus completed an economic circuit based entirely on unfree labor: slaves produced the raw materials, which convicts then converted to textiles, which then ingloriously covered those same slaves toiling in the fields. The directors proclaimed the arrangement beneficial to planters, beneficial to the South, and beneficial to the Texas treasury. Bearing out their enthusiasm, the mill generated $16,000 more in revenue than was expended for raw materials in the first year.[108] This went a long way toward covering the state's initial investment, but it was small change compared to what lay ahead. Within six years of the factory's opening, southern demand for textiles suddenly exploded, and the Walls emerged as the only facility west of the Mississippi River capable of meeting it.

The Civil War began in Texas several months before the shelling of Fort Sumter—and with prophetic carnage. In the summer of 1860, as the nation's political parties campaigned toward Armageddon, a series of fires broke out in Dallas and other towns. Although no hard evidence connected the conflagrations, jittery whites detected conspiracy. "Great excitement" soon swept the state. "A thousand and one rumors [are] afloat," sputtered one newspaper, while another warned that "the woods . . . seem alive with runaway slaves." Under what we might call "stress interrogation" today, several slaves confessed to "the most diabolical plot that the wickedness of man could invent." Following the instructions of abolitionist white preachers, slave insurrectionists were to torch towns, "poison the inhabitants, assassinate the aged females, and . . . seize and appropriate the young and handsome for their villainous purposes." They would enact precisely the doomsday scenario that feverish ultrasoutherners had been envisioning for years.

In response, Texas's "best citizens" acted swiftly and decisively, showing little patience for cumbersome courtroom justice. In town after town, popular assemblies established committees of public safety, rounded up "any and all suspicious persons," staged hurried tribunals, and carried out summary executions. No precise tally of the dead exists, but the historian who investigated the supposed rebellion most carefully found newspaper accounts of more than hundred extrajudicial hangings. One victim was found "suspended to a pecan tree," his execution posthumously endorsed at a show trial that same evening. Another alleged conspirator "was summarily disposed of by the use of a 'two bit' rope." As in 1835, when rumors of a slave revolt swept through plantations along the Brazos, a mostly imagined rebellion generated reprisals all too real.[109]

In the war itself, white farm boys soon joined the dying. Many would have to make the ultimate sacrifice to settle "the great question . . . of slavery," declared Oran Roberts, chief justice of the Texas Supreme Court and chair of the secession convention. They would do so in great numbers. In the first seven months of combat, some twenty thousand Texans signed up to prove their "Southern valor." Four years later, an appalling number failed to return home. All told, twelve thousand to fifteen thousand men died in the field, about a quarter of Texas's total recruits. "I don't know what will become of us," mourned a woman who lost four relatives in battle. "We are surely scourged if any people were."[110]

If blood constituted Texas's greatest contribution to the "Lost Cause," however, production at the penitentiary was not far behind. Although the South was abundant in cotton and field hands, it had few facilities for weaving the fabrics necessary for tents, supply bags, and uniforms. Once the Union blockaded southern ports, therefore, Huntsville became the number-one textile supplier in the trans-Mississippi West.

"Application upon application is daily being made for Penitentiary goods for the use of the troops," complained Texas's second wartime governor, Francis Lubbock, adding that the state could not hope to "satisfy a tithe of these demands."[111] Already by August 1862, requests from the field sounded notes of desperation. "Their destitution is truly distressing," wrote a commander of some 50,000 troops. "Hundreds of them are almost in a state of nakedness." Other officers were grateful for whatever they received. "But for your noble state it is difficult to see how the war could be successfully prosecuted," observed Major General Theophilus Holmes. "She not only sent her brave and chivalrous men in disproportionate numbers, but she is now feeding the whole Army, and has the means of clothing [it]."[112]

Although much controversy erupted between citizens and soldiers over the distribution of textiles—in 1863, a sodden Confederate unit went so far as to attack the penitentiary in order to seize cloth they needed to make tents—full-scale production continued throughout the war.[113] Between 1861 and 1863, the prison mill churned out more than two million yards of cotton and woolen fabrics, much of it confederate gray. The result was not only a better provisioned army but a healthy bursary. "The financial condition of the institution . . . [is] most flourishing," reported the penitentiary directors in late 1863—this at a time when the wider Confederacy was careening toward economic collapse. So lucrative was the convict textile business that the penitentiary covered all of its costs and deposited net profits into the state treasury. By 1864, the Walls became Texas's leading source of revenue.[114]

Breakneck milling required not just raw materials but a steady supply of labor, a resource that became increasingly scarce as the war tightened the job market. Between 1861 and 1863, the convict population declined from 211 to 157, and officials had to scramble for factory hands. In December 1863, the legislature authorized directors to start hiring workers to keep the machinery in motion, but Huntsville's superintendent, Thomas Carothers, warned against introducing free labor into the prison setting. "The men employed with [the inmates] *must* remain with them," he argued. "Hired labor must be like convicts excluded from intercourse with the world." In order to keep prison workers "docile and obedient," he insisted, "only one kind of labor would be at all admissible within the Walls . . . slave labor."[115]

Acquiring slaves for prison production, however, proved costly and challenging. Contracting with prominent citizens around Huntsville allowed the warden to secure at least two dozen. But because slave prices remained high until the bitter end, prison officials were constantly on the lookout for alternate suppliers. With increasingly audacious entrepreneurship, they bartered rolls of cloth for black POWs, handed out rewards to mercenary slave catchers, and compensated county sheriffs for transporting runaways to Huntsville, where, if unclaimed for six months, they became property "of the keeper of the penitentiary for life."[116] By the conclusion of the war, Huntsville had become not only a profitable depository for convict workers but a center of slave commerce.

The mingling of slave and convict labor confirmed the original fears of southern penitentiary opponents—that imprisonment would ultimately break down the sacred barrier between honor and dishonor, freedom and bondage, white and black. Indeed, by 1863, white men convicted of criminal offenses were not only laboring, like slaves, without pay under threat of the lash, but they were doing so shoulder-to-shoulder with actual slaves. The prison at Huntsville thus became the state's first racially integrated public institution, not by bestowing rights on bondsmen but by stripping them from citizens.

This was but one of many perplexing compromises that southerners made in defending their "peculiar institution." In order to check "a fanatical [northern] government drifting toward centralism," the Confederacy created a powerful and increasingly centralized government of its own. In the name of individual liberty and property rights, southern statesmen silenced their opponents, conscripted thousands of their citizens, and, toward the end, began expropriating slaves to labor on public works. In order to safeguard the basis of their prosperity, white southerners marched headlong into ruin.

In the end, Texas and its confederates were not just defeated but destroyed. More than 250,000 white southerners gave their lives but for naught. Cities, hamlets, and plantations smoldered. With their economies shattered, demographics altered, independence lost, and "domestic institutions" torn asunder, Texas and other conquered states looked toward an uncertain future. If slavery had served, as Chief Justice Roberts claimed, as "the controlling influence that characterizes the civilization peculiar to the southern states," then what would take its place?[117]

This postbellum reckoning touched every corner of southern society, but it raised particularly acute challenges in the realm of crime and punishment. In the war's wake, Texas retained more of its infrastructure than other southern states, including its penitentiary. Whereas other southern prisons had been burned to the ground, the Walls at Huntsville had prospered. Even so, Texas was ill prepared for the aftershocks of total war. Thousands of veterans limped home, spirit broken and destitute but well armed and accustomed to violence. The result, according to Governor Pendleton Murrah, was "fearful demoralization [and] crimes prevailing throughout the state." "In some sections," he declared ominously, "murder, robbery, theft, outrages of every kind against property, against human life, against everything sacred to a civilized people, are frequent and general. Whole communities are under a reign of terror."[118]

Texas's legal system also had to deal with an entirely new population of citizens—and potential offenders: men, women, and children who for the most part possessed nothing but the fragile prize of freedom. By 1865, there were some 250,000 former slaves living in Texas, including more than 30,000 who had been hastily transported to the state for safekeeping during the war. What would be the fate of this propertyless class so recently held as property? How would the courts engage newly independent persons who had previously been subject to private rather than public discipline? These were among the weighty questions raised by what one governor called that "unholy war."[119]

# 3

# "WORSE THAN SLAVERY"

Neither slavery nor involuntary servitude, except as a punishment for crime whereof the party shall have been duly convicted, shall exist within the United States, or any place subject to their jurisdiction.
—THIRTEENTH AMENDMENT TO THE U.S. CONSTITUTION

Edward H. Cunningham was a Texas phoenix. Although he rode through some of the worst conflagrations of the Civil War at the head of his own regiment, the "Mustang Greys," he surrendered nothing upon defeat. As other prominent confederates nursed their wounds, he diversified his investments. Near San Antonio, he expanded a farm and ranch operation and before long began devouring real estate along Oyster Creek, twenty-five miles southwest of Houston. One of the farms was called Sugar Land, which Cunningham took as the name of his broader estate. The spread had once belonged to Stephen Austin himself, and according to the empresario's beloved cousin Mary it was *splendid* country," "exceeding even [the] best lands in productiveness."[1]

Defenders of Texas's "domestic institutions" had predicted planter ruin in the wake of emancipation, but Cunningham proved them wrong. In the decades after Dixie's debacle, he coaxed fantastic new wealth from the Gulf Coastal Plain's deep alluvial soil. From a wraparound porch on his sprawling whitewashed plantation house, he looked out on a moneymaking enterprise that stretched for miles in every direction. The colonel, as underlings called him, had grazing pastures for Texas Longhorns, fields devoted to cotton and corn, and timber patches in the distance. He operated his own private railroad as well as two mills, one for raw sugar, the other to make paper from the refuse. At the heart of it all was sugarcane, impenetrable thickets of tough, magically sweet grass, tall enough to swallow a farmer on horse-back, thousands of acres across.

Like the slaveholding aristocrats he emulated, Cunningham pursued a life of genteel repose, the southern version of the American Dream. Standing well over six feet tall and weighing nearly three hundred pounds, he projected a formidable presence. "The Colonel was an impressive sight as he towered above his cronies," observed one contemporary. When he traveled, he "dressed in black, with a wide brimmed hat to match, and a white ruffled shirt resplendent with a great diamond stud." On the grounds of his estate, he indulged fanciful hobbies, tending banana trees and raising Belgian hares for his table. Most of all, he enjoyed food and spirits, for which he had an unrivaled hunger. Drinking binges could last a month, reported associates, while sit-down meals, even breakfasts, were Roman affairs. The "Colonel [would sit] at the head of the table" and "polish off the whole bowl . . . of strawberries," remembered one Sugar Land manager. After that, "he would get away with 4 or 5 cups of coffee, a quart of milk, half dozen eggs with ham, and a dozen plate sized pancakes. The old gentleman was a lusty trencherman."[2]

Such landed indolence was supposed to have expired with the Civil War, but Cunningham not only succeeded in carrying on the Bourbon lifestyle; he did so as a master of unfree labor. Harvesting sugarcane is one of the most grueling tasks in agriculture, as the stalks have to be cut, stripped, crushed, boiled, and processed in a blistering race against spoilage. Yet Sugar Land's field hands received neither specie nor company scrip for their work. Locked at night into fetid barracks or the old slave quarters, they were doled out corn bread and fatback but nothing more. Like the bondsmen who had cultivated these same fields before them, they labored because they were so ordered, because they dreaded the lash more than toil.

Although slavery had been abolished more than a decade before the colonel first ensconced himself in the Oyster Creek bottomlands, a loophole in the Thirteenth Amendment, which prohibited slavery "except as punishment for crime," allowed him to command forced labor just as surely as his compatriots had before the war. Texas and other cash-strapped southern states took full advantage of this exemption in the postbellum years. Rather than housing convicts in expensive penitentiaries, they hired them out to the highest bidder. The practice, known as "convict leasing," developed into the most corrupt and murderous penal regime in American history. In the Lone Star State, it reached its apex—and there stood Edward Cunningham, the "Texas Sugar King."[3]

## "THE WAR IS NOT OVER YET"

That southern planters would be able to carry on like slave masters through the second half of the nineteenth century scarcely seemed imaginable at the close of the Civil War. Although Texas was less ravaged than other Confederate states, its ruling class had been trounced. By the summer of 1865, Governor Pendleton Murrah had fled, and U.S. soldiers were streaming into the state. Union general Gordon Granger arrived at Galveston, and on June nineteenth, or Juneteenth for short, a date forever celebrated by African Americans, he stood on the balcony at Ashton Villa and issued a proclamation that white Texans had feared and fought against since their first scuffles with Mexico. "All slaves are free," read his General Order No. 3. With those words, Texas's bedrock social and economic institution was swept away. Some 250,000 state residents suddenly gained control over their lives, a prospect that terrified slaveholders but elated the emancipated. "We was free. Just like that, we was free," exclaimed Felix Haywood, who had been a slave cowboy in Bexar County. "Everyone was a singin'. We was all walkin' on golden clouds. Hallelujah!"[4]

Echoing forth from Galveston, "freedom cried out" in Texas from mouth to mouth, household to household. "The old master didn't tell us about freedom until after the crop was in," explained Alice Rawlings. But "a friendly planter talked with my father in the road one day. . . . I guess that's how we heard about it." Many slave owners were officially notified by mail, and the more scrupulous among them made announcements, however grudgingly. After dinner one evening, reported Lewis Jenkins, the master gathered all the slaves on the gallery and gave them a speech. " 'This is military law, but I am forced to tell you.' He says, 'This law says free the nigger, so now you is just as free as me.' " However the word arrived, slaves rejoiced. "We was the happiest folks in the world when we knowed we was free," recalled Annie Hawkins. "We couldn't realize it at first but how we did shout and cry for joy when we did."[5]

General Granger advised freedpeople "to remain quietly at their present homes and work for wages," but to women and men who had

spent their lives in bondage, freedom signified independence and mobility. "Nobody took our homes away," acknowledged Haywood, "but
right off colored folks started on the move. They seemed to want to get
closer to freedom, so they'd know what it was." After quitting their former masters, many former slaves joined the burgeoning cattle industry
or moved to towns. Most settled back into agriculture, working either
for wages or better yet as tenants or sharecroppers, which allowed them
greater control over their lives and labor. Whatever their vocation,
slaves remained poor. "We soon found out that freedom could make
folks proud," observed Haywood," but it didn't make 'em rich."[6]

For their part, dispossessed whites reacted bitterly to emancipation, occasionally voicing paternalistic concern but more often rage.
Indeed, freedom's halting march unleashed the most virulent paroxysm of antiblack violence in Texas history. When ex-slaves weren't being unlawfully maintained in bondage, they were frequently attacked
on the roads, whipped by vigilantes, beaten with wrenches, chased
down by dogs, shot, or occasionally hung. A former slave named Susan
Merritt reported that in Rusk County, where Texas's second walled
penitentiary would go up years later, planters employed every means to
keep their field hands at work. "You could see lots of niggers hangin' to
trees in Sabine bottom right after freedom, 'cause they cotch 'em swim-
min' 'cross Sabine River and shoot 'em."[7]

Labor conflicts precipitated most of the violence. According to records of the Freedmen's Bureau, which the federal government set up to
assist former slaves, black workers were assaulted for taking too long to
eat breakfast, hoeing too slowly, or simply trying to collect their pay.
Other factors provoked wrath, too. Petty thievery or violations of deferential etiquette—addressing a white man by his first name rather than
an honorific, for instance—might do it. Sometimes mere existence was
enough. One white man reported that he and two friends murdered
three freedmen because they wanted to "thin the niggers out and drive
them to their holes."

All told, more than five hundred former slaves were murdered in
Texas between 1865 and 1868, almost all of them by whites. In per capita terms, postbellum Texas had a homicide rate nearly twice as high as
the most dangerous American cities in the twentieth century; in just
three years, roughly 1 percent of working-age black men in the state
were killed.[8] Even so, Texas's legal system, which remained under the
exclusive control of conservative whites in early Reconstruction, did

little to intervene. Noting that whites were often indicted for homicide but rarely convicted, one visitor remarked, "No white man in that state has been punished for murder since it revolted from Mexico . . . Murder is considered one of their inalienable state rights."[9]

Postwar violence raised troubling questions about the meaning of emancipation. As African Americans were busily asserting their personhood—searching for sold-off loved ones, building churches and schools, and trying to scratch out a living for themselves—unrepentant Confederates were organizing with equal determination, as one woman put it, to "persecute them back to slavery." The perils were immediately apparent in Huntsville, where "nearly every night some outrage [was] committed." When local slaves first heard about Granger's proclamation, "they were plum thick hollering and shouting," remembered Andy McAdams, "but that merriment did not last long." A white man on horseback appeared. He had "a rag tied over his face" and a sword, and when he "rode by a Negro woman, [he] just leaned over in his saddle and cut [her] nearly half in two." "Something like an hour passed" before anyone dared retrieve the body, and in that time, freedpeople may have wondered what Union victory had wrought. Would deliverance from bondage lead to equal rights and better lives or would Reconstruction unravel into a "frightful story of blood"?[10]

In the contest to shape Texas's postbellum society, conservative whites held the upper hand, at least initially. Under the lenient terms of federal occupation set by President Lincoln's successor, Andrew Johnson, himself a southerner, right-wing unionists and embittered ex-confederates were able to gain control of Texas's first postwar administration. Their goal, according to the archreactionary Oran Roberts, was to form a "white man's government" and to "keep Sambo from the polls."[11]

The critical task facing the fledgling government was to define the legal rights of former slaves and to lay the groundwork for a new political economy. Fearful of provoking federal troops, the lawmakers renounced secession and acknowledged the end of slavery. Yet conservative politicians had no intention of yielding to what postbellum governor James Throckmorton called "the hell-hounds of radicalism." Instead, leading Texans hoped to follow Stephen Austin's example when he had sidestepped abolitionist decrees from Mexico, complying with the letter but not the spirit of the law. Their aim, explained Throckmorton, was to "adopt a coercive system of labor" to replace slavery.[12] Their instrument would be a new body of civil and criminal laws known as the "black codes."

Like other vanquished states, Texas promulgated black codes to reconstitute white supremacy and perpetuate an economy based on command labor relations. Planters had seen "their personal authority over blacks destroyed," explains Eric Foner, the dean of Reconstruction historiography, so they "turned to the state to reestablish labor discipline." Texas's codes acknowledged that former slaves had rights, to own property and petition the courts, for instance, but the emphasis was on constricting them. African Americans were excluded from juries, elected office, public rail transportation, and, of course, voting. They were prohibited from owning guns, no small matter in a state wracked by racist violence. To enforce poverty and dependence, the legislation also barred freedpeople from public schools and homesteading benefits.[13]

Former masters wanted tractable hands back in the fields, and the most exacting regulations aimed to oblige. Convinced that "indolence, dishonesty, and general unreliability" were immutable "characteristics of that race," white lawmakers required black workers to sign comprehensive labor contracts that would govern every facet of their lives. Entire families were bound to work at least six days a week. Ex-slaves were required to "obey all proper orders," with fines or "moderate corporal chastisement" imposed for any infraction, from "leaving home without permission" to "impudence." In certain cases, judges could order terms of apprenticeship for minors, under which black youths would labor for white families without any payment whatsoever. According to one contemporary, Texas's legislation aimed "to reenslave the negroes."[14]

While the black codes outlined a legal framework for black subjection, the criminal justice system put muscle behind it. A vagrancy statute allowed any "idle person" to be fined, jailed, or forced to labor on public works. The revised penal code promised stiff discipline. Rape became a capital crime; petty theft garnered lengthy sentences. Free blacks had greater legal rights than they had as slaves, but in courtrooms controlled exclusively by whites those rights guaranteed no justice. "What chance do they stand with rebel judges, rebel lawyers, sheriffs, & jury?" asked one Republican. "No show at all."[15]

Small wonder that Texas's prisoner demographics turned full circle in the postwar years. Although lawbreaking by whites, from contract fraud to homicide, was by most accounts rampant, it was former slaves who flooded into the penitentiary. A handful landed prison sentences for violent felonies (not infrequently crimes of self-defense against whites), but the vast majority lost their newfound freedom for trifling offenses, often convicted on the flimsiest of evidence. One fellow received five years for stealing a bushel of corn, another two years for taking a pair of shoes.[16] All told, Texas's prisoner population nearly quadrupled between 1865 and 1868. Whereas Texas's penitentiary had been chartered for whites, it fast became an institution for the "colored man," a development, some contemporaries acknowledged, that had less to do with crime than prejudice. "In my opinion, white men could not be convicted, in any county of Texas, for crimes that a great majority of colored men now here are undergoing sentence," remarked a disquieted prison official in 1870. "Had this place of punishment justice, they would not be here now."[17]

Freedpeople themselves quickly grasped the ramification of their new relationship to the legal system. "It seem like the white people can't git over us being free," observed Allen Manning, "and they do everything to hold us down all the time." Another former slave foresaw imprisonment as a growth industry. "I think the old master learned me the wrong trade," the man reportedly remarked. "He ought to have made a brickmason out of me, for as sure as Negroes go to prison for stealing they will have to build a prison reaching five miles out on the prairie to hold them all."[18]

Texas built no such prison infrastructure, of course, at least not in the nineteenth century. Instead, officials turned to antebellum traditions of servitude to resolve the state's first prison-crowding crisis. African American women arriving at the penitentiary were hired out to local families as live-in domestics. Male prisoners, by contrast, were divided into two groups. As stipulated in an 1866 "convict labor" law, "first-class" felons convicted of serious crimes, the greater portion of them whites, would stay on at the Walls. A larger number of "second-class" convicts, most of them African Americans convicted of low-level offenses, were to be treated like impressed slaves during the war. They were to be deployed around the state on "works of public utility." Significantly, "public utility" was defined broadly, opening the door for any "company or individual" to hire convicts for railroad construction, mining, iron smelting, or irrigation. Thus began the leasing of convicts in Texas. In February 1867, the Air Line and Brazos Branch railroad took possession of the first shipment of 250 prisoners.[19] Hundreds more would follow.

The public utility system opened a new chapter in Texas punishment, but before it had a chance to fully develop, events in Washington overtook it. After the 1866 elections, congressional Republicans began asserting new authority over Reconstruction. Fed up with Andrew Johnson's accommodation of former rebels, they began passing legislation over the president's veto. They devised a Fourteenth Amendment to the Constitution, which guaranteed "equal protection of the laws," mandated black participation in politics, and divided the South into military districts. "The whole fabric of Southern society *must* be changed," exhorted Thaddeus Stevens, leader of the Radical Republican faction in the House, "and never can it be done if this opportunity is lost."[20]

In Texas, ruling Democrats remained impenitent, hewing to the same self-destructive zeal that led them into the Civil War. In "an address to the people," Governor Throckmorton railed against the Freedmen's Bureau, nonwhite juries, and "despotic rule." When General Griffin, the Union commander in Texas, ordered him to crack down on racist violence and release 227 black convicts from the penitentiary, he refused, prompting the army to remove him from office on July 30, 1867.[21]

This set in motion what Foner has called "a stunning and unprecedented experiment in interracial democracy." Under the stewardship of local Republicans backed by an emboldened Congress, Texas got a new constitution in 1869, the most inclusive in its history. Two years later, a reconfigured multiracial electorate, including some forty thousand black voters, sent a Galveston attorney and former Union officer named Edmund J. Davis to the Governor's Mansion. A rail-thin Republican with porcelain features and a fiery disposition, Davis moved Texas closer to the ideal of equality before the law. Committed to activist government and economic diversification, Davis and his allies nullified the black codes, mandated free, compulsory education, and amassed sweeping powers to protect black life.[22] Though cut short, Davis's regime represented what Texas might have become had Reconstruction been allowed to run its course.

Among Davis's boldest initiatives was to restructure Texas law enforcement. To shore up his "civil authority" and prevent the state from being "overrun by desperadoes," the governor organized two armed forces under his command, both comprised partly of freedmen. Outraged by racist massacres, including the slaughter of some twenty-five African Americans in Brazos County, Davis raised a state militia. To tamp down everyday violence, including a growing number of assaults by a new secret society, the Ku Klux Klan, Davis and his allies created a new State Police force, a Republican counterweight to the Confederate-allied Texas Rangers. "The war is not over yet," warned Davis. "I tell you there has been a slow civil war going on here . . . since the surrender of the Confederate armies."[23]

One of the most explosive clashes of this "slow civil war" took place in Huntsville, which Governor Davis accused of "overbearing lawlessness" beyond any place "where the English language is spoken." In those tempestuous times, the "Walker County affair" began routinely enough. In early December 1870, the body of Sam Jenkins, a former slave who Democrats accused of making "himself obnoxious to white people," was found on the outskirts of town, bearing "unmistakable signs that he had been foully murdered." The State Police rounded up three suspects, but before the defendants could be tried their supporters staged a mutiny at the courthouse, "fir[ing] upon the officers," "yelling like savages," and escaping en masse. In response, the governor declared martial law and eventually tried twenty Huntsville residents before a military commission, sending one to the penitentiary for five years.[24]

According to Governor Davis's police commander, his force was "a vigilant, untiring enemy to all evil-doers." To most whites, however, armed enforcement of black civil rights amounted to "a succession of wrongs, mingled with blood." Nearly half of State Police officers were African American and the majority Republican. Most of the seven thousand persons they arrested by 1872 were white, and for the first and only time in Texas history conservative Anglos found themselves bewailing police misconduct and discrimination. "The police [are] . . . at war with the principles of civil liberties," declared the 1873 Democratic Party platform. "They never trouble themselves in pursuing real offenders," editorialized the *Texas Star Gazette*, "but devote all their precious time and talents in hunting up imaginary Ku Klux Klans."[25]

Until recently, historians of Texas have followed this same line of interpretation. Walter Prescott Webb, Texas's most celebrated historical author, dismissed the State Police as a "carpetbag . . . political machine" with a record "of official murder and legalized oppression." T. R. Fehrenbach, author of the canonical *Lone Star,* the state's most popular one-volume history, asserts that "no institution in Texas ever aroused so much hostility and hatred as the Davis police." The governor not only "gave the badge to Negroes and paranoids," he argues, but aimed to establish a prototypical "police state" "founded on Union bayonets and Negro votes." In reality, the State Police inspired such vitriol because it was the most racially integrated and antiracist law enforcement body in Texas history. Singularly, it worked against white supremacy rather than in its service.[26]

When they first came to power, it looked like Republicans might revolutionize the fast-growing penal system as well. Within months of Governor Throckmorton's removal, federally backed authorities released scores of dubiously convicted inmates and began canceling public utility contracts, which, by that time, had been extended to "farms, mills, butcher shops, etc." At the Walls, the first Unionist managers talked of importing northern-style penitential idealism. They prohibited whipping and proposed erecting a hospital, chapel, and separate barracks for women and boys. Governor Davis considered moving the entire operation out of Huntsville, a town he regarded as fatally compromised by Confederate sentiment.[27]

As is so often the case, however, good intentions soon gave way to expediency. Despite their differences with Democrats, Republicans, too, sought to boost state revenue by hiring out prisoners. Under wise stewardship, the state's new leaders reasoned, convict labor could be used to extend railroads and produce money for schools.[28] Instead of victimizing freedmen, scalawags, and carpetbaggers, their penal code would discipline rebels and Ku Kluxers.

Guided by such thinking, moderate and radical Republicans alike voted to retain and redesign the public utility system. Instead of hiring out groups of convict workers piecemeal, however, they decided to privatize the entire state penal system, felons and facilities alike. A well-connected firm from Galveston, Ward, Dewey & Co., submitted the winning bid, and in July 1871, in exchange for $325,000 over fifteen years, the company took possession of every state prisoner in Texas, 737 persons in all, more than half of them former slaves.[29]

This first all-encompassing convict lease lasted only six years, but it nonetheless produced every fault of its successors. According to the contract, Ward, Dewey & Co. was supposed to refurbish the Walls' textile mill, pay the salaries of state supervisors, and treat "all convicts with care and humanity." In reality, the pursuit of profit overwhelmed every aspect of prison management. "Instead of a penitentiary," observed legislative investigators a few years after the lease got started, "there exists only a system of vilest slavery for the benefit of the lessees."[30]

Because the lessees benefited by maximizing prisoner toil while minimizing expenses on their upkeep, the new arrangement produced spartan hardships. This was especially true of work sites outside the penitentiary, which received more and more convicts after the economic panic of 1873 weakened demand for textiles and other products manufactured at the Walls. Seeking the greatest possible return, Ward, Dewey & Co. started subcontracting prisoners to other employers, such that by the mid-1870s, three quarters of Texas's prisoners had been handed over to forty-nine separate businesses scattered all over East and Central Texas.[31]

State supervisors rarely visited these "outside camps," but when they did they were appalled. At the Lake Jackson Plantation, near several present-day prisons along Oyster Creek, a government inspector, J. K. P. Campbell, reported that convicts were expected to labor through every daylight hour despite illness, hunger, and "inhuman treatment." "The convicts had not changed their clothes for ten weeks," he wrote, and "the lower extremities of some of them were naked." Provisions, as a rule, were scant if not spoiled. "The meat ration was only hog chidings with the excrement still on them, and only half cooked." By contrast, the guards at Lake Jackson dispensed punishments "very freely." "I found convicts whose backs were cut to pieces in the most shocking manner," Campbell complained. Although 65 out of 185 prisoners were ill, many of them seriously, the inspector noted, none were given medical care.[32]

Conditions at the Walls provoked criticism as well, particularly with respect to female prisoners. From the start of their lease, Ward, Dewey & Co. had promised to eliminate the "evil" of having women and men in the same facilities, which they "regard[ed] as incompatible with a good moral discipline." They had failed to do so. Instead, the lessees hired out some women to local residents and kept others incarcerated with the men, an arrangement that fostered both consensual and coerced sexual relations. Punishments abounded. For getting pregnant while incarcerated, one woman was "put in the dungeon and her head shaved" (her suspected paramour was "put in the stocks"). For more pedestrian infractions, women got "punished in the back ally" where "the night buckets were emptied." Others endured a contraption called the horse, which investigators labeled a "barbarous" "instrument of torture." Consisting of an ax-handle-sized peg driven into a vertical wooden stake, the horse earned its name when prisoners were hoisted up onto the peg and forced to straddle it, sometimes for hours. Guards fastened their victims to the stake so they could not squirm away and let gravity press the peg into their genitals. When a woman was put up on the wooden horse one night, a witness testified, "[I] heard her cry and scream as though she was being terribly punished."[33]

The principal lessees, A. J. Ward and E. C. Dewey, countenanced not just torture, critics charged, but "licentious conduct." According to Charlotte Green, an African American woman sentenced to "five years for stealing blankets," both men regularly visited female prisoners at the Walls. "Ward has intercourse with that 'yellow' girl often," she claimed, and sometimes took "two or three of them . . . down to their cells." After interviewing prisoners, guards, and townspeople, a legislative committee concluded that "Messrs. Ward and Dewey were . . . guilty of a drunken debauch with the convict women at night."[34]

All this proved too much for conservative Democrats, who were already clawing their way back to power by the mid-1870s. Ward and Dewey hung on through the power shift, but successive scandals, soaring escape and death rates, as well as late lease payments, eroded their political support. In 1876, lawmakers concluded the lessees were guilty of "inhumane and deliberate cruelties," as well as corruption and mismanagement. The legislature called for "speedy, radical, and permanent" change, and on April 2, 1877, the state annulled the lease.[35] Texas's first experiment in for-profit punishment thus fell apart. Worse would follow.

## REDEMPTION

For all their avarice and misconduct, Ward and Dewey fell victim less to humanitarianism than politics. By the mid-1870s, Reconstruction was in retreat. Despite passage of the landmark Civil Rights Act in 1875, railroad scandals and the ravages of depression enervated the federal government's commitment to full black citizenship. Lawmakers killed the Freedmen's Bureau in 1870, and the Supreme Court subsequently curtailed the reach of the Fourteenth Amendment. Finally, after a contested presidential election, Republicans regained the White House only by agreeing to restore southern states to "home rule." This Bargain of 1877 marked the end of federal Reconstruction and portended a bitter future for African Americans. As W. E. B. DuBois described the turning point in his monumental *Black Reconstruction in America,* "The slave went free; stood a brief moment in the sun; then moved back again toward slavery."[36]

In Texas, Reconstruction had faced serious challenges from the start. Tens of thousands of southern Anglo immigrants poured into the state in the 1870s, overwhelming the Republican electorate.[37] Revanchist Democrats assailed the Davis administration for "plac[ing] us beneath the feet of brutish negroes," and after recovering from the shock of federal displacement they rebuilt their base. Gathering at a statewide Taxpayers' Convention in 1871, they railed against excessive taxation, gun control, the public school fund, and what they called Governor Davis's attempt "to emasculate the strength of the citizens of Texas."[38]

While appeals to white supremacy remained a favorite Democratic harangue, the party also staked out seemingly race-neutral positions that nonetheless reinforced social inequities. With calls for local control, limited government, and constitutional originalism, former rebels during Reconstruction pioneered the sort of racially coded rhetoric that would bind southern conservatives through much of the twentieth century. Rather than revisiting the hated issue of emancipation, which Democrats acknowledged was "a fixed fact," they maligned the "odious, unconstitutional acts" of "Radical . . . misrule" and called for the "strictest economy" in government.[39]

Given that whites outnumbered blacks by four to one in Texas by 1880, political campaigning entirely within the law would almost surely have returned Democrats to power. As in other southern states, however, they were in no mood to wait. All through the elections of the 1860s and 1870s, Democrats relied not just on a swelling electorate but fraud, vote buying, intimidation, and murder. In 1871, notwithstanding the efforts of the State Police, gangs of disguised white men roamed across Bastrop County burning churches, whipping black schoolteachers, and generally hunting, as they put it, "mean negroes and Radicals." In Limestone County, whites advised that trouble "with the freed negroes" had escalated into "race war." The *Waco Times-Herald* reassured its readers that "only the insolent, impudent, worthless negroes . . . are in danger," but African Americans took little comfort. "The raid on the colored people . . . continued for several weeks," reported Governor Davis, resulting in the deaths of "some forty or fifty men, women, and children."[40]

Buoyed by sectarian violence, the Democratic Party recaptured the legislature in 1872. A year later, a Democratic hard-liner from Waco, Richard Coke, prevailed in such a bitterly contested gubernatorial election that Edmund Davis was driven out of the executive mansion under threat of arms.[41] Although Coke represented the interests of the Klan and had been involved in the slave hangings of 1860, he depicted his victory as popular liberation. "Let the hearts of the patriot throb with joy," Coke proclaimed in his inaugural address, "for the old landmarks of constitutional, representative government, so long lost, are this day restored, and the ancient liberties of the people of Texas reestablished."[42] White conservatives christened this moment "Redemption."

Once they returned to power, Redeemers set about reinforcing the white-planter power structure just as surely as Radical Republicans had tried to dismantle it. Their most lasting achievement was a new constitution. To replace the 1869 document that Governor Coke described as "repugnant," a constitutional convention controlled by Democrats drafted a legal framework devoted to local authority and white supremacy. To ensure that radicals would never again try to remake Texas society through government, the document curtailed executive and legislative powers, capped spending and tax increases, and enacted a beggarly funding scheme for public schools. To block African Americans from exercising their full rights as citizens, it devolved voter registration and jury selection to local officials and required judges to run for office in partisan elections, thus guaranteeing that most black defendants would face justice in white courts. An unwieldy amalgam of some sixty-three thousand words, the new constitution was the product of white rage and conservative retrenchment, yet it has demonstrated remarkable staying power. Although Texas had been in the habit of rewriting its organic law every few years—in 1836, 1845, 1861, 1866, and

1869—the Redeemer constitution of 1876 outlasted the twentieth century. It remains Texas's bedrock code today.[43]

Another Democratic milestone was the termination of the racially integrated State Police. "The people of Texas are today delivered from as infernal engine of oppression as ever crushed any people," heralded the *Texas State Gazette*. In its place, lawmakers resurrected the Texas Rangers, who took aim at freedmen, Indians, and Mexicans rather than white mobs and die-hard rebels. In the 1870s and 1880s, the all-white Rangers fought Mexicans in the Skinning and Salt Wars, participated in racist violence against black voters, and helped break the first strikes of the Knights of Labor. As had their forebears, they rode as the armed enforcers of white rule.[44]

New criminal justice institutions produced new prisoners—and of predictable hue. Under Governor Davis, for the first and only time in Texas history, black and white imprisonment rates reached parity; each group went to prison in numbers commensurate with their share of the state's population. After Redemption, traditional inequality returned. Between 1871 and 1880, the rate of black imprisonment shot up by 500 percent, compared to 60 percent for whites.[45]

One aspect of Texas government that Redeemers did not change was the mode of prison management. Although Democratic salons had argued that convict leasing, as practiced by Republicans, "degrades humanity, shocks sensibility, and breaks down the barriers between civilized and savage man," they pursued the same course. The system they called a "most terrible evil" continued as before, only this time its beneficiaries were loyal Confederates rather than hated scalawags. First in line was the husky businessman from Sugar Land, Edward H. Cunningham.

Although some lawmakers recommended "that the State resume control of its penitentiary and convicts," Cunningham managed to strike a deal comparable in scope to the Ward-Dewey lease.[46] To justify the renewal of the very arrangement politicians had just annulled, the revised contract included stricter provisions. Under the stewardship of a new superintendent—the former slaveholder and Confederate officer Thomas J. Goree—the government would exercise greater control over the guard force and would supervise every subcontract. Texas also negotiated better financial terms. Instead of turning over convicts for a lump sum, the state would lease prisoners to Cunningham on a per capita basis ($3.01 a head per month), thus allowing the treasury to benefit from future population growth.[47] Even so, the agreement gave Cunningham the hard labor of every convict in the system, more than 1,500 people in all, at a bargain price—much lower than he would have had to pay in wages and with less capital investment than antebellum slavery would have required.[48] The Sugar King had negotiated a sweet deal.

Cunningham proved himself an abler prison profiteer than Ward and Dewey, notwithstanding his contractual obligations. Sugar farms had languished all along the Gulf since emancipation, but under the colonel's leadership—with convicts swinging the machetes and rolling the cane—the industry experienced a resurgence. With the assistance of a partner, Littleberry A. Ellis, another Confederate veteran and former slaveholder, Cunningham expanded his holdings to twenty thousand acres and eventually built a mill that could process one hundred thousand pounds of dry white sugar a day.[49]

Although his cane patches have since given way to tract homes and prisons, Cunningham's hulking refinery still towers over Sugar Land's landscape. Known as the Imperial Mill, it continued to operate throughout the twentieth century. In 1990, eighty-two years after Cunningham's passing, his Imperial Sugar Company made the Fortune 500 list. It ranked as one of Texas's largest nonenergy companies and the biggest sugar refiner in the United States. Founded with slave capital, Imperial was built by convicts.[50]

Despite the considerable needs of their personal enterprises, Cunningham and Ellis turned to subcontracting as the convict population climbed 1,500 percent between 1865 and 1880.[51] Among their most eager clients were railroads. From the Houston and Texas Central, which first connected Texas's cotton belt to eastern markets, to the Texas and Pacific, the state's first line to California, leased prisoners helped construct Texas's most important transportation routes, laying the groundwork for a second cotton boom that drove economic development into the next century.[52]

For the companies, prisoner proletarians provided multiple advantages. Although they constituted only a minority of their workforce, they helped depress free wages, reduce recruitment costs, and provided a ready pool of strike breakers to confront the South's first industrial unions. Along with massive land grants, convicts provided railroad builders a critical government subsidy, helping expand Texas's total track mileage from 395 in 1865 to 1,650 in 1874. By 1877, with thousands of convicts having worked on its tracks, Texas led the nation in railroad construction.[53]

Laboring like slaves, without pay and in the worst conditions, impressed convicts played a vital role in assembling the infrastructure of what boosters called the New South. Although historians have dismissed the practice as a "barbarous relic," in fact, forced labor helped propel Texas and other southern states down what one analyst labels "the Prussian Road" to industrial capitalism, a development model predicated on the strong-arm tactics of capital more than the unleashed productivity of free labor. Convict leasing was not a "retrograde step," as most critics have suggested. Alas, like slavery before it, it constituted what historian Alex Lichtenstein has called one of "the region's first tentative, ambivalent, steps toward modernity."[54]

Edward Cunningham especially appreciated the virtues of convict leasing. From his lavish estate in Sugar Land, he presided over a lease system larger than any other in the United States, with some 2,300 convicts at its peak, the majority of them former slaves. Splitting the force between his personal operations and legion subcontractors, he and his partner made a substantial fortune over the course of their five-year contract, at least $500,000 in "clear profit." By some measures, the state of Texas made out even more handsomely. While most governments expect their penal systems to incur significant expenses, Texas's, for much of the nineteenth century, provided steady revenue, more than $300,000 a year by the early 1880s.[55]

Superintendent Goree occasionally expressed misgivings about the arrangement—convict leasing "is an evil," he admitted—but money had a way of soothing doubts. As the profits piled up, Governor Coke's successor, Richard Hubbard, beamed, "I cannot but regard the State as fortunate in securing for lessees gentlemen of such high integrity, business capacity, and energy." Against his better judgment, the superintendent fell in line: the lessees are "kind hearted and humane," he reported, and they are making the convicts "cozy and comfortable." A few months later, Ellis and Cunningham built Goree a stately new home adjacent to the Walls.[56]

• • •

In the prison business, parties always bring hangovers. Although Cunningham and Ellis basked in the praise of powerful Democrats, scandal stalked them from the shadows. One of the most serious developed at an out-of-the-way wood-chopping camp near Mineola, east of Dallas. To fill an order for fifty thousand railway ties for the Texas and Pacific, local residents charged that prisoners were being worked beyond human limits, even to death.[57]

State officials launched an investigation and soon discovered what they described as "the Mineola Horror." Despite paltry rations, verminous housing, and epidemic illness, the sergeant in charge, J. H. Randle, tolerated no excuses for missing quotas (three quarters of a cord of wood per day for white men, a full cord for blacks). According to a guard, Randle whipped men with persimmon branches for claiming sickness. When a Native American convict slumped over a log one day and said he was too weak to go on, Randle reportedly kicked him viciously and forced him to work anyway. The next morning, the prisoner was dead. Another fellow got pummeled with an ax handle. "His name was Cooper [and] he died afterwards," explained an officer. "He was beat because he could not find his hat." His was a common fate at Mineola. On a force of roughly eighty prisoners, eighteen had died in four months.[58]

Facing death, many convicts attempted to escape. If runaways were recaptured, however, they suffered still more torments. Guards and prisoners testified that escapees were beaten, "eat[en] up with dogs," even murdered. Sergeant Randle made special use of homemade stocks that hoisted prisoners off the ground by their neck and arms. Witnesses said that convicts dangled in the contraption for hours, sometimes vomiting or losing control of their bowels. Other prisoners asserted themselves in rash, self-destructive ways that recalled slave resistance. One man tried to make a dash for freedom, despite the fact that a long spur was bound to his ankle to hobble him. He was shot down. Two convicts used their axes to "cut their hands off on purpose." Randle made the men "work right away with their well hand[s]."[59]

Conditions at Mineola, largely because a number of white convicts were involved, attracted a great deal of attention, but they were not especially aberrant. Black prisoners—who many whites believed "were formed for the climate of Africa" and were therefore concentrated on the lessees' muggy cane farms—experienced similar hardship but found little sympathy. In the Mineola case, prison officials took remedial action, firing Sergeant Randle and prohibiting the stocks.[60] But when it came to corporal punishment and convict neglect generally, Redeemers remained silent.

In defense of Texas's system, Superintendent Goree pointed out that "the prison population in the older Northern States differs very materially from that in the Southern States." "There, the majority of men are white," he instructed, eager for education and industrial training. In Texas, on the other hand, "a large majority of our population have been raised on farms . . . having neither the capacity or inclination to learn a [skilled] trade." Such prisoners, the bulk of them "colored," "can be made to work," he explained, "but they cannot be made to think intelligibly." As for physical punishments, the superintendent asserted glibly, "there are, of course, many men in the penitentiary who will not be managed by kindness." Many, it turned out, would not be managed at all. During the five years that Colonel Cunningham, with Goree's able cooperation, lorded over Texas's convicts, 1,151 of them escaped. Another 633 met their demise.[61]

## "BRUTAL AND WICKED COMPACTS"

Texas was not the only state to create a penal system in the image of slavery. With their penitentiaries in ruins and criminal convictions on the rise, every southern state handed over prisoners to for-profit contractors in the decades after the Civil War. In North Carolina, state officials stuffed convicts into padlocked boxcars and shipped them off to Appalachian railroad camps. In Florida, they contracted with turpentine distillers and dispatched prisoners to such miserable swamps that some gouged out their eyes in order to be sent back to the penitentiary. In Tennessee, efficient lessees figured out how to eke profits from prisoners even in death. They lowered convicts into coal mines, collected barrels of their urine for sale to tanneries, and when the workers expired, by the hundreds, they sold the bodies to the medical school at Nashville.[62]

Everywhere the results were the same: corruption and cruelty, calcified racial divisions, broken bodies, and ghastly death rates. The social costs were enormous, especially for recently delivered slaves, who made up the overwhelming majority of brokered inmates. Yet leasing's benefits gave the system life: lower taxes, infrastructure development at little cost, and, most of all, profit. As with chattel slavery before it, convict leasing took hold—surviving countless efforts at abolition—principally because it made men rich. Not just any men, but prominent planters and industrialists, the captains of commerce in the New South. Men like Colonel Edmund Richardson, a Mississippian known as "the largest cotton planter in the world." Like Nathan Bedford Forrest, a slave trader turned ruthless Confederate general, who rebuilt his fortune with convict railway workers and founded the Ku Klux Klan. And men like Joseph E. Brown, one of Georgia's most illustrious politicians—a long-serving governor, U.S. senator, and supreme court justice—as well as the founder of the Dade Coal Company, one of the largest convict operations in the South.[63]

Bound up as it was with the bank accounts of giants, convict leasing proved remarkably difficult to dislodge. Even so, there were homegrown critics, among them one of the region's most celebrated novelists, George Washington Cable. A forerunner of southern literary realism, Cable was praised in *Scribner's Monthly* as the first southern writer since Poe to make "a contribution of permanent value to American literature." Not long after going on a "Twins of Genius" tour with Mark Twain, however, Cable found himself denounced as a traitor to the South, a heretic as reviled by whites as John Brown of Harper's Ferry. Longtime friends turned against him; his credit dried up. For fear of violence, he moved his family north.[64] Against the advice of his friends and editors, Cable had spoken out against convict leasing and southern race relations generally. He paid dearly for it.

The son of a New Orleans slaveholding merchant, Cable was an unlikely candidate for literary greatness, much less apostasy. At the age of fifteen, he had dropped out of school after his father died. When the Civil War broke out, he enlisted in the Confederate cavalry. Although he was puny and bookish—he weighed less than one hundred pounds as an adult—he recalls that he was "reeking with a patriotism of the strongest pro-slavery type."[65]

In the carnage that followed and during his dejecting experience as a prisoner of war, Cable nursed doubts about the cause he was fighting for. "The practice of slavery became an Institution," he realized. "It grew, until every element of force in our civilization—the political arena, the sacred desk, the legislative hall, the academical chair—all—

were wrapped in its dark shadow." The result, he came to believe, was clouded thinking, retarded development, and, ultimately, ruination. The South had fabricated "guns that shoot backward."[66]

After returning home, Cable initially consigned his social criticisms to the imaginative realm of fiction. But this began to change in 1881, when he sat on a grand jury investigating the Orleans Parish Prison and Insane Asylum. The conditions "would bring the blush to the cheek of a murderer," he said, and long after the jury's term expired Cable refused to let the matter rest. He wrote columns for the *Times-Democrat*, cajoled prominent citizens into joining a prison aid association, and began researching penal operations across the country.[67] The abuses he discovered stemmed not just from neglect, he concluded, but from the unholy union of imprisonment, profit, and white supremacy.

Cable thus redirected his attention from New Orleans to southern justice writ large.[68] In particular, he began gathering official documents on convict leasing, which he denounced as "the worst prison system in Christendom." After amassing a riverboat of data, Cable traveled to Louisville, Kentucky, and presented his findings in a lengthy and impassioned speech before the National Conference on Charities and Corrections in 1883, later published in *Century Magazine*. Proceeding state by state, he exposed a record of deception, degradation, and death. Lessees are "men whose profits are coined from the flesh and blood of human beings," Cable railed. Their "brutal and wicked compacts" must be declared void if ever the South is to reclaim its "honor" and "humanity."[69]

One of the most entrenched lease regimes, admitted Cable, had developed in his own Louisiana. Since 1869, every prisoner in the state had been turned over to the exclusive control of just one man, Major Samuel James. On a wide bend in the Mississippi River, James had set up his own penal colony. The place was called Angola, named for the provenance of its first African slaves, and its master lived in grand antebellum style. At the big house and on his personal steamboat, convict servants attended to his every need. In the surrounding fields, prisoners picked cotton, while subleased convicts worked up and down the state on levees.

When James first assumed command of Louisiana's prisoners, he had agreed to make steadily increasing payments to the treasury, but he rarely bothered. Instead, in characteristically Louisiana fashion, he wove a web of influence that allowed him to manage convicts as he saw fit—and at river-bottom prices. Legislators objected, those not on the payroll most strenuously. James blithely ignored them. Louisiana's key players went along.[70]

Seven years after Cable's speech, Major James's contract expired. A Texas partner of Edward Cunningham put in a counter bid but, as always, James prevailed.[71] A few years later, the master of Angola, a pear-shaped man with swamp moss sideburns, stood up in the gallery of his plantation home, stumbled to the railing, sputtered blood, and died. A granddaughter claimed, in vainglorious slaveholder fashion, that "a few hundred of our Negro[es] . . . were crying softly, others wailing," but they had little cause for mourning. Convicts had made the bulky planter one of the richest men in Louisiana, but he had provided them only hardship in return. Over the full span of his lease, which extended through heirs into the twentieth century, some three thousand prisoners lost their lives, nearly 90 percent of them black.[72] Cable proposed that "one word: Aceldama—the field of blood" be engraved over the door of James's "sumptuous home."[73]

While Cable reserved his harshest words for his own birthplace, he regarded leasing as even more disheartening in comparably developed states like Alabama. On a visit to the teeming city of Birmingham, Cable marveled at the sight of "crude ore, so long trampled under foot, now being turned by great burnings and meltings into one of the prime factors of the world's wealth." In Cable's view, Birmingham's awesome mills were engines of the future. That Alabama's convict lease system recalled the pharaohs, therefore, struck him as all the more disgraceful. Citing the complaints of an unusually candid warden, Cable reported that on the outskirts of the South's most industrial city, convicts were "filthy . . . as dirt," "poorly clothed and fed," and "cruelly punished." "The [lease] system is a . . . reproach to civilization and . . . ought to be swiftly abandoned," he contended.[74]

But it was not. Instead, five years after Cable launched his crusade, a mishmash of leases were consolidated under the control of one company, Tennessee Coal, Iron, and Railroad, or TCI, the biggest corporation in the South. Under TCI's leadership, Alabama convicts worked off their sentences underground. Stooped in dank shafts and inhaling dust, they were each required to mine between one and four tons of coal a day, depending on their physical capacity, which invariably diminished over time. Since convicts tended to be less efficient than experienced free miners, lessees kept them on task longer, from twelve to sixteen hours a day. In 1889, a legislative committee reported that "many convicts in the coal mines . . . have not seen the sun shine for months."[75]

An Alabama inspector scribbled terse observations in his notebook ("Filthy—crowded—lice," "convicts ragged—many barefooted—very heavily ironed"), but he didn't expect much to change. Convict leasing served as a principal source of state revenue; in 1898, prison contractors covered fully 73 percent of Alabama's state budget.

For TCI, convict labor proved indispensable as well. Unlike wage workers, prisoners refused no task and took no holidays. TCI's chief engineer observed that "convicts mined the cheapest coal ever produced by the Company." Even more so than in Texas, prisoner labor could be used to depress free wages and bludgeon unions. "The chief inducement for the hiring of convicts," explained the president of TCI, "was the certainty of a supply of coal . . . in the contingency of labor troubles." Indeed, convicts played a key role in the racially divisive miners' strike of 1894, which forever weakened the United Mine Workers of Alabama.[76] Convict labor not only built the New South but helped ensure that it would remain relatively union free, a pattern that holds into the present.

Pliant prisoner labor and its externalities provided vital competitive advantage to TCI. In 1907, the company merged with U.S. Steel, a pillar of American industry founded by the likes of Andrew Carnegie and J. P. Morgan. Over four decades of leasing, tens of thousands of unpaid, abused, and overworked convicts cycled through the mines of TCI and then U.S. Steel. By 1918, nearly four thousand of them had perished, with countless others maimed. Recorded mortality rates in excess of 20 percent, in some instances, put U.S. Steel on par with German and Japanese companies that profited from slave labor in World War II. But while these corporations have been held to account, U.S. Steel has escaped unscathed. Although the *Wall Street Journal* recently probed the company's shameful history, no reparations movement has emerged among former convicts or their descendants.[77]

In taking on the convict lease system, George Cable challenged powerful and deep-pocketed adversaries, but in the course of his campaign he widened his circle of criticism. In daring commencement addresses and a series of essays, he began to question not just the practices of southern justice but their underlying presumptions. He started targeting the South's most sacred covenant, white supremacy.

Corrupt punishment was but a symptom, argued Cable. The real issue, "the greatest social problem before the American people to-day is . . . the presence among us of the negro." This dubious formulation—black existence as social problem—was a common refrain among whites. But in his groundbreaking 1884 essay, "The Freedman's Case in Equity," Cable went well beyond it. America's preeminent moral failing, he contended, was to "lose sight of the results of African-American slavery," which continued to "work mischief and injustice." The problem was not really race, in other words, but racism. "We have had a strange experience" in the South, he posited. "The withholding of simple rights has cost much blood; such concessions of them as we have made have never yet cost a drop."[78]

In assailing the lease system, Cable enlisted many allies, but in this quixotic campaign against white domination he rode mostly alone. African Americans wrote letters of support. "I hope that you will continue the work you have begun, and may God bless you," offered one reader. But whites, even Cable's erstwhile friends, responded with silence or more often vitriol. One critic accused Cable of "blind hatred of the Southern white race." In directing his arguments to white southerners, Cable had hoped to give voice to what he called a "silent South," but he encountered the "solid South" instead.[79]

From exile in Massachusetts, Cable finally tired of his lost cause. He returned to fiction but not with the same force of his first novels. At his debut, Cable had been lauded as a literary genius on a par with Henry James, but his later historical romances never again reached that "plane of excellence," observes his biographer. Like many white southern dissidents, Cable spoke out and suffered banishment. The cult of white supremacy not only subjugated African Americans but suffocated free thought.[80]

## "LIGHTED BY THIS LAW OF LOVE"

Despairing of prison practices in the South, Cable detected glimmerings of hope in the North. Prisons that merited the nation's pride "may be counted on the fingers of one hand," he said, but in those few he admired a "grave and silent decency." In Massachusetts and other northern states, he believed that the best prisons maintained a "perfection of order." They emphasized training over avarice and administered dispassionate discipline "free from brutalizing tendencies." In sharp contrast to leasing, well-managed penitentiaries showed "wise benevolence . . . toward bad men" while "upholding the integrity and honor of the state."[81]

By the early 1880s, the country's leading penologists—pioneers in the new field of penitentiary science—agreed that only a handful of institutions embodied "the reformatory idea." Like their southern counterparts, most northern prisons scraped for funds and sought profits from captive labor.[82] Although less intensively than in the South, they similarly incubated abuses. Because whipping invited humanitarian censure, managers devised novel methods of punishment, both unusual and cruel. At Sing Sing, officials rigged up pulley devices that hoisted inmates into the air and dangled them painfully by the thumbs. In Kansas, inventive disciplinarians built a "water crib," a coffin-sized box that gradually filled with water while a strapped-down inmate struggled to keep from drowning.[83]

While the Civil War alleviated population pressures on northern prisons, diverting unruly young men from crime to cannon fodder, it also unleashed a new wave of humanitarian activism. Although the fighting began, from a northern perspective, as a philosophically modest effort to preserve the Union, it evolved into a moral crusade, not only against slavery but for national regeneration. "As never before, the war mobilized the energies of Northern reformers, imbuing their lives with a renewed sense of purpose," writes Eric Foner.[84] After victory, these armies of charity took on new causes: temperance, school building for freedmen, and, in many cases, prison reform.

The challenges were daunting. Soon after the war, Enoch C. Wines, a former minister, along with Theodore Dwight, a blue-blooded law professor, undertook a massive survey of American prisons, more ambitious than anything since Beaumont and Tocqueville's effort three decades earlier. They visited every northern state and compiled seventy volumes of documentation but found every prison wanting. "There is not one . . . which seeks the reformation of its subjects as a primary object," they regretted.[85]

Even so, Wines and Dwight were not without hope; like many penal reformers, they had a boundless supply, undiminished by disappointment. Having discovered a small number of fledgling but worthy institutions scattered about the states, they decided to bring together the most prominent criminal justice officials in the nation to help set a new course. Their purpose was nothing less than the reinvention of the penitentiary ideal, "not only in every state of the American Union, but . . . in every country of the civilized world."

Three years later, in October 1870, Ohio's governor and future U.S. president, Rutherford B. Hayes, opened the National Congress on Penitentiary and Reformatory Discipline in Cincinnati. After a determined organizing campaign by Wines, more than two hundred delegates attended—prison managers, charity workers, politicians, physicians, and chaplains. The South as a region was scarcely represented, but historians nonetheless regard the gathering as a watershed national event, the birthplace of America's second penal reform movement.[86]

Among the standouts at the gathering was Zebulon Brockway, the superintendent of the Detroit House of Correction, one of the few institutions singled out by Wines and Dwight for approbation. For nearly a decade, Brockway had been innovating in his "own quiet corner." Now the prison congress thrust him onto center stage. He delivered a rousing address that became the first draft of the congress's statement of principles, which would themselves serve as the blueprint of American corrections for a century.[87]

Not prone to modesty, Brockway said that he felt himself strengthened by "a mysterious, almighty, spiritual force." The challenge for penal reformers, he said, was not only to diagnose the "social disease" of crime but "to cure criminals" with modern methods that embodied "the *christian ideal*." "Let prisons and prison systems be lighted by this law of love," he preached, and "we shall have found God's plan for saving the race."[88]

Under the influence of Brockway and Wines, delegates adopted the Declaration of Principles—the founding charter of the National Prison Association, today known as the American Correctional Association—on the sixth day of the congress. Consisting of thirty-seven articles, the principles contained a welter of recommendations: professional guard training, education and religious instruction, the replacement of "physical force" with "organized persuasion," and an end to all kinds of private contracting, especially full-scale leasing. Philosophically, the points went well beyond organizational retooling. The "supreme aim" of prison "treatment" was not "vindictive suffering," the charter began, but the "moral regeneration" of criminals. The nation's first penitentiaries—noble creations though they were—had worked "only [on] the inert and obedient body." In the next generation of scientific institutions, the delegates prophesied, "the living soul must be won."[89]

To "gain the will of the convict" and bring it into "harmony" with society would require a comprehensive approach, instructed the founders, one that combined the millennial zeal of the first penitentiary builders with the organizational vigor of the Union army. States would need to construct an array of charitable and disciplinary institutions, from truant homes to industrial-training facilities for adults. Within them, inmates would have to be carefully "classified or graded," according to not only "conduct" but "character," a deeper, more elusive quality to be measured by well-trained penitentiary scientists. Critically, expert keepers would need the augmented authority to determine when an inmate had sufficiently internalized obedience and good work habits to be released. "When you show yourself a reformed man, when you convince us by satisfactory evidence that it will be safe to let you be at large, you can go," admonished Wines, "but not before."[90] This became known as the "indeterminate sentence."

In Detroit, Brockway boasted, many of the congress's principles were already under development, most ambitiously in the women's annex, which he called the House of Shelter. "Wayward women must be won to virtue by their own sex, if they are won at all," Brockway believed. And so, pinning his faith to the Victorian notion of nurturing, civilizing femininity, Brockway employed "refined and virtuous women" to staff every position beneath him, from matron to guard. To head up the experiment, he had tapped Emma Hall, whom he described as the embodiment of "true womanhood": "large-hearted," self-abnegating, and tireless. Under her leadership, the House of Shelter broke sharply with penitentiary conventions of solitude and martial discipline. Cell isolation gave way to "family life," and education overshadowed employment. Because middle-class reformers tended to believe that lawbreaking women were victims of male vice, that they had fallen from their proper pedestal, Hall's regime also included enactments of genteel femininity. On Thursday evenings, inmates would don their "neatest and best attire" and "assemble in our parlour" to sip tea and listen to poetry read aloud. Although most incarcerated women would return to low-wage domestic service or the mills, Hall took pride in habituating them to the mores of "refined society."[91]

As the first adult reformatory in the country—a fact overlooked by historians too focused on male institutions—the House of Shelter was one of the gentlest locations in America to complete a prison sentence. But there was another side to the story. Women were often committed for petty crimes that rarely snared men, notably prostitution. Moreover, on Brockway's urging, Michigan adopted the nation's first indeterminate sentencing law, which effectively extended prison terms. The statute applied exclusively to women and allowed them to be held for up to three years depending on their progress toward reformation, much longer than they would have served under regular sentencing.[92]

Undermined by crowding and political disputes, the House of Shelter lasted only until 1874, but its example lived on. Indiana, then Massachusetts and New York, built more elaborate prototypes, completely separate institutions staffed exclusively by women. Although most African American women continued to be dispatched to conventional prisons, white women inmates experienced radically upgraded penal environments in these early reformatories. In New York, the housing looked more like family cottages than austere cell blocks, and well-behaved inmates were allowed to tend their babies in live-in nurseries. While most northern prisons were urban fortresses, these facilities were surrounded by forests and rolling farmland. In the South, plantations remained sites of forced-labor production, but to gilded-age reformers in the North, rural reformatories became curative retreats from the temptations and pressures of the city.[93]

Institutions for women and juveniles came closest to the National Prison Association's ideal of "generous parental care," but after 1876 the reformatory model was applied to male offenders as well, again at the hands of Zebulon Brockway. The setting was a new prison built in the style of a Romanesque Revival palace in upstate New York. Although Brockway had clashed with politicians in Michigan, he was given free rein and generous resources at the Elmira Reformatory, which he turned into the preeminent penological laboratory in the nation. In accord with NPA principles, he devised a prison plan to fit the criminal rather than the crime. He conducted personal interviews with each incoming prisoner and then prescribed individuated courses of training and character reformation. For most of each day, inmates labored—in the broom factory, on the farm, or elsewhere—but in the early evening, they participated in a smorgasbord of enriching activities: mandatory schooling, team sports, guest lectures, and religious services. According to Brockway, Elmira resembled less a conventional prison than a "hospital" or a "college on a hill."[94]

By all accounts a dedicated warden, Brockway was also a master of public relations. Each year, some three thousand copies of Elmira's illustrated reports were mailed to politicians and prison professionals around the world. The superintendent gave personal tours to visiting delegations, claiming (unverifiably) that 84 percent of his graduates were "reformed in the broadest sense of the word." Impressed by Elmira's ornate facade and orderly operations, these visitors returned accolades by the train load. One prominent penologist described Brockway as a "master of reformatory discipline," while the Prison Association of New York asserted confidently that "all the world is looking to this reformatory prison for a solution of some of the most involved problems of criminal treatment."[95]

Look they might, but admirers of the Elmira system saw only what Brockway allowed. In practice, the reformatory dispensed tamer punishment than most regular prisons, certainly compared to any southern lease camp. Yet beneath Elmira's veneer of benevolence lurked a new sort of totalizing discipline. Over his twenty-four years at Elmira, Brockway amassed almost complete control over every aspect of prison management, including disciplinary hearings and the parole board. He alone determined who worked at Elmira, who advanced, who got out and on what terms. Loyal inmates who pleased him could do extraordinarily well; one rose to the top of the prisoner ranks and was then rehired upon release as Brockway's second in command. Those who didn't might find themselves chained to the floor, prodded with hot iron rods, and threatened with death. Although Brockway said he ran his prison according to "God's plan," a wide-ranging investigation in 1894 revealed that he personally administered "spankings" in Elmira's feared "Bathroom #4," not just occasionally but hundreds of times a year. Inmates accused of sexual misconduct sometimes had metal rings surgically implanted over the heads of their penises to prevent erections.[96]

Although Elmira's superintendent came in for stiff criticism in his later years—a state inquest at one point found him guilty of "cruel, excessive, degrading, and unusual punishment of the inmates"—Brockway's allies in the field of penology stuck by him. In 1897, he was elected president of the National Prison Association, and after his retirement (finally engineered by Governor Teddy Roosevelt in 1900), he wrote and lectured extensively. At an NPA tribute in 1910, one disciple described him as the "Nestor of American penology," another as "the greatest warden America has produced."[97]

Historians, by and large, have repeated these panegyrics. Conceiving the evolution of criminal punishment as a saga of halting progress, a "history of good intentions," they have figured Brockway as "the father of prison reform," his Elmira as the prototype of modern corrections. Elmira served as "a sterling example of successful application of rehabilitative techniques," offers one history, while another notes that the "College on the Hill" became "the model for other reformatories, demanding not originality but repetition."[98]

In recent years, historians have more often recognized that the practices of penal institutions rarely match the trumpery of their annual reports. Andrew Pisciotta titled his recent assessment of Elmira *Benevolent Repression*. Others have gone further, assailing the "failure of reform," or suggesting, as does Michel Foucault, that reformatory discipline represented only an insidious new technology of dehumanizing power.[99] Yet even critics have hewed to a genealogy of punishment grounded almost entirely in the North. What this geographic parochialism ignores is that another punishment tradition was taking shape simultaneously in the American South. This alternative regime, which made only passing claims to humanitarian or scientific progress, was larger and more cost efficient. Based on forced labor, repression, and racism, it was in the process of becoming more politically and socially entrenched.

### "THIS IS NO BIBLE"

While New York innovated, Texas elected the arch-Confederate Oran Roberts governor in 1878. An angular, awkward man whose long face melted into his white beard as he aged, Roberts had migrated to Texas from Alabama in 1841 and had worked his way through the most important posts in the polity: supreme court justice, president of the secession convention, U.S. senator, and now governor. Throughout, he stood for obdurate conservatism. He railed against "the reckless fanaticism" of abolitionists and defended the "beneficent and patriarchal system of slavery," which he called "the revealed will of the Almighty Creator." After the Confederacy's defeat, he labored mightily to restore that natural order. He helped draft the black codes, condemned "the military government" of Edmund Davis, and rallied behind every effort to reestablish white supremacy.[100]

The end of slavery, Roberts warned, would ultimately precipitate a "war of races," resulting either in the extermination of blacks or worse, in his view, their persistence as "a demoralizing, degrading element, dragging us down in the scale of civilization." This grim fate was only avoided, he explained in a book he wrote on Texas history, when saviors on horseback appeared. "Dressed in white flowing shrouds and tall paper hats," these knights of southern honor sent superstitious "negroes . . . dart[ing] into the first house they came to" and finally compelled them to recognize "the precedence and superiority of the white man." Afterward—once the "debasing doctrine of the equality of man" was laid to rest—Roberts announced with satisfaction that "whites and blacks were at peace, the same as they were in slavery times."[101]

With the "white man's government" restored, Roberts turned late in his career from the judiciary to the executive. Although he was by all accounts a "long and tedious" speaker, he handily won the 1878 governor's race. Over the next four years, he racked up dubious accomplishments—hobbling public schools, cutting taxes, and selling off wide swaths of public land to speculators at fifty cents an acre—but he nonetheless ranks as one of Texas's preeminent statesmen. Although less revered than Stephen Austin or Sam Houston, he more than any-one shaped Texas law and politics in the turbulent decades around the Civil War. With a vision that encompassed limited government, states' rights, and legally enshrined white supremacy, Roberts stands out as the founding father of Texas conservatism.[102]

In criminal justice, Roberts has a significant legacy as well. In re-sponse to what he ambivalently called "the changed condition of a large colored population," he favored vigorous law enforcement. Because he opposed most government spending, he also supported convict leas-ing, which "incur[red] . . . little expense to the state." As Roberts famil-iarized himself with the details of Texas's profitable penal regime, however, he felt "constant uneasiness." In particular, he worried about poor whites who ended up on the wrong side of the law. At prisoner work sites managed by some subcontractors, whites were worked side-by-side with blacks like slaves. After reading through a batch of citizen com-plaints, Roberts wrote to Superintendent Goree in 1881. "An impression has been forming in my mind that the treatment of the convicts . . . is not what it should be," he advised. "[Let us] take some steps [to] fore-stall the coming storm."[103]

Under the leadership of the state's preeminent reactionary, Texas thus embarked on its most concerted round of penal reforms since 1848.

An ideological purest, the governor accepted only "practicable" adjustments "without too great a sacrifice of means." Still, on paper, the
changes looked significant, especially for white prisoners "not inured
to outdoor hard labor."[104] A prison reorganization bill that Roberts pushed
through in 1881 aimed "to secure to the convicts humane treatment" by
increasing state oversight, prohibiting labor on the Sabbath, separating
women from men, and regulating physical punishments. Most important, the legislation promised to concentrate "as many convicts as can
be comfortably and profitably employed . . . within the Walls . . . as soon
as possible." More aggressively than any other southern state, Texas began importing some of the ideas of northern penology—though on its
own terms.[105]

Roberts's plan was to create a system of Auburn-style penitentiaries—
but not for all convicts. Given the costs involved, he believed that most
nonwhites should continue moiling in the fields. As his superintendent
explained, "there is a very large class of convicts in Texas, as in other
Southern States, who, being totally unfit for skilled labor, can never be
profitably employed in the Walls." The profits derived from these unfree black field hands, Roberts hoped, would support an industrial penitentiary system for the supposed benefit of whites. "Outside labor can
be operated without any investment of capital, and is the most profitable," Goree explained. "The policy of the State is to increase the inside
force at the expense of the outside."[106]

Roberts's segregationist program was reform at its most cynical;
George Washington Cable dismissed it as "very inadequate [and] super-
ficial." Yet the new Texas model—combining, as it did, penitentiary
confinement with profit and slaveholder nostalgia—would prove enormously influential. By 1890, Texas was presiding over the biggest penal
system in the South, the second largest in the nation.[107] Already, the
state was emerging as a colossus in American punishment, and as other
southern states began retooling their own troubled penal systems around
the turn of the century, many of them looked to Roberts's plan for
guidance.

Although the governor described his hybrid program as humanitarian and efficient, the record shows that prisoners thought otherwise. In
piecing together the origins of Texas punishment, historians have had
to rely almost entirely on official sources, from biennial reports to
legislative investigations. From the 1880s, however, the archives include

a richer assortment of documents written by convicts themselves. Among them are clemency appeals and protest petitions, as well as book-length convict memoirs, most of which have escaped the notice of historians. As convict leasing's mainstream political legitimacy quavered, nearly a dozen of these unauthorized autobiographies were published by local presses or the authors themselves.[108] Angry, muckraking, sometimes introspective and sentimental, the texts vary in style and literary merit, but together they provide a bottom-up challenge to official whitewashing.

One of the period's most compelling memoirs was also its first, *The Texas Convict,* published in 1893. Authored by a luckless white farm boy from the gulf coast, Andrew George, the book is a prisoner bildungsroman. It begins with a tragic, love-starved youth. Orphaned and separated from his siblings at a tender age, George was passed from relative to relative and earned his keep picking cotton "at trifling wages." As soon as he was able to buy a horse, he set off on his own, drifting between farm jobs and picking up whatever schooling he could. Seeking refuge from the loneliness at his core, he fell in with "rough acquaintances" and soon met "a most . . . diabolical fate."[109]

One day, George and his companions stopped in a general store owned by German immigrants for "a pint of good whisky" and a meal. Quarreling broke out, then gunfire, and the proprietor was killed. Our protagonist claimed he had nothing to do with the fight but, as he described it, false testimony before a stacked jury got him convicted of murder. The sentence was death, commuted to life in prison by the governor. Thus, at the age of twenty-one, George stepped through the "big iron doors" at Huntsville "never to return."[110]

Although saddled with a lifelong sentence, George would experience the best penology Texas had to offer; he was the direct beneficiary of Roberts's reforms. At the Walls, where most white long-timers did their time, inmates had access to church services, basic education, a physician, and occasional entertainments; for Christmas one year, the prison hosted "Dark Town Fun," a blackface minstrel show.[111] In the year that George arrived, 1884, Superintendent Goree reported, "the discipline of the prison is excellent. The convicts have been well fed and clothed and kindly treated." Compared to other prisoners, George's ordeal was almost benign. He was never sent to an outside camp, never attacked by other inmates, and never whipped. Even so, he claimed the

Walls almost broke him as a person. "My horrible experience of most abject and cruel slavery," he wrote, was "seldom if ever equaled by any human being."[112]

Like convicts elsewhere in the system, George grumbled about ill-fitting clothes, exhausting labor, and the "cheapest and plainest of food." While prisoners on plantations and railroad projects struggled for their very survival, however, George bemoaned above all the diminution of his personhood. As a white southerner who had jealously guarded his honor in the free world, he greeted each step of his transformation from citizen to convict with shock and indignation. After being paraded through the streets, chained at the neck to other prisoners, he arrived at the Walls humiliated and afraid. Passing beyond its "terrible threshold," he went through intake rituals not unlike those that dismay prisoners today: he was stripped, prodded, sheared, and outfitted in "a suit of stripes . . . habiliments of shame and disgrace." That night, George was led through dark hallways to "seven row." The guard opened an iron door, and George entered his "new lifetime home," a musty four-by-six two-man cell furnished with nothing more than bedsteads, a couple of buckets, and a wash pan. Overcome with anxiety and exhaustion, he "passed the night in fitful slumber and gloomy meditation."[113]

In the morning, George discovered that his new world was not only constricted but tightly regulated. Although northern lockups were fast abandoning the silent system, Huntsville officials still scripted every movement in hopes of replacing bad habits with military discipline. At dawn, upon the ringing of a "small triangle," inmates were "required to walk out of their cells and fall in line." After a "large triangle sounds," the prisoners then "march forward, three abreast, each man having his right hand on the shoulder of the man in front."

Mealtimes were similarly choreographed. In groups of eight, prisoners filed into the dining room, stood for the count, and, in response to further chimes, sat down and ate for no more than twenty minutes. "From the time a convict enters until he leaves . . . he is not allowed to speak." Instead, the subject diner was instructed to signal his wants to convict servers with approved gestures: "If he wants a piece of bread he holds up his knife; if it is meat, he holds up his fork."[114]

After breakfast, a factory "whistle blows, announcing time to go to work." Assigned to the shoe shop, George chafed under the constant "eye of a master" and the "monotonous" labor. "Allowed to converse in a quiet tone" for only "a few moments" between shifts, the young prisoner envisioned a dreary life of stupefying servitude. Although George had long known hardship, he complained that imprisonment robbed him of what little he held dear: his self-respect and racial privilege, his freedom to speak, move, and manage his own time. "It was indeed especially trying on me, in the very spring of my early manhood, to spend my life in this . . . abject manner, as a slave."[115]

Lest the "kind reader" think that only menacing outlaws suffered such "horrible and appalling . . . misfortune," George cast himself as a sympathetic specimen of Victorian manhood. Emphasizing his refinement and sensitivity, virtues then much prized by the middle class, he contrasted the brutish dehumanization of imprisonment with his own "painful feelings." In chivalric form, he dedicated his story to the devoted mothers of errant boys. Imprisonment not only wounds the felon, he pointed out, but abuses his "tender, loving . . . guardian angel" as well.[116]

Like the first southern critics of the penitentiary, George also appealed to the bonds of white supremacy. In jail, he suggested that one of his most degrading experiences was to share a bed with "three negroes [on] a very cold night." Not long after, he was "neck[ed] . . . to a negro" for transportation—"just think of that, will you?" These prejudices notwithstanding, George developed a certain empathy for the few African Americans held at the Walls. While visiting the inmate hospital, he was especially moved by the suffering of a black man who had been brought in from a farm after a severe beating by guards. The fellow had been flayed for missing his cotton quota, George explained, and once a "fever set in," he grew delirious, believing he was "still under and crowded by his task masters." George tried to comfort him, but in a death scene out of *Uncle Tom's Cabin*, the patient slipped into unconsciousness, muttering, " 'Getting cotton here, boss; getting a move on myself.' Then all was still." Toiling to the end, the man was soon "breathing his last."[117]

Although George eventually secured a pardon and walked free, he refused to see any justice in Texas's penal system. Rather, he turned the official depiction of the prison topsy turvy. Whereas Huntsville's managers touted its "flourishing" industries and "kind" treatment, George conjured a dungeon of "sorrow and misery" run by "a pack of dogs."[118]

• • •

While the Walls served as the nexus of prison industries, a second component of Governor Roberts's scheme hinged on completing another penitentiary eighty miles to the north. Like the antebellum textile mill at Huntsville, this new facility was supposed to jump-start manufacturing and alleviate dependency on the North, this time in iron production. Squads of convicts and free hands labored on the project for years, and midway through Roberts's term the hulking Rusk ironworks was ready for business. It was Texas's most ambitious attempt at industrialization through forced labor.[119]

A complex of sandstone buildings surrounded by thick East Texas pine forest, the Rusk prison had cells for 1,056 inmates, almost double the capacity of Huntsville.[120] It boasted the penal system's first electrification plant, and when the furnace ignited, the facility stood out as an illuminated fortress of modernization. On any given day, curious visitors could watch gangs of convicts chopping wood outside the walls while the foundry blazed. "To the lovers of the beautiful, a night visit to the blast furnace will repay them," a state senator noted. "When the runs are being made the heavens are lit up for miles around."[121]

Truth be told, there wasn't much of a market for iron products in Texas; driving cattle and baling cotton required only so much hardware. Just as politicians were beginning to realize they had erected a "sinkhole for money," however, a fire at the state capitol gave the prison an unexpected boost. Orders for iron columns, dome castings, and ornamental finishings poured in. Despite the opposition of organized labor, hundreds of convicts cast arches, cut wood, and quarried granite for the Renaissance Revival facade.[122] The result was a lovely public building but also a monument to command labor relations. Texas's original capitol had been built by slaves, its replacement largely by convicts.

But the completion of Texas's sunset-hued statehouse marked the beginning of Rusk's corrosion into obsolescence. Edward Cunningham, the principal lessee, had never embraced Governor Roberts's dream of industrial penitentiaries, and as convicts arrived at the new prison he had many of them diverted to better-paying pursuits, namely, farming. Other problems plagued the foundry as well. In no time, the surrounding forests went up in smoke. Transportation costs for materials soared, so much so that officials decided to build a special railway, a boondoggle that cost many prisoners their lives and ate up half a million dollars.[123] In short, the largest iron manufactory of any kind in Texas amounted to, in the words of legislative investigators, "stupendous folly."[124]

Perhaps because Rusk's glorious promise so instantly begot failure, the convict memoirs it produced are even more acerbic than those conceived elsewhere. One of the fieriest is Charles C. Campbell's *Hell Exploded: An Exposition of Barbarous Cruelty and Prison Horrors*. The story begins, as most prisoner stories do, with hard luck. Campbell lost both parents, and at fourteen he "drifted out on the cold mercy of the world." He traveled from town to town. He blackened his face with cork and played his banjo in order "to keep up the habit of eating." He drank, he fought, he forged a check, and a "thick headed" jury sent him to prison for two years. In no time, he had a "substantial ornament around [his] neck" and was delivered by state railway to the prison ironworks. In this way, Campbell mimics the plot structure of Andrew George's *Texas Convict*, though he replaces noble didacticism with unbridled rage. This work is no "treatise on kindness and good morals," he advised. "The language used is a mixture of scrap iron, broken glass, barbed wire, and fragments of rusty thunder bolts strung together with fish hooks and prickly pears."[125]

As did George, Campbell described his initiation into prison life as a harrowing descent from manliness to dependence, civilization to savagery, whiteness to slavery. After surrendering his property and donning a suit of "big blue stripes" (a supposedly less stigmatizing color than the conventional black, another Roberts reform), he exclaimed, "Subjection! Oh, the terrible, the awful import of that word! The pride and ambition of a man brought to the ground and trampled upon. . . . Every refining attribute smothered with complete humiliation."[126]

At the Walls, George had focused on what Erving Goffman would later call the rituals of social mortification, but at Rusk, Campbell's concerns quickly shifted from the mind to the body. Arriving at the ironworks in the morning, his first task was to load wood into a wagon, move it across the complex, and then restack it next to a charcoal kiln. The lifting itself wasn't so difficult, but hauling the loaded wagon was another matter. "We had to hitch ourselves to it and get down and paw the sand just the same as mules," he explained. The demeaning assignment was meant to underscore the initiate's new status; it also left "the palms of [his] hands . . . a solid blister."[127]

The next morning, Campbell naively requested a "lay in" based on the condition of his hands, but he received curses and a reassignment to the ore beds instead. Handed a "rusty crow-bar and a rough handled pick," he was instructed to start pounding. This was Campbell's real introduction to prisoner powerlessness. "My first impulse was to grab up a pick and dig out his macaroni brains, but a strange choking sensation came over me, and I felt like I wanted to die."[128]

In the months ahead, Campbell faced even more wrenching ordeals. In the style of many slave narratives, he escorted the reader through an escalating series of trials before finally regaining his self-respect and liberty. Assigned to a brush-clearing "roustabout squad," he insulted a field boss and was stripped, tied down, and lashed until his back and legs were shredded. Transferred to a wood-chopping detail, he lost three fingers to an ax and was then punished for shirking. The prison surgeon, an "old dispenser of death," peeled back the skin, clipped the bone to the joint, and sewed him up "like he was repairing a saddle"— all without painkillers of any kind. Afterward, Campbell was cast into "the 'loony's cell' and chained . . . to a ring in the wall," where he remained for the next forty days and forty nights, subsisting on "a little okra soup and some water." When his arm swelled to "twice [its] normal size," he lanced his wounds with a shard of broken glass. "If ever there was or ever will be a soul in hell that suffered or will suffer greater agony," he railed blasphemously, "heaven is a farce and God a tyrant."[129]

Campbell survived this Dantean descent into Rusk's circles of agony. He remarked, "When I was finally taken out, I was the most cadaverous looking object one might well care to look upon."[130] Still, he had enough fight in him to attempt escape and finally write his screed after his release. Notwithstanding his claims to singularity, other prisoners suffered as much or more than Campbell. The difference is that most convicts left behind nary a trace of their existence, much less their hardships in prison. Except for perfunctory court records, census tabulations, or an occasional notation in a "whipping ledger," they did their time and vanished to history.

## "GO DOWN OL' HANNAH"

Most convicts—and almost all nonwhite convicts—were sent to outside camps, which generated the highest returns for lessees. Although Governor Roberts had proposed to centralize and industrialize Texas's penal system, in reality, it became more dispersed and agricultural. In

1884, with Rusk blazing, some 48 percent of Texas's 2,539 convicts occupied cells in one of the penitentiaries, with the remainder working all over eastern Texas on railroads, mines, and plantations. Twenty years later, as the total prisoner population approached 4,000, the penitentiary portion had declined to 30 percent.[131] By reforming and segregating the convict lease system, Governor Roberts and his successors, in the end, only strengthened and expanded it.

After the Panic of 1893 depressed railroad construction, plantations increasingly came to dominate Texas punishment, yet we know comparably little about them. Journalists, legislative investigators, and prison officials wrote extensively about conditions at the penitentiaries but recorded few details about the farms. This lack of documentation extends to prisoner writing as well, largely because the walled institutions more often confined literate whites. State and university archives contain hundreds of records written by white convicts at Huntsville and Rusk; by contrast, prisoners of color concentrated on the farms—and women prisoners generally—are poorly represented. Although Texas has always punished African Americans and Mexicans most intensely, historians are largely reliant on the voices of Anglos with respect to the early years.

Until the civil rights era, no woman or person of color published a substantive convict autobiography or book-length exposé in Texas.[132] Even so, a variety of sources can be used to piece together a sense of plantation life at the height of the leasing era. Records of the Penitentiary Board dwell overwhelmingly on harvest figures, lease payments, and capital improvements, but they also include telling statistics, from demographic indicators to death tallies. Newspaper articles, legislative inquests, and occasional letters by prisoners help fill in the blanks. None of these scattered and self-interested sources provide a full reconstruction of the convict experience, but they do open a window on daily life. They allow us to imagine the career of a representative Texas prisoner around the turn of the century.

A typical convict, according to admission charts, was born in rural East Texas, the son of former slaves. He grew up poor, probably in rickety sharecropper housing. He might have attended church or school but not enough to qualify as literate. Nor did he claim, when queried by a prison clerk, to have a "trade or profession," though he had almost surely worked for wages or shares. With a constricted economic horizon and a thirst for cash, drink, or respect, this fellow ran afoul of the law. Before the age of twenty-four, he showed up in prison records, a first-timer convicted of a property offense, most likely horse theft or burglary. His sentence probably ranged from two to three years, though escape, pardon, or death might cut it short.[133] The limited statistics available suggest that this unremarkable prisoner bears striking similarities to the typical convict today. From the end of slavery forward, Texas's prisons have predominately and disproportionately disciplined the same sort of people: poor black men living on the margins of society.

For most African American prisoners, the road to prison was unobstructed by legal niceties. In the days before *Powell v. Alabama* (1932) and *Gideon v. Wainwright* (1963), low-income defendants had no right to counsel; verdicts were returned swiftly and usually guilty. "It has come to be axiomatic that the defendant who has means . . . can escape punishment," observed Tom Finty, a prominent Dallas journalist, "and it is equally true that a man without means stands practically no chance." Low-income African Americans had the deck twice stacked against them. By the 1880s, white Democrats had regained control of almost every Texas county, with the result that the vast majority of criminal defendants stood alone before white judges, white prosecutors, and all-white juries. "Have not the rich and influential white murderers been acquitted, while the colored hog thief has been sent to Huntsville?" asked a political pamphlet circulated among eligible black voters. Throughout the South, "it was not . . . a question of crime, but rather one of color, that settled a man's conviction on almost any charge," argued W. E. B. DuBois.[134] Although the black codes were gone, African Americans in Texas were nonetheless going to prison at seven times the rate of whites.[135] By 1890, Texas was imprisoning more African Americans than any other state in the Union.[136]

Most of these prisoners began their incarceration in jail. Conditions varied by county, but local lockups were generally even more disorganized and unequipped than their state counterparts. As jail populations rose, many sheriffs set up their own cozy relationships with nearby employers: renting out prisoners, enforcing peonage, or rounding up hapless travelers for the harvest. Rural work sites set up for jail inmates by smalltown proprietors ranked even lower "in the scale of degradation than the state convict camps," averred John Henderson, an appellate judge who became a prominent leasing critic. "In the one, oppression and cruelty are regulated somewhat by law." In the other, "the supreme law . . . is the unbridled will of the private lessee."[137]

County inmates rarely made themselves heard, but here and there a letter survives in a governor's papers to corroborate Henderson's charges. A prisoner on a Nacogdoches County road gang complained that local officials "just do as they please just make thir on rules." I work "from sun up till sun down," he wrote, and for no good reason, they "tied me to a tree an liked to whipped me to death." An inmate in the Liberty County jail pleaded that he was wasting away in an "eight foot cell," surrounded by "prisoners that have got the scurvy so bad that their teeth are falling out."[138]

For some prisoners, transfer to the state meant an improvement in living conditions, though few would have looked forward to it. Disabled prisoners and white long-timers usually went to a penitentiary, but most convicts were headed for more lucrative work sites. Because the labor was regarded as semiskilled, railroads took possession of the healthiest Anglos and Mexicans.[139] African American convicts, by contrast, were generally chained up and hauled by wagon or train to a plantation, perhaps a cotton farm like Eastham but more likely a bottomland spread nearer the gulf. Throughout the last two decades of the nineteenth century, the owner of this property, more than likely, was Edward Cunningham, Texas's lessee extraordinaire.

Between 1878 and 1883, Cunningham and his partner Littleberry Ellis had run Texas's penal system as a private kingdom. Governor Roberts sometimes criticized them, arguing that subcontracts were poorly supervised and that too few white inmates were sent to work at the penitentiaries. Despite his uneasiness, however, Roberts always settled on the penurious course. When Cunningham's lease headed toward expiration in 1883, the governor ultimately endorsed full renewal. "This is no time for costly experiments," his superintendent advised the legislature. Many lawmakers agreed. Advancing arguments in favor of prison privatization that echo into the present, Representative James Chenoweth insisted that "business matters are never controlled by . . . governments with the same economy and good management as by individuals." A colleague warned that an end to leasing would result in "extravagant expenditures . . . for the state."[140]

The Sugar King no doubt appreciated this show of support, but he took no chances. According to *Texas Siftings*, an Austin newspaper, he also ran an aggressive if illicit lobbying campaign. Near the Capitol, he set up a private club for legislators, stocked with "whisky . . . cigars and other luxuries." To avoid the impropriety of outright bribery, he invited salons to games of "jack-pot poker," in which even the most hapless card player could win handsomely.[141]

The strategy backfired. The senate voted to renew Cunningham's lease, but after the *Texas Siftings* articles appeared, a "tidal wave of . . . public sentiment" swamped the vote in the house. Seeking to sidestep obloquy, Cunningham preemptively withdrew his bid and allowed his lease to expire on May 15, 1883.[142]

In the wake of what became known as "the poker legislature," Texas never again leased out its entire penal system to a single enterprise.[143] But this was hardly the end of prisoner contracting. After 1883, the state assumed full control over its two penitentiaries, but almost immediately Goree and the Penitentiary Board started signing labor deals with a variety of employers, most of them experienced with convicts. Some proprieters signed up to run workshops at the penitentiaries, while a larger number arranged to take possession of prisoners at their own mines, wood camps, or plantations. Texas thus canceled one lease but continued leasing.

From the point of view of prisoners, this administrative reorganization made little difference. Because Cunningham's subcontractors were the first to negotiate new deals with the state, most convicts stayed put, working for the same masters as before. Even the Sugar King managed to stay in the game. Although he had lost his exclusive lease, Cunningham soon received a fresh allocation of 243 convicts for his properties along Oyster Creek. In some ways, this comparatively modest contract was more beneficial to the planter. As the sole lessee, Cunningham had been responsible for the entire system: the profitable plantations but also the unprofitable penitentiaries; the healthy and hardworking but also the aged and sick. As one labor contractor among many, Cunningham could now take his pick of convicts. Accordingly, he began to accept only "first-class" black field hands, men he could work to the bone with little fear of public outcry. Even better, his new contracts stipulated that burdensome sick or injured inmates had to be quickly replaced by the state. In this way, the productivity that Cunningham wrested from convicts actually increased after his monopoly expired. A full ten years following his ignoble defeat at the legislature, he remained the largest prison contractor and the most successful sugar planter in Texas.[144]

• • •

With no principal lessee, state officials had to figure out what to do with those prisoners contractors rejected, inmates that Goree described as "old men, boys, [and] cripples." At Rusk and the Walls, private companies operated the foundry and a few manufacturers, but this solved only part of the problem. Texas's prison population was steadily growing, and while physically robust "first-class" men were easy to rent out, "surplus labor," or "deadheads," were not.[145] As a solution, state officials decided to acquire land and take up cash-crop convict agriculture themselves.

Texas's first state-owned prison farm, Wynne, fell into state hands almost by accident. As part of a complicated severance deal with Cunningham, the Penitentiary Board acquired 1,900 acres along the northern border of Huntsville. Administrators originally intended to grow only prison-use crops with "invalid convicts who otherwise would have been a dead expense to the state," but within two years, the farm's productivity inspired grander ambitions.[146]

The prison system's next purchase—inspired by Cunningham's "grand success" in the sugar business—was the Harlem Farm, a "truly magnificent . . . plantation" situated "in the Brazos bottom and on Oyster Creek." The operation was an "experiment," said Superintendent Goree, to see whether the state could profitably work "second-class negroes" on its own lands.[147] To get started required a sizable outlay for a sugar house and sundry equipment, including guns and ammunition. Even so, "the test [was] pronounced a decided success." Within four years, Harlem's swampy canebrakes—later dubbed a "burning hell"—had produced a net gain of $20,000.[148] More impressively, the prison system's financial agent calculated that Harlem's supposedly weaker inmates were earning more profit per head than "first-class, able-bodied negro convicts employed on contract farms," $501.39 per capita annually versus $178. Forced labor, it turned out, could generate income just as surely for government bosses as for private ones.

Buoyed by financial gain, prison officials requested permission from the legislature to buy more farms, "some on the Brazos . . . and Colorado rivers, where the land is rich, on which to work negro convicts, and some . . . upland places on which to work white men."[149] Lawmakers agreed, and in 1887 the state bought land just north of Gatesville to serve as a reform school for boys.[150] In 1899, the Penitentiary Board purchased the Clemens Farm, 8,212 acres in the "Sugar Bowl District of Brazoria County."[151] Although costly, officials saw these purchases as sound investments.[152] By banking the extraordinary profits of forced labor—first from leasing and secondarily from the state farms—they aimed to gradually buy themselves out of the lease system. Just as slavery had served as the inspiration for convict leasing, in turn, convict leasing funded and fashioned its replacement, state-managed convict farming.

Although private profiteering was absent on the state farms, prison records and investigative reports indicate that living and labor conditions hardly changed. In most cases, the Penitentiary Board purchased plantations from lessees and then carried on operations in the same manner and with the same personnel as before. On every farm, whether private or public, daily life was harsher than in the penitentiaries. "Rusk prison is a paradise compared to the camps," asserted John Shotwell, who did fourteen years all across the system.[153]

Whether they were sent to private or government farms, convict field hands encountered deprivation of every kind. Prison rules stipulated that prisoners be "comfortably clad," "substantially" fed, and "treated with humanity," but these idealized pronouncements bore little resemblance to reality.[154] Almost universally, convicts reported that they wore the same tattered, filthy uniforms day after day. "The new clothus which we Braught with us was taken away," wrote a group of African American prisoners at the state-owned Clemens Farm, leaving us to work "in all kinds of wearther [with] nothing . . . to ware . . . but Rags." As for food, some prisoners said they received "better than most . . . farmers get on the outside," but the majority groused about monotonous, rotten, bug-infested meals. "We were fed on spoiled hog head," a convict wrote from a lease farm, supplemented by "stale corn bread and coffee made of burned corn bread crust."[155]

At night, prison officials promised "secure and commodious" housing, but in reality convicts slept in squalid twenty-by-fifty-foot plank houses stuffed with double bunks. Up to fifty men jammed inside, sleeping on corn husk mattresses, relieving themselves in common buckets, and washing themselves in a trough of grimy water. Barred windows and a bolted door kept prisoners locked in, but biting insects were free to come and go as they pleased. "The mosquitoes are so bad the convicts have to war gunny sacks over their heads," reported one prisoner.[156]

Sleeping was difficult, but it came easier after a day in the fields. Six days a week, convicts returned to the quarters after dark and woke to the bell before dawn. The rest of the time they worked: felling trees, digging ditches, hoeing weeds, cutting cane, or picking cotton. On the largest farms, the day began with a "fast trot" to the fields, up to five miles away.[157] Once they arrived, prisoners worked in task gangs, a tightly constricted form of labor organization that had been widespread under slavery but had given way to tenancy and sharecropping in the free world.[158] As under slavery, an overseer on horseback supervised each squad, while a convict "lead row" set the pace and sometimes led a work holler. The shifts were long, up to fifteen hours in summer, and the quotas difficult to meet. On a "number one hoe squad" made up of the most able-bodied prisoners, each field hand might be expected to pick four hundred pounds of cotton a day.[159]

Because they spent so much time outdoors, convicts' well-being depended largely on the weather. Prison rules prohibited work in darkness or rain but, as with other directives, they were ignored. Testifying before legislative inquiries, many camp supervisors admitted they had never seen a copy of the rules, much less tried to enforce them. One convict described working in "mud . . . so deep and heavy that I had to pull off my shoes." Other convicts had no shoes. "One particularly severe winter they did not furnish half of us with shoes," wrote John Shotwell about a lease camp west of Huntsville. "My feet were frost bitten and I almost suffered death."[160]

In the summer, prisoners bewailed the heat and humidity, especially on the sugar farms. "Down there in the jungles," wrote one prisoner, "a man at work . . . would almost gasp for breath." In "Go Down Ol' Hannah," a popular field song, convict singers recalled a summer "on de Brazis" so hot "we wuz almos' dyin'." With "the cap'n . . . holl'in" and "the mens . . . fallin'," the workers turned to the sun itself for mercy, begging "Ol' Hannah" to set and stay set forever:

Go down, ol' Hannah, doncha rise no mo',
Go down, ol' Hannah, doncha rise no mo';
Ef you rise in de mornin', bring Jedgment Day.[161]

Indeed, Texas prison farms did bring Judgment Day to many prisoners. Apologists for prison agriculture insisted that "employing the negro and the Mexican convict on farms" was necessary because of "the limited capacity of these races to acquire technical knowledge." They claimed that "the Negro is more likely to die within the walls than working outside."[162] Actual death figures suggest the opposite. Huntsville often recorded more deaths than any other site, but a prison physician estimated that "50 percent of those who die within the walls are worn out and broken down on the farms and then sent back to the prison to die." "The policy of management," asserted one convict, is "to send only the most robust out upon the farms, and to bring back to the walls the mutilated and sick to be exchanged for well ones." Overall, African American convicts in Texas perished at nearly twice the rate of whites.[163]

The causes of death varied, but the prison system's own tallies suggest that exhaustion, filth, and violence predominated. Among the top killers in a typical biennium were dysentery (17), sunstroke (15), typhoid (14), malaria (12), gunshot wounds (8), and, more generally, "killed trying to escape" (10). "In many cases sick convicts are made to toil until they drop dead in their tracks," complained a black citizens' convention.[164] Whatever the causes, the totals were ghastly, especially considering the fact that roughly 90 percent of enumerated prisoners were under the age of fifty.[165] On any given year, 112, 84, or 150 convicts passed away.[166] Between 1866, when leasing began, and 1912, when the last contracts expired, at least 3,558 prisoners lost their lives, most from unnatural causes.[167] The numbers show that in Texas alone imprisonment in the leasing era took a larger toll than the horror of southern lynching, which has attracted much greater attention. According to research conducted by the Tuskegee Institute, 3,220 African Americans were lynched in the South between 1880 and 1930.[168] Over the five and a half decades, the death total associated with convict leasing across the South probably exceeds 30,000.[169]

Death was the ultimate consequence of southern justice, but some prisoners more dreaded survival. "Young man, old men,—men! Don't go to that place!" exclaimed Charles Campbell. "If Fate ever says you must go—die first! Welcome death instead of worse than death." Prison punishments terrified convicts, especially those administered with "the bat," a thick leather strap that became Texas's instrument of choice from the 1880s forward. "Down here in Texas we do not know how to manage without the strap," explained Huntsville's warden to a national audience. "We have been trying to reduce it as much as we could. . . . But there are men that will not allow you to be kind to them." Asked by legislators whether or not "Negroes can be ruled without the strap," a captain at the Borden Farm replied, "No, sir; I am positive they can not."[170]

Much prison discipline aimed to extract labor, but as a set of leather-bound "whipping ledgers" stored at the state archives reveal, punishments were also inflicted to assert supremacy and debase prisoners. Violations of prison hierarchy—"disobedience," "impudence," and "misconduct"—were more frequently punished than labor infractions like "laziness." "I have heard [a] hardened . . . guard say 'he loved to see a damn convict suffer, and gloried in their misery,'" wrote Andrew George.[171]

Carried out in the fields or back in the quarters at night, whippings were perversely intimate affairs. Guards and convicts shared the noise, sweat, blood, and smells, though not the pain. For some bosses, lashing flesh took on twisted, even sadistic homoerotic qualities. When officers wanted to convey special dissatisfaction, they stripped off a convict's clothes and let loose on the "naked hide." Other prisoners were made to watch or help pin the naked victim to the ground. After one particularly bloody episode, a manager had other convicts parade before him to "smell . . . the bat."[172]

This stagecraft of dominion and degradation did not stop with whipping. A prisoner on the Johnson Farm claimed he was forced to "eat his own droppings." On the Clemens Farm, several convicts charged that Captain Grace punished sodomy by forcing suspects to engage in humiliating public sex acts. After being caught "playing man and wife," reported one prisoner, the captain "whipped me about 45 licks" and then "made me kiss the other fellow's tail." Calling other prisoners to gather around, Grace had one "Negro hold a light," while he made "me drag my tongue right through the hole." "Now, don't that taste good, you G-d-m-f-s-of a b-," he asked, "and I would say, yes sir; Captain."[173]

Although prisoners were censored, retaliated against, legally barred from testifying in court, and assailed as liars ("Some of these darkeys down here can make the best speeches you ever heard," remarked one warden), their complaints nonetheless spilled into the public arena. Against great adversity and at great risk to themselves, convicts mailed incendiary letters to church leaders and governors, wrote their own stories, and contradicted their masters in legislative hearings. None of these efforts reached a mass audience, but they effectively countered official pronouncements and increasingly influenced skeptical reporters and politicians. By the turn of the century, prisoners were helping shape the terms of debate. As convict grievances piled up in the public record, reformers in the free world began echoing the wide-ranging criticisms of for-profit punishment developed by educated convicts. While state officials insisted that Texas had "a pretty good penitentiary system," prisoners depicted it as corrupt, sadistic, and spirit-breaking, dedicated to avarice rather than public safety, staffed by ignorant, brutish guards, and incompatible with an "advanced and enlightened age."[174] Bourgeois humanitarians adopted these conventions wholesale, such that by the dusk of the lease era convicts, clergymen, club women, journalists, and dissident politicians seemed to be speaking in one voice. Texas prisons are "gruesome and satanic," declared one newspaper, while lawmakers excoriated the system as "a disgrace to Christian civilization."[175]

While prisoner writers and witnesses influenced the thinking of reformers, they also went several steps farther. In the free world, leasing opponents like George Washington Cable tended to look to the North for leadership. In accordance with the principles of the National Prison Association, their goal was not to relax prison discipline but to make it more effective. Convicts, by contrast, tended to regard prison improvement schemes with skepticism. Reform is nothing but "a grim joke" played by every "'bone head' that chances to get into the Legislature," scoffed Joe Wilkinson, a prisoner at Rusk.[176] Although convicts favored many of the same administrative fixes put forward by reformers—better food, less whipping, and shorter work hours—their concerns went much deeper.

Convicts depicted a prison world perfectly inverted from free-world concepts, a world impossible to redeem by simple retooling. Where outsiders imagined tough but orderly institutions in which hardscrabble public servants watched over unruly and menacing criminals, convicts conveyed bastions of lawlessness lorded over by "brutes of the most savage kind." In representing guards as "incarnate fiends" and the penal system as a "bifurcated hell," in assailing the depredations of state farms as zealously as leasing camps, convicts signaled they wanted to upturn the foundation of Texas criminal justice. "The only reform" I seek, declared Charles Campbell, will be complete "when the form of the devil is seen clambering up out of his bed of hot ashes and takes the entire gang by the neck and slams it into hell."[177]

Together with escapees, rioters, work strikers, and letter writers, angry autobiographers like Campbell would play a pivotal role in the final dismantling of convict leasing, but they would not necessarily embrace its replacement.

# 4

## THE AGONIES OF REFORM

> Let it be no more written over the doors of our prisons, as was written
> over the portals of Dante's Inferno, "He who enters here leaves hope
> behind."
>
> —JUDGE JOHN N. HENDERSON, AUSTIN, TEXAS[1]

When Lula Sanders got out of prison in August 1907, she faced daunting prospects. She was only thirty-one years old but had no education,
no high-dollar skills, and no husband with whom to pool resources.
Many African American women worked as domestic servants in those
days, but Sanders lacked the deferential temperament. A tall, thickset
woman with a combustible demeanor, she had trouble holding her fists
much less her tongue. Assault to murder had landed her in prison, and
she had once received "20 licks" for fighting with a razor.[2]

Sanders would have had better luck finding a job picking cotton, as
she had done in prison, but like many ex-convicts she wanted to leave
field labor behind. Collecting her discharge money, she traveled to Fort
Worth, where she had worked previously as a cook. There, she might
have pushed three harrowing years of imprisonment into the closet
of her memory. But Sanders remained haunted by the women she left
behind at the Johnson Farm, a privately owned cotton plantation near
Huntsville, the home of Texas's women prisoners since 1883. Before her
release, she recalled that other inmates "got . . . on there kneese and
begged" her to make public their plight.[3] And so, although prison records listed Sanders as illiterate, she sat down on October 2 and struggled through a letter that would, as the first link in a chain of events,
change Texas history.

Prison officials claimed that women at Johnson were "exceptionally well . . . cared for," that they benefited from "wholesome exercise, plenty of well-cooked provisions, and an enforcement of regular habits." By contrast, Sanders wrote that "there were never a more inhumane place in the world." "We have had to cut down trees and build roads like we were men," she reported, adding that when inmates "fall out" from heat exhaustion "they were dragged out under a tree and throwed water on like a dog." If any woman refused to work or angered her bosses, they had their "nackedness [exposed] to all the guards" and were "whipped so bad" that blood had to be scrubbed off the floor.[4]

But this was not the only sort of nakedness going on at Johnson. According to Sanders, guards had the power to take "any woman in any squad for their convenience." The result was a greenbrier thicket of sex relations: assaults, semiconsensual affairs, and jealous rivalries. She wrote that officers regarded some prisoners as "too pretty to work" and made other women pick up the slack, thus instigating many fights. Prisoners also started getting pregnant. "Two thirds of the Children that have been borned down there is the guards'," charged Sanders.

Although she penned a long letter in careful strokes, Sanders could not have expected much to come of it. She had seen inspectors visit Johnson, and she knew they reported that "they treat the convicts nice." What Sanders didn't know was that a new governor, Thomas Campbell, had only days before received a packet of papers detailing similar charges. Not far from Huntsville, alleged one John Tardy, guards "are raising themselves some convicts out on a farm [for] convict negro women."[5]

This was the stuff of first-class scandal, and Governor Campbell ordered all women prisoners transferred to Eastham, regarded at the time as a capably managed lease farm.[6] With that, the matter might have ended had not another official, Jake Hodges, the prison pastor, become aware of Sanders's charges.

Reverend Hodges had been on the job only a few months, but he knew what Sanders said was true—and worse besides. Not six weeks before, he had ministered to a dying inmate who had been "whipped with a rope . . . stripped, and put in an ant bed."[7] As the chaplain at Huntsville, he made it to the women's farm only one Sunday a month, but what little he saw troubled him deeply. On one occasion, he discovered an infant who had been born in the fields. According to prisoners, the mother's squad mates had "begged the captain" not to make her work, "for her water had already broke." But the boss ignored them, assigning the woman to haul potatoes in a croker sack. Later that day, she squatted down and gave birth in "the sand of the cotton field." (Not long after she was transferred to Eastham, the baby died.)[8]

As Hodges's misgivings grew, his relations with prison officials grew tense. He tried to report problems to his immediate supervisor, Assistant Superintendent R. H. Underwood, but the man was dismissive and not infrequently drunk. The reverend had only a tenuous hold on his job; he had once worked as a college president but was lucky to have landed the prison post after a mental breakdown. Now Hodges felt anxiety creeping over him again. During whipping sessions, he retreated from his office to "where [he] couldn't hear." He tried to focus on his preaching and evening classes, but the chair of the prison board, William Ramsey, nonetheless warned the governor about his "sensitive nature." Hodges must "mend his ways," Ramsey advised, for "we cannot stand for anything that will undermine the discipline or cause trouble."[9]

But Hodges did not mend. He agonized. He withdrew into himself. Ultimately, he broke ranks. Even though, as one admirer put it, the pastor risked "his position, if not his life," he finally decided that no man worthy of the cloth could remain silent. When it became clear that the governor would take no further action in response to Sanders's letter—there would be no criminal charges and no new regulations—Reverend Hodges called on an idealistic young reporter, George Waverly Briggs. On December 5, 1908, Briggs began a long series of stories in the *San Antonio Express*, one of the state's leading newspapers. Convict leasing had weathered countless storms over the previous four decades, but it would not survive this one.[10]

## "THE WILL OF THE PEOPLE"

Although Texas has long been regarded as a stronghold of reaction in American politics, there has always been more to the story. If the Lone Star State has produced its share of Ku Kluxers and Texas Regulars, it has also given rise to agrarian socialists, borderland revolutionaries, and prison reformers.[11] This was particularly true toward the end of the nineteenth century, when a host of grassroots movements sprung up to challenge an increasingly stratified social order. Before Lula Sanders mailed her thunderclap, these movements had been gathering force. Together—sometimes working in harmony, other times apart—they finally mustered enough power to counter all the dollars commanded by lessees.

Among the first popular movements to take aim at convict leasing was organized labor. During the 1880s, a coalition of unions organized a boycott to protest the use of contract prison labor in building the State Capitol, which they denounced as a "scab job."[12] The effort failed—as did a much larger campaign organized by the Knights of Labor—but the Penitentiary Board nonetheless got skittish about approving contracts in the mechanical trades.[13] Heeding the "howl . . . against 'competing with free labor,'" prison officials turned their backs on industrialization, including the ironworks, wrote a Dallas journalist. Instead, they "inaugurate[d] a back-to-the-farm movement."[14] Ironically, organized labor helped derail Oran Roberts's plans for skilled-labor penitentiaries, the very system that was supposed to restore fallen white men to free-labor citizenship.

Another movement that had a pronounced impact on Texas's prison politics was agrarian radicalism. Around the turbulent turn of the nineteenth century, the state's struggling farmers became increasingly politicized. Tens of thousands of them had pinned their hopes to cotton, which sat "on the throne as a money crop." But as production soared and prices plummeted, they harvested not yeoman independence but desiccated dreams. Battered by droughts, boll weevils, and repeated economic downturns, smallholders increasingly lost their land and went to work as tenants or sharecroppers. In 1880, 38 percent of Texas farms had been operated by tenants; by 1900, the portion had grown to 50 percent. "We are just alive and that is all," lamented one African American tenant. "We never get out of debt, no matter how we toil."[15]

Out of these fields of disappointment grew some of the most powerful movements in American history: the Grange, Greenbackers, Farmers' Alliance, People's Party, and the Farmers' Union, in turn. They rallied against miserly creditors and monopolistic railroads and eventually took aim at the very structure of American society. Instead of a gilded age, they set out to build a "cooperative commonwealth." As the fastest-growing cotton producer in the nation, Texas served as a hothouse of agrarian radicalism. Lampasas County, where overconfident immigrants had pushed cotton beyond Central Texas's blackland prairie and onto more arid plains, gave birth to the Farmers' Alliance, a cooperative movement that eventually grew to some four million members, including two hundred thousand in Texas. Forced to organize separately by whites, African Americans in Houston County, site of the Eastham plantation, chartered what became the Colored Farmers' National Alliance, a group that eventually counted more than a million members and led a daring but ill-fated cotton pickers' strike in 1891. At their most inclusive, both alliances struggled against the odds to organize proletarians and tenants, whites and blacks, westerners and southerners into "one united brotherhood" standing against "power and plunder."[16]

Like their unionized comrades, farm organizers spoke out forcefully against Texas's "faulty, vicious, and corrupt convict system." As early as 1878, the Greenback Party argued that "the honest mechanic and laborer . . . should not be forced into competition with gangs of convicts sent to the penitentiaries for crimes."[17] By the 1890s, agrarian leaders pushed the matter further. Turning conventional conceptions of crime and criminals upside down, activists affiliated with the People's Party declared, "Wealth belongs to him who creates it, and every dollar taken from industry without an equivalent is robbery." Society's criminal "enemies" lurked not on the social margins, in other words, but at the centers of power, where "the fruits of the toil of millions are boldly stolen to build up colossal fortunes for a few." The Populists, as partisans of the People's Party were known, demanded that convicts be paid for their work and provided "intellectual and moral instruction."[18]

Populism had more staying power in Texas than organized labor—largely due to the state's overwhelmingly rural character—but its influence on leasing ultimately produced a similar result: the growth of convict agriculture. Because organized farmers fancied themselves independent proprietors rather than agricultural proletarians, they spoke out more forcefully against profiteering lessees and railroads than against the use of unpaid prisoner field hands. They didn't worry about depressing agricultural wages because they regarded themselves, however naively, as potential employers. Even as Populists articulated a radical critique of convict leasing's role in solidifying an unholy social order, therefore, they ended up countenancing the expansion of prison plantations. Under fire from the left, prison officials reinforced just the sort of institution that convicts dreaded most.

Populism scared the wits out of Texas's ruling Democrats, provoking violence and electoral fraud in many cases but also forcing them to sail the ship of state leftward. Railroad regulation, loose monetary policy, homesteader rights, and the abolition of convict leasing all showed up in Democratic platforms by the end of the century.[19] At the same time, a more genteel sort of social movement gained sway that ultimately played a more direct role in crafting criminal justice policy: middle-class progressivism.

Progressivism never exerted the same influence in Texas as it did in the Midwest and Northeast, but by the early 1900s growing ranks of Texas townsfolk were developing progressive-style campaigns to file down the jagged edges of modern living. Kindergartens, food safety, child labor regulation, and natural parks ranked among their core issues, as did penal reform. As champions of efficient government and careful management of the "dangerous classes," respectable reformers recoiled at the lease system, which they regarded as a "wasteful . . . inheritance of our earliest savage ancestors." In contrast to Populists, however, progressives tended to worry less about social inequity than instability. Texas's privately run prison camps were nothing but "schools [for] cut-throats, rapists, and murderers," warned a University of Texas professor. Progressives advocated more humanitarian punishment, but they also wanted more effective discipline. They sought modern methods that would lead to the "suppression of crime and the extinction of the criminal class."[20]

Homegrown progressives were often drowned out by economizing conservatives, but in 1897, the National Prison Association held its annual congress in Austin and gave Texas reformers a boost. Lucius Whatley, the superintendent, hoped the gathering would showcase his administration's improvements. "I am not afraid to ask you to go to Huntsville" and even "some of our outside camps," he announced. "If we are a new state, we have a pretty good penitentiary system." In the months leading up to the congress, however, national organizers made contact with local progressives—chaplains, physicians, and judges— and choreographed an event that would deliver more castigation than kudos. The NPA's president, Roeliff Brinkerhoff, a former Union general from Ohio, assured local delegates that "we are not here to criticize," but in reality, nearly every session celebrated the northern innovations, like indeterminate sentencing and women's reformatories, that Texas lacked. Rather than refining the system Texas had in place, NPA luminaries urged administrators to adopt wholesale Zebulon Brockway's Elmira model, which they said was "going over the country like a wave."

Your "evolution" may be costly and difficult, President Brinkerhoff conceded, but such were the demands of science and "God's law."[21]

Shrewdly, NPA organizers left it to Texans to deliver the most blistering criticisms of their home state. A judge on the Texas Court of Criminal Appeals, John Henderson, delivered a damning keynote. Whipping by whipping, scandal by scandal, death by death, he condemned the regime Superintendent Whatley was trying to showcase, comparing it to the "horrors inflicted on the Siberian exiles." Fifty years had passed since the founding of the Walls, the judge pointed out, but the state's first penitentiary builders had "understood . . . prison management . . . better than their descendants." Let us change direction, he implored. "Let it be no more written over the doors of our prisons, as was written over the portals of Dante's Inferno, 'He who enters here leaves hope behind.' "[22]

As the applause abated, Whatley gamely rose to challenge some of Henderson's claims, but President Brinkerhoff shut him down. Elsewhere, too, Texas loyalists fell back. On the platform committee, southerners inserted a plank on states' rights, but no one spoke in favor of convict leasing, the principal penal institution everywhere in the region. Former superintendent Goree, who had devoted his life to Texas prisons and bore as much responsibility as anyone for their condition, managed only this: "While our system may not be perfect we have done the very best we could."[23]


By the end of the NPA congress, it seemed that no one supported the convict lease system in Texas. Labor leaders, agrarian radicals, and middle-class progressives were all denouncing the practice, while prisoners, by escaping, sowing mayhem, and publishing exposés, kept their warders constantly off balance. Even as the forty-year-old institution started to teeter, however, another species of grassroots social movement was giving it legs. That movement was white supremacy, an ideological force that had long shaped American social relations but that experienced a virulent resurgence around the turn of the century. While the "Age of Reform," as Richard Hofstadter christened it, gave us national parks, the eight-hour day, women's suffrage, and, ultimately, the New Deal, this pivotal era was also characterized by vicious labor repression, the country's first imperial war, and, not least, an epidemic of lynching and race riots—fateful clashes that ultimately cast a new racial order, one that would mock the promises of emancipation for three generations: Jim Crow segregation.[24]

Even at the National Prison congress—where reformers pledged themselves to the "grander cycles of human destiny"—hardening racial attitudes were on display. Although Texas's official delegates found themselves outmaneuvered on most questions, their grumblings about the "colored element" elicited support. In the middle of a debate on whipping, Frederick H. Wines, son of the NPA's founder and a prominent penologist in his own right, rose to the South's defense. "You gentlemen in charge of northern prisons who may have a few negro prisoners, do not know anything at all about the situation here where the great mass of prisoners are negroes," he said. "The negro prisoner . . . has not the sense of shame and degradation that the white man has" and is thus difficult to rehabilitate without corporal punishment. Moreover, "the negro is a man who is not very well adapted to mechanical pursuits. . . . The natural place for [him] is the farm, the plantation."[25]

Such commentary was mostly confined to floor discussions. But on the final weekend night of the convention, before an "immense audience" at the University of Texas, a keynote speaker rose to give white supremacy a full hearing. The lecturer was George T. Winston, UT's first regular president, and his topic, "The Prevention of Crime," turned into a broadside against two threats to civilization, "foreign [and] negro criminals."[26]

These two groups were responsible for most crimes in America, Winston asserted, dubiously conflating prisoner demographics with actual lawbreaking, and while the first could be easily controlled by "properly restricting further immigration," the second would prove "far more difficult." The origin of the problem, as he saw it, reached back to emancipation: the "restraints . . . peculiar to slavery . . . have been cut loose but not replaced by others." As a result, the "impulse"-driven Negro, puffed up with "new ambitions," had not advanced toward civilization but had wallowed in "the freedom of vice, prostitution, gambling, drinking, [and] fighting." He warned, "the Negro problem has not ended, but has only begun."[27]

"To protect their property and civilization," the president argued, "the Southern white population" would have to adopt stern measures. More incarceration and the forcible removal of black children from "depraved, vicious, and cruel" homes would have to be considered. Advanced education, by contrast, would only make matters worse; for what "the negro needs [is not] intellectual culture with freedom of conduct," but "industrial and moral [training], enforced by severe restraints." The only true solution, he declared, was an aggressive, government-managed program of racial separation and subjugation. "These views may seem paternalistic," he admitted, but only to "those who confound liberty with license, who glorify personal freedom at the expense of social progress and civilization."[28]

Such pronouncements were eminently respectable among southern whites when President Winston spoke. Three decades removed from the conflagration of the Civil War, white employers still depended on cheap black labor, but many of them displayed even less tolerance than had their fathers for black independence and politics. Angry about crime, spooked by Populism, and dissatisfied with what they saw as the racial accommodationism of their forebears, a new generation of white politicians rose to prominence at the close of the century and sought to draw clear lines between whites and blacks, lines to be enforced not by custom but by law.[29]

Legal restrictions on free blacks date back to the sixteenth century, but from the 1880s they proliferated, coalescing into a new system of racial governance. In Texas, as elsewhere in the South, railroad depots, schools, prisons, hospitals, and all sorts of public amusements were segregated by legislation. The purpose was to formally divide the world into separate spheres, one dominant, one subordinate, thus adapting the social order of slavery to the modern era. "Lest I be misunderstood, I have no prejudice against the negro in his place," explained Texas's U.S. senator Joseph Bailey, "but I think his place is the white man's kitchen and not the white man's dining room."[30]

Segregation went hand in hand with the exclusion of black men from electoral politics (women, both black and white, were already excluded). Rallying against political corruption, which they associated with "the lowest and most degraded type of the human race," white politicians employed familiar tactics to "purify the ballot box": fraud, literacy tests, and intimidation.[31] In counties where whites controlled law enforcement and the courts, black elected officials found themselves investigated, indicted, and sometimes imprisoned. In majority black districts, Democratic hacks established partisan militias that slashed and burned their way to power. Around Edward Cunningham's spread in Fort Bend County, an all-white Jaybird club terrorized political opponents, ordered African American leaders to leave the area, and finally seized control of local government in a bloody shoot-out at the courthouse as the Texas Rangers stood idly by.[32]

The culmination of this exclusionary crusade was the passage of the poll tax in 1902, a disenfranchisement measure that affected not just blacks but low-income Tejanos and whites. Reinforced by terrorism and trickery, it produced striking results. Into the 1890s, some one hundred thousand black men had continued to cast their ballots in major elections. By 1906, their turnout had dropped to five thousand. This was a demoralizing turn of events for activists on the left. As John Rayner, one of the most influential black populists in the state, put it, "The South loves the Democratic Party more than it does God."[33]

As it had during the Texas revolution, the Civil War, and Redemption, racial violence stands out as a defining feature of this repressive age. Amid the turbulence of the Mexican Revolution, the Texas Rangers, reinforced by vigilantes, local law enforcement, and a contingent of U.S. soldiers, conducted ethnic cleansing along the Rio Grande, killing at least three hundred in response to an aborted uprising in 1915 and driving thousands more from their homes.[34] In eastern Texas, African Americans remained the most common victims. One of the worst incidents occurred in Palestine, just a horse ride away from Rusk. "[I] hastened to the scene and found men running around killing negroes apparently without any . . . provocation," reported the local sheriff. By the end of the day, eighteen African Americans had been murdered without a single loss among whites. This "was no race war," explains Bruce Glasrud, a historian of Texas race relations. "It was a pogrom in which . . . black citizens of the county were hunted down and killed."[35]

Whispers of black rebellion sometimes unleashed these killing sprees, but from the 1880s forward, accusations of rape gained prominence. "Atrocious, diabolical, and shocking" Negro crimes "destroy the reason of the white community . . . driving them almost to a frenzy of summary vengeance," explained UT president Winston. No evidence exists that assaults on white women by black men actually increased during the period, but white commentators nonetheless claimed that extraordinary measures were required to deter what newspapers called the Negro "beast." "If rape and murder by brutish negroes are to become common, the negro must expect extermination," warned an editorial in Longview. "Nothing else will do."[36]

In the first decade of the twentieth century alone, approximately one hundred black Texans were murdered by white vigilantes. Those numbers pale beside the carnage that erupted during and after the Civil War, but in this new cycle of killing, theatrical elements added symbolic force. Unlike the KKK's quasi-secretive assassinations, this new cadre of angry white men sought to redeem their honor by staging public executions of unprecedented ritual and gore. Alongside the Age of Reform, they ignited an Age of Lynching.[37]

"Southern Horrors," as the crusading journalist Ida B. Wells called them, were legion in those days, yet each depraved act seared itself into public consciousness. Take the 1893 lynching of Henry Smith in Paris, Texas. Accused of sexually assaulting and killing a four-year-old white girl, Smith accreted all the lurid fears of new southern racism. A slow-witted fellow who did odd jobs about town, he morphed in the white imagination into a "brute . . . of gorilla ferocity." After being captured near Hope, Arkansas, he was dragged back home, where "indignant" Parisians sidestepped the courts and prepared a spectacle of punishment befitting an eighteenth-century regicide. Ignoring the pleas of a local black minister, white townsfolk fastened Smith to a "carnival float," and paraded him though "a surging mass of humanity 10,000 strong," their numbers augmented by free rail tickets and a mayoral holiday proclamation. The organizers hoisted the man onto a hastily erected scaffold, where the little girl's male relatives took turns burning the accused "inch-by-inch" with "red-hot iron brands," while the throng cheered. After nearly an hour of "slow torture," they doused Smith with oil and set him on fire. From a blurred photograph taken from the back of the crowd, we can make out one word scrawled across the base of the wooden scaffold: "Justice."[38]

To many fin de siècle white southerners, this was justice, terrible but warranted, irregular but effective. Apologists for lynching claimed that "the delays, reversals, and failures of the courts" made such extrajudicial executions necessary. In reality, Texas's conventional halls of justice dispatched African Americans accused of serious crimes with nearly as much haste as the mob. Few black defendants found peers in the jury box, and few hired attorneys. In cases that animated the public, district attorneys issued their own demonizing calls for blood. "If you turn a deaf ear to the thousands of mothers who have daughters [the victim's] age, haven't you formed . . . a covenant with hell?" one prosecutor implored jurors in a capital rape trial. "This Negro is a lustful animal, without anything to transform to any kind of valuable citizen, because he lacks the very fundamental elements of mankind." Such harangues sent sixty-five black Texans to their deaths in the 1890s alone, many fewer executions than would take place a century later in the 1990s but enough to keep pace with lynching.[39] For every rope strung over a tree branch by vigilantes, Texas officials used a legally sanctioned noose at the local jail.

Lesser offenders landed in prison, a state farm, or most likely a lease camp, and here, too, the numbers suggest that racism was gaining strength. Between 1890 and 1904, Texas's white imprisonment rate fell by almost half, but it climbed 27 percent for blacks.[40] Pinpointing the reasons for this widening disparity is difficult, but the internal economy of imprisonment likely played a role. Partly in response to humanitarian protest, prison officials concentrated as many white convicts as they could at Rusk and the Walls. Since neither work site was profitable, a new Board of Pardon Advisors had every incentive to send white prisoners packing. Black prisoners, by contrast, went mostly to outside camps, both lucrative and capacious.[41] When Oran Roberts passed away in 1898, therefore, only half of his prison scheme survived him. While industrial penology for whites was withering away, his unyielding racism—institutionalized on retooled slave plantations—carried on into a new century.

The increasingly disproportionate punishment of African Americans shored up convict leasing's shaky supports among white politicians but not enough to survive the aftershocks of Lula Sanders's letter. Governor Campbell, its recipient, was not especially sympathetic. Like most other elected officials, he showed little regard for black life. Although he was at Texas's helm during particularly egregious outbreaks of racist violence—the public torching of two black amusement parks in Beaumont, a massacre of African Americans in Sabine County, and the twentieth century's peak year for lynching in Texas, 1908—the governor's most notable effort to reduce racial tensions was to ban prizefight films after Jack Johnson, the "Galveston Giant," became the first black Heavyweight Champion of the World, thus provoking nationwide rioting.[42] Even so, Campbell had no tolerance for the debauchery described in Sanders's letter. Nor was he a fan of convict leasing, which he worried drove "free labor from the mines, the factories and farms of Texas."[43] Unlike so many of his predecessors who had assailed the lease system while allowing it to expand, Campbell was determined to take real steps toward its replacement.

Born and raised in Rusk, Campbell had seen penitentiary problems firsthand. A serious-looking man with a receding hairline offset by a feral brow and lustrous mustache, he had worked his way to prominence as a railroad executive. After falling out with his company's owner, Jay Gould, however, he quit his post and entered politics as a progressive. Corporations generally and convict lessees in particular "rob the people and defy our laws" while making "government . . . the instrument of avarice," he declared. Under his watch, Campbell pledged that prisoners would no longer compete with the "free and honest toiler."[44]

True to his word, Campbell took an active interest in prison matters once he became governor in January 1907. Although he appointed a former lessee, Jacob Herring, as his superintendent, he turned against punishment profiteers. Shortly after taking office, he ordered a "close inspection" of all "farms leasing convicts and railroad camps." Any camp found in violation of state rules was to be closed down. "I want this done, even if you have to do it in the middle of the crop and without regard to the damage done to the [proprietor]," he instructed.[45] That August, when inspectors discovered shoddy housing on the Trinity and Brazos Valley Railway, Campbell's Penitentiary Board took the unusual step of voiding the company's lease.[46]

Governor Campbell opposed the private exploitation of prisoners rather than forced labor per se, and his most substantitive innovation was to approve the government's purchase of additional farmland. In May 1907, the Penitentiary Board bought the eight-thousand-acre Ramsey Farm along Oyster Creek in Brazoria County.[47] A year later, the state added one thousand acres to the Harlem Farm and acquired one of Ellis and Cunningham's prized possessions, the five-thousand-acre Imperial Farm.[48] Taking advantage of these new properties, Superintendent Herring more than doubled the percentage of convicts working on government lands between 1907 and 1908. For the first time, Texas was assembling a robust alternative to leasing.[49]

There prison innovations might have stopped had Campbell had his druthers. With state land opening up, the governor hoped that leasing would gradually fade away as the "penitentiary system lift[ed] itself by its own bootstraps." By moving women prisoners from Johnson to Eastham, moreover, the governor hoped not only to protect inmates from the most predatory guards, including Jerry Borden, the warden's son, who apparently maintained a covey of convict concubines, but also to put them "deeper into the woods," beyond the reach of Reverend Hodges and urban reporters. Like all prison prelates, he prayed for quiet.[50]

But his prayers went unanswered. A year after filing away Sanders's letter, all her charges came raging back, this time in George Waverly Briggs's *San Antonio Express* series. Although he was only twenty-seven years old, Briggs was well trained for battle against the prison system. Like his primary informant, Reverend Hodges, his father was a free-minded minister; at the 1897 NPA congress in Austin, he had delivered a sermon against "covetousness, oppression, [and] misrule." Having studied in Galveston, San Francisco, and Austin, young Briggs was also well acquainted with the principles of progressivism. Stirred to indignation by his interviews with Hodges, as well as by personal visits to the women's farm and other camps, the reporter began his series with excoriation. "Texas fails signally to achieve" anything of value from its penal system, he declared. It does only the "very minimum" to protect society and reform criminals and succeeds only in "money-making" and "political spoiling." If the system has a motto, it ought to be "Fear, Force, and Leather."[51]

Briggs wrote with special vehemence about the mistreatment of female prisoners, which he called a "grave inhumanity to womankind." Making Sanders's charges public for the first time, he described the field birth incident, as well as another prison delivery sure to vex opponents of race mixing: a jailhouse infant "fair of complexion" born to a "coal-black" mother who had been in prison for seven years. Although conditions had improved at Eastham, Briggs contended that female wards were still treated like "dumb, driven cattle." Superintendent Herring had tried to cut down on whipping, he acknowledged, but "the general belief [among the guards] is that a woman should 'have the hell knocked out of her' with the same dispatch and severity that the men receive." Corporal chastisement had deep roots in Texas, but the young reporter pronounced the "whole idea . . . obnoxious to the Southern man."[52]

In camp after camp, Briggs found similar deficiencies, but in addition to cataloguing horrors, he put forward a passel of remedies. He proposed that modern road camps replace backward plantations, that professionals take over from cronies, that parole take the place of determinate sentencing, and that reformation supplant "vindictive justice."

Reformatories like Elmira in New York rather than state-owned plantations should form the backbone of a new system, he argued. Only by relying on proven techniques could Texas's prisons "result in golden achievement to society."[53]

Although Briggs's most ambitious proposals lay beyond the imagination of most lawmakers, his series had a profound impact. Newspapers around the state reprinted his findings, and when legislators returned to Austin in January 1909, they discovered a bound copy of Briggs's articles on their desks. Startled into action by "the white light of publicity," lawmakers demanded a wide-ranging investigation, the fourth since 1883. Governor Campbell initially resisted; he fired Reverend Hodges and hoped the tornado would pass. When it touched down and looked to stay awhile, however, he conceded that "the good name of the State demands . . . [a] searching, sweeping, and effective" probe.[54] Texas prisons thus threw open their gates, setting in motion convict leasing's endgame.

### "MAN'S REDEMPTION SHALL SURELY COME"

As Texas's fact finders got to work, convict leasing in the South was everywhere under fire—sometimes literally. In the aftermath of the Civil War, every southern state had delivered its prisoners into the hands of for-profit contractors, and by the turn of the century every state was scrambling to get them back. From Raleigh to Baton Rouge, Tallahassee to Little Rock, lawmakers hurled accusations and then compromised, issued regulations and then ignored them, stepped forward and then back, nonetheless moving haltingly toward abolition. In Tennessee, one of leasing's most profitable domains, this jousting between profit and reform came to a head first, and with the most furious results.

Like Alabama, Tennessee hired out its convicts as coal miners, and principally to the very same company, Tennessee Coal, Iron, and Railroad (TCI). Founded by a "prophet of the New South," Arthur St. Clair Colyar, a Confederate congressman turned industrial entrepreneur, TCI started out as a slave concern but had shifted deftly to convicts after emancipation. If Tennessee had developed its coal deposits by relying exclusively on free labor, Colyar warned, its mining camps would have turned into nothing but "outposts for Pennsylvania tramps whose principal business was to strike."[55]

By 1890, TCI had become Tennessee's exclusive lessee. Hundreds of convicts pounded rock underground in the company's mines, while hundreds more were subleased to smaller outfits. The practice produced outsized profits, and TCI began gobbling up competitors in the style of Standard Oil. But what made men like Colyar rich sapped the life from their toilers. In 1883, George Washington Cable had described Tennessee's prison conditions as "too revolting for popular reading," but the situation only worsened under TCI's monopoly. Exhaustion, hunger, filth, fear, disease, and death—all the standard fruits of convict leasing—flourished in the mines. Legislative investigators decried the company's "rough-board shanties [as] unfit for the habitation of human beings," and denounced "inhuman whipping . . . for failure to get out tasks." One committee member worried that if he didn't speak out, the "haggard faces and emaciated forms of some of those prisoners would have haunted me to the grave."[56]

But TCI carried on. By 1892, it controlled three-fifths of the coal and iron reserves in Tennessee and Alabama. Free workers generally extracted higher quality coal for the company, but they, too, felt the chains of imprisonment. In the battle between labor and capital, convicts served as TCI's favorite cudgel: they depressed wages during booms, maintained core operations during slowdowns, and thwarted organizing all around. "For some years after we began the convict labor system," explained Colyar, "we found that we were right in calculating that the free workers would be loath to enter upon strikes when they saw that the company was amply provided with convict labor." Prisoners, he boasted, allowed for "absolute control."[57]

This strategy paid handsomely but only until July 14, 1891, Tennessee's own Bastille Day. On that moonlit summer night, agitated free miners and their hometown supporters embraced a new tactic in the long struggle against convict competition. Instead of signing petitions or withholding their labor, they gathered up their shotguns and hunting rifles and prepared a military assault. Assembled into a force some five hundred strong, they marched on a convict stockade, overwhelmed its guards, herded its bewildered inhabitants onto a commandeered train, and sent them off to Knoxville. "We the miners, farmers, merchants, and property holders of Briceville and Coal Creek have come together to defend our families from starvation . . . and our people from the contamination . . . of convict labor," read the movement's first communiqué. "[We] do hereby beg you [the governor] to prevent their introduction and thus avoid bloodshed, which is sure to follow if their taking of our livelihood from us is persisted in."[58]

In the ensuing months, miners, mining companies, and the governor engaged in fitful negotiations. But when a special session of the legislature failed to abolish leasing, free miners again picked up the gun. Late that fall and again the next summer, hundreds of protesters drilled in military tactics and laid siege to convict camps—burning barracks, chasing off company guards, and taking possession of prisoners, sometimes dispatching them to Nashville's penitentiary and other times fitting them with fresh clothes and setting them free. State officials raised a militia and placed the most restive hamlets under martial law. Even so, Tennessee's insurgent miners succeeded where so many other dissidents had failed. By suppressing coal production and forcing the state to field and fund an army, they took the profit out of convict leasing and thus sealed its fate. Although politicians and city newspapers vowed to stamp out "red handed anarchism," lawmakers allowed TCI's lease to expire in December 1895 with no replacement bidders in sight.[59]

Thus unfolded the first popular victory against convict leasing, albeit one with pyrrhic elements. TCI had to retreat from Tennessee, but it compensated by expanding in Alabama, where leasing continued well beyond the company's absorption by U.S. Steel in 1907. Miners and national labor leaders exulted in driving convicts from the mines, but after a roundup of organizers, Tennessee's unions ended up weaker than before, their best organizers imprisoned or exiled, their allies turned out of the statehouse by law-and-order conservatives. As is often the case in prison rebellions, convicts ended up worse for the wear. Rather than being transferred to a penitentiary, by 1896 they were sent back underground, this time into the dusty bowels of an immense new coal mine owned and operated by the state. At Brushy Mountain, Tennessee's convicts labored as they had before, only for new taskmasters. Not until the 1930s did prisoners get out of the Appalachian coal business altogether.[60]

Nowhere outside the mountains of Tennessee did convict leasing face organized armed resistance. Nonetheless, a broad and multifaceted anti-leasing movement steadily gained ground, not only in the South but nationwide. Propelled by the winds of populism, as well as leasing's never-ending outrages, the movement rekindled the righteous scorn of abolitionism. African Americans, in particular, declared moral war against what they called "the new system of slavery in the South." "In the . . . convict lease camps of the South to-day are thousands of colored people, men, women, and children, who are enduring a bondage, in some respects more cruel and crushing than that from which their parents were emancipated forty years ago," argued Mary Church Terrell, the first president of the National Association of Colored Women. A minister with Christian Methodist Episcopal church in Washington agreed: "Go to a Southern court house; watch the progress of the trials; . . . hear the sentences imposed; . . . go to the prison records; and you will see to your astonishment, no doubt, that the Southern white people are slowly but surely restoring slavery in that section which is far worse in its subjective and objective effects than that which cursed the country for nearly three centuries."[61]

Such impassioned denunciations garnered little sympathy among southern whites, even less than had the section's literary race traitor George Washington Cable. Nevertheless, to many northerners, convict leasing came to symbolize everything backward about the former Confederacy: its unmanly hostility to free labor, its suspicions of modernity, and its irrational negrophobia. "The toleration of [contract prison labor] will be regarded by posterity with puzzled horror," asseverated Frederick H. Wines in his landmark *Punishment and Reformation*. After a national survey, the U.S. Industrial Commission concluded that "the lease system . . . should not be tolerated in any civilized community."[62]

Within the South itself, white women drew upon this rhetoric of civilization and shame with special force. Although they were denied the vote, politically oriented women used the language of Victorian femininity to speak out on a variety of issues, particularly those involving families and wards of the state. If women were held up as guardians of virtue in the home, then why shouldn't they demand greater virtue in society?

Among the most outspoken southern penal reformers was Rebecca Latimer Felton, a country-bred politician's wife known for rousing oratory and a razored pen. An advocate of temperance, women's suffrage, and public education, she became especially exercised about convict leasing, which she labeled "the shame of the great commonwealth of Georgia." In a choleric broadside published in the *Forum* in 1887, Felton not only condemned leasing as cruel, wasteful, and crime-producing but made it personal. Georgia's own governor, John B. Gordon, and one of its U.S. senators, Joe Brown, were profiting from convict labor, she pointed out, "farming out criminals for [their] own private emolument." So that corrupt politicians could line their pockets, she charged, "women are placed in normal schools of degradation" and "children are propagated in wickedness and graduated in villainy." Felton reveled in such taunts. When lease supporters "showed their heads above the ramparts," she remembered in her memoirs, "this sharp shooter in woman's form deliberately picked them off for public amusement and feminine revenge."[63]

Having lost her family fortune, which consisted mainly of slaves, during the war, and having buried four of her five children by the age of thirty-nine, Rebecca Felton had anger to spare. But she also exhibited deep sympathy for folks down on their luck, particularly Georgia's growing ranks of landless farmers. What most troubled her about convict leasing, she wrote, was that it amounted to "the selling of the poor to the highest bidder." While Felton took up the torch of populism, however, she wielded it not only against the Bourbon establishment but against the "new Negro," who she believed had morphed in freedom into a "black fiend." In 1897, she amplified this theme with a vengeance, and with hideous results. Rural women faced numerous challenges, she told the Georgia State Agricultural Society, but none so serious as the black rapist. "A crime nearly unknown before and during the war had become an almost daily occurrence," she asserted without evidence, adding that abominable crimes required terrifying sanctions. "If it takes a lynching to protect woman's dearest possession from drunken, ravening human beasts," she raged, "then I say lynch a thousand a week if it becomes necessary." In an interview, she recalled that "good, true men cheered me to the echo."[64]

Picked up by the northern press, Felton's call to arms sparked a lively debate across the country, but before long the fire spread beyond newspapers. A year later, Felton's remarks emerged as a precipitating factor in the Wilmington, North Carolina, race riot, in which white reactionaries overthrew the city's fusion government, murdered at least twenty-two African Americans, and torched the offices of a black newspaper that had dared assail Mrs. Felton in print. Unfazed, Felton continued to press the case for lynching in her regular column in the *Atlanta Journal*. After an African American man named Sam Horse reportedly raped a white woman and murdered her husband, she urged his pursuers to forgo the sheriff's reward and take justice into their own hands. On the very morning her essay appeared in print, a white mob sprang the captured suspect from jail, hurried him to the edge of town, cut off his genitals, and burned him alive.[65]

To Felton, there was no contradiction between lynching and progressive penal reform. In her view, each cause complemented the other; each aspired to crime control and justice. Like many white progressives in the South, Felton perceived Prohibition, prison reform, white women's suffrage, and racial segregation as harmonizing efforts. The shared objective was good, clean government for an orderly, modern society. Historian C. Vann Woodward called this "progressivism for whites only." [66]

Rebecca Felton proved more effective as an instigator of homicide than a prison reformer. For decades, railroads, mining companies, and brick factories successfully weathered her spirited attacks. As repeated economic downturns sapped lessee profits, however, more and more states regained control of their convicts. Yet almost nowhere in the region did the ethos of prison moneymaking die out. In Georgia, where lessees finally hoisted the white flag during the Panic of 1907, as well as in North Carolina and Florida, state officials simply redeployed forced convict laborers from the private sector to the public. In response to the powerful "good roads movement"—another progressive campaign—they put prisoners to work on state chain gangs.

Strange as it seems, the chain gang, in which thousands of prisoners, most of them black, were loaded onto cattle trucks and carted around the state to pound rocks and shovel dirt, was celebrated as a humanitarian advance. Counties had long employed misdemeanor chain gangs; now the state would systematize and improve the process for the good of everyone, even convicts. "Good roads make good men," proclaimed Joseph Hyde Pratt, a geologist and convict labor advocate in North Carolina. "Life in the convict road camp . . . is more conducive to maintaining and building up the general health and manhood of the convict than when he is confined behind prison walls." This was particularly true for blacks, chain gang boosters believed. "The negro is accustomed to outdoor occupations . . . [and is] experienced in manual labor," explained the assistant director of the U.S. Office of Public Roads, and he "does not possess the same aversion to working in public . . . as is characteristic of the white race."[67]

Most importantly, politicians rallied to the chain gang because it provided public works on the cheap. Between 1904, when state felons first began working on its roads, and 1915, convicts were primarily responsible for expanding Georgia's surfaced road grid from two thousand to thirteen thousand miles, making its state highway system the most advanced in the South. "The magnitude of the work being done in Georgia by the convicts, and the results being accomplished, are almost beyond comprehension," marveled legislators.[68] Just as leasing had jump-started postbellum railroad construction, sugar milling, and coal mining, chain gangs helped lay the infrastructure for twentieth-century rural development. The American South was built not only by slaves but by convicts.

While states with strong progressive movements turned from leasing to convict road gangs, most governments fell back on a more familiar model, the plantation. Texas had taken an early lead in state-managed agriculture by acquiring the Wynne Farm in 1883, but it was George Washington Cable's home state of Louisiana that first made the switch completely.[69] Although leasing was as entrenched in Louisiana as anywhere else, its identification with one oversized personage, Major Samuel James, made its abolition almost as simple as changing letterhead. Cosmetic changes, alas, were about all that convicts noticed when the state wrested back control in 1901. Government officials erected new buildings, including a sturdy brick barracks for white prisoners, but the vast majority of convicts trudged forward in filthy stripes as they had for their previous master: picking cotton, cutting cane, or building levees to control the mighty Mississippi. James's overseers kept their jobs as well. The state's warden at Angola held the same post as under leasing; at the helm of the new Board of Control was the executor of James's estate.[70]

Following Louisiana's lead, Mississippi and Arkansas similarly replaced leasing with government plantations. In important ways, this represented a significant advance over private contracting, which Felton had described as "a cankerous sore on the body politic." Convict death rates invariably declined, the most objective measure we have of prison conditions. In the ensuing decades, however, the new state institutions pieced together from the remnants of leasing—vast plantations like Angola, Parchman, Cummins, and Eastham—all vied for the title of "America's worst prison."[71]

To reformers, the establishment of these government farms represented an important advance: better treatment, better facilities, a be-lated embrace of modernity. In other respects, though, the birth of the state plantation owed as much to the past as to the future. Along with segregation and disenfranchisement, it symbolized the New South's idealization of the Old South's social order; it signaled that government would assume powers once held by masters. More than any other American institution, the plantation prison delivered the ghosts of slavery alive and well into the twentieth century.

## ABOLITION

"Old Joe" Wilkinson had his own reasons for being skeptical of prison reform. A crippled, shriveled, and ornery white man, he had been a Texas prisoner since 1899, convicted of killing three men he called "half breed" hog thieves. Over the years, he had seen inspectors come and go, and he was none too impressed. So-called fact finders typically gave advance notice of their arrival, he wrote. The superintendent rushed to greet them and then escorted them to his office, "where the decanter, clink-ing glasses and . . . cigars made conversation easy and a brotherly feeling grow." Convicts were given their chance to speak, "but they, under-standing they would be beaten if unfavorable reports were made, had no grievances to present." After "a stroll into the flower garden" and a quick visit to a work site, committee members caught the train back to Austin, "where they reported everything . . . in apple-pie order, with the nicest and most capable men they ever met in charge."[72]

Old Joe exaggerated but not by much. Over four decades of convict leasing, Texas had racked up an inglorious record of prison oversight. Since 1883, two full-time inspectors had supposedly kept watch on the system, and both houses of the legislature had launched periodic in-quests. But conditions had scarcely improved. Although government investigators voiced criticisms more commonly than Wilkinson admit-ted—in 1902, legislators had reported that "men are shot down like dogs and are worked until they drop dead"—words on the page rarely trans-lated into action.[73] Whatever policy changes investigators proposed were generally dismissed as impractical or excessively expensive. Other times, their complaints were buried or ignored.

As a new set of surveyors got to work in the wake of George Waverly Briggs's fiery newspaper series, even convict cynics like Wilkinson sensed that change was in the air. Convicts and keepers alike began to realize that "for the first time . . . an investigating committee . . . would go to the bottom of things." Unlike previous efforts, the 1909 team received a substantial budget of ten thousand dollars, the assistance of professional accountants, and, with Briggs and other reporters in tow, planned to visit nearly every private and public work site in the state. Guards, officials, and community members contributed to nearly one thousand pages of testimony, as did convicts, who for the first time "felt reasonably safe" from reprisals. "During the entire sitting of the committee," Wilkinson reported, "only one convict was whipped, and he was a Negro."[74]

"The occasion seems ripe for genuine prison reform in Texas," observed Tom Finty, political editor of the *Dallas News*. Governor Campbell and key legislators were speaking out against leasing, and events elsewhere in the South seeded expectations. By 1909, Tennessee, North Carolina, South Carolina, Louisiana, Mississippi, and Georgia had all abandoned prisoner contracting, and lawmakers imagined the winds of history behind them. "Now that the public has again been advised of these conditions," wrote the investigators, "we confidently believe that the humane, patriotic citizenship of Texas will not longer delay such steps as are necessary to place our penal system upon that high ground . . . of her sister States."[75]

Texas's Penitentiary Investigating Committee had a simple but sweeping mandate, remarked one of its members: they were "looking for trouble, hoping that no trouble will be found." But trouble they did find, and plenty of it. Beyond Rusk and Huntsville, the committee discovered that "not one thing is being done looking to the reformation of the men." Instead, "excessive work" predominated, carried on seven days a week in some cases, from first light to last. In tone, the lawmakers strived for moderation, but as the testimony piled up, some of them started to sound like wrathful prisoner memoirists. "The evidence will show that . . . the convicts were poorly fed, half clothed, and that they were driven to their work with the lash, like galley slaves," blasted Senator Claude Hudspeth. "The whole system is devilish and corrupt."[76]

At virtually every stop, committee members found "brutal treatment" and "flagrant violations of the rules." At Texas's one convict coal mine in Calvert, which received predominantly white convicts because the work was considered semiskilled, investigators discovered conditions not unlike those in Tennessee or Alabama. Convicts spent their days wading through muck fifty feet underground, their uniforms so "smutty" that their "stripes [were] obliterated." Those who made task (seven tons a day) could retire to the "extremely filthy" barracks; those who didn't first got the strap. So abject were the chained white men—toiling without pay for a private master, caked in coal dust, clothed in rags—that one legislator seemed to fear they were losing their racial identity. Their feet are "scaly and . . . as black as a negro's," observed Representative Bowman. "They are brown . . . and shriveled."[77]

The examiners stopped twice at Eastham, the new women's farm. Two years had passed since Lula Sanders mailed her grievance, but the committee found few improvements. Hard labor in rain-soaked fields, dirty quarters, and recurrent beatings remained facets of everyday life, according to prisoners and some guards. Punishment logs, notorious for undercounting, confirmed twenty-four women had been whipped at Eastham. A fifteen-year-old girl testified that the warden had kicked her "in the spine of my back right in my kidneys," knocking her "down the steps."[78]

Just as Reverend Hodges had feared, sexual mischief had carried over from Johnson to Eastham. The prison's two white women voiced no complaints, but several black women admitted having sex with guards, sometimes in groups, in "the hospital," "back behind the wood pile," or "out in the weeds somewhere." Although they recognized these encounters as exploitative, many convicts refused to play the victim. They described having sex for money, better treatment, or just for fun. "I was a convict and in prison and didn't know," testified Rosa Brewing, "and I thought if I got that chance . . . of being with a man . . . I would do it." She added, "I like white men, on account of my father was a white man."[79]

Such forthright discussions of interracial sex proved "too shocking and repulsive" for inclusion in the final report, but lawmakers showed less reticence in describing the physical abuse of men. "Atrocities [are] daily heaped upon this mass of . . . breathing, human souls, wards of the state," asserted Senator Hudspeth, whose previous employment as a newspaper editor came through in his breathless prose. In hearing after hearing, witnesses described how men had been attacked by dogs, dangled from building rafters, "whipped until they couldn't walk no more," and even killed. At the Herring and Whatley Farm, which Superintendent Herring had managed prior to taking over the entire system in 1907, witnesses described a string of murders officially attributed to "sunstroke." In one case, a heavy "Dutchman" was reportedly dragged to death by a horse because he refused "to run on the turn row." H. W. Johnson swore that he dug the grave for another convict who had been whipped to death. In a macabre twist, he charged that a supervisor made one of the shovelers "get up and dance on his coffin."[80]

In the face of such damning testimony, prison guards attempted exculpation but only dug themselves deeper holes. One squad boss explained that he had broken no rules because he had never seen any written rules. "Here is all the rules that I know," he told dismayed lawmakers, "for guards to take them out at daylight," "work them" all day with a single meal break, "work them until night," and to "see that they are doing the work properly." Other prison employees offered only the feeblest defenses. "We have never done anything to reform the men," admitted Captain Grace at Clemens, but "I always tell them to do the right thing."[81]

Prison officials and lessees tried their best to intervene. Presented with evidence of spoiled food and shoddy housing, top officers reminded legislators that they received very little money from the state. Accused of cruelty, they countered that hardened criminals, "who are adepts at intrigue as well as in crime," required stern discipline. Convicts were habitual prevaricators, they asserted, motivated by "hatred" of their keepers. "Sometimes I use profane language . . . I have called a Negro a s—of a b—," grudgingly acknowledged Captain Grace, "but that is about as far as I went."[82]

A dose of racism, either coded or explicit, added potency to these apologias. While reform advocates urged lawmakers to keep in mind that white prisoners, too, suffered the indignities of leasing, hard-liners spoke almost exclusively of blacks. "Some of the negroes you could reform by kind treatment and some you could not," remarked a longtime employee of Edward Cunningham. "I don't believe that teaching them to write and read would help them, for some of them would come back for forgery." Allowing convicts to testify in court posed similar dangers, suggested Superintendent Herring. If convicts gain civil rights, "no guard . . . could afford to take any chances on trying to stop a man who attempted to escape."[83]

R. H. Underwood, Reverend Hodge's old nemesis at the Walls, was perhaps the most effective defender. In August 1909, while the investigators were on recess, he traveled to the American Prison Congress in Seattle to speak on "The Warden and His Work." With Tom Finty of the

*Dallas News* on hand to report his every word, Underwood urged prison officials to seek reform within the limits of security. A warden's responsibility is "the uplifting of his unfortunate fellow-men," he conceded, but "firm discipline" and "safety" were necessary prerequisites. Too much indulgence and "our prisoners would become uncontrollable and dangerous." An element of coercion was essential, he advised. "Some [convicts] can be controlled by appeal to their moral natures, some by love, and others through fear only."[84]

This sort of managerial conservatism gained sway as legislators moved from fact finding to policy formulation. With lessees, prison officials, and Governor Campbell counseling restraint, leading lawmakers sought ways to substantially change the prison system without significantly raising costs or giving over too completely to northern-style penology, which they saw as appropriate, perhaps, for white prisoners but not for blacks and Mexicans. Texas would have to "steer safely between the two extremes," advised Finty, who served as the press's establishmentarian voice. The prisoner should no longer be treated as a "revenue bearing animal," but neither, he added hyperbolically, should the prison be converted into "a summer resort with perfumed baths, long pile carpets, Parisian paintings, [and] Italian orchestras."[85]

When the investigative committee finally presented its report in late November 1909, this middling view prevailed. Although the members came down resolutely on the main issue before them—"We recommend that the contract . . . system be abolished," they wrote—the most ambitious proposals for progressive reform were already fading. Gone from the final report was Governor Campbell's plan to use able-bodied prisoners to improve public roads. Sidelined were calls from the American Prison Association (previously the National Prison Association) to base a system on treatment rather than production. Ignored were prisoners' hopes for fairer trials, shorter sentences, and looser discipline.[86]

Instead, investigators recapitulated remedies that lawmakers had bandied about for more than a generation. To replace scattered leasing camps, they proposed more state farms, preferably split between coastal sugar and upland cotton properties, with the latter providing greater comfort for whites. To improve "repulsive" living conditions and "hazardous" labor, committee members dusted off regulations first drafted in the 1870s: limited work hours, better food, cleaner housing, and professional medical care. To foster "refinement and high ideals," they called for a new women's prison and the retirement of degrading striped uniforms. On the question of whipping, which had generated some of the most impassioned testimony, the majority voted to place new restrictions on the bat but not to lock it away.[87]

These were significant but modest fixes. Too modest, cried many observers. The "findings are not so drastic nor its recommendations so sweeping as the circumstances seem to justify," counseled Finty. Reporter Briggs, who had been writing feverishly on prison reform for more than a year, was particularly crestfallen. "Commercialism not the lease system is the root of the penitentiary evil," he argued, and on that basis, "the state farms [too] must go."[88]

But Briggs's was a lonely voice. By the time lawmakers began drafting bills in the winter of 1910, pro-plantation moderates had dug in. Governor Campbell argued against major legislation, claiming that he was retooling the system well enough on his own. Leasing was already being scaled back, he pointed out, and the state farms were making money.[89] Only in August did Campbell relent, agreeing to convene a special session of the legislature.

After a month of contentious debate and fevered press coverage, an Act Establishing a Prison System arrived on the governor's desk and received his signature on September 17, 1910. It represented a dramatic break with the past but fully satisfied no one. Having dominated criminal punishment in Texas since just after the Civil War, convict leasing was henceforth illegal—or would be when current contracts expired, a significant concession to lessees. In its place, the legislation mandated that administrators "work all prisoners within the prison walls and upon farms owned by the State."[90]

Although field work would remain the principal vocation in the new regime, the reform act spelled out major changes in prison labor relations. In response to prisoner complaints, the law limited workdays to ten hours, banned all labor on Sundays, and threatened prison officers with removal or even criminal prosecution for violations. More important, the act included provisions to pay prisoners for their work. All "first class" prisoners would be paid a ten cent per diem "from the earnings of the State prison," the law stipulated, with higher rates paid for "overtime," Sunday work during "an extreme or unavoidable emergency," for example.[91] Texas convicts would no longer be slaves but agricultural proletarians.

Living conditions, too, came in for an overhaul. Within seven years, every prison camp was to provide "good and wholesome food," medical care by physicians and dentists, and "modern, fire-proof, well-ventilated buildings." Most ambitiously, legislators encouraged prison officials to confine each inmate in a separate cell, a nod to the isolating idealism of the first penitentiaries.[92]

Troubled by recurring iniquity at Eastham, lawmakers devoted special attention to female prisoners. Even before the investigators filed their report, Governor Campbell had moved the women again, this time to the Goree Farm, named after the old superintendent.[93] But legislators remained skeptical. They mandated permanent separation from male prisoners and issued strict regulations meant to foster moral rectitude. Taking a page from the women's reformatory movement, they ordered the appointment of a prison "matron," who would "give her personal attention to the welfare of . . . female prisoners." To stamp out impropriety, they required guards at the women's farm to be married and live with their families less than a hundred yards from the barracks. Proximity, they believed, would help male employees resist the temptations of "yellow women," whom lawmakers imagined as wily seductresses. To bandage their most embarrassing wound, then, lawmakers called on the paternalistic logic of slavery. To replace a debauched lease farm run by lower-class miscreants, they envisioned a model plantation ruled by a mocked-up master family. Wholesome married men would maintain order and keep women prisoners, 94 percent of them black, busy in the fields, while a hired lady and dutiful wives would provide moral instruction and keep their men out of the quarters.[94]

While politicians thus drew on the heritage of slavery, they also borrowed selectively from scientific penology. All prisoners were to be provided "opportunity, encouragement, and training in the matter of reformation," the act stipulated. Texas would not try to emulate Elmira, even allowing for its failings, but the legislation did mandate reformatory programming within the limits of plantation production. Sunday religious services, evening reading classes, libraries stocked with "good and wholesome literature," as well as "suitable recreation," including music, would all provide "moral training."[95]

Classification was also restructured. Under leasing, brute strength had served as the principal criterion in divvying up convicts, but under the revised system a more elaborate scheme took hold, one based on not only race and gender but age, offense, and perceived corrigibility.

Through "orderly, industrious, and obedient" conduct, convicts could advance among three classes, earning "privileges according to their deserts," and pushing up the date of their release. Although Texas's "good time" credits did not amount to indeterminate sentencing as championed by the APA, politicians nevertheless hoped that everyday rewards and the promise of early release would elicit more cooperation than had the lash alone. "When a man keeps the key to his own prison," postulated a UT professor, "he is soon persuaded to fit it to the lock."[96]

All these innovations notwithstanding, Texas's reform act maintained core elements of the old regime. The vast majority of convicts would continue toiling in the sun, often for the same field bosses since the state frequently retained lessees' personnel. Racial segregation was actually strengthened under the law, institutionalizing the popular belief among whites that strict separation fostered social peace and clean government. Most important, Governor Campbell refused to attach any appropriation to the act, thus requiring state managers to fund every improvement just as their predecessors had, by extracting proceeds from forced labor. Even as lawmakers finally buried convict leasing, therefore, they retained its funding scheme and basic infrastructure. They accommodated the past in ways that portended trouble in the future.

## "MANY TRYING AND VEXING PROBLEMS"

The monumental task of building a new penal system fell not to Governor Campbell but to his successor and political rival Oscar Branch Colquitt. A number-crunching former railroad commissioner who had started out as a tenant farmer, Colquitt was more conservative than Campbell. He opposed Prohibition, antagonized organized labor, and lambasted "needless legislation" advocated by progressives. When it came to the prison system, however, he campaigned convincingly as a reformer. Reverend Hodges made the rounds with the candidate, and once Colquitt became governor in January 1911, he took an active interest in implementing the abolition act. "Kind treatment and a ray of hope to the forsaken felon is more potent and effective in his reformation than the lacerations made by the inhuman application of the strap," he said."[97]

The challenges facing the new governor were formidable. Because the legislation ordered a phaseout rather than an annulment of labor contracts, his administration had to supervise and inspect thirty separate work sites, some of them reachable only by rutted tracks that turned to impassable mud traps in a heavy rain. Not even the two walled penitentiaries promised trouble-free management. Iron production at Rusk had sputtered to a halt. Huntsville had "practically no sewerage" and needed extensive repairs.[98]

The difficulties notwithstanding, Colquitt found three able administrators to sit on the restructured Board of Prison Commissioners. Two of them, Robert W. Brahan and Louis W. Tittle, were friendly with lessees and advocates of no-nonsense corporal discipline. But the third, Ben E. Cabell, Colquitt's choice for chair, was a progressive-leaning former mayor of Dallas whose father had once been held as a prisoner of war. Although Cabell had once been a sheriff—not a post that normally engenders sympathy toward criminals—he emerged as the most prominent supporter of convict reclamation in the post-leasing period. In response to early flare-ups, he investigated guards as avidly as convicts, and he urged the governor to complete a "right-thinking" prison system.[99]

Under Cabell's leadership, the prison commission took steps beyond those required by statute. Convinced that privatized punishment was "iniquitous, out of date, and . . . brutal," the commissioners voted in May 1911 to cancel all remaining labor contracts by December 1912, thus bringing the lease system to a close a full year ahead of schedule. Reformers welcomed the move, but it wreaked havoc on prison finances. The prison system is living "hand to mouth . . . just like a tenant farmer," griped Colquitt. Even so, the new prison chiefs managed to improve food quality, erect "very substantial buildings," and start paying prisoners menial wages. "We have done more in the past year toward making improvements than other administrations did in two or three years," boasted Commissioner Brahan.[100]

Determined to turn prisoners into "better men than when they entered," the commissioners made basic efforts at reformation. Prison schools and libraries opened, despite "an empty treasury," while a greater number of prison clergymen, including the system's first full-time African American pastor, took the gospel to previously unreachable camps. Because Cabell believed that "every human being is a potential criminal" and "every criminal is a potentially honest man," his administration also retired time-honored rituals of degradation.

Half a century after most northern institutions, Huntsville and Rusk relaxed their codes of silence. Tattered stripes gave way to smart, duck-cotton whites, the uniforms still in use today. By treating convicts with greater dignity and doling out rewards, Texas's new prison administration sought not only to "atone for the heartless disgrace" of leasing but to grasp one of the most coveted if elusive prizes in prison management: the consent of the kept.[101]

But convict consent ran in short supply. What sources we have suggest that prisoners greeted reform with high hopes. Joe Wilkinson, for one, wanted "to bless the day of [the investigative committee's] appointment," while Commissioner Cabell observed that "many convicts felt that the law . . . was passed entirely in their interest." What Texas had in store for convicts, though, was not necessarily what they had in mind. To be sure, the legislation addressed convicts' most acute concerns—for shelter, nourishment, rest, and physical safety. Even as the material conditions of everyday life started to improve, however, convicts found their personal autonomy diminished. Prisoners were happy to discard stigmatizing stripes, for instance, but were dismayed by new rules prohibiting the use of any civilian clothes, even free-world underwear. Likewise, they welcomed the security and privacy of new cell blocks but not the curtailment of nighttime recreation: craps games, sex, and drinking.[102]

The most favored prisoners had the most to lose. In the interest of consistency, the commissioners shut down the "little shops" operated by convicts that had sprung up under leasing and ordered all inmates, "including trusties and office men" to "eat in the general dining room . . . and receive the same treatment." On direct orders of the governor, female trusties, some of whom had worked around town as domestics, had their day passes revoked and were locked up at Goree, where they would supposedly stay out of trouble.[103] To the administration, such adjustments seemed sensible, even inconsequential. But to convicts, petty entitlements made prison life livable. Their sudden elimination inspired the visceral rage of the arbitrarily dispossessed.

Prisoners also discovered that, in certain ways, their keepers wielded augmented powers under the reform act. Officers were prohibited from striking and cursing inmates, but at the top ranks they gained authority to determine the length of imprisonment. Under the new "good-time" system, officers could both give and take away. First-class convicts might earn fifteen days a month toward early release, but the commissioners could also erase good time in thirty-day installments or wipe the slate clean, thus taking on the powers of judge and jury.[104]

From the perspective of convicts, then, the 1910 act imposed a conflicted bargain. Prisoners looked forward to limited work requirements and greater opportunities, but each gain seemed to carry with it new liabilities. Besides survival and safety, freedom is what prisoners wanted most. "It is not the work that hurts," explained the convict editors of Huntsville's *Prison Bulletin*. "No, it is the constant, galling sense that every movement is restricted, that freedom is lost." Yet in this all-important arena, prisoners gave ground; prison life became more orderly but more circumscribed. As one lawmaker put it, "firmness and kindness" now served as the new prison system's "beautiful hand-maidens."[105]

Ambivalence toward the new regime showed up in a blizzard of convict writing in the first years of state control. Whereas punishment had been the most common response to prisoner complaints in the past, Governor Colquitt actively solicited convict feedback, promising protection from reprisal.[106] The result was an outpouring of letters, often written in the deferential idiom of prison power, yet also containing the seeds of radical and potentially destabilizing critique.

The most common documents in the state archives are appeals for executive clemency. Partly because each additional prisoner now cost the state money, the number of pardons granted annually more than doubled after abolition.[107] Each success invited still more appeals so that hundreds of letters flowed into the governor's mansion—a trove of desperate life stories and also a window into convicts' perceptions of crime, punishment, and reform.

In clemency appeals, prisoners shared their hardships and solicited favor, sometimes with remarkable intimacy but within a template stamped by dominion. In an accommodating tone, they praised the system's revamped mission, underscored their own worthiness, and appealed to the governor in the style of feudal supplicants. "May God's richest blessings come to His Excellency," concluded one letter. "Thank to God, we have on the State Executive a man of human sentiments, and a tru[e] friend of the helpless and unfortunate," offered another.[108]

In almost every letter, prisoners poured out their sorrows. One recalled losing his father to gunfire at a young age, while another pointed to his "wife and six young children, who are dependent upon me for their support." Pedro Rodriguez, who had served nineteen years on a life sentence, begged to "go to mine mother's bed side and see her just once more" before she died.[109]

Because the prison system, according to one lawmaker, now dispensed "the milk of human kindness," many inmates claimed already to have suckled to redemption. I have been "reformed . . . through punishment," proclaimed Peter Donnell. "Give me that which is so precious and dear to me—my liberty," and "I shall then prove my worth. . . . The law [will be] vindicated."[110] Such crafty reasoning might have enhanced Donnell's prospects for release but, inadvertently, it also served to legitimate his imprisonment. In dogged pursuit of freedom, many pardon applicants depicted a prison environment just as administrators liked to imagine it. To showcase contrition, they felt compelled to admit criminal guilt. To spotlight worthiness, they had to affect receipt of what the institution purported to offer, rehabilitation, instead of what, in reality, it still offered, toil and degradation.

Yet frustration bubbled to the surface even in obeisant pleadings. "[I made] a most horrible decision," admitted prisoner John McGill, who torched his boss's house in revenge for withheld wages, "but please stop right here and consider my age which was fifteen—all my life spent with rough men who knew no law but force." When Samuel Kaufman had his repentant appeal rejected, he warned ominously that "uncharitable conditions . . . bring out the brute passions in men, when the thirst for blood becomes inevitable."[111]

This tense balancing act between prostration and indignation was also present in prisoner grievance petitions. Scrawled on odd scraps of paper, seeking "some ray of hope" from the powerful, these documents likewise appealed to penal paternalism. "We, the undersigned, most humbly beseech you, as an administrator of mercy . . . to look into our trouble, and see that we get justice," read one. Yet grievances were inherently confrontational. Prisoners complained about abuse or substandard care and with increasing confidence that state employees were breaking the law. An appeal from "Negro convicts . . . on the Clemens state farm" began with an itemization of ignored legislative mandates: "We ar working over time and can't get our pay and is worked in all kinds of wearther and has not surfishian clothes to ware." Emboldened by two years of public scrutiny, some petitioners started to sound more like constituents than convicts: "[We] know our complaints are legitimate and want a thorough investigation before [the] citizens of Texas."[112]

After 1910, many convicts believed that "the law was on their side," and they maneuvered to secure whatever advantages they could. Free-world reformers told themselves that decently treated inmates would take advantage of fresh opportunities to repent and seek redemption. But many, perhaps most, convicts had nursed uncontainable fury. When expressing themselves in unguarded forums, they bemoaned their persecution rather than take responsibility for their faults. In work songs, autobiographies, and protest writings, they valorized resistance rather than submission, thirsted for revenge rather than reformation. For Joe Wilkinson, the most satisfying part of Texas's reform effort was to watch guards sweating through interrogation by lawmakers. "Of all the squirming you ever saw; we had it," he remarked, marveling that "many of them could be put into the penitentiary, and possibly some of them hung." At last, he wrote gleefully, "It looked like the convicts themselves had the whip hand."[113]

Although many prisoners fantasized about trading place with their persecutors, in reality, their lives scarcely changed—and sometimes for the worse. Perhaps the most noticeable difference was that more and more prisoners were sent out to the fields. Under leasing, multiple industries had bid for convicts, but under state control the reliable returns of plantation labor ruled. By the end of 1911, 2,910 of 3,471 prisoners were working in the fields, a higher proportion than at any point in Texas history. This came as a shock, especially to white prisoners who had believed "they would not be taken from the factories," reported Cabell. The quality of farm living was supposed to be improving, but convicts took little note of this. Swore one man recuperating from illness at the Walls, "I rather take my life and be in my grave as to geth transferd bake to the Farmes."[114]

Wages were supposed to mitigate the hardships of field work, but these were paltry and short-lived. Overtime pay and per diem allowances were designed to protect prisoners from exploitation while encouraging inmates to develop an honest work ethic. They were to serve as a bridge from bondage to freedom, allowing prisoners to prepare for success on the outside. But the bridge never had stable trusses. A few months after passing the reform act, the legislature appropriated

$310,000 for the prison system, but the entire amount vanished almost instantly, mostly to pay off debts.[115] By March 1911, with no further resources at their disposal, the commissioners voted to suspend all payments to convicts except for Sunday overtime. As one prisoner put it, "We are nothing but slaves, for the state."[116]

Additional disappointments lurked in the new parole system. In order to qualify, "meritorious convicts" had to line up a job, but employers with offers, many of them recently repudiated lessees, were looking for tractable field hands at below-market rates.[117] J. T. Campbell, the state's first parole agent, vowed to "place every . . . convict in a good home and under the influence of one of the very best men in Texas," but employer bids preserved in the archives suggest that cupidity overshadowed charity. One petitioner said she could afford to pay Gregorio Luera only $8 a month—well below farmer and servant wages—but she agreed "to keep him comfortable and take care of him." Another hinted that he intended to work his parolee into the dust. Committing to pay "Jeff Williams, #14554, Negro . . . $10 per month and board as a farm laborer," F. B. Martin also pledged, "in case of death, burial expenses not to exceed $25."[118]

Ben Cabell knew that rollbacks on wages and early releases would have "a bad effect" on prisoner morale. Just how bad, he had no idea. Like most progressives, he expected the overthrow of leasing to usher in "good order and harmony." Yet as his new administration ran up tensions and ran out of cash, he encountered nothing of the kind. As one group of disgruntled lawmakers scolded, penal reform seemed only to invite "more disobedience," "more mutinous conduct," and "more escapes."[119]

Dissent and defiance are difficult to measure in prisons. Officials have neither the time nor inclination to keep track of every disturbance, and poorly educated convicts, condemned to civic death, have few opportunities to record their actions or opinions for posterity. Of the imperfect indicators available, however, all of them point to an upsurge of prisoner-staff conflict in the wake of leasing's demise. Official punishment tallies jumped by a third in 1911 and then by a third again in 1912. Some of this can be explained by more assiduous record keeping, but however you parse the numbers, they show no signs of social peace.[120]

Escape numbers, which are generally quite reliable, also soared. Between 1911 and 1914, the total number of annual runaways nearly doubled, from 88 to 167.[121] Greater opportunities afforded by outside labor contributed to this upsurge, but some convicts politicized their escapes, claiming that broken promises and continued abuses gave them no choice but to run. In an open letter to the *Houston Chronicle*, Posey Griffith asserted that he had every intention of serving out his sentence but could no longer endure his "steel driving Captain." He pledged to "voluntarily surrender any time I hear that [the officer in charge] is discharged."[122] In the meantime, he held himself hostage at liberty.

A rising tide of punishments, escapes, and grievance petitions signaled an aggressive turn in prisoner politics. Their hopes buoyed and then swamped, scores of prisoner leaders, sometimes called "convict congressmen" by their compatriots, began mobilizing to rework Texas's penal system on their own terms.[123] Increasingly, they embraced a tactic that brought the contradictions of Texas's new regime to a head: mutiny.

On a small scale, convict mutinies, or "bucks" in prison argot, broke out almost immediately as the prison commission took control. Trouble struck first at Eastham. In early February 1911, seven protesters demanded to meet with the new commissioners and then refused to march out to the fields. Under the previous management, such impudence would have been swiftly and severely punished, but the commissioners decided to conduct an inquest before taking action. They dispatched two trusted aides from Huntsville, who ultimately pronounced the "mutiny a stubborn one" but with blame to go around. They suggested changes to the plantation's disciplinary procedures but no punishments.[124]

Such evenhandedness quieted no one. Two weeks later, at least twenty prisoners bucked at Clemens. Then, in March, prisoners revolted again at Eastham, where veteran officers were as frustrated with the commissioners as with their unruly field hands. Work strikes followed at Ramsey and Imperial, while mysterious fires broke out, first at Rusk, then on several farms, and finally at the Walls, where the penitentiary's new schoolhouse crumpled in the flames.[125]

During the summer, the prison commission reported no serious incidents, but "mutiny after mutiny" resumed during the harvest season, especially once the cane rolling began. From Goree to Rusk, Clemens to Eastham, hundreds of prisoners rioted, taunted guards, locked themselves in their barracks, and fired off still more grievance letters. Over just nine months in 1912, legislative investigators counted at least "thirteen mutinous demonstrations in which a total of 283 men participated." A self-satisfied Jake Herring, the last superintendent under leasing, commented, "They had more mutiny and hell-raising all over this country than ever in the history of [Texas]."[126]

One of the most serious rebellions took place at Imperial in August. Following a week of agitation and a slowdown in cotton picking, some fifty-seven white men sawed through prison bars, orchestrated a diversion, and then, in the overwrought prose of one reporter, "struck out like scampering mice for a dim-horizoned liberty." Within two days, one of the men had been shot down and most of the others recaptured. But the "ringleader[s]" remained defiant, refusing to work, threatening guards, and "hurling any throwable object . . . shoes, knives, forks, etc." "I will not do a lick of work until I have presented my case before the commissioners," declared one prisoner. Meanwhile, the Imperial guards claimed "they [were] powerless to cope with the men" and demanded a "phase of rigid discipline."[127]

Successive uprisings demonstrated solidarity among convicts but also forged unity among their keepers. When the first protests began, administrators insisted on getting the facts straight, with the result that guards were sometimes disciplined rather than convicts. As strikes and arson spread, however, the commissioners increasingly closed ranks with farm managers. To prevent coordinated outbreaks, the administration ordered tighter censorship of prisoner mail and called for the creation of a high-security labor camp to concentrate all convicts "who show no appreciation of [their] privilege[s]." Inexorably, Cabell and the other commissioners began devoting more attention to reinforcing their authority than reforming inmates. "The energy of the convict is expected," they pronounced; "rules must be obeyed."[128] When black convicts at Clemens disrupted the all-important cane harvest to protest a bigoted warden they called "a 'slave driver' of great notoriety," Cabell and company ordered no inquest. Rather, just as their predecessors would have, they counted up the names on the prisoners' grievance petition and sent an underling to the plantation with twenty-seven presigned whipping orders, one for each man who had dared affix his signature.[129]

This show of force notwithstanding, veteran bosses grew increasingly dissatisfied with their new superiors. Trained under the old order and generally suspicious of reform, they saw bucks and fires as the misbegotten fruit of outside interference and relaxed discipline. "A great many old employees of the system . . . felt that the law . . . was a reflection on their past services and that it was too lenient toward the convicts," observed Cabell.[130] Especially among the higher ranks, prison officers chafed against restrictions on their authority and belittled programs they regarded as costly do-gooding. With bedlam on the rise, they sought to restore obedience, hard work, and what they saw as managerial common sense.

Not every employee opposed the post-leasing reforms, of course; many had eagerly testified before the committee and did their best to make the new system succeed. In general, however, low-ranking guards joined experienced supervisors to form a conservative bloc in prison politics, hostile to unruly convicts and meddling outsiders alike. Insularity and wariness, in fact, were defining features of Texas's guard culture. This related partly to the nature of prison work: wielding absolute power over degraded though sometimes dangerous subordinates fosters tight bonds among keepers. But it also stemmed from geography. Texas's prisons were all located in the eastern slavery belt, where a turbulent history incubated potent strains of regional chauvinism, racism, and anti-governmentalism. Moreover, because prison plantations offered meager wages for thankless work in isolated, swampy locales, they tended to attract and retain personnel only from nearby farms, thus cultivating a guard force cross-sectioned by community and kinship ties. Locals in prison towns like Huntsville, Rusk, and Richmond might disagree about punishment matters among themselves, but they generally regarded hard-won experience passed down from father to son as a better guide to convict management than high-minded schemes dreamed up in Austin.[131]

Even before the Board of Commissioners got to work, Texas's inward-looking guard force was riled. During the investigation, a parade of witnesses had depicted prison employees as ignorant, sadistic, low-class soakers, while progressive reporters declared the lot of them "unfit for service," calling for "an infusion of new blood." Such characterizations naturally antagonized prison personnel, tapping into working-class and rural resentments, and almost everything the prison commission did made matters worse. From the start, Commissioner Cabell vowed to root out "laggards in the system." "I don't believe the managers or sergeants have any more right to violate the rules than have convicts," he insisted. Under leasing, employees had faced censure only for egregious offenses like murder, if that, but in the first years of state control, line bosses and captains alike incurred sanctions for a gamut of rule violations, from cursing and slapping to unauthorized whipping and sexual misconduct. During at least one inquest, commissioners asked convicts to evaluate the job performance of their custodians, surely an infuriating role reversal.[132]

As if restrictions, regulations, and convict rioting weren't enough, personnel after 1912 also faced threats to their livelihood. When the system ran out of money, the commissioners responded first by cutting payments to prisoners, then by going after the guards. "We must . . . face the new year, 1912, with a depleted treasury," instructed Cabell, and "economy in every line . . . must be practiced." Department heads were ordered to trim expenses and prepare lists of employees for wage reductions and layoffs. "In every case where salaries are thought to be larger than they should be they should be reduced," Cabell advised.[133]

Small wonder that most guards, as journalist Tom Finty put it, were "not in sympathy with the new law or its purposes." They thought of prison reform not as an advance toward Christ but a leap toward chaos. "Under the laws at present in force . . . negroes are very much more rebellious than before," warned one farm manager, while another lamented that forced labor had degenerated into nothing but a "general frolic." Convinced that prisoners had previously obeyed only out of fear, officers charged that they had lost control of their prisons and that their hands were tied by inexperienced administrators and ill-conceived legislation. In response to "the constant shirking on the part of convicts, the indifference, the contempt," the *Houston Chronicle* reported, "the guards are throwing up their hands in disgust."[134]

Sensing political opportunity in this "frightful . . . uproar," William T. Eldridge, a former partner of Edward Cunningham, invited a reporter from the *Houston Chronicle* to visit Imperial, where he interviewed outraged employees. The result was a bombastic two-part series that so precisely matched Eldridge's public statements that Commissioner Brahan "suppose[d] he dictated the article[s]" himself. "'Prison reform' had made [convicts] masters and guards mere prisoners," complained the author. "Instead of the convicts being prisoners they are governors; and instead of the guards and officers being in power they are practically subservient to the will of mob rule." Convict insurrectionists had put "the new system on trial," concluded the newspaper, and only Texas's political establishment could return a verdict.[135]

The verdict came swiftly. Although lawmakers in both houses had orchestrated the abolition of convict leasing, a more conservative bunch of politicians had come to power with Colquitt, and they regarded Texas's experiment in reform penology with suspicion verging on contempt. Even before the law took effect, a transition team dispatched by the thirty-second legislature suggested preemptive budget cuts and an elimination of per diem payments to prisoners. Afterward, as some $40,000 a month in lease payments dried up, politicians became increasingly exercised. By the end of 1912, Texas's once profitable penal system had devoured every cent appropriated by the legislature and had racked up $1.5 million in debt.[136]

To set matters right, the legislature in 1913 approved up to $2 million in funding. Over Colquitt's protests, they also launched a full-scale investigation of prison finances. This time around, fact finders devoted only passing attention to prisoner welfare. Instead, they sought ways to make the state's penal system "self-sustaining." In place of "lax and inefficient" management, they favored "experienced business judgement" and "practical humanitarianism."[137]

After assembling some four hundred pages of testimony, none of it from convicts, this second round of surveyors drafted a report that echoed nearly every complaint of the revanchist guard establishment. Dismayed by an "uninterrupted record of financial disaster," the committee suggested that the Rusk ironworks and other industrial-style workshops be shut down and that prison managers focus their attention on producing "money crops." "Enough expensive experiments have been indulged," admonished Representative R. B. Humphrey. "The system should, for a time at least, follow such work as is known to be profitable."[138]

Exhortations to shutter the remaining convict industries and shift fully to plantation agriculture raised awkward questions about Texas's commitment to prisoner reformation and, in turn, white supremacy. As had other policy reviews dating back to the 1870s, the investigators endorsed "complete separation of the white convicts from the negroes." African Americans and Mexicans should go straight to the fields, lawmakers insisted. With respect to nearly a third of the prison population classified as white, however, the salons equivocated. In part of the report, they looked forward to employing "the greater portion of the white convicts in manufacturing enterprises." In another, they suggested concentrating Anglos on "healthful" land "considerably north of the [sugar] farms." For neither scheme did they suggest funding. On the contrary, legislators urged "extreme conservatism in . . . factory undertakings." In the meantime, white convicts continued in their peculiarly auxiliary roles: laboring in workshops to supply the farms with equipment, shuffling down the cotton rows in segregated but second-tier field gangs, or lending a hand to blacks and Mexicans bringing in the sugar crop.[139]

This downward social leveling suggested novel developments in early-twentieth-century race and class relations. While sharecropping, border troubles, and Jim Crow had hardened the barriers of subjugation around African Americans and Mexicans, the bonds of whiteness were starting to fray along economic lines. With record numbers of white farmers reduced to tenancy and excluded from voting by the poll tax, poor whites were assuming their place alongside what one author called the "scrubs and runts" of civilization.[140]

This is not to say that politicians were abandoning white supremacy as a principle of prison management. In a state system reoriented toward plantation production and strict discipline, however, they were, finally, abandoning the segregationist idealism of Oran Roberts, who had envisioned but failed to deliver a reformatory, industrial penal system for whites. With wide agreement that unruly prisoners of every color needed to be put down, forced to work, and subjected to discipline, lawmakers were advocating, paradoxically, a more equitable prison system, one of "perfect control and obedience" for all.[141]

Jealous like all governors of his executive authority, Oscar Colquitt vetoed the legislature's retrenchment plan but then proceeded to implement most of its recommendations. Everywhere, the new regime crumbled into the old. The Rusk ironworks, once the vision of convict industrialization, finally shut down for good, its foundry roof collapsed, its machinery exposed to scavengers and the elements. Budget cuts across the system forced managers to fall back on methods devised by lessees and their slaveholding predecessors.[142] Work hours and picking quotas crept back up. Oversight of field bosses declined. Convict compensation, even for Sunday work, vanished.[143]

What few reformatory initiatives the prison commission had managed to launch also faltered. Schools succumbed to cutbacks or fires. Restrictions imposed in response to prisoner unrest ossified into permanent regulations. Whereas progressives had fancied reformed prisons as cooperative institutions, in which philanthropic volunteers and professional keepers would counsel and uplift the downtrodden, the prison commission increasingly redrew sharp lines between citizens and convicts, freedom and bondage. "In order that better discipline be had," the administration advised "citizens . . . not to hold conversations with prisoners inside of the Walls or elsewhere." They ordered guards to avoid chatting with prisoners "except [when] giving instructions." Such rules were virtually unenforceable, but they signaled an exasperated, unyielding attitude toward prisoners. In the turbulent wake of reform, top administrators no longer thought of inmates as "unfortunate creatures" training to become "better citizens" but as wily criminals to be contained and disciplined.[144]

Prison punishments, too, turned back toward severity. A year into his term, Ben Cabell had successfully persuaded Governor Colquitt to "buil[d] a monument to himself" by abolishing whipping.[145] Reluctantly, the other commissioners had gone along, voting to lock away the bat in March 1912 for the first time since Reconstruction. As disorder escalated, however, farm managers began enhancing the system's main alternative penalty—dark celling—and with gruesome results.[146]

Dark celling, a form of solitary in which inmates were temporarily locked in a small, pitch-black box and sustained on bread and water, was supposed to be a modern alternative to the strap. "I, myself, never regarded the dark cell . . . as a place of torture or . . . physical punishment," Cabell remarked. Rather, "it is a place of extreme isolation, giving the offending convict . . . a chance to meditate and think over his condition."[147]

But prison veterans regarded simple isolation as insufficiently terrifying to keep prisoners at work. "The dark cell . . . is of very little value," complained Captain Addison at Imperial, "particularly among the negroes, who regard it with good-natured contempt." To intensify the sanction, farm managers began extending the term of confinement from several hours, as prescribed by prison regulations, to several days. In some cases, they packed more than one prisoner into a box made for one.[148]

On September 6, 1913, in response to a cotton strike by African American prisoners on the Harlem Farm, prison guards used both enhancements. Into a single enclosure, they stuffed a full gang of twelve field hands. The men made a tight fit. Harlem's contraption was

a freestanding wooden box, elevated off the dirt by short stilts and ventilated with six auger holes in the ceiling and four pipes in the floor.
Witnesses testified later that even a single occupant stumbled out of
the "putrid vat of deadened air" bathed in sweat and "half-asphyxiated."
With twelve prisoners inside, the chamber, which measured seven by
seven by nine feet, afforded each occupant less space than an individual coffin.

On the captain's orders, Harlem guards gathered the chosen prisoners together. They stripped them down to their underwear, pushed
them inside, closed the solid wooden door behind them, locked it, and
walked away. No one reported hearing sounds of struggle, but when
the guards returned and opened the door sixteen hours later, eight
men were dead, their naked corpses piled one on top of the other. Four
survivors crouched in each corner, their mouths wrapped around the
floor pipes, gasping for air.[149]

Ghastly as it was, the sacrifice of eight black convicts was not enough
to arrest the state's drift toward plantation moneymaking. *Century Magazine* called the incident "the darkest night" in American punishment.
Prisoners talked of the killings as far away as Oklahoma, according to
one convict writer. Yet among free-world Texans, the matter passed
mostly in silence. Only the embittered guard establishment spotlighted the tragedy for political advantage, arguing that the suffocations
proved the wisdom, even the mercifulness, of bringing back the whip.
Completing a familiar box step in the history of punishment technologies, they called for the bat to replace the dark cell, which only the year
before had replaced the strap.[150]

If the Harlem deaths snuffed out the vestigial hopes of convicts,
then the "boiling Brazos" soon drowned the ambitions of administrators. Tropical storms and river overflows had long ruled the lives of
farmers on the Gulf Coastal Plain, enriching the soil but also, periodically, destroying crops in the bargain. Under the contract system, lessees
bore the risks of weather, but now the state alone shouldered the costs—
and they could be considerable. Since the 1880s but especially after
abolition, prison administrators had concentrated the bulk of their convicts on low-lying farms along the Brazos River and Oyster Creek. In
1913, those waterways burst their banks with unusual force.[151]

As the waters rose, farm managers had just enough time to evacuate.
Some 2,700 prisoners gathered what they could carry on their backs
and marched, in some cases thirty miles, to higher ground, where guards

set up military-style encampments, surrounded by whatever livestock they had been able to save. After three weeks, this ragged force made its way back, traveling by chartered train, wagon, boat, and foot. "They had to walk awhile and swim awhile to reach Ramsey Farm," explained one of the commissioners in a letter to the governor. But when they returned, they found everything ravaged. Crops and food stores had been washed away. Prison buildings were covered in silt. "Not a single bridge or culvert [is] left standing on any of the state farms," officials reported, leaving the properties more isolated than ever. The economic losses were staggering: some twelve thousand bushels of Irish potatoes, a year's supply of corn for the entire system, ten thousand cords of stacked wood, all of which would have to be purchased on the open market lest convicts and guards starve or freeze.[152]

Whatever remained of the legislature's 1913 funding package disappeared in that December flood, thus returning the system to deficit only five months after its rescue. Then, between February and June 1914, the Brazos and its siblings overflowed three times more, destroying additional cotton and corn crops at Ramsey, Imperial, and on prison lands rented from the House Farm. "While [the first flood] was bad enough," remarked an administrator, "[it] was not so disastrous to the interests of the System as the floods that we have experienced during the past Spring."[153] As precious capital washed away, so did the remnants of reform.

Roughly five months before the floods and one month before twelve prisoners crawled into the fatal dark cell at Harlem, the chair of the Board of Prison Commissioners, Ben E. Cabell, lost his job. Governor Colquitt renominated him for another term but quickly folded when senators balked. Having more exhausted himself in two and a half years of prison management than he had in two decades of law enforcement, Cabell was not without bitterness. "Political conditions are in a very queer way in our great state," he wrote to the Galveston rabbi Henry Cohen, a noted humanitarian. "The prison proposition was opposed and antagonized from many angles." Under the chairman's watch, the lease system had finally given way to state farms infused with reformatory hopes, if not the resources or will to realize them. A new penal system had been inaugurated amid great fanfare, only to slip, fitfully and painfully, onto a punishment foundation laid in slavery.

And yet Cabell, like any prison reformer worth his salt, clung to hope. "The pioneer was always laughed at and sneered at until his work had proved a success," he wrote a month after his removal. Striving to divine achievement from the embers of defeat, he told Cohen that "in sensible and practical prison reform this administration was the pioneer." "We had to clear the timbers," he wrote. "Others, I hope, will reap the benefit."[154]

# 5

# THE PENAL COLONY THAT WASN'T

[Prison reform] is a frightfully big piece of work . . . and it can easily absorb all that all of us are and have and still be unfinished unless the Lord Himself will perform a miracle.

—MINNIE FISHER CUNNINGHAM[1]

On August 15, 1919, at the height of the sweltering harvest season, a barrel-chested cotton picker known as Walter Boyd reached the end of his rope. Compared to other prisoners at the Shaw Farm, Walter had it relatively easy. He had a girlfriend and three children waiting for him on the outside; his parents were so devoted that they had sold their farm to hire him an attorney. As a muscular "man of terrible energy," he worked hard enough to avoid the strap, which Texas prisons had re-introduced in 1915. "They didn't bother me too much 'cause I was the number one roller on the number-one gang," he explained.[2]

Yet to Walter prison life was insupportable. "I wasn' used to it an' didn' like it," he told his employer in the free world, a folklorist who tran-scribed his remarks so as to emphasize his colorful dialect. "Couldn' do widout women 'tall. I been used to lots o' women, an' I couldn' stan' de penitenshuh." Nor could he stand the men running the place. Walter hadn't grown up around white people; his parents had sharecropped for a black landowner near Shreveport, Louisiana, before buying their own place in northeast Texas. But now he endured racist taunts from sun to sun, followed by fitful nights in filthy barracks. Possessing a de-cent education and hearty pride, Walter harbored grander dreams than his thirty-year sentence allowed.[3]

So he made a run for it. He and a buddy "slip behin' a brush pile" and sprinted down a dirt road until they were heaving for breath. His friend "fell out" from exhaustion, but Walter outran the hounds. "I don' b'lieve they would ever got me, if hadn' some hard luck come," he said. When he stopped to rest that evening, "down in de rushes by a pon' of water," a white man spied him and notified the sheriff. He awoke surrounded by dogs, with a pistol pointed at his head.[4]

A fellow prisoner, a "dog boy" trusty, approached him first. But Walter, who "was known to have an ugly temper," said he wasn't going anywhere. "I tol' him, 'Naw, nigger, I ain' goin' back to dat place no mo'.'" The head of the chase team took aim and barked out a warning. "Get up there an' walk, you damn nigger . . . or I'll shoot your black heart out." But Walter didn't comply. He stood up and then strolled calmly into the water, although he couldn't swim. "I just keep on walking in right up over my eyeballs, drinking up that nasty river."[5]

Walter survived to face another day in prison, and he gradually, grudgingly accommodated himself to it. He spent five and a half years locked up in Texas, most of it at Sugar Land, always as a pace setter or "lead row." Not long after his release, he went down for another four and a half years at Angola, this time for knife fighting.[6] Untold thousands of African American men living on the borderlands of freedom suffered similar fates in the first decades of the twentieth century; they did their time, either survived or didn't, and faded from the historical record. But Walter was different. Not only did he have a boundless capacity for work and a seemingly inexhaustible supply of confidence and charm, but he was blessed with exceptional musical talent.

Walter's real name (the alias had allowed him to sidestep another rap) was Huddie Ledbetter, and he earned the sobriquet Leadbelly in prison. With a booming voice and quick fingers on his Stella twelve-string guitar, he sung his way to a pardon and eventually to stardom—if not riches. "Huddie was an extraordinary man," observed Gordon Parks, who made a feature film about his life. He was "the rarest of American folklorists who composed, sang, hollered, and shouted some of the greatest folk music and blues ever written."[7]

Leadbelly is a legendary bluesman; in 1988, he was inducted into the Rock and Roll Hall of Fame. But he was also Texas's first black convict to record his experiences in the sort of rich detail previously found only in white prisoner memoirs. He told his story to John and Alan Lomax, both prominent folklorists, and related elements of his life in dozens of work songs and field hollers.

Even as Texas entered the age of radio and the automobile, the conditions Ledbetter described harked back to leasing and its inspiration, chattel slavery. Gang labor in the fields, routine brutality, and minimal comfort were part of the equation. So was an entrenched institutional culture of masters and minions—one characterized not only by total authority and racism but by convict solidarity, subterranean resistance, and subversive song.

As had their precursors, Texas's state-run prison plantations generated widespread opposition. A decade after Ben Cabell beseeched Henry Cohen to continue the work he had begun, the rabbi led, along with a coalition of white women progressives, an even more ambitious movement for penal reform. This second generation achieved remarkable success, virtually taking over Texas's prison system in 1927. But they encountered so many difficulties that they began to think that East Texas's soil was itself to blame, that the region's tortured history could produce only more of the same.

## "THE NEXT BIG JOB"

As Leadbelly's recollections suggest, Texas prisons had continued backsliding after Cabell's removal from the Board of Prison Commissioners. During a long period of reaction and neglect that followed the collapse of the state's post-leasing reforms, operating budgets declined, education and recreation programs withered, and physical punishments rallied. Echoing their predecessors, lawmakers concluded in 1918 that "no system of prison operations could be worse than the one now carried on by the state." Three years later, another set of investigators found that "prison authorities were manifestly indifferent to the spiritual welfare of their prisoners."[8]

Instead of reclamation, prison administrators through most of the 1910s and 1920s aimed for retribution, deterrence, and most of all production. They conceived of prison properties as for-profit state enterprises, and, as had lessees, they sought to wrest maximum exertion from convicts. According to Leadbelly, who traveled widely with the Lomaxes as they recorded folk songs for the Library of Congress, hard labor was hardest of all in Texas. "Now I been to Lou's'ana, an' Arkansas, Georgia, and Alabama, an' all dem odder states, . . . but in Texas dey got 'em all beat for workin'."[9]

One indicator of severity was the condition of women prisoners at Goree, the most reform-oriented farm in the system. According to administrators, Goree's "enforcement of regular habits" led to a "wonderful improvement [among the inmates] in a very short period." When an expert in reformatories investigated, however, she concluded that Texas "continued to maintain a prison farm for women of the lowest rank."[10]

Dr. Carrie Weaver Smith visited the institution in 1916, and she noted few improvements since Lula Sanders's day. The prison held twelve white and seventy-eight black inmates, but there was only one "woman connected officially" to the administration. According to the 1910 reform act, a matron was supposed to be in charge of the women's prison so as to "temper justice with mercy." Under Governor Colquitt, however, a former lessee, Mr. R. H. Cabiness, had been installed as warden, with his uncredentialed wife hired as an assistant. Dr. Smith noted that "armed white men" were back in charge, most of them "hardened against human sympathy."[11]

In every other way, Goree had degenerated as well, Smith reported. "The negro women were . . . herd[ed] together [like] animals." "The food was inadequate," the sanitation ghastly, the schooling nonexistent. The dangerous and the docile, the old and the young associated at all hours, she observed; one girl she met had been sentenced to forty years at the age of eleven. "There is no inspiration," she scolded, "only neglect and exploitation."[12]

Goree housed both white and black women, but they lived in different worlds, one bad, one worse. "The white women are paid very little attention," explained one inmate. "We are set out here in this house and absolutely forgot." African American women, by contrast, hardly relished the attention they received. They labored in the fields, endured more frequent and more severe punishments, and contended with the same sort of sexual predation that had characterized Texas women's imprisonment for decades. During a legislative inquest in 1921, inmates reported that Boss Robinson passed secret notes to women he favored, telling one that "he loved her for his own use." If his squad wanted a smoking break, he made one of the women feel around in his front pockets for cigarette papers.[13]

"There has been investigations and investigations, . . . but the system has not improved," lamented Dr. Smith. Yet still she grasped for hope. "Women are [now] in politics," she pointed out in a speech to women's groups, and it was time they take a stand. "The appeal of Humanity and Progress is a ringing clarion," she intoned, "and I call you, Women of Texas, to the Fellowship."[14]

To an astonishing extent, women in Texas heeded Smith's call. Since the turn of the century, prominent women reformers, Dr. Smith among them, had been involved in campaigns to set up a juvenile court system and establish a female counterpart to the delinquent boys' school at Gatesville.[15] These efforts emphasized the care of women and children, thus conforming to Victorian norms. In the late 1910s, however, as women activists mobilized successfully for suffrage and Prohibition, many of them began thinking beyond the confines of female charity; they set out to upturn society and politics generally. As one historian put it, "a great age of women in politics" had dawned.[16]

In these "piping times of victory," women's groups took on causes ranging from child labor to "pure food." But for many activists, prison reform loomed as "the next big job." Women were disproportionately the victims of male vice and violence, they reasoned, which meant that all women stood to benefit from effective crime prevention and criminal rehabilitation, even if relatively few women ended up in prison. Moreover, many women's advocates believed they were better equipped to run charitable institutions than their male counterparts: that they were less corruptible, less prone to violence, and more nurturing. "Men have . . . made a terrible mess of prison work," one clubwoman wrote in 1921. "It is time we women had more to say about such matters, for there is certainly more of women's emotions and heart needed in such work."[17]

Having lived through the rollback of the 1910s, experienced women's leaders knew that prison reform was daunting. Rather than advocating specific legislation right away, therefore, a coalition of women's organizations—including the Texas State Federation of Women's Clubs, the Women's Christian Temperance Union, and the Texas League of Women Voters—joined forces with a union-affliated, left-leaning brain trust based in New York, the National Committee on Prisons and Prison Labor, or CPPL, to conduct a sweeping "scientific survey" of the state's penal institutions. The goal, in typical Progressive-era fashion, was not only to devise "a new and modern prison plan" but to advance the "prevention and cure of crime."[18]

A prominent lineup of bankers, physicians, and humanitarians endorsed the effort, among them Rabbi Cohen, whom Woodrow Wilson once called "the foremost citizen . . . of Texas," but the brains and brawn of the operation was a woman named Elizabeth Speer, who became the CPPL's local executive secretary. An experienced social worker, Speer "had a thorough training in criminology and penology," commented Robert Holmes Baker, the CPPL's titular chairman in the late 1920s. Having cut her teeth in the suffrage movement, she was a capable organization builder—meticulous and indefatigable—as well as a daring activist; during the war, she had once dressed up like a maid to infiltrate and expose a brothel catering to servicemen. Although she has been almost entirely ignored by historians, Elizabeth Speer would mastermind the most powerful citizen movement for penal reform in Texas history.[19]

After extensive planning and fund-raising, which allowed the CPPL to build a statewide network of supporters, the prison survey got under way in 1923.[20] By any measure it was an exhaustive undertaking. Accountants pored over prison ledgers, while agricultural experts walked the farms. Convicts themselves were only occasionally interviewed, but more than 3,800 of them were poked, prodded, diagnosed, and classified by teams of physicians, dentists, psychologists, and educators. Phrenologists from the University of Texas took measurements in search of innate markers of criminality, among them "flat feet," "prevalence of hair on body," and "prognathism," which, they noted ominously, affected "practically all negroes." Overall, the CPPL boasted in a press release, it was conducting "the most exhaustive, far-reaching investigation of prison systems ever carried out in the United States."[21]

Although staid in tone, the final product, the four-hundred-page *Texas Prison Survey,* brimmed with indignation. "Our prison population is practically half white," consisting mainly of "young people . . . native Texans," the authors pointed out, hoping to elicit support from otherwise unconcerned lawmakers. Most inmates are salvageable but have been converted into "human wrecks," they argued. Syphilis, tuberculosis, and eye infections ravaged prisoners' bodies, while the state did almost nothing to enlighten their minds, this despite a 1921 law requiring "each prison, farm, and camp" to establish schools. Even in the arena most prized by wardens—revenue generation—CPPL experts described "complete failure." Three generations earlier, the institution of slavery had brought only shame and ruination to Texas, opined the authors, and yet the state "has endeavored to carry over the plantation system, despite its admitted failures, and to retain its convicts in a slavery status, despite the weaknesses of that system."[22]

In place of "almost unbelievable backwardness," the CPPL called for "a prison system new from start to finish." Revisiting recommendations put forward at the end of leasing, the surveyors proposed that schooling take precedence over stoop labor, that parole replace determinate sentencing, that expert penologists train guards "of high character," and that prisoner wages supplant the strap as an incentive to toil. Going further, the investigators proposed that Texas shutter the Walls and sell off its swampy plantations in order to erect an entirely new, scientifically designed "penal colony" near Austin. Complete with a diagnostic center, a mental hospital, a women's reformatory, and an honor camp for "promising white men," this thoroughly modern campus would more resemble a university or sanitarium than a traditional prison. Its construction would be "a great undertaking for the citizens of Texas," acknowledged the CPPL. "But this state is great enough and her citizens wise enough to demand the best that can be had."[23]

Backed by women's groups and other progressives, the *Texas Prison Survey* landed with a potent thud on each legislator's desk, but the CPPL's program faced formidable obstacles. Among them was Governor Pat Neff, a former prosecuting attorney from Waco with fine Grecian features and a reputation for Baptist rectitude. Neff had promised, "I will welcome ANYTHING from ANY source which will lead to better treatment of prisoners," yet it soon became clear that he perceived the politics of crime very differently than his reform-minded supporters.[24]

As crime rates climbed after World War I—partly the result of demobilization and new categories of illegality created by Prohibition—Governor Neff spoke not of social defectives in need of repair but of "cold, cruel, calculating" "evil-doers" who needed to be punished and deterred. Whereas penologists likened anticrime work to medicine—with inmates requiring professional diagnosis and treatment—Neff favored martial metaphors. "To win against [criminals] . . . good citizens must organize and fight," he declared. "The conflict is on in Texas for law and order."[25] Although elected as a progressive, Pat Neff was the first Texas governor to make hard-fisted, no-nonsense crime fighting a central part of his political identity.

This no-holds-barred attitude toward crime spelled trouble for prison reformers and criminal defendants. Arguing that "the law no longer had terror for evil-doers," Neff proposed tougher penalties for bootleggers, an expansion of the Texas Rangers, and the abolition of the state's suspended sentencing law, an innovation enacted at the end of leasing. He also radically curtailed executive clemency. Complaining that "the free use of pardoning power . . . robs the courthouse of its victory over the lawless," he abolished the Board of Pardon Advisors, and vowed to scrutinize every application himself, few of which he found deserving. Whereas Neff's two predecessors had pardoned more than four thousand convicts between them, he extended clemency to just over two hundred during his two terms in office. Just as the CPPL was pushing a massive overhaul, the governor was inflating the prisoner population and thereby complicating any fixes.[26]

Walter Boyd, aka Leadbelly, was himself caught in Neff's clutches. "'Dat man ain' gonna tu'n you loose, ol' Walter,'" his fellow convicts told him. "'He wouldn' tu'n his own mammy loose.'" Since his escape and transfer to the Imperial Farm in 1920, Leadbelly had tried everything but running to regain his freedom. Through hard work on the line, he had convinced a captain to request that his escape record be expunged, which under a different governor would have enhanced his chances of parole. About a year after his arrival at Sugar Land, Leadbelly's father showed up carrying a "fat roll of bills." He had sold the family's last parcel of land and tried, rather brazenly, to buy his only son's freedom, but the warden turned him down. "They mus' think you's a mighty bad boy an' needs lotsa punishment, Huddie," his father remarked.[27]

But Leadbelly still had cards to play. At Imperial, he was well known as a musician and was allowed to travel from camp to camp after work. When he heard that Governor Neff was planning a personal inspection, he composed a special song. Neff was "a big, fine-lookin' man," he recalled, and "sho was crazy about my singin' an' dancin'. Ev'y time I'd sing a new song or cut a few steps he'd roll me a bran-new silver dollar 'cross the flo'" Once his audience warmed, Leadbelly presented his unusual appeal.

> Please, Governor Neff, be good and kind,
> Have mercy on my great, long time.

With his boot tapping and strings blazing, the musician hit all the conventional clemency notes. He called himself Neff's "servant," pleaded on behalf of his wife Mary (in reality his girlfriend), lamented his thirty-year sentence, and even offered an oblique critique.

> Some folks say it's a sin,
> Got too many women and too many men.
> . . . In de pen.

Neff himself remembered the encounter almost as vividly. In his autobiography, *The Battles of Peace*, he painted the singer as a happy minstrel and himself as the benevolent master. "On one of the farms . . . was a negro as black as a stack of black cats at midnight," he wrote. "This negro would pick his banjo, pat his foot, roll his eyes, and show his big white teeth as he caroled forth in negro melody his musical application for a pardon." In his paternalistic way, the governor was moved, or at least amused. He announced that he would grant the supplicant's request but in his own time. "Walter, I'm gonna give you a pardon," Leadbelly remembered Neff telling him, "but I ain' gonna give it to you now. I'm gonna keep you down here to play for me when I come, but when I get out of office I'm gonna turn you loose." True to his word, the governor enjoyed Leadbelly's high-spirited performances on command whenever he visited the lower farms, then set him free on his last day in office.[28]

Few other convicts were as fortunate. Despite the costs to taxpayers, almost a thousand more convicts entered Texas prisons than were allowed to leave during Neff's four-year reign. Inmates sentenced to death, most of them African Americans and Hispanics convicted of rape or murder, found especially little sympathy. Largely in response to lynching, which the governor condemned, Texas centralized the death penalty in 1923. Previously, every county had carried out its own executions, usually in the form of public hangings. Progressives hoped that by sequestering such events at the Walls, they would discourage mob sentiment and encourage reverence for "the majesty of the law."[29] But the site and method of execution did not alter its racial dynamics.

Following the lead of New York and other states, lawmakers also ordered prison officials to carry out executions by a new technique, one they perceived as "more modern and humane," the electric chair. Huntsville officials thus built a new death house, the very same in use today, and by the end of the year a squat, straight-backed throne—soon

christened Ol' Sparky—was ready for operation.[30] Governor Neff wasted
little time in authorizing its use.

On a visit to the Walls in January, the governor stopped in to visit
with five men he would soon send to their deaths. "A queer feeling
creeps over you as you pass the death cell and pause," he wrote. "They
knew, and I realized, that I held within my hand the power to save
them from the electric chair. How feeble were words, both theirs and
mine, at such a time."[31] Not long after the governor departed, the men,
all of them African American, ranging in age from twenty to thirty-
nine, were approved for elimination.

In a dramatic gesture of conscience, Huntsville's warden, R. F. Coleman, resigned his post only days before. "It just couldn't be done," he
told reporters. "The penitentiary is a place to reform a man, not to kill
him." But a replacement was quickly found, and the Walls' inaugural
electrocutions went forward as scheduled. At nine minutes after midnight, the first condemned man, Charlie Reynolds, was escorted by
two guards into the brightly lit death chamber. He blinked rapidly,
reported a witness, was speedily strapped in the chair, and then stiffened violently when the new warden threw the switch. Within the
hour, four other men met the same fate.[32]

Governor Neff hoped this efficient new machinery of final justice
would sate the mob. In 1920, the year before he took office, Neff noted
that Texas carried out more lynchings than any other state. "We led the
civilized world in this species of savage lawlessness," he chided.[33] Even
as the governor struggled to make Texas law enforcement more professional and potent, however, a counterforce was rising up in the name of
popular retribution—the reanimated Knights of the Ku Klux Klan.

Having flared out during Reconstruction, the KKK roared back to life
in 1915, with a spectacular cross burning atop Georgia's Stone Mountain, the South's most hallowed shrine to the Lost Cause. In 1920, the
second incarnation of the Klan arrived in Texas, not long after a Houston
race riot resulted in the military execution of nineteen black soldiers.
Like the Confederate forebears they revered, the new Klansmen pledged
themselves to the "noble principles" of white supremacy, patriarchal
family values, and fire-and-brimstone Protestantism. Whereas the postbellum Klan was conceived to restore southern governments to their
rightful guardians, however, this new generation of Grand Dragons, Ti-

tans, and Cyclops sought not only to wield political power but to hold it. According to Hiram Wesley Evans, a Dallas dentist who rose up through the ranks to become the Klan's nationwide Imperial Wizard, the modern Klan would evolve from a secret society into "a great militant political organization" capable of getting its best "citizens" elected to office.[34] In the interwar period, Klansmen became America's homegrown Fascisti.

True to this wider calling, the KKK of the 1920s embraced a diversity of causes, as symbolized by the banners present during the Klan's first march up Congress Avenue in Austin: "All Native Born," "We Stand By Old Glory," "Bootleggers, Beware," "Lewd Woman, This Is Your Only Warning"—plus the no doubt reassuring message to any African American spectators, "Good Niggers Need Not Fear Us."[35] Such eclectic pronouncements, all wrapped together with the slogan "Pure Americanism," allowed the Invisible Empire to attract a wide range of Anglo followers, including uneasy middle-class strivers who generally supported both Prohibition and Progressivism. Indeed, unlike the third Klan, formed in response to the later civil rights movement, this second wave coveted mainstream respectability. "The charter members," reported one Houston observer, "were silk-stocking men from the banks, business houses, and professions."[36]

Organizationally disciplined and bolstered by white middle-class anxieties—about crime, Mexican (mostly Catholic) immigration, flapper hedonism, and destabilized postwar race relations—the KKK spread faster than Johnson grass through East and Central Texas. At its peak, it counted more than 170,000 dues-paying members and became a more potent political force than the Democratic Party, which it largely controlled. In 1922, the Knights elected one of their own to the U.S. Senate, Earle B. Mayfield, and captured a majority of seats in the state legislature. Overall, concludes one historian, "Texas was the number-one Klan state politically."[37]

As they moved into positions of governmental authority, Klan leaders claimed they were transcending the organization's "original necessary *modus operandi*." The KKK "stands for law enforcement" not "mob violence," asserted an organizer in Plainview. Like the Redeemers, who had claimed they fought merely for equal citizenship and states' rights, the savviest leaders of the second Klan insisted, "We make no fight on races or religions."[38]

Despite the rhetoric, the second Klan relied almost as much on force and intimidation as had its predecessor. In 1921 alone, Texas newspapers reported some eighty KKK whippings, not including ghastlier incidents: the castration of an African American dentist in Houston and the branding of *KKK* into the forehead of an African American bellhop in Dallas. In 1922, the organization was suspected of involvement in nine mob killings, though police departments—themselves riddled with Klansmen—were unable to solve the crimes. In less guarded moments, Klan leaders suggested that still greater wrath lay in store. When a "large group of negroes" protested a KKK speaker in Temple, he turned to them and warned that if they "kept on listening to insidious propaganda of mongrel negro uplift societies, . . . the modern Knights of the Ku Klux Klan will have to rise up as our fathers did and . . . everyone of you will be swept from the earth."[39]

Klan excesses galvanized opponents, who gained strength in step with the hooded order. But in the early 1920s, more Texas politicians knelt before the burning cross than tried to extinguish it. Governor Neff, whose tenure coincided with the Klan's meteoric ascent, spoke out regularly against mob violence but declined to criticize the KKK by name. So close were many of his policy positions to the Invisible Empire's, in fact, that critics suspected him of cultivating a secret alliance.[40]

In the realm of crime and punishment, Governor Neff and Texas Klansmen marched almost perfectly in sync. In recruiting pamphlets, the organization identified vigorous law enforcement as its paramount concern. "Law and Order" served as a unifying cry, by which, explained one contemporary, Klansmen meant "not overscrupulous observance of the forms of justice, . . . not squeamishness about the legal rights of guilty defendants, but unceremonious and drastic 'cleaning up' of the community." In the field of policing, the Klan posted its most impressive institutional gains. Well before the order began putting up candidates for statewide office, it took over judgeships, jury commissions, sheriff departments, and prosecutor offices in communities large and small. Indeed, Klansmen made no exaggeration when they paraded under the banner "We Are the Law."[41] For longer than anyone could remember, Texas lawmen had turned a blind eye to vigilante violence. Now, with the rise of the Klan, law enforcement and vigilantism simply merged.

In his own campaign for "law and order," Neff's words echoed the Klan's almost verbatim. Criminals were not errant citizens, he suggested, but enemy marauders, a designation that recalled earlier crusades against Indians and Mexicans. Like his hooded countrymen, he had little regard for "faint-hearted sentimentalists" or legal formalities. "The genius of man has never found any better way to prevent crime than to punish criminals," he blasted. "Punishment must follow crime as night follows day."[42]

A nasal-voiced teetotaler who had reportedly "never shot a gun [or] baited a fish hook," Pat Neff did not exhibit rough frontier masculinity in the style of Texas's heroes. Yet by waging war against "gamblers, bootleggers, thieves, thugs, [and] murderers," he developed a swagger. "While I am governor," he growled, "no band of criminals will ever take charge of a community as long as a Texas Ranger can pull a trigger."[43]

Unsurprisingly, the CPPL made little headway under Neff and the Klan-dominated legislature. More disappointment followed the election of Miriam Ferguson, Texas's first woman governor, who functioned mainly as a stand-in for her husband, the former governor Jim Ferguson, a corrupt and ideologically scattershot populist who had been impeached and removed from office in 1917. Like Neff, "Ma" Ferguson opposed the CPPL's prison relocation proposal as impractical and costly.[44] So as the 1926 elections approached, women's organizations decided to shift from lobbying to electioneering.[45] They drafted a constitutional amendment to reorganize the prison administration and mobilized on behalf of a youthful, reform-minded candidate for governor, a "red-headed whirlwind" from Tyler named Dan Moody.

A sharp-minded, serious-talking prosecutor, Moody had made a name for himself by going after the Klan; in a sensational 1923 case, he had sent four prominent Klansmen to prison for tarring and feathering a traveling salesman accused of adultery. The clean-cut young counselor also pledged himself to prison reform, higher education, and graft-free government. So stark was the contrast with the freewheeling Fergusons, who were mired in contracting and pardon-selling scandals, that many progressives came to think of Moody as their "political Moses."[46]

Women's groups played a vital role in Moody's campaign. The CPPL mailed out tens of thousands of leaflets and organized speaking events across the state. Jessie Daniel Ames, founder of the Texas League of Women Voters, said she campaigned "to the limit of [her] endurance," while Jane McCallum, a women's lobbyist, ran herself so ragged her doctor ordered her to bed. Moody himself visited up to a dozen towns a day. To the amazement of reporters, he always appeared at dusty outposts in a pressed white linen suit with white polished shoes, thus casting himself as an unblemished, incorruptible "Idol of Texas."[47]

The Fergusons ran a characteristically ugly campaign. They used convict trusties to distribute literature and accused Moody of unholy alliances—with oil companies, Negro rights activists, and "ammonia-spraying highbrows." Jim said his wife was going "to electrocute [Moody] on July 24," but when primary day came around, it was Ma who got fried.[48]

Modernizers of all stripes were exultant. "Texas has recovered her self-respect," trumpeted the *El Paso Times and Herald*. Moody's victory signaled "a new day," opined the *New York Evening Post*. "A new Texas of the public schools, of the universities, of growing industries, of immigration, and of a widening future is doing its best to turn its back on the demagogy and 'hill-billyism' of the old Texas."[49]

To mark the transition from ignominy to modernity, Moody's supporters staged an inauguration extravaganza on January 18, 1927, said to attract the largest crowd in Texas history. All told, some fifty thousand spectators turned out to watch the new governor accept the people's "sacred trust." Moody spoke only briefly but sounded resonant notes. He would "restore public confidence" in government and set a new course in Texas politics.[50]

For Elizabeth Speer and her colleagues, the inauguration marked their political arrival. For the first time since the end of leasing, a chief executive was promising to do everything he could to clean up Texas prisons. The CPPL's constitutional amendment had curtailed the authority of the Board of Prison Commissioners, which had become a bastion of the plantation establishment, and a majority of incoming lawmakers, including Klansmen, expressed support for the CPPL program. Governor Moody, it seemed, had only to dip his pen in the inkwell and await a comprehensive reform and relocation package. After a decade of unceasing agitation and repeated disappointments, the women at the helm of the most powerful free-world movement for penal reform in Texas history were poised to take over the state's far-flung prison system and make it anew.

## "IT IS LIBERTY ALONE THAT FITS MAN FOR LIBERTY"

As had previous generations of southern penal reformers, the CPPL looked north for guidance. New York, in particular, stood out for innovation. In the nineteenth century the Empire State had devised Auburn and Elmira. In the twentieth, breakthroughs occurred at two institutions just up the Hudson from New York City. Under the leadership of charismatic progressives, these prisons hosted some of the most ambitious experiments ever attempted in rehabilitative penology, before or, arguably, since. For a brief, exhilarating interval between the Spanish-American and world wars, they seemed to illuminate, as one partisan put it, the "prison of the future."[51] In Texas, when Speer and her compatriots spoke idealistically of the penal colony, it was these experiments they hoped to replicate on southern soil.

The first institution to chart a new course was the women's reformatory at Bedford Hills, opened in 1901. Situated on two hundred leafy acres in Westchester County, the facility's residential cottages more resembled prep school dormatories than dreary gaols. Each inmate had her own room, and there were no walls or gun turrets to signal the loss of freedom. All of the women had to work, often in gardening or the laundry, but education and job training predominated. Every summer, volunteers poured in from the Seven Sisters, prestigious colleges in the Northeast, allowing Bedford Hills to offer a wide-ranging curriculum. There were classes in gymnastics and singing, sexual hygiene and current events, history and geography, carpentry and mechanical drawing, as well as domestic science, the last representing the field most likely to offer employment to former prisoners. "Our efforts," explained Superintendent Katherine Bement Davis, "are to fit girls for life" and then "parole [them] as rapidly as they are found to be fitted to go out."[52]

With a doctorate from the University of Chicago, Davis epitomized the more professional outlook of this second generation of women's prison administrators. In contrast to her gospel-inspired forebears, she and her cohort approached their work with more confident detachment than missionary zeal. They tended to conceive of their wards not as wayward sisters but as "clients or subjects of research." Their responsibility, as they saw it, was not so much to rescue fallen women from sin as to treat women criminals for physical and especially mental disease.[53]

This psychologization of inmate care came to full fruition at Bedford Hills. With the support of John D. Rockefeller Jr., who had become exercised about the "social evil" of prostitution, Davis set up an advanced research institute adjacent to the prison and employed some twenty female social scientists, who analyzed her wards more rigorously than perhaps any group of human captives in history.[54]

With generous financing and pliant subjects, the Bedford Laboratory of Social Hygiene marked the coming of age of women's criminology. It helped refine the nascent field of intelligence testing and cast new light on the complex interplay between heredity and environment. Compared to the crude typologies of positivists like Cesare Lombroso, who argued that squat, dark-haired women with dull eyesight and misshapen skulls were programmed for perverse wickedness, the research was remarkably sophisticated. Yet it was anything but disinterested. The scientists' purpose was not simply to gain greater understanding of incarcerated women but to devise new techniques of categorization and control.[55] They studied inmates' minds to reorder them.

This applied dimension to the Rockefeller research took concrete form in the creation of two auxiliary institutions, both charged to isolate "defective delinquents" from those deemed more capable of reformation: the Division of Mentally Defective Women and the Bedford Psychopathic Hospital. In neither place did much treatment take place. Women designated as "feeble minded," a diagnosis that connoted both mental retardation and biological propensity to crime, were, by definition, beyond reach, while so-called psychopaths seemed to grow only more resentful in response to fanciful remedies involving ice packs and water submersion.[56] The failure to cure, however, tended to legitimate as much as undermine the facilities. Their function was to constrict troublesome women, and under New York indeterminate sentencing laws they could do so indefinitely. While Dr. Davis and her colleagues at Bedford Hills broke down the walls between women inmates and the community, they also amassed formidable new powers as penological experts.

On September 28, 1913, just as the laboratory at Bedford Hills was exercising its greatest influence, a different sort of experiment was getting under way two hundred miles away at New York's oldest penitentiary, Auburn. It was Sunday morning, and some thirteen hundred male convicts had assembled in the chapel to consider a remarkable proposition. Before them was Thomas Mott Osborne, a millionaire industrialist and part-time philanthropist. He had been appointed chair of the State Commission on Prison Reform, and he proposed to study their aging institution "from the inside looking out." If convicts and their warders would kindly go along, he would shed his finery and live among them for a week as a common prisoner.[57]

Standing before "rows and rows of men in gray trousers and faded shirts," Osborne addressed his "sad audience" in a way that visitors from the free world rarely if ever did. "Somehow, deep down, I have the feeling that after I have really lived among you, marched in your lines, shared your food, gone to the same cells at night, and in the morning looked out at the pieces of God's sunlight through the same iron bars— that then, and not until then, can I feel the knowledge which will break down the barriers between my soul and the souls of my brothers." The prisoners paused, as if to apprehend the full meaning of this potentate addressing them as brothers, and then applauded heartily.[58]

The next morning, Osborne presented himself at the front gate and became "Thomas Brown, No. 33,333x." His experience would hardly be typical—everyone was on their best behavior around Tom—but it was harrowing nonetheless. Like other convicts, he surrendered his property and contacts with the outside world and took up residence in a "stone vault" so cramped that it reminded him of getting locked in a closet as a child. Along with the others, he marched, labored, and submitted to petty rules that governed prisoners' every move and prohibited almost every utterance; on the first day, he was rebuked for turning his head in the dining hall. "The rule is always, 'Eyes Front,'" the captain told him. To get the full treatment, Tom also spent a night in solitary, which he described as "a spot haunted by the spirits of evil."[59]

Although his incarceration was a sham and his reprieve certain, Tom nevertheless felt the prisoner role overtaking him. In his journal, he expressed solidarity with convicts over "screws" and quickly "learned the first duty and only pleasure of the convict—to deceive a keeper and get away with it." As his dignity slipped, a "torrent of rage" surged up within him. By the end, he was describing the prison system in the same bombastic terms as convict muckrakers. "An aching, overwhelming sense of the hideous cruelty of the whole barbaric, brutal business sweeps over me," he wrote. "This is worse than a negation of God, it is a betrayal of God."[60]

At the end of seven days, Osborne was more transformed than he expected. He had gained new respect for the inmates, whom he praised for "their courtesy, sympathy, and understanding" and new contempt for the prison system. The current regime "tends to crush slowly but irresistibly the good in" each prisoner, he concluded, and needed to be organized on fundamentally new principles. Most of Osborne's suggested remedies had been tried before—indeterminate sentencing, schooling, and classification by psychological testing—but he added a fresh element to the mix. In order to prepare prisoners for successful lives in freedom, he proposed they should be given "as much freedom as [they] can stand" in prison. Quoting William Gladstone, he proclaimed, "It is liberty alone that fits man for liberty."[61]

With the consent of the warden—an old friend and political ally—Osborne launched a radical overhaul of prison management. After meeting with a council of inmates, he helped set up a prisoner-led Mutual Welfare League, which he hoped would eventually take over Auburn's basic governance. The association started off modestly—presenting everyday requests to the warden, staging entertainments, and organizing sporting contests, sometimes pitting prisoners against guards—but soon took on more serious responsibilities. In the workshops and on the yard, guards pulled back to the perimeter, allowing league "sentries" to maintain order. A tribunal system was set up, in which petty rule breakers were judged and punished by convict juries rather than prison officials. If Osborne was not exactly "the Emancipator of the Prisoner," as one supporter claimed, he was certainly taking the deregimentation of the penitentiary further than any of his predecessors. One commentator called it "democracy under a humane despot."[62]

When the new Auburn didn't tear itself apart, Osborne was asked to take on an even more challenging assignment, the wardenship of Sing Sing. Since its construction on the banks of the Hudson by lash-driven convicts in the 1820s, the penitentiary had operated as a crowded catacombs of "uninterrupted silence and uninterrupted labor." Its marble cell blocks were "damp, cold, poorly lighted, and poorly ventilated," reported investigators in 1914, distilleries of vice and tuberculosis. Although he would have preferred to raze it, Osborne set out to transform this "Bastille on the Hudson" into a showcase of what he and his allies were calling the "New Penology." Even more dramatically than at Auburn, he hoped to assemble a walled-in facsimile of free society. Not only would a Mutual Welfare League represent convict interests and police the ranks, but a host of auxiliary institutions, from a prison banking system to an internal parole board, would mimic their counterparts beyond the walls. "The prison indeed, ought, as far as possible, to represent a real community," Osborne insisted. "It is the duty of the state to make a prison a school where men can be trained for citizenship."[63]

As had Katherine Bement Davis at Bedford Hills, warden Osborne cultivated a web of outside contacts to fortify his "self-government system." With the support of Henry Ford, he coordinated an extensive job placement program. With funding from Rockefeller, Sing Sing opened its own research laboratory, this one more concerned with ferreting out "sexual perversion" than feeblemindedness. Most important of all was the National CPPL. In coordination with Columbia University and the American Federation of Labor, the committee set up educational programs, helped revamp prison industries, and assisted a national public relations campaign. All together, these overlapping initiatives showed early signs of success, though reliable data are scarce. Injuries, assaults, heroin smuggling, and escapes all reportedly declined under Osborne's leadership, while sales from Sing Sing's workshops soared. One writer labeled Osborne's first year in office an *"annus mirabilis."*[64]

Miraculous or not, the new Sing Sing failed to make converts of its most vital parishioners, state politicians. Although Osborne seems to have mastered the challenges of internal prison governance, and although his publicity savvy made him the most celebrated warden in America, powerful figures in Albany came to regard him as excessively autonomous. Republicans and Tammany Hall Democrats maneuvered to remove him from office, at one point charging him with "unnatural and immoral acts with the convicts." The courts delivered vindication, but Osborne never regained his footing. In 1916, he resigned. A succession of replacements promised to carry on his legacy, but the "prison of the future" steadily fell back on its past. The Mutual Welfare League hobbled on, for a time, but ersatz prison democracy was dead.[65]

Similar reversals took place at Bedford Hills. With her "nerves . . . strained almost to the breaking point" from dealing with overcrowding and inadequate funding, Dr. Davis departed in 1914. Four years later, Rockefeller shut down his laboratory, and in 1920 Bedford's prisoners rioted with such force that the state police had to be called in to restore order. In the aftermath, Amos Baker, a psychiatrist previously posted at Sing Sing, took over the institution, the first man to lead a women's reformatory in New York. Investigators soon concluded that Bedford Hills was "in the main not a reformatory at all."[66]

To a certain extent, this retreat from innovation marked a regular turn in prison management's version of the business cycle—with reform and reaction always following on each other's heels. But Davis's and Osborne's work also fell victim to a deeper shift in American politics.

Although Progressivism expanded in Texas in the years surrounding World War I, a variety of social dislocations—among them, increased immigration, the Great Migration of African Americans northward, as well as the rise of the New Woman, the New Negro, and the Bolsheviks—enervated the movement in the Northeast and Midwest. Anxiety and anger eclipsed state-building idealism, while conservatism, both moral and corporate, enjoyed a resurgence. Although many progressive ideas would reappear in the New Deal, they lost oxygen in the Roaring Twenties.[67]

The politics of crime played a critical role in this conservative revival. Although the numbers are unreliable (the federal government didn't start tracking crime statistics until 1929), many commentators believed the United States was experiencing an upsurge of illegality in the postwar period. "The United States is the most lawless nation on the globe, barring only Russia under Bolshevist rule," exclaimed one observer, echoing the frightening hyperbole of Governor Neff and the Klan. During the Progressive Era, social scientists had convinced many Americans that hereditary or environmental factors primarily caused crime, explanations that favored preventative and rehabilitative remedies. In the age of the gangster, however, a more traditional view gained sway. The criminal was not so much defective or deprived as immoral and avaricious. What America needed to defend itself was not "floppy-minded" theories peddled by "blithering sentimentalists," argued a new generation of anticrime crusaders, but swift, severe punishments.[68]

With the ground shifting beneath their feet, penological visionaries in the mold of Davis and Osborne gained little traction in the so-called lawless decade. Prison reformers, notes one historian, had to grapple with a new "sense of uncertainty if not disillusionment." Compared to previous years, death sentences increased in the 1920s, while reformatories languished. Stripes and silence passed from the scene as prisons became less absolutist, but critics saw chaos as the consequence. In 1929, prisons from New York to Colorado erupted in the nation's first coordinated wave of convict rioting.[69]

A bundle of national prison surveys came out in the period, almost all of them dour. Most comprehensive was the fourteen-part Wickersham Commission report, released in 1931. Although primarily concerned with Prohibition and law enforcement, it included a hefty—and damning—volume on criminal punishment. More than sixty years had lapsed since the rebirth of reformatory penology at the national prison congress in Cincinnati, but the surveyors found not a single prison in the nation that lived up to the "reformatory idea." America's penal system was "unwieldy [and] unorganized," they determined. Its prisons were overcrowded, "insanitary, and degrading"; its prisoners largely idle (outside the South), untouched by education, and subject to severe, often capricious discipline. Overall, the assessment was nearly as categorical as the CPPL's *Prison Survey* in Texas. "We conclude that the present system is antiquated and inefficient," wrote the commissioners. "It does not reform the criminal. It fails to protect society. There is reason to believe that it contributes to the increase of crime by hardening the prisoner."[70]

Although the Wickersham Commission report ended up recapitulating the main tenets of scientific penology, it appeared at a low point for the field. The CPPL had achieved its greatest influence more than a decade earlier, with Osborne's efforts at Sing Sing coming closest to the full realization of its vision. In the years after World War I, however, the organization's credibility ebbed. Its most prominent supporters lost their posts; its union allies fell back under withering anticommunist attack. Thus, when the Texas chapter announced in 1926 that a new governor was poised to implement the full slate of recommendations put forward by the *Texas Prison Survey*, the national organizers jumped. Not only would the foundation of an industrial-scientific penal colony mark a new direction for Texas but a chance for the movement to redeem itself nationwide. Suddenly, a weather-beaten CPPL had the opportunity to revitalize rehabilitative penology by carrying it to a new frontier.

## "A NEW SPIRIT SEEMS TO BE STIRRING"

True to his campaign for honest, efficient government, Dan Moody proposed a far-reaching prison agenda when he became governor in January 1927. "Fundamental evils" plague the current system, he told legislators, requiring "comprehensive reorganization." As a first step, Moody stacked his Prison Board with CPPL progressives, among them Rabbi Cohen and Robert Holmes Baker, a Houston insurance executive, who became chair.[71] Elizabeth Speer came along as executive secretary to the board, and just as she had at the CPPL, she parlayed a diminutive title into considerable clout. Together, the new administration promised to "save the State [from] humiliation" and to harvest "the souls of men."[72]

Although the legislature declined to grant the Prison Board authority to relocate the penal system, Moody's team undertook substantial changes on the existing properties. Under the direction of Speer and a new general manager, a Yale-educated engineer named W. H. Mead, authorities drafted new rules for convicts and guards alike and enforced them more consistently. Ten-hour work limits were back, as was classification by corrigibility rather than physical strength. Schooling, sanitation, and crop yields all started to improve, administrators claimed, despite the challenges of "old, obsolete, badly located, and entirely unfit" infrastructure. Philosophically, Texas's penal system was turning a corner, declared Cohen. No longer would convicts be returned to freedom "more brutalized and more anti-social than before." Instead, they would be prepared "for a life of useful citizenship."[73]

Although the CPPL-dominated board adapted to the existing landscape—whipping, racial segregation, and forced labor remained institutional mainstays—it also pushed against its boundaries. After sending administrators on two cross-country junkets, the board reiterated proposals for indeterminate sentencing, industrialization, and relocation.[74] Most dramatically, prison chiefs took steps toward convict democracy, allowing inmates to set up a Prison Welfare League, an attenuated version of Osborne's creation at Sing Sing. The response was overwhelming. By September 1929, almost half of Texas's prisoners had signed up, two thousand in all. In coordination with Cohen, who chaired the board's "welfare committee," the league set up schools, recreational programs, and even a postrelease job placement program. The purpose, explained prisoners at the helm—all of them white male trusties at the Walls—was to "promote the welfare of the inmates" and to foster "corrective rather than punitive incarceration."[75]

As in New York, the league started out by organizing holiday entertainments. For Thanksgiving in 1928, the group staged a "vaudeville show" at Huntsville, featuring "a fine turkey dinner," comedy sketches, and an a cappella rendition of "Down South Everybody's Happy." Convicts gave up "3 cheers for the warden," and league officers reported "a new spirit . . . stirring in the State prison system." "Formerly, the conversation was . . . about jails, crimes, length of sentences, and effective methods of escape," noted Eugene V. Simons, the league's first president. "Now . . . the boys are discussing the trades they would like to learn . . . and their plans for the future."[76]

In the welfare league's newspaper, the *Echo*, which remains in print today, convict leaders put forward an expansive vision, albeit cautiously. In the first issues, they praised their keepers and exhorted inmates, "KEEP YOUR RECORD CLEAR." But they also developed a shrewdly independent voice. "The paper . . . shall be the echo of prison life, prison thoughts and aspirations," intoned the editors, "an echo, thrown from the four walls of this prison, which will grow in resonance until its vibrations are felt, and heeded."[77]

Beyond page 1, dissident notes sounded more prominently. In a satirical column, "Plain Hokum," a writer took on the voice of a crotchety old-timer to broach taboo topics like torture and sexual assault. Prisoners writing in Spanish enjoyed greater license. "Remember that because we live under the same roof, suffering together . . . we are one family," instructed an ardent reporter in his mother tongue. Study, work hard, and stay true to your "noble hearts," and you will become "soldiers in this immense army."[78]

Of all the *Echo* writers, President Simons demonstrated the greatest moxie. A charismatic, college-educated Jewish man who had once worked in a Pennsylvania settlement house, Simons took sole credit for founding the league, and he labored tirelessly for its success.[79] He printed a glowing self-portrait in the *Echo* and explained in private correspondence to Cohen that he was single-handedly establishing schools on the farms and struggling to keep "the penitentiary . . . entirely clear of dope." "I am very busy these days," he announced in a May 1929 letter. "We are meeting with success wherever we go." In the margin, the rabbi scribbled, "This man is ok!"[80]

As his stature and mobility within the prison system grew, so did Simons's ambition. In chatty correspondence with Cohen, he began recommending coworkers for clemency and weighing in on disciplinary matters—interventions that made Speer nervous.[81] More audaciously, Simons proposed to set up an entirely new "honor farm" for "worthy men," where traditional prison rules would not apply. Only two state employees would work at the new unit, he recommended, a school principal and an expert in "scientific farming." Prisoners themselves, organized into paramilitary ranks by league officers, chief among them Simons, would take care of everything else, including the guarding. "I am anxious to put my Welfare League Farm Plan in operation," he beseeched Cohen in one of his last letters as president. "It will set the pace of penal work for the entire nation."[82] What had started out as a club for trusties was now poised, in its founder's mind, to take over the prison system.

Simons's dynamism earned him the wary admiration of top administrators—Baker called him "one of the very best prisoners we have"—but his chutzpah boded ill for the penal reform movement. With progressives controlling the Prison Board, a feminist social worker setting top-level policy, and a Jewish convict plotting prisoner self-government, Texas's prison administration was fast getting ahead of the political establishment, not to mention the guard force. Chairman Baker insisted, "We are not running this institution to please . . . disappointed politicians" and "old-time prison men trained under the old-time methods."[83] He failed to realize how quickly the prison system's outdated "political machine" could derail his administration.

Prison farm managers had historically exercised nearly absolute power in Texas. Their plantations were isolated, their field hands rightless, their job performance evaluated, above all, by crop yields. So, when the greenhorn Prison Board began issuing new guidelines from headquarters, many wardens simply chucked them in the bin. In turn, the Speer-Baker team started terminating personnel, thus kicking up a dust storm. After Captain McLoed lost his post at Retrieve farm for "beat[ing] up a negro contrary to law," for instance, the president of Brazoria County State Bank reminded Governor Moody that the officer "stands very high in the esteem of this community." "If McLoed had not conquered that negro," he went on, echoing the stock advice of antebellum slaveholders, the warden "would have lost the respect of every convict in the building and would have had never been able to regain it."[84]

As a rule, Elizabeth Speer came in for special excoriation. "Mrs. Speer is a real *menace* to the system," counseled the pastor of Huntsville's First Methodist Church. A farm manager added that "Speer seemed to interest herself in picture shows, ball games, . . . and music for convicts, and she didn't want [work] to interfere with this either." Public safety was threatened, warned prison neighbors. A "mollycoddling attitude . . . has done much to break down discipline in the camps," asserted a Brazoria man, while a resident of Huntsville postulated that the "lack of discipline in the System is largely responsible for the crime wave in Texas today."[85]

Convicts did little to dispel this impression of "inadequate management." Their immodest expectations collided with modest, slow-moving reforms, and frustrations, then turmoil, followed.[86] Just as they had at the end of leasing, convicts disappointed by the pace of change regularly filed grievance petitions. Four women at Goree begged the governor to "send one of your Texas Rangers to investigate how the Women's Penitentiary of Texas is being run." Men at Darrington warned that unless an imperious supervisor backed off "he is going to get hurt."[87]

Even as some convicts appealed for redress through conventional channels, however, far greater numbers took advantage of overcrowding, understaffing, and recalcitrant, inattentive guards to run for the rivers. Every few weeks, the general manager prepared a disorder report that included terse descriptions of each escape. A trusty at Blue Ridge "was last seen going out to bring in the cows," while another got away while "acting as a dog boy on [a] practice chase." One entry inadvertently revealed the limits of medical care at Retrieve: "Small pox patient, isolated in shack, chained to bed, broke lock, ran."

Most convicts absconded on their own, but when opportunity knocked large groups sometimes answered. On May 6, 1928, twenty prisoners escaped from Blue Ridge after "cutting [a] hole in the building with hacksaw blades." Six months later, thirty-one men crawled through a window at Clemens. All told, Texas's escape rate climbed steadily under the reformers, continuing a trend that had started under Ma Ferguson. In 1928, fully 17 percent of Texas's prison population escaped, 760 prisoners in total—an all-time record.[88]

Prisoners tested the grip of their keepers in other ways as well. Not long after General Manager Mead took the reins in March 1928, convicts at Eastham, complaining that they were "being cursed in the field and run on by guards' horses," refused to work, as did protesters at Harlem, Ramsey, and Ferguson. "[We] encountered an apparent epidemic of mutinies," Mead wrote in his annual report, "fourteen . . . in the month of May" alone. In response, officials tried dialogue, transfers, and work rule changes but soon resorted to stiffer measures. Mead ordered employees to target practice and warned, "Our guards shall shoot to hit." After successive bucks and breakouts at Blue Ridge—the first documented uprising by Hispanic convicts in state history—the general manager "talked to the Mexicans, made them admit [fault]," and then left whipping orders with the farm manager.[89]

But beatings brought no more peace than talk. Not long after a series of whippings at Clemens, a gang of convicts smuggled in six-shooters, took three guards hostage, and escaped en masse, setting off running gun battles through the "swamps and cane breaks."[90] Even the Wynne Farm, "where cripples are kept," got in on the action. Over the course of several weeks, an interracial team of convicts confined to the TB ward excavated a seventy-foot tunnel, working at night and using blankets to haul dirt to an attic. On September 27, eighteen men wriggled their way to liberty. A month later, prisoners torched the main building at Wynne Farm, inspiring one inmate, according to a local newspaper reporter, to pick up his banjo and commit the occasion to song. " 'It ain't gonna burn no more,' " the man warbled, "as the old wooden building crumbled under the onslaught of flames." It was the tenth fire to strike Wynne since 1927.[91]

Trusties proved no more trustworthy than tuberculars. For a year, Eugene Simons had been lobbying Cohen and other officials for a furlough. First, he explained that he wanted to celebrate Yom Kippur at a synagogue, then that he needed thirty days to patent an airplane motor he said would "revolutionize the industry."[92] In August 1929, he finally got his leave. As promised, he stopped by Galveston to visit Cohen on his way out—but just long enough to borrow money, cash a bad check, and swipe a pair of spectacles. Then he vanished, only to be discovered weeks later in San Francisco, "where he was working for a business college."[93]

A month later, two other *Echo* writers made a break for it. While visiting the offices of Huntsville's main free-world paper, the *Item*, they bludgeoned a guard with a wooden mallet, stole his car, and made for Houston.[94]

By the end of their second year in power, everything was going wrong for Texas's prison leadership. Like penologists elsewhere, the CPPL-dominated Prison Board had promised convict cooperation and lower costs but had delivered neither. In 1927, good weather and higher cotton prices had provided a healthy balance sheet. But flooding, arson, escapes, increased operating costs, and a shift from cotton to food crops ensued, so by 1928 the prison system was hemorrhaging cash.[95] With expenses exceeding revenue by more than a hundred thousand dollars a month, board members promised Governor Moody they would stanch the bleeding. They proposed consolidating departments, selling off equipment, cutting the guard force by 10 percent, and reducing starting salaries by a third—this despite the record number of escapes. Without a dramatic increase in paroles, warned the general manager, the prison system could expect "much dissatisfaction and unrest."[96]

But Governor Moody was in no hurry to open the gates. On the campaign trail, he had promised to clean up Ma Ferguson's "pardon orgy," and in office he proved no more lenient than Pat Neff. Whereas Governor Ferguson had granted clemency to 3,595 prisoners during her two-year term, Moody released fewer than 2,000 over four years, most of them on time-limited furloughs. The result was that Texas's prison population rose sharply under Moody's leadership, from 3,053 to 5,069, an increase of 67 percent, with little expansion of infrastructure or personnel.[97]

At any time, lawmakers could have come to the rescue, but they were in no mood. In the fortieth and forty-first legislatures, politicians approved record budgets for the prison system, but when the money fell short they offered no more. Modernists to the end, Speer and her allies clung to the hope that relocation would solve their problems. "Little permanent progress can be made until the System is reorganized, centralized, and relocated," argued Baker. When a Texas Prison Centralization Commission presented its findings in 1929, however, lawmakers looked favorably on a "minority report" that proposed consolidating prison properties in the old slavery-sugarcane belt. As always, race and cost loomed large. "Negroes and Mexicans must, as a rule, be given outdoor occupation," argued the dissident commissioners. "The removal of our entire central prison plant [to] Austin would be a useless and extravagant waste of public funds." Four times, Moody submitted CPPL-style relocation bills to the legislature. None became law.[98]

With chaos regnant and the penal colony lost, Texas's prison progressives began plotting their own getaways. Robert Baker fell deathly ill during the 1929 legislative session and resigned in the spring. Elizabeth Speer soldiered on but quietly disappeared from the letterhead sometime in October, her duties consolidated under the general manager, who himself cut out in November.[99] Rabbi Cohen persevered but drafted a series of resignation letters between June and December, finally begging the governor to relieve him. "I am not pleased at the action of the legislature throughout," he remarked. It "is cutting the very Institutions that should be supported. What's the use?"[100]

At Baker's suggestion, another wealthy progressive, W. A. Paddock, took over as chairman of the prison board. But a traumatic personal experience soon hardened his outlook. After stopping to chat with an ex-convict outside his bank office one day, he found himself kidnapped, robbed, and dumped on the side of the road outside Houston. "A convict like that," bellowed the "kindly" gentleman, "you ought to take him out in the Gulf, tie a rock around his neck, and pitch him overboard."[101]

## "THE BIGGEST PRISON SHOW ON EARTH"

Prison pandemonium invites reaction, and under pressure from "business interests" and the legislature, Governor Moody delivered on March 24, 1930. Although he continued to support relocation, he selected one of the CPPL's most caustic critics to take over as general manager.[102] The man was Lee Simmons, a businessman and former sheriff, and although he had served on the Prison Board since 1927, he had never embraced its reformatory mission. He championed the system's veteran farm managers and clashed regularly, if congenially, with Cohen, whose welfare plans he regarded as "not practical" and contrary to the legislature's mandate to make "the System self-sustaining." In one meeting, he introduced a motion to cut Speer's salary in half, a move (though voted down) that earned him Baker's lasting enmity.[103] "Over the first two years of our Board's experience . . . recall that every constructive act was vigorously opposed by Mr. Simmons," Baker wrote to the governor, beseeching him to reconsider the appointment. "My own feeling is that whatever I have accomplished . . . will go for naught if the System is now turned over to [him]." In reply, Simmons blasted Baker and Speer's "misdirected sympathy" toward convicts and their ignorance of farming.[104]

Although Moody may have sympathized with Baker, he sided with Simmons. After three years of budget overflows, mayhem, and legislative stalemate, he and other power brokers yearned for "a strong hand." Simmons promised "fairness and common sense," in contrast to what he called the "fantastic" and "theoretical" proposals advanced by the CPPL. Prisons under his watch would be managed "on a business and humanitarian basis," he told reporters, with business taking precedence. "This is a time that a man has got to work if he has a job," he instructed prisoners, alluding to the depression then tightening its grip on the nation. "You may not agree with me, but when we keep you at work, now this means work, . . . we are rendering you a service."[105]

Although Simmons had a meager frame and a long, sad face, he fancied himself a rugged frontiersman and responded accordingly when convicts first probed his resolve. Unlike his predecessor, he reached readily for the bat, which he claimed worked just like "spurs on [an] old horse." When the cotton-picking and bucking season began, he vowed to use "pitchforks and baseball bats" to suppress any mutinies. Some protesters might have to be "carried out feet first," he growled, but "I had already made up my mind who was running the prison system." Under Simmons, New Woman penology was out; manly planter justice was back.[106]

Even as convicts grumbled—one prisoner decried a "rule of tyranny" propped up by "inhuman abuses"—Simmons gained support in the free world. Farm managers liked him for rehiring veterans and restoring their sovereignty. Prison communities praised his "business efficiency" and newspaper reporters his restoration of discipline.[107] Most important, the new general manager pleased his paymasters. By reemphasizing cash-crop agriculture, dispensing with convict work restrictions, and restoring the whip hand to bosses, he managed to show improvement by almost every indicator tracked in Austin. Cotton production rose, at least initially, per capita expenditures steadily declined, and escapes continued to fall from their 1928 peak.[108]

With support from the statehouse, Simmons was finally able to undertake overdue capital improvements, though what took shape in no way resembled the CPPL penal colony. Rather than breaking new ground in the Hill Country, his administration decided to revamp and consolidate regional farming operations at Imperial, soon to be renamed Central, once the domain of Edward Cunningham. The legislature approved $575,000 for the effort, and a host of new buildings went up along Oyster Creek, some of them still in use today: dormitories, warehouses, and, as a compromise between agriculture and industry, a canning and meatpacking plant.[109] The new complex would have been dwarfed by the envisioned Austin plant, with its grandiose plans for forty-eight-foot walls surrounding cell blocks, schools, and factories, but it was considerably more secure than the "antiquated wooden firetraps" originally built by lessees. The "Central State Farm . . . is halfway between the two extremes of prison theory," observed a Houston weekly, "a fenced-in group of splendid, modern industrial buildings, yet located on a great tract of land."[110] Rather than building from the CPPL's blueprint, conceived in New York, the new facility signaled that

Texas's penal system would develop on its own terms, rooted in the Texas slavery belt and devoted, above all, to plantation production.

If returning to Sugar Land nodded toward Texas's past, in another way Lee Simmons leaned into the future—with an embrace of modern public relations. He added progress-dramatizing photographs to annual reports, hosted banquets for prison communities, and charmed visitors with his folksy wisdom. This, indeed, would be his most lasting contribution to Texas prison administration: whatever the actual conditions inside Texas prisons, Colonel Simmons (like many southern men, he brandished a military title throughout his career) proved that concerted publicity management went a long way toward shoring up administrative legitimacy. "Texas prison inmates are well in hand," concluded a lionizing series in the *Houston Chronicle*. "As respects bodily wants and needs, they fare better in the prison system than they did out of it."[111]

Simmons's PR wizardry included an aggressive overhaul of prisoner after-work activities. Whereas Speer and company had allowed inmates to develop their own programs, the new general manager shut down the Prison Welfare League and asserted new controls. Baseball leagues, boxing, bands, and even Juneteenth celebrations all continued, even expanded, but under Simmons's close supervision. "I am a strong believer in recreation," he wrote, "when it is rightly handled." The convict newspaper, the *Echo,* carried on as well, though it became a mouthpiece for the administration. The names of officials rather than inmate editors graced the masthead; a typical article praised "Colonel Simmons's . . . policy of fairness to all."[112]

Simmons's most spectacular innovation was Texas's "Fastest and Wildest Rodeo," an event that transformed him into a showman to the nation. Although the welfare league had helped organize a rodeo at Eastham two years earlier, the general manager moved it to Huntsville, built a grandstand, and produced what would become one of the state's preeminent tourist attractions for half a century, "the biggest prison show on earth."[113] Held every Sunday in October, the rodeo raised money for the inmate welfare fund, which Simmons controlled, and provided welcome diversion for convicts, as both spectators and participants. Simmons claimed the goal was simply to stage "entertainment for the prisoners and for the prison employees and their families." But as the press coverage spread from local dailies to *Time* and *Collier's*, management benefited as well.[114]

Governors, legislators, and spectators generally—fifteen thousand by 1933, twenty-five thousand by 1938—flocked to the rodeo, and what they witnessed was not just a rip-roaring display of bulldogging and bronc riding but a scripted, sweat-varnished performance of Texas justice. With illustrated brochures and pious opening speeches, prison officials depicted a secure system in which convicts worked hard to earn their keep but were provided every opportunity for reformation. Yet everyone knew more than charity drove the show. Like all rodeos, the event appealed as a blood sport, with the prison setting intensifying the element of lurid fascination. Unlike professional cowboys, "daring inmate buckaroos" generally had little experience riding; they commanded attention not for their extraordinary skill but their lack of it. Outfitted in stripes, lest anyone forget their transgressions, they took risks that free-world rodeo hands wouldn't tolerate. Conventional entries like bareback riding and goat roping appeared on the program, but what made the prison rodeo famous were uproarious events like "Wild Mare Milking" and the "Mad Scramble," a sort of demolition derby on ornery mounts of every description. At the prison rodeo, visitors took in not just a primordial contest between man and beast but a gladiatorial spectacle, in which convicted criminals took their licks.[115]

Racial hierarchy, too, took center stage. In the early years, only white men competed as "cowboys," with African Americans and Mexicans relegated to farcical free-for-alls like "Convict Poker," in which prisoners sat gambling around a table with an angry bull loose in the arena (the last man seated won a prize). White women only occasionally appeared, usually to sing patriotic carols. Black women, by contrast, could sign up for the sexualizing "greased pig sacking contest," in which participants hitched up their skirts and rolled around in the mud in pursuit of ornery swine, all to the hooting delight of spectators, free and convict alike.[116] In this way, the Texas Prison Rodeo exhibited nostalgia for not just the frontier but the Old South. It brought the minstrel show to the cattle drive.

One of the acts regularly featured at the rodeo was an all-black singing troupe that Simmons affectionately named the Cotton Pickers' Glee Club. Although white prisoners at the Walls had long been organized into musical groups, including an orchestra, the general manager believed that a "wealth of dormant material" remained untapped.

"Twenty-two hundred Negroes meant talent," he remarked, "and I meant to see it developed." So with the help of two assistants, he selected the best musicians throughout the system and had them transferred to the Walls. "Such singing!" he exclaimed. "No white-skinned folks can equal it."[117]

"At length we had assembled forty Negroes in the chapel, where I made them a pep talk," he recalled. "I [don't] want any hifalutin' music," he told them, just the music "as it came naturally." When he finished, he asked, "You boys like to get in the game with us on that?" To which they replied, in Simmons's telling, "Yassah, Boss! Yassah, Cap'n! We's wid you!"

At the rodeo, Simmons presented the Cotton Pickers with theatrical flair. "I had the boys rig up an old one-horse wagon" filled with "a few old quilts and like plunder," to which "we hitched a large angular mule," he explained. A "385-pound singer [with] an unusually powerful voice of wonderful quality" led the haggard steed into the center of the arena. There he paused wearily, then stood and belted out, "Goin' Down Dat Lonesome Road." Here, a forlorn freedman was reincarnated in the prison, linking present-day bondage to its past. The crowd thundered, Simmons recalled. "I got as big a kick out of it as anybody."[118]

As Simmons gained renown as a prison ringmaster, another Texan with a fondness for "plain people's" music came calling at the Walls. Although nationally respected as a folklorist, John Lomax had fallen on hard times. He had lost his academic post during the governorship of Jim Ferguson and his fortune in the market crash. "I was worth less than nothing," he remembered. "I was heavily in debt, I had no job."[119]

Improbably, African American folk music came to the rescue. Toting a sheaf of song lyrics he had gathered over the years along the Texas Gulf Coast—where, he said, "the Negroes are thicker than mustang grapes"—Lomax traveled to New York and landed a book contract to collect authentic American ballads before "the spread of machine civilization" wiped them out. Funding from the Rockefeller Foundation ensued (the same that built the Bedford Laboratory of Social Hygiene), and thus began one of the most storied folkloric expeditions in American history. With his son Alan in tow and five hundred pounds of recording equipment lodged in the trunk of an "overburdened Ford," Lomax traveled along winding dirt roads from Appalachia to the river deltas, compiling scores of mining and military tunes but placing special emphasis on the roots of a uniquely African American style: the blues. The two Lomaxes recorded, for the first time, such future hits as "Rock Island Line" and "Midnight Special," and preserved a vital chapter in America's culture of song.[120]

In search of "the best and most genuine Negro folk songs," the portly ex-professor and his gangly son trolled levee and lumber camps. They descended into "the jungles of Negroland," as the father put it, sleeping outdoors and swatting off "malaria mosquitoes." (The latter may account for his fevered imagination, which periodically transported him to the "turgid, slow-moving rivers in the African jungle," where he listened to "the tom-toms of savage blacks.") Everywhere, the duo lamented that "gang songs of labor" were "fast disappearing." Everywhere, that is, except on "the Negro prison farms of the South," where they found "such songs in greatest number, variety, and purity."[121]

The Lomaxes had never been to a prison before, but with Simmons's support they hit pay dirt at the newly consolidated Central Farm. "We heard such dynamic singing of work songs," the father wrote, that "[we] worked with those men until we both were exhausted from the long nervous tension." With their aluminum disk-making machine set up in the new infirmary, the folklorists found just the sort of "sinful songs" they were looking for—unpolluted, they believed, by jazz, the radio, "churchly community," and "the white man." Whereas free-world blues often injected humor into doleful verses, the Lomaxes detected little but anguish in this older music. "Only one song is recalled that reflected unrestrained abandon to joyous emotions," Lomax senior wrote. The others "were dominated by brooding sadness," with slow, pounding rhythms—often punctuated with ax or hoe strikes—and rhyming, long-voweled lyrics that gave voice to "the tragedies of imprisonment, cold, hunger, heat, the injustice of the white man."[122]

One of the songs they recorded at Central, a hoe chant led by a quick-witted singer named Lightnin', alluded to generations of suffering in Imperial's broiling fields.

Oughta come on de river in 1904,
You could fin' a dead man on every turn row.

Oughta come on de river in 1910,
Dey was drivin' de women des like de men.

As did several songs, "Ain' No Mo' Cane on de Brazis" referenced the tribulations of convict leasing but slid effortlessly into the present tense, suggesting a punishing continuity of deprivation and toil. Joined by three companions, Lightnin' decries a field boss who keeps cursing no matter how hard his convicts work.

> Cap'n, cap'n, you mus' be blin'
> Keep on holl'in an' I'm almos' flyin'.[123]

In another song, "Great God A'mighty," Lightnin' describes a guard so merciless that his squad prays for otherworldly deliverance. The music begins with a boss riding up on a gang of woodcutters with a "bullwhip in one hand and a cowhide in the other." "Cap'n, let me off, suh," the protagonist begs through several verses. But the horseman is unmoved. As the precisely measured tree-chopping song progresses, with more voices added along the way, the boss tells the prisoner to "low down yo britches" and orders the others to "hold him." He then lets loose with the leather.

> Cancha hear th' bully squallin'?
> Cancha hear th' bully screamin'?

So asks the lead singer, to which the chorus, now four strong, replies, "Great God A'mighty."

There was a "terrible sweep" to the music, observed the elder Lomax. "Even outside in the adjacent iron-barred dormitory, the chatter and clamor of two hundred black convicts became stilled into awed and reminiscent silence as the song swept on, gaining power to the end." The attending guard, too, grew quiet. "The goose pimples always come out along my spine when I hear that song," he whispered.[124]

Deeply affected by their "unforgettable experiences" at Central, the Lomaxes determined to visit as many southern prisons as they could. Next on their list was Angola, where they encountered Huddie Ledbetter who provided their richest material and helped them interpret it as well. Officials had given Leadbelly a laundry job at Angola, so he would be close at hand to entertain visitors, and he did so regularly. By the time the Lomaxes met him in July 1933, he knew some five hundred songs by heart, about one hundred of them genuinely "folky" or unrecorded.

Even more impressive than his playlist were his performances. Leadbelly "crouched over his guitar as he played, as his fingers made the incredibly swift, skillful runs," the Lomaxes wrote, "and he sang with an intensity and passion that swayed audiences who could not understand a single word of his songs. . . . His whole being focused in a song."[125]

Contrary to legend, Leadbelly never sang himself to freedom in Louisiana as he had in Texas. After he accumulated sufficient good time and secured early release, however, he met up with Lomax Sr. in Marshall, Texas, and the two began a strained partnership that propelled both of them toward stardom. A year later, *Time* magazine celebrated the "Murderous Minstrel's" debut in New York City.[126]

Money, as well as the veil of race, as DuBois called it, constrained their relationship. Both men fell into roles assigned by wealth and white supremacy. Leadbelly went to work as Lomax's driver and "body servant," dutifully laying out his clothes and drawing his bath each morning. His employer patronizingly exhorted his hireling to better himself and took to doling out his "allowance" in "fixed amounts" so as to keep the ex-convict from nighttime carousing.[127]

Yet despite these inequities, Leadbelly was more of a guide than a chauffeur. Over hundreds of miles on the road, sometimes with Alan joining them in the front seat, other times with big John alone in the back, the ex-prisoner churned out countless songs, explained their context, and served as an invaluable interlocutor at every stop. Alan recalled a certain "embarrassment" involved in "break[ing] the ice" with a new group of potential performers, but when Leadbelly was present he took the lead, translating the folklorists' wants and warming up the crowd with performances of his own. "Always the nimble fingers of his guitar and his singing helped to bring out the best talent," Lomax wrote. "I began to see how useful he might prove to be."[128]

Through Leadbelly, the Lomaxes began to appreciate the layered complexity of African American prison songs, how they could be both wistful and wry, stabilizing and subversive. Like slave songs, from which so many of them derived, work songs and field hollers survived partly because they served a valuable function, to both laborers and bosses. Even as they bemoaned the slow arc of the summer sun across the sky, they helped pass the time. They set a steady work pace—with guards sometimes telling a lead singer to pick up the tempo—and they synchronized dangerous tasks like wood chopping. (African American squads could safely put more men with axes around a single big tree than could whites or Mexicans, who had no such singing tradition.)[129]

Yet prison music was more than utilitarian. Lyrics about hard bosses, long sentences, loves lost, and spectacular crimes enabled prisoners to pool their sorrow, revel in past exploits, and enigmatically mock their keepers. Field bosses generally tolerated and sometimes enjoyed the music, so long as their squads made task, but many work songs went beyond the boundaries of dissent permissible in regular speech. They allowed convicts to voice their grievances, even their rage, and to forge bonds that could coalesce, in the right circumstances, into political solidarity.[130]

One of the most popular work songs that Leadbelly learned in Texas was "Ol' Rattler." The Lomaxes believed that it derived from a tune composed amid the violence of Reconstruction, "Run Nigger Run!" But the story line also bore a striking resemblance to Leadbelly's own escape. The song depicts a prized chase dog, Ol' Rattler, who is outsmarted and outrun by a tireless convict, Riley. When Riley makes a break for it, a guard blows an alarm horn, and the dog team puts Rattler and his pack on the trail. "Ketch that nigger, ketch that nigger," the singers chant, beginning in the voice of the guards. With famous speed, the "huntin' dog" barrels through the canebrakes after the escapee. But Riley proves too strong, thus embodying a potency that, in reality, convicts rarely experienced. He runs from "sun to sun," and Rattler falls out. Then, "like Christ," the man comes to the banks of the Brazos and glides across, with the singers switching voice from the pursuers to the pursued at the moment of apotheosis.

> Ol' Riley los' ol' Rattler,
> Riley walked the water,
> Ol' Rattler couldn't walk it.
> Bye, bye, Rattler.[131]

Such musical glorifications of escape bound mutiny to mirth, a sort of insurgent ecstasy that father Lomax, for all his slumming, couldn't hear. They didn't provoke convict protest, but they did keep freedom dreams alive in the most inhospitable soil.

**• • •**

With more secure housing and tighter management, official tallies of convict disorder declined in the early 1930s, but breakouts and bucks remained commonplace, especially when compared to today's prisons. During Simmons's five years at the helm, there were some six hundred escapes. Some of these were opportunistic; in 1932, twenty-seven inmates ran off during a category-four hurricane.[132] Others involved plotting and violence. One of the most sensational took place at the Eastham Farm on January 16, 1932. On a cold, foggy morning, two guards drove a squad of white convicts out to the woods for clearing. Before they started working, however, two of the men—both notorious outlaws doing 288 years between them—pulled out smuggled pistols and shot one boss in the hip, the other in the gut. On cue, two outside conspirators sprang from the trees and opened fire with BAR machine guns, sending everyone scurrying for cover. Five prisoners ran, four of them to a waiting V-8 with a young woman named Bonnie Parker pounding the horn to signal her location. Her famously fast-driving boyfriend, Clyde Barrow, stowed his rifle and took the wheel. In a flash, they were gone. The *Dallas Morning News* called it "the most spectacular prison delivery in Texas history."[133]

With the help of a special investigator hired by the prison system, law enforcement eventually tracked down and killed Bonnie and Clyde, but that was not the end of Colonel Simmons's troubles. In 1933, Depression-related budget cuts forced him to slash salaries by 20 percent, thus undermining morale and raising fresh questions about his own sizable paycheck.[134] Compared to his predecessors, he endured only tepid criticism from politicians, but, as reports of abuses trickled out, some journalists turned negative. Accusing Simmons of buck passing, cover-ups, and excessive emphasis on profit, the *Houston Press* labeled his management "a disgrace to civilized people."[135]

Largely because of Simmons's censorship rules, few grievances survive in the archives. In letters smuggled out to the *Press* and Henry Cohen, however, many prisoners expressed the same complaints they had had for half a century. Although the quality of housing was improving and death rates had declined, convicts reported fifteen-hour workdays, substandard food, "innumerable brutal beatings," even summary executions. Simmons ran the prison system with "an Iron Hand," contended prisoners at Darrington.[136]

With traditional protest outlets blocked, many convicts turned to a desperate tactic that had once been popular during slavery and convict leasing: self-mutilation. Clyde Barrow, who had chopped off two toes in the hope of getting himself transfered from Eastham to the Walls, was one of the first to turn his work tools against himself, but others followed. "Self-mutilation is prevalent throughout the state prison system," admitted a board member. "It's no surprise to find convicts injecting kerosene or gasoline into their legs and arms," agreed Simmons. Others used cane knives or axes, particularly at Retrieve, the only Brazos bottomland farm worked exclusively by whites. There, more than twenty-one prisoners maimed themselves in the spring of 1935, two by chopping off a lower leg. When asked why they had hurt themselves, many of them answered simply, "I can't make it."[137]

With wounded white boys involved, the legislature launched an intrusive investigation, the first under Simmons's watch. The committee reported "utterly inadequate" housing, unauthorized field beatings with "ropes and pieces of rubber hose," and miserable work conditions, with the fields "badly poisoned with Johnson grass." So rough was Retrieve that lawmakers proposed "to operate [it] with negro prisoners." White men, they suggested, should be moved to a modern "dormitory now under construction" at Darrington.[138]

But Simmons was unconvinced. He made his own inspection at Retrieve and pronounced "everything as it should be." Prisoners were just angling for sympathy and trying to avoid work, he told a reporter. "It all boils down to one thing. It just doesn't suit the convicts to be controlled." Rather than making concessions, he proposed sterner measures. Put the offending inmates "back to work on the farm," he said. "As long as they want to . . . chop themselves," he told guards, "I say give them more axes."[139]

The Walls, Huntsville, 1890s. *(Texas Prison Museum)*

Guards and convicts at the Imperial Farm, 1908. *(Texas Prison Museum)*

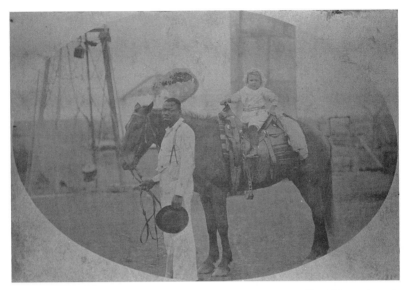

"Higher-ranking officers were assigned 'houseboys,' usually African American trusties who could be used for cooking, cleaning, or even child care." Barracks captain Veale's daughter with trusty, Imperial Farm. *(Texas Prison Museum)*

Just as slaves built Texas's first state capitol, leased convicts constructed its replacement. Prisoner stonecutters, 1893. *(Texas State Library and Archives Commission)*

"Because whipping invited humanitarian censure, managers devised novel methods of punishment, both unusual and cruel." Georgia road camp. *(Henry Ransom Humanities Research Center)*

Women prisoners at the Goree Farm, early 1930s.

Prisoners in neck chains arriving for processing at the Walls, circa 1950.
*(Texas State Library and Archives Commission)*

Chow hall at the
Ramsey Farm, 1955.
*(Texas Prison Museum)*

On the farms, prisoners lived in overcrowded barracks, or "tanks," circa 1950. *(Texas Prison Museum)*

TDC director George Beto posing with the bat, 1965. *(Texas Department of Criminal Justice)*

Hoe squads turning out to work at the Clemens Farm, 1970. *(Texas Prison Museum)*

"We had total control, absolute literal control," said former guard Steve Martin. Prisoners being searched at the Ellis Unit, 1968. *(Danny Lyon)*

David Resendez Ruíz, lead plantiff in Texas's epic prison rights lawsuit, leaving federal court, 1978. *(Alan Pogue)*

The Polunsky Unit, home of Texas's death row. *(Texas Department of Criminal Justice)*

Emmerson Rudd, Ellis Maximum Segregation Unit, 1994. Rudd was executed in 2001. *(Alan Light)*

Supermaximum-security cell block at the Ellis Unit. *(Robert Perkinson)*

Fifteen-year-old boy in isolation, Juvenile Justice Center, Laredo. *(Steve Liss)*

# 6

# "BEST IN THE NATION"

I live in mortal fear of a convict-run prison.
—GEORGE J. BETO, DIRECTOR, TEXAS DEPARTMENT OF CORRECTIONS[1]

If General Manager Lee Simmons thought he had "stopped the . . . epidemic" of self-mutilations with threats and punishments, he was grievously mistaken. Roughly three dozen Texas prisoners intentionally wounded themselves under his watch, but after he retired in 1935, the grisly tactic became even more commonplace. Administrators recorded 174 acts of self-mutilation between 1936 and 1940, 273 between 1940 and 1944, and 341 between 1944 and 1948. What started out as scattered acts of defiance "acquired the proportions of a cultural pattern," observed a researcher in Huntsville. In cutting and chopping themselves, prisoners were turning an age-old form of self-destructive rebuke into a new sort of social movement—a "revolt against the system," as one guard put it— one that eventually spread to Georgia and Louisiana. Self-mutilation, warned Austin MacCormick, a protégé of Thomas Mott Osborne and one of the most prominent penologists in the country, "has attacked Texas like a peculiar tropical disease; it is as contagious as can be."[2]

Acting alone or in groups, prisoners most commonly mutilated themselves by severing their Achilles tendons, thus rendering them-selves unable to walk—or work—for several weeks. They became known as "heel-stringers." Other protesters tried "bugging," which involved slicing open the skin with a razor blade and packing the wound with lye to create a festering sore. Still others resorted to bone breaking or amputation. The infirmary at Huntsville "resembled a 'Chamber of

Horrors,'" cried one visitor. "The bare legs of men, after amputation of feet, were in full view. Men with broken arms and otherwise mutilated filled . . . the building."[3]

When they were interviewed at the Walls, the men—and they were all men—spoke of exhaustion and exasperation. A nineteen-year-old at Eastham claimed he chopped off his fingers with an ax because "he had been sick and forced to work by the guard and could not get any relief." Another fellow, also at Eastham, was "forced to run 2½ miles to the fields" while recovering from pneumonia. He collapsed and declared he couldn't keep up. Later, he broke his arm. After being returned to the farm, he broke the same arm again.

Some inmates said they acted out of fear. "I lived in constant dread of being killed or suffering serious bodily injury a goodly portion of the time I was in the penitentiary," said the arm breaker. Others struck in anger, directing violence against the only target they could reach, themselves. Treated as beasts of burden, they directed a blow against the only facet of their personhood that prison officials seemed to value, their capacity for labor. After a field boss coldly rejected a prisoner's request to "lay in sick," the man retreated to the back of his barracks, amputated his lower leg, and then "threw his bloody foot and leg out to the captain." "Now can I lay in?" the fellow reportedly asked.[4]

As the maiming metastasized, prison officials put forward a mishmash of explanations. The perpetrators were "drug addicts," "perverts," and "emotionally unstable psychopaths," they asserted. Some prisoners were angry that a new warden at Eastham had "discontinued the practice of giving convicts coffee in the fields twice a day," proposed O. J. S. Ellingson, Simmons's replacement as general manager. Most of all, they were malingerers. After disclosing a round of bone breaking and foot chopping in March 1940, Ellingson announced that there would be no investigation because "there is nothing to investigate. This thing is merely rebelling against work."[5]

But there were investigations, and their conclusions, for the most part, echoed the convicts. Social scientists noted that most of the mutilators were Anglo or Mexican, suggesting that black convicts had little faith in their ability to rouse the public by wounding their bodies. The researchers found few signs of mental illness. Instead, because most outbreaks occurred during the harvest season and on the farms, they determined that heavy work, "cruel treatment by guards," and "unsanitary, very unhealthful" living conditions were to blame. "Self-maiming was largely a product of the system itself," argued MacCormick, who was called in to offer remedies.[6]

Dissidents had assailed Texas's prisons before, but they gained a wider hearing in the 1940s. While the United States was fighting tyranny abroad, critics charged, Texas was practicing the techniques of tyranny at home. Penologists posited similarities between prison plantations and Axis concentration camps, at one point publishing in the APA's journal, *Prison World*, a photograph of a naked, emaciated Texas inmate who looked like a victim of the Holocaust.[7] When legislators inspected prison farms near Houston, they made similar linkages. Texas convicts were "underfed," sent to work in shoes "that barely [hung] on their feet," and "made to live in a state of deathly fear and violence," reported one group. At the Darrington farm "brutality was very prevalent," remarked a war veteran turned lawmaker, "far worse than a German or Jap prison camp."[8]

Such claims carried special punch in the postwar years, as the full scope of wartime atrocities came to light and an international human rights movement, headquartered at the new United Nations, gained its footing. During the ill-fated reform efforts of the 1910s and 1920s, Texas convicts had rebelled against the penal system. But this time—with new tactics that involved committing violence against the self to spotlight the violence of the state—their protests yielded more lasting results. In the aftermath of war and in the wake of the heel-stringers, Texas undertook yet another experiment in prison reform, one that, for the first time, propelled the state to national prominence. More so than before, prisoners were responsible for this change, but in no way could they have anticipated its outcome.

## THE REHABILITATION FACTORY

Texas was not the only state to overhaul its prisons in the 1940s; the Second World War had aligned the stars for penal reform. During the Great Depression, crowding and idleness had characterized the nation's lockups, but as the economy roared back to life and the armed forces sopped up potential criminals, prison managers' most intractable problems melted into air. Crowding eased as prison populations declined by a quarter between 1939 and 1945, and once the president waived New Deal restrictions on the interstate commerce of prisoner-made goods, industrial prison production soared.[9] In Michigan, prisoners made pontoon boats; in West Virginia, bandoliers; in California, submarine nets. Between 1942 and 1943 alone, the value of prisoner output increased from $34 to $41 million, with patriotism, skilled job training, and a sense of purpose reportedly boosting inmate morale.[10] Of all the crime-control and prisoner-uplift initiatives attempted by government since the days of Benjamin Rush, none proved so effective as total war.

With convicts hard at work and crime on the wane, public antipathies shifted from domestic to foreign enemies, from felons to fascists. Whereas profiles of menacing gangsters had sold papers in the 1920s and 1930s, depictions of patriotic inmate unfortunates—giving blood, buying war bonds, or sewing flags for the navy—proved more popular in the early 1940s. As America transitioned from hard times to fighting times, prisoners seemed more deserving of a second chance. Through the prison branch of the War Production Board, "numbers are made back into men again," exulted a reporter for the *Atlanta Constitution*. *Time* magazine suggested that American inmates, more than anyone, appreciated the stakes. "They Know What Freedom Means," began one article.[11]

Redemptive story lines coupled with full employment encouraged inmate rehabilitation efforts, and as prison managers braced themselves for the surge of institutional admissions they knew would accompany demobilization, several states dug out their penal reform toolkits. New York overhauled its juvenile justice system. The Federal Bureau of Prisons expanded classification and treatment programs. Georgia abolished its infamous chain gang system.[12] Of all the nation's criminal justice jurisdictions, however, none metamorphosed as completely as California's. By the late 1940s, observes one historian, the state was "undisputedly in the forefront of American prison developments." "Californian corrections [became] a byword for decency and order," argued an admirer, "a model for emulation throughout the world."[13]

Although wealthy and dynamic, the Golden State hardly stood out for penological innovation before World War II. Its flagship institution, San Quentin, was monumental in scale and its guard towers provided sweeping views of San Francisco Bay, but little inspiration took place behind the walls. An eccentric prison doctor, Leo Stanley, tried to reclaim inmates by removing stigmatizing blemishes through plastic surgery and, more oddly, by injecting them with paste he made from the ground-up testicles of executed convicts. But for the most part, life at San Quentin mirrored the regimentation, monotony, and quotidian terrors of big houses across the country. The institution was a "house of fear and forgotten men," asserted Clinton Duffy, a reform-minded warden who took over in 1940.[14] As in Texas, though with less severity, California's prewar prisons were crowded, haphazardly managed, and ruled by "convict bosses." The principal difference was that Texas's convicts toiled to exhaustion, while California's rotted in boredom.

Before the war, a handful of prison administrators experimented with reformatory initiatives, and in 1943 a new governor lent them vital support.[15] At first glance, Earl Warren seemed like an implausible trailblazer. His father had been murdered in a robbery, and he had started out his own career as a tough-on-crime prosecutor. After Pearl Harbor, he had campaigned aggressively for the internment of Japanese Americans, a policy that ultimately created a nationwide incarceration complex twenty times larger than California's regular prison system.[16] Warren, though, was an old-fashioned progressive as much as a pro-business Republican, and he had become increasingly skeptical of prisons' social utility. "Caging men like animals . . . then expecting them to become better men is fallacious," he once remarked.[17]

In his first inaugural address, Warren called for crime policies to emphasize "prevention instead of suppression." "We must make certain that those who are paying their debt to society are not ground further into the mire," he implored. Shrewdly political, the governor dealt first with the juvenile justice system and waited for a crisis to take on the state's four adult prisons. He did not have to wait long. In late 1943, he learned that a cunning bank robber known as "the yacht bandit"—a man Warren himself had prosecuted—was weekending in the city while he was supposedly locked up at Folsom. This was just the sort of scandal Warren needed, and he asked the police to apprehend the man with as much publicity as possible. This "case is the most outrageous thing I have ever heard of in prison management," he railed at a press conference. He ordered a full investigation.[18]

Warren's inquest generated familiar policy recommendations— indeterminate sentencing, "scientific" classification, and psychological treatment—but in fast-growing California, they were implemented as never before. Under an all-encompassing reorganization statute passed in 1944, every facet of California's postconviction criminal justice system, from sentencing to prison management to parole, came under the coordination of a single agency, the California Department of Corrections (DOC), so named to underline its reformatory mission.[19] "We will always have a crime problem," the governor admitted before the APA, but "it has long been my belief that we should attack it as *one* problem." Although most biographers have downplayed this aspect of Warren's career, the man who became one of America's most renowned chief justices of the Supreme Court first distinguished himself as a crusader for institutional change by overhauling California's prisons.[20]

To apply "the most modern techniques" to an "antiquated system," Warren tapped an outsider to lead his new superagency, Richard McGee, a wiry and well-respected administrator who had previously directed penal systems in Washington and New York. With solid political support and the help of the booming postwar economy, McGee was able to throw tremendous amounts of money at the prison problem. He launched a $60 million building program, raised guard salaries, and attracted a "brain trust" of social workers, psychologists, and penologists. If California wants "to raise the standards of its prison service above . . . public embarrassment," the new director told legislators, it "surely would cost more."[21]

As a spender and experimenter, McGee represented the antithesis of Texas-style conservatism. His passion, though, was not for inmate reclamation so much as organizational administration. Procedures manuals, accounting protocols, in-service training guidelines, staff and inmate rule books—all of these were redrafted and formalized under the director's guidance. Recognized nationally for his attention to both structure and detail, he was selected by the APA to rewrite its *Manual of Correctional Standards* in 1954. As testament to his political and bureaucratic acumen, three governors retained McGee's services, extending his leadership beyond two decades. Earl Warren recalled that in "more than half a century of public service, [he] never had a better administrator."[22]

McGee created a correctional apparatus that collected and sorted data of every description. Upon arrival at a reception and guidance center, new prisoners submitted not only to the standard searching, photographing, and fingerprinting but to scholastic evaluations and personality profiles. Staff members sought out additional information from family members, high-school principals, and local law enforcement, painstakingly assembling a master file on each inmate that would track individuals through their institutional careers. "In the prison bureaucracy any scrap of hard data remains relevant," noted one long-serving convict. "The ink never fades."[23]

Over time, more pages were added to prisoner files: disciplinary write-ups, notes on church participation, even the titles of books checked out of the library. In theory, all of this information allowed prison professionals to make dispassionate, scientifically grounded decisions on unit placement, job assignment, programming, and, ultimately, release. At final sentencing, which took place after several weeks of observation, and again at parole hearings, a panel of prison officials reviewed each inmate's file, conducted a cursory interview, and determined who went free and when. Almost a century after Zebulon Brockway pioneered indeterminate sentencing in Detroit, his dream came to full fruition in postwar California. For the first time, penological experts grasped all the keys to the kingdom.

The stated purpose of California's data gathering and discretionary release system was to encourage criminals to change for the better. "It was assumed we were here because of our psychological problems, and our task now, by which we could expect to be judged, was to isolate and come to terms with them," recalled Malcolm Braly, a prisoner at San Quentin who became a successful novelist. Counseling and programming supposedly tailored to each individual were "designed to change inmate attitudes," observed a UCLA researcher. A contrary disposition or disruptive behavior would result in extended imprisonment, whereas compliance would more quickly and successfully return inmates to the free world. "The message was clear," explained sociologist and former prisoner John Irwin. "You conform or you will not be paroled."[24]

Because the history of prison reform was so littered with failure, McGee and company knew they would have difficulty "winning inmate acceptance." In 1940, a noted prison administrator and sociologist, Donald Clemmer, had proposed that the profound psychological and social effects of imprisonment on inmates were "inimical to reform." "The prison world is a graceless world," he wrote. "Its people are thwarted, unhappy, yearning, resigned, bitter, hating, revengeful." "The apparent rehabilitating effect which prison life has on some men," he concluded, "occurs in spite of the harmful influences of the prison." But McGee had too much drive, too much faith in government and institutions to accept such bleak pronouncements. If prisons incubated a corrosive culture of "bitter emotion" among inmates and "indifference" among guards, as he acknowledged, then prison culture would have to be restructured.[25]

To reach deeper into the "prison community," McGee and his underlings relied on extensive study and surveillance, as well as positive and negative incentives. To cooperative inmates, the new regime offered college classes, trade training, and token wages. To recalcitrants, officials threatened transfer to more dangerous prisons, confinement in "Adjustment Centers," the department's euphemism for solitary, and, ultimately, protracted incarceration, sometimes for decades, even for comparably pedestrian crimes like second-degree robbery, which in California carried an indeterminate penalty of one year to life.[26]

As the industrial prison boom petered out after the war, penologists turned from production to psychology. By 1960, fully half of California's inmates had undergone counseling in prison, mostly in groups, which were cheaper to sustain than individual sessions with licensed professionals. Some California prisons evolved into "therapeutic communities," in which every facet of daily life was organized to inspire wholesome transformation. Little hard evidence suggested that such counseling reduced recidivism, but staff members (especially at the higher ranks) nonetheless came to believe that psychological treatment improved prisoner personalities and enhanced the prison environment.[27]

California's most treatment-oriented facility was Chino, a minimum-security facility outside Los Angeles. This was "a new kind of institution," "deservedly famous," asserted a prisoner who arrived there after a long bus ride from San Quentin. "At Chino the man serving his term encounters trained personnel genuinely interested in helping him be successful when released," he wrote. "He isn't surrounded by high walls, bristling gun towers. Custodial regimentation doesn't smother his individuality. Everything isn't figured out for him down to the last tiny detail." Life at Chino, prison officials claimed, approximated life on the outside. Its motto, later adopted by the Department of Corrections as a whole, was: "There can be no regeneration except in freedom."[28]

At Chino, and to a lesser extent elsewhere, imprisonment as treatment seeped into the institutional marrow. Custody personnel continued to hold up "security of the institution" as the paramount concern, regarding convicts with world-weary suspicion. But with pay raises tied to educational credits and group-counseling participation, most of them fell in line. Prisoners continued to harbor the dreams of captives everywhere; "Each of us had only one motive here, how to get out as quickly as possible," said Malcolm Braly. But to convicts with experience in other prison systems, California represented a different world. Words like "pleasant," "relaxed," and "tolerant" scarcely appear in the archives of Texas punishment, but they crop up regularly in prisoner writings about postwar California. "We who were doing time were treated like human beings, not caged wild animals," wrote Caryl Chessman, who nonetheless ended up on death row.[29]

Although prisoners were coerced into counseling, John Irwin suggested that many inmates nonetheless pinned their hopes on its success. "We began to believe we were sick, and we started searching for cures," he recalled. "Staff promised . . . and we believed that they were going to make new people out of us." But convicts also held on to their subaltern skepticism. Because prisoners recognized that disclosures of any sort could end up in their parole file, they tended to remain circumspect with staff. They played roles in search of freedom rather than sharing feelings in search of healing. Staff members likewise pursued ulterior motives in treatment sessions. "The persistent concern at all levels [is] getting through each day with a minimum of ruckus," observed an on-site researcher. This was the real purpose of California's therapeutic programs, he concluded: they were "strategies of control."[30]

Clear-eyed convicts and clever keepers no doubt recognized their strategic insincerity. But so long as treatment programs delivered—order to officers and parole to prisoners—most everyone went along with what Braly called the "artful shuck." Over time, however—as embryonic idealism settled into institutional routine and as many counseling graduates returned to prison with new convictions—McGee's treatment regime began losing its luster. "Hope shaded to cynicism and then turned to bitterness," wrote Irwin.[31]

A "competently managed prison is a very orderly place," instructed Richard McGee in a how-to manual he wrote for corrections officials. Over the course of his long tenure, however, he found that ideal increasingly out of reach. During his first six years in office, California's prisons remained commendably calm. But in the early 1950s, when riots "exploded like a string of firecrackers across the nation," McGee's facilities ignited as well. In the words of one warden, there was an "outbreak of hooliganism" from Soledad to Folsom to San Quentin's death row.[32]

Even in McGee's most far-reaching programs, fractures started to appear. In the prison system's celebrated "bibliotherapy" experiment, for instance, inmates not only bathed in "inextinguishable light and wisdom" but started to ask hard questions. "We began reading more and more serious literature," Irwin recalled. "We developed a relatively firm foundation in world knowledge . . . [and] with this new perspective, we saw through things: our culture, society, the prison system." "Rehabilitation," he argued, "inadvertently contributed to mounting criticism of itself by promoting a prison intelligentsia."[33]

One measure of this emerging intelligentsia was the proliferation of convict writing. In 1947, the prison system's head librarian and official censor, Herman Spector, reviewed 395 manuscripts for possible publication; by 1961, the annual total reached 1,989. A number of these works, the jailhouse fiction of Malcolm Braly, for instance, was of high literary quality. Much of it was also bitter and contentious, despite Spector's best efforts to bury "undesirable material."[34] Some prisoners developed an audience, and McGee's beneficent regime came under fire not only from convict intellectuals but from their free-world fans.

Of all the products of California's "rehabilitation factories," none attracted so much attention or so relentlessly pointed out the system's contradictions as Caryl Chessman. A graduate of Chino, from which he escaped, Chessman arrived at San Quentin's death row in 1948, convicted of robberies and sexual assaults in a trial marked by irregularities. He was an avid jailhouse lawyer and so troublesome to staff that the prison psychiatrist suggested he write out his life story as a diversion. The result was *Cell 2455: Death Row,* a compelling and carefully reasoned prison memoir that, much to the chagrin of prison officials, became a runaway best seller.[35]

Transformed by the power of the word, just as bibliotherapists intended, Chessman was able to attract tremendous attention to his case and to California's death penalty, which he assailed as shamefully inconsistent with the DOC's rehabilitative mission. Prison officials, as they are wont to do, overreacted. Chessman's remunerative writings were declared property of the state and confiscated. McGee and his minions tied themselves in knots trying to explain why Chessman should be silenced. Meanwhile, their star pupil continued to write, smuggling three more books out of death row, all wildly successful. Although the DOC enjoyed remarkable bipartisan support, the Chessman case helped turn the era's incipient left and counterculture against the prison system.

A contemporary of the San Francisco beats, Chessman became an outlaw-intellectual folk hero, inspiring prolific press coverage and a worldwide movement against the death penalty. McGee admitted that on "many days, I spent from one-third to two-thirds of my time dealing with this particularly difficult case." On one occasion, he accepted "two large suitcases filled with petitions" from Brazil; on another, he carried out a stay to allow President Eisenhower to travel safely abroad. After Chessman lost his final appeal, *Time* magazine put him on the cover, calling him "the world's most famous prisoner."[36] Although California's treatment model was supposed to guarantee quiet, it was generating lots of noise. In the years after Chessman calmly stepped into the gas chamber on May 2, 1960, it would generate more noise still. What Earl Warren and Richard McGee had created in the name of rehabilitation would soon be churning out revolution.

## A DYNASTY OF CONTROL

While California tried to secure prison peace through counseling and co-optation, Texas settled on an entirely different approach. As always, scandal provided the impetus for change. In response to the prisoner self-mutilation movement, the state launched a series of probes during and after the war that revealed not only overwork and mistreatment but alarming levels of brutality among the prisoners themselves. Although Texas had mostly retired the wooden barracks built by lessees, it still held prisoners in collective dormitories, or "tanks," that incubated conflict and predation. "Most of your trouble is due to the whole life in the tanks, . . . which resemble the hold of a ship," reported Austin Mac-Cormick, who conducted an outside review in 1944. "You have got men who should be in cells at night because they are wolves," he explained. "Most of us would not permit [it]."[37]

Texas's tanks encouraged "every form of perversion," warned Mac-Cormick, who, like many prison officials, expressed increasing anxiety about homosexuality in the 1940s, as churches and government agencies struggled to reconstitute the nuclear family fractured by wartime mobilization. Picket guards "can't see any distance into [the dormitories]," he said, and prisoners "can crawl from one bunk to another." Most sexual encounters were consensual, but legislative investigators concluded in 1947 that many were not. "One man related he was attacked at night by twenty-eight men—had been held at point of a knife at his throat and made to submit."[38]

As during previous upheavals, salacious revelations generated considerable outcry. "Our penal system" exercises "power without pity" and "cruelty without conscience," declared Dallas reformer C. V. Compton in a civic education pamphlet. "We . . . expect and will appreciate a humane, sane, and Christian Prison," argued a member of the Texas State Council of Methodist Women, which organized public lectures and a letter-writing campaign. "For our sakes, for Texas, and for the sake of your own conscience," one letter writer beseeched the governor, "be . . . as brave where prison reformation is concerned as Gov. Warren of California."[39]

In response to renewed public criticism, prison officials implemented a variety of reforms. Having already abolished whipping for the third time in 1941, the Prison Board approved an ambitious postwar construction program and revisited ideas that had languished since the days of the CPPL, expanding education efforts and experimenting with "scientific classification," at least for white inmates.[40]

This halting modernization got a boost from Beauford Jester, a forward-looking petroleum plutocrat who became Texas's governor in 1947. Although Jester was ferociously antilabor and capable of race- and red-baiting alike, he was not opposed to state spending on prisons, so long as the coffers were full, which, as the wartime recovery marched onward, they often were. Shortly after taking office, he invited MacCormick to give him a personal briefing. Over the summer, he shook up the prison board and launched a national search for a new general manager. "I have had a feeling for a long time that our prison system is perhaps antiquated and needs revising," he told reporters. Although he had campaigned against a "new, radical, and expensive form of government," Governor Jester embarked on a prison overhaul that would yield longer-lasting results than any effort since the abolition of convict leasing.[41]

The man he tapped to head up his new regime was Oscar Byron Ellis, a lifelong southerner who had made a name for himself running Shelby County Penal Farm, an immaculate moneymaking penal institution outside Memphis, Tennessee. When members of the Texas Prison Board visited, they liked everything about the Shelby farm. It had job training and a literacy school but was largely "self-supporting" and scandal free. Ellis, a husky, plainspoken professional, impressed them not only with his commitment to "reclaim men for society" but with his tough-minded conservatism. All prisoners should be made to work at least ten hours a day, he said. He believed in "firm and just discipline."[42] This was exactly the sort of "practical thinking" Texas needed, board members agreed. Without dissent, they offered Ellis the job, and on New Year's Eve 1947 he arrived in Huntsville to choreographed acclaim. "Sam Houston and Davy Crockett came to Texas from Tennessee and made their names immortal," proclaimed the chair of the Prison Board. "Mr. Ellis has a similar opportunity, and it is my belief that he will fulfill our greatest expectations."[43]

Ellis was not a man of new ideas. By Texas standards his program, announced in March 1948, was far-reaching, but it drew heavily on Mac-Cormick's proposals and included provisions that had been on the table since the late 1870s: diversification of prison industries, guard professionalization, and improved inmate welfare. Where Ellis would distinguish himself was in his ability to implement changes without the system slipping from his grasp. He was more technocrat than visionary, more versed in cash-crop agriculture than scientific penology. Whereas penal progressives like Elizabeth Speer and Ben Cabell had attempted to break from the state's plantation base, Ellis favored limited adjustments to the system at hand: the state's farms should be mechanized rather than sold off; the guards instructed rather than replaced. With respect to inmates, Ellis reassured an anxious lawmaker, "I believe in rigid discipline. . . . I believe in prisoners working and . . . producing more."[44]

More than anything, what set Ellis apart from his predecessors were the resources available to him. In 1949, after a yearlong lobbying campaign in which he delivered some 250 speeches statewide, Ellis received a record $4.2 million for capital improvements, plus a higher operating budget. Compared to California, this was chicken feed, but Ellis made every penny count. He was a fiendish economizer. "If you wanted something you grew it," remembers Jack Kyle, whom Ellis recruited to take over the Ferguson farm. "We made our own hoe handles. We had our own lumber. We cut the trees off the land that we had, sawed them into material. Everything was aimed at being self-sufficient."[45]

With convicts baking and laying the bricks, money went further in Texas than it did in other states. Dairy barns, grain silos, and a textile mill went up. For the first time, tractors and combines appeared in the fields. Almost all of the money went to farm and security upgrades, but convicts, too, noticed new comforts. Electricity, hot water, and indoor plumbing finally reached every prison in the system; sanitation and food quality improved markedly. "These are the days of a 'new deal,'" remarked a reporter in Austin.[46]

Although Ellis never put much stock in psychological treatment—he listed "do[ing] something for the criminal" as the third priority of prison administration, behind security and punishment—he nonetheless ramped up what he called "a sensible, vigorous program of rehabilitation."[47] Tapping rodeo proceeds, he encouraged after-work programs like Alcoholics Anonymous and the Dale Carnegie self-improvement course. By the 1950s, a point incentive program allowed inmates to accumulate credits toward parole by attending church or taking classes in their time off. Such efforts charted a new course, Ellis contended, and in 1957 the legislature made his reorientation official with a symbolic name change. Following California, the Texas Prison System became the Texas Department of Corrections, or TDC, with Ellis serving as director.[48]

If Texas followed California in nomenclature, however, Ellis's approach to prisoner management contrasted sharply with Richard McGee's. In the Golden State, administrators tried to maintain order and transform inmates through information gathering and psychological treatment; in the Lone Star State, they continued to rely on work and force. Illustrative of these rival approaches were the two states' building programs. In California, McGee's first priority had been to construct a new medium-security prison, Soledad, which offered Chino-style frills to a rougher class of inmates; the trend was toward less regimentation not more. In Texas, by contrast, Ellis's first and most expensive request was for a maximum-security "Segregation Unit" at Huntsville. His plan was to quarantine "hopeless cases" indefinitely, perhaps "for the rest of their lives." Sardonically christened the "Shamrock" by convicts—after a lavish hotel in Houston—the stand-alone lockup represented both a precursor to the supermax and a throwback to penitential solitude. Complained a liberal-minded officer, "There is no zoo in the United States in which animals are as desperately caged as are the men in Huntsville's maximum security."[49]

Only the hardest cases were booked into the Shamrock, but Ellis built smaller solitary blocks on six other units. His motto: "Discipline and Respect." Whereas convict autonomy had expanded during the 1920s, particularly during the run of the Prison Welfare League, it shrank under Simmons and shrank further under Ellis. Prisoners were expected to work from "light enough to shoot till too dark to shoot," recalls Redbird McCotter, a convict who began his first term in 1955. They were to respond to officers with obedient snap and observe a version of the silent system in the chow hall. Ellis himself showed up for work carefully attired in a double-breasted suit and he expected his underlings, both free-world and felon, to present a neat, soldierly appearance. Every prison building was to be "exceptionally clean."[50]

Like Simmons, Ellis had little tolerance for dissent. Confronted with a buck during his first week in office, he declared that if "able-bodied inmates refused to work, . . . they would not be allowed to eat." When self-mutilations occurred, he ordered the wounded patched up and put back to work on the same farms; heel-stringing, he instructed, should not provide a ticket to Huntsville. Such measures did not eliminate conflict—as we will see, officially sanctioned violence remained commonplace—but by expanding solitary and backing up his officers in almost any confrontation, Ellis brought Texas's prisons more forcefully under control. During the 1950s, an average of twenty-two convicts escaped annually, down from ninety-eight in the 1940s. Self-mutilations evidently decreased as well, though these numbers are harder to trust. Not long after taking office, Ellis requested "permission to not count mutilations or other disciplinary infractions committed by irresponsible or insane persons in making statistical returns." The Prison Board agreed.[51]

Fewer bucks meant fewer headlines, but what politicians cared about just as much was prison productivity—and here, too, Ellis excelled. Thanks partly to modern agricultural management and partly to greater convict exertion, cash-crop output soared in the first years of Ellis's rule, with cotton proceeds topping $2 million annually during the Korean War. Cattle raising and dairying, as well as corn, rice, and potato planting, also climbed, enabling TDC to become increasingly autarkic in food production. Prison officials liked to boast that Texas's convicts were the "best fed in the country"—indeed, prisoners complained less frequently about food quality than in previous decades—and at little cost. Although the prison population and guard force swelled, the state's cost per inmate dropped by more than half under Ellis's watch, bottoming out at $1.24 per convict per day in 1958.[52]

Lower budgets and fewer scandals made Ellis exceptionally popular

in Austin. Governor Allan Shivers, Beauford Jester's right-wing successor, praised the director's "record of progress," and the legislature regularly approved his budget requests—though they were always modest.
Within the prison system, Ellis achieved even higher stature. Administrators respected his work ethic and open-door policy, while the rank-
and-file appreciated his sometimes futile efforts to win them better
salaries and benefits. "He was a giant of a man," says Jack Kyle, who
worked closely with him during his final years in office, "the best overall prison administrator I've had the opportunity to meet." In 1951, the
Prison Board voted to increase Ellis's salary by 25 percent and build
him a five-thousand-square-foot Georgian mansion across the street
from the Walls.[53]

By the end of the decade, Ellis was at the top of his career. Newspaper editors heralded "the Miracle within the Walls" and praised Ellis
for doing a "remarkable job of filling one of the most difficult jobs
any man ever faced." Although subsequent investigations revealed that
TDC's order and efficiency were the products of systematic intimidation by staff and legion inmate trusties, or building tenders, the director nonetheless basked in the national limelight more than any of his
predecessors. *Reader's Digest* feted Ellis as a "builder of men and soil,"
"the best prison man in America." "Texas's prison system [has moved]
from the bottom of the ladder to near the top," argued a reporter in the
*American Journal of Correction*. With impressive speed unexplainable by
legislative largesse, TDC was steadily closing the public relations gap
with California. Then, on November 12, 1961, while having dinner at
the Houston Club with members of the corrections board, the architect
of Texas's triumph slumped over in his chair and died.[54]

"Ellis literally killed himself building the system," Jack Kyle remembers, but the system he built outlasted him. Throughout the ranks,
Ellis had cultivated hardworking devotees to what penologists termed
the Texas "control model." At the top, he had surrounded himself with
"clean-cut, thoughtful businessmen," and on the farms he had given
free rein to experienced wardens who knew how to subdue convicts and
bring in the crop. Like a prudent monarch, Ellis had also anointed a successor, George Beto, a college administrator and ordained minister who
had served six years on the corrections board. Within hours of Ellis's
death, the powerful chairman of the board, H. H. "Pete" Coffield, was
on the phone with Beto, sounding him out on the job. Four months

later, Beto drove to Huntsville, family in tow, and moved into his mentor's stately home.[55]

In a condolence note to Ellis's family, Beto called himself a "disciple." He told reporters he "simply wanted to continue the progress that O. B. Ellis had begun." Yet the new director fit awkwardly into the Texas prison mold. He had served on both corrections and parole boards, but he had never worked professionally in a prison. He was a hulking man—six foot four with penetrating eyes and an oversized balding head—but he was unathletic and unabashedly intellectual. He had lived in Texas for years, but he was a Midwesterner by birth and a Lutheran rather than a Baptist or Methodist. He was politically conservative but ambivalent about white supremacy. In 1953, he had provoked Austin by integrating the boys' school he administered; he threatened to leave his church if his new pupil wasn't allowed in a front pew.[56]

As an academic and clergyman, Beto necessarily brought new emphases to the job. Religious counseling and basic education expanded dramatically under his watch, with the TDC chartering its own school district in 1968. Thanks to a state-use law passed in 1963, industrial sales to other government agencies shot up tenfold during his tenure.[57] By the height of Beto's influence in the late 1960s, TDC had all the trappings of a modern correctional system: psychological testing at intake, vocational training and group counseling on the main units, regular parole evaluations, and a work-furlough program.[58] "We believe we are making progress in achieving the goal of rehabilitating a large number of the broken lives committed to us," Beto observed. To a reporter for the *Lutheran,* he commented, "I would like to believe that I am attempting to fulfill the words of our Lord when he said, 'I was in prison and you came to me.'"[59]

In contrast to Ellis, who imposed order on mayhem, Beto inherited a mature, stable penal system and was able to devote greater attention to program building. He decommissioned the Shamrock, believing that "toughies" should be disbursed and made to work like anyone else, and he encouraged groundbreaking (by Texas standards) experiments in openness and treatment. At Ferguson, a four-thousand-acre farm adjacent to Eastham, he inaugurated a new prison for young first-time offenders, where officials pioneered what they called a "progressive yet realistic approach" to reducing recidivism.[60] At Goree, the long-serving

warden, Velma Dobbs, developed a program of "training and treatment," claiming, "We do everything we can inside and out to make it
seem less like a prison." In 1965, she was elected president of the Wom-
en's Correctional Association. Privately, Beto remarked that "we could
turn every woman we got in the Texas prison system loose and nobody
would know the difference."[61]

Beto considered enacting even deeper changes. Not long after his
appointment, he spoke out against the convict guard system, staff violence, and an overreliance on agriculture, which he saw as out of step
with the state's rapidly urbanizing demographics. The director made
progress in these areas, yet Beto was ultimately changed as much by
the institution he inherited as he was able to change it. Although the
bat had been retired, physical discipline persisted, especially in the
fields. Although the civil rights movement was in full bloom, Beto
made only token efforts at racial integration, hiring a handful of African
American guards who usually got posted to dead-end jobs on outside
pickets.[62] Although prison industries expanded, field work still dominated; in 1966, 1,500 out of 12,000 inmates had factory jobs, about the
same proportion as under convict leasing. Although the prison system
received regular, biennial appropriations and was no longer expected to
be fully self-supporting, Texas's spending on corrections remained
among the lowest in the nation: $1.50 per prisoner per day in 1963
compared to $3.50 nationally.[63] Although Beto expanded and modern-
ized Texas's penal system, it remained southern at heart.

What really differentiated the Texas system was its mastery of
control—and here Beto outstripped even his mentor.[64] "Whenever a
social group is without rules, anarchy prevails," he warned in the 1964
prison rule book. To Beto, a central task of corrections—the central
rehabilitative task, in fact—was "to furnish discipline to previously un-
disciplined lives." Criminals spring from chaos, he believed, from "dis-
integrated families" and wanton greed. In prison, he aimed to introduce
them to routine and restriction, as well as the "dignity and necessity of
labor."[65]

Even more so than Ellis, Beto insisted that prison properties be me-
ticulously kept. "Texas prisons employ the philosophy that if something can be cleaned or polished or painted, it should be," says former
warden Jim Willett, who started off his thirty-year corrections career
under Beto. "In those days you didn't see any Johnson grass or other
weeds sticking up through the cotton, corn, or vegetables growing in

the fields," remembers a veteran who started in 1966. "The ends of the rows were scraped clean, and the turnrows . . . were always flat-weeded by the convict hoe squads."[66]

Respect for authority was another Beto maxim. Staff underlings addressed him as "Dr. Beto" (he had earned a doctorate in educational administration at UT Austin), and he made clear that he would "not be satisfied with anything less than complete compliance with orders." "Whatever the rules, enforce them," commanded a TDC training manual. Any officer who fails to do so "is not only useless . . . but a positive menace."[67]

From inmates, Beto demanded complete submission. He mingled freely on the yards but never extended his hand to convicts. Day in and day out, prisoners were held to a standard of regimentation that had faded from most prisons with the nineteenth century. Personal appearance standards looked to boot camp—neat, unadorned, and closely shaved. In the fields, convicts had to "deuce it up" and march two abreast; in the buildings, they were to stay on either side of bright green lines painted down the middle of the floors. At Eastham, a sign read, "No Smoking, No Talking, No Loitering, Single File," and enforcers, both guard and convict, took each commandment seriously. John DiIulio, one of the most influential criminal justice scholars of the late twentieth century and a great admirer of Beto, called the Texas approach to order and obedience "most rigorous (even fetishistic)."[68]

"We had total control, absolute literal control," recalled Steve Martin, who started out as an officer at the Ellis Unit, which opened near Huntsville in 1965. "Inmates could not even get letters out. It was all censored, and the inmates knew that. . . . There was no recourse." Critics would denounce the control model as "authoritarian," but Beto made no apologies. "There are two . . . kinds of prisons," he told a reporter in 1967, "prisons run by the prisoners and prisons run by the administration. These prisons are run by the administration." Above all, Beto dedicated his career to keeping them that way. "I live in mortal fear of convict-run prison," he once told a federal judge.[69]

Maintaining stability in a sprawling prison system required constant vigilance, and Beto carried more than his weight. He was a force of nature, colleagues recall. Racing down the highways in his Plymouth Fury, hopping from one unit to another in the TDC plane he purchased in 1962, Beto managed to hold together Texas's far-flung prisons through constant locomotion and force of will; he accomplished, through technology and travel, some of what progressives had sought through centralization. Putting in longer hours than convicts—albeit not with a hoe—and subsisting largely on cigarettes and coffee, Beto planned and politicked, inspected and inspired. Because he was always on the move, staff members began referring to him as "Walking George." Guards and convicts alike learned to stay on their toes.[70]

With unbounded energy and unshakable conviction, Beto led mostly by example, but he was also remote and physically intimidating. He towered over his associates, his bald head topped with a fedora or Stetson, his probing eyes framed by thick-rimmed glasses. He seemed immune to tear gas, Willett recalls, and unflappable in a crisis. After only two days on the job, he ordered officers to put down a buck at Harlem by whacking protesters with pieces of wet rope. "He was a preacher but a practical preacher," explains Esso "Woody" Woods, who rose up through the ranks under Beto's leadership. "He was a pretty tough guy." Convicts grumbled that he came to Texas "with a Bible in one hand and a baseball bat in the other." They called him "The Man."[71]

Hard-nosed and devout, sympathetic but stern, Beto was a natural hit in Texas. Like Ellis, he cultivated feverish staff loyalty. "We all loved and respected him," says Woods. In Austin, most lawmakers lined up in support. "He was an educated man of God, a wonderful guy," says A. R. "Babe" Schwartz, who served in the legislature from 1955 to 1981. "We tried to get him as much money as we could."[72]

Beto was a skillful lobbyist, and with the help of Pete Coffield, the wealthy chairman of both the corrections board and the Texas Democratic Party, he squeezed more money out of the statehouse than anyone had before. In 1965, his annual budgets surpassed $20 million, still modest compared to other big states but enough (with convict labor) to build three new prisons and undertake other construction projects.[73] Because censorship and control kept outbreaks and embarrassments to a minimum, politicians further rewarded Beto by staying out of his business. Except for polite inquiries during budget hearings, he operated TDC's fourteen separate prisons with almost no oversight. He became the most influential prison director in Texas history.

With a record of success—as defined by efficiency, economy, and official tallies of disorder—and a knack for promoting it, Beto attracted even more national attention than had Ellis. Out-of-state delegations regularly showed up in Huntsville, seeking to figure out what made Texas tick. Dozens of newspapers, from Levittown to Panama City to Long Beach, profiled the "tall, tough minister," who had turned a bastion of brutality into "a clean, highly disciplined industrial dynasty." Paul Harvey, the radio personality, called Beto "an uncommonly dedicated man," who was doing the whole nation a service by "rebuilding character and integrity in these evildoers." DiIulio joked that his hope for the future of American corrections "rests entirely on a 'technological fix'—clone George Beto 51 times; put each clone in charge of a corrections dept. (and the Bureau of Prisons)."[74]

For most of American history, Texas had languished on the margins of the penological establishment. Since its founding, the American Correctional Association had regularly assailed the state's plantations as anachronistic and criminogenic. Yet all of this changed in the latter half of the twentieth century. In 1958, the ACA bestowed upon O. B. Ellis its highest honor: he was elected president of the organization, the first man south of Virginia to hold the post. Austin MacCormick, an apostle of Thomas Mott Osborne and a consultant to prison systems across the nation, became a friend to both Ellis and Beto and lavished upon them increasingly unqualified praise. "I saw the Texas Prison System come up from close to the bottom of the rating list to its present position [near] the top," he wrote after a visit in 1967. One year later, George Beto was himself elected ACA president.[75]

For almost one hundred years, Texas prison chiefs had either ignored the ACA or looked to it for inspiration. Starting in the 1950s, however, first Texas and then other southern states began exerting influence over the organization; they began giving advice rather than simply taking it. The South had long imprisoned a greater portion of its citizenry than northern states; now the section began to exercise its clout.[76]

During Beto's presidency, the ACA assembled in Cincinnati for its centennial congress, and the adopted Texan charted for the association a more pragmatic, more southern course. With respect to forced labor, he argued, "Our prisons will become more productive," not only because "excessive idleness is the bane of many penal institutions" but because "the tax-conscious constituent will demand it." With respect to rehabilitation—the founding creed of the ACA—he levied more skepticism than praise. He called on his colleagues to eschew "undocumented fads" and devise "bold, imaginative, and yet realistic programs."[77]

Among the weighty tasks that fell to President Beto was the redrafting of the ACA's Declaration of Principles, originally promulgated in 1870. With characteristic grace, he paid homage to his distinguished forefathers and lauded their "visionary" ideals. When Beto's committee presented its final revisions, however, they marked a significant retreat from that vision. Whereas the original document telegraphed Christian idealism, the rewrite choked on bureaucratese. In 1870 the "great object" was "moral regeneration"; a hundred years later, the objective was "the strengthening and expansion of the correctional methods [that] . . . are the presently recognized methods of preventing and controlling crime and delinquency." Everywhere, the updated principles marked subtle steps away from the association's messianic origins. Whereas the founders called for "fallen men" to be treated with "generous parental care," the revisionists proposed that "the offender . . . be accorded acceptable standards of decent living." Where Wines and his acolytes had stressed that "brute force may make good prisoners [but that] moral training alone will make good citizens," Beto's principles advised that "control and management of offenders should be by sound scientific methods, stressing moral values and organized persuasion, rather than primarily dependence upon physical force." Whereas education was once extolled as "a vital force in . . . reformation," the new goal was to "improve . . . vocational competence and skill."[78]

The 1970 principles signaled a creeping pessimism in the field, a gathering suspicion among prison professionals that they might hope to effectively contain some criminals but not to cure them. Just as America's prisoner population was about to embark on a meteoric ascent, the original rationale for imprisonment was starting to falter. Prisons were poised to become, for the first time, central institutions in American life just as they were drifting from rehabilitation toward punishment, from a northern ethos to a southern one.

## BEYOND THE FENCE LINE

Texas's journey from backwater to beacon was propelled by a carefully crafted image of Texas corrections. On paper TDC was among the cleanest, safest, and cheapest penal systems in the nation—qualities that became increasingly desired amid the turmoil of the 1960s.[79] What outsiders read in the newspaper or saw at the rodeo, however, was not a full account of what went on inside. To a certain extent this disconnect was true of every prison; walls not only keep prisoners in, they keep the public out. But the Texas control model achieved an exceptional mastery of information. Through surveillance, censorship, staff cohesion, and relentless self-promotion, TDC's top managers were able to present only what they wanted to the world. Texas's prisons were quiet, disciplined, and economical, administrators proclaimed at every turn. What they seldom, if ever, acknowledged was that Texas's prison peace was purchased just as it always had been, with force and fear. Beto may have toted a Bible in one hand and a baseball bat in the other, but it was the bat that made his prisons run.

To newly recruited corrections officers, TDC's modus operandi was not immediately apparent. "The floors, be they tile or concrete, shone like countertops," remembers Willett. The prison ran so smoothly that "[I began to think] if I kept this job, there would be a lot of this gazing off into nothing." Only after catching their breath did "new boots" begin to realize that prison order had to be continuously regenerated. Prisons are not inherently quiet places but require constant stifling. "Ahm tellin' yew, son, hyere's what you got to know," reportedly explained a warden at Wynne to a new officer, who recorded the exchange in exaggerated dialect. "Yew got yew some mean sonsabitches on this cheer farm and they gonna' stomp on yew ever chance they get. Yew know what yew goin' to do? . . . Yew ain't never goin' to give them the chance."[80]

Prison guards received almost no formal training in how to carry out this advice. In 1962, Beto set up a training program at Ferguson, but nearly all of the instruction took place on the job. To the surprise of new boots, much of the teaching was done by convict trusties: building tenders, turnkeys, porters, bookkeepers, and lead rows who taught novice bosses how and when to open doors, how to conduct the count, how to file a disciplinary report, and how to supervise agricultural work. Longtime trusties reported directly to senior officers and accreted significant authority as their surrogates. "Those suckers told you how to do things," remarks Willett.[81]

Experienced officers watched from a distance, but when a recruit demonstrated promise, they reached out. Around the major's office or after hours at a barbecue, TDC veterans swapped buck and chase stories and let new hands know what it meant to be considered a "good officer." It might take years to be accepted into what two guards-turned-sociologists labeled the "inner core" of TDC's "strong officer subculture," but the remoteness of many units, combined with the unique pressures of the job, fostered cohesion in the ranks. "We had super camaraderie among the employees back then," says Willett. "The staff was strong," agrees Kyle. "They were loyal to Beto, the state, and each other."[82]

When O. B. Ellis first took on the job, one of his first priorities had been to professionalize the guard force. The prison system had "fill[ed] its rolls with incompetents, uneducated persons, sadists, and drifters," noted a TDC pamphlet; Ellis wanted "to make prison work a career." Better pay was a necessary first step—the starting salary in 1948 was $120 a month (about $1,000 today)—but when legislators agreed only to modest raises, Ellis began piling on as many benefits as the prison system could produce itself. Rent-free convict-built housing on prison properties, for both bachelors and families, was the most important bonus, but free meals, haircuts, shoe shines, and laundry service sweetened the pot. "I was finding out that there were definite perks to this job," marvels Lon Glenn. "If a man wanted to save money, all he had to do was stay on the unit and bank his paycheck, as there were no living expenses."[83]

Carrying forward plantation tradition, higher-ranking officers were also assigned "houseboys," usually African American trusties who could be used for cooking, cleaning, or even child care. After his four-year-old son wandered off one day, Willett decided to have his convict groundskeeper look after the little fellow. Official policy discouraged such practice; one Beto directive prohibited houseboys from babysitting, watching television with the family, and, for good measure, laundering "women's undergarments." But by the time Willett was assigning convicts to take care of his son (and later his daughter), he was a warden and could do pretty much as he pleased. "Like the captain of a warship at sea," he writes, the warden "was the final authority in almost every situation."[84]

All of these emoluments were supposed to attract "competent personnel." Ironically, they had the consequence of intensifying the prison system's historic insularity. Into the 1970s, three-quarters of prison officers hailed from within fifty miles of their units. Living and working on the farms, they tended to socialize mainly with each other, gradually developing a wariness toward outsiders. After several years on the job, Willett realized that he felt at home. "In some ways, I'd grown as institutionalized as an old convict."[85]

Benefits and close-knit community offered a powerful draw to many employees, but, in order to move up through the ranks, bosses had to make a strong impression on their superiors. Not surprisingly, given the long hours, a formidable work ethic was one of the requisite character traits. Glenn recalls that when he dismounted after spending ten hours in the saddle for the first time, he "had to grab the fence in order to remain standing." But when he got up the next morning before dawn and turned out his squad, he earned the respect of his older colleagues.[86]

Because of the tensions with inmates, as well as potential outside scrutiny, personal loyalty was equally prized. "If you work for a man, in Heaven's name work for him," instructed the employee manual, a rule book nearly as exacting as the convict version. "Speak well of him and stand by the institution he represents. Remember an ounce of loyalty is worth a pound of cleverness." Successful officers took this advice to heart, striving to gain the respect of more experienced officers and expecting to be backed up, when the time came, in return. "I was loyal to [my] warden . . . first and TDC second," reported an officer. "That's the way people were. . . . If there was trouble, we was all in trouble."[87]

Although serious rebellions were rare under the control model, officers were also expected to maintain a cool head in a crisis and not shrink from physical confrontation. Beto's manual prohibited "using force . . . except in case of actual self-defense or in an emergency," but insiders report that "coercion was deeply entrenched in the guard subculture." Clashes with inmates were important to employee status, as a new boot at Eastham learned after defending himself and forcibly subduing a prisoner in the hall. "After the incident, . . . co-workers saw [me] in a new light," he wrote. "Veteran officers on the same shift who had not even deigned to speak to [me started asking] the whereabouts of 'Joe Palooka.' "[88]

Violence could usually be avoided, experienced officers believed, if employees developed good "convict sense," an intangible quality that connoted the ability to predict trouble before it started and compel prisoners to work and obey without assistance. Among old-timers, convict sense was also called "knowing your niggers." It was a skill that could not be easily taught, but recruits soon realized that they were constantly being tested for it. In the fields, veterans watched greenhorn riders to see if they could keep their squads on task and avoid being "hogged," or duped, by inmates. In the tanks and cell blocks, ranking officers scrutinized the comportment of newcomers before assigning them to posts with more responsibility, where they had to "have nuts." Convict trusties, too, were watching on behalf of management. When Jim Willett once tried to save time by allowing his inmate bookkeeper to complete some paperwork, he got berated by the major the next morning, having been ratted out by a prisoner. "Everyone was under surveillance," reports Steve Martin. "The intelligence system was unbelievably sophisticated. And that meant control."[89]

Successful prison guards also learned to play the part, to project strength and hide weakness. "You had to prove that you were the Man . . . the *baddest of the bad*," recollects a CO. To intimidate inmates, officers growled and cursed in a practiced "convict voice." One fellow felt compelled to sew up his own cuts without anesthetic after breaking up a knife fight, lest his coworkers detect sensitivity. One of the first female wardens took to chewing Days Work tobacco whenever she made her rounds.[90]

New boots learned that every interaction with inmates should reinforce the unbreachable divide between keeper and kept, free and unfree. On the one hand, guards were supposed to keep their distance. "Employees . . . shall not become familiar with inmates or permit familiarity on the part of inmates," instructed the staff manual. On the other, they were supposed to exhibit dominance at every turn. They were constantly reminded "of the necessity for security and discipline in all relations with inmates." As had always been the custom on Texas plantations, forced laborers were expected to treat their superiors with reflexive deference. Prisoners were to remove their caps when passing by an officer, and every employee was to be addressed as "boss" or by rank. Guards, by contrast, wielded the power of naming, referring to convicts as "ol' thangs" or bestowing upon them a grab bag of demeaning nicknames, like Saddlehead, Bugeye, Goat, Flea Brain, Tarbaby, Wetback, or Cowfucker.[91]

Convicts were universally dishonored under the control model, but by all accounts African Americans were most intensively debased. Although Beto made an effort to cut down on profanity and name-calling, racial epithets remained a staple of guard speak in some units, especially in the fields.[92] "I got called a nigger every day," recalls James "Yogi" Yeager, who went to prison in 1972. Not long after starting out as a guard, Steve Martin remembers, he made the mistake of referring to a turnkey as a "tall, slender black guy," to which the shift lieutenant objected. "Boss Martin," he said, leaning into the control station, "we got coons, speer-chuckers, apes, darkies, jigaboos, and niggers, but I'll be damned if there's a 'tall, slender black man' on the Ellis farm."[93]

Keeping convicts in their place was one challenge facing officers. Getting them to obey and work was another—and here the control model refined a variety of time-worn techniques. As in treatment-oriented systems like California's, TDC offered positive incentives for good behavior. Points toward parole and "good time" were the most important, but there were other inducements as well: better job assignments, eligibility for vocational classes, or access to the craft shop, which could provide a smidgen of income. Prison officials distributed off-the-books perks as well. Field hands on number-one squads had first run of the showers and sometimes got special steak dinners after a successful harvest. Prisoners working in the woods with axes were allowed to keep whatever they could kill—"possums, coons, rabbits, squirrels, [or] armadillos"—for subsequent preparation by the inmate cooks. When a "varmint" popped up, an inmate hunter would yell, "Getting it over heah, Boss!" and take off after his prey.[94]

For convicts and officers who coexisted on a unit for years, working relationships could blossom into full-fledged paternalism, if not friendship. Albert "Racehoss" Sample, a champion cotton picker, wrote that when he went back to prison on a parole violation in 1962, his warden made him a bookkeeper, figuring he had filled more than his share of sacks. When Willett became warden at Diagnostic, he remembers watching out for an agreeable sixty-three-year-old convict named Crump, who, he said, had "black-as-midnight skin" and "could out-work men half his age." Crump took care of the flower gardens and had been on the unit so long that "he rested under the shadow of trees he had planted himself." One day, a lynx-eyed picket boss noticed that the old-timer was sneaking off under a bridge for contraband smokes. Willett said he would take care of it, and he did—by transferring the officer to another station. Years later, after he buried Crump at Captain Joe Byrd cemetery and took over at the Walls, Willett continued to bend the rules for favored inmates, sometimes authorizing off-hours family visits or providing a condemned man a last cigarette before leading him down the final hallway.[95]

If TDC offered a fistful of carrots, however, it maintained a larger pile of sticks. Solitary confinement and revocation of good time were the standard penalties for serious rule violations, but ranking officers also devised alternative sanctions that could be dished out on the spot and without paperwork. For "bad-eyeing" a guard or picking "dirty cotton," a prisoner might be ordered to balance for three hours on an elevated two-by-four, the Rail. Or he might be forced to stay up all night shelling peanuts, only to be hauled out to the fields again at daybreak without supper or breakfast. "If a man was caught eating tomatoes or cantaloupes that he was supposed to be tending or picking, he would have to carry one around with him everywhere he went, every day, until it literally rotted," explained Michael Jewell, who has been behind bars since 1970. Willful cons might buck, but their circumstances only worsened. "I refused to stand on the rail . . . one evening," remembered Jewell. "So I had to do thirty-three days in solitary and then I still had to do my three hours on the rail my first night out."[96]

Convicts and officers alike say that informal, swiftly administered punishments acted as a significant deterrent. But they by no means exhausted the control model's methods of repression. After 1941, legally sanctioned whipping never again took place in Texas, but prisoners report that laggards in the fields were regularly struck with reins or knocked over by a boss's horse. Inside the building, insubordinate convicts were subjected to "tune ups," which involved, according to former guards, "verbal humiliation, profanity, shoves, kicks, and head and body slaps." If a convict fought back, he would get an overhaul, or "ass-whipping," a more serious beating with clubs and boots that often resulted in hospitalization. Although less frequent than in previous decades, homicides by staff still occurred under murky circumstances. Albert Sample claimed that his supervisor at Retrieve, "Boss Band," shot and killed two prisoners while he was there, both for "tryin ta 'scape." Band was a "traveling executioner," the inmates whispered. He had been transferred "cuz he kilt a whole squad over on anutha camp."[97]

Although staff members periodically got in their licks, the overwhelming majority of disciplinary blows delivered within TDC were administered not by guards but by convict trusties. This was probably true from the beginning. In 1874, the lessees Ward and Dewey promoted their best convicts to serve as "sub-bosses." Four years later, the governor prohibited the practice, thus inaugurating a cycle of scandal, failed containment, and persistence that rolled forward for more than one hundred years.[98]

Both Ellis and Beto tried to curtail the use of trusty enforcers. In 1948, Ellis complained that "for years inmates armed with dirks and blackjacks have been used to rule the tanks," and he vowed to abolish the practice. Twenty, even thirty years later, they were still there, still armed, still ruling, despite a similar order issued by Beto in 1963. The trouble was that a full-strength guard force cost more money than the State of Texas was willing to spend, so administrators had to make do. In order to maintain a high level of internal discipline, they came to accept the fact that only convicts were plentiful enough to carry out the core functions of the prison system. "Paperwork, counts, monitoring, and security—we ran the whole thing," claims a former building tender, or BT, who first went to prison in the 1950s. Low-level employees like "picket bosses didn't have to lift a finger. They just sat down and read a western."[99]

Defenders of the "BT system," as the reliance on convict guards was euphemistically called, acknowledged that trusties allowed TDC to maintain fewer employees. "We used to hold more than a thousand men at Ferguson with as few as twelve paid staff on duty," says Esso Woods, who used to oversee the selection of state-approved trusties. Critics charged that the system fostered abuses, but high-ranking officers from the period generally offer no apologies. "We selected them carefully and kept them in line," asserts Woods. "They kept order, and they did it well." Jack Kyle, who rose to the position of assistant director under Beto, agrees. "The idea that you can do a better job with more employees is a fallacy," he argues. "What matters is the quality of your people and your operation. . . . We had the most stability of any system."[100]

Administrators often claimed that trusties did menial jobs: building tenders swept the tanks, turnkeys opened the doors under supervision, and porters ran errands. If they helped enforce the rules, Woods says, "they used more bluff than brawn." Convicts and many officers tell a different story. "Building tenders were used as police," says James Yeager. "Two or three [of them] would run in and attack inmates" for fighting, mouthing off, or even for "talking loud when the mail was called." Immune from shakedowns, BTs—and to a lesser extent lower-status trusties like porters or "water boys"—carried a variety of weapons. This was against written policy, but officers looked the other way and counted on it during a crisis.[101]

When Lon Glenn confronted his first riot at Clemens—a hooch-induced melee in one of the tanks—the assistant warden's first order was to "call all the day-shift BTs . . . and tell 'em to come packing." "Within three minutes, there were ten building tenders standing under the swing picket in the center hall, and they were ready for battle," Glenn writes. "They had cut-off baseball bats, slapjacks, axe handles, links of trace chain, and various other implements of destruction." In less than an hour, all of the drunken rebels were subdued, stripped naked, and crowded into solitary, which was managed by another trusty. "The BTs were dangerous and mean," admits Walter Siros, a former convict guard, "but the job made them that way."[102]

With convict sentries always at the ready, corrections officers operated in a safer environment than they would have otherwise. The trouble was that BTs and their auxiliaries amassed extraordinary powers and then wielded them not just for official purposes but for their own. Certain privileges came with the job—better cell assignments, clean-pressed uniforms, and limited freedom of movement—but the most powerful BTs, those who worked closely with a major, for example, took considerably more. "We skimmed money off the top at commissary," recalls Siros. Others collected protection payments or took a cut from gambling winnings. Indeed, as one long-termer notes, "building tenders controlled much of the illegal activity that goes on in a prison, drugs, homosexuals, etc."[103] Indeed, one of the most coveted benefits was first choice of "punks," young, slender, often broken-spirited inmates who would do a BT's laundry, keep his cell clean, cook special meals on his hot plate, and provide other services on demand.

TDC officials knew that sex—both consensual and non—was a vital cog in the BT machine; Beto once rejected trusty status for an aggressive prisoner he said "would rape a snake through a brick wall."[104] So long as BTs remained loyal to their patrons, however, they were generally allowed to "turn out" whoever they wished. "Most of the building tenders had punks," says Willie Redis, an inmate at Wynne who has been in prison since 1962, but, according to him, they were "too cowardly" to assault "fresh fish" on their own. That's where Freaky Willie came in. By his own account, Redis was thuggish and out of control during his first years in prison, and he became a sort of sexual tamer for the building tenders. "They would say, 'A new boy just come in, man. He's sittin' right over there. You want him?' I was crazy, so I said, 'I don't care, man. Open the door.' So they would open the [cell] door and gather around to watch the fight. . . . I would hit the guy in the solar plexus, then try to break his nose. I would take off his clothes and tell him, 'If you say a thing to anyone I'm gonna kill you.' . . . After I was finished with him," Redis says, "the building tenders could move in."[105]

Some officials tried to stop prison rape; Redis eventually had the top bunk in his cell removed because "everyone that they put in my cell, I'd rape him." Others came to regard sexual assault as sport. When a "gnat liver," or young first offender, showed up at Retrieve one day, Albert Sample recalls that the captain paraded him before the building tenders and bantered with them about who would take him first. "Cap'n, you knows I been heah a long time. . . . Pleeze, lemme have 'em," one of the BTs pleaded, while the others "crowded up to the bars, . . . shouting obscenities at the 'new one.'"[106]

"You nigguhs dry up them ol' mouths an git back away frum them bars!" the officer hollered. "You sonsabitches ack lak you ain' never had no boar pussy befo. Hell, this heah ain't the first little ol' mare niggah ya'll done seed." Once the clamor died down, Sample writes in his memoir (the first full-length autobiography published by an African American convict in Texas), the captain organized a little contest on the spot. Listen up, he said, "I'll put this little ol' nigguh on the nigguh's tank what cums up wit the best name fer 'em."

"Captain Sir, I ain' no punk, sir," protested the newcomer, but the officer carried on. "Name 'em Sweet Meat, Cap'n," one of the BTs shouted out. "Betty Grable," offered another (this drew a "sharp stare" from the boss, who didn't like black convicts talking about white women). From a welter of suggestions, the captain finally settled on the name "Ol' Dumplin," and delivered the terrified inmate into the clutches of the winner, Bull, a BT "nicknamed for his brawny wide chest and big arms." As if according to a twisted script, Bull led Dumplin back to his bunk, gave him a snack and a cigarette, and later that day demanded a blow job in return. "Man, . . . I ain' doin but two years an I don' wanna git involved in no stuff lak that," Dumplin said. He received a fist in reply. "Bull fiercely stomped him," Sample remembers, then splashed some water in his face and forced "his prick . . . into Dumplin's bloody mouth."

Thus began a daily routine. "Nearly every night after Dumplin pulled his shift, Bull lay on his bunk in the back and forced Dumplin to play with his pecker until he raised a hard. Then he'd make Dumplin suck him off while anybody in the tank who wanted to, looked on." Such exploitative relationships formed across the system, but this one ended badly for Bull. One night, Dumplin smuggled a razor blade back from the kitchen and cut off his tormenter's penis. Afterward, Sample points out, "Dumplin could pull his shift in the kitchen, return to the tank, and get on his bunk without anybody bothering him. . . . He had earned his right to sleep in hell."[107]

## THE LONG SHADOW OF SLAVERY

In the decades since Texas first set up its network of prison farms, the Lone Star State had undergone social changes worthy of a revolution. Well into the twentieth century, the state remained primarily agricultural, with cotton still on the throne; in 1920, two of every three Texans still lived in places with populations of fewer than twenty-five hundred. After World War II, however, Texas became a different state. The gusher at Spindletop spawned refineries, pipelines, and boom towns, first in East Texas, then across the central plains to the panhandle. Smelters, steel mills, petrochemical plants, shipyards, and aircraft factories had all sprung up during the war, and, before long, industry outstripped agriculture as the primary engine of economic growth. By 1950, the census classified Texas as a majority urban state, with Houston, Dallas, and San Antonio closing in on or surpassing the half million mark. Old Texas—both the reality of tenant farming and the myth of the cattle drives—was fast fading away. "The Metropolis swallowed the Frontier like a small snake swallows a large frog," observed Larry McMurtry in 1968, "slowly, not without strain, but inexorably. And if something of the Frontier remains alive in the innards of the Metropolis it is because the process of digestion has only just begun."[108]

Texas's prisons had changed, too. By the 1960s, there were tractors in the fields and televisions in the dayrooms. Inmates took IQ tests at Diagnostic and psychopharmaceuticals at Wynne. Yet for all the innovations of the control era, prisoners stepping off the chain bus and onto a Texas prison farm felt that they were shuffling into the past. "They delivered me in leg irons, chained to other convicts by the neck," recollects Norris Trevenio, who first went to prison in 1950. Having grown up in Dallas, Trevenio had never worked in agriculture, but he had the misfortune of arriving at Clemens Farm during the harvest season and was expected to pick two hundred pounds of cotton a day. "No way I could make that," he chuckles in a gravelly voice, recalling that he had to miss supper a number of times before catching on. Urban convicts experienced profound "culture shock," wrote another prisoner. "They learned quickly that . . . there was nowhere to turn for assistance if they got on the wrong side of their masters. They had been removed from the civilized world."[109]

This removal was perhaps even more bewildering for white prisoners than their black counterparts. Having come of age in the Jim Crow South, white Texans were accustomed to a measure of respect, even if they hailed from broken, impoverished homes. They might be "crackers" or "white trash," but they weren't "niggers"—and for some, this was about the only mark of social distinction they had. When white convicts were delivered into the hands of TDC, however, they soon discovered that "the wages of whiteness" didn't buy as much as they might hope.[110]

"I was a middle-class boy from Houston," remembers Walter Siros, who became a BT on his second sentence. "No one in my family could have imagined what it was like to be a Texas prisoner." On his first day in the fields at Eastham, Siros was dumbstruck by the conduct of the guards. "They called me 'ol' thang' and asked me how many dicks I had sucked. They said my mother was a whore with a mattress tied to her back. I had never heard that kind of stuff before." When Siros fell behind on the line, the field boss dropped cotton bolls behind him and then struck him with a rope for sloppy picking. "It was murderous out there," he says. Explains another white prisoner, "Picking cotton with that horse and rider over me with a gun and a whip was the most degrading and disrespectful experience I have had down here so far." Michael Jewell remembers, "We were treated like chattel."[111]

Still, compared to African Americans, white convicts received lighter work quotas, fewer ass whippings, lower security classifications, and higher-status inmate jobs, including BT and bookkeeper positions. "Los Chicanos were treated real bad," says Arturo Aranda, who caught the chain for the first time in 1966, but "the white bosses called them niggers their 'real slaves' . . . and beat them the old slave way." When "Freaky Willie" Redis arrived at Central he recalls that the warden advised him, "You're a nigger now, and you're gonna be a nigger every time I see you."[112]

At Retrieve, which had been worked by convicts since the 1870s and by slaves dating back to the time of Stephen Austin, Albert Sample reported that black convicts had no rights their bosses were bound to respect. When he went to work there under Boss Bands, the man laid down his rules with a "death sermon": "I'm gonna tell ya'll one time, an one time alone how I'm gonna deal," the sinewy officer growled, never raising the flattened brim of his hat high enough for the convicts to catch his eyes. "First off, if airy one uv you tries to run off, I'm gon' kill ya. If airy one uv you 'sputes my word, I'm gon' kill ya. If airy one uv you don' do lak I tell ya, I'm gon' kill ya. If you lay th' hammer down under me, I'm gon' kill ya. And if I jes take a notion to, I'm gon' kill ya." Unsatisfied with the TDC's conventional honorifics, Bands reportedly demanded that his "nigguhs" address him as "Oh Lawd," lest any of them seek mercy elsewhere. If a prisoner wanted to speak, he was to say, "Oh Lawd! Speakin ta you, Boss." If he wanted to urinate, he was to holler out, "Oh Lawd! . . . Pourin it down over heah, Boss."[113]

Although a cold January wind was blowing, Sample writes that he worked so hard that first day under Bands that his shirt was sticking to his back. Even so, he got chained to the bars all night for slacking. By summertime, the officer had his squad working with such frenzied desperation that a corn-pulling contest was arranged against four new John Deere combines. Firing shots into the dirt behind them, Bands drove his squad to victory, thus allowing the tickled prison warden, who regularly received commendations for his winning harvests, to send the machines away to "sumwhere they need 'em."

By that time, Sample had been promoted to lead row. Bands was so impressed with his subject's terror-driven speed that he nicknamed him "Race Horse," or "Racehoss," a moniker that stuck with Sample for the rest of his days. Out of earshot, the convicts bestowed their own names. The warden was "Big Devil." Bands's horse was "Ol' Satan." The prisoners didn't dare nickname Bands himself, but when he fell off his horse and clawed at his chest one day, Sample claims the squad sat down under a tree and let their boss die rather than go for help. "That muthafucka sho died hard," said one of the squad members afterward.[114]

Although the Texas control model piled up accolades in the free world, prisoners continued to describe the conditions of their confinement as akin to slavery. "When I was picking cotton under the gun . . . [and] learning those old plantation songs, I thought, 'This is really slavery,'" recalls Trevenio. Elements of modern corrections permeated the buildings, but forced field labor still predominated. "Each farm had schools," says Jon Reed, who started at Darrington in the early 1970s and today sits on death row, but they "were geared toward agriculture. . . . Everything else was secondary." Almost as important as production, argues Jewell, were the "old ways," which some officers clung to like "the rebel armies who fought so stubbornly to preserve . . . the Old South." "Prison officials had a way of life to protect," he says. Like an "old plantation master," each warden "revels in his role as lord of his manor. He has a black 'house boy' and a black 'yard boy,' just like the house niggers of Old Savannah." Another prisoner referred to Texas's penal system as "the largest slave plantation in the United States."[115]

While the metaphor was commonly invoked, the continuities between enslavement and imprisonment were often overstated. Unlike chattel slaves, prisoners were not born into bondage but had lost their freedom after being convicted of a crime, no matter how roughshod the proceedings. Although there are more persons incarcerated in Texas today than were enslaved before the Civil War (223,195 in 2005 versus 160,467 in 1860), the total draws from a much larger population base.[116] Texas has never been a prison society in the same way it was once a slave society.

The role of racism also represented another important difference. In antebellum Texas, black subjugation was relentlessly codified into law. "Negroes are, in this country, *prima facie* slaves," ruled Chief Justice Oran Roberts in 1859.[117] Afterward, racism remained potent but not so totalizing. From 1865 forward—through the black codes, Redemption, Jim Crow, and on into the present—African Americans (and to a lesser extent other nonwhites) have been disproportionately arrested, indicted, convicted, and imprisoned. Nonetheless, the majority of nonwhite Texans have always maintained their civic liberty.

Institutional culture also differed. Under slavery, men and women, young and old, endured together, suffering lifelong debasement and exploitation but also, to the extent that sales didn't interfere, partnering, raising children, and burying their dead. Prison farms, by contrast, generally housed young and middle-aged men for limited periods of time, usually apart from incarcerated women and children. This gave rise to transitory, homosocial subcultures, in some ways more akin to "total institutions" like military and migrant labor camps than slave plantations.[118]

Notwithstanding these critical differences, Texas prisons carried forth many of slavery's core practices and cultural traditions. Convicts were not off the mark when they complained that their daily grind harked back to slavery. On the farms, they worked long days in the hot sun or the biting cold without compensation. They cut cane and picked cotton on plantations that had never been touched by free labor. They toiled according to a gang-task system that, outside of southern penal plantations, had disappeared shortly after the Civil War. And they did so under the command of what prisoners called "white country boy bosses," who could beat or even kill them with impunity. If all of this added up to slavery from the perspective of convicts, some officers saw the parallels as well. "When I first took a job at Ramsey," says a former guard, among the first African Americans hired into the system, "I thought to myself, 'Man, this ain't prison. This is slavery.'"[119]

In his sweeping cross-cultural study *Slavery and Social Death,* the sociologist Orlando Patterson defines slavery as the "permanent, violent domination of natally alienated and generally dishonored persons." Convicts were juridically rather than natally alienated (though many thousands of felons tangled with the criminal justice system from adolescence until death), and they were generally deprived of their liberty for specific periods of time. Inside Texas prisons in the control years, however, no one could doubt that prisoners were violently dominated and generally dishonored. In accord with the historic legal decision *Ruffin v. Commonwealth* (1871), a Texas prisoner "not only forfeited his liberty, but all of his personal rights except those which the law in its humanity accords to him. He is for the time being a slave of the state."[120]

In the case of chattel slavery, it took a civil war to force Texas and other southern states to yield. Texas's prison plantations resisted change similarly, and it took federal intervention, at the tail end of the civil rights movement, to upend the Texas control model. The results, while nothing like the conflagration wrought by the blue and gray, proved similarly divisive—empowering to some, embittering to others, explosive all around.

# 7

## APPEAL TO JUSTICE

Old hands in the mule business say that the best way to get a mule's attention is to hit it hard, right between the eyes.

—WILLIAM WAYNE JUSTICE, FEDERAL DISTRICT JUDGE[1]

Behind three sets of double-locking doors and at the end of a long basement hallway sat the solitary cell of David Resendez Ruíz, Texas's most famous prisoner for much of the last thirty years. The occupant was the lead plaintiff in a fantastically expensive and bitterly contested lawsuit that laid waste to the TDC control model, but when I first visited him in 2002 his circumstances bore no trace of glory. His cell, sunk halfway underground, was cramped and dank. In summer, it was a steam room, in winter a walk-in refrigerator. The space provided amounted to about three airplane bathrooms, but boxes of legal documents reduced it further. Although Ruíz was sixty years old and no longer a disciplinary problem, he was allowed out of his cage only once a day. At the designated time, he stuck his thick forearms through the bars for cuffing and was led upstairs to an outdoor recreation pen, where he paced or lifted weights for an hour, before descending back to "the hole."[2]

Prison officers spoke poorly of Ruíz. The warden at the Goree farm was reluctant to let me visit him. "I don't want to give him any more attention," she explained, though she finally agreed to let me "walk by" his cell. On the way, my escort, Captain Ken Jones, a stiff-backed, broad-shouldered marine type, told me that Ruíz was a troublemaker and a whiner with a "second-rate legal mind" to boot. Throughout the system, employees and not a few prisoners agreed. Over coffee at the Café Texan in Huntsville, Jim Willett shook his head when I brought up Ruíz. "He doesn't realize, even today, what damage he's done," he said. "He's sorry. He's a sorry human being."[3]

It is no small irony that Ruíz was by then housed at the historic Goree farm, a short drive from headquarters. Rebuilt and expanded under Ellis and Beto, the main building showcases a bygone nod to rehabilitation. The dormitories and dayrooms face internal gardens. Decorative lattice-work takes the place of vertical bars. One visitor described it as "more or less like a college dormitory."[4] Since its conversion to a male facility in 1982, however, there has been noticeable tightening. Wire mesh now covers many of the windows. The gardens are off-limits. A double peri-meter fence, buttressed by coils of concertina wire, closes in the once open landscape. Living in Goree's dungeon, Ruíz was presented with the best of what he helped destroy and the worst of what he helped create.

Despite his circumstances, Ruíz remained upbeat. He cut a veteran convict profile, with slicked-back silver hair and a muscular upper body covered with roughly drawn tattoos, but he had bright eyes and was quick to laugh. Whereas many long-timers withdraw into a cara-pace, Ruíz reached out his hand and spoke warmly, like we were old friends. Although he was no longer in and out of federal courthouses, he was still a fighter. "I'm working on a case now that is going to expose all of their illegal activities," he reported. Ruíz had spent all but four-teen years of his life behind bars, but still he hurled himself against them.[5]

With Captain Jones hovering, we didn't talk long that first day. But a series of letters followed, in which Ruíz wrote about his new lawsuit and complained about the prison system's "cave man" medical care. On occasion, he enclosed a blazingly colored pencil and ink drawing, often an allegorical fantasy of sex and defiance. A year after we first met, after getting official approval as a prison system researcher, I managed to arrange a longer visit. This time, Ruíz was allowed out of his cell, and we met in an empty, sweltering visiting room, shouting through holes in the Plexiglas over the noise of an industrial fan. Although he was suffering from a variety of ailments—gallstones, cataracts, back pain, and hepatitis C—he demonstrated remarkable stamina.[6] Outfit-ted in the standard whites, with his hands cuffed before him, he sat down on a hard stool and, without water or rest for six hours, told me his life story: how he journeyed from East Austin to Eastham, how he brought a constitutional lawsuit against the most powerful prison system in the nation, how he helped dislodge Texas's traditions of plantation punishment, but how he, indirectly, helped create an equally severe and infinitely larger prison system in its place. Like so many prisoner rebels before him, David Ruíz fought the law and the law won.

## "A HARDHEADED LITTLE SON OF A BITCH"

As far back as David Ruíz can remember, he has drifted toward trouble, like a moth to flame. His parents were migrant farmworkers who tried their best to emphasize education, but David, one of the youngest of thirteen, never took to schooling. He says the Anglo teachers in Austin looked down on Mexicans and punished them for speaking Spanish. "When I got up early," he explains, "it was to rob the paperboy."[7]

After a series of arrests for shoplifting, fighting, and finally a car theft, young David got sentenced to the reformatory at the age of twelve. Skinny and scared, he had never been away from his family, and tears ran down his cheeks as the transport car pulled away. With the exception of a few months here and there, he would never regain his freedom.[8]

David's destination was Gatesville, the hilly cotton farm one hundred miles north of Austin that had served as Texas's main lockup for juveniles since 1889. State leaders had celebrated its opening as a great advance, promising "reformation of the mind" and "religious regeneration," but it didn't take long for the polish to wear. Even before construction was completed, reformatory officials were complaining that they were "overrun with colored convicts," whom they saw as incapable of reformation. The state's appropriation was always insufficient, and as more boys arrived the buildings filled beyond capacity and became filthy and infectious. Work trumped education, as the assistant superintendent made clear in his 1900 biennial report. "This year our crops have been abundant. It has been my endeavor to have boys do as much of the work about the place as possible . . . without employing more outside help than necessary."[9] Gatesville had been created to emulate New York's Elmira, but it ended up replicating Texas's prison plantations instead.

On the streets, David had heard stories of beatings, stoop labor, and sexual exploitation, and upon his arrival in 1954 Gatesville confirmed his fears. At intake, he was snickering with a boy behind him when an officer walked up and punched him in the face. "Some of the guards just enjoyed inflicting pain on kids," he remembers. "There were some good officers who would help a Latino brother out. But most of them I wouldn't trust with my cows or pigs."[10]

No doubt the officers—trained in agriculture rather than youth counseling—found young Ruíz equally exasperating. From the start, he fell in with "hard core kids" from Austin and San Antonio and imbibed a crude set of jailhouse ethics that became his lifelong creed: "Don't tattle tale. . . . Don't take any bull honk from anybody. And if you have to fight, you know, fight." Over the course of four stints at Gatesville, he escaped thirteen times—with each attempt ending in recapture and thirty to ninety days in the "bull pen." Even as a kid, remarks a friend, David was "a hardheaded little son of a bitch."[11]

After finishing a final term at Gatesville, Ruíz passed the fateful age of seventeen and thereafter tangled with a meaner breed of Texas justice. One cool night, he and four friends flipped a stolen Oldsmobile 88 on the road to Houston and soon had multiple confessions of robbery beaten out of them by the police. David got twelve years, and on February 2, 1960, at the threshold of adulthood, he was delivered to the Texas Department of Corrections.[12]

Ruíz's first stop was Huntsville, where he chummed around with other graduates of the reformatory. But after two weeks, he caught the chain down south to the Ramsey Farm for his real introduction to TDC. "They put me on No. 3 hoe," he recalls, "and, man, I didn't think I was gonna make it. I mean, it was like slaves." Ruíz was used to hard labor but not the pace and regimentation of an adult farm. "The officers were all racists," he says. "They'd call you 'meskin' and 'wetback.' " The enforcement was relentless. "They'd yell at you for talking too loud or if you stood around like you were taking a little break." For a city boy, even one who had spent thirty-nine months at Gatesville, "everything about Ramsey was a shock."

David got tight with his squad. "We all stuck together, especially the Chicanos," he says. "You get three or four of us together, and you got an army." But he clashed with the bosses and building tenders. For participating in a work strike, he got beat up and sent to the hole. When a BT stole some packets of instant coffee from a care package, Ruíz swiped a file from the tool shed and later plunged it into the man's chest and neck. On another occasion, he nearly decapitated a prisoner he believed was plotting to kill him. "I think I could have cut his head off, you know, I was in good shape," he explains with perverse pride. "But he must have seen the ax 'cause he ducked, and I hit his shoulder instead, cutting it up to here," motioning to the middle of his collar bone.

For these and other rule violations—some gravely serious, others "bullshit," as he puts it—Ruíz experienced the gamut of TDC tortures. After stabbing the BT, he was clubbed so severely that he ended up with a broken hand, two broken knees, and several fractured ribs. For lesser infractions, like "talking in the dining room" or "slow picking," he had to stand for hours on a Coke box or carry around a greased watermelon. "When they took you to [disciplinary] court, you were always guilty," he explains. "There was no innocence. The only question was how much punishment you'd get."

Ruíz did seven years on his first adult sentence. When he got out, he was even less adaptable to the free world than when he went in. In prison, he was "trained to be a criminal and to hate authority," he says. With his discharge money, he made it back to the barrio, where he hooked up with his friends and courted a woman whose snapshot had sustained him in solitary. Her parents objected, but Rose Marie and David began a passionate romance and were soon married.[13]

Ruíz had the makings of a new life for himself, but within no time, money and drink intervened, as they always did. Rose Marie got pregnant, but David couldn't find a job. "I had obligations and no kind of trade or education," he explains, "so I returned to what I knew. I picked up the gun." Within thirteen months, in July 1968, Ruíz was returned to TDC with a twenty-five year sentence.[14]

Missing the birth of his first child, Ruíz took this sentence harder than the others. Assigned to Eastham, he fell into a familiar routine— work, eat, sleep—but he also began plotting an escape worthy of Clyde Barrow, whose exploits, as depicted by Warren Beatty, had garnered ten Academy Award nominations that spring. With four friends from reform school, David made knives from bunk bed parts and had a friend on the outside send him hacksaw blades sewn into book bindings. The plan was to wait for a quiet night just before Christmas, cut through the bars in the dayroom, climb over two perimeter fences, and then steal away in a car filled with clothes, money, and guns. Like so many of David's schemes, however, nothing turned out as he had hoped. Only four of the escapees made it over both fences; the fifth fell to high-powered rifle fire from the tower. When the survivors reached a designated spot in the woods, the getaway car was nowhere to be found. "I put my trust in a man," he says, "but I was betrayed."

Their minds spinning, the four decided to split up. David raced off alone through the dark, tumbling over stones and underbrush, until he made it to the Trinity River, where he plunged into the water to throw off the search dogs. Once the chase team moved on, however, he was soaked, freezing, and lost. "A cold front had moved in, and it was about 17 degrees," he remembers. "Oh, man, it was cold."

To survive the night, David crawled into a rotting tree trunk and covered himself with dry leaves. The next day, he wandered aimlessly and might well have died on his second night out if he hadn't come face-to-face with two quail hunters and their shotguns. He asked them to let him go, but they gave him hot chocolate and a bath and then called the police.

About noon, his warden appeared, accompanied by none other than George Beto. On the ride back, "I thought [the warden] was going to kill me," Ruíz says, but Beto made him stop after a few blows.[15] Two nights in the freezing cold was punishment enough, he figured. Little did Beto know that the scraped-up, hungry, exhausted, and pathetic-looking inmate riding in the backseat would, over the next several years, help tear down much of his life's work.


Upon his return to Eastham, Ruíz spent a week in the hospital, then went to solitary, where he languished in the pitch dark for forty-five days, with bread and water his only sustenance. In the stillness, he mulled over his years behind bars and the many years that lay ahead. He thought about the rebelliousness that got him sent to reform school and about his mother, who had passed away. Most of all, he thought of his wife, Rose Marie, and their infant daughter, who he had never touched.

Both the escape and its meditative aftermath transformed Ruíz, but not into the docile inmate officials hoped for nor into a cynical con determined to do his own time. Rather, with no prospect of freedom any time soon, Ruíz decided for the first time to start fighting for principle rather than prisoner prestige. As the civil rights and antiwar movements raged on the outside, he decided to become a revolutionary.[16]

Revolution was in the air in 1968. While Ruíz had been committing armed robberies from Austin to Toledo, the Viet Cong had launched the Tet Offensive, Texas's "favorite son" Lyndon Johnson had withdrawn from the presidential race, and Martin Luther King Jr. had fallen to an assassin's bullet in Memphis, setting off riots nationwide. In August, not long after Ruíz was arrested, the Democratic National Convention degenerated into chaotic street battles, prompting Director Beto to send Chicago mayor Richard Daley a note praising him for "meeting insolent disrespect for law and order with force." A few weeks later, students rose up in Mexico City—just as they had earlier that year from Paris to Prague to Tokyo—only to be slaughtered by the hundreds in the Tlatelolco district. Bill Moyers, the Texas journalist and LBJ confidant, worried that "the country . . . [was] on the verge of some kind of national nervous breakdown."[17]

Texas managed to sidestep some of the pyrotechnics of the sixties, but the state had long figured prominently in the civil rights movement, especially in the legal arena. In 1944, after a twenty-year campaign by local and national activists, the Supreme Court invalidated Texas's white-only political primary system, thus rolling back a significant restriction on black voting rights in the South. Six years later, in *Sweatt v. Painter,* the court stepped to the brink of overturning the "separate but equal" doctrine by ordering the University of Texas law school to admit a black student—the line was actually crossed, of course, in 1954 in *Brown v. Board of Education*.[18]

As in other southern states, Texas authorities resisted and resented these federal intrusions. After *Brown,* Governor Shivers vowed "to keep the system that we know is best," declaring that "no law, no court, can wreck what God has made." When three black students tried to integrate an all-white high school south of Fort Worth, Shivers sent the Texas Rangers to stop them. However, with the exception of hard-line holdouts like Huntsville, which resisted desegregation until the bitter end, Texas surrendered somewhat more gracefully to civil rights than Alabama or Mississippi. In 1969, the legislature voted to sweep away scores of segregationist statutes that had piled up over the years.[19] For the first time since the brief, tumultuous reign of Edmund Davis, Texas's top officials, on paper at least, dedicated themselves to equality before the law.

Mexican Americans like Ruíz were legally classified as "white," but they suffered many of the same indignities as African Americans: entrenched poverty, substandard schooling, job discrimination, and mistreatment by the criminal justice system. For more than a hundred years, since the ink dried on the Treaty of Guadalupe Hidalgo, Mexicans in the United States had struggled against Anglo dominion. But in the 1960s, the movement developed a sharper edge. Students and labor organizers staged school walkouts and city council takeovers. After the

Rangers suppressed a wildcat strike against agribusiness in the Rio Grande Valley, union leaders organized a ragtag, three-hundred-mile march to Austin to demand a state minimum wage. This new generation of activists called themselves Chicanos to emphasize their indigenous rather than Hispanic heritage, and they laid claim, in quasi-nationalist terms, to all of the territories of the Southwest, which had fallen long ago to "brutal gringo invasion."[20]

As a hard-fisted convict with little faith in white man's government, Ruíz gravitated toward the more militant strains of the movement. At Eastham, he observed the Black Muslims with wary admiration, as they drilled and proselytized despite severe reprisals.[21] In his clique of Chicano toughs, there were few politicized role models. He and his compatriots fought for what they called "respect"—a street variant of the old southern honor system—but generally against other prisoners and without much attention to larger struggles going on outside.[22] But when David got out of the hole, having lost twenty pounds, he announced that he was no longer going to work like a slave. Building tenders told him they would club him all the way to the hoe line, but David went back to his cell, unscrewed the straight razor from his shaver, and cut through his Achilles tendon.[23]

Heel-stringing signaled a new moral outlook for Ruíz; rather than slashing other prisoners, he was slashing himself—and for symbolic effect. "I cut the two tendons in front and the two in back," he reports, lifting up a leg to show me the scars. No reporters or legislative investigators came calling, as they had in the 1940s, but Ruíz's protest changed the course of his life. Exempted from work because of his injuries, he bounced between medical and disciplinary facilities, descending into the bowels of TDC as never before. Along the way, he encountered a different sort of convict: bitter, vengeful, and uncompromising like himself but less reckless and more focused. They, too, saw themselves as insurgents, but they were using a new weapon, one that the state had previously used only against them: the law.

One prisoner in particular had a profound impact on David's thinking: Fred Cruz, a dogged jailhouse lawyer who had spent even more time in solitary than Ruíz. The two men had entwined histories. Cruz hailed from San Antonio and had run in Ruíz's set at reform school. Both had repeatedly lost their freedom, but as adult inmates their lives had taken different paths. Whereas Ruíz craved action and stirred up conflict, Cruz sought serenity and devoted himself to social transformation. Inspired by Martin Luther King and Malcolm X, he read avidly, kept a meticulous diary, and practiced Buddhist meditation. "Fred was a serious dude," recalls Redbird McCarter, a white lifer who knew him well in the 1960s. "Most of us convicts had tunnel vision. We focused on only one thing, ourselves. But Fred was different. He was always encouraging us to think from society's point of view. He wanted convicts to better themselves."[24]

With self-discipline and the ability to lead others, Cruz might have become a model prisoner had he enrolled in an officially sanctioned group like the Toastmasters. But Fred dedicated himself to prisoner rights rather than his own privileges and suffered mightily for it. Texas's control model had no place for legal dissidents; any civil rights complaint was regarded as a "pernicious . . . threat to . . . security," observed a TDC staff attorney.[25] So when Fred started filing federal lawsuits against the prison system in the early 1960s, his custodians tried everything to stop him: lowly work assignments, sham disciplinary cases, periodic beatings, and extended stretches in solitary. Those who aided Cruz also faced reprisals. When Redbird tried to help Cruz on a religious freedom case involving the Black Muslims, he was punished with reassignment to the number-one black hoe squad. "I was the only peckerwood there," he chortles. "The guards thought those Black Muslims were gonna tear me up, but they knew I was friends with Fred so they didn't pay me no mind."[26]

Cruz's stature grew throughout the late 1960s, especially as some of his lawsuits gained traction in federal court. Along with Allen Lamar, another writ writer, Cruz helped launch a suit against racial segregation that attracted the support of the Department of Justice's Civil Rights Division. In *Cruz v. Beto*, Fred sued for the right to collaborate with other prisoners on civil and criminal legal work. After an initial setback in district court, he took the case to the Fifth Circuit Court of Appeals and won, thus becoming a celebrity in the tanks. "Fred was an amazing guy, a great lawyer really," says William Bennett Turner, a pioneering prisoners' rights attorney. "He had to endure these awful conditions in solitary, but they could never break him."[27]

Since the courts prohibited Texas from silencing Fred, prison officials did their best to quarantine him. In November 1971, Beto ordered Cruz and other writ writers from across the system isolated at the

Wynne Farm in Huntsville. As a cover, many of them were diagnosed with schizophrenia, claims one inmate, a favorite state tactic in the Soviet Union but a new one in Texas.[28] Because David Ruíz had racked up so many disciplinary violations—for stabbings, escape, and, now, refusing to work—he, too, got transferred from Eastham to Wynne, and he landed on the same work detail, the disciplinary "eight-hoe squad." It was a field assignment that changed Ruíz's life and TDC along with it. In effect, the eight hoes would become one of the most successful prisoners' rights law firms in the country.[29]

## EIGHT HOE

At Wynne, Ruíz joined a corralled team of convict activists—chronic recalcitrants in the administration's view—who had been struggling to improve prison conditions by filing lawsuits against TDC in federal court. For the first time in his life, David applied himself to his studies. He pored over a prisoner rights litigation handbook, but he felt outclassed by his comrades. Many of the eight hoes were well educated and versed in the law. One was a bank president turned bank robber; Cruz was fond of quoting Blackstone and Montesquieu in his legal briefs. Ruíz was so embarrassed by his first effort to draft a constitutional case based on his own mistreatment that he threw it away without showing anyone. "I wanted to fight with my mind," David explains, but "I didn't know the law, and I didn't really even have a command of the language." As guards and building tenders retaliated against the eight hoes with periodic beatings and petty disciplinary write-ups that effectively pushed back parole dates, Ruíz says he considered giving up writs and getting back into the mix, where at least the dangers were accompanied by visceral pleasures.[30]

Yet Ruíz quit thinking that way when he met one of the few women who ever got past the visiting room at Wynne, Frances Freeman Jalet. A New York attorney just as headstrong as her clients, Jalet became a kind of muse and motivator to the eight hoes. Already in her fifties, she had followed a long, winding road to the TDC. She had degrees from Radcliffe and Columbia but had spent most of her adulthood as a housewife in Darien, Connecticut—a "cozy enclave of Republicans and anti-Semites," as her daughter Vanessa described it, hardly a breeding ground for radicals. After she and her husband divorced in 1957, Jalet returned to the law, but as a single mother with five children in tow she had a rough go of it. She tried opening a private practice but attracted few clients, then followed tedious research jobs to Lincoln, Nebraska, and Ithaca, New York. Wherever she landed, she excelled, but only through tireless effort. Vanessa remembers that her mother got up every morning at six and continued working long after the children went to bed. Even now, she tends to picture her mother bent over a rolltop desk, concentrating on a tall stack of papers, twisting a lock from her silvery mane around her left index finger. "She had more energy than anyone I've ever met."[31]

Finally, when the last daughter left the nest in 1967, Vanessa explains, her "mother followed her star." Interested in providing legal assistance to low-income defendants, who had only recently won the right to counsel in the landmark *Gideon v. Wainwright* decision, Frances applied for and won a national fellowship sponsored by the Office of Economic Opportunity, an LBJ Great Society program. After training in antipoverty law at the University of Pennsylvania, she had her pick of two legal aid assignments, one in New Mexico and the other in Texas. Fatefully, she chose the latter, and in late August Frances packed her belongings into her car and set out across the country. For the first time in thirty years she was alone. The freedom was exhilarating.[32]

At the Legal Aid and Defender Society in Austin, Frances plunged into a thicket of legal disputes over evictions, child custody, divorce, and debts. A local reporter, who found her an unusually well-bred crusader for social equality, called her Austin's "Portia of the Poor." In truth, Frances had always been idealistic and a bit of an insurgent. As a child, she had fearlessly stood up to her dictatorial father, a quality he came to admire. "She disliked taking orders, and she never took no for an answer herself," Vanessa reports. "She was a rebel with a patrician accent."[33]

What Frances lacked was an all-consuming cause, and in Texas she found one. One day in early October 1967, she opened a letter from a prisoner who had seen her profile in the newspaper and wanted to request outside legal assistance. His name was Fred Cruz. Frances had never been to a prison, and she knew little about prison law. But something about Fred's letter caught her eye.[34]

Despite a full plate of responsibilities at Legal Aid, Frances arranged to take a day off and drive 170 miles to the Ellis Unit, near Huntsville, where Cruz was then held before getting transferred to Wynne. Her

first stop was to meet Director Beto, who had a knack for charming
first-time visitors to TDC. He had just returned from deer hunting, a
favorite pastime, and was in a buoyant mood. Still wearing his hunting
garb, he gave Frances an enthusiastic overview of his orderly, efficient
prison domain and made a favorable impression. But Jalet's visit with
Cruz rattled her. The prisoner spoke so softly she had a hard time making out his words, but he related events of astonishing severity: blackjack
beatings by building tenders, arbitrary disciplinary hearings followed
by sadistic sanctions, retaliation against prisoners for doing legal work,
and constant racial taunting by guards. Always a bit claustrophobic
since a near-drowning incident as a child, Frances found Cruz's depictions of pitch-black solitary especially affecting. She had been warned
by Beto to watch out for convict storytelling, but she believed Cruz's
stories.[35]

Riveted by his descriptions of injustice and institutional lawlessness,
Frances was also fascinated by Fred as a person. Although he had grown
up on San Antonio's meanest streets, he made warm eye contact and
spoke with a hint of southern charm. His calm devotion to principle
and meditation made him seem more like a spiritual guide than a re-
cidivist drug addict. For his part, Fred found Jalet equally captivating. In
almost every way, she was his opposite. She was twenty-nine years older,
an Anglo with an East Coast pedigree, refined and politically committed. In the stilted prose of his diary, he noted only that Ms. Jalet "seems
to have a vast resource of understanding and compassion for the plight
of man."[36] Although it would be a long time before either would admit
it, Frances and Fred were smitten.

Over the next few months, as Jalet visited Cruz and other prisoners
dozens of times, her relationship with Beto deteriorated. At first, the
director hoped to convert Jalet into an advocate, as he had other northern liberals.[37] But as her criticisms became more vitriolic—she accused
Beto of "obscuring the truth from interested eyes" and compared the
Ellis Unit to Auschwitz—and as the quality of her clients' legal work
improved, he changed tactics. In March 1968, he tried to have her disciplined for practicing law before passing the Texas bar and then worked
his political connections to have her discharged from Legal Aid. Jalet
found another job at a Houston law clinic and dug in her heels. "My
mother prayed every night before she went to bed. She believed in
turning the other cheek," explains Vanessa. "She did not hate easily,
but I know that she hated George Beto."[38]

At various points, Beto the master bureaucrat thought he had Jalet licked. Twice, he banned her from the prison system, and when she used court orders to wriggle back in, he arranged for three trusties to sue her in federal court, claiming that she was inciting revolutionary violence and thus putting their lives in danger. When judges got around to examining the evidence, however, the director was soundly defeated. Not only were TDC's restrictions on prisoner legal work unconstitutional, a federal appellate court ruled, but Dr. Beto was personally liable for ten thousand dollars in attorney's fees. "The turning point for Beto was when he had to pay all of that money out of his own pocket to Frances Jalet," recalls Jack Kyle. "After that, Beto quit thinking about his future at TDC."[39] In early 1972, he announced his resignation.

When she wasn't battling Beto, Jalet devoted most of her attention to helping Fred Cruz. She became his personal attorney and confidante, helping him craft numerous civil suits and advise other eight hoes. Prison records show that between 1967 and 1970, she visited him seventy separate times. In struggle they formed a tight bond, and when Fred finally made parole in March 1972, they quietly traveled across the border and were married in Mexico. Vanessa describes the news as "a jolt to the family."[40]

While Cruz had the greatest impact on Jalet's life—and not always for the better once he went back to heroin—it was his apprentice who imprinted his name on TDC. At first, David Ruíz was a bit skeptical of "Saint Frances"—Anglo attorneys had never done him much good in the past—but as she stayed true in the face of harassment, he came to idolize her. "Mrs. Cruz is the one who motivated me most," Ruíz recalls, using her married name. "She was always doing little things for us. . . . I had a lot of respect for her. She was like a big sister or a second mom."

With Frances's encouragement, Ruíz redoubled his legal research and began drafting an ambitious case that would combine multiple constitutional and civil rights violations into one. Through the fall and winter of 1971 and 1972, Ruíz worked feverishly. After ten hours digging ditches in the fields, most convicts looked forward to dominoes or movies in the dayroom, but Ruíz and his fellow eight hoes gathered up their legal materials and headed straight to the writ room, a windowless storage area that had been converted into a woefully understocked law library. After the final count, most of the writ writers kept working alone in their cells, sometimes until morning. "There was no useless talk, no yelling in our cell block," Ruíz recalls. "We were all working on something, and we all wanted to win."[41]

Because David did not have much background in case law, Frances urged him to stick to his own story, which, she believed, exemplified most of the illegal practices that would convince federal courts to act. The result was a legal autobiography of torment. Ruíz recalled that he was once clubbed so severely by BTs that he suffered chronic headaches. He explained how, following a roughshod disciplinary hearing, he was confined naked in a dark, freezing solitary cell for weeks on end. Desperate for a transfer to a hospital unit, Ruíz described sharpening his shirt buttons and slicing open blood vessels in his forearms, then getting stitched up without anesthetic and thrown back in the hole. Most sensationally, Ruíz charged that Carl "Beartracks" McAdams, a legendary warden who had ruled at Ramsey, Eastham, and Wynne, had threatened him with death if he didn't sign a letter discharging Jalet as his attorney. He took the threats seriously, he wrote, because he had seen Beartracks's henchmen murder other inmates with impunity.

Altogether, Ruíz's ordeal touched on myriad legal issues, both statutory and constitutional: racial segregation, due process, access to the courts, right to counsel, negligent medical care, and cruel and unusual punishment. Ruíz acknowledged that he was a prisoner with limited legal rights, but he insisted that Texas imprisonment went far "beyond constitutional sanction." Although built around the story of one individual, Ruíz's writ constituted a searing indictment of TDC operations from top to bottom.[42]

In an earlier era, such a lawsuit would have landed straight in the courthouse rubbish bin. For most of American history, courts adhered to the "hands-off" doctrine, allowing prison authorities to run their facilities as they saw fit. State facilities, in particular, lay beyond the reach of the federal courts, based on federalist principles reinforced during the retreat from Reconstruction.[43] In isolated instances, federal judges had broken precedent and intervened in postconviction practices. In *Johnson v. Dye* (1949), for example, the Third Circuit Court of Appeals held that conditions on Georgia's chain gangs were so "cruel, barbaric, and inhuman" that an escapee in Pennsylvania should be released rather than extradited. The case was reversed on appeal, however, thus reestablishing the standard of judicial restraint. As late as 1956, the Seventh Circuit rejected a prisoner's appeal in the starkest terms: "The Government of the United States is not concerned with, nor has it power to control or regulate the internal discipline of the penal institutions of its constituent states."[44]

Although buttressed by precedent, the hands-off doctrine began to crumble under the leadership of Earl Warren, whom President Eisenhower plucked from California and made chief justice of the Supreme Court in 1953. Although the first Republican president since the Great Depression hoped his appointee would nudge the court rightward, the opposite occurred. Building on the pragmatic progressivism that had characterized his governorship, Warren—along with allies on the bench, the bar, and the streets—charted a new direction in federal jurisprudence, expanding the reach of the Constitution and reanimating civil rights statutes that had lain fallow since the aftermath of the Civil War. In what liberals took as high praise, Eisenhower later regretted that appointing Warren was "the biggest damn-fool mistake I ever made."[45]

Even before Warren's ascension, the Supreme Court had grown increasingly frustrated with southern criminal justice and voting practices. In addition to the Texas white-only primary case, the court made a series of rulings in the 1930s and 1940s to curtail jury discrimination, police torture, and lynching-influenced trials. These cases aspired to blunt the excesses of southern justice, but the Warren Court went much further, ultimately seeking to destroy Jim Crow "root and branch" and challenging many of the basic practices of government nationwide. "For the first time in American history," argues Harvard law professor Morton Horwitz, "the Supreme Court demonstrated its concern and support for the weak and the powerless, the marginal and the socially scorned."[46]

Because of its moral clarity and expansive scope, the *Brown* case is the Warren Court's most famous decision. But throughout the 1950s and 1960s, many of its criminal justice rulings were comparably ambitious and, in the long run, more contentious. In *Hernandez v. Texas* (1954), the chief justice, writing for the majority, extended Fourteenth Amendment protections against race discrimination to "persons of Mexican descent" and placed new restrictions on racial bias in jury selection, an issue that remains unresolved to the present. In *Monroe v. Pape* (1961), a warrantless search and interrogation case, the court held that citizens can sue state officials for civil rights violations committed "under color of law" even if those violations are not expressly sanctioned by statute; what matters is conduct not code.[47] Reinforced in landmark decisions like *Mapp v. Ohio* (1961), *Gideon v. Wainwright* (1963), and *Miranda v. Arizona* (1966) were fundamental rights that many Americans take for granted: the freedom from arbitrary arrest, search, and coercive interrogation; the right to privacy, due process, and to be represented by counsel in criminal proceedings, regardless of one's ability to pay.[48] Many of these civil protections were present in the Bill of Rights, but until civil rights protesters, joined in no small part by aggrieved criminals and convicts, approached the federal bench and gained a hearing, they had not always applied to the states and had not protected equally.[49]

Because so many of these decisions dusted off statutes and constitutional doctrines crafted in the aftermath of slavery, historians sometimes refer to the modern civil rights movement as America's Second Reconstruction. In 1964, it arrived at the jailhouse door. The pivotal case pitted one of the country's most entrenched prison regimes, Illinois's Stateville, which operated with the same authoritarianism as Texas's control model, against a fast-growing inmate group that corrections officials from coast to coast regarded as a dire threat to security: the Nation of Islam, or the Black Muslims. At Stateville, which Joseph Ragen, a close friend and mentor of Beto's, had ruled with an iron fist for a quarter of a century, a young prisoner named Thomas X Cooper had been locked up in solitary for years, denied access to the Koran. With the help of the *Nation* and the ACLU, he filed a religious freedom complaint and, to almost everyone's astonishment, he triumphed at the top of the judiciary. Ragen warned that "any concession is a step toward chaos." But the Warren Court in *Cooper v. Pate* (1964) decided that the wall that had grown up between prisoners and the Constitution had stood long enough. As Justice Byron White later commented, "There is no iron curtain drawn between the Constitution and the prisons of this country."[50]

Before *Cooper*, most prisoners had approached federal courts by filing writs of habeas corpus, the venerable common-law protection against arbitrary imprisonment that predates even the Magna Carta. This ancient legal procedure gave jailhouse lawyers in Texas their name—"writ writers"—but because habeas petitions generally required a prisoner to exhaust all state remedies before turning to the federal courts, they rarely resulted in redress. Starting in the 1960s, however, prisoners increasingly turned to a provision of the 1871 Civil Rights Act that allowed citizens to sue the states in federal court for violations of their constitutional rights. The provision, codified as section 1983, had gone unused by detainees for most of a century, but after its revitalization by *Monroe v. Pape*, it became the principal gateway to the federal bench for state prisoners. With the help of civil rights standard-bearers like the NAACP and the ACLU, section 1983 litigation exploded in the late 1960s.[51] In 1966, only 218 inmates filed civil rights lawsuits in federal court against their keepers. By 1972, the yearly total surpassed 3,000; by 1984, it exceeded 18,000.[52] Although neglected by most historians, prisons were fast becoming the new frontier of the civil rights movement.

Although prisoners' rights lawsuits first gained traction in the North, they had a greater impact in the South. The landmark southern case, which involved the complete reconstruction of a state prison system, concerned Arkansas's Cummins farm, a sixteen-thousand-acre cotton plantation not unlike those in Texas, though without the benefit of the Ellis-Beto reforms. At Cummins, convicts were crowded into fetid, perilous barracks at night and worked to exhaustion by day under the watch of convict trusties, who, even more so than Texas's building tenders, beat, raped, or even killed "rankers" with impunity. Federal judges all the way up the line were aghast. "For the ordinary convict," wrote the first trial judge, "a sentence to the Arkansas Penitentiary amounts to banishment from civilized society to a dark and evil world." In *Holt v. Sarver* (1970), he ruled that the state's entire penal system dispensed "cruel and unusual punishment," and he began devising remedies that would require comprehensive reorganization.[53]

Nothing of the sort had ever been attempted by a federal judge before, but this far-reaching style of "institutional reform litigation," based on the Eighth and Fourteenth Amendments and crafted through section 1983, soon became a trend. Other judges ruled prison systems unconstitutional in Mississippi, Oklahoma, Florida, Louisiana, and Alabama, and before long the process broke out of Dixie.[54] A century after the founding of the National Prison Association and half a century after the demise of convict leasing, American prisons were once again in for an overhaul, this time at the hands of the federal judiciary rather than the executive agencies of the many states. The prisoners' rights revolution had begun.

• • •

The goal of David Ruíz and his counselor, Frances Jalet, was to do to Texas what *Holt* had done in Arkansas. The critical difference was that prisons in Arkansas were almost universally regarded as abominations. They provided virtually no education or medical care and were so understaffed that trusties actually carried shotguns and manned the pickets. By contrast, Texas's prisons were promoted as among the "best in the world." In 1970, a respected federal judge in Houston dismissed one of Fred Cruz's complaints, noting that "the Texas Department of Corrections is an outstanding institution in every respect. The court is further convinced that Dr. George J. Beto, Director, is a fair, kind and just man and an excellent administrator."[55] To succeed, Ruíz and his allies would have to turn this view on its head.

To increase Ruíz's chances, Jalet advised him to focus largely on Eastham, which lay in the federal judiciary's Eastern District of Texas. She had heard good things about the new judge presiding at Tyler, the auspiciously named William Wayne Justice. A homegrown Texas populist with a quick wit and ferocious work ethic, Justice had been nominated by Texas's most liberal U.S. senator, Ralph Yarborough, and was one of Lyndon Johnson's last judicial appointees. From the start, says one admirer, "he embraced the struggles of ordinary people to bring life to the law." In one of his first cases, he ruled that Tyler Junior College had to admit qualified male applicants no matter how long their hair—a decision that so rankled the conservative town, he remembers, that "it was as if I had gotten out in the middle of the public square and announced that I was a communist . . . or in favor of peddling dope." Soon after, he vexed Tyler's cultural guardians in a desegregation case, in which he ordered Robert E. Lee High School not only to bus in black students but to take down the Rebel flag and quit playing "Dixie" at sporting events—no small matter in a state where, as John Steinbeck once observed, "football games have the glory and the despair of war." In no time, Justice became a pariah among Tyler whites; hundreds signed a petition calling for his impeachment.[56] Although he had made no prison rulings, he seemed just the sort of judge that Frances Jalet and her clients had been waiting for.

Although Justice, in his previous career as a defense attorney and prosecutor, had both delivered defendants from prison and sent them there, he admits that until he became a judge he "wasn't particularly concerned" about prison conditions. "My attitude toward TDC at that time was probably similar to that of most Texans," he noted later in a speech at Stanford. "I thought that the system was efficient." But this started to change when his court began receiving what he described as "bushel baskets of letters from prisoners." Reading through them, Justice started to suspect that more was going on at TDC than met the eye. Accordingly, he directed his two law clerks to keep an eye out for a case that addressed major legal issues. "I decided that I'd have a little test case," the judge remembers. "I wanted to find out if there was any substance to what [the prisoners] were saying."[57]

Ruíz had been writing up just such a case, but despite the Fifth Circuit's protective order, getting it outside the fence was no easy task. To file, Ruíz needed to get his suit notarized, but the designated notary was one of his named defendants, Billy McMillan, a stiff-necked TDC loyalist. According to Ruíz, Major McMillan read only the first page of his complaint before looking up. "I'm gonna tell you what I think of prisoners' rights," he said calmly. Then he tore the hand-printed lawsuit into eight pieces and dropped it at David's feet. Minutes later, BTs escorted Ruíz to solitary, where he spent twenty-one days in the dark, subsisting on the usual bread and water.[58]

During the winter and spring, David rewrote and revised, working secretly in his cell and hiding the case amid reams of legal papers. Finally, in late June 1972, he got the second petition notarized without incident during one of Jalet's attorney visits and entrusted it to her for mailing. That night, alone in his quiet cell, he lay back on his bunk and let himself relax for the first time in months. Despite a lifetime of bad luck and poor choices, he maintained exceptional self-confidence. He saw himself as a Chicano warrior, and even though he had lost most of his battles, he imagined himself winning this one. Yet not even in David's grandest dreams did he envision the journey his fifteen-page writ was about to take.[59]

From the disciplinary block at Wynne, Ruíz's document traveled first to Judge Justice's courthouse in Tyler, where a clerk stamped it June 26, civil action 5523, and filed it away. At the time, Justice's docket was one of the busiest in the nation. In addition to the standard load of criminal and civil proceedings, the judge was managing the school integration case, the statewide reapportionment of legislative districts, and a class-action lawsuit against the Texas Youth Commission, which had scarcely improved since Ruíz's days at Gatesville. Already up to his receding hairline in work, Justice was in no hurry to take on TDC, one of the most powerful and respected agencies in the state. Nevertheless, the judge and his clerks selected eight illustrative prisoner complaints—with Ruíz's headlining—and sent them to the New York offices of the NAACP's storied Legal Defense Fund to solicit representation for the indigent plaintiffs.[60]

The "first-class lawyer" Justice hoped would take the case was William Bennett Turner, a premier expert in prison law whom Justice had met at a symposium in Dallas. Turner was no longer in New York, so Ruíz's writ and its companions flew from New York to San Francisco, where Turner had opened an LDF branch office, and then across two oceans to a spare, concrete-block hotel room in Kathmandu, where the attorney was on holiday.[61]

Turner says that a wave of disquiet washed over him as he read through Justice's packet. He was unquestionably the right man for the job; he knew prison law backwards and forwards and had already worked with Jalet on other Texas cases. But Turner was also restless. He didn't like a case or even a girlfriend that hung around too long, and he was itching to get into other lines of litigation. He was born in Fort Worth but had gladly left Texas behind—for a middle-class upbringing in Saginaw, Michigan, for college at Northwestern and law school at Harvard—and he didn't relish returning. Civil rights was a passion, but he wasn't sure he was up for a protracted lawsuit against TDC. In the Arkansas case, which Turner had helped formulate, a reform-minded prison administration had secretly welcomed litigation as a way to pry resources out of the legislature.[62] From Beto's bare-knuckled tactics against Jalet and the eight-hoe squad, however, Turner knew Texas would fight against federal intervention like it had during the Civil War. The more he thought about it, the more he wanted to say no. But respected federal judges are hard to turn down, and Turner reluctantly said yes.

Once he returned to the United States, Turner filed an amended lawsuit under section 1983 that extended the case from Eastham to all fourteen TDC units and from a handful of plaintiffs to every prisoner in the system. He agreed to forgo any monetary damages, which allowed Justice to try the case alone, without a jury. In this amended form, Ruíz's civil action 5523 became known as *Ruiz v. Estelle,* with Ward Jim Estelle, Beto's handpicked successor as TDC director, standing as the named defendant.[63]

Judge Justice then went further by asking the Department of Justice's

Civil Rights Division to join the case as a "friend of the court," or amicus curiae. Ruíz's original complaint thus traveled to Washington, where it was examined by a group of eager young lawyers who were already investigating TDC as part of the racial discrimination case *Lamar v. Coffield*, which had been initiated by another writ writer. After conducting its own fact-finding, the Justice Department requested to expand its role to full partner, or "plaintiff intervenor," a request Judge Justice granted in December 1974. In no time, FBI agents were poking around Texas prisons looking for evidence to corroborate the writ writers' charges.[64] What had started out as a roughly drawn petition by a repeat armed robber was now a class-action lawsuit backed by the virtually limitless resources of the federal government.

## "GET YOUR GUNS"

Once Bill Turner and the Justice Department got involved, Judge Justice recalls, "it is fair to say that the State of Texas began to raise hell." Director Estelle, an impeccably dressed organization man, had started out in corrections under Richard McGee and had once extolled the virtues of treatment over retribution. But he was also a lifelong prison insider, the son of a San Quentin screw and a devoted proselyte of the Texas control model. "I don't think I was brought in here to revolutionize or dramatically change a system that had already some proven success," Estelle told a newspaper reporter. Come what may, he was not about to let "pathologically maladapted inmates" tear down what his predecessors had so painstakingly built. In most states, administrators struck a rather cooperative posture when confronted with federal litigation. Not Texas. Estelle's attitude, says a Huntsville attorney, was, "Fuck you, go get your guns, and let's fight."[65]

Insecure about his outsider status—he joked that he was TDC's "carpetbagger" director—and with a convert's zeal, Estelle was even more uncompromising than Beto. Two months after taking office in September 1972, he broke up the eight-hoe squad, which had produced synergy rather than surrender, but in every other way his administration kept up the pressure on the writ writers.[66] Ruíz was transferred to the Ramsey Farm, where he was beaten and maced in solitary, sent to the fields with a cast on his leg, subjected to digital rectal probes every time he visited the writ room, and stripped of his good time just before a parole hearing.[67]

In its public pronouncements and legal filings, TDC was equally combative. Estelle's duty was to defend "the finest large Department of Corrections in America" against "institutional anarchy and . . . community terror," he told a gathering of criminal justice professionals. The strategy was pure Texan—defend the Alamo at all costs—and a succession of state attorneys general, who represented TDC in court, played along. Over six years of pretrial wrangling, they did everything they could think of to derail the case. They sought to ban FBI investigators from TDC facilities, then tried to have the Justice Department removed as a plaintiff. They demanded a change of venue, hoping to displace Judge Justice, and sought to discredit "lying convicts." Amid a flurry of briefs and counterbriefs, Texas did manage at one point to elicit a spirited defense from Supreme Court Justice William Rehnquist, who in those days still voted in the minority.[68] But when the pretrial rulings came down, the state lost in every forum. Delay, admit nothing, fight everything—this constituted the whole of TDC's playbook, but none of it was enough to hold off *Ruiz*.

As TDC battened down the hatches, the plaintiffs were assembling a gargantuan case. Attorneys and federal investigators fanned out to collect hundreds of depositions and official documents. Frances Jalet Cruz turned over her materials, as did a growing army of writ writers scattered across the system. "We started out under President Nixon, but we never had any budget problems," remembers Patricia Gail Littlefield, one of the Justice Department lawyers. In order to prove systematic unconstitutionality, Littlefield says they put up a wall chart divided by unit and violation. "We wanted every issue for every prison," she explains. "It was one of the biggest cases that ever went to trial."[69]

In preparing for battle, the rival sides developed diametrically opposed visions of the case. They disagreed about principles of law: What, precisely, constitutes "cruel and unusual punishment" and "due process," as guaranteed by the Eighth and Fourteenth Amendments, and just how far should federal courts intrude into the traditional domain of states? They differed equally about the purpose of prisons: Should they stress deterrence, security, and hard work, as Texas's did, or should they emphasize rehabilitation—perhaps giving way, over time, to alternative institutions "more consistent with . . . the ideals of civilized society," as Justice once suggested?[70]

From thousands of pieces of contested evidence, each side conjured its own penal system. After an extended tour, an expert witness for the state pronounced TDC "superior to any other state system," while an expert for the plaintiffs, after taking the same tour, recoiled at what he called "the best example of slavery remaining in the country."[71] More than any other case, *Ruiz* brought into direct conflict two competing traditions of American discipline—reformatory versus plantation justice—with both sides determined to fight to the last strike of the gavel.

On October 2, 1978, more than a decade after Ruíz's vow to become a revolutionary, his writ finally got its day in court. Because Judge Justice had granted the state's request for a change of venue—and then, to TDC's horror, followed the case—the proceedings took place in Houston's downtown federal building, a white concrete monolith with cubic windows. In the shaded entryway, a phalanx of protesters greeted the attorneys as they hustled inside. "W. J. Estelle Is a Slave Master," "Prisons Are Concentration Camps," announced their signs. At nine o'clock, a heavy brass knocker sounded in the spacious courtroom, signaling the audience—a full house—to rise.[72] After the clerk's proclamation, Justice entered, fully robed, and took his commánding seat. *Ruiz v. Estelle,* the most wide-ranging prisoners' rights trial in American history, was under way.

David Ruíz, decked out in a wide-lapelled, three-piece suit, which he wore cholo style, buttoned up without a tie, sat attentively at the plaintiff's table, along with two other convicts.[73] They would be joined in the coming weeks by a succession of other inmate witnesses, whom TDC transported to court in shackles, as well as by ex-cons who made their way to Houston on their own. According to Littlefield, felons were notorious for missing court dates, but in this case all but one of forty ex-prisoner witnesses showed up as requested, eager to testify.[74] Having lived under the control model—a system built on inmate silence—they were ready to talk back.

Within the confines of TDC, convicts not directly involved with the lawsuit were determined to be heard as well. On the first day of the trial, prisoners at Ellis refused to work. Hundreds of them gathered on the back slab and, although authorities cut off water and food, they refused to budge; when news helicopters passed over, they spelled out "NO FOOD" with black socks. Soon after, the bucking spread to Darrington, Ramsey, Clemens, Coffield, and Eastham. As if to confirm all of Jim Estelle's fears, TDC was wracked during the first two weeks of the trial by the most stubborn convict protests since the 1920s. They abated only when Judge Justice issued a statement urging prisoners to cooperate and allow their advocates to speak for them in court.[75]

Prisoners had the most at stake—they had suffered mightily to sustain the case and remained at the mercy of TDC regardless of the outcome—but for most of the attorneys, the trial would similarly mark a defining moment of their lives. Bill Turner, who acted as "captain of the ship" in terms of strategy, admits he felt a bit trapped by the lawsuit's magnitude, but for the other plaintiff lawyers—seven in all—*Ruiz* was not just a case but a cause. David Vanderhoof, lead counsel for the Justice Department, regarded it as the most important civil rights suit in the country. Littlefield and Donna Brorby, who, like women activists in the 1920s, avoided the limelight but did much of the heavy lifting, saw the lawsuit as a "crusade for right." "We were totally committed," says Brorby. "It was like David versus Goliath."[76]

It fell to Ed Idar, Texas's assistant attorney general, to play the unlikely role of Goliath. A Tejano born and raised along the Rio Grande, Idar had once worked for the Mexican American Legal Defense and Educational Fund, but as the Chicano movement radicalized, he left public-interest law and went to work for the state.[77] He had little firsthand knowledge of the prison system, but he came to believe fervently—"blindly," his detractors say—in TDC's version of events. "I am very concerned that [this] highly disciplined, well-organized prison system may yet be torn wide open by well-meaning people who, as the good Lord said, know not what they are doing," he admonished. In court, he put on a pugnacious performance—"Ed was a bulldog," says Littlefield; "completely humorless," chides Justice—but from the first day to the last, he had difficulty making his punches connect.[78]

Although judges generally present themselves as disinterested arbiters, William Justice had a stake in *Ruíz v. Estelle* as well; to no small extent, he had created it. In the style of a judicial activist, he had selected the original plaintiffs, recruited the attorneys, provided them resources by involving the feds, and set the parameters of discovery.[79] It was Justice who had set this "little case" in motion. Now he was going to find out where it went.

• • •

As lead counsel for the named plaintiffs, Turner rose to give the first opening argument. He was a master of the courtroom, colleagues say, and with precision and confidence he outlined the main factual and legal issues of the case. He promised to provide overwhelming evidence of unconstitutionality in five main areas: physical safety, living conditions, medical care, disciplinary procedures, and access to the courts. "While corrections in Texas may be cheap," he concluded, "the System exacts intolerable costs to the human rights of the citizens in its custody."[80]

David Vanderhoof, for the feds, followed up with a bit more drama. Texas's may be the biggest prison system in the nation, he contended, but it is really the "leader in overcrowding . . . [and] constitutional deprivation." More than fifty years ago, he intoned, producing a tattered copy of the CPPL's 1924 *Texas Prison Survey,* the citizens of Texas carefully examined their penal system and suggested sensible remedies. At last, it was time to heed their wisdom.[81]

Ed Idar spoke for the defense, but he was already having a rough morning. After dodging the protesters outside, he had started off by pleading yet again to delay the case, provoking derision from the judge. As the trial progressed, he hardly fared better. The plaintiffs produced scores of witnesses, some of them convicts but many of them TDC employees and nationally renowned experts, but Idar responded mainly by objecting at every turn—usually unsuccessfully. On cross-examination, he was plodding but artless, often making witnesses repeat their testimony word for word. Is this "some kind of filibuster?" Justice broke in at one point. The plaintiffs found it maddening—"They took four times as long on cross-ex as we did on direct," grouses Turner—but ultimately useful. Idar and his deputies asked so many questions that new violations often came to light. "We got as much positive material from their case as we did from ours," sniggers Littlefield.[82] In the topsy-turvy world of Justice's courtroom, the Texas Department of Corrections was suddenly reliving the experience of many of its inmates: reluctant to go to trial, probably guilty as charged, and ineffectively represented by counsel.

Due partly to Idar's laborious style and partly to the case's intrinsic complexity, the trial moved forward at an agonizing creep. But from time to time, particularly unsettling testimony riveted the courtroom. A recent escapee from Eastham described how he had quickly surrendered after being shot in the groin but how the pursuing officers nonetheless thrashed him with a bullwhip and made him fight the dogs. It was the "worst case of brutality I have ever seen," the doctor told the court. Had he seen other incidents of abuse? the plaintiffs asked. "Hundreds," he replied.[83]

Abuses by building tenders figured prominently. A BT named Butch Ainsworth, for instance, whom a former warden described as the most violent inmate he had ever known, decided after sniffing paint thinner one day to "turn out," or punk, a new inmate on the wing. When the young man resisted, an eyewitness testified, Butch and another trusty beat him up and made him stand in a toilet while zapping him with the exposed ends of an extension cord. Then they raped him and stole his commissary goods.[84]

Since the 1870s, the hospital at Huntsville had offered respite from the terrors and toil of regular prison life, but according to patients, physicians, and outside experts, the modern facility provided no such sanctuary.[85] Despite TDC's spic-and-span reputation, the medical facility was "woefully inadequate," testified a specialist in hospital accreditation, "crowded, dirty . . . just a very, very shoddy situation." If the hygiene was wanting, however, the actual treatment, much of it administered by poorly trained med techs and convict orderlies, was worse. In one instance, a newly hired doctor fished around in a patient's abdominal cavity for two hours looking for the appendix before an assistant called for outside help. Medical personnel testified that prison officials were more interested in ferreting out "malingerers" than dispensing quality medical care, an age-old complaint. In one case, a prisoner was forced to drag himself around with his hands for several weeks because officers thought he was faking paralysis. In another, a guard yanked a urine catheter out of a man's penis after he got up without permission to empty his waste bag.[86]

Neglect at the infirmary also led to depredations by inmates. A young man named Euris Francis, for example, almost died when he lost both arms in a threshing machine, which he had been ordered to use without proper safety equipment. At the hospital, he underwent emergency surgery and had his amputations bandaged. He was then left alone on the ward, where another patient took advantage of his helplessness and raped him. "The man without the arms was crying," testified a witness.[87]

The daily recitation of horrors notwithstanding, Judge Justice says that one of the most sensational episodes took place outside the trial. In his chambers one day, he got a call from Houston's flamboyant district attorney Johnny Holmes, who announced that David Ruíz was being indicted for raping an inmate at the county jail. The plaintiff attorneys were instantly suspicious. The sheriff in charge of the jail was Jack Heard, a TDC veteran who had helped apprehend Ruíz after his 1968 escape; the only outside witness was a former TDC building tender. Not until the alleged victim testified at a special hearing, however, could they be sure of Ruíz's innocence. Everyone in the court braced themselves as the young man took the stand. He spoke in Spanish, but once the translation came through the prosecutor's case collapsed. The witness denied being raped and said he had agreed to the story only to wiggle out of a murder rap. Ruíz and his lawyers were overjoyed, but Justice was disgusted. Over the summer, he arranged for every inmate witness to have the option of transferring to a federal prison.[88] What little faith Justice had in Idar and his client was fast evaporating.

During the trial itself, Justice says the most captivating moment was Director Estelle's appearance. A handsome, well-spoken man, Estelle tried, against the odds, to strike a convivial tone. "He was kind of slick," recollects Littlefield. "He wouldn't just say 'yes.' He would say, 'You bet.'" Bill Turner tried to keep the exchange civil, but he wove facts around Estelle like a spider wrapping up its prey. In their pretrial research, the plaintiffs had discovered that the director himself had regularly highlighted the same deficiencies now being pursued in court. Texas's staff-to-inmate ratio—the lowest in the nation—was "extremely dangerous," he had told the legislature in requesting additional funding. The crowding situation was "severe," the medical facilities inadequate, the assault rate rising "dramatically." In its legal filings, TDC had steadfastly denied problems in all of these areas, but Estelle now had to eat his words, bite by distasteful bite. "Estelle just told the truth," Justice states, but "the truth was devastating. . . . It was one of the best cross-examinations I'd ever heard. Turner nailed him to the cross."[89]

Everyone but the named plaintiffs, who were headed back to prison, were relieved to see the trial come to an end, almost a full year after it started. "The trial of this action lasted longer than any prison case—and perhaps any civil rights case—in the history of American jurisprudence," Justice noted. There were 349 witnesses who testified and 1,530 exhibits submitted. Afterward, attorneys from both sides drafted voluminous posttrial briefs, while Justice and his five clerks got to work on the opinion.[90] All of this took another year, but when the ruling came down, in December 1980, it was what everyone expected: a stinging rebuke to the state.

To a remarkable extent, Justice accepted the plaintiffs' version of the case. Texas's prisons might be clean and secure, he conceded—this was not Arkansas—but they were riddled with "constitutional infirmities." They were intolerably overcrowded, staffed largely by "auxiliary guards," and pervaded by brutality. Over 125 pages, he reviewed the factual record, assessed its legal significance, and came to an expansive conclusion: the "totality of conditions" within TDC "contravene[ed] the Constitution."[91]

In tone, Justice struggled for restraint over fury but finally gave way. "It is impossible for a written opinion to convey the pernicious conditions and the pain and degradation which ordinary inmates suffer within TDC," he wrote in closing. "No human being, regardless of how disfavored by society, shall be subjected to cruel and unusual punishment or be deprived of the due process of the law within the United States of America," he observed. "Regrettably, state officials have not upheld their responsibility to enforce these principles," leaving the court to do it for them.[92]

If such vehemence took Texas officials aback, Justice's final remedial order, issued in May 1981, took their breath away. The *New York Times* called it "the most sweeping reform [order] in the history of federal court intervention in state prison systems." Justice himself recognized that it would be "extremely difficult" for the state to meet all the requirements he laid out, but in order to comply with the law of the land, he insisted, it would have to. Within two years, he ordered, TDC was to completely eliminate the BT system and double the size of its guard force. It was to hire hundreds of health-care professionals, upgrade all of its facilities, and rewrite its operating procedures from A to Z. To alleviate overcrowding—and to meet Justice's safety requirement that all medium- and maximum-security prisoners be single celled—the state would have to either turn thousands of inmates loose or build many more institutions to hold them. All together, the judge from Tyler was going to cost the taxpayers of Texas hundreds of millions of dollars.[93]

But even substantial funds would not be enough to make Texas's penal system lawful, the judge had come to believe; a fundamental philosophical reorientation was also in order. For too long, Texas's prisons had stressed only work and discipline. To keep up with what constitutional jurists called "evolving standards of decency," the state would have to shift substantially toward treatment, adhering more closely to standards like those set by the American Correctional Association, which Beto had helped dilute, but not enough to match his practice at home. Future TDC units, the judge advised, would have to be smaller, less regimented, and located closer to major population centers.[94] Like Elizabeth Speer and the CPPL, Judge Justice aimed to dislodge Texas prisons from their slaving foundation.

To the plaintiffs, Justice's opinion and ruling came as delicious vindication. "I was amazed at the scope," remembers Turner. "It was a great feeling." Convicts, not surprisingly, were even more enthusiastic. "The first word of it came on the radio," writes Robert Lee Mudd, who had participated in the work stoppage at Ellis. "It was like a volcano had erupted. A lot of yelling from one cell to the next."[95]

The defendants, meanwhile, reacted with anger and disbelief. "Catastrophic," sputtered Idar. "It would be difficult to describe how this could get any worse," agreed the attorney general. For his part, Director Estelle nursed personal bitterness. Judge Justice had "vilified one of the finest prison staffs in the U.S.," he complained; his opinion "read like a cheap dime store novel."[96]

Having been trounced in court, state officials might have turned pragmatic and started planning for compliance; instead, they bet the farms on appeal. In posttrial negotiations, TDC did agree to address health care and crowding. But when it came to security, building tenders, and overall philosophy, the agency just dug in deeper. To lead the charge to the Fifth Circuit, the state hired a white-shoe firm from Houston that billed upwards of two hundred thousand dollars a month.[97] A damning factual record had accumulated, but the new attorneys argued that Judge Justice had stretched too far from "hands off" to "hands on," that his remedial order exceeded precedent and constituted excessive interference in state affairs. Because the Reagan administration was just then setting up shop in Washington, state officials also hoped to convince a more conservative Justice Department to withdraw from the case. Even as Texas's lawyers drafted their double-barreled appeal, a top-level state delegation quietly opened talks with William Bradford Reynolds, the new Republican head of the Civil Rights Division.[98] The state's plan was to bog down the plaintiffs on appeal while cutting off their federal funding.

## "ACCOUNTABLE TO NO ONE"

Texas's corrections officers "would have charged Hell with a bucket of water if [Estelle] had asked them to," wrote former guard Lon Glenn, but as TDC's costs and courtroom losses mounted, politicians started asking questions and a handful of TDC executives began edging toward the exits.[99]

Part of the problem was that the control model itself was coming unglued, not least because of excessive crowding. During the long course of the *Ruiz* case, Texas's prison population had started to climb, increasing in aggregate and per capita terms at a faster rate than at any time since the end of World War II. In 1972, when Estelle took office, there were 16,000 inmates in TDC; a decade later, there were 36,149. To cope, prison authorities resorted to extraordinary measures: double, triple, then quadruple celling; mattresses on the floor; tents in the yard. All of which, noted Judge Justice, had "a malignant effect on all aspects of inmate life."[100]

Since the late 1940s, Texas's prison chiefs had stressed order above all, but, under Estelle, order became increasingly difficult to maintain. Not long after the start of his tenure, in July 1974, a group of convicts led by Fred Carrasco, a borderlands drug runner, took hostages at the Walls and held off authorities for eleven days—the longest prison siege in American history.[101] In the aftermath, the director hired more guards and allowed a tremendous expansion of the BT system—but to no avail. Under Beto, bucks and homicides had been relatively rare, but they became increasingly frequent on Estelle's watch. In 1981, there were twelve separate work strikes or riots; in one of them, convicts responded to a volley of tear gas by hurling Molotov cocktails at the guards.[102] That spring, an African American trusty named Eroy Brown killed both the warden and the farm manager at Ellis. Then, in a succession of sensational trials, in which still more evidence of TDC brutality and corruption came to light, he managed to escape punishment, finally being acquitted by reason of self-defense—a verdict unimaginable just a few years before. After ten years in office, Estelle was losing what his mentors had valued most, his grip on convicts. "The Texas prison system is not only slipping but has already slipped," observed

Beto, who had directed the criminal justice program at Sam Houston State University since his departure. "It is only a matter of years, maybe months, before we hear the crash and see the rubble."[103]

While Estelle's troubles brewed in Huntsville, his trips to Austin turned perilous as well. Thanks in no small part to the federal courts, which had prohibited white-only primaries, poll taxes, and segregationist gerrymandering, fresh faces had started showing up at the statehouse in the late 1960s and 1970s, most of them from urban areas and many of them African American and Mexican American. After a colossal bribery scandal brought down the governor and the Speaker of the House in 1972, some of these newcomers got a shot at power. "The standard bourbon-swilling mossbacks who had run things" suddenly had to start negotiating with blacks, Hispanics, and women, observed a veteran capitol correspondent. The result was the "biggest political upheaval in Texas since Reconstruction," cried the *Dallas Morning News*.[104] None of this boded well for TDC.

The 1973 session, with its huge freshman class, "may have been the most progressive legislature before or since," claims Carlton Carl, who worked as a staffer at the time. It is most remembered for restricting big-money lobbyists and for launching an ambitious if ultimately futile attempt to rewrite the Redeemer constitution of 1876. But it also challenged the prison system, first by outlawing the use of convict guards—a dictate TDC simply ignored—and then by launching a thorough investigation, the first to seriously criticize racial discrimination in Texas's prisons since the Reconstruction Convention of 1868.[105]

Initiated by Senator Babe Schwartz at the request of the NAACP, the Joint Committee on Prison Reform held sixteen hearings and produced scores of briefing papers. It also chartered a Citizens Advisory Committee that mobilized inmate-friendly witnesses and agitated for better prison conditions. One senator called the unique public-private partnership "the most grotesque collection of radicals ever put together under one roof."[106]

To lead the citizens committee, progressive lawmakers tapped an energetic community activist and former priest, Charles Sullivan, who, along with his wife, Pauline Sullivan, a former nun, advocated full time for prisoners and their families. After meeting at a Catholic seminar in 1969, the couple had fallen in love and decided to dedicate themselves to what Pauline called "the revolution in the world." They had traveled the country in a rusted-out VW bus, working odd jobs and participating in all sorts of civil rights and antiwar protests. In San Antonio, during a stint in jail for civil disobedience, Charlie found himself drawn to the wry humor and wrenching life stories of his fellow inmates, and upon his release he and Pauline had thrown themselves into a new cause. "We just felt very strongly that if we were going to do something with our lives . . . it should be something that was going to really be for the people at the bottom," Pauline explained.[107]

At first, the Sullivans concentrated on providing direct services to inmates and their families—setting up a charitable bus service between San Antonio and TDC's rural prison units—but they inevitably drifted into politics. They started observing meetings of the corrections board, much to the chagrin of Chairman Coffield, and organized a beggarly prison reform group called Citizens United for Rehabilitation of Errants, or CURE. During the investigation of the Joint Committee on Prison Reform, the Sullivans ensured that inmate voices were heard and that the final report's criticisms stung. TDC's health care and disciplinary practices were grossly deficient, concluded the lawmakers, previewing much of the evidence that would be introduced during the *Ruiz* trial. "Discrimination, prejudice, and segregation" were entrenched; when queried about his inmate houseboys, one warden casually complained that it was difficult to find "good house niggers now." "The joint committee revealed what was really going on inside TDC," says Charles Sullivan. It would fall to the courts to change it.[108]

While the community and legislative investigations of 1973 signaled crumbling support for TDC on the left, unexpected opposition surfaced on the right as well. The Republican Party had not figured prominently in Texas politics since getting chased out of office at gunpoint at the end of Reconstruction. As the national Democratic Party antagonized many white voters by gradually embracing the cause of civil rights, however, the GOP seized the opportunity to gain lost ground, not by carrying forth the legacy of Lincoln but by appealing to the ideological progeny of the Confederacy. Once the party of freedmen and carpetbagger Yankees, the southern GOP reinvented itself in the 1950s and 1960s as the proper home of states' rights conservatives.

Governor Allan Shivers began the movement with his "Texas Democrats for Eisenhower" campaign, but the migration picked up speed after 1961, when John Tower took over LBJ's Senate seat and then spearheaded

Texas's resistance to civil rights legislation, marching arm in arm with Dixiecrats (and future Republicans) like Strom Thurmond. Tower was the first Republican elected to statewide office since 1870, but he gradually picked up compatriots from smaller districts, among them George Herbert Walker Bush, who won a House seat in 1966. In 1979, the party staged an even more historic victory by installing the oil magnate Bill Clements in the governor's mansion, the first Republican to lead the state since Edmund Davis.[109] None of these politicians cared particularly about convicts, but as outsiders they weren't necessarily content to carry on business as usual—and this is precisely what threatened TDC.

By his own admission, Clements knew next to nothing about prisons when he took office during the Ruíz trial. Like most politicians, he liked his prisons cheap and secure, and he was inclined to support Estelle. One of the governor's first appointments to the corrections board, however, took a less sanguine approach—and with far-reaching consequences. Harry Whittington, who many years later became famous for getting shot in the face by Vice President Dick Cheney, was a conservative real estate attorney who Charlie Sullivan feared would be another "country club Republican." He had an independent streak, however, and as an urbane Austinite he made an awkward addition to the Democrat-dominated board. Hoping to fit in at the annual rodeo, he bought a pair of cowboy boots, but they hurt his feet, and he cared less for the performance. At one of his first board meetings, he ruffled feathers by casting the first recorded "no" vote in twenty years after he grew skeptical of a proposed TDC land purchase.[110]

At first, Whittington spoke out mainly on financial matters, but he soon started asking more elemental questions: Why was "rehabilitation" not listed as one of the agency's strategic objectives? Why did TDC favor maximum-security prison farms over cheaper community corrections centers? One of Whittington's daughters was mentally retarded, and he was particularly disturbed to find that TDC was "mainstreaming" mentally and physically disabled inmates with minimal support, punishing them for rule violations and leaving them vulnerable to exploitation. When he had been mulling over his appointment, Estelle had assured him that board meetings rarely took longer than two hours every other month. "We're a tight-knit group, like one big, happy family," the director had said. After Whittington joined, the meetings began to stretch on for hours; Estelle's family was not happy at all.[111]

As his own misgivings deepened, Whittington cleared out a room for TDC business at his offices in the downtown Vaughn Building, which he owned, and started compiling materials on all aspects of TDC management. He became friendly with the Sullivans, despite their peace-and-justice radicalism, started hiring ex-cons to work on his rental properties, and gradually morphed into a most unexpected role: "agitator." "He's one of us; he really is," exclaimed Charlie. "He's the one who taught me that prison reform can be bipartisan." In public forums, Whittington began to challenge not only TDC's traditions but its legal posture. "What [are] we trying to gain by taking such a hard line against the inmates and the court?" he asked a group of Rotarians. The result, he asserted, was only wasted dollars and wasted opportunities.[112]

With "the judge and the politicians and the newspapers . . . all over [him] like stink on a skunk," Jim Estelle's quality of life deteriorated in the wake of the *Ruiz* verdict. Despite record spending on legal fees, the state's losses kept mounting in court. Governor Clements had high hopes that his allies in the Reagan administration would pull the Justice Department out of the case, but after a series of settlement meetings in December 1981, William Reynolds announced that he found his own attorneys more credible than TDC's; the federal government was going to continue as a co-plaintiff. Seven months later, the Fifth Circuit delivered its appellate verdict. In certain instances, Judge Justice had overstepped, the three judges ruled. Requiring TDC to put every inmate in an individual cell and to build smaller, urban, lower-security facilities was too "intrusive," they instructed. In every other way, however, the Fifth Circuit validated Justice's conclusions. "The totality of conditions" within TDC indeed violated the constitution. State officials could no longer defer compliance by engaging in "ceaseless guerrilla war."[113]

Compounding the damage, lawmakers subjected TDC to withering scrutiny when it came begging for cash. Legislators wanted to know why existing projects were running over budget and how the prison system kept track of noncash emoluments like food, housing, and servants. "Fiscally that place stinks over there," grumbled one senator; the lieutenant governor complained that TDC was becoming a "bottomless pit." Top officials in the executive branch were particularly incensed when Judge Justice's chief inspector and compliance officer, or "special master," reported that staff violence was still endemic and that the BT system was alive and well, despite Estelle's repeated denials. The prison system "desire[s] to be accountable to no one," observed one politician. In 1982, to comply with Justice's mandates and build new prisons, TDC requested a budget of $1.5 billion. Lawmakers balked. In the end, they would spend many times that, but they weren't about to shovel cash to a man they no longer trusted.[114]

Convinced he had become a "lightning rod," Estelle announced in September 1983 that he was planning to step down. The man associates invariably described as charismatic and confident sounded battered and embittered in his resignation speech to the board. "There are some areas where my intransigence makes me a difficult client . . . to defend," he acknowledged. "Maybe a different perspective than mine would better serve the department." While Estelle offered a few phrases of conciliation, he still had plenty of scores to settle: with the attorney general for being "more concerned with compromise" than defending the state's interests, with the legislature for micromanaging and withholding funds, and with TDC's legal opponents, who were bent on ruining what he still believed was "the greatest prison system in the nation."[115]

Originally, Estelle intended to stay on the job through a six-month transition period, but as Whittington and other officials hounded him about financial improprieties, he lasted only three weeks. Abrupt termination was "a painful and frustrating experience," he admitted afterward. Back in 1972, when Beto handed over the reins, Estelle had believed he was inheriting the nation's top penal system, and that he, like his predecessors, would ride it to the top of the American Correctional Association (in fact, he lost his presidential bid in 1980, just before Justice issued his verdict). Now, after twelve exhausting years, he was out of work and having a hard time nailing down another job; one search committee told him he was a "political liability." Worse yet, he had to defend himself against what he called "baseless allegations" that he had misappropriated funds for personal gain. Like President Nixon, he was reduced to differentiating himself from criminals. "I have never knowingly or willfully broken a law," he implored. "I do not lie or steal." Once heralded as "the crown prince . . . of American corrections," Estelle was dethroned by convicts and outside radicals.[116] After a thirty-six-year reign, the Texas control model came to an inglorious conclusion.

# 8

---

# RETRIBUTIVE REVOLUTION

If you say you're not scared, then you're either stupid or crazy.
—TEXAS PRISONER[1]

The year before Jim Estelle's forced resignation, a landmark election swept a host of progressive Democrats into office, portending still deeper changes at TDC. The state's once-proud penal system was getting pummeled in court and in the press. Slack oil revenues, combined with a steadily increasing prisoner population, convinced many lawmakers to consider low-cost alternatives to incarceration. Locking up criminals in maximum-security facilities is not "a luxury we can afford anymore," observed Dallas Republican Ray Keller.[2]

At the start of the 1983 legislative session, during his last months in office, Director Estelle requested a whopping budget increase, but TDC no longer had the clout to move legislation. Instead, politicians developed their own plan to comply with federal court orders. They diverted tens of millions of dollars from regular prisons to probation, parole, and "restitution centers," in which nonviolent felons held day jobs in the community. To arrest growth in the prison population, the legislature loosened good-time provisions, eliminated the governor's veto over paroles, and even relaxed the state's habitual law, which had been on the books since before the Civil War. Charlie and Pauline Sullivan, who had practically moved into the statehouse to shepherd through sixteen bills, two resolutions, and a constitutional amendment, called it "the most productive legislative session in criminal justice reform in Texas history."[3]

In the wake of Estelle's departure, TDC itself embraced change. An outsider, Raymond Procunier, or "the Pro," an experienced prison hand who had started out under Richard McGee in California, became the new permanent director and set out to dismantle the control model.[4] Building tenders, officers, and nearly half the system's wardens lost their jobs, while an "explosion [of directives] from the central office" sought to enforce what Procunier called a "more sophisticated organizational approach." The new director was supposed to lead the agency "out of the dark ages," commented one writer.[5]

Under new leadership, TDC and Texas's attorney general finally entered into serious settlement negotiations. Prodded by successive defeats in court, the state had already signed consent decrees on health care, the BT system, and the use of force. In early 1985, both sides reached further agreements on facilities upgrades, staffing ratios, and population caps, measures that would cost the state at least $173 million. The deal by no means closed the *Ruiz* case (Judge Justice would maintain judicial supervision over Texas's penal system for another seventeen years), but for the first time both sides agreed on the necessary steps to make Texas's prisons constitutional. The Republican chair of the corrections board called the consent decree a turning point. "The war is over," he announced. "The side of reform has won."[6]

The Sullivans saw the settlement as a promontory achievement. "We have moved closer to the possibility of a humane prison system with opportunities for rehabilitation," Charlie wrote. "The *Ruiz* case set this course in motion, but in the last four years most of the political leaders in the state have come around to it." With significant victories in hand, the couple organized their most successful fund-raiser ever and decided it was time to take their group, CURE, national. The plan was to mobilize a coast-to-coast network of ex-prisoners and their families and to replicate in Washington what they had already accomplished in one of the most conservative states in the union. With high hopes and good cheer, they packed their meager belongings into a U-Haul and set off. "Turning back the clock is impossible," Charlie wrote.[7] What they could not know was that the very anatagonists they thought they had vanquished in Texas had also set their sights on the nation's capital.

## SOUTHERN STRATEGY

The 1983 victories in Texas were hard-won but had seemed almost inevitable to reformers. They felt the winds of change had been at their backs. Despite water hoses and church bombings, the civil rights movement had marched from milestone to milestone; with Judge Justice's help, it had reached East Texas's most resistant hamlets. In 1972, Texas voters approved the Equal Rights Amendment. In 1973, the United States began withdrawing from Vietnam, a retreat brought about largely through popular protest. Not since Reconstruction had so many non-white faces populated the Capitol; for the first time ever, one of them showed up for work in a dashiki.[8]

Prisons were challenging venues for social justice activists—few convicts had the unimpeachable credentials of Rosa Parks—but the trajectory seemed preordained. "Community corrections" was the mantra of the day, just as "indeterminate sentencing" had been previously. Conventional big houses and prison farms were nothing but "warehouses of human degradation," chanted Ramsey Clark, whom President Johnson had recruited from Dallas to become the most left-wing attorney general in American history. Previous generations of penal reformers had wanted to centralize criminal control in benevolent institutions run by expert government administrators—hence the CPPL's campaign for the Texas penal colony. In the skeptical era of Vietnam and Watergate, however, deinstitutionalization came to the fore. "Community corrections [means] decentralizing the monstrous state penal system that is TDC," wrote Charlie Sullivan. "The Prison of the Future," predicted criminologist Daniel Glaser, will be small, urban, humane, and have "extensive links with community organizations." "Custodial emphasis [will be] mainly peripheral and invisible," he argued, overshadowed by "work, study, and play activities."[9]

Some critics went further. If "the prison, the reformatory, and the jail had achieved only a shocking record of failure," as concluded a federal study, then perhaps they should be done away with altogether. "There is something basically wrong with the idea of forcibly removing lawbreakers from society, bringing them together in a single location, and placing them under the domination of keepers for long periods," argued Robert Sommer in his provocatively titled book *The End of Imprisonment*. Sommer and his fellow travelers called themselves "abolitionists," and although their campaign had more success closing mental hospitals than prisons, they made significant inroads. In 1972, the National Council on Crime and Delinquency called for a halt to new prison construction. Three years later, activists launched the National Moratorium on Prison Construction, which opposed new prison building of any sort. Even George Beto caught the bug. Although prisons will always be required for "hard core" offenders, he wrote in 1974, they "are largely obsolete as treatment centers for criminals." The massive Coffield Unit, he mused, could well be the last prison built in the United States.[10]

But even as penologists prepared for what Norval Morris called "the decline and likely fall of the 'prison,'" the political landscape was shifting under their feet.[11] In Texas, a convergence of factors—including reapportionment, political scandals, the *Ruiz* case, and a transitional period of partisan depolarization—had allowed the progressive coups of 1973 and 1983. Yet, as an insurgent political force known as the New Right gained strength in response to civil rights, the antiwar movement, and the Great Society, such breakthroughs became increasingly scarce, not only in Texas but nationwide. Decarceration, once a destination, withered to a dream.


No one understood the politics of backlash better than Lyndon Johnson, Texas's most legendary politician since Sam Houston and the White House's most determined champion of civil rights since Ulysses S. Grant. Although Johnson had started out as a segregationist, as president, his social programs extended the New Deal and went further toward alleviating economic inequality than any policy regime before or since. His deployment of federal power in the interest of civil rights retraced the footsteps of Reconstruction, and for the first time gave genuine credibility to the age-old American credo of equal justice before the law. "I'm going to be the President who finishes what Lincoln began," Johnson pledged—and to a certain extent he was. Even as his Great Society ushered new voters into the Democratic Party, Johnson increasingly antagonized his traditional white southern base. After the passage of the Civil Rights Act in 1964, he confided to Bill Moyers, "I think we just delivered the South to the Republican party for a long time to come."[12]

The Great Society's fiercest critics indeed came from Johnson's own section of the country, often from his home state. In 1960, he and Lady Bird had been jostled and spit on by a right-wing mob in Dallas. After the passage of the Civil Rights Act, J. Evetts Haley, a wealthy rancher and far-right rabble rouser, denounced the president as a "traitor" to the South whose policies would result in "race and national suicide."[13]

By the mid-1960s, however, neo-Confederate obstructionists were in retreat. A strong majority of white poll respondents nationwide said they accepted the basic justice of civil rights demands; even whites in the South were no longer responding to racial venom with the same fervor they once had. Critics of the Johnson administration, therefore, had to refine and redirect their ire. Anticommunism remained at the ready, but, with the president dispatching hundreds of thousands of combat troops to Vietnam, partisan red-baiting was losing its zing. A fresh issue on the home front, however, held unusual promise. Not only would it allow the right to tap into smoldering fears and frustrations without resorting to outmoded racist demagoguery but it suggested a way to reclaim the populist mantle from redistributionist liberals. The issue was crime, and after 1964 it became one of the most divisive forces in American politics.[14]

Since crime had traditionally been a mayoral or at most gubernatorial concern—with the notable exception of Prohibition—Johnson was slow to grab hold. "A visitor coming to America for the first time might have been forgiven for assuming that the President of the United States commanded all the city police departments and that control of the courts was his personal responsibility," he explained "[But] crime is a local problem. . . . The federal government has little or no power to deal with the problem . . . nor should it have."[15] From the mid-1960s, however, Johnson's foes increasingly ignored his civics lesson. As the president himself was sabotaging his experiment in social democracy by diverting resources and attention to Southeast Asia, the New Right began ravaging it from within in the name of public safety and just deserts.

A pioneer in this effort was George Wallace, the sharp-tongued segregationist who ran four times for president between 1964 and 1976. When first elected governor of Alabama in 1962, he epitomized southern demagogy. In his first inaugural address, he lambasted federal enforcement of civil rights by invoking the Civil War. "From this cradle of the Confederacy, this very Heart of the Great Anglo-Saxon Southland," he thundered, "I draw the line in the dust and toss the gauntlet before the feet of tyranny, and I say segregation now, segregation tomorrow, segregation forever." As most Americans accommodated themselves to legal equality, however, Wallace was one of the first Dixiecratic firebrands to figure out how to talk about race without hurling racial epithets. Instead of "White Man's Government," he championed states' rights, public order, and perceived white victimhood. Crime proved to be especially fruitful terrain, as it enabled him to stoke subterranean fears of integration while assailing what he called the fanciful theories of liberal elites. "If a criminal knocks you over the head on your way home from work," he complained, "he will be out of jail before you're out of the hospital and the policeman who arrested him will be on trial. . . . Some psychologist will say, well, he's not to blame, society is to blame."[16]

Much of the trouble, in Wallace's view, stemmed from the federal judiciary. "The same Supreme Court that ordered integration and encouraged civil rights legislation," he blasted, is now "bending over backwards to help criminals." Affirmed by an outpouring of national support following a carefully choreographed standoff with the Justice Department over admissions to the University of Alabama, Wallace believed he glimpsed the fuming, fearful soul of a nation. "They all hate black people, all of them," he mused, according to NBC news. "They're all afraid, all of them. Great God! That's it! They're all Southern! The whole United States is Southern!"[17]

Crime served as a perfect surrogate for Wallace's brand of racial resentment. As an issue, it had the respectability that old-fashioned "Negrophobia" lacked. It was also an undeniable social problem, even if the ballyhoo surrounding it sometimes outstripped the reality. Over generations, most historians agree, U.S. crime rates had been steadily declining, culminating in a precipitous drop during World War II. In the 1960s, however, both property and violent crime rebounded. In 1960, there were 9,110 murders and 17,190 rapes recorded in the United States; by 1975, the toll had mounted to 20,510 murders and 56,090 rapes. In per capita terms, the national homicide rate increased by 88 percent. "Today, we are in the midst of a crime wave of unprecedented proportions," warned *U.S. News & World Report.*[18]

Pundits blamed their favorite villains. Social critics on the left labeled property crime "reparations" and depicted rising illegality as the result of pent-up frustrations in the face of persistent injustice. On the right, Wallace and other foes of social liberalism blamed legalistic permissiveness, moral degeneration, and a "culture of welfare." Academic criminologists put little stock in such explanations. They pointed out that local and state crime reporting became much more systematic during the 1960s, thus inflating the numbers. They also noted that the first baby boomers hit their teens and twenties in the 1960s, thereby expanding the most crime-prone demographic. Two other factors stand out to crime researchers in retrospect. First, during the wartime and post-war economic expansion, millions of Americans, many of them low-wage African American workers from the South, moved to cities in search of jobs; more affluent white Americans, in turn, followed the new inter-state highway system out to the suburbs, taking resources with them. Second, starting in the late 1960s, the phenomenally productive U.S. eco-nomic engine started to sputter, wracked by increasing competition from Japan and Germany, declining profits, inflation, rising unemployment, and finally the oil crisis. Together, stagnation and suburbanization con-centrated poverty in the inner cities, where crime rates climbed most steeply.[19]

Most experts believed that the expansion of civil liberties by the federal courts had little to do with the baby-boom crime wave. Court decisions like *Miranda* have had as much of an effect on crime rates "as aspirin on a brain tumor," argued a former prosecutor. But public per-ception was another matter. Opinion polls showed that Americans were becoming increasingly concerned about crime in the 1960s, especially as politicians spotlighted the issue. They also disagreed sharply about what should be done. Ironically, those groups that were most vulnerable and most often victimized, notably women and African Americans, had the least punitive attitudes; they tended to favor preventative and rehabilitative solutions to crime. White men, although they were less often victimized and less personally fearful of crime, favored the harsh-est penalties.[20]

Such differences help explain George Wallace's potency. His hyper-ventilating style never got him elected to national office, but Wallace secured a legacy by splitting votes, coaxing white voters, especially in the South but also in northern cities with growing black populations, away from their traditional homes in the Democratic Party. Wallace mapped out a racially charged "southern strategy" that his ideological heirs followed to victory. The ultimate beneficiary, of course, was not the party of Jefferson Davis, where Wallace began and ended his career, but that of Abraham Lincoln.

Barry Goldwater, the archconservative senator from Arizona, was one of the first Republicans outside the South to recognize the potential of Wallace's right-wing racial populism. The Democrats increasingly had a lock on the black electorate, he acknowledged, but this represented an opportunity rather than a liability. "We're not going to get the Negro vote," he told a southern audience, "so we ought to go hunting where the ducks are." To Goldwater, this meant bagging frustrated, fearful white voters not by hurling racial slurs but by honing a message of states' rights and crime control. "The abuse of law and order in this country is going to be an issue," Goldwater pledged at the start of his rousing 1964 presidential bid, which ultimately won Wallace's endorsement. "At least I'm going to make it one."[21]

Goldwater placed crime fighting front and center when he accepted the Republican nomination at San Francisco's Cow Palace. "Security from domestic violence, no less than from foreign aggression, is the most elementary and fundamental purpose of any government," he bellowed, "and a government that cannot fulfill this purpose is one that cannot long command the loyalty of its citizens." Here the candidate privileged martial over social governance and chained street crime to the cold war. In both cases, he argued, the enemies were socialist ideas. "If it is entirely proper for the government to take away from some to give to others," he mused, conflating progressive taxation with theft, "then won't some be led to believe that they can rightfully take from anyone who has more than they? No wonder law and order has broken down, mob violence has engulfed great American cities, and our wives feel unsafe in the streets."[22] Goldwater thus wielded crime as a dagger to strike at the heart of social democracy. In his view, Johnson's myriad antipoverty programs not only failed to prevent crime; by cultivating a pathological culture of dependency and permissiveness, they actually caused crime.

Such obdurate pronouncements proved too ideological for the 1964 electorate. When a journalist asked Goldwater what it might feel like to become president one day, he had replied, "Frankly, it scares the hell out of me." Voters agreed, and he picked up just 52 of 538 electoral votes. Even as the Arizona senator fell far short in his drive for national power, however, he proved an able revolutionary within his own party. Unlike any politician since Prohibition, he made crime a galvanizing national campaign issue. By winning five ex-Confederate states plus his own, he proved that Republicans could compete in the solid South, and he shifted the party's center of gravity to the Sunbelt. Proclaiming famously that "extremism in defense of liberty is no vice," he drove liberals like his primary opponent Nelson Rockefeller into Republican exile. Within a single election cycle he repositioned the Grand Old Party as the standard-bearer of opposition to civil rights. Only two years earlier, poll respondents had perceived almost no difference between the two major parties when it came to race. By late 1964, however, Americans overwhelmingly identified Democrats with civil rights and Republicans with a go-slow, states' rights approach. The sea change was apparent at party gatherings, where the conservative journalist (and future *Cross Fire* pundit) Robert Novak was dismayed to hear a new cadre of GOP activists conversing freely about "niggers" and "nigger lovers." Under Goldwater's leadership, he concluded, the Republican Party "was now a White Man's Party."[23]

Despite his commanding 1964 victory, Johnson recognized his vulnerability on the crime front. In his second term, he built whopping additions to the Great Society, adding Medicare and Medicaid, as well as Head Start, the National Endowment for the Arts, and the Public Broadcasting System. When he spoke of social welfare programs, however, he increasingly framed them as anticrime initiatives. Crime is a "malignant enemy in America," he warned, borrowing Goldwater's combative and paternalistic imagery. "I will not be satisfied until every woman and child in this Nation can walk any street [and] enjoy any park . . . at any time of the day or night without fear of being harmed."[24]

Although he continued to believe that crime fighting was best left to local authorities, the president got in the game by creating the Bureau of Narcotics and Dangerous Drugs (precursor to the DEA) and the Law Enforcement Assistance Administration (LEAA), which funneled money and matériel to police departments. Hoping to generate more policy proposals before the next presidential election, he also chartered a blue-ribbon commission to investigate the crime problem under the leadership of his first attorney general, Nicholas Katzenbach. "I hope that 1965 will be regarded as the year when this country began in earnest a thorough and effective war against crime," he said in announcing the appointments.[25]

The Katzenbach commission was supposed to reclaim crime control as a Democratic issue. It acknowledged the scope of the problem— "There is . . . far too much [crime] for the health of the nation"—but tried to steer the debate back toward liberal solutions. "Warring on poverty, inadequate housing, and unemployment is warring on crime," the final report insisted. "More broadly and most importantly every effort to improve life in America's 'inner cities' is an effort against crime. . . . We will not have dealt effectively with crime until we have alleviated the conditions that stimulate it."[26]

After nineteen months of study, the Katzenbach commission sent more than two hundred recommendations to the president, many of which got incorporated into an omnibus bill with an appealingly nostalgic title: Safe Streets. While Johnson was typically unbeatable on Capitol Hill, however, the crime issue was already slipping from his grasp. In 1966, his party lost seats in the midterm elections, and a conservative coalition of southern Democrats and rebounding Republicans rewrote the legislation. As the president had requested, there was more money for research, training, and modernization, but most of it was provided through "block grants" to states, a concession to southern federalists. In a rebuke to the Supreme Court, the bill expanded police wiretapping authority and made it easier for cops to interrogate suspects without the bother of defense attorneys. One writer called the legislation "a piece of demagoguery devised out of malevolence and enacted in hysteria." The president's advisors agreed, labeling it "repressive" and "obnoxious," but Johnson, ever the political operative, held his nose and signed.[27]

If nothing else, the Safe Streets Act was supposed to keep the president safe. By the end of Johnson's first full term, however, no legislative accomplishment could protect his right and left flanks. After his momentous victory over Goldwater, *Time* magazine had described LBJ as "fresh as a daisy and frisky as a colt"; four years later, he was wilting and hobbled. With some four hundred American GIs dying every week, he was sinking ever deeper into the quagmire he had created in Vietnam.[28] At home, violent crime continued to tick upward, while vitriolic street protests and full-fledged riots erupted like perennials in the long hot summers. Watts, Detroit, and Newark started to look like Hue and Saigon.

"Disruption and disorder will nourish not justice but repression," warned the last of the president's study groups on lawlessness, the Kerner Commission. Indeed, hard-liner stock soared. In March 1968, Johnson withdrew from the presidential race, passing on his liabilities to would-be Democratic successors, the most eligible of whom, Robert Kennedy, was promptly shot dead. Opinion polls suggested the electorate was veering right even had the Democrats been able to field a unifying candidate, which they were not. For the first time since the 1930s, a majority of Americans listed crime as the most important domestic issue facing the nation. In large cities, more than 40 percent said they felt afraid to go out at night in their own neighborhoods. Increasingly, they distrusted liberal solutions, no matter how eloquent or well credentialed the White House's commissioners. Most Americans contended that the courts were "too soft" and that criminals were getting off "too easily." Eighty-one percent of respondents told pollsters that law and order had broken down, with a majority blaming "communists" and "Negroes who start riots."[29]

"Our nation is moving toward two societies, one black, one white— separate and unequal," the Kerner Commission famously warned. The process "is not inevitable," the authors wrote. It could be reversed by "a commitment to national action—compassionate, massive, and sustained, backed by the resources of the most powerful and the richest nation on earth." But in March 1968, when the report went to press, it was already too late for such talk. A month later, cities across the country ignited after the assassination of Martin Luther King Jr. The Great Society was burning to the ground.[30]

By decrying lawlessness and social protest in one breath—by replacing the GOP's patrician golf club with a populist pitchfork—Goldwater had positioned his party to take advantage of white America's fears. But it took an abler politician, a scrappy, red-baiting schemer from another Sunbelt state, to thrust that pitchfork to victory—Richard Milhous Nixon.

Having launched his career in the divisive, fear-laden waters of McCarthyism, Nixon quickly grasped the zap of crime. In a 1967 article for *Reader's Digest,* "What Has Happened to America," the former vice president lamented that "in a few short years . . . America has become among the most lawless and violent [nations] in the history of the free peoples." While "decent people" cower in their homes, he complained later in the campaign, the Johnson administration was offering handouts to no-accounts and making excuses for criminals. "In a civilized nation, no man can excuse his crime against the person or property of another by charging that he, too, has been a victim of injustice," he admonished, dismissing the Katzenbach and Kerner commissions' social explanations for lawbreaking. "To tolerate that is to invite anarchy." A Nixon administration would be different. Foreseeing a "showdown with anarchy," the candidate pledged to expand police powers, appoint tougher judges, and "curb [criminal] appetites" by punishing criminals. "Doubling the conviction rate in this country would do more to cure crime in America than quadrupling the funds for [the] war on poverty," he jabbed.[31]

While Nixon was not as reactionary as Goldwater or as segregationist as Wallace, he, too, indulged in the alchemy of race and crime in pursuit of white votes. "I believe in civil rights," he explained shrewdly, "but the first civil right of every American is to be free from violence." Suggesting that civil disobedience was partly to blame for urban crime, he postulated that "the deterioration [of law and order] can be traced directly to the spread of the corrosive doctrine that every citizen possesses an inherent right to decide for himself which laws to obey and when to obey them." Although the candidate disavowed any covert appeal to racism—"Our goal is justice, justice for every American," he insisted—Nixon's advisors suggested otherwise. "We'll go after the racists," the president's special counsel John Ehrlichman wrote about the 1968 campaign. "The subliminal appeal to the anti-black voter was always present in Nixon's statements and speeches." After the election, H. R. Haldeman, Nixon's chief of staff, confided in his diary that "[the president] emphasized that you have to face the fact that the whole problem is really the blacks. The key is to devise a system that recognized this while not appearing to."[32] Crime, then, was not just about fear but racial fear. Emphasizing it enabled Nixon to tap visceral prejudices that had divided Americans since before the birth of the republic.

Nominated behind barbed wire, with tear gas wafting through the Chicago air, Johnson's vice president, Hubert Humphrey, proved an easy target in a campaign dominated by "law and order." On Election Day, the Nixon and Wallace tickets combined won nearly 60 percent of the popular vote (and a higher portion of the white vote).[33] Nixon, having been humiliated by John F. Kennedy and Pat Brown in 1960 and 1962, was suddenly a winner. By pursuing a southern strategy first outlined by Wallace, he strangled the Decade of Love and moved back to Washington.

### "A TIME TO DIE"

Richard Nixon promised to "restore order and respect for the law" at home, but in office he had to come to terms with the fact that Johnson's federalist admonition on crime policy was essentially correct: there was relatively little the president could do about street crime because most of it occurred outside his jurisdiction. "I was cranking out that bullshit on Nixon's crime policy before he was elected," recalls former White House counsel John Dean with characteristic bombast. "And it was bullshit, too. We knew it. The Nixon campaign didn't call for anything . . . that Ramsey Clark wasn't already doing under LBJ. We just made more noise."[34]

Finding his options limited, the new president initially stood tall atop the shoulders of his predecessors. Funding for Johnson's LEAA increased thirteenfold during Nixon's first term, with much of the money earmarked for riot control, police hardware, and corrections. Revisiting the turf of Robert Kennedy, Nixon signed an aggressive organized crime bill, which included provisions for vaguely defined conspiracy prosecutions that were soon turned against Black Panthers and antiwar protesters. The president also backed a harsh anticrime bill for Washington, D.C., a facsimile of legislation LBJ had vetoed in 1966. So severe were its provisions for no-knock warrants, preventative detention, and life sentences for third felony convictions (an early version of three strikes) that Senator Sam Ervin denounced it as a "blueprint for a police state." The legislation nonetheless sailed through Congress and became a blueprint for the nation.[35]

These efforts had a comparatively modest policy impact—and next to no impact on crime—but in two areas the Nixon administration broke new ground. At the Supreme Court, Earl Warren and three associate justices stepped down not long after Johnson's departure, thus giving the new president a rare opportunity to shape interpretations of the law. Warren Burger, whom Nixon made chief justice, and his other picks confirmed by the Senate (two southern reactionaries were rejected) declined to move the court as far as he would have liked; regarding Watergate, his own appointees would turn fatally against him. Nonetheless, Nixon's judges set a rightward course that continued long after his own ignominious departure. His most ideological appointee, William Rehnquist, moved up to chief and dominated the court for almost twenty years. With the help of additional justices appointed by Gerald Ford, Ronald Reagan, and the Bushes, the liberal judicial activism of the Warren era began reverting to the conservative judicial activism that had characterized the third branch for most of its history.[36]

In law enforcement, the Nixon administration similarly left its mark, mainly by homing in on an area of well-established federal authority under the Constitution's commerce clause: illegal drug trafficking. If poverty and racism had served as the preeminent social maladies to Great Society liberals, drug addiction and lax morality came under fire from the "silent majority." Although drug addiction was more implicated in property crime than violence, the president declared illegal drugs "the number one public enemy" and ramped up a new war at home even as he lost one abroad.[37]

Although he provided funding for drug treatment, including methadone maintenance, the president's antidrug initiatives tilted heavily toward the hard end of criminal justice: policing, prosecution, and imprisonment. Through statute and executive order, the Nixon administration moved drug classification authority from medical experts to law enforcement; pushed through aggressive forfeiture provisions that eventually allowed prosecutors to seize any asset involved in drug sales, including family homes; and hired three hundred more drug enforcement agents to target mainly low-level street dealers, described as "the very vermin of humanity." Despite the fact that as many Americans died choking on food as from drug overdoses (2,227 versus 2,313 in 1971), the president declared illegal drugs a "growing menace to the general welfare of the United States." During Nixon's years in office, federal drug enforcement spending climbed from $65 to $719 million.[38]

Just as criminologists predicted, none of these policies effectively curbed crime, which continued to escalate under Nixon's watch. Nonetheless, the White House's crime war set the tone for the nation. Under Republican leadership, crime and drug abuse became linked in the public imagination with civil rights, failed social programs, and especially with urban blacks. Law-and-order advocates successfully convinced a majority of Americans that individual irresponsibility rather than social inequality breeds crime; that the government was going "too easily" on criminals; and that old-fashioned punishment rather than "squishy soft" programs would better keep the country safe.[39] In short, after following a southern strategy to the White House, Republicans began making American criminal justice a lot more southern.

In the helter-skelter politics of the late civil rights era, Nixon conservatives weren't the only ones questioning the presumptions of criminal justice liberalism. The left, too, wondered whether genuine transformation was really possible inside cages. Although Quakers had helped invent the penitentiary, the progressive American Friends Service Committee called for its abolition in 1971. "It would be naïve not to acknowledge the blunders that an uncritical faith can produce," they wrote. "The horror that is the American prison system grew out of an eighteenth-century reform by Pennsylvania Quakers. . . . This two-hundred-year-old experiment has failed."[40]

Such criticisms gained strength among prisoners as well. Pioneered by convict authors like Caryl Chessman, writ writers like Fred Cruz, and the day-in, day-out organizing of the Black Muslims, a radical prison movement took root in America's cell blocks in the late 1960s. Champions of rehabilitative corrections like Richard McGee and Ramsey Clark had hoped that humane, treatment-oriented prisons would encourage criminals to repent and go straight. Instead, as "Black Power" drowned out "We Shall Overcome" and antiwar radicals posed as domestic Viet Cong, educated, empowered, and enraged convicts began to think of themselves not as errant miscreants in need of liberal mending but as lumpen proletariat revolutionaries. Rather than validating penal benevolence, politicized convicts lambasted imprisonment and American society writ large. "Don't be shocked when I say that I was in prison," instructed Malcolm X, who inspired the movement in life and martyrdom. "That's what America means: prison."[41]

The radical prison movement blossomed most spectacularly in sunny California, where the nation's best correctional education program produced the most eloquent convict critics. There the sixties began with Chessman's measured, best-selling pleadings to save his life, and there the sixties ended as revolutionaries like Eldridge Cleaver, Huey P. Newton, and Angela Davis geared up for battle against Ronald Reagan and the shock troops of the New Right.

The battle was joined mostly with words. Governor Reagan, who took office in 1967 and promptly chased out McGee, vowed to "put down riot or insurrection wherever and whenever the situation required," while George Jackson, the prison movement's most insurrectionary voice, boasted that he was ready to send cops to the "big pig pen in the sky."[42] Real bullets were also exchanged. In August 1970, George's younger brother Jonathan staged a brazen takeover of the Marin County Courthouse, only to perish by fusillade, along with two comrades and a judge. A year later, George, whose incendiary memoir through letters, *Soledad Brother,* had made him a national celebrity, was shot down during a bloodbath at San Quentin.

While traveling the country in their blue VW bus, Pauline and Charlie Sullivan attended the younger Jackson's funeral. It was a stirring event, with fiery speeches and a Black Panther honor guard. But it was also a perplexing moment: the country's prison politics seemed to be moving in two directions at once. On the one hand, convict rebels were joining with criminologists to call for the abolition of America's "concentration camps."[43] On the other, a new breed of politician was clamoring to unshackle the police and brick up the cell doors. Only days after the fateful melee at San Quentin, these countervailing forces— law-and-order conservatism versus convict radicalism—came together most cataclysmically of all. The setting was a quiet town in upstate New York named after the Athenian province that gave rise to democracy: Attica.

Built in the early 1930s, the prison at Attica was a crumbling fortress surrounded by thirty-foot walls: on the outside, a monument to the awesome power of the law; on the inside, a mass of urban convicts lorded over by rural guards. As in most northern lockups, the prisoner population had steadily darkened in the postwar decades, largely the result of migration from the South. By 1971, Attica's population was 54 percent black and 9 percent Latino; the guard force remained exclusively white. In January of that year Governor Nelson Rockefeller had brought in a new commissioner to implement reforms, but prisoners were unimpressed. "For inmates, 'correction' meant daily degradation and humiliation," concluded a massive investigation of the institution in 1972. "[T]he promise of rehabilitation had become a cruel joke."[44]

By the time George Jackson was shot dead—provoking an outpouring of rage from prisoners across the country—Attica had become, according to the state's investigative commission, a "lethal crucible in which the most explosive social forces in our society are mixed with the pettiness and degradation of prison life, under intense pressure of maintaining 'security.'" On September 9, 1971, the crucible ignited. Would-be convict revolutionaries took hostages, freed comrades, and seized the yard, where they were joined by nearly two-thirds of the prison population, 1,281 inmates in all. Five days of national media coverage and tense negotiations ensued. At one point, Bobby Seale of the Panthers and the radical lawyer William Kunstler were brought in to help resolve the standoff. But despite moments of hope, negotiations collapsed. Governor Rockefeller ordered the prison retaken by force, and on September 13, an army of white state troopers and corrections officers—armed with hunting rifles and backed up by helicopters dropping tear gas—did just that. By all accounts, they performed miserably. When the gas and smoke dissipated, thirty-two inmates and eleven hostages lay dead, almost all of them shot by officers. It was the bloodiest prison riot in American history, the deadliest act of state-ordered domestic violence since the massacre at Wounded Knee in 1890.[45]

Attica shook American corrections to its foundation. It came to symbolize everything rotten about prisons. The trouble was, few people agreed on what precisely was rotten, much less what should be done about it. Liberals and leftists tended to regard the uprising as the tragic result of thwarted dreams and overly authoritarian prisons. *Time* magazine argued for community correction centers to replace aging "Bastilles" and for the revitalization of parole. Such reforms "will not solve the large social problems of racial prejudice, inadequate housing, poor schools, and lack of jobs, which breed so much of the nation's violent crime," the authors conceded. "But reform might at least prevent more prisons from becoming ugly, brutalizing battlegrounds where the tensions of society, racial and political, redouble in the claustrophobic air." As the dust settled, however, a sterner view took hold. President Nixon came to Governor Rockefeller's defense, as did the *Atlanta Constitution,* which called for the "animals of Attica" to be executed. America needed not prisoner liberation but inmate obedience, rallying conservatives believed, not gentler prisons but tougher ones. "What has happened here is but the sound before the fury of those oppressed," read a prisoner statement released during the standoff. What it unleashed was the fury of the oppressors.[46]

The next year, 1972, marked another milestone in the history of American imprisonment, though it passed unnoticed at the time. For as long as consistent records had been kept, the nation's per capita imprisonment rate had remained remarkably stable. It fluctuated with the turns of history, rising in the Great Depression, declining during wars. But overall, the rate hovered close to 100 per 100,000 residents, or 0.1 percent of the population. In 1972, however, the imprisonment rate broke free from this historical baseline and started to climb, at first gradually, then arithmetically.[47] Just as the legitimacy of prisons as public institutions tottered, their perimeters expanded.

This upswing in imprisonment began first and took hold most intensely in the South. Whereas per capita imprisonment in the North, Midwest, and West generally declined in postwar decades, in the South the rate surged in the 1950s, retreated in the 1960s, and rebounded in the 1970s. All through the twentieth century, southern states had disproportionately incarcerated their citizens, but in the civil rights era the regional differential widened. In 1950, before the demise of Jim Crow, the South's imprisonment rate was 40 percent higher than the North's; by 1980, it was 75 percent higher. In aggregate terms, the South was locking up more than twice as many individuals as any other region, with Texas at the head of the pack. The reason, according to a 1979 report by the Texas legislature, had less to do with crime or population growth than politics.[48] Prisons were full because lawmakers made them that way.

## LAW AND ORDER, TEXAS STYLE

As they did nationally, Texas's politics of crime and punishment exhibited signs of schizophrenia in the late civil rights era. In one sense, the Lone Star State seemed to be veering left. Two Texans, Johnson and Ramsey Clark, were emphasizing "root causes" and rehabilitation as never before, while nonwhite voters were reshaping the state's Democratic Party. Another Texas, though—the more powerful one, it turned out—was already catching a stiff conservative wind.

That Texas politics leaned to the right was nothing new. Although the uniformity of the electorate is often overstated, conservatives have commanded the state—with fleeting exceptions during Reconstruction, Populism, and the late Progressive Era—since the days of Oran Roberts, the godfather of what U.S. Senator Lloyd Bentsen has called "the Texas point of view." Albeit less zealously than other southern states, Texans joined "massive resistance" to integration and flirted with race-baiting national politicians like George Wallace and Strom Thurmond. In "my poor old state, they haven't heard a real Democratic speech in thirty years," lamented President Johnson. "All they ever hear at election time is, 'Nigger, Nigger, Nigger.'"[49]

Although the Texas Democratic Party remained under the control of segregationists into the late 1960s, opposition Republicans courted white racial resentment with increasing effectiveness. After Republican John Tower took over Johnson's vacated Senate seat in 1960, he became one of the GOP's first crusaders against civil rights, a pioneer of the "southern strategy" before it had a name. Along with George H. W. Bush, Tower campaigned avidly for Goldwater and helped defeat a pro-integration plank at the Republican National Convention. "I have always been proud to be a southerner, but never so proud as I am today," he boasted. None of this was sufficient to loosen the Democrats' grip on Texas politics, but it did reconfigure the Republican Party itself, which gradually became, as one political historian put it, "the party of the white race." Although the GOP had once depended largely on black support, by 1978 African Americans and Mexicans made up less than 1 percent of the party's primary voters. "Blacks supporting the Republican Party is like a bunch of chickens getting together to support Col. Sanders," quipped a Texas congressional representative.[50]

As in national politics, race and crime combined into a potent elixir. Establishment politicians conflated civil rights, communism, and lawlessness, while rabble-rousers reached for the bullhorns. J. Evetts Haley asserted that Johnson's attention to the social causes of crime only encouraged "the lawless, shouting, sitting, marching, rioting negroes [to step] up their violence." In response to pro-defendant, pro–civil rights rulings of the Supreme Court, the Houston-based *Southern Conservative* mused that "we are fast approaching the place where an American citizen, in order to get justice from our highest court, will first have to paint his face with a piece of burnt cork."[51] As in the aftermath of the Civil War, embattled whites began depicting themselves not as supremacists but as victims of discrimination.

Countervailing pressures from the civil rights movement and white reactionaries tore apart the Democrats' big tent in the 1960s and 1970s, producing inconsistent policy making. On the one hand, the ascent of the party's liberal wing (bolstered by the defection of conservatives to the GOP) gave activists like the Sullivans critical allies in the legislature; during a transitional period of genuine bipartisan competition, they also picked up support from the other side of the aisle. On the other hand, increasing numbers of political candidates—would-be district attorneys, judges, lawmakers, attorneys general, and, not least, governors—came to believe that they could improve their prospects by talking tough on crime.

Compared to their national counterparts, Texas's so-called Tory Democrats were less vulnerable on the crime issue. Texas's laws had always been strict and its prisons unforgiving. "We didn't hear as much about tightening up on crime as some other places," recalls Carlton Carl, a veteran Democratic operative in the state. "Our laws were pretty tough already. Our politicians always wanted to lock criminals away forever—and those were the Democrats." From the late 1960s, however, just as the civil rights movement institutionalized its most historic gains, Texas politicians found numerous ways to make those laws tougher still. Under Governor John Connally, who broke with Johnson over civil rights and later joined the Nixon administration, the state cut back on prisoners' "good time," curtailed parole eligibility, deployed the Texas Rangers to bust unions and quell protests, and broke ground on what would become the highest-capacity prison in the state, the Coffield farm. Under Connally's successor, Preston Smith, who railed against "long-haired weirdoes" and Negro rioters while making "vigorous enforcement of laws" a top campaign issue, juveniles began receiving adult sentences for the first time since 1906, and elected judges handed down astonishingly long terms to politically unpopular drug users. Lee Otis Johnson, for example, "the swaggeringest Black Power advocate in Texas," received thirty years for passing a single joint to an undercover officer at a party in Houston.[52]

The politics of marijuana exemplify the contradictions of the era. In response to the Johnson case, civil rights protesters called for a repeal of Texas's draconian 1925 anti-cannabis statute, which had been drafted during the heyday of the KKK. What ended up changing the law, however, according to a reporter for the *Texas Monthly*, was the tendency of grass to "jump the tracks from the barrios and black neighborhoods to River Oaks, Highland Park, and Alamo Heights." Most of "the upper-class white kids . . . convicted under the law never spent so much as two days in jail," recalls a UT medical professor who dealt with admissions at the time, "but the fact that they had a felony on their record was still a problem. . . . Something was clearly going to have to be done about it."[53]

In 1973, the legislature took up the cause. The result was a dramatic reduction in penalties for low-level pot possession. After several lawmakers admitted that they were regular valium users (Babe Schwartz brandished his pills on the Senate floor), they also voted to limit restrictions on certain prescribed pharmaceuticals. In order to placate hardliners in the House and Governor's Mansion, however, the legislature simultaneously augmented penalties associated with numerous other drugs, from speed to heroin. Getting caught with one hit of LSD, for example, could result in a life sentence. What had started out as an effort to mediate severity thus ended up enhancing it, a pattern repeated many times over the next two decades. To avoid the "political peril of seeming 'soft' on anything," observed one journalist, most lawmakers anted up and played "get the pusher."[54]

Even the marijuana provision was opposed by Governor Dolph Briscoe, a massive landowner turned oil magnate who made crime fighting a top political issue. He lost that battle, but in other ways he contributed substantially to the state's rapidly rising prisoner population. During his second term, he vetoed record numbers of prereleases recommended by the Board of Pardons and Paroles. In 1977, he pushed through a hulking anticrime package that kept more defendants in prison during appeals and created new types of "aggravated felonies" that required convicts to serve at least one-third of their sentences without good-time reductions, an early version of "truth in sentencing," which would become a conservative cause célèbre in the 1990s. Although reformers like the Sullivans made progress in certain areas like probation, the legislative pattern of the 1970s became increasingly clear. "When they're in session, we're in trouble," remarked a longtime prisoners' rights activist in Houston. "The first thing the legislature does when it meets every two years is to increase the penalties for everything."[55]

Against Democratic incumbents like Briscoe, Texas Republicans had difficulty capitalizing on race and crime, but this didn't stop them from trying. During his three campaigns for governor (two of them successful), Bill Clements—oil driller extraordinaire and Nixon's former deputy secretary of defense—played the game both to suppress votes and to attract them. In one contest, his secretary of state tried to purge thousands of felons from the voter rolls; on Election Day, Clements's campaign reportedly posted menacing signs in Dallas's black precincts, warning potential voters they could be imprisoned for various types of voter fraud. To bolster his support among crime-fearing whites, Clements lambasted the Democratic incumbent, Mark White, for releasing "hundreds of prisoners" and ran a TV ad accusing him of paroling predatory rapists. (Two years later, Clements's friend George H. W. Bush used a similar ad to great effect against Michael Dukakis.)[56]

Governor Clements had no great love for TDC, which he regarded as corrupted by longtime Democratic rule, but he had no qualms about committing more and more Texans to its care. During his first legislative session, he vetoed $29 million for new prison construction but nonetheless pursued policies to create more prisoners. On the front end of the criminal justice system, he favored expanded wiretapping, adult penalties for juveniles, and prosecutor-friendly revisions to the rules of criminal procedure. Although a Blue Ribbon Commission he appointed recommended various ways to reduce the already bulging prisoner population, the "crotchety old curmudgeon," as one rival called him, nonetheless vetoed even more board-recommended paroles than his predecessor. Although he started out trying to save corrections dollars, by the end of his first term he was soliciting them by the hundreds of millions. Already Texas's inmate population had breached the thirty thousand mark—more than the entire U.S. prison population a century before—and under Clements, TDC was laying plans to accommodate ten thousand more.[57]

As with his political mentor in Washington, Richard Nixon, Governor Clements left his most lasting marks in the netherworld of narcotics. Not long after taking office, he asked H. Ross Perot, the paranoid tech billionaire and future presidential candidate, to lead the Texans' War on Drugs Committee. With the help of a government task force and his own staff—one of whom he dispatched to Central America on a secret mission to sabotage drug exporters—the eccentric businessman interviewed scores of experts and produced a battery of recommendations: educational programs for parents, military-style border interdiction, and a variety of sentencing enhancements to be piled on top of the already severe 1973 statutes. There should be life without parole for selling pot to a minor, he advised (a partial return to the 1925 law), as well as bans on drug paraphernalia, greater police search and interrogation powers, and new restrictions on pharmacists. "We want to make Texas an absolutely awful place in which to be a major drug dealer," Perot explained, "and an even worse place to be as an adult caught selling one marijuana joint or one pill to a teenager."[58]

To ensure consent at the legislature, Perot's employees fanned out across the state to rile suburban mothers and bus them to the Capitol; the *Dallas Morning News* obligingly printed a drug-war Sunday supplement that included the article "How to Get Your Child Off Marijuana." Although the costs would be high and the benefits negligible, Democrats and Republicans alike lined up to pledge their "yes" votes. Governor

Clements called the package the "crown on the head" of the "law enforcement session." Not long after, Perot was hobnobbing with Ronald
and Nancy Reagan, who wanted to reenergize President Nixon's war on
drugs nationally and take it to new heights.[59]

In the realm of pharmaceuticals, Governor Clements secured his legacy
in another way as well. In 1977, Governor Briscoe had signed a new
death penalty statute (it had to be rewritten after the Supreme Court
temporarily abolished capital punishment in *Furman v. Georgia*), and it
fell to Clements to carry it out—by a new method: lethal injection. Just
as the electric chair had been introduced some six decades earlier as a
modern replacement for hanging, the needle was supposed to represent
a humanitarian advance over the jolt. The first recipient—the patient
of sorts—was a man named Charles Brooks. A young-looking, forty-
year-old African American man, Brooks had been convicted four years
earlier of participating in an execution-style slaying of a car salesman
who had escorted him on a test drive. His lawyers filed a flurry of
appeals, but Brooks's options ran out on December 7, 1982.[60]

Before dawn, he submitted to shackling and climbed into the back
of a TDC vehicle for transport from the Ellis Unit to Huntsville. He
clinched his eyes shut for the entire trip—what would have been his
last glimpse of the free world—and then paced through a tedious day at
the Walls. On the outside, protesters and counterprotesters gathered.
"Many of the men had shaved necks; some had ponytails," recalls Jim
Willett, who worked the late shift that day. On the inside, the condemned man had an awkward chat with two chaplains, one Christian,
one Muslim. He visited with his niece and played a few games of chess
with a specially assigned guard (Brooks won handily).[61] In the early
evening, he showered, changed into street clothes, and had his last
meal—not what he ordered (fried shrimp and oysters), but the best
TDC had on hand: a T-bone steak, french fries, and peach cobbler.[62]
Just before midnight, the pastors, surrounded by guards, arrived at his
cell door.

Since Governor Neff had presided over the execution of five black
prisoners in 1924, Ol' Sparky had awaited condemned inmates down
the hall, but now a hospital gurney had been rolled in, with slender,
sheet-covered boards extending from either side. Charlie remained
calm as he stepped up onto the bed, but his eyes flashed with fear as

the execution team strapped him down and opened a vein. He called out, "I love you," to his fiancée, who was watching on the other side of the glass, and began a chant from the Koran. At 12:09, the warden gave his signal and the "triple dose" began to flow. Charlie's chest heaved and his fingers trembled, but in a few seconds he was quiet.[63]

Willett's job was to accompany the hearse to the Huntsville Funeral Home. It was his first execution, and already he felt conflicted. "I knew that Charlie Brooks had committed a horrible crime," he writes, reconstructing his thoughts as he waited outside the death house. "But I also knew that he was alive and was—right this very minute—being made dead." Many years later, when Willett presided over his own executions—eighty-nine of them—the ambivalence returned each time. He never came to peace with what he called "the worst part of [his] job," but he never stopped, either.[64]

## "SURVIVE OR PERISH"

About a year after Charlie Brooks lay down to die, in 1984, penal reforms set in motion by *Ruiz v. Estelle* reached a high-water mark in Texas with the arrival of Raymond Procunier as TDC director. Dubbed "Mr. Fix-It," the rumpled and garrulous bureaucrat represented a stylistic departure from his control-model predecessors. Whereas Jim Estelle had been tightly wound, circumspect, and intensely loyal to TDC traditions, the Pro freely criticized old-timers and made policy adjustments on the fly. Like Walking George Beto, Procunier regularly toured the units but in his own style; much of what he said was too "salty" for trailing reporters to print, and he "pressed the flesh" with inmates and guards alike. When the Sullivans invited him to speak at a CURE convention, he stayed the entire day, hugging inmates' family members and promising to improve the lives of their loved ones. Governor Mark White, Clements's Democratic successor, welcomed "the beginning of a new era in criminal justice policy in Texas."[65]

Director Procunier pledged far-reaching changes at TDC: better staff, better procedures, better conditions. "Every place I've been the place works better when I leave," he assured inmate reporters at the *Echo*. Almost as soon as he turned up for work in Huntsville, however, he began to have doubts about his prospects for success. TDC's transitional administration was in "chaos," he charged. "Texas spent too much time saying, 'Ain't it awful,'" when it came to the *Ruiz* case, instead of planning for compliance. "They had not anticipated the resources that would be required."[66]

In ordering the BT system dismantled, Judge Justice had warned that hundreds of new, well-trained officers would be needed to fill a "vacuum of authority." But the agency had done more fighting than hiring. The result, observed Procunier's spokesperson, was a "long, hard row" to hoe for the new administration. "The last three months," sighed the director in September 1984, "have been tougher than my first thirty-five years in corrections, put together. I am not sure I am going to be able to pull this off."[67]

As Justice had predicted, one of Procunier's most daunting challenges was to hire and motivate staff. By the end of his tenure, TDC had some nine thousand security officers, up from twenty-five hundred at the start of the Ruíz trial. Every new boot was desperately needed, but many of them did not fit into the mold cast by Ellis and Beto. "Before we hired country people," explained a farm warden. "Now . . . we're hiring mostly kids from the city." Increasingly, women, African Americans, and Chicanos populated the guard force, and as the personnel started to resemble prisoners, TDC old-timers complained about lax standards and lack of respect for rank. "A lot of the bosses here don't care nothing about the job," grumbled one veteran. "They come in, put in their eight hours, and go on about their business. They don't realize how dangerous it can be."[68] Although TDC's troop strength was growing fast, its famous esprit de corps was starting to fissure.

Because so many long-timers followed Estelle out the back gate—some of them hurried along by Procunier—the new guard force lacked experiential depth even as the daily demands of prison work were becoming more onerous. Under the control model, select convicts filed reports, provided intelligence, and maintained security. Under Procunier's leadership and court supervision, however, free-world personnel had to turn the keys, conduct the counts, and handle every disciplinary infraction by themselves. Headquarters regularly updated procedures, eventually filling a two-volume manual, causing officers to complain they were buried in paperwork. "Used to be I did something," groused a sergeant who started out in 1972. "Now I got to tell you what I did, put it down on paper."[69]

Even with battalions of new hires, TDC remained perpetually understaffed; its guard-inmate ratio was still one of the lowest in the country. Under the BT system, outnumbered guards were rarely in danger, but that started to change. "All of a sudden the boss was out front all by himself," explained Procunier.[70] The BTs no longer provided backup, and new policies limited the ability of staff to conduct "tune-ups." "It's changed because you can't put that boot in their ass," explained a veteran. "Ain't no fear no more." Many convicts relished the change. While new boots hesitated, confused by the limits on their authority, convicts started to stand up straight, their resolve stiffened by victories in court. Once obsequious, prisoners turned obstreperous. "Quit harassing me you old country punk," went a typical retort. "Fuck all you whores, you can't tell me what to do anymore." Other convicts went further. Between 1983 and 1986, reported assaults on officers more than quintupled, from 733 to 4,144 a year.[71]

Terror, once the companion of inmates, began creeping into the guard force. "I've been struck several times, been bitten by inmates," reported one officer. "Some of them, I'm afraid of. I'm afraid to say something to them because I know what I'm going to get. . . . A lot of times, . . . if I see an inmate do something wrong, I just completely ignore it. I just walk off." "Nobody felt like keeping it up," lamented another officer, referring to the discipline and cleanliness of the control model. "So we let go, let everything go."[72]

In the old days, it was the camaraderie more than the meager pay that bound officers to TDC. They had working-class pride in their jobs, a sense of purpose. They were "protecting the frontier against the imprisoned savages," as one writer put it, and they had decent benefits besides: discount housing, food, laundry, and servants. In any confrontations, superior officers stood by their underlings. Under the new court-monitored regime, however, the central administration was as likely to send out internal affairs investigators as commendation letters; in several use-of-force cases, staff members got indicted. Legislators demanded that TDC employees give up their irregular emoluments—the backbone of O. B. Ellis's personnel system—and the press derided veterans as "dinosaurs," on the verge of extinction. The morale was low, admitted one officer. "Three or four years ago, I liked it. I came in and felt fresh and ready to work. I felt like somebody." Some guards started to sound envious of convicts, calling themselves "gray slaves." "The convicts got W. Wayne and Ruíz," remarked one guard, "but the bosses ain't got shit."[73]

• • •

Convicts expressed little sympathy for their disheartened keepers. "They had it made in the shade under the old system," chided Albert "Racehoss" Sample, the prisoner memoirist who got out in 1972. "They could sit around all night cracking peanuts and reading *Playboy*. It's eating their lunch, just killing them, that they have to go out and patrol the cell blocks now."[74] But it wasn't only staff that found the new regime unsettling. During a transitional period, prisoners enjoyed greater personal autonomy and less intimidation by staff and BTs; they looked forward to improved conditions and new opportunities for early release. As TDC's authoritarian power structure crumbled in the mid-1980s, however, many convicts turned not only on their former masters but on each other as well.

Officially sanctioned violence had been endemic (if seldom reported) under the control model, but it was freelance violence that grew up from the rubble. "Everyone I knew had a shank," recalls a long-serving prisoner. "When Judge Justice ordered the BT system abolished, it opened the door for others to seize the power." TDC became a "war zone." A lieutenant remembers that one of his first jobs as a twenty-year-old at Ellis was to watch the warden's car during an emergency. No one told him what had happened, but he soon noticed pieces of skin and bone splayed across the trunk—both his warden and farm manager had been killed. Four years later, his task was to videotape a crime scene. His friend Minnie Houston had been stabbed at least ten times in the chest with a carving knife. "There was a huge hole, and her fingers were missing," he says flatly.[75]

Overwhelmingly, the victims were inmates. There was the case of Calvin Williams, who was doused with lighter fluid and set on fire by two members of the Aryan Brotherhood. Michael Jewell recalls a deadly scuffle over television programming. "A black guy wanted to watch 'Roots,' which was then a rerun, when something else had been voted in," he writes. After a tense series of channel changes, a white prisoner "pulled a knife about nine inches long and stabbed him once through the heart." With feuds escalating into fatalities, prisoners reported that convict fights became increasingly desperate. "In those days fist fights had become obsolete," says Jewell. "If it was a matter worth fighting for, it was worth killing for. You couldn't afford to kick the shit out of someone and let him walk away. Odds were that he would be back." "You're on your own," observed another convict. "You're either going to survive or perish."[76]

Many assaults emanated from a deadly mix of race, rackets, and gangs. "They didn't have no gangs under the old system; we were the gang," remarks a captain at Jester, formerly the Harlem Farm. That may have been true when BTs prowled the tiers but not in their absence. In search of protection and prison spoils (drug running, gambling, and prostitution), gangs and rival gangs, usually organized by ethnicity, proliferated across the system. There was the Texas Syndicate, the Aryan Brotherhood, the Mexican Mafia, the Mandingo Warriors, and even, for a time, the Seeds of Idi Amin.[77] Together, they were the most powerful convict organizations to take root in Texas prisons since the ill-fated Prison Welfare League of the late 1920s.

Director Procunier made squashing gang violence his top priority and tried everything he could think of to stop it. TDC bought metal detectors and high-tech listening devices. Administrators made greater use of lockdown and formed Special Operations and Reaction Teams (SORT) to quell disturbances. When prisoners sharpened their dinnerware, TDC switched over to plastic; when convicts figured out how to harvest brass rods from their toilets, the agency spent five hundred thousand dollars on sturdier, stainless steel replacements. Regular shank sweeps turned up formidable arsenals; a single search at Coffield produced 489 weapons. Still the killing continued. In 1979, there had been three homicides in TDC; in 1985, there were 27.[78]

As had besieged prison reformers in the 1910s and 1920s, Procunier became exasperated and combative. "What we have to establish in this department is that we are the tougher of the two groups," he declared. "There is no room for negotiation in a time of insurrection." Even as the Pro channeled his control-model predecessors, however, guards, convicts, and politicians turned on him. After only a few months on the job, Governor White warned the director to "end the violence or else." After a year, Procunier packed up and moved back to California. The job was too much for him, he admitted. He had "just run out of gas."[79]

Procunier fell more quickly than had previous reform-minded administrators, but with similar consequences. His replacement, Colonel Lane McCotter, had deep ties to the old control-model establishment—the *Houston Post* called him "a protégé of George Beto"—and his marching orders were to restore authority at all costs. In another time, this would have meant a sheaf of whipping orders. But according to the courts' "evolving standard of decency," McCotter had to rely on an equally weather-worn alternative: solitary confinement. Under Procunier, the state had already started concentrating the most "unruly inmates" on six special units and confining them to their cells for extended periods. Under McCotter, this became a core operating procedure. In September 1985, after a triple stabbing involving the Texas Syndicate and the Mexican Mafia, he ordered seventeen thousand inmates locked down in their cells.[80] For many of them, the status became permanent.

At first, segregation blocks only concentrated the violence, but TDC steadily tightened the controls. Since most fights broke out at congregation points, officers started taking prisoners to recreation and the showers individually, which, given the staff shortages, meant that many inmates rarely left their cells. Some convicts then figured out how to make spears and hurl them at rivals as they passed by their cell fronts; in response, prison officials installed wire mesh screens. "We're caging them in," explained a warden. "They won't see much more than wire and steel." Carrying forth the retaliatory logic, enterprising convicts started dousing bosses with urine and feces (an offense known as "chucking"), so that officers began wearing slickers and finally crept down the halls behind trundling Plexiglas shields. Each insurgent innovation invited repressive countermeasures, and before long thousands of inmates found themselves living in "isolation chambers." "24 hours a day in a 9-by-6 cell, it's degrading, humiliating, it's sick," complained one occupant. But also effective. What one journalist wryly called the Quaker Solution finally brought TDC's gang war under a semblance of control. In 1986, the number of convict homicides dropped back to five.[81]

Traditionally, solitary confinement in Texas had lasted only a few weeks (during the sweatbox days, only a few hours); longer stays, wardens knew, interfered with agriculture. In the emerging legalistic-bureaucratic order, however, the "pisser" got a new name—"administrative segregation," or ad-seg—and it became a permanent classification status. The role of convicts with the highest security designations thereafter shifted from farmhand to something closer to farm animal. TDC's infrastructure changed shape accordingly. "Super segregation" cell blocks were created at Eastham and elsewhere, from which convicts never turned out to work. As new prisons went up, large sections were set off for idle ad-seggers. In 1987, the agency opened the Michael Unit near Palestine, not far from the old Rusk ironworks. Hailed as the "model for the future," just as Rusk once was, Michael dispensed with the traditional telephone-pole layout, which was cheap to build but difficult to police without hordes of unpaid building tenders, in favor of a modular pod design, which facilitated visual surveillance and riot control. Some pods were set up as dormitories, like the old tanks, but most featured reinforced concrete, double-bunk cells with enhanced security features, like bolted-down metal toilets and slit windows.[82] Most Texas prisoners continued toiling in the fields, but an increasingly large minority never went outside.

Officials said that Michael's extended lockdown capabilities were modeled on the federal government's highest-security prison at Marion, Illinois, a replacement for Alcatraz, which had itself resurrected the total isolation of Pennsylvania's Eastern State Penitentiary. If forced labor had historically governed TDC operations, confinement, separation, and complete architectural control were stepping up. In response to chaos and court orders, Texas's prisons were morphing from workhouses into warehouses.[83]

## TEXAS ROUNDUP

As Texas's penal system passed through a paroxysm of violence while devouring tax dollars as never before, conservatives and not a few liberals vented their frustrations at Judge Justice, whom the Speaker of the House accused of "working on behalf of the criminal element of this state." Segregationists and the top brass at TDC had always despised the judge, but as the state's "cell blocks became killing grounds," as *Newsweek* put it, many Texans, especially white Texans, came to share the sentiment. *Texas Monthly* ran a feature titled, "How They Ruined Our Prisons." After a Houston TV station aired a special on the judge's career, his chambers were flooded with vitriol. "You are a horrible man—may you rot in hell for your decisions," read one letter. Politicians shouted, too. A House representative from Rusk introduced a bill to build a juvenile detention center across the street from Justice's home. It would serve him right, the lawmaker said, for going "too far in looking at the rights of hoodlums and outlaws" (the bill died in the Senate).[84]

Texas conservatives were angry not only about judicial intervention in their state's prisons but about crime generally, which had steadily worsened; between 1960 and 1980, Texas's murder rate almost doubled.[85] The *Ruiz* case had almost nothing to do with it—crime was up across the country, not just in Texas—but because Judge Justice placed limits on overcrowding and thus forced officials to expedite releases if they wanted to continue accepting record numbers of incoming inmates, the case served as a handy scapegoat.

Many Texans came to see easy paroles rather than excessive sentencing as the state's most pressing criminal justice problem. Early releases eased population pressures and made it easier for the state to comply with federal court orders. But many discharged felons ended up back in the clink (in the mid-1980s, Texas's three-year reincarceration rate ranged between 35 and 44 percent), most for technical violations, but a fraction for committing horrible new crimes. Amid the ascendance of law-and-order conservatism, these depredations attracted widespread attention. "The Board of Pardons and Paroles, through some arcane twist of reason, concluded that rapists and murderers" should be released "from Texas prisons to relieve crowding," bemoaned the *Waco-Tribune Herald*. "The horror stories are beginning to emerge."[86]

The most horrifying story maker of all was Kenneth McDuff. Well before he came up for parole, McDuff had been well known in Central Texas. In 1966, he was convicted and sentenced to death for abducting and murdering three teenagers. In 1973, *Furman v. Georgia* rescued him from the chair, and he became "just a number," as one journalist put it, just another dim-witted lifer big and mean enough to get promoted to building tender. Years later, he became eligible for parole, and in 1989, under murky circumstances, he got the two votes he needed to walk. Soon after, women started vanishing. At a late-night car wash in Austin, McDuff grabbed a woman by the throat and threw her in the backseat of his car. He and a buddy took turns raping her. Then McDuff said he was "gonna use her up" and drove off with her alone; her body wasn't found for years. In Waco, he abducted a clerk at a convenience store. He raped her, too, then bound her with the shoelaces of her tennis shoes and threw her in a flooded gravel pit to drown.[87]

The latter crime got McDuff another death sentence—a post-*Furman* first—and it fell to Jim Willett to carry it out. By 1998, Huntsville's death chamber was a well-lubricated machine, and McDuff didn't get special attention like Charlie Brooks. Instead of T-bone steaks, he got "broiled hamburger patties"; gone were the niceties. By 6 p.m., McDuff was on his way to Joe Byrd Cemetery, where a white cement cross, marked only with his prison number and an X for execution, is today sinking into his grave. Willett, for once, slept easily. Investigators suspect that McDuff was responsible for a dozen murders over the course of his life. "Tonight, no matter what the opponents of capital punishment might say," Willett wrote, "I knew that we've ridded the world of a man that it will be better off without."[88]

Even before McDuff's killing spree came to light a new sort of social movement was lending legitimacy to the law-and-order cause: victims' rights. Outraged by "revolving-door" parole policies and bound by common grief, such groups took hold across the country in the 1980s and 1990s. They demanded victims' services and tougher penalties, especially for repeat offenders. "The situation is out of control," scolded the chair of People Against Violent Crime, Bob Sterns, whose son had been murdered in Houston. "The system is not able to protect law-abiding citizens from known felons. The battle is not being won."[89]

Victims of violent crime had always been angry, of course, at the perpetrators, most of all, but also at defense attorneys, plea bargains, and insurance companies. As the violent crime wave crested, however, they found a public voice. Conservative politicians invited victims into the halls of power, and from one emotional hearing to another they helped shift the debate. Tough-on-crime lawmakers were not mean-spirited, as civil libertarians claimed, but compassionate champions of the aggrieved. They weren't racists but crusaders for a new class of rights. "We must stand for . . . equal rights for the victims of crime," declared victims' rights leaders in the *Dallas Morning News*.[90] Suddenly, the language of injustice and equal rights—used to such powerful effect in the civil rights movement—could be deployed to curtail parole, extend prison sentences, and send children to jail as adults. A new age was in the making.

Both Democrats and Republicans vied for seats on the victims' rights bandwagon. Governor Mark White called for a Victims' Bill of Rights. But it was his archrival, Bill Clements, who wielded the rhetoric of crime victimhood to greater effect. In 1982, White, a conservative Democrat, had chased the pathbreaking Republican out of office. Four years later, Clements came roaring back on an antitax, get-tough-on-crime platform. In a dagger-thrusting campaign designed largely by an up-and-coming political operative named Karl Rove, Clements accused White of mismanaging the prison system and releasing precisely 2,070 "murderers, rapists, and sex offenders."[91]

During his first term, Clements had racked up a conflicted criminal justice record. He stiffened laws and threw dollars at the prison system, but he had also appointed. Harry Whittington to the corrections board and chartered a crime commission that recommended many of the reforms championed by Pauline and Charlie Sullivan. After an interregnum of prison pandemonium and what sociologists call "crime panic," however, Clements mounted his second governorship in the style of a frontier lawman. Under legislation signed during his second term, prisoners were required to serve a greater portion of their sentences before parole eligibility, and prosecutors were granted new powers to try more juveniles as adults and introduce illegally obtained evidence. On the narcotics front, the governor kept up the fight he had launched with H. Ross Perot. His administration allowed police departments to keep the loot they seized in drug busts and set up regional narcotics task forces, which fattened on federal pork and eventually dragged the state into a series of embarrassing scandals, including the racist Tulia debacle, in which a corrupt cop sent forty-six people to jail based on perjured testimony.[92]

By the time Clements returned to power, Texas politicos had already been defining new crimes and ramping up penalties for almost two decades. The result—exacerbated by general population growth and high crime rates—was a massive influx of felons to TDC. In 1972, 7,725 persons had caught the chain to Huntsville; by 1987, annual prison admissions had climbed to 35,007. At first, the agency coped by stuffing them in—hence the quadruple celling assailed during the *Ruiz* trial. Under court-ordered crowding limits, however, the state had to make greater use of politically risky parole, which expanded sixfold over the same period. "We were kickin' prisoners out the back door every time we let one of them in through the front door," remembers Babe Schwartz.[93]

Because new sentencing laws had a disproportionate impact on low-level defendants (murderers and rapists were already getting long sentences under the old rules), a growing portion of new commitments to TDC were nonviolent, first-time drug offenders. To make room for them, the parole board had to bump up the percentage of applications it approved, with the result that, as two UT researchers concluded, "the pool of eligible persons became more hard core." "We're going to have to release worse and worse people to keep the prisons" in compliance with court mandates, warned one board member, making the case for more prison space. By the late 1980s, when McDuff slithered out, first-time parole approval rates had climbed to almost 80 percent. As more and more chain buses arrived from the city jails, the pressure only mounted.[94]

Social scientists found that early releases were having a negligible impact on crime rates. But politicians knew that something had to give. Texas was discharging murderers, in some cases, to make beds for potheads, and the news media were having a heyday. If Texas wanted to continue using its growing arsenal of penalties, the state was going to have to get serious about prison construction.

In his first term, Clements had been an avid prison builder. He added five new units and sundry cell blocks to TDC (Mark White then continued at a slightly slower pace). During his encore performance, however, Governor Clements embarked on prison expansion on an unprecedented scale.[95] In 1987, he and the legislature approved $530 million for prison construction, much of it borrowed, and broke ground on 12,500 new beds, equivalent to the entire prison population in 1968, the year David Ruíz decided to become a writ writer. Attorney Bill Turner, the Sullivans, even Clements's friend Harry Whittington warned against such massive growth. "To think that they can handle a third bigger system is crazy," cried Turner, who continued to lead the plaintiffs in the drawn-out settlement phase of *Ruiz*. "They can't manage it. They can't afford it." But when the governor convened a Texas Criminal Justice Summit in 1988, law enforcement and prison officials told him he hadn't gone far enough. In the 1989 legislative session, Clements and his allies redoubled their efforts, providing $324 million for another 10,800 beds.[96]

TDC "has embarked on the largest construction program in the history of the state," boasted Clements's chair of the corrections board, Charles Terrell. Yet even a total of 24,000 new prison slots—as large as the entire prison system when Clements first took office in 1979—would be insufficient, hard-liners advised. "Despite the passage of twenty-nine anti-crime bills [and] unparalleled increases in prison beds . . . we are still being forced to release monsters back to our streets," complained Terrell in his outgoing message. "I'm not sure, today, . . . that we don't need 50,000 more prison beds to protect our citizens."[97]

Terrell's outlandish prediction proved too modest, but already Texas's prison boom was profoundly reshaping TDC. Between 1979, when Clements started out, and 1991, when he finished, the agency's inmate count doubled, its staff sextupled, and the number of prisons under its management jumped from nineteen to thirty-seven. For the first time, some of these units sprang up outside of the state's historical East Texas slavery belt, and for the first time, they weren't all surrounded by cropland. Secure custody began to overshadow agriculture, and in 1984 prison officials had to hire outside contractors to bring in the full cotton crop. Around Sugar Land, pressure mounted to sell lowland fields that convicts had worked for more than a century to suburban real estate developers—all the better to fund still more construction, politicians reasoned.[98] The credo "self support" had governed Texas prisons since before the Civil War, but now the system's historic work ethic was evaporating in the hot sun.

Even as agriculture receded from primacy, however, the profit motive remained prominent. During the old days, wardens had been evaluated based on the success of their crops, based on how much money they could haul in for the state. Under Governor Clements, the money haul got redirected outward. Prison demand was outstripping supply, so Clements and company, like their forebears after the Civil War, turned to the private sector to lend a hand.

Thus began what *BusinessWeek* described as a "free-for-all" in "Texas' next ten-gallon business." In the early stages, construction firms and equipment suppliers were the big winners, but in 1987 lawmakers invited a new set of vendors to play: private prison companies. For-profit jailers like Edward Cunningham's outfit had once controlled all of Texas's convicts, but under the new regime they would get, in a sense, an even better deal. Rather than paying the state for the right to exploit convict labor, corporations would collect payments from the state to lock up inmates in their own private brigs. This is where the smart money was, as it involved both construction and renewable contracts, and by 1989 two of the smartest moneymakers in the emerging human confinement industry, Corrections Corporation of America (CCA) and Wackenhut, had both opened two prisons in the state.[99]

The benefit to politicians was that they could avoid up-front investment, thus alleviating short-term pressure to raise taxes; the arrangement also created a new class of generous campaign donors. The danger was that private contractors would try to boost their profit margins by cutting services to inmates, just as lessees once had with deadly consequences. Indeed, the first state audit of the new for-profit facilities found them riddled with age-old deficiencies, including inadequate medical care, understaffing, and lack of promised educational and drug-treatment programming.[100] Nevertheless, after a few adjustments, Wackenhut and CCA had their contracts renewed—and soon multiplied.

Private prison lobbyists proved enormously effective under the elegant capitol dome partly cast by leased convict laborers; by the turn of the century, Texas hosted the largest private prison industry in the nation, just as it had once hosted the largest lease system. A government report in 1994 fretted about the emergence of a "prison industrial complex," a set of "self-perpetuating interest groups" that were "in business to keep [their] empire growing," but like so many state inquests going back to Reconstruction, the report gathered more dust than policy influence. What one Texas historian called "penology for profit" was back.[101]

The Clements administration gestured toward Texas's prison past in another way as well, by stripping a moniker from the penal system's official title that had always been more inspirational than operational: "corrections." With backlogged admissions and early releases both causing headaches, lawmakers decided in 1989 to combine probation, parole, and imprisonment functions under one big bureaucratic roof, the Texas Department of Criminal Justice, or TDCJ. The Texas Department of Corrections thus ceased to exist, its sprawling domain folded into TDCJ as the "Institutional Division." "Rehabilitation of felons" remained a stated goal of the super agency, but "confinement" and "supervision" came first.[102] In truth, they always had.

A different sort of politician moved into the Governor's Mansion in early 1991. While Clements had been drilling for millions in the Gulf of Mexico, his successor had been teaching school and raising kids. Whereas the outgoing governor represented the new face of the Texas right, the newcomer stood for what passed as the Texas left. Ann Richards had started out in politics campaigning for liberal politicians like Ralph Yarborough and Sarah Weddington, the Roe v. Wade attorney who won a Texas House seat in 1972. In 1976, Richards won a county commissioner seat in Austin, and in 1988 her folksy vernacular made her a star at the Democratic National Convention. She mocked the priviledged vice president as having been "born with a silver foot in his mouth." In the 1990 governor's race, her GOP opponent, Clayton Williams, had a tendency to put his manure-encrusted boot in his mouth. He joked about "getting serviced" south of the border and once boasted he was going to "head [Richards] and hoof her and drag her through the dirt" like a cow on election day.[103] Women voters, including many suburban Republicans, herded over to Ann, and she became Texas's last Democratic executive of the twentieth century.

A champion of feminism and civil rights, Richards leaned further left than any Texas governor since the Progressive Era. In criminal justice policy, she favored rehabilitation over revenge. "The public wants to believe there is a way to incarcerate anyone who's committed a crime and keep them there until they won't do it again," she told an interviewer. "Well, that's obviously not true. . . . I believe people deserve punishment," she said, but "you have to take advantage of these people while you have them, and focus on what they're going to be like when you release them." Having gone to what she called "drunk school" in 1980, Richards recognized something of herself in the struggles of many inmates. On a prison visit, the governor sat down with a group of convicts and said, "My name is Ann, and I am an alcoholic."[104]

One of Richards's proudest accomplishments was to build what she called "the largest drug-and-alcohol treatment system in the world" within TDCJ. In every other way, however, the new governor found herself sailing the retributive winds with as much tilt as her predecessor. During her first year in office, Texas's overall violent crime rate, as reported by the FBI, hit an all-time high, and it was under her watch that Kenneth McDuff showed up on *America's Most Wanted*, becoming an icon of accursed second chances. The parole rate was still climbing, and counties were suing in federal court to force TDCJ to accept their backlogged felons. "Governor Richards really had no choice but to build more prisons," says Tony Fabelo, former director of the Criminal Justice Policy Council. "She got caught in a perfect storm."[105]

Although vestiges of her rehabilitative efforts still exist within TDCJ—the Substance Abuse Felony Punishment and therapeutic community programs both started under her watch—the defining contribution of Richards's administration was to increase the amount of time prisoners spend behind bars and to provide the necessary space for them to do so. Although Clements had bellyached about parole leniency, it was Richards who finally brought the first-time approval rate back down to historic norms, from 79 percent in 1989 to 29 percent in 1994. On the entry side, Richards toughened up as well. In 1991, she signed a bill to abolish the state's discretionary sentencing code in favor of fixed penalties to be set by a sentencing commission. The purpose was to cut down on racial and jurisdictional disparities, but the actual impact was to push sentences up across the board and to shift discretion from judges and the parole board to prosecutors. In 1993, Richards and the legislature reworked the sentencing system again, doubling the amount of time "aggravated offenders" had to serve before parole eligibility, mandating that capital lifers serve at least forty years before coming up for consideration, and creating a new state jail system, in which low-level, nonviolent offenders would serve short sentences with no good-time reductions whatsoever. Texas had always dispensed long sentences, but they had been mitigated by relatively generous good-time and clemency policies. No more. Said the chair of the Senate Criminal Justice Committee, "We're fixin' to have a lot of very old prisoners in Texas."[106]

Sentencing and parole changes would require many more beds—or "shelves," as TDCJ called them—and Governor Richards built plenty, more than anyone before her. In 1991, she approved construction to accommodate 25,000 new prisoners, including her 12,000 slots for drug treatment. In 1993, voters rejected a $750 million bond issue for schools but approved a cool billion for prison construction. The result was 22,000 new shelves for the felony state jail system, a new branch added to TDCJ, plus 15,000 more regular beds. All told, the size of Texas's already hulking prison system more than doubled under Richards's watch, a notable accomplishment for a liberal governor. In this way, Richards's program offered a punitive twist on the New Deal politics of her youth. By the end of her term, she was managing one of the biggest public works projects in Texas history, what the Criminal Justice Policy Council called "the largest correctional construction project in the world."[107]

With the parole spigot tightened and prisons springing up from Beaumont to El Paso, Richards would seem to have earned her crime-fighting bona fides. In the 1994 elections, however—the year that Newt Gingrich masterminded a Republican takeover of Congress—there was virtually no way for a southern Democrat to sufficiently fortify her right flank. Four years earlier, she had trounced a bumbling oil rancher who, as Molly Ivins delicately put it, "was as useless as ball moss."[108] But going for reelection, she faced the affable scion of a U.S. president and a disciplined disciple of Bill Clements's direct mailer and dirty tricks master, Karl Rove.

Texas's crime rate had finally started to fall during Richards's tenure, but that didn't stop Rove's candidate from attacking the governor in what she thought was an area of strength. Drawing on cherry-picked statistics, the challenger warned that "crime in Texas is becoming more random, more violent, and the criminals are getting younger while she has been in office." Because she had vetoed a concealed carry bill, the National Rifle Association put her in its sights. Menacing GOP attack ads flooded the cable lines. In one spot, made to look like real-life closed-circuit television feed, a woman was set upon by two masked assailants. "Crime is out of control" went the tag line. "Ann Richards is out of touch if she thinks Texans feel safer than they did a few years ago."[109] With 60 percent positive approval ratings, the folksy incumbent took to ridiculing her opponent, dismissing him as "some jerk," but George W. Bush was no joke.[110]

# 9

# THE TRIUMPH OF TEXAS TOUGH

The consequences will be tough and certain.
—GEORGE W. BUSH[1]

In 1999, four years into George W. Bush's governorship and twenty-one years after Judge William Wayne Justice first consolidated the case, *Ruiz v. Estelle* went back to trial. In 1985, the parties had signed a comprehensive settlement agreement, and in 1992 the court had agreed to begin releasing the state from supervision. In the meantime, TDCJ had expanded exponentially, and prison officials were having a hard time keeping up with their commitments. Plaintiffs were concerned the state was backsliding, but it was the defendants who hauled the case back into court. In 1996, Congress had passed the Prison Litigation Reform Act (PLRA), which placed new restrictions on prisoners' rights cases, and the Bush administration sensed an opportunity. With the help of an increasingly conservative judiciary, Texas could possibly regain full control of its prisons and put an end to *Ruiz v. Estelle* for good.[2]

Bill Turner had extricated himself from the lawsuit in 1991, but his assistant Donna Brorby had kept at it. *Ruiz* was her first case out of law school, and it had consumed most of her life. "I'm a one-horse lawyer," she says from her disheveled San Francisco living room. Since the lead-up to the first trial, Brorby had "lived and breathed Texas prisons." Now she faced another showdown—this time without the backing of the Justice Department and the NAACP, which had withdrawn from the case after the main settlement.[3]

The Bush administration was in a strong position going into the rematch—Texas's congressional delegation had helped craft the PLRA specifically with *Ruiz* in mind—but Brorby still had Judge Justice, and if she could get compelling evidence into his courtroom, she figured she had a chance. Based on her correspondence with convicts, Brorby was convinced that TDCJ remained unconstitutional and would only deteriorate without judicial oversight. To prove it, she needed to conduct extensive discovery and hire outside experts, all on her own dime. To pay the bills, she ate through her life savings and became increasingly terrified of losing. "I felt the full lives of the prisoners on my shoulders," she says, "and I was afraid of debt and poverty for myself. The work was totally exhausting. I got boils and a staph infection."[4]

By her own estimation, Brorby has a plodding and pedantic style, more suited to research than trial work. She has a deep voice and unshakable convictions but lacks Turner's oratorical charisma and lightning wit. "Bill would have done a better job in court," she admits freely, "but I *would* do it." Luckily for her, the testimony itself supplied the necessary drama. The attorney general's office had tried to avoid a full-blown hearing by having the appellate court shut down the case by fiat—and for good reason.[5] Once the trial began, it became clear that conditions within TDCJ remained abysmal.

In his 274-page ruling issued in March 1999, Judge Justice acknowledged that Texas prisons had changed significantly over the years. "TDCJ-ID [Institutional Division] has remade itself into a professionally operated agency," he offered. In two critical areas, however, Justice concluded that "systematic constitutional violations" remained. Inmates still lacked basic physical safety, he regretted, despite the fact that he had been issuing protective orders for twenty-five years. In crowded, poorly supervised cell blocks and dormitories, prison gangs preyed on the weak, reducing some to sexual enslavement, while officers themselves continued to engage in "sadistic and malicious" violence, largely unchecked by supervisors. Even more disturbing, in Justice's view, was the system's principal remedy for conflict—administrative segregation—which was itself cruel and unusual. Ad-seg had become the dumping ground not only for troublemakers but for the mentally ill, experts testified. "Smeared feces, self-mutilation, and incessant babbling and shrieking are almost everyday occurrences," Justice observed. "The administrative segregation units of the Texas prison system deprive inmates of the minimal necessities of civilized life." They "are virtual incubators of psychoses."[6]

With the same vehemence that had long characterized his rulings, Judge Justice gave Texas's prison system one last whack between the eyes. In the changed political and legal circumstances of the 1990s, however, the strike no longer stung. Governor Bush hardly acknowledged the verdict, despite the trial's revelation of hellish mistreatment. Instead, he and his aides turned their heads expectantly toward appeal on the Fifth Circuit, which was no longer a citadel of civil rights enforcement. As during the days of Jim Estelle, prison officials made scarcely any effort to comply with the ruling. What thundered inside the courtroom barely echoed within the increasingly fortified walls of TDCJ.

At seventy-nine, Justice was as energetic and indignant as ever, but he had few allies, so politicians no longer had to bow to him. He had once been described as "the most powerful man in Texas," but George W. Bush held that title now.[7] The governor's idea of prison reform was to build new prisons and tighten their hold, and in late-twentieth-century America there was little an isolated district judge could do about it.

## BIRTH OF A PRISON NATION

By the time Bush became governor and set about trying to shut down the *Ruiz* case, the whole country was engaged in what one researcher called a "race to incarcerate." The South was winning. In 1995, the region accounted for 34 percent of the U.S. population but was locking up 44 percent of state prisoners. Sunbelt states in the West were rushing forward on the same track, as were comparably lenient, ethnically homogenous, and predominately rural jurisdictions. In Wyoming, for example, the modest murder rate hardly budged through the 1970s and then started to decline in the early 1980s. The state's imprisonment rate nonetheless soared by 344 percent between 1970 and 1995. Texas was leading the way, but America generally, from the red hills of Georgia to the curvaceous slopes of California, was following close behind.[8]

States with long-standing commitments to the "reformatory idea" were by no means immune. New York had bequeathed to the world Auburn, Elmira, Bedford Hills, and the Mutual Welfare League. Yet between 1970 and 1995, it jettisoned rehabilitative programming and erected fifty-three warehouse prisons; the state's imprisonment rate shot up from 66 to 326 per 100,000 residents.[9] Governor Nelson

Rockefeller, whom Barry Goldwater had beaten into submission in 1964, was at the helm when this punitive turn began. He was a Republican moderate, but after Attica he championed sterner prisons and endorsed the "toughest anti-drug program in the country." The resulting legislation surpassed even Texas's in severity. Drug dealers and many second-time felons were incarcerated for life; defendants possessing as little as four ounces of narcotics spent at least fifteen years behind bars.[10]

The Rockefeller drug laws churned out prisoners by the brigade; by 1985, the state's inmate population more than tripled. But when the payments came due, taxpayers balked. In 1981, they rejected a $500 million bond initiative. Governor Mario Cuomo thus decided to raid the state's Urban Development Corporation (UDC), an agency created to provide public housing to the poor. The scheme eventually cost taxpayers $700 million, but it got the cement mixers churning. Although he was a Great Society liberal who opposed capital punishment and mandatory minimums, Cuomo ended up fabricating more prison beds than all of New York's previous governors combined.[11]

There was a tortured logic to using the UDC—an entity chartered in 1968 to honor the memory of Dr. King—to build prisons. Corrections was becoming America's public housing program for the urban poor. Indeed, the Empire State's expanding constellation of cell blocks and caged dormitories contained mostly indigent felons sent upstate from New York City, many of whom had come of age in government housing complexes built by postwar liberalism. Overwhelmingly, they were nonwhites snared by narcs. As late as 1980, only 11 percent of the state's inmates were drug offenders, but by 1995 the portion had grown to 45 percent. Of those, more than 90 percent were African American or Latino.[12]

In another way, the UDC was retooled for rural development, this time in the interest of upstate whites. In the struggling Adirondack counties known as the North Country, imprisonment has supplanted farming, logging, and manufacturing as the economy's mainstay. Seventeen new prisons have gone up in the area, and their annual operating expenses top $400 million—a yearly subsidy to the North Country that adds up to more than $1,000 per resident. Almost everyone there seems to have a relative working in corrections, just as everyone in rough parts of Brooklyn or the Bronx has a relative in prison. The North Country has become New York's Siberia.[13]

• • •

Across the continent in the Golden State, a similar sort of prison ar-
chipelago has taken shape. In California, the pendulum had swung
furthest toward rehabilitative justice, and in the post–civil rights era it
swung back with equal force. Group counseling, bibliotherapy, and deinstitutionalization had spawned only gangs and revolutionaries, critics charged, and politicians began coalescing around simpler, stricter
alternatives. In 1976, in response to criticism from the left and right,
Governor Jerry Brown agreed to do away with indeterminate sentencing and parole—the pillars of California's postwar system—and replace
them with longer fixed terms and good-time reductions. Blotting out
the legacy of Earl Warren and Richard McGee, the legislation also stipulated that the primary purpose of imprisonment should be "punishment" rather than "rehabilitation."[14]

Brown's successor, Republican George Deukmejian, went further.
During his two terms as governor, he appointed more than a thousand
conservative judges, secured $3.5 billion for prison construction, chris-
tened a new generation of high-tech supermaxes (Pelican Bay was California's version of the Michael Unit), and signed 350 separate bills to
extend sentences for an array of crimes. The results were breathtaking.
When he took office in 1983, California's prison population had
climbed to 35,000; by the time he left in 1991, the total exceeded one
hundred thousand.[15]

Deukmejian's heir, Pete Wilson, then elevated punishment to a central strategy of governance. Over the course of an illustrious career in
state and national politics, Wilson had long advocated stiff criminal
justice policies, but during his eight years in office—a tumultuous period
marred by earthquakes, fiscal crisis, and the Los Angeles riots—he
made crime fighting and, to a lesser extent, immigrant exclusion his
top political issues. During his campaign against Dianne Feinstein in
1990, he hammered incessantly at the law-and-order theme, following
in the footsteps of his political mentor, Richard Nixon. Bolstered by
generous financing from the state's powerful guard union, Wilson
pledged to curtail plea bargaining and save money by hiring out inmates to private companies, an updated version of convict leasing. "Pete
Wilson [has] been an outstanding leader in the war against crime,"
wrote the first President Bush in an open letter to voters. "He is the co-
author of federal legislation that imposes the death penalty on drug

kingpins and the cop-killers they employ." Once in office, Wilson signed a flurry of anticrime bills, ratcheting up penalties for everything from gang membership to drive-by shootings. But it wasn't until the heat of his reelection campaign in 1994 that he found the policy that defined his governorship: three strikes.[16]

California's three strikes initiative was born in the parking lot of a late-night diner in Fresno. There, in June 1992, two ex-cons gunned down the daughter of an energetic wedding photographer who had once campaigned for Barry Goldwater. The man was Mike Reynolds, and within weeks of his daughter's death he contacted prominent GOP operators and launched a statewide movement to put third-time felons away for life, no exceptions.[17]

Prominent politicians initially ignored Reynolds's radical proposition, fearing it would bankrupt the state. Then along came Richard Allen Davis, a two-time felon with a mile-long rap sheet. On a brisk October morning in 1993, Davis abducted twelve-year-old Polly Klaas from her family home in a sleepy northern California town and managed to elude capture for nine anxious weeks. After a massive manhunt and saturation news coverage, Davis was finally apprehended in early December. Californians soon learned the worst. Polly had been raped and strangled to death.[18]

Pete Wilson was energized. Seizing on the Klaas murder, his reelection campaign honed its message and kicked into high gear. Speaking at the girl's enormous memorial service, the governor declared, "We must join Marc [Klaas] and take action by supporting the 'three strikes, you're out' initiative, the work of another California father driven by grief and anger over the wanton murder of his beautiful daughter." Although Polly's father ended up speaking out against three strikes as dangerously broad, Wilson plowed ahead. "I endorse [three strikes], and I hope you'll join me in supporting it," he said in his weekly radio address. "It's time to make these career criminals career inmates."[19]

As the election approached, Wilson turned crime fighting into high political theater. He proposed a roster of new initiatives: adult sanctions for teenagers, harsher prison conditions, even a one-strike law for rapists and child molesters. He called a special session of the legislature to deal exclusively with crime, produced scary sexual-predator ads, and hosted a lavish Hollywood crime summit. Despite the fact that California's overall crime rate had been declining for two years, Governor Wilson stoked a sense of public crisis, conjuring a California of law-abiding citizens under siege. With the help of media outlets more interested in grisly crime scenes than socioeconomic analysis, he successfully redirected public attention from budget cuts to personal safety. In November, along with Republicans nationwide, he won by a landslide.[20]

During the same election, Californians overwhelmingly approved three strikes, as well as a host of punitive add-ons. The resulting legal bulwark ensured that murderers with criminal records like Richard Davis stayed off the streets, but the statute's broad wording also mandated protracted imprisonment for thousands of individuals convicted of relatively minor third felonies. One case upheld by the U.S. Supreme Court involved a man who received twenty-five years to life for shoplifting golf clubs (a crime that can be defined as either a misdemeanor or a felony, at the discretion of the prosecutor). Another unlucky defendant landed a life sentence for swiping a piece of pepperoni pizza.[21]

Catch-all statutes like three strikes, piled on top of punitive legislation enacted all through the 1980s, ensured that California's prison population continued its breakneck ascent. By the late 1990s, when the inmate population hit 160,000, the size of the state's prison system for a time surpassed Texas's. Once a beacon of the decarceration and treatment movements, California had created one of the largest, most expensive, and most seriously overcrowded prison systems in the United States.[22]

Demographic and unemployment patterns, persistently elevated crime rates, the heroin and crack waves, around-the-clock news coverage, partisan realignment, and the rebirth of racial conservatism on the resting place of civil rights—all of these contributed to America's watershed transition from rehabilitative to retributive justice. So, too, did developments within the country's factories of ideas: its universities and think tanks. For some two hundred years, since Benjamin Rush first introduced his "house of repentance" in Benjamin Franklin's Philadelphia salon, intellectuals had embraced the cause of criminal reclamation. Starting in the 1960s, however, increasing numbers of professional researchers turned their backs on this venerable ideal. Sociologists on the left spoke out first, questioning the ethics of coercive treatment and looking forward to "a nation without prisons." In the wake of Nixon's law-and-order triumph in 1968, another set of thinkers then hitched themselves to the conservative express and began advocating what they called a realist approach to the crime-related social sciences. Instead of social engineering, they stressed rational choice and moral condemnation.

George Beto was something of a forerunner in this intellectual revolt. In his pronouncements as president of the American Correctional Association, he extolled "custody and discipline" and scorned "allegedly rehabilitative practices [that] have little evidence to show that they are successful." Outside the prison profession, a new school of conservative crime theorists took these arguments and ran with them. Even more stridently than progressives, they began questioning the core assumptions of crime prevention and prison-based rehabilitation efforts. Instead of antipoverty programs and counseling sessions, they posited, perhaps America needed more police officers and tougher, bigger prisons. Perhaps criminals would respond more to handcuffs than handouts. Proclaiming that dangerous felons "are going free in droves," an influential 1968 book, *The Lawbreakers,* predicted that soaring crime rates could be cut in half if only convicts were made to serve out every day of their sentences.[23]

A vanguard figure in this intellectual counterrevolution was Harvard political scientist James Q. Wilson. In a landmark 1975 book, *Thinking About Crime,* he ridiculed liberals' obsession with the "root causes" of illegality and questioned the evidentiary basis of rehabilitation. Like the Kerner Commission, he suggested that America was "becoming two societies." But for Wilson this was a call to arms over reconciliation, for the "affluent and worried" needed to defend themselves against the "pathological and predatory." Suggesting that GOP voters were far ahead of fuzzy-headed academics, he proposed scaling back the founding objectives of the penitentiary. Rather than trying to turn criminals into virtuous citizens, he argued, the purpose of the prison should be to "isolate and to punish." These no-nonsense rationales for imprisonment—particularly the notion of "incapacitation," by which wrongdoers would be prevented from committing new crimes simply by being incarcerated—became the guiding lights of America's expanding penal state.[24]

Wilson served as the don of this neoclassicist school, but the movement's most influential article, "What Works," published by *Public Interest* in 1974, was drafted by an upstart named Robert Martinson. A young, ambitious, emotionally troubled sociologist, Martinson had been hired during Governor Rockefeller's early push toward rehabilitative reform. The task of his research group was to examine every treatment program in the country and suggest best practices for New York. After reviewing some 231 studies on various rehabilitation initiatives, however, the team was dismayed to find that very few programs had hard data to prove success. "With few and isolated exceptions," Martinson wrote, "rehabilitative efforts that have been reported so far have had no appreciable effect on recidivism." Although other social scientists questioned his bluntly worded findings, demonstrating that some of the programs he investigated had indeed reduced recidivism, the take-home message of "What Works" was that nothing works. Martinson appeared in *Newsweek* and on *60 Minutes*, and his study was cited by a generation of policy makers diverting funds from rehabilitative programming to security and prison construction.[25]

Building on Martinson's success, an angrier criminological clique turned from basic research to policy advocacy in the 1980s and 1990s. Chief among them was Wilson's star pupil John DiIulio. An admirer of Beto, DiIulio launched his career by publishing a celebratory analysis of Texas's control model. The book, *Governing Prisons*, condemned Judge Justice for unleashing "malevolent anarchy" and concluded that hard labor and rigid discipline formed the bedrock of "safe, civilized" prison conditions. Seeking influence, DiIulio then distilled his findings into fiery sound bites and took them on the road. He warned that America needed to build hundreds of rigidly disciplined, Texas-style prisons in order to cope with a coming generation of "fatherless, Godless, and jobless . . . teenage predators"—rhetoric that harked back to the racial coding of George Wallace. The price should be no object, he asserted, citing dubious studies about the wanton proclivities of "known felons," for "it costs society at least twice as much to let a prisoner loose than to lock him up."[26] Crisscrossing the country and rubbing shoulders with presidents, DiIulio became one of the most influential public intellectuals of his generation. Preaching Texas tough, DiIulio became Rasputin to America's punishment czars.

In the postwar years, such dragon slayers of liberal wisdom howled against the wind, at least outside the South. As morning dawned in conservative America, however, they were invited in from the cold. When James Q. Wilson previewed his ideas in the *New York Times Magazine,* John Ehrlichman clipped the article for the president. Before long the Harvard man found himself leading the National Advisory Commission on Drug Abuse and Prevention. When conservative administrators at the Federal Bureau of Prisons got hold of John DiIulio's hard-line treatise on prison management, they ordered copies for every warden in the system.[27] Politicians and prisoncrats from Albany to Austin to Sacramento listened attentively to criminological realists, distilling their abstracts into lockdown policy innovations that reworked the country's criminal justice system from top to bottom. With the election of Ronald Reagan, this punitive priesthood returned to national power and pressed the politics of law and order further than Richard Nixon could ever have conceived.

Although he sported a sunnier personality, Reagan was more of an ideologue than Nixon. In 1964, he had campaigned passionately for Barry Goldwater and against civil rights legislation, which he pronounced "humiliating" to the South. As governor of California, he had often compromised with Democrats but he had never missed a chance to send out the Praetorian guard against Black Panthers and campus radicals.[28]

Exhibiting little of Nixon's personal bile toward Jews and blacks, Reagan nonetheless played white racial resentments to his political advantage. On the stump in 1976, he complained about "welfare queens" and a "strapping young buck" buying T-bones with food stamps (his aides prevailed on him to drop the "buck" lingo, but the subtler imagery remained). When it came time to launch his third bid for the presidency in 1980, he dusted off Nixon's southern-strategy road map and decamped to Philadelphia, Mississippi. During Freedom Summer, three civil rights workers had been abducted and murdered in this torrid little hamlet, and Reagan chose it as a venue to endorse "states' rights." To southerners, both white and black, the message couldn't have been clearer. As Andrew Young remarked caustically, "It's going to be all right to kill Niggers when he's President."[29]

Like his friend Goldwater, Reagan favored individual over social explanations for crime. "Choosing a career in crime is not the result of poverty or of an unhappy childhood," he claimed. "It is the result of a conscious, willful choice made by some who consider themselves above the law, who seek to exploit the hard work and, sometimes, the very lives of their fellow citizens." The solution, he insisted, was not more welfare, which Reagan depicted as "a crippling poverty trap," but "stiff penalties and swift and sure punishment."[30]

In some ways, this clarion call for government intervention represented an ideological contradiction. "Government is not the solution,"

Reagan was fond of saying, "government is the problem." True to what biographer Garry Wills describes as his almost religious faith in unfettered free markets, President Reagan pursued regressive tax cuts and regulatory rollbacks, coupled with massive curtailments of Medicare, welfare, school lunches, and other programs that had been set up to alleviate poverty. When it came to the bellicose branches of government, however—what Reagan called the "legitimate functions"—he countenanced bureaucratic bloat at every turn.[31] The crime war became his domestic equivalent of the cold war.

Although the White House still had little effect on the local station house, Reagan found numerous ways to escalate the fight. His Justice Department reassigned hundreds of agents from white-collar to street crime, even as they handcuffed the Civil Rights Division. In the judiciary, the president appointed almost half of sitting federal judges, including three Supreme Court justices, thus accelerating the third branch's long march backward. In speeches, he invoked "a frightening reality of our time: the face of the human predator."[32]

In retrospect, Reagan's most lasting impact came in the rather arcane realm of sentencing schedules. In 1984, Congress swept aside one of the oldest rehabilitative ideals, indeterminate sentencing, and chartered the U.S. Sentencing Commission to set fixed penalties. Democratic cosponsors hoped the shift would ensure greater fairness and rationality, but as lawmakers began piling on mandatory minimums, arbitrary severity won the day.[33]

As always, illegal drugs represented the most tempting field of federal action. In 1982, President Reagan redeclared the "war on drugs," thereby exempting law enforcement from across-the-board budget cuts. H. Ross Perot and Nixon-era hangers-on contributed recycled ideas, while the First Lady initiated an ambitious if startlingly ineffective public education program under the banner "Just Say No." More substantively, the president signed three massive drug bills in 1984, 1986, and 1988, each more ambitious and expensive than the last. The result was not the "drug-free America" Reagan's drug warriors promised, but an unprecedented expansion of federal drug prosecutions, which climbed by 99 percent between 1982 and 1988, while nondrug prosecutions increased by just 4 percent.[34]

Most of Reagan's statutes dealt exclusively with federal crimes, but his administration also found ways to bestow fresh funding on the states, generally with strings attached. Once upon a time, state agencies had been required to curtail discrimination and augment prevention and rehabilitation programming to qualify for federal largesse. Under Reagan, the terms changed. Suddenly, asset forfeiture, mandatory minimums, parole curtailments, and privatization came into federal favor. In order to stay on the dole, states had to launch crime wars and prison booms of their own.

Most invidiously, jurisdictions across the country began replicating the federal distinction between different types of cocaine, a move that Jim Crowed the drug war to an astonishing extent. By treating crack a hundred times more harshly than powder cocaine, Reagan's 1986 drug laws eventually condemned thousands of low-income, generally African American crack addicts to prison, while their coke-addicted, more often white counterparts remained free. By the early 1990s, nearly 90 percent of crack prosecutions targeted blacks, most of them low-level street dealers. In 1995, the average federal prison term for a crack offense surpassed that for murder.[35]

Reagan's successor, Texas's George H. W. Bush, built on the rhetoric and spending priorities of his mentor. He came to power not only by riding Reagan's coattails but by depicting his opponent Michael Dukakis as soft on crime and "lost in the thickets of liberal sociology." Most dramatically, his campaign borrowed from Bill Clements by sensationalizing the case of Willie Horton, a convicted murderer who escaped from a Massachusetts furlough program and raped a white woman. The incident provided a perfect opportunity for wedge advertisements, according to an aide, because it was "a wonderful mix of liberalism and a big black rapist." Several months later, in the Oval Office, Bush captivated television audiences by famously brandishing a bag of crack that DEA agents had purchased across the street in Lafayette Park. Drugs are "our nation's most serious domestic problem," he declared.[36]

Such theatrics had a powerful impact on public opinion. Although the crack trade had stabilized and crime had declined since the early 1980s, in the wake of Bush's PR offensive, 64 percent of poll respondents listed drugs as the country's number-one problem, up from 15 percent when he took office. Capitalizing on success, Bush proposed what the Fraternal Order of Police called "the toughest crime bill in our history." Democrats blocked many of its provisions but settled for breathtaking spending boosts, $8.8 billion for antinarcotics efforts in 1990 alone. Although he served only one term, Bush managed to spend more on the drug war than every president since Richard Nixon combined.[37]

Together, Reagan and Bush built an unrivaled punitive legacy. Between 1981 and 1992, the federal inmate population more than doubled, from 28,133 to 80,259. By the end of Bush's term, 60 percent of federal inmates were in for drug crimes, up from 26 percent in 1981. Roughly 60 percent were black or Hispanic.[38] Across the nation, every state in the union save Kansas was exceeding prison capacity. In 1991, for the first time in American history, there was a greater total number of blacks in prison than whites—a startling milestone given that African Americans made up only 12 percent of the U.S. population.[39]

True to his campaign promises, President Reagan had reinvented government. After his and his veep's twelve years in office, he not only left behind stratospheric deficits and a tattered social safety net but a more federalized, racialized, and punitive criminal justice system, one that would expand even more rapidly in his wake. Following his death in 2004, commentators memorialized Reagan's buoyant optimism; in reality, he set America on a path from social democracy to mass imprisonment.

By the early 1990s, two decades of right-wing advocacy, combined with a booming high-tech economy (which meant the bills hadn't come due), had converted pugilistic crime fighting into common sense. Candidate William Jefferson Clinton signaled as much when he rushed back to his home state Arkansas in the heat of the 1992 presidential campaign to preside over the execution of Ricky Rector, a man so brain damaged that he set aside his pecan pie for later before shuffling off to the death chamber. "I can be nicked a lot," Clinton said afterward, "but no one can say I'm soft on crime."[40]

A New Democrat trying to hold together a center-left coalition, Clinton occasionally sounded Great Society themes. "We have to rebuild families and communities in this country," he implored in 1993. "We've got to take more responsibility for these little kids before they grow up and start shooting each other." His attorney general, Janet Reno, was fond of arguing that "prenatal care is more important than prisons."[41] But such words dematerialized in the political ether. Overall, Clinton's administration sought to neutralize Republican advantage by supporting severe changes to the penal code, as well as enormous funding for law enforcement and prison construction.

The president's first crime bill took shape during the midterm 1994 election cycle, when Californians passed three strikes, Bush Junior became governor of Texas, and Democrats everywhere got kicked like stray dogs. Trying (in vain) to stave off disaster, Clinton appropriated as much as he could of the populist GOP crime agenda, repackaging it with liberal frills. The result was a $30 billion behemoth known as the Violent Crime Control and Law Enforcement Act. Hailed as "the toughest, largest, smartest federal attack on crime in the history of our country," the law significantly expanded funding for prevention programs, but it delivered more than two-thirds of the money pot to cops and corrections. As with Reagan's crime laws, the package came with barbed strings attached. In order to qualify for federal support, states had to augment their own prison and policing budgets, while simultaneously cutting back on good time and parole so that prisoners everywhere would serve more time behind bars.[42] In this way, Clinton's crime act not only funded prison growth; it mandated it.

Beyond its record-breaking appropriations, the 1994 law represented the final abandonment of penal rehabilitation. Not only did the legislation include a federal three-strikes law, thus abandoning the promise of redemption, but it greatly expanded the scope of capital punishment, eliminated Pell Grants for model inmates, authorized the imprisonment of thirteen-year-olds as adults, and ordered the Federal Bureau of Prisons to "provide prisoners the least amount of amenities and personal comforts consistent with Constitutional requirements." Despite spirited protests by the Congressional Black Caucus, lawmakers refused to include the Racial Justice Act, which would have mitigated racial bias in the death penalty. Liberals did manage to tuck in an assault weapons ban and funding for preventative programs like after-school basketball, but as a whole the package was so overwhelmingly punitive that Democrats spoke sheepishly off the record. "You can't appear soft on crime when crime hysteria is sweeping the country," said one administration official. "Maybe the national temper will change, and maybe, if it does, we'll do it right later."[43] Liberals had said the same when Johnson signed the Safe Streets Act in 1968.

Although centrist Democrats gushed that for the first time since Nixon they had "wrest[ed] the crime issue from Republicans and made it their own," President Clinton kept checking the White House locks.

In the run-up to his reelection campaign, he presided over the assembly of four more criminal justice packages. In 1995, he sided with congressional Republicans to squash a recommendation from the sentencing commission to do away with the crack-cocaine disparity, despite mounting evidence of its discriminatory impact. In 1996, in the wake of the Oklahoma City bombing, he signed the Antiterrorism and Effective Death Penalty Act, which limited capital appeals and, in the words of the ACLU, constituted "one of the harshest attacks on civil liberties in the nation's history." That same year, the president approved legislation making it easier to deport immigrants, including long-term legal residents, if they had ever been convicted of certain crimes, including failure to properly complete INS paperwork. Finally, Clinton squeezed in the Prison Litigation Reform Act. Billed as a sensible limitation on frivolous convict lawsuits, the PLRA in fact shut down virtually all federal prisoner litigation, no matter the merits. Included among its legion restrictions were miserly fee caps for plaintiff attorneys, filing fees for inmates, limitations on court-appointed special masters, fixed expiration dates on consent decrees, and permanent legal bans on previously unsuccessful litigants—all measures that would have made *Ruiz v. Estelle* and most constitutional lawsuits like it impossible.[44] The "hands-off" doctrine was back.

All this crime fighting had far-reaching consequences. On the one hand, New Democrats insulated themselves from Willie Horton–style ambushes; after the 1994 crime law, polls suggested that Republicans no longer held an advantage on crime. On the other, by embracing right-wing retributionism and funding prisons as public works, centrist Democrats fundamentally undercut liberal principles, locking down resources that might have been used to mitigate social inequities and rolling back gains of the civil rights movement. Although Clinton tried to chart a more moderate course than Reagan or Bush I, he presided over—indeed, he funded and facilitated—the most intensive incarceration boom in U.S. history. By the time he left the White House in 2001, there were 645,135 more Americans living behind bars than on his inauguration day, equivalent to having rounded up the entire population of Washington D.C. Roughly 60 percent of these new inmates were black and Latino, reflecting an alarming level of racial disparity.[45] While Clinton fans describe him as a pragmatist in pursuit of progress, a master tactician who tacked right to sail left, in fact, he supervised the construction of more prison cells than Nixon, Reagan, and Bush put together.[46] More than any other twentieth-century president, he built a prison nation.

## TEXAS'S JAILER IN CHIEF

In Texas, Ann Richards had set state records for punitiveness in almost every category during her one-term governorship, but she was no match for her successor. By the end of his executive leadership, first in Austin, then in Washington, George W. Bush managed to eclipse every punishment champion before him, not just Richards and Clements but Nixon, Reagan, Clinton, and his own father. Although Bush was a blueblood aristocrat, the product of Andover, Yale, and Harvard, he was a true-believing southern conservative. He had come of age in Midland, Texas, which Michael Lind describes as "the most reactionary community in English-speaking North America." Its ethos had sunk into his marrow.[47]

When Bush became governor in January 1995, he took over a criminal justice system that was already the largest and arguably harshest in the nation. His most enduring accomplishment was to make it tougher still. Although he had once struggled with alcohol like his predecessor, one of his first acts was to convert most of Ann Richards's drug-treatment beds to regular prison slots.[48] In 1995 and again in 1997, he approved harsher drug penalties, resulting in a surge of nonviolent prison sentences. By the end of his tenure, some ninety thousand Texans were being incarcerated for nonviolent offenses, including more than thirty thousand for drug crimes and over three thousand for marijuana possession alone. So unbending were the Bush statutes that one woman, Melinda George, got ninety-nine years for possession of less than one-tenth of a gram of cocaine.[49]

On the campaign trail, Bush had pledged to crack down especially hard on teenage defendants. "It's always been normal, when a child turns into a criminal, to say it's our fault—society's fault," he chided. "Well, under George W. Bush, it's your fault. You're going to get locked up because we aren't going to have any more guilt-ridden thought that says we are somehow responsible." True to promise, Bush redirected drug treatment money to juvenile incarceration and approved legislation that extended sentences and allowed fourteen-year-olds to be prosecuted as adults. By the end of his second term, the number of incarcerated juveniles in Texas had increased by 150 percent.[50]

Most convicted teens were held by the Texas Youth Commission, which generated a series of sex and abuse scandals in the years after Bush left office, but a growing minority were sentenced as adults and sent to TDCJ.[51] By 2000, some three hundred persons under the age of eighteen were doing adult time in Texas. Most of them got sent to the Clemens Farm, a state plantation inherited from lessees. Compared to other adult prisons, the unit offered more schooling and programming, but in the disciplinary blocks, the rhythm of daily life harked back to the nineteenth century. A slight seventeen-year-old told me through his cell door that he was doing ninety-nine years and had been assigned to a hoe squad after losing his schooling privileges. The boy was black, his field boss white, and he picked cotton under the gun for several hours a day. As he understood it, this was his fate: a life of penal servitude, lost to the world.[52]

During Bush's governorship, the adult prison system expanded dramatically as well. In his first year in Austin, Texas opened a new prison at the astonishing rate of nearly one per week. Even as he was honing his message of "compassionate conservatism," the governor's budgets suggested punishment was his top priority. Imprisonment became the fastest growing area of state government, with spending up 60 percent compared to 33 percent for higher education. During the course of his tenure, Texas's prison budget swelled from $1.4 billion to $2.4 billion. Total prison beds jumped from 118,195 to 166,719. "We were throwing up prisons so fast we couldn't find wardens to run them," recalls a criminal justice professor in Huntsville. "It was like building the Pyramids."[53]

While Bush stood out among governors nationwide as a prison builder, his unwavering support for capital punishment put him in a class by himself. In 1995, Bush signed a bill that expedited executions and limited capital appeals. Thereafter, he presided over the busiest death chamber in the nation. Over the course of six years in office, Bush oversaw the execution of 152 people, a modern American record. "We're a death penalty state," the governor explained. "We believe in swift and sure punishment."[54]

Bush expressed certainty that only the guilty got the needle. "I'm confident that every person that has been put to death in Texas, under my watch, has been guilty of the crime charged, and has had full access to the courts," he told NBC news. But outside analysts were unconvinced. "At every stage of the death penalty process," concluded an expert with the American Bar Association, "Texas is far below any measure of adequacy in terms of the legal representation it provides." In another study, the Texas Defender Service found that many court-appointed attorneys were "unqualified, irresponsible, or overburdened" (three of them had slept through long portions of their clients' trials) and that the state's elected appellate judges were more likely to side with prosecutors than any in the nation.[55]

Texas's noncapital defense system was broken as well; a State Bar of Texas survey found that 87 percent of trial judges regarded the quality of indigent defense work as deficient. But when the legislature passed a bill that would have created a statewide public defender system (Texas was one of the few states in the nation without one), Governor Bush vetoed it.[56]

Juvenile and mentally retarded defendants were particularly vulnerable to inadequate counsel, but Bush opposed expanded protections for either group. In 1999, the Texas Senate passed a bill that would have prohibited executing retarded offenders, but Bush torpedoed the measure in the house. "I like the law the way it is," he explained. As a result, several Texas defendants went to their deaths without a clue about their grim fate. One inmate repeatedly asked his legal-aid lawyer what he should wear to his funeral.[57]

A final check against executing the innocent is the executive clemency process, but Texas's system was riddled with faults. As a 1998 lawsuit revealed, the state's Board of Pardons and Paroles never actually convened in person. Instead, individual members, all of them appointed by Bush by the end of his term, simply faxed in their votes (almost always "no" votes), sometimes without reviewing the paperwork. The governor himself then considered each capital case on the fateful morning of scheduled executions. According to an in-depth investigation by the *Atlantic Monthly*, however, Bush generally allocated only half an hour to decide whether a defendant should live or die. Moreover, the clemency memos he reviewed were consistently biased toward prosecutors, often leaving out the best arguments for clemency and omitting material submitted by defense attorneys. Accordingly, Bush commuted a death sentence only twice during his governorship and only after overwhelming evidence of actual innocence surfaced.[58] The man charged with preparing those execution dossiers was Alberto Gonzales, Bush's future attorney general.

By the end of Bush's governorship in 2000, Texas had emerged as the unequivocal leader of a nationwide lockdown. With more than seven hundred and fifty thousand Texans under some form of criminal justice supervision, including those on parole and probation, the state was operating the largest punishment system in the country and had the nation's second-highest per capita imprisonment rate.[59] Texas led the United States in handing down lifelong prison terms, relying on supermax control units, locking up juveniles, and outsourcing incarceration to private contractors.[60] Accounting for only 7 percent of the U.S. population, the state was locking up more than 12 percent of the nation's prisoners, managing one in four of its supermaxes, and dispatching half of its executed.[61] With the largest, fiercest prison system in the United States, the Lone Star State had become America's punishment heartland. In 2000, its chief executive took Texas-style justice to Washington and, after 9/11, to the world.

George W. Bush's ascension to the White House in 2001—an Electoral College feat facilitated by felony disenfranchisement in Florida, which banned a third of the state's black men from voting—marked the coming of age of Texas tough.[62] As the culminating act of the retributive revolution, nearly half of American voters elected the country's harshest crime-fighting governor—a hard-line conservative who stood out, above all, as a prison builder and executioner—to lead the nation.

Ironically, in some ways the Texas tendency in criminal justice seemed to be losing ground at the start of a new century. As crime rates dropped and the tech bubble burst, politicians of all stripes started trying to rein in their runaway prison bureaucracies; by 2000, states were spending nearly $40 billion on corrections, one of every fourteen general revenue dollars. Faced with wrenching choices between prisons and schools, many states began rolling back some of the most punitive innovations of the past quarter century. California was one of the first to act. In 2000, voters approved a ballot measure to divert petty drug offenders from prison to community-based treatment programs. During President Bush's first year in office, at least six other states followed suit, expanding parole or scaling back "truth in sentencing" laws that required offenders to serve some 80 percent of their terms. Among them was Louisiana, the one state in the union with a higher per capita imprisonment rate than Texas. "We were pouring money into a bottomless pit," complained State Senator Donald R. Cravens. Louisiana had reached the point where "we had half the population in prison and the other half watching them."[63]

Over the next two years, more than two dozen other states—from Connecticut to Alabama, Arizona to Washington—enacted similar changes, eliminating mandatory minimums, accelerating parole, or expanding alternatives like drug treatment.[64] Overall, the reforms were modest, especially compared to the radically punitive laws pushed through in the 1980s and 1990s. One measure of their modesty was that the nation's inmate population continued to grow, adding two hundred thousand beds between 2000 and 2004. Still, a host of legislative changes suggested that cash-strapped politicians might be willing to touch what had become "a third rail in American politics." Increasing numbers of politicians, both Democrats and Republicans, seemed to agree with Reagan-appointed Supreme Court justice Anthony Kennedy, who declared before the American Bar Association in 2003, "Our resources are misspent, our punishments too severe, our sentences too long."[65]

Texas, too, got clobbered by rising corrections costs and the tech bust. By 2003, the state faced a $10 billion revenue shortfall, a quarter of it attributable to the rising prison budget. With the right wing of the Texas Republican Party ascendant, however, politicians stuck to their guns. State leaders cut back on parole revocations and diverted a small number of drug offenders to treatment programs, but, by and large, they responded to fiscal crisis by curtailing costs rather than the prison population.[66] They thus fell back on a favorite tactic of Texas prison bosses since the Civil War.

To cope with the fiscal crisis, Bush's successor, Rick Perry, undertook $230 million in cuts to TDCJ, even as the prison population continued to grow. The state's independent criminal justice auditor, Tony Fabelo, warned that the prison system might not be able to fulfill its mission under such budgetary strain. But Governor Perry plowed ahead, promising to save money through another round of prison privatization. Then, at the end of the legislative session, he eliminated Fabelo's office, so no one would be around to count. "They wanted me to cook the books," the veteran civil servant recalls bitterly, "and when I said no, the bastards fired me."[67]

Because prison health care costs were rising and security was exempted from Perry's cuts, education and treatment programs took the hardest hits. Over the summer of 2003, the prison system's independent school district, one of Beto's crown jewels, began eliminating electives from its curriculum and focusing exclusively on basic math and literacy. Once inmates received their GED, they hit the end of the road. On the treatment side, although tens of thousands of inmates were in line for program slots, the state froze capacity and cut back the duration of therapeutic communities from nine months to six—too short, many counselors believe, to have a genuinely transformative effect. In a move that aggravated prisoners across the board, TDCJ also axed the inmate food budget, first eliminating dessert and then setting a ceiling on total caloric intake. "Life in prison is hard no matter what," explained Jon Reed, who has been doing time since 1978, "but until this year, I rarely went to bed hungry. Now it's sometimes hard to think about anything else."[68]

Combined with a host of administrative changes that rolled back writ-writer victories of the 1970s and 1980s, including new limitations on prisoner correspondence, subscriptions, and legal access, the Perry cuts exacerbated tensions among guards and convicts. "Lots of these guys carrying long sentences don't have anything to lose," explains a beleaguered officer, "and if we don't keep them busy, they take it out on us." A long-serving inmate states it more bleakly. "It used to be that rehabilitation meant something, but now they just kennel us." In letters, several prisoners warned that their units were on the brink. "Now we're not much better off than we were before *Ruiz*," writes Robert Lee Mudd, a drug offender who has been in and out of Texas prisons since 1969. "The courts have shut the doors, and we're headed to another Attica."[69]

Adding to the pressures, Governor Perry and his fellow travelers cooked up new definitions of crime and fresh sentencing enhancements for every election cycle, with the result that Texas had 2,324 separate felonies on the books by 2007. "When God sat down to author His list of forbidden acts . . . He could only come up with ten," quipped Scott Henson, the state's leading criminal justice blogger. Anticrime legislation provided drop-in text for direct mailings, but as Perry's governorship stretched across a decade—in 2008, he became the longest-serving executive in Texas history—legislators on both sides of the aisle started sobering up and looking to cut costs. In 2005, House and Senate leaders passed a major overhaul of the probation system, making it more of an alternative than a gateway to prison. Perry vetoed the measure, but two years later he relented. In the same session, he approved yet another prison expansion bill, funding 8,590 new beds. Because of the probation reforms, falling crime rates, and subsequent steps to curtail prison growth taken by leading lawmakers, however, there is some hope the slots won't fill.[70] Having grown steadily, and often steeply, since the late 1960s, Texas's prison population began leveling off in Perry's second full term. With more than 170,000 individuals in prison—and more than 800,000 under state criminal justice supervision in the state, counting those in jail, juvenile detention, and on probation and parole—Texas tough showed signs of reaching a plateau.[71]

On capital punishment, Perry was also forced to step back. Like his predecessor, the governor demonstrated personal fondness for the needle. In 2001, he shot down bills that would have protected juveniles and the mentally retarded from execution, and in 2007 his administration pushed successfully to make certain types of aggravated rape a capital offense—a throwback to pre-*Furman* southern justice.[72] But because Texas had become such an outlier on capital punishment—with its severe statutes, hard-charging prosecutors, listless court-appointed defenders, and merciless appellate justices combining to produce not only bumper crops of condemned inmates but a steady stream of embarrassing death-house exonerations, some of them posthumous—the state came under increasing scrutiny by the Supreme Court, dominated though it was by pro–death penalty conservatives. In 2002, the high court barred the execution of mentally retarded offenders and later extended the protection to juveniles, thus overruling Bush and Perry's vetoes. In 2004 alone, the court rebuked Texas in four separate criminal cases, at one point censuring the Texas Court of Criminal Appeals for upholding a rape conviction despite two exculpating DNA tests.[73]

Although there were signs that the country was developing second thoughts about criminal justice severity, George W. Bush in Washington played Texas tough as avidly as he had in Austin. Since Clinton had given congressional Republicans nearly everything they wanted in the mid-1990s, the new president initially had few opportunities to make crime a priority issue. Instead, the younger Bush set out to consolidate conservative gains. To do so, he scattered Texas conservatives among top posts, among them his execution dossier handler, Alberto Gonzales, who became White House counsel and later attorney general. He appointed scores of law-and-order judges, some of them (Texas's own Priscilla Owen, for instance) with extremist views on civil rights and corporate power. When given the opportunity—in the case of identity theft and so-called unborn child murder, for example—the president extended criminal penalties.[74] Overall, however, Bush's most telling early contribution to national criminal justice policy was to appoint the fiercely ideological John Ashcroft, former senator from Missouri, to the nation's top law enforcement post.

Although Ashcroft's political legitimacy was unstable beyond his fundamentalist base—in his most recent election campaign, he had been defeated by a dead man—he emerged as the administration's point man on criminal justice, staking out unyielding positions that echoed his boss's pronouncements as Texas governor. "I believe that when a predator commits a crime, he should do the time," Ashcroft proclaimed, summing up his philosophy with allusions to the Old Testament and Wild Kingdom.[75]

As attorney general, Ashcroft supervised significant policy changes in three major areas: drugs, the death penalty, and plea bargaining. On drug policy, despite the fact that Bush made nods to treatment during his campaign, Ashcroft prioritized imprisonment above all else. "I want to escalate the war on drugs. I want to refresh it, relaunch it, if you will," he told Larry King on CNN.[76] True to promise, the attorney general recommended against mitigating crack-cocaine disparities, despite successive recommendations from the U.S. Sentencing Commission. At the same time, Ashcroft stepped up the government's campaign against marijuana—on the one hand, blocking research that might demonstrate the drug's relative harmlessness, and on the other, going after low-level users, including state-approved medical marijuana patients.[77] Despite three decades of proven ineffectiveness, as well as mounting budget deficits, the attorney general, along with the nation's drug czar, John Walters, managed to secure massive drug-war spending increases during Bush's first term: nearly $2 billion for notoriously corrupt counterinsurgency warfare in Colombia, a $563 million annual boost for the DEA, and nearly $1 billion more annually for antidrug law enforcement across the board. All told, the Bush administration exceeded Clinton's already inflated baseline on drug-war spending by at least $9.5 billion.[78]

Ashcroft also devoted himself to a cause close to the president's heart, capital punishment. Shortly after taking office, Bush presided over the executions of Timothy McVeigh and convicted killer Juan Garza—for him, merely the 153rd and 154th lethal injections of his career, but for the federal government, the first executions in nearly four decades. In addition, Bush's attorney general took steps to make the federal death penalty more efficient and routine—in other words, more like Texas's. Centralizing capital indictment powers in his office, Ashcroft recommended death in nearly half of all eligible cases, including at least twenty-eight in which local prosecutors recommended against it (in one instance, federal prosecutors had already struck a tentative plea arrangement with a defendant before being ordered to seek his execution instead).[79]

Worried that federal judges might overturn the federal death penalty because of racial disparities, Ashcroft also commissioned a narrow study that faithfully concluded there was "no evidence of racial bias in the administration of the federal death penalty." When outsiders analyzed the same data, however, they concluded that racial disparities were actually worsening. During Ashcroft's tenure, the Justice Department was three times more likely to seek the death penalty for black defendants accused of killing whites than for black defendants accused of killing nonwhites.[80]

Overall, the administration tried to expand the use of capital punishment, even as opinion polls suggested growing ambivalence about its fairness. "The pattern that's developing under the Ashcroft regime is running counter to the national trend, which is to place more restrictions on capital punishment," observed a federal defense attorney. "I think there's a conscious attempt here to federalize the death penalty."[81]

Less widely discussed but more broadly significant, Bush's first attorney general also tried to increase the severity of federal punishments across the board, first by tracking judges who deviated downward from federal sentencing guidelines and, second, by fundamentally altering the business of plea bargaining. With respect to pretrial negotiations, Ashcroft tried for months to convince U.S. attorneys to take a harsher approach. Then, in September 2003, he simply ordered it. In almost all cases, he directed federal prosecutors to refuse any deals and to instead seek the maximum allowable penalties for the most serious possible charges; those who balked were among those targeted for dismissal. In defending the order, Ashcroft claimed it would guarantee stiffer penalties for "child predators, criminal bosses, drug kingpins, and violent gun criminals." Outside analysts agree that the most profoundly affected were low-level drug users—already more than half of all federal prison inmates.[82]

Having advanced policies that produced record numbers of prisoners, the Bush administration haltingly endorsed efforts to treat inmates more humanely behind bars and to lend them a hand upon their release. In 2003, the president signed legislation to study and help prevent prison rape, a problem more pronounced in Texas than anywhere else.[83] In his 2003 and 2004 State of the Union addresses, he embraced mentoring for children of prisoners and federal grants for adult reentry programs, the latter codified as the Second Chance Act. When opportunities arose to limit the use or duration of imprisonment, however, the Bush team reverted to form. After the U.S. Sentencing Commission at long last voted to mitigate the racially charged disparities between crack and powder cocaine penalties, for instance, Bush's third attorney general, Michael Mukasey, urged Congress to pass emergency legislation to prevent what he called "violent gang members" from being released "into communities nationwide."[84]

This persistent federal commitment to protracted incarceration was all the more remarkable given that so many states were trying to figure out ways to reduce their prison populations. "The states and the federal government are moving in quite different directions," said Frank Bowman, an Indiana University law professor. At the Justice Department "you have a group of people in control who are really true believers in incarceration. They have an almost religious zeal to see that people get sentenced to prison for a long time." Indeed, despite precipitously falling crime rates, the federal prison population continued to grow rapidly under Bush's watch. Between 2001 and 2008, the federal prison population swelled by 56,000, accounting for more than a quarter of new inmates nationwide. In 2002, for the first time in American history, the federal government was locking up more people than any single state, having cleared California and Texas's high bar of 163,000. Remarkably, Mr. Bush twice presided over the largest and fastest-growing prison system in the nation, first as governor, then as president.[85]

## PUNISHMENT EMPIRE

George W. Bush's career in Austin and his early actions in Washington previewed his punishing response to the attacks of September 11, 2001. In his first remarks following the deadly attacks, he framed the country's response in criminal justice terms: "Make no mistake: The United States will hunt down and punish those responsible for these cowardly acts." On that same evening, he pledged to direct "the full resources of our intelligence and law enforcement communities to find those responsible and to bring them to justice." Indeed, in the months after September 11, the president recast government bureaucracies to fight a new and particularly virulent strain of political crime. He prosecuted a "War on Terror"—an elastic and potentially unending offensive that at times has included everything from hunting down al Qaeda to busting street-level drug dealers—with millennial zeal, casting himself as defender of "all that is good and just in our world."[86]

Although Bush's doctrine of preemption, backed up by his invasions of Afghanistan and Iraq, will most define his presidential legacy, his retooling of U.S. law enforcement was similarly transformative. At home, the shock of September 11 allowed the president to enact far-reaching changes to both the structure of government and the law. Administratively, the Bush team not only reorganized Byzantine agencies internally, forcing the FBI to reprioritize and purging naysayers from the CIA, but also conglomerated huge government entities, from the Secret Service to the Coast Guard, into a new bureaucratic super-colossus, the Department of Homeland Security. At the same time, lawmakers approved immense budget increases for all types of law enforcement. Between 2001 and 2004, the FBI's budget grew by 50 percent. In aggregate, the agencies managed by Homeland Security saw their budgets more than triple, rising to more than $35 billion a year.[87]

Local law enforcement likewise cashed in on the 9/11 bonanza. Although state and local security agencies spent heavily to keep up with Homeland Security's bewildering color-coded alerts, they also took advantage of billions in new federal aid. Federal spending on first responders alone, mostly police departments, increased sixteenfold in Bush's first term to almost $4 billion annually.[88] Although federal crime-fighting efforts had grown steadily since Prohibition and rapidly since Johnson's presidency, such a gigantic infusion of funds augmented the national policing infrastructure in ways that no previous president could have imagined.

While legion government agencies were hiring new law enforcement officers, the Bush administration also redesigned the laws they were sworn to enforce. The most ambitious efforts came together in the USA PATRIOT Act, a smorgasbord of police empowerment initiatives and civil liberty limitations, many of which had been kicking around Washington since the Nixon era. The president claimed the legislation would strengthen the fight against terrorists, "while protecting the constitutional rights of all Americans." In fact, the 342-page act contained a thicket of constitutional abridgements, among them provisions authorizing secret searches and electronic surveillance with minimal judicial oversight; a breakdown of legal barriers between domestic law enforcement and international intelligence agencies; and a host of measures curtailing the rights of noncitizens, including the authorization of secret deportation hearings and indefinite detention of immigrants suspected of terrorist involvement.[89] In short, the Patriot Act rolled back half a century of federal court rulings on government searches, seizures, and due process. In countering the threat of al Qaeda, the Bush administration marched toward a fortress America with two tiers of constitutional rights and an unchecked executive.

While it is too early to assess the historical significance of antiterrorism legislation passed during the Bush administration, a host of media revelations and public investigations point to a profound impact. Despite assurances that new law enforcement powers would be used judiciously, federal agents in the first years after 9/11 infiltrated mosques and other houses of worship without evidence of criminal conduct, undertook "sneak and peek" searches on homes without first notifying residents, listened in on privileged conversations between defendants and their lawyers, and electronically monitored wide swaths of telecommunications without warrants. Remarkably, the government deployed its new legal muscle not only against suspected al Qaeda sleeper cells but, as a Justice Department spokesperson proudly put it, against "garden-variety criminals," from drug dealers to computer hackers. "What the Justice Department has really done," explains Elliot Mincberg, legal director of People for the American Way, "is to get things put into the law that have been on prosecutors' wish lists for years. They've used terrorism as a guise to expand law enforcement powers in areas that are totally unrelated to terrorism."[90]

The new approach had an especially pronounced effect on immigrants. In the weeks after September 11, federal authorities rounded up thousands of noncitizens, holding most of them on the basis of enhanced immigration powers. Attorney General Ashcroft insisted, "We have used these tools to prevent terrorists from unleashing more death and destruction on our soil." But when Georgetown law professor David

Cole surveyed the cases of more than four thousand persons jailed in the two years after September 11, he found that only one of them was convicted of conspiring to support terrorists. On September 2, 2004, that one conviction collapsed on appeal. The remaining thousands have languished in a legal netherworld, in which mere suspicion of terrorist involvement, even on the flimsiest of evidence (anonymous, unsubstantiated tips by disgruntled neighbors, for instance), denied them nearly all legal rights.[91]

Although the vast majority of immigrants were eventually cleared of all charges, the conditions of their confinement, often supermax-style lockdown followed by deportation, were frequently severe. After 9/11, constitutional watchdog groups were flooded with complaints of abuses at immigration detention facilities—another arm of the U.S. incarceration complex, one that holds some thirty thousand inmates scattered across the country, a large portion of them in Texas.[92] In one of the best-documented cases, involving a federal holding facility in Brooklyn, Justice Department investigators turned up some three hundred videotapes showing how "officers slammed and bounced detainees against the wall" and subjected them to punitive and gratuitous strip searches. One former detainee, who later pled guilty to nothing more than credit card fraud, testified in federal court that he was repeatedly punched and kicked, paraded naked in front of female guards, cursed as a "Muslim bastard," and anally violated with a flashlight.[93]

Texas tough went national after September 11 but achieved its greatest virulence abroad. As early as September 17, 2001, the president had warned that a war against terrorists was "going to require a new thought process. . . . This is a different sort of enemy than we're used to," he asserted. "It's an enemy that likes to hide and burrow in. . . . There are no rules. It's barbaric behavior." In his loftiest speeches, Bush claimed to be leading "civilization's fight" for "all who believe in progress and pluralism, tolerance and freedom." Yet we now know that his administration plotted from the earliest days to adopt the "no rules," "barbaric behavior" approach as its own.[94]

In gearing up for the invasion of Afghanistan, Bush's war cabinet developed a radically new policy for dealing with enemy combatants captured on the battlefield. Although numerous advisors suggested maneuvering within existing legal structures, namely the Geneva Conventions, which had governed U.S. treatment of POWs for half a century, Bush's counselors devised an untested approach. They worried that POW protections, regular criminal prosecutions, or international tribunals like those set up after the slaughters in the Balkans and Rwanda would be too cumbersome for dealing with a secret, decentralized network like al Qaeda.[95] More important, ideological neoconservatives in the administration saw the conflict as an opportunity to advance historic goals: expanding presidential authority, disentangling the United States from international accords, projecting American military power more aggressively across the globe, and generally extending the punitive reach of government.

Accordingly, the White House, led by Bush's trusted Texas counselor Alberto Gonzales, began drafting unprecedented policies on detentions, interrogations, and trials that would govern American military and law enforcement operations in Afghanistan and beyond. To maximize presidential flexibility, the Gonzales team, reinforced by ideologues from Justice, Defense, and the vice president's office, first recommended suspending the Geneva Conventions, regarded by international jurists as a cornerstone of international human rights law. Although Secretary of State Colin Powell prophetically warned of endangering U.S. troops and undermining military discipline, Gonzales argued for maximum leeway to extract information from "captured terrorists." In an age of terror, he concluded, the Geneva Conventions were "obsolete" and its exacting protections "quaint." The president agreed, officially suspending the conventions in January 2002 and decreeing that the United States would treat detainees as he saw fit.[96]

To deal with prisoners once they had been interrogated, the Gonzales group developed a plan for military tribunals that would prosecute prisoners and perhaps even sentence them to death under new rules designed exclusively by the president. Under the initial order, any detainee whom the president determined to have "engaged in, aided or abetted, or conspired to commit" terrorism could be tried before a military tribunal. Defendants would have no right to independent counsel, no presumption of innocence, no right to review or counter evidence, and no right to appeal to any court, foreign or domestic. The roles of judge, prosecutor, defense advocate, and juror would all be played by American military personnel—their name badges blocked out by tape—and a mere majority of soldier-jurors could condemn the accused to life imprisonment (a death sentence would require a unanimous vote).[97] In short, only two months after September 11, the Bush administration began assembling an entirely new criminal justice system in which the Constitution would not apply and the president would reign supreme.

Critics, including uniformed military lawyers, the State Department, and occasionally even the attorney general, worried that tribunals weighted so overwhelmingly toward prosecutors would undermine American moral authority. "What several of us were concerned about was due process," explains a former National Security Council staffer. "There was great concern that we were setting up a process that was contrary to our own ideals." But the president's men were unmoved. In Texas, Bush had never much fretted about prosecutorial overreach or bias, and he wasn't about to start now. Vice President Dick Cheney remarked obliquely, "We think [our system] guarantees that we'll have the kind of treatment of these individuals that we believe they deserve."[98]

As the military campaign in Afghanistan yielded thousands of prisoners, U.S. officials began using Bush's new justice system even before it was fully formulated. High-value detainees, including suspected leaders of al Qaeda, were whisked off to top-secret CIA detention sites, a shadowy network of supermax torture and interrogation centers where prisoners had no rights of any kind and no contact with the outside world, not even the Red Cross. Other prisoners were outsourced to allied autocratic governments, so they could be brutalized while officially outside of U.S. custody. A third group, the largest, consisting of thousands of low- and mid-ranking detainees, were held at U.S. bases or other way stations and then sent to Guantánamo Bay, Cuba, a legally ambiguous piece of real estate that the administration hoped would be beyond the reach of any court.[99] Dressed in fluorescent orange jumpsuits, hobbled by triple shackles, their vision obscured by hoods or blacked-out goggles, the inmates made an eerie spectacle as they arrived at Guantánamo, the newest member of America's rapidly growing prison family. At first, the prisoners languished in makeshift open pens. But over the next year and half, tents gave way to trailers and then to a $50 million concrete and steel prison complex, complete with medium-security dormitories, dayrooms, an expansive supermax, and soundproof interrogation chambers.[100]

Although the facility's initial imperviousness to any law made it unique, the island penal colony quickly settled into familiar carceral routines: counts, feedings, searches, cell extractions, endless tedium, and myriad mind games—all punctuated by lengthy interrogation sessions. Tim Conover, a writer and onetime prison guard, said that Guantánamo reminded him of maximum-security lockups stateside, only harsher. Another worried that a corrosive prison culture was taking root. "Guantánamo is a huge problem for Americans," said a foreign intelligence official. "Even those who were not hard-core extremists have now been indoctrinated by the true believers. Like any other prison, they have been taught to hate."[101]

As the months stacked into years, almost everything that can go wrong in a prison did: the inmates resisted, revolted, and attracted sympathy, while the evidence against them came to look increasingly flimsy (in 2002, a CIA investigation concluded that most Guantánamo prisoners were low-level fighters of limited intelligence value; one of them was thirteen years old). The prison's administration consumed itself with internal spy hunts and swung wildly from coercion to accommodation and back again.[102] Foreign governments demanded their citizens back, and human rights organizations became vociferous in their criticism (Amnesty International condemned the United States for setting up "the gulag of our time"). Eventually, five former secretaries of state called for the prison to be shuttered; candidate Obama called Guantánamo and its tribunals "an enormous failure."[103]

While the prison became a focal point of international and judicial opprobrium, U.S. detainees elsewhere were subjected to greater levels of depravity. Without the Geneva Conventions tying their hands, the administration approved long lists of coercive interrogation techniques, among them dietary manipulation (including food withdrawal followed by rotten meals), prolonged hooding, exposure to extreme temperatures, threats with attack dogs, stress positions, religious humiliation (including forced shaving and public nudity), moderate beatings, wall throwing, chaining, and "waterboarding," or near drowning.[104] Although the Pentagon and the CIA used the most severe techniques rather sparingly, most famously against Khalid Sheikh Mohammed, allegedly a key player in the 9/11 plot, the same clique of Bush loyalists that had dreamed up the military tribunals argued that intelligence agents had a free hand to engage in even more aggressive conduct. In a flurry of memos, administration lawyers advanced a tightly constricted definition of "torture" permitting almost any coercive technique, so long as the inquisitor's primary purpose was to seek information rather than to inflict pain and so long as the threshold of that pain fell somewhere below "serious physical injury, such as organ failure."[105]

With such directives emanating from the top, the treatment of prisoners soon degenerated on the ground, just as Secretary Powell had warned. Reports of abuses, including severe beatings and imprisonment in freezing shipping containers, began filtering out of Afghanistan almost as soon as U.S. boots hit the dirt.[106] But it wasn't until snapshots taken by gung ho reservists on the night shift at Abu Ghraib were published that the full extent of American debauchery came into public focus. A hooded prisoner wired for electric shock teetering atop a wooden crate, a stripped and cowering detainee held at the end of a smirking private's dog leash, naked prisoners piled up like death camp corpses—these banal images of degradation became the instant icons of America's new global prison establishment.[107]

A series of high-level investigations and low-level court-martials followed. They documented dog attacks, chemical burns, naked parading, psychoactive drugging, savage beatings, sexual assaults, and even murder—with much of the abuse carried out by reservists who had previously worked as prison guards in the United States. According to the Pentagon's own investigators, dozens of officers and soldiers had committed "egregious acts and grave breaches of international law."[108]

Overall, a pattern of mistreatment emerged that was so prolonged, pervasive, and officially countenanced, not only at Abu Ghraib but in Guantánamo, Afghanistan, and beyond, that one has to travel back through American history to find incidents of comparable severity. It is Texas that provides the richest archive of such examples. By managing racially divisive prisons on the cheap, insulating them from public scrutiny, and imposing order above all by physical force and sexual degradation, Texas had, over the course of its history, incubated all of the abusive practices that sprouted with such vengeance in the new century. The criminal justice frameworks and belief systems that allowed such misconduct to flourish dated back to the legal bifurcations and systematic cruelties of slavery. Through the second Bush administration—with its darkly polarized view of humanity, its contempt for compromise and the rule of law, and its fondness for raw displays of power—the harshest elements of Texas tough were fused with the machinations of a new American empire.

# CONCLUSION

Man's capacity for justice makes democracy possible; but man's inclination to injustice makes democracy necessary.

—REINHOLD NIEBUHR[1]

At the end of a long interview on a suffocating day in July 2003, I ask David Ruíz about his legacy. "Do you think Texas's prisons are better for your efforts? Was it worth it?" Through the shatterproof pane of glass between us, he looks almost wounded by the question, with its implication that his hard-fought life, almost all of it spent behind bars, might have been for naught. "The system is the best it's ever been," he replies. "The facilities are better. The guards aren't beating on people like they used to, not as much. There's more respect for the law."[2] He leans forward, as if preparing to enumerate a litany of improvements, but the list is short, and he delivers it hesitantly.

In a poem published in the *Texas Observer,* he later answered the same question in more personal terms. In a defiant holler against the guards, he proclaims:

I'm the huevon Mexican, cell-taught,
self-taught, the original writ-writer,
chained up and locked down
for a lifetime. I'm the Mexican
who never gave up, who fought till
every prisoner, guard, and lawyer
in America knows me, I taught myself

> to use your tools: I'm Ruiz,
> unbroken for all your torture.

Face-to-face, though, David struggles against his own doubts to find glory in what his lawsuit has wrought. "They never could accept that Mexicans beat them," he says after a pause. "So they never kept their agreements." During the 1980s, after the main settlement agreement of *Ruiz v. Estelle*, and into the early 1990s "the system was better," he recalls. "It wasn't a Holiday Inn, but they started to treat us like human beings." But after the PLRA and the Fifth Circuit closed the case for good, he says the prison administration started "slacking off." "They're not following their own procedures," he regrets. "You can see a lot of new shiny buildings, but the insides are the same."[3]

For almost twenty years, since he returned to TDC from protective custody in the federal system, Ruíz has been held in administrative segregation. He says he "trains his mind" to stay alert and stay positive, but the isolation and dim prospects for freedom are weighing on him as he enters his sixties. When he was an unruly kid growing up in the barrio, a wild-eyed escapee tearing through the underbrush to outpace the hounds, a movement celebrity after his court victory, Ruíz never imagined that he would end up back in the hole, counting down his golden years in a boxcar tomb halfway underground. "I have accepted Jesus Christ as my savior. I have to have hope," he says intently. "But if I knew that I had to spend my whole life caged like an animal, I'd want to die now."[4]

For all his bravado, Ruíz desperately wanted to live. As his health deteriorated after a hepatitis C diagnosis, he filed grievance after grievance to get more attentive medical care. In 2004, prison doctors told him he had colon cancer, and he started writing old friends asking for help with an illness-based parole request. Like many ailing lifers, Ruíz had an acute fear of dying in prison, a fate that would seem to obliterate every hope, to define him finally, forever as a convict.[5] In an earlier time, when sentences were shorter, when capacity for toil mattered most, and when paternalism still reigned, Ruíz might well have gotten his medical release. But not now, not from the legalistic bureaucracy he unwittingly helped install. Not from skittish politicians in the post–Kenneth McDuff, post–Willie Horton era, who feared nothing more than taking a chance on the wrong man.

As far as I know, Ruíz never got a hearing. In late 2004, he requested a little money for his commissary account, which I sent. If he got out, he wanted me to come to Austin to meet his family and tour his childhood hangouts. Then he quit writing. Several months later, he transferred to TDCJ's prison hospital in Galveston, a facility his lawsuit helped to build. On November 12, 2005, he died.[6]

Despite the fact that he had spent a total of only four years in the free world since his first adult conviction in 1960, Ruíz's family had stuck by him, even Rose Marie, who divorced him once but married him twice. His relatives spared David's body the indignities of Huntsville's Joe Byrd Cemetery and organized a service at Austin's Cristo Rey, a limestone, mission-style church just a few blocks from where he had grown up. A throng of activists, ex-prisoners, and family members gathered. When Judge Justice unexpectedly appeared, eyes welled up not just for the departed but for the passing of an era.[7]

The *Austin American-Statesman* set up an online guestbook, and people from around the country logged on to pay their respects. "Against all odds Mr. Ruíz proved himself to be a winner," read a typical tribute. "Many of us strive to touch one life," wrote a prisoners' rights activist in Huntsville. "You have changed hundreds of thousands." Charlie Sullivan, who had known David since the early 1970s, praised Ruíz as a courageous advocate whose case "basically ended torture in Texas" and who "gave his life to the cause." "He was such a mixture," he added, obliquely referencing David's fondness for alcohol and armed robbery. He "was a victim of the prison system he brought down."[8]

If the people who knew David best have a hard time assessing the meaning of his troubled life, they similarly struggle with the legacy of the case that bears his name. Not surprisingly, those who devoted long sections of their lives to crafting, fighting, and winning the lawsuit are the most sanguine. "Prison conditions remain disappointing," Donna Brorby stated after the Fifth Circuit ordered Judge Justice to terminate the case in 2002, but she remains proud of her life's work. "We created a system based on rules, bottom line." Her old boss, Bill Turner, agrees. "There was no way for us to stop them from building all those prisons," he says ruefully, "but we made them more habitable, more civilized." William Wayne Justice, who was still on the bench forty years after his appointment by Lyndon Johnson, stands by the case with even stronger conviction. "My only regret is that Congress passed the PLRA and that the appellate court ruled the way it did," he says in his Austin chambers. Asked about the charges, widely promulgated by John DiIulio and state officials, that he unleashed "malevolent anarchy," he bristles. "The court gave the state ample time to replace the building tenders with officers," he insists, but it "refused to take advantage." He adds, "Texas's prison system still has a long way to go to become a truly rehabilitative instrument," but "the most revolting aspects were abolished in the case I tried."[9]

TDC's defenders see matters differently, though they too equivocate. "We used the *Ruiz* case as a lever to get full budgets," recalls Woody Woods, the former head of prisoner classification. "The system is more professionalized now, but I believe it's more dangerous for inmates." More dangerous for officers as well, contends Jim Willett. Some good came out of the case, he admits. "We learned to use video cameras and paperwork to protect ourselves against false allegations." But overall, he believes that Ruíz "created a monster," too big to manage, too beset by idleness, too reliant on ad-seg. "To tell you the truth, I wish they had shot him when he escaped" in 1968.[10]

Most prisoners are too young to have any sense of what *Ruiz* created; the average inmate in 2006 was just three years old when David penned his writ. Convicts who have spent a generation or more behind bars, however, are of mixed minds. Most say that judicial intervention improved prison life. TDCJ "still needs to change," asserts James Yeager, who first went to prison when O. B. Ellis was director, but it "is not as brutal or inadequately manned as it was back then." A minority, though—more often whites, who lost privileges with the collapse of the control model—voice as many regrets as their keepers. "The old system was an evil," remarks a former building tender, "but all in all, it ran a lot better." Splitting the difference, Michael Jewell perhaps speaks for the majority on both sides of the bars: "*Ruiz* helped this system in many ways; it is still shit sorry in others."[11]

This glib pronouncement might do for the whole of Texas's prison history. At every stage, managers have claimed they were ringing in the dawn. Constructing a penitentiary will secure "our ultimate bright destiny," promised the state's first generation of penal reformers. At the start of the lease era, commentators waxed that "a politic humanity has waved its wand over [Huntsville] and the brutes have become men again." We have arrived at "an historic turning point," officials boasted in 2002. "We will never go back."[12] In only scattered instances, however, have any such promises been kept.

To be sure, there is evidence of advancing technology and gradually improved living conditions within Texas's prisons. In the early days, convicts lived in fetid firetraps and labored through every daylight hour under the gun. Today, they are kept in comparably hygienic concrete structures with electric lighting and indoor plumbing. They have access—albeit restricted and contested access—to relatively modern medical facilities.[13] Although hoe squads still turn out at the older units, prisoners these days are as plagued by tedium as by toil. Perhaps the most reliable index of prison amelioration is the inmate death rate, which has dropped from 2 to 7 percent annually under leasing to 0.3 percent today—this despite longer sentences and a surge in executions.[14]

Even in areas of obvious betterment, however, ambiguities remain. Take internal prison sanctions, which have become less physically painful but more prolonged. From the 1850s through the mid-1980s, prisoners writhed under the whip or got smacked upside the head, but they rarely spent more than thirty days in the hole; now, they might spend years there, even decades. As prison management has become more bureaucratic, another paradox has emerged. Inmates are less likely to be treated capriciously by staff, but they are also commensurably less likely to get treated favorably, less likely to exercise anything like personal autonomy. In the old days, even at the height of the exacting control model, strong, hardworking convicts could hunt, make spirits, gamble, and have sex with some impunity; the toughest or wiliest could jockey for BT or bookkeeper positions. These days, prisoners are more apt to be treated equally: as bodies to contain and count. "Sure, they . . . worked you till you dropped, but when you got back to the building you could do whatever you wanted," recalls one prisoner a bit too fondly. Now "the guards perceive us as animals . . . and view the pods as livestock pens."[15] The most notable difference of all is that there are so many more pens.

This conflicted assessment of historical change runs against the American grain. Since John Winthrop proclaimed his Puritan settlement a "city on a hill," Americans have treated progress as a covenant. The notion that each generation will be richer than the last, that each adversity will be overcome by pluck and hard work is a national creed. Prisons, though, present a stark challenge to this manifest destiny. They are built in progress's name; their architects have promised to cure crime, to reclaim fallen citizens, and to supplant barbarism with humanitarian correction. But more often they have delivered everything they were built to overcome: lawlessness, cruelty, abomination. "Penal history is littered with unfulfilled promises, abandoned hopes, and discarded institutions," observes one historian.[16]

This legacy of disappointment is most pronounced in the North, where the prison's virtues were promoted most rapturously. Benjamin Rush set the tone when he predicted that his "house of repentance" would unite "humanity, philosophy, and Christianity . . . to teach men that they are brethren; and to prevent their preying any longer upon each other." Southerners were always suspicious of such Panglossianism. They built prisons hesitantly in the nineteenth century and avidly in the twentieth but charged them with a more modest purpose: to punish criminals. In prison management, they emphasized subjection over salvation and, until recently, hard labor and white supremacy above all. From the beginning, southern progressives recoiled at this rejection of institutional idealism. They denounced southern penal institutions as "sources of disgrace" and tried to remake them in a northern image. When forward-thinking Texans built the Walls, for instance, they spoke of Auburn. When they opened the Gatesville reformatory, they invoked Elmira. When they dreamed up the Austin penal colony, they referenced Thomas Mott Osborne at Sing Sing and Katherine Bement Davis at Bedford Hills. In bringing the *Ruiz* case to trial, civil rights activists believed they were nudging the state toward "community supervision," which Ramsey Clark called "the future of corrections."[17]

To almost everyone's surprise, the opposite sort of geographic diffusion has taken place. After 180 years of failing to fulfill its founding promise—as crime rates reversed their historic decline and as the New Right clawed its way to power over the wounded body of civil rights—the northern prison became more southern rather than the other way around. In this unforeseen punitive turn, race has played a pivotal role. During the extended epoch of American penal innovation from the Revolution through the Great Society, northern penitentiaries overwhelmingly imprisoned whites. But as migration transformed these Yankee prisons into demographic facsimiles of their southern counterparts, Dixie-style management migrated north as well. Programs oriented toward social reintegration, like counseling and parole, remain on the books, but they have been eclipsed in recent years by sanctions that permanently differentiate criminals from free citizens: "real life" sentences, adult penalties for juveniles, and lifelong restrictions on ex-felons.[18] If northern prisons once gestured toward freedom and southern penal farms toward bondage, the whole Union is in alignment now, pointing back toward the eternal bifurcations of slavery.

About the only northern penological innovation that has truly flourished in recent years is what Charles Dickens once called "rigid, strict, and hopeless solitary confinement," the brainchild of Benjamin Rush. Modern-day supermaxes have achieved a technical mastery of isolation that Cherry Hill's warders could only have dreamed of but with none of the founders' idealism. Today, the country's most regimented lockups—high-tech überprisons like Pelican Bay in California, ADX Florence in Colorado, and Estelle High Security Unit in Texas—aspire not to "cure . . . the diseases of the mind," as Dr. Rush once dubiously envisioned, but to secure perfect discipline by excluding troublesome inmates from all human contact, by exiling them from the land of the living without actually extinguishing their breath.[19]

This resurgence of hard-edged, permanently debasing punishment coincided with a renewal of southern political potency in the latter third of the twentieth century. Before secession, the South dominated American politics from the presidencies of George Washington to Zachary Taylor. Northerners and midwesterners commanded for a century thereafter, but since the mid-1960s a majority of presidents have been southerners, and the exceptions mostly southern-strategy sunbelters. Each of these late-twentieth-century presidents, in his own way, pushed the country further away from the New Deal consensus. After the unlikely reign of Texas's most famous liberal, Lyndon Johnson, the social safety net frayed while the policeman's net widened; Keynesianism gave way to trickle down economics; the helping hand of government closed into a fist. Although regional distinctiveness is generally on the wane—with homogenization driven by interstates and the Internet— the North has become more southern over the past generation than the South has become northern. As we approach the sesquicentennial of the Civil War, it's not always clear which side came out on top.

One of the symptoms of "Dixie rising" is an uneven hardening of American race relations. Even with the disappearance of formal segregation and the election of an African American president, the United

States by some measures, like family income and unemployment, is more separate and unequal today than it was at the end of the civil rights era. According to other indicators, there has been progress, but at an agonizing creep. At the present rate of convergence, for instance, the white-black poverty gap is expected to close in 2152.[20]

Nowhere is the persistence of inequality more visible than in the criminal justice system, where the "color line" has widened into a moat.[21] Why this is and how it came about becomes clear over the long march of Texas history. From the very beginning, the territory's legal and criminal justice institutions were bound up with racial subjugation. According to the first constitution, basic rights were allocated by race. According to the first penal codes, so were criminal sanctions, with wayward whites sent to the penitentiary and blacks to the whipping post or gallows. In law enforcement, racial and labor repression took precedence over traditional crime fighting. The consequence was that nonwhite Texans between the 1830s and the 1960s had little say in crafting or enforcing the laws. They were nonetheless readily punished for disobeying them.

Within the penal system itself, Texas started out by copying from Auburn but soon fell back on a more familiar mode of forced labor. Every effort was made to extract wealth from convict bodies, most mercilessly from black ones. At times, Texas made concerted efforts to break with this "penology for profit": in the 1910s after the abolition of leasing and in the 1920s under the progressives. In each case, however, lawmakers failed to appropriate the necessary funds, largely because they could conceive of no other fate for Negro convicts than picking cotton or cutting cane. From 1867, when the governor signed the first convict lease, through 1983, when the *Ruiz* rulings began taking effect, Texas's prison plantations thus carried forth the lifeways of chattel slavery. They served as racially segregated bastions of a seemingly bygone era, one that, in the distorted mirror of late-twentieth-century conservatism, started to look not backward but ominously modern.

The civil rights movement—and its offshoot the prisoners' rights movement—presented a serious challenge to this divisive racial order. Despite significant victories in court and in the political arena, however, Texas's legal institutions continued dispensing unequal justice. As Jim Crow finally collapsed, criminal justice emerged as a final bulwark of "white man's government." Under assault from Washington, the judiciary, and the streets, Texas and other southern polities eventually yielded on integration. But as they did so, they set a higher premium on public order and law enforcement and began assembling an incarceration apparatus of unprecedented scale. Although such talk was no longer polite, tough-on-crime politicians at the end of the century started institutionalizing the viewpoint of Texas's antediluvian, arch-segregationist U.S. senator Joseph Bailey, who once remarked, "I want to treat the negro justly and generously as long as he behaves himself, and when he doesn't I want to drive him out of this country."[22]

Prison proliferated in response to myriad variables, of course, among them crime, demographic shifts, and economic restructuring, especially at the bottom of the labor market. In Texas and the wider South, however (and subsequently elsewhere), prison growth proceeded according to a time line governed significantly by race relations. As Jim Crow acted out its death throes, imprisonment rallied. Between Redemption and the triumph of civil rights—that is to say, for ten decades of de jure segregation—Texas's imprisonment rate remained remarkably stable, never exceeding 200 per 100,000 residents. Between 1968 and 2005, however, the rate septupled. Over the same period—even as civil rights organizations and convict plaintiffs scored innumerable victories—Texas's prison population grew by 1,300 percent; its prison budget ballooned from $20 million to $2.6 billion.[23]

This astounding growth has put people of all sorts behind bars—but not equally. While the white prisoner population has increased eightfold since 1968, the African American prisoner population has grown fourteenfold; the Mexican American prisoner population has jumped even faster, increasing twenty-five-fold.[24] The sobering consequence is that young African Americans and Latinos today are more likely to spend time in prison—and less likely to get out—than their parents or grandparents were before the civil rights movement. A black baby boy born just after World War II faced roughly a 10 percent chance of ending up in prison by his midthirties. If he were born in the late 1960s, by contrast, the odds had increased to 20 percent, with the likelihood climbing still higher from the 1980s.[25] By the turn of the century, black Texans were being incarcerated at five times the rate of whites—a degree of racial disparity not seen since the early 1920s, when the KKK was the most powerful political force in the state.[26]

Since Stephen Austin first cleared his domain of its native inhabitants and proclaimed it a "slave country," almost everything about Texas has changed. Once dominated by subsistence farmers, the state became a cotton and then an oil kingdom. Today, it boasts the Texas Technology Corridor. Once overwhelmingly rural, it now hosts two of the five largest metropolitan areas in the United States; many Texans still don cowboy boots but rarely to ride horses.[27] Through it all—from the Texian Revolution to the Confederate insurrection to the first and second incarnations of the Klan to Massive Resistance and beyond—white supremacy has served as a mainstay of Texas politics. Over time, the language and methods have changed. But to an astonishing extent, the historic black-white divide (and to a somewhat lesser extent, the Anglo-Mexican divide) has stood fast, nowhere with greater prominence than in the prison system. Although the ghosts of the Confederacy have been, to a considerable extent, chased out of schools, lunch counters, and city buses, they continue to prowl Texas's cell blocks with relentless fury.

While racism has laid down one disheartening line of continuity in Texas's criminal justice history, crisis has another. Drop into the official archives at the start of any new management regime, and you will find uplifting reports of wrongs righted, problems fixed, and prisoners well treated. "The efficiency of the Superintendent . . . cannot be too highly appreciated," beamed prison directors in 1855, as Huntsville's textile mill went up. Thanks to "wholesome changes in management," officials trumpeted at the start of the Cunningham lease, "the convicts [are] comfortably clad, well fed, . . . and well treated." Even as the Texas control model flew off a cliff in the early 1980s, the attorney general and future governor Mark White was touting TDC as "one of the best in the nation."[28]

Such is the ebullience of official reporting. Drop into the same archives a few months or years later, however, and you find promises broken, scandals erupting, and officials scurrying for the exits. At the Walls, it turned out, obstreperous prisoners in the 1850s were being branded and maimed. Under the Sugar King, independent investigators soon agreed, prisoners received "devilish treatment" and were driven to the point of death, as one newspaper put it, like "the galley slaves of Southern Europe."[29] Not long after Mark White heaped praise upon TDC, a vicious gang war broke out in the cell blocks. At every turn, Texas officials claimed they saw the light only to descend into darkness. The state's prisons were constantly on the mend but needed ever more mending.

Like their national counterparts—if less ecstatically—Texas prison officials always claimed they were nudging their institutions forward, that they were participants in a steady if frequently rough-going march from the pillory to the modern penitentiary, from savagery to civilization. In reality, however, prison history has been characterized less by advancement than corrosive cycle. From the birth of the penitentiary forward, prisons over the long haul have followed a distressingly predictable sequence: crisis begets reform; reform (plus cutbacks) unleashes unrest; unrest bleeds into disappointment; failure leads to rollback; retrenchment gives way to neglect, or worse, which finally generates crisis anew. Like a spin on the treadmill—an invention, incidentally, of the English penitentiary that was meant to underscore the futility of dishonorable labor—these historical loops have developed over and over again in Texas's prisons and elsewhere. What Nathaniel Hawthorne called the "black flower of civilized society," it turns out, is a hearty perennial.[30] It resists every effort at beautification even as its ugliness inspires another.

Cycles of reform, rebellion, and retrenchment generate their own circles of blame—and there is plenty to go around. Corrupt administrators and guards, who gave themselves over to graft, sadism, or sexual predation, share some of it, as do irascible convicts, who responded to openness by filing a shank or running for the river. Texas's political leadership shoulders a greater share of responsibility for strangulating reform efforts in the 1880s, 1910s, 1920s, and 1980s. Such failings go a long way toward explaining the perpetual rupture and reinvention of the penitentiary, but history over the *longue durée* suggests that an incarnate agent is implicated as well—the prison itself.

Prisons are peculiar institutions. In all their forms, they lend themselves readily, almost inexorably, to trouble. This has partly to do with their purpose: to hold individuals involuntarily, to coerce them in confined spaces. It has partly to do with their demographic composition. Overwhelmingly, prisons herd together quick-tempered young men and contain them not just with walls but with haphazardly trained, inexperienced, and poorly paid personnel. These factors, combined with generally shoddy oversight, make prisons intrinsically difficult to manage, even for a day, even under the best of circumstances. Over time, they tend to get worse. In pursuit of order, they set in motion dialectical tensions between the kept and their keepers that often produce disorder.

One vital reason that prison environments tend toward deterioration is that they not only hold people but transform them. Most completely metamorphosed are their involuntary residents. Inmate initiates show up at the gates in all flavors, but over the course of depersonalizing initiation processes, they tend to develop characteristics institutionally selected for survival: circumspection, canniness, coldness, and cruelty. On the surface, they become masters of sycophancy; underneath, they seethe. Although both retributive and rehabilitative prisons aspire to convert criminals into law-abiding subjects, they most successfully manufacture convicts. "The prison may have its monks," advises one, "but it breeds no penitents."[31]

Although less completely, prison employees are remade by the prison experience as well. This was especially true in the old days, when officers hailed from similar backgrounds and more often lived on the units. But even today the unique qualities of the job—the rigid hierarchies, the geographic isolation, the forced intimacy mixed with contempt, the undercurrents of violence, the social stigma associated with prison work—foster staff insularity and individual transformation. During training, new boots learn to keep their distance from "offenders"—to use the currently favored nomenclature—to remain constantly vigilant, and to regard every interaction as potentially treacherous. Over time, as convicts test them, most guards develop a self-preserving callousness toward their charges, whom they come to regard as duplicitous, potentially dangerous, and deserving of their fate. "I'd rather work at a dog kennel," one veteran says, "they mind better."[32]

Symbiotically, convicts react by hardening further; they come to view their keepers not as honorable gray-collar stiffs struggling to make their truck payments but as "a species of humanity coated with moral filth." On both sides of the bars, then, prisons nurture the sort of personality traits that forensic psychologists associate with one of the most dangerous diagnoses, psychopathy.[33] Prisons punish empathy and reward cold calculation. On most days, the resulting mistrust and mutual hostility floats through the tiers like a toxic miasma. At flash points—often during transitions from one management regime to another—it can easily ignite, as the history of prisons in Texas and almost everywhere else makes clear. Predicated on violent containment, to violence prisons regularly return.

From the earliest days, prison managers grappled with the Manichaean tensions that took root in their shrouded domains. Many of penology's most vaunted innovations—from indeterminate sentencing to the Mutual Welfare League to group counseling—were attempts to mitigate prison polarization, to win the grudging consent of the damned. When those, too, failed to produce docile inmates, prison professionals, as well as a growing cadre of prison sociologists, surrendered to a deeper skepticism. "In spite of the many ingenious programs to bring about modification of attitudes or reform," wrote Donald Clemmer, one of the leery forerunners, "the unseen environment in the prisoner's world, with few exceptions, continues to be charged with ideational content inimical to reform."[34]

Such world weariness later undergirded the community corrections and decarceration movements, but prison boosters like John DiIulio rejected such institutional pessimism. In his influential paean to the Texas control model, *Governing Prisons,* DiIulio ridiculed what he called the "sociological understanding" of prisons, and argued that stern, consistent, Texas-style discipline could make prisons "safe" and "civilized," "no more likely to fail than . . . schools, armies, state hospitals, [or] regulatory agencies."[35] History, though, contradicts the political scientist. Although certain well-honed management regimes, including the authoritarian control model, have demonstrated above-average stability and staying power, most prisons in most places have proven remarkably entropic, incubators of not just misery but mayhem. Even in the most effective administrations—those managed by Zebulon Brockway, Joseph Ragen, and George Beto—subsequent investigations and lawsuits revealed that much villainy was going on behind closed doors.

Not all prisons are alike, of course. Some are much safer, for both inmates and staff, as DiIulio rightly points out. Some are more restrictive, others less. In the highest-security lockups, danger virtually disappears, as does human contact. At the other end of the spectrum, some minimum-security, treatment-oriented facilities bear a striking resemblance to outside life; they can seem almost pleasant. The very best prisons may help some residents turn their lives around and prepare for successful reentry to free society. By and large and over the long haul, however, the prison as an institutional form has fostered more criminogenesis than moral regeneration, more debasement than redemption, more scandal than success. Were the prison, with its lengthy record,

judged by the same standard as its inhabitants, it would surely be classified as a repeat offender, perhaps a candidate for the death penalty.

For most of American history, this recurrent bankruptcy of the prison—
its unremitting racism, its soul-scarring cultural dynamics, its limitless
capacity for depravity, its stunning inability, despite repeated over-
hauls, to reclaim criminals—had, for all its horrors, a comparably minimal impact. Reformers and their rivals designed and redesigned
penitentiaries, entrusting them with utopian hopes or sealing within
them their darkest fears. For all their philosophical portent, however,
prisons touched few lives directly. In the early twentieth century, when
Osborne shook up the field, the total U.S. prisoner population stood at
69,000, about the size of Wilkes-Barre, Pennsylvania, then the nation's
eighty-third largest city. By O. B. Ellis and Richard McGee's day, the
prison head count had grown to 178,000, but that still amounted to
just one-tenth of one percent of the larger population.[36] From the invention of penal rehabilitation to the beginnings of its demise, prisons
were peripheral institutions.

Not so today. In 2008, the U.S. prison and jail population exceeded
2.4 million, equivalent to the nation's fourth largest city, outdone only
by New York, Los Angeles, and Chicago. In per capita terms, the incarceration rate has reached 788 per 100,000 residents, seven times above
the historic norm; in Texas, the rate is 991 per 100,000. Across the
country, one out of nine young African American men is currently
in prison or jail, with a greater portion on parole or probation.[37]
Once marginal, prisons have emerged as pillars of American government, core institutions in the management of an increasingly diverse
society.

Even as prisons have extended their reach, however, most people
have lost faith in their ability to promote public good. Once erected in
grand architectural style and imbued with grand hopes, prisons today
are spare concrete boxes with confused missions. The most compelling
contemporary argument for their large-scale deployment is that they
keep crime-prone individuals off the streets. This incapacitation effect,
most criminologists agree, has contributed to perhaps a quarter of the
decline in U.S. crime rates over the past decade. Because this sort of
postconviction preventative detention costs so much and deprives so
many of their liberty, however, few want to acknowledge incapacita-

tion as the primary objective of incarceration; to do so seems too utilitarian, too contrary to the principle of individuated justice. Instead, alternative explanations continue bouncing around in the popcorn popper of public ideas, no matter how weakly buttered by evidence. There is the moral, frequently biblical, injunction to punish wrongdoing, although no one agrees on how much or for how long. There is the old canard, deterrence, which remains as unverifiable as ever (in truth, burglars rarely stop to consult sentencing statutes before breaking a window in search of the next score). There is the victims' rights rationale, an update of the ancient eye-for-an-eye credo. Even rehabilitation still gets invoked, although robustly funded, well-designed programs are fewer and further between. At TDCJ, the agency mission statement pledges to "promote positive change in offender behavior," though the administration makes no more effort than it ever did.[38] The sum total of these cacophonous, often contradictory rationales for mass incarceration is incoherence. Prisons are among the country's most structurally solid and historically resilient institutions, but they operate on a shaky philosophical foundation.

With the mission uncertain, the results dubious, the headaches chronic, and the costs mounting, many policy makers at the start of a new century are beginning to ask themselves, Is there a better way?

This book doesn't detail specific alternatives but, as we come to the end of this rather sorrowful tale, it's worth pausing for a moment to consider where we've been and where we might go from here. We have traveled far in these pages, from the Indian wars of Stephen Austin to the terror wars of George W. Bush, from the slave plantation to the supermax. Along the way, my hope is that readers have tucked away a few lessons. We have seen that inequitable societies produce unequal justice, that criminal justice has as much to do with subjection as safety, that good intentions can easily go awry (though not so quickly as bad ones), and that the modern prison owes as much to slave masters as to Quaker reformers. My hope is that these insights will help us contend with the challenges ahead.

As we peer into the fog at the end of this extended prison journey, it seems to me that three possible pathways present themselves. One option is to stay the retributive course. America's criminal justice juggernaut currently consumes more than $200 billion a year and employs 2.4 million individuals to keep 7.3 million others under formal state supervision. Such might be the limit, but the United States is a rich country, and there's no reason to think that prosecutors and lawmakers can't keep filling new prisons as they've been doing for almost forty years.[39]

Because of the incapacitation effect, further expansion would most likely continue to curtail crime, especially if greater numbers of young repeat offenders were kept locked up into middle age. To provide space for, say, much of the country's unemployed (assuming this as a natural stopping point) would require at least quadrupling the size of our current incarceration infrastructure. This might sound outlandish, but it's precisely what the United States did between 1985 and 2000.[40]

There would be costs, of course, fundamental ones. Criminal justice expenditures would close in on the trillion-dollar mark, devouring money for schools, health care, and free-world infrastructure. America's tattered promise of equal citizenship would give way as incarceration rates for young African American men crept into majority territory. If the Confederacy at its peak held almost 4 million Americans in bondage, this new carceral Union would imprison twice as many; it would represent the Rebels' final vengeance. Increasingly, the United States would come to resemble not the social democracies it once defended in western Europe but their foes. Somewhere on this road toward an American gulag, Leviathan will slay liberty.

A more probable course, perhaps, if America's destiny is more democratic than authoritarian, is that policy makers will rediscover the "fond hope" of criminal rehabilitation. In the face of bulging budgets and persistently high recidivism rates, lawmakers may turn, as they have before, to prisoner education, job training, drug treatment, psychological counseling, parole, and aftercare. There are signs that the Obama administration, state lawmakers, and even politicians in Texas are considering this approach, shifting resources from incarceration to research-based prevention and treatment programs.[41]

But there is promise as well as peril along this well-trodden thoroughfare. Another round of penological innovation will alleviate suffering and may enhance public safety. On the other hand, if retooling proceeds without scaling back; if the criminal justice net widens rather than retracts, we may unleash further cycles of reform and reaction. On the backside of another reformatory romp, we could end up with a prison establishment even larger and more entrenched than the one we have now. Leviathan lurks down this path as well.

Finally, Americans may consider taking a road less traveled. More than four decades ago, in the closing days of the Great Society, Lyndon Johnson's crime commission suggested that the nation shift its mighty resources from punishing crime to preventing crime. "A country's most enduring protection against crime is to right the wrongs and cure the illnesses that tempt men to harm their neighbors," offered the final report.[42] In the political arena, the Katzenbach Commission's unwieldy policy recommendations were mocked by the rising right and soon forgotten. As we grapple with the formidable consequences of that mockery, however, we would do well to take another look.

Continuously fighting the "war against crime" in late-twentieth-century style—an approach that circles the wagons and opens fire against criminal enemies—is not the only way to deal with lawbreaking and seemingly intractable social problems. Instead, we could reinvigorate a rival, equally misnamed campaign of the same vintage, the War on Poverty. Its methods and even its goals are strangely foreign to us now—after four decades of the New Right counterrevolution—but they are worth rekindling, especially now that we know what their antitheses have wrought. Amid a broad democratic renewal of the sort that has swept through American society from time to time—during Reconstruction and the New Deal, for instance—we could embark on a long-neglected pursuit of justice, defined in social as well as individual terms. Rather than demanding order above all, we might prioritize hope and economic opportunity, especially in downtrodden neighborhoods that lack all three. In addition to securing the rights of crime victims, we might make amends for historic wrongs and finally, at long last, make good on the promise of equal citizenship. Rather than crafting a more punitive response to every infraction, we might provide a richer set of choices to the refractory. Rather than getting even, we might endeavor to minimize harm. Rather than clamping down, we might lift up. Such a redirection of public policy may not lead us to a "nation without prisons," as the most far-reaching reformers of the late civil rights era hoped, but it would almost certainly lead toward a nation with many fewer.

Such an optimistic trajectory might seem unlikely. Lest we consign ourselves to overly modest dreams, however, let us remember that slavery and segregation, too, once promised to rule forever. Even the widely unpopular convict lease system took half a century to dismantle. Yet unforeseen historical developments, along with dedicated people working together—some bonded, some free—ultimately toppled these ignominious institutions. In the century that followed, prison reformers time and again prevailed over harsh regimes. In most cases, they created flawed institutions in their stead. Rather than harvesting regret alone, however, we can learn from their missed opportunities and partial successes. Only by taking honest stock of the full history of the prison can we plot our escape from it.

# NOTES

## SELECT ARCHIVES AND MANUSCRIPT COLLECTIONS

**Beto Papers**   George John Beto Papers. Newton Gresham Library, Sam Houston State University. Huntsville, Texas.

**BPL**   Records, Texas Board of Public Labor. Texas State Library and Archives Commission (hereafter TSLAC). Austin, Texas.

**Briscoe Papers**   Dolph Briscoe Papers, 1940–1980. Center for American History, University of Texas at Austin (hereafter CAH).

**Campbell Papers**   Thomas M. Campbell Papers, 1898–1923. CAH.

**Campbell Records**   Records, Texas Governor Thomas Mitchell Campbell. TSLAC.

**Clemency Records**   Texas Secretary of State executive clemency records. TSLAC.

**Cohen Papers**   Henry Cohen Papers, 1850–1951. CAH.

**Coke Records**   Records, Texas Governor Coke R. Stevenson. TSLAC.

**Colquitt Papers**   Oscar Branch Colquitt Papers, 1873–1941. CAH.

**Colquitt Records**   Records, Texas Governor Oscar Branch Colquitt. TSLAC.

**Davis Records**   Records, Texas Governor Edmund Jackson Davis Records. TSLAC.

**Estelle Papers**   W. J. Estelle Papers, 1927–1984. Cushing Memorial Library. Texas A&M University. College Station, Texas.

**Hardin Papers**   John Wesley Hardin Papers, 1870–1895. CAH.

**Hubbard Records**   Records, Texas Governor Richard Bennett Hubbard. TSLAC.

**Jalet-Cruz Papers**   Frances Jalet-Cruz Papers, 1966–1986. CAH.

**Jester Records**   Records, Texas Governor Beauford Halbert Jester. TSLAC.

**KKK Papers**   Ku Klux Klan Papers. TSLAC.

**Lomax Papers**   James Avery Lomax Family Papers, 1842, 1853–1986. CAH.

**McCallum Papers**   Jane Y. and Arthur N. McCallum Family Papers, 1910–1982. CAH.

| Moody Records | Records, Texas Governor Daniel James Moody. TSLAC. |
| PBM | Board of Criminal Justice minutes and meeting files, Texas Department of Criminal Justice. TSLAC. |
| Pope Collection | Lawrence C. Pope Collection, 1961–1989. CAH. |
| Ring Papers | Mrs. Henry F. "Elizabeth L." Ring Papers, 1920–1930. CAH. |
| Roberts Records | Records, Texas Governor Oran Milo Roberts. TSLAC. |
| Rodeo Records | Texas Prison Rodeo records, TDCJ. TSLAC. |
| RRP | Records Relating to the Penitentiary. TSLAC. |
| Ruíz Files | Ruíz Litigation Administrative Files and Court Records, TDCJ. TSLAC. |
| Ruíz-GC Files | General Counsel's Office Ruíz litigation case files, TDCJ. TSLAC. |
| Ruíz-SM Records | Ruíz Case Office of Special Master Records, 1979–1992. CAH. |
| Sánchez Papers | Ricardo Sánchez Papers, Benson Latin American Collection, University of Texas at Austin. |
| Sterling Records | Records, Texas Governor Ross Shaw Sterling. TSLAC. |
| TDCJ Records | Records, Texas Department of Criminal Justice. TSLAC. |
| Wallace Papers | John F. Wallace Papers. TSLAC. |

## INTRODUCTION

1. Friedrich Nietzsche, *Thus Spake Zarathustra* (London: George Allen & Unwin, 1923), 118.
2. Thomas Paine, *Common Sense* (New York: Peter Eckler, 1918), 37, 22; John S. Jenkins, ed., *Life and Public Services of Gen. Andrew Jackson* (New York: Miller, Orton, and Mulligan, 1855), 371; Barack Obama, inaugural address, January 20, 2009, http://www.nytimes.com/2009/01/20/us/politics/20text-obama.html.
3. Jennifer Warren, *One in 100: Behind Bars in America 2008* (Washington, D.C.: Pew Center on the States, 2008); Heather C. West and William J. Sabol, *Prison Inmates at Midyear 2008*, Statistical Tables, NCJ 225619 (Washington, D.C.: Bureau of Justice Statistics [BJS], March 2009), 3; Todd D. Minton and William J. Sabol, *Jail Inmates at Midyear 2008*, Statistical Tables, NCJ 225709 (Washington, D.C.: BJS, March 2009), 3; Roy Walmsley, World Prison Population List, 5th ed., Findings 234 (London: Research, Development, and Statistics Directorate, Home Office, 2003), 4.
4. U.S. Census Bureau, "2000 Census: US Municipalities Over 50,000," http://www.demographia.com/db-uscity98.htm; William Spelman, "The Limited Importance of Prison Expansion," in Alfred Blumstein and Joel Wallman, eds., *The Crime Drop in America* (New York: Cambridge University Press, 2000): 97–129; Franklin E. Zimring, *The Great American Crime Decline* (New York: Oxford University Press, 2007). Some economists estimate a more pronounced impact. See Steven D. Levitt, "Understanding Why Crime Fell in the 1990s: Four Factors That Explain the Decline and Six That Do Not," *Journal of Economic Perspectives* 18, no. 1 (2004): 163–90.
5. BJS, "Justice Expenditure and Employment Extracts" (2006), http://www.ojp.usdoj.gov/bjs/eande.htm#selected; "My Global Career 500," http://www.myglobalcareer.com/my-global-career-500/; James J. Stephan, *Census of State and Federal Correctional Facilities* (2005), NCJ 222182 (Washington, D.C.: BJS, October 2008), 1.
6. Thomas P. Bonczar, *Prevalence of Imprisonment in the U.S. Population, 1974–2001*, NCJ 197976 (Washington, D.C.: BJS, August 2003), 1; National Center for Education Statistics, *Literacy Behind Prison Walls*, NCES 1994–102 (Washington, D.C.: U.S. Department of Education, 1994), 17; Caroline Wolf Harlow, *Education and*

*Correctional Populations*, NCJ 195670 (Washington, D.C.: BJS, January 2003), 1; David Cole, *No Equal Justice: Race and Class in the American Criminal Justice System* (New York: New Press, 1999), 66. See also Bruce Western, *Punishment and Inequality in America* (New York: Russell Sage Foundation, 2006); John Hagan and Ruth D. Peterson, *Crime and Inequality* (Stanford, Calif.: Stanford University Press, 1995).

7. Gustave de Beaumont and Alexis de Tocqueville, *On the Penitentiary System in the United States and Its Application in France*, trans. Francis Lieber (Philadelphia: Carey, Lea & Blanchard, 1833), 44. Racial disparity estimates based on: Patrick A. Langan, *Race of Prisoners Admitted to State and Federal Institutions, 1926–1986*, NCJ-125618 (Washington, D.C.: BJS, May 1991); Campbell Gibson and Kay Jung, *Historical Census Statistics on Population Totals By Race, 1790 to 1990, and By Hispanic Origin, 1970 to 1990*, Working Paper Series No. 56 (Washington, D.C.: U.S. Census Bureau, September 2002), table 1; Allen J. Beck and Paige M. Harrison, *Prisoners in 2000*, NCJ 188207 (Washington, D.C.: BJS, August 2001), 10; Jesse McKinnon, *The Black Population: 2000*, Census 2000 Brief, C2KBR/01–5 (Washington, D.C.: U.S. Census Bureau, August 2001), 3; Elizabeth M. Grieco, *The White Population: 2000*, Census 2000 Brief, C2KBR/01–4 (Washington, D.C.: U.S. Census Bureau, August 2001), 3.

8. Western, *Punishment and Inequality in America*, 29. See also Jason Ziedenberg and Vincent Schiraldi, *Cellblocks or Classrooms? The Funding of Higher Education and Corrections and Its Impact on African American Men* (Washington, D.C.: Justice Policy Institute [JPI], August 28, 2002).

9. BJS, "Justice Expenditure and Employment Extracts" (2005); Susan B. Carter et al., *Historical Statistics of the United States*, millennial ed., vol. 5 (Cambridge: Cambridge University Press, 2000), pt. E, 5–311; Henry W. Bragdon and John C. Pittenger, *The Pursuit of Justice* (New York: Crowell-Collier, 1969), 91, x; Norval Morris, "Prison in Evolution," in Edward Eldefonso, ed. *Issues in Corrections: A Book of Readings* (Beverly Hills, Calif.: Glencoe Press, 1974), 250. See also Norval Morris, *The Future of Imprisonment* (Chicago: University of Chicago Press, 1974).

10. M. Stanton Evans and Margaret Moore, *The Lawbreakers: America's Number One Domestic Problem* (New Rochelle, N.Y.: Arlington House, 1968); William John Bennett, John J. DiIulio, and John P. Walters, *Body Count: Moral Poverty–and How to Win America's War Against Crime and Drugs* (New York: Simon & Schuster, 1996); James Q. Wilson, *Thinking About Crime*, rev. ed. (New York: Basic Books, 1983).

11. Anne-Marie Cusac, *Cruel and Unusual: The Culture of Punishment in America* (New Haven, Conn.: Yale University Press, 2009); Sasha Abramsky, *American Furies: Crime, Punishment, and Vengeance in the Age of Mass Imprisonment* (Boston: Beacon Press, 2007); Jonathan Simon, "Fear and Loathing in Late Modernity: Reflections on the Cultural Sources of Mass Imprisonment in the United States," *Punishment and Society* 3, no. 1 (2001): 21–34; David Garland, *The Culture of Control: Crime and Social Order in Contemporary Society* (Chicago: University of Chicago Press, 2001). For rival explanations, see Christian Parenti, *Lockdown America: Police and Prisons in the Age of Crisis* (New York: Verso, 1999); Jonathan Simon, *Governing Through Crime: How the War on Crime Transformed American Democracy and Created a Culture of Fear* (New York: Oxford University Press, 2007); Michael Tonry, *Thinking About Crime: Sense and Sensibility in American Penal Culture* (New York: Oxford University Press, 2004).

12. See Paulette Thomas, "Making Crime Pay: Triangle of Interests Creates Infrastructure to Fight Lawlessness," *Wall Street Journal*, May 12, 1995, A1, A6; J. Robert Lilly and Paul Knepper, "The Corrections-Commercial Complex," *Crime and Delinquency* 39, no. 2 (April 1993): 150–66; Joel Dyer, *The Perpetual Prisoner*

*Machine: How America Profits from Crime* (Boulder, Colo.: Westview Press, 2000); Ruth Gilmore, *Golden Gulag: Prisons, Surplus, Crisis, and Opposition in Globalizing California* (Berkeley: University of California Press, 2007).

13. Notable exceptions include: Katherine Beckett, *Making Crime Pay: Law and Order in Contemporary American Politics* (New York: Oxford University Press, 1997); Marc Mauer, *Race to Incarcerate* (New York: New Press, 1999); Loic Wacquant, "Deadly Symbiosis: When Ghetto and Prison Meet and Mesh," *Punishment and Society* 3, no. 1 (2001): 95–134. More recently, see Glenn C. Loury, *Race, Incarceration, and American Values* (Cambridge, Mass.: Boston Review/MIT Press, 2008); Naomi Murakawa, "The Origins of the Carceral Crisis: Racial Order as 'Law and Order' in Postwar American Politics," in Joseph E. Lowndes, Julie Novkov, and Dorian Tod Warren, eds., *Race and American Political Development* (New York: Routledge, 2008); Loïc Wacquant, *Punishing the Poor: The Neoliberal Government of Social Insecurity* (Durham, N.C.: Duke University Press, 2009).

14. There are numerous long-range historical surveys of American criminal justice, of course, but these typically minimize the South and marginalize race. See James Q. Whitman, *Harsh Justice: Criminal Punishment and the Widening Divide Between America and Europe* (New York: Oxford University Press, 2003); Lawrence Friedman, *Crime and Punishment in American History* (New York: Basic Books, 1993). Exceptions include: Scott Christianson, *With Liberty for Some: 500 Years of Imprisonment in America* (Boston: Northeastern University Press, 1998); Mark Colvin, *Penitentiaries, Reformatories, and Chain Gangs: Social Theory and the History of Punishment in Nineteenth-Century America* (New York: St. Martin's Press, 1997).

15. There are numerous books that deal with the cruelties of southern justice, but they tend to move no further forward than the Progressive Era. See Edward L. Ayers, *Vengeance and Justice: Crime and Punishment in the Nineteenth-Century American South* (New York: Oxford University Press, 1984); Alex Lichtenstein, *Twice the Work of Free Labor: The Political Economy of Convict Labor in the New South* (London: Verso, 1996); David M. Oshinsky, *"Worse Than Slavery": Parchman Farm and the Ordeal of Jim Crow Justice* (New York: Free Press, 1996); Douglas A. Blackmon, *Slavery by Another Name: The Re-Enslavement of Black People in America from the Civil War to World War II* (New York: Doubleday, 2008).

16. West and Sabol, *Prison Inmates at Midyear 2008*, 3; BJS, "Justice Expenditure and Employment Extracts" (2006); Google, FY2007 results, January 31, 2008, http:// investor.google.com/releases/2007Q4_google_earnings.html; U.S. Census Bureau, "State and County QuickFacts" (2008), http://quickfacts.census.gov/qfd/ index.html. California and Texas both held 173,000 prisoners in July 2008, but California's numbers have decreased while Texas's are still increasing.

17. Paige M. Harrison and Allen J. Beck, *Prisoners in 2005*, NCJ 215092 (Washington, D.C.: BJS, November 2006), 1; Paige M. Harrison and Allen J. Beck, *Prison and Jail Inmates at Midyear 2004*, NCJ 208801 (Washington, D.C.: BJS, April 2005); Walmsley, *World Prison Population List*.

18. *The Fair Defense Report: Analysis of Indigent Defense Practices in Texas* (Austin: Texas Appleseed Fair Defense Project, December 2000); *Public Safety, Public Spending: Forecasting America's Prison Population 2007–2011* (Washington, D.C.: Pew Center on the States, 2007); West and Sabol, *Prison Inmates at Midyear 2008*, 13; Kevin Johnson, "From Extreme Isolation: Waves of Felons Are Freed," *USA Today*, December 11, 2002, http://www.usatoday.com/news/nation/2002– 12–11-prison-cover-usat_x.htm; *One in 31: The Long Reach of American Corrections* (Washington, D.C.: Pew Center on the States, March 2009), 42; Death Penalty Information Center, "Executions in the United States, 1608–1976, by State," http://www.deathpenaltyinfo.org/executions-united-states-1608–1976 -state; Joseph T. Hallinan, *Going Up the River: Travels in a Prison Nation* (New York: Random House, 2001); xii.

19. See Michael Lind, *Made in Texas: George W. Bush and the Southern Takeover of American Politics* (New York: Basic Books, 2003); James McEnteer, *Deep in the Heart: The Texas Tendency in American Politics* (Westport, Conn.: Praeger, 2004).

20. On the Byrd lynching, see Ricardo C. Ainslie, *Long Dark Road: Bill King and Murder in Jasper, Texas* (Austin: University of Texas Press, 2004); Mike Berryhill, "Prisoner's Dilemma: Did the Texas Penal System Kill James Byrd?" *New Republic*, December 27 1999; Dina Temple-Raston, *Death in Texas: A Story of Race, Murder, and a Small Town's Struggle for Redemption* (New York: Owl Books, 2003).

21. On Texas's populist tradition, see Lawrence Goodwyn, *Democratic Promise: The Populist Moment in America* (New York: Oxford University Press, 1976); V. O. Key and Alexander Heard, *Southern Politics in State and Nation*, new ed. (Knoxville: University of Tennessee Press, 1984); Chandler Davidson, *Race and Class in Texas Politics* (Princeton, N.J.: Princeton University Press, 1990). Ronnie Dugger, "The Texification of the USA," *Texas Observer*, December 3, 2004, 6.

22. "Pontesso Sees State Prisons as Failing to Rehabilitate Cons," *Houston Chronicle*, September 4, 1978.

23. "Declaration of Principles Adopted and Promulgated by the Congress," in Enoch C. Wines, ed. *Transactions of the National Congress on Penitentiary and Reformatory Discipline, Held at Cincinnati, Ohio, October 12–18, 1870* (Albany, N.Y.: Weed, Parsons & Co., 1871), 541; "Convict Camps," *Dallas Morning News*, November 2, 1909, 6.

24. Patrick A. Langan et al., *Historical Statistics on Prisoners in State and Federal Institutions, Yearend 1925–1986*, NCJ-111098 (Washington, D.C.: BJS, May 1988), 10; Beck and Harrison, *Prisoners in 2000*; Kathleen Maguire and Ann L. Patore, eds., *Sourcebook of Criminal Justice Statistics 2002*, NCJ 203301 (Washington, D.C.: BJS, 2004), 495. James Marquart, interview by author, Huntsville, Texas, March 19, 1999.

25. See Margaret Werner Cahalan, "Historical Corrections Statistics in the United States, 1850–1984" (Washington, D.C.: BJS, 1986); Roger Lane, *Murder in America: A History* (Columbus: Ohio State University Press, 1997).

26. See, for example, Norval Morris and David J. Rothman, eds., *The Oxford History of the Prison: The Practice of Punishment in Western Society* (New York: Oxford University Press, 1995); Thomas G. Blomberg and Karol Lucken, *American Penology: A History of Control* (New York: Aldine de Gruyter, 2000); Blake McKelvey, *American Prisons: A History of Good Intentions*, rev. ed. (Montclair, N.J.: Patterson Smith, 1977).

27. Even the most critical thinkers have typically followed this forward march from sanguinary to supple discipline. See Michel Foucault, *Discipline and Punish: The Birth of the Prison*, trans. Alan Sheridan (New York: Vintage Books, 1979); Georg Rusche and Otto Kirchheimer, *Punishment and Social Structure* (New York: Columbia University Press and the Institute of Social Research, 1939).

28. Another reason that northeastern prisons have dominated the historiography is that the nation's elite universities afford ready access to their archives.

29. Enoch Wines, "Reformation of the Criminal" (1895), in Corinne Bacon, ed. *Prison Reform* (New York: H. W. Wilson Company, 1917), 1.

30. Plato, *Republic*, trans. Francis MacDonald Cornford (New York: Oxford University Press, 1951), 18.

31. Republic of Texas, *Constitution* (1836), secs. 6–10.

32. Manning Marable, *Race, Reform, and Rebellion: The Second Reconstruction in Black America, 1945–1982* (Jackson: University Press of Mississippi, 1984).

33. Erving Goffman, *Asylums: Essays on the Social Situation of Mental Patients and Other Inmates* (New York: Doubleday, 1990).

34. Here, my work is influenced by a long line of prison sociologists and anthropologists. See Donald Clemmer, *The Prison Community* (Boston: Christopher

Publishing House, 1940); Gresham M. Sykes, *The Society of Captives* (Princeton, N.J.: Princeton University Press, 1958); Donald R. Cressey, ed., *The Prison: Studies in Institutional Organization and Change* (New York: Holt, Rinehart and Winston, 1961); John Irwin, *Prisons in Turmoil* (Boston: Little, Brown, 1980); Lorna Rhodes, *Total Confinement: Madness and Reason in the Maximum Security Prison* (Berkeley: University of California Press, 2004).

35. Teri Crook, "Texas Prisons—'A Bad Situation,'" *Galveston Daily News*, March 6, 1984.

36. For an overview of reform efforts at the start of the new century, see Daniel F. Wilhelm and Nicholas R. Turner, *Is the Budget Crisis Changing the Way We Look at Sentencing and Incarceration?* (New York: Vera Institute, June 2002); Marc Mauer, *State Sentencing Reforms: Is the 'Get Tough' Era Coming to a Close?* (Washington, D.C.: Sentencing Project, October 2002). On the death penalty debate, see Scott Turow, *Ultimate Punishment: A Lawyer's Reflections on Dealing with the Death Penalty* (New York: Farrar, Straus and Giroux, 2003); David R. Dow, *Executed on a Technicality: Lethal Injustice on America's Death Row* (Boston: Beacon Press, 2005). Fox Butterfield, "States Ease Laws on Time in Prison," *New York Times*, September 2, 2001, http://www.nytimes.com/2001/09/02/us/states-ease-laws-on-time-in-prison.html.

37. On Mississippi politics during my grandparents' youth, see Neil R. McMillen, *Dark Journey: Black Mississippians in the Age of Jim Crow* (Urbana: University of Illinois Press, 1989). On the modern civil rights movement and white resistance to it, see John Dittmer, *Local People: The Struggle for Civil Rights in Mississippi* (Urbana: University of Illinois Press, 1994).

38. Numan V. Bartley, *The Rise of Massive Resistance: Race and Politics in the South During the 1950's* (Baton Rouge: Louisiana State University Press, 1969). Henry's father worked for Mississippi's U.S. senator Pat Harrison, one of the more progressive politicians in the state.

39. On James Meredith's quixotic March Against Fear, which culminated in the beginnings of "Black Power," see Stephen B. Oates, *Let the Trumpet Sound: The Life of Martin Luther King, Jr.* (New York: Harper & Row, 1982), 404–6. On the southernization of American politics, see Peter Applebome, *Dixie Rising: How the South Is Shaping American Values, Politics, and Culture* (New York: Times Books, 1996).

40. Jared Bernstein, Elizabeth McNichol, and Andrew Nicholas, *Pulling Apart: A State-by-State Analysis of Income Trends* (Washington, D.C.: Center on Budget and Policy Priorities, April 2008).

## 1: PRISON HEARTLAND

1. David Dewhurst, inaugural address, January 16, 2007, http://www.ltgov.state.tx.us/Speeches/?speech=0016&PHPSESSID=faa9cb1ee0d529287ee2293. Dewhurst was speaking in favor of a measure to impose the death penalty for heinous crimes other than murder for the first time since *Furman v. Georgia*, 408 U.S. 238 (1972).

2. John Gibbons, Nicholas Katzenbach, et al., *Confronting Confinement: A Report of the Commission on Safety and Abuse in America's Prisons* (New York: Vera Institute, June 2006), 11; Peter Wagner, e-mail to author, August 6, 2009.

3. Herman Lee Crow, "A Political History of the Texas Penal System, 1829–1951" (PhD diss., University of Texas, 1963), 36–37; Jim Willett, e-mail message to author, December 9, 2006.

4. The prisons in the immediate Huntsville area include Byrd, Ellis, Estelle, Ferguson, Goree, Holliday, Huntsville, and Wynne. In 2005, they collectively held 16,227 inmates. TDCJ, "Unit Directory," http://www.tdcj.state.tx.us/stat/unit

directory/all.htm; Huntsville's estimated 2003 population was 35,567. U.S. Census Bureau, State and County QuickFacts, Huntsville, Texas (2003), http://quickfacts.census.gov/qfd/states/48/4835528.html.

5. Carol Blair Johnson, director, Human Resource Division, TDCJ, e-mail to author, February 15, 2006; Paige M. Harrison and Jennifer C. Karberg, *Prison and Jail Inmates at Midyear 2003*, NCJ 203947 (Washington, D.C.: BJS, May 2004), 1; Walmsley, *World Prison Population List*, 5; Simon Beardsley, interview by author, July 20, 1999.

6. Jim Willett, interview by author, July 19, 2002; Jim Henderson, "Ghostly Sightings Put Walls Unit Inmates on Edge," *Houston Chronicle*, January 9, 2000, A1.

7. William P. Barrett, "The Town Where Crime Pays," *Forbes*, October 28, 1991, 178–79; "Huntsville Prison Blues," produced by Daniel Collison for National Public Radio (NPR), aired on September 10, 2001; Chuck Hurt, interview by author, July 17, 2002. To save transportation money, the legislature in 2009 ordered TDCJ to begin releasing inmates from units other than Huntsville. Grits for Breakfast, "Texas Criminal Justice Reform Legislation Passed in 2009," June 29, 2009, http://gritsforbreakfast.blogspot.com/2009/06/texas-criminal-justice-reform.html.

8. See Peter Carlson, "It's All in the Execution, There's No Getting Out—Without a Stop at the Gift Shop," *Washington Post*, November 29, 2004, C1; Scott Nowell, "A Guarded Past: Texas's Impressive New Prison Museum Engages in a Little Escapism of Its Own," *Houston Press*, January 9, 2003, http://www.houstonpress.com/2003-01-09/news/a-guarded-past/.

9. James W. Marquart, Sheldon Ekland-Olson, and Jonathan R. Sorensen, *The Rope, the Chair, and the Needle: Capital Punishment in Texas, 1923–1990* (Austin: University of Texas Press, 1994), 20.

10. Carlson, "It's All in the Execution"; Jim Willett, interview, July 19, 2002; Jim Willett and Ron Rozelle, *Warden: Prison Life and Death from the Inside Out* (Albany, Tex.: Bright Sky Press, 2004); *Witness to an Execution*, CD, produced by Stacy Abramson and Dave Isay, Sound Portraits Productions, New York, 2000.

11. William Faulkner, *Requiem for a Nun*, quoted in M. Thomas Inge, ed., *William Faulkner: The Contemporary Reviews* (New York: Cambridge University Press, 1995), 341; Barrett, "The Town Where Crime Pays," 178; Johnson, e-mail to author, February 22, 2006; Huntsville-Walker County Chamber of Commerce, "Huntsville and Texas Prisons," http://chamber.itemonline.com/area_information/prisons/.

12. BJS, "Justice Expenditure and Employment Extracts" (2006), tables 9, 5; Stephan, *Census of State and Federal Correctional Facilities* (2005), 9; TDCJ, "Unit Directory," http://www.tdcj.state.tx.us/stat/unitdirectory/all.htm.

13. Lauren Glaze and Thomas Bonczar, *Probation and Parole in the United States, 2007*, NCJ 224707 (Washington, D.C.: BJS, December 2008), 2; West and Sabol, *Prison Inmates at Midyear 2008*, 3; U.S. Census Bureau. State and Country Quick-Facts, Austin, Texas (2008), http://quickfacts.census.gov/qfd/states/48/4805000.html.

14. Michael Jewell, letter to author, June 5, 2005; Frank Smyth, "Bankrolling Beltway Badges," *Texas Observer*, July 30, 2004, 4–7; FBI, "Crime in the United States, 2007," tables 4, 5, http://www.fbi.gov/ucr/cius2007/index.html. The Justice Department suspended the UCR Crime Index program in June 2004. To estimate overall crime rates, I totaled the UCR's violent and nonviolent rates.

15. Jim Henderson, "Arresting Discovery Puts Dallas Ahead in Crime," *Houston Chronicle*, August 9, 2003, 1A; FBI, "Crime in the United States, 2006," tables 1, 8; http://www.fbi.gov/ucr/cius2006/index.html; TDCJ, *Fiscal Year 2004 Statistical Report*, 19; Tanya Eiserer, "Developers, Residents Are Fearful About Building for the Future if South Dallas Is Not Safe," *Dallas Morning News*, special report,

"Dallas at the Tipping Point—Going South," 2004, http://www.dallasnews. com/s/dws/spe/2004/dallas/crime2.html. Dallas's prison admission figures do not include another five thousand inmates convicted in Tarrent County.

16. John Wesley Hardin, *The Life of John Wesley Hardin, as Written by Himself* (Norman: University of Oklahoma Press, 1961), 15, 13; Bruce McGinnis, *Reflections in Dark Glass: The Life and Times of John Wesley Hardin* (Denton: University of North Texas Press, 1996).

17. Anne Dingus, "Deadline," *Texas Monthly*, July 2002, 96.

18. Gene Hathorn, letter to author, August 23, 2004; *Hathorn v. State*, 848 S.W.2d. (Tex.Cr.App. 1992), 105–6; Dale Lezon, "Rampage Killer Loses His Chance for Early Release," *Houston Chronicle*, February 23, 2004, A17; Roger Lane, "Murder in America: A Historian's Perspective," *Crime and Justice* 25 (1999): 220–21.

19. Gary M. Lavergne, *Bad Boy from Rosebud* (Denton: University of North Texas Press, 1999); Ray Surette, *Media, Crime, and Criminal Justice: Images and Realities* (Pacific Grove, Calif.: Brooks/Cole Pub. Co., 1992); West and Sabol, *Prison Inmates at Midyear 2008*, 3; TDCJ, *Statistical Report* (2008), 1; Donald F. Sabo, Terry Allen Kupers, and Willie James London, eds., *Prison Masculinities* (Philadelphia: Temple University Press, 2001), 49. Calculating the exact breakdown of violent to nonviolent offenders in Texas is complicated by different counting methods employed by state and federal authorities. My estimate relies on the total number of Texas prisoners as tallied by the BJS, divided according to offense data reported by TDCJ.

20. TDCJ, *Statistical Report* (2008), 19; TDCJ, *Statistical Report* (2006), 15; Lauren Glaze and Thomas Bonczar, *Probation and Parole in the United States, 2006*, NCJ 220218 (Washington, D.C.: BJS, December 2007), table 5; TDCJ, "Technical Revocations of Probation FY 2006," http://www.tdcj.state.tx.us/publications/cjad/Technical%20Revocation%20Report%20Fact%20Sheet%202007.pdf; Richard Watkins, interview by author, February 8, 2006. In order to curtail the numbers of community-based offenders going to prison on technical violations, Texas enacted much-delayed probation and parole reforms in 2007. See Patrick Michels, "Politically Correct: New Prisons, Tougher Sentences, with a Little Love Thrown In," *Texas Observer*, June 15, 2007, 20–21.

21. TDCJ, *Statistical Report* (2008), 1; West and Sabol, *Prison Inmates at Midyear 2008*, 3; Peter Wilkinson, "Assault with a Deadly Elbow," *Rolling Stone*, June 22, 2000, 51–55; "Texas Judge Declines to Cut 5-Year Term in Sports Case," *New York Times*, March 11, 2000, A12.

22. Robert J. Sampson and John H. Laub, "Life Course Desisters? Trajectories and Crime Among Delinquent Boys Followed to Age 70," *Criminology* 41, no. 3 (2003): 301–39; Cole, *No Equal Justice*, 147; Adam Liptak, "To More Inmates, Life Term Means Dying Behind Bars," *New York Times*, October 2, 2005, 1, 18–19.

23. Jewell, letter to author, June 5, 2005; January 8, 2006. Although releasing longserving violent offenders is politically unpopular, recidivism data suggest they pose less of a threat than released short-timers. Marc Mauer, Ryan S. King, and Malcolm C. Young, *The Meaning of 'Life': Long Prison Sentences in Context* (Washington, D.C.: Sentencing Project, May 2004), 3.

24. Jewell, letter to author, June 5, 2005.

25. Jewell, letter to author, July 1, 2005; January 24, 2006.

26. Jewell, letter to author, June 5, 2005.

27. Kimberly Leavelle, interview by author, May 27, 2006; Leavelle, e-mail to author, January 5, 2006; Helga Dill, e-mail to author, December 17, 2006.

28. Kimberly Leavelle, "An Autobiography" (unpublished manuscript, Gatesville, Texas, 2001); Leavelle, letter to author, October 22, 2004; Leavelle, e-mail to author, January 5, 2006.

29. Leavelle, "An Autobiography."

30. Leavelle, "An Autobiography"; Leavelle, e-mail to author, January 6, 2006.

31. Leavelle, letter to author, November 21, 2004.
32. Kathleen Daly, "Women's Pathways to Felony Court: Feminist Theories of Law-breaking and Problems of Representation," *Southern California Review of Law and Women's Studies* 2 (1992): 11–52; Lawrence A. Greenfeld and Tracy L. Snell, *Women Offenders*, NCJ 175688 (Washington, D.C.: BJS, December 1999); Caroline Wolf Harlow, *Prior Abuse Reported by Inmates and Probationers*, NCJ 172879 (Washington, D.C.: BJS, April 1999). See Joanne Belknap, *The Invisible Woman: Gender, Crime, and Justice*, 3rd ed. (Belmont, Calif.: Thomson/Wadsworth, 2007). Some researchers argue that the Justice Department's survey underestimates the portion of women prisoners who have been violently or sexually abused. See Angela Browne, Brenda Miller, and Eugene Maguin, "Prevalence and Severity of Lifetime Physical and Sexual Victimization Among Incarcerated Women," *International Journal of Law and Psychiatry* 22, nos. 3–4 (1999): 301–22.
33. Janet L. Mullings, Deborah J. Hartley, and James W. Marquart, "Exploring the Relationship Between Alcohol Use, Childhood Maltreatment, and Treatment Needs Among Female Offenders," *Substance Use & Misuse* 39, no. 2 (2004): 288, 292; Texas Commission on Alcohol and Drug Abuse, "Study Indicates High Drug Use Among Texas's Female Inmates," *Alcoholism and Drug Abuse Weekly* 7, no. 20 (May 15, 1995): 7.
34. Greenfeld and Snell, *Women Offenders*, 5, 7; Maguire and Patore, eds., *Sourcebook of Criminal Justice Statistics 2002*, table 6.22; West and Sabol, *Prison Inmates at Midyear 2008*, 5; Minton and Sabol, *Jail Inmates at Midyear 2008*, 5.
35. TDCJ, *Statistical Report* (2008), 18, 32; Vincent Schiraldi and Jason Ziedenberg, *Texas Tough: Three Years Later* (Washington, D.C.: JPI, April 23, 2003), 7; Beth E. Richie, "The Social Impact of Mass Incarceration on Women," in Marc Mauer and Meda Chesney-Lind, eds., *Invisible Punishment: The Collateral Consequences of Mass Imprisonment* (New York: W. W. Norton, 2002), 141. See also Christopher J. Mumola, *Incarcerated Parents and Their Children*, NCJ 182335 (Washington, D.C.: BJS, August 2000); Lauren Glaze and Laura Maruschak, *Parents in Prison and Their Minor Children*, NCJ 222984 (Washington, D.C.: BJS, August 2008).
36. Jamie Watson et al., *A Portrait of Prisoner Reentry in Texas* (Washington, D.C.: Urban Institute, March 2004); Schiraldi and Ziedenberg, *Texas Tough: Three Years Later*, 7; Fox Butterfield, "Parents in Prison: A Special Report: As Inmate Population Grows, So Does a Focus on Children," *New York Times*, April 7, 1999, A1, A18. To coordinate and augment federal efforts to assist released prisoners and their family members, Congress passed the Second Chance Act in 2008. See Bruce Western, "Reentry: Reversing Mass Imprisonment," *Boston Review*, July/August 2008, 7–12.
37. Doris J. James, *Profile of Jail Inmates*, NCJ 201932 (Washington, D.C.: BJS, July 2004), 1.
38. Kenneth Broussard, letter to author, October 21, 2004.
39. Ibid.; Broussard, "Family" (unpublished manuscript, 2003).
40. Broussard, letter to author, October 21, 2004.
41. Broussard, letter to author, December 5, 2005.
42. Broussard, letters to author, October 21, 2004, December 5, 2005.
43. Broussard, letters to author, October 21, 2004, January 17, 2006.
44. Broussard, letter to author, December 5, 2005.
45. Broussard, letters to author, October 21, 2004, December 5, 2005.
46. Broussard, letters to author, October 21, 2004, November 28, 2005.
47. Broussard, letter to author, January 17, 2006; Jewell, letter to author, January 14, 2006.
48. Jewell, letter to author, February 10, 2006.
49. Eric Cummins, *The Rise and Fall of California's Radical Prison Movement* (Stanford, Calif.: Stanford University Press, 1994), 13–14.

50. William Sabol and Heather Couture, *Prison Inmates at Midyear 2007*, NCJ 221944 (Washington, D.C.: BJS, June 2008), 18.

51. TDCJ, "Offender Orientation Handbook" (2004), chap. 1; Becky Price, interview by author, January 19, 2006.

52. Willett, e-mail to author, January 21, 2006.

53. Allen Leskinen, letter to author, February 14, 2006; Charles Brown, letter to author, July 3, 2004; Norris Trevenio, interview by author, August 7, 2003; Broussard, letter to author, January 17, 2006.

54. Jorge Antonio Renaud, *Behind the Walls: A Guide for Families and Friends of Texas Prison Inmates* (Denton: University of North Texas Press, 2002), 2; Jewell, letter to author, January 12, 2006; Erving Goffman, Charles C. Lemert, and Ann Branaman, *The Goffman Reader* (Cambridge, Mass.: Blackwell, 1997), 56.

55. TDCJ, "Offender Orientation Handbook," 18; Leavelle, e-mail to author, January 26, 2006.

56. TDCJ, "Offender Orientation Handbook," 19; Renaud, *Behind the Walls*, 20.

57. Leavelle, e-mail to author, January 26, 2006. For an account of intake from the perspective of corrections officers, see Willett and Rozelle, *Warden*. Like many female inmates, Leavelle started out at the Plane State jail rather than at a massive transfer unit like Holliday.

58. TDCJ, "Offender Orientation Handbook," chap. 1.

59. Renaud, *Behind the Walls*, 111, chap. 17.

60. Vivian Elizabeth Smyrl, "Gatesville, Texas," *Handbook of Texas*, http://www.tsha.utexas.edu/handbook/online/articles/GG/hfg2.html; Mavis Kelsey and Donald Dyal, *The Courthouses of Texas* (College Station: Texas A&M University Press, 2007), 80.

61. City of Gatesville, "Welcome to the City of Gatesville," http://www.ci.gatesville.tx.us/; TDCJ, "Unit Directory"; TSLAC, "2000 Census: Population of Texas Cities," http://www.tsl.state.tx.us/ref/abouttx/popcity12000.html. Gatesville's prisons include the Gatesville, Mountain View, Hilltop, Woodman, Murray, and Hughes units. The town's Web site also boasts of a diverse population without mentioning that most of the nonwhite population resides in prison.

62. "Reformatory for Vicious Boys," *Dallas Morning News*, April 4, 1887, 4; Jewell, letters to author, February 10, 2006, July 1, 2005, February 10, 2006. *Morales v. Turman*, 383 F.Supp. 53 (1974), 77. Virginia opened a state boys' school in 1890. Vernetta D. Young, "Race and Gender in the Establishment of Juvenile Institutions: The Case of the South," *Prison Journal* 73, no. 2 (1994): 252.

63. Leavelle, e-mail to author, January 27, 2006; J. W. Campbell, interview by author, August 5, 2002.

64. Campbell, interview by author, August 5, 2002.

65. James F. Anderson, Laronistine Dyson, and Tazinski Lee, "A Four-Year Tracking Investigation on Boot Camp Participants: A Study of Recidivism Outcome," *Justice Professional* 10, no. 2 (1997): 199–213; Leavelle, e-mail to author, January 27, 2006.

66. Leavelle, e-mail to author, December 15, 2006; Leavelle, letter to author, October 22, 2004.

67. Campbell, interview by author, August 5, 2002.

68. Pamela Baggett, interview by author, July 18, 2002.

69. City of Livingston, "Civil War Reenactment," http://www.cityoflivingston-tx.com/community/civilwar.asp; TDCJ, "Unit Directory: Polunsky," http://www.tdcj.state.tx.us/stat/unitdirectory/tl.htm.

70. Amnesty International, "Death Sentences and Executions in 2008," http://www.amnesty.org/en/library/asset/ACT50/003/2009/en/0b789cb1-baa8–4c1b-bc35–58b606309836/act500032009en.pdf; Death Penalty Information Center (DPIC), "Execution in the United States, by State," http://www.deathpenaltyinfo.org/article.php?scid=8&did=1110; TDCJ, "Executed Offenders," http://www.tdcj.

state.tx.us/stat/executedoffenders.htm. Houston's Harris County alone has sent 108 defendants to their deaths since 1976, more than any state besides Texas. TDCJ, "County of Conviction for Executed Offenders," http://www.tdcj.state.tx .us/stat/countyexecuted.htm.

71. TDCJ, "Death Row Facts," http://www.tdcj.state.tx.us/stat/drowfacts.htm.

72. Jonathan Reed, interview by author, August 7, 2003; Jonathan Reed, letter to author, October 21, 2003. For basic information on Reed's case, see 269 F.Supp.2d 784 (N.D.Tex 2003); TDCJ, "Offender Information: Jonathan Reed," http://www .tdcj.state.tx.us/statistics/deathrow/drowlist/reedj.jpg. Against the odds, Reed won the right to a new trial in early 2009. Steve McGonigle and Diane Jennings, "Texas Death Row Conviction Tossed; Biased Jury Selection Cited," *Dallas Morning News*, January 13, 2009, http://www.dallasnews.com/sharedcontent/dws/dn/ latestnews/stories/011308dntexconvictionreversed.1434cb1.html.

73. Reed, letter to author, October 21, 2003.

74. Cameron Todd Willingham, letter to author, September 11, 2003.

75. Steven Woods, letter to CURE, June 2004; Reed, letter to author, October 21, 2003.

76. On the long-term effects of severe isolation prisons, see Jesenia Pizarro and Vanja M. K. Stenius, "Supermax Prisons: Their Rise, Current Practices, and Effect on Inmates," *Prison Journal* 84, no. 2 (2004): 248–64; Craig Haney and Mona Lynch, "Regulating Prisons of the Future: A Psychological Analysis of Supermax and Solitary Confinement," *New York Review of Law and Social Change* 23 (1997): 477–570; Stuart Grassian, "Psychopathological Effects of Solitary Confinement," *American Journal of Psychiatry* 140, no. 11 (1983): 1450–54; *Out of Sight: Super-maximum Security Confinement in the United States* (New York: Human Rights Watch, 2000).

77. Woods, letter to CURE, June 2004; Jonathan Reed, untitled poem, December 5, 2004; Jon Reed, letter to author, March 6, 2006; TDCJ, "Offenders No Longer on Death Row," http://www.tdcj.state.tx.us/stat/permanentout.htm; Richard Cartwright, "Uncensored from Death Row," unpublished open letter, February 6, 2005.

78. See Carroll Pickett, *Within These Walls: Memoirs of a Death House Chaplain* (New York: St. Martin's Press, 2002).

79. TDCJ, "Final Meal Requests," http://www.thememoryhole.org/deaths/texas-final-meals.htm, Claude Jones and Keith Clay. Condemned prisoners can order whatever they like, but TDCJ only honors requests for items on its regular menu. T-bone steaks, for instance, are not provided, though hamburgers are. Whatever they order, most prisoners don't eat much, mentally retarded offenders excepted. Says Pickett, "Despite the popular myth, most condemned men who order an elaborate meal only pick at it. The mentally challenged always display a voracious appetite." Pickett, *Within These Walls*, 176.

80. Despite regulations, Warden Jim Willett says he sometimes allowed condemned men to have a smoke or two before their last walk down the hall. Willett and Rozelle, *Warden*.

81. Texas has executed three women in recent years. None of them ordered more than a salad. TDCJ, "Final Meal Requests." Out of eleven female prisoners executed nationwide since 1976, seven of them ordered nothing, very little, or simply the standard prison menu of the day. Bill Hayes, e-mail to author, February 4, 2006.

82. Jim Willett, interview by author, July 19, 2002; *Witness to an Execution*; Willett and Rozelle, *Warden*. Until the 1990s, prisoners in Texas were executed at midnight, but TDCJ changed the procedure to make the process easier on staff.

83. Mike Graczyk, in *Witness to an Execution*.

84. TDCJ, "Executed Offenders, Last Statement: Richard Cartwright," http://www

.tdcj.state.tx.us/stat/cartwrightrichardlast.htm; "Cameron Todd Willingham," http://www.clarkprosecutor.org/html/death/US/willingham899.htm; Maurice Possley, "Report: Inmate Wrongly Executed: Arson Experts Say Evidence in Texas Case Scientifically Invalid," *Chicago Tribune*, May 3, 2006, http://www.chicagotribune.com/technology/chi-060502willingham,0,6033976.story.

85. TDCJ, "Executed Offenders, Last Statement: Hilton Crawford," http://www.tdcj.state.tx.us/stat/crawfordhiltonlast.htm; Karla Faye Tucker, http://www.tdcj.state.tx.us/stat/tuckerkarlalast.htm; John Moritz and Jim Brazille, in *Witness to an Execution*.

86. Melvin Wayne White, http://www.clarkprosecutor.org/html/death/US/white990.htm; Leighanne Gideon in *Witness to an Execution*. The drug combination pioneered by Texas and used by most other states has come under criticism from human rights advocates, death penalty opponents, and anesthesiologists because the initial dose may provide insufficient sedation to prevent intense pain. See TDCJ, "Death Row Facts," http://www.tdcj.state.tx.us/stat/drowfacts.htm; Adam Liptak, "Critics Say Execution Drug May Hide Suffering," *New York Times*, October 7, 2003, A1; Louis Sahagun and Tim Reiterman, "Execution of Killer-Rapist Is Postponed After Doctors Walk Out," *Los Angeles Times*, February 21, 2006, http://www.latimes.com/news/local/la-me-morales21feb21,0,246025.story?coll=la-home-headlines.

87. Sara Rimer, "Working Death Row: In the Busiest Death Chamber, Duty Carries Its Own Burdens," *New York Times*, December 17, 2000, 1, 32; Kenneth Dean and Fred Allen in *Witness to an Execution*. See also Bob Herbert, *Promises Betrayed: Waking Up from the American Dream* (New York: Times Books, 2005), 92–94.

88. Rimer, "Working Death Row"; "News About Gary Etheridge," http://www.ccadp.org/garyetheridge-aug2002news.htm; Michael Graczyk, "Man Convicted of Killing Four, Including His Mother, Put to Death," Associated Press, February 18, 2005.

89. Rimer, "Working Death Row"; Mike Graczyk and Leighanne Gideon, in *Witness to an Execution*.

90. Robert Lee Mudd, letter to author, March 10, 2006; TDCJ, "Unit Directory"; Bill Habern, interview by author, July 19, 2002.

91. TDCJ, "Unit Directory: Eastham"; Fred King, "6 Units to House Unruly Inmates," *Houston Post*, August 30, 1984; "The Recent Eastham Prison Breaks," *Sheriffs' Association of Texas Official Magazine* 6, no. 8 (August 1937): 18–19; Fred Roe, "Willie's Story: The Beginning," *Hill n' Holler Review*, April 16, 1999.

92. "Eastham Rodeo Thrills," *Echo*, August 1929, 9; E. R. Milner, *The Lives and Times of Bonnie and Clyde* (Carbondale: Southern Illinois University Press, 1996); Texas, Joint Legislative Committee Investigation of the State Penitentiary System, Hearing Transcripts (1925), 88–106; Louise Adams Fulsom, *Prison Stories: The Old Days* (Huntsville, Tex.: privately printed, 1998); Bruce Cory, "The Old Days at TDC Are (Almost) Over," *Corrections Compendium* 11, no. 6 (1986): 1, 6–10; Texas State Penitentiary Board, *Biennial Report* (1896), 10–11. The Eastham family bought the farm in 1891 and started using convict labor shortly thereafter, perhaps before an official contract showed up in the official reports. "Eastham folder," Texas Prison Museum. Jim Willett, e-mail to author, February 14, 2004.

93. Jane Howe Gregory, "Persistence and Irony in the Incarceration of Women in the Texas Penitentiary, 1907–1910" (master's thesis, Rice University, 1994); Prison Commission, *Annual Report* (1921), 7; James Robert Reynolds, "The Administration of the Texas Prison System" (master's thesis, University of Texas, 1925), 115.

94. Walter Siros, interview by author, July 24, 2002; Aric Press et al., "Inside America's Toughest Prison," *Newsweek*, October 6, 1986.

95. John Massingill, interview by author, July 19, 2002.
96. Massingill, interview by author, July 19, 2002. See James W. Marquart and Ben M. Crouch, "Judicial Reform and Prisoner Control: The Impact of *Ruiz v. Estelle* on a Texas Penitentiary," *Law and Society Review* 19, no. 4 (1985): 557–86.
97. Anonymous convicts, interview by author, July 19, 2002.
98. Massingill, interview by author, July 19, 2002.
99. Massingill, interview by author, February 17, 2006; Massingill, interview by author, July 19, 2002.
100. Massingill, interview by author, July 19, 2002. On the complaints of the un-recognized guards' union, see Nate Blakeslee, "The Gray and the White," *Texas Observer*, March 31, 2000, 10–15; Diane Jennings, "Violence Erupts Again at South Texas Prison," *Dallas Morning News*, December 21, 1999, 31A.
101. Massingill, interview by author, July 19, 2002; TDCJ, "Unit Directory: East-ham"; Chris DeGrate, letter to author, November 18, 2004.

## 2: PLANTATION AND PENITENTIARY

1. Beaumont and Tocqueville, *On the Penitentiary System*, 79.
2. Carleton Beals, *Stephen F. Austin, Father of Texas* (New York: McGraw-Hill, 1953), vi; Eugene C. Barker, *The Life of Stephen F. Austin, Founder of Texas, 1793–1836: A Chapter in the Westward Movement of the Anglo-American People* (Nashville, Tenn.: Cokesbury Press, 1925), 2.
3. Austin to James F. Perry, May 10, 1834; Austin to James F. Perry, August 25, 1834, in Eugene C. Barker, ed. *The Austin Papers*, 3 vols. (Washington, D.C.: U.S. Government Printing Office, 1924–1928); 2:1049–54, 1075–84.
4. Austin to James F. Perry, May 10, 1834; Barker, *Life of Stephen F. Austin*, 444–45.
5. Austin to Perry, May 10, 1834; Austin's address at Brazoria, September 8, 1835, in Barker, *Austin Papers*, 3:116–19; Texas Declaration of Causes for Taking Up Arms Against Santa Anna, San Felipe de Austin, Texas, November 7, 1835, in Ernest Wallace, David M. Vigness, and George B. Ward, eds., *Documents of Texas History*, 2nd ed. (Austin, Tex.: Steck Company, 1994), 91. See also Barker, *Life of Stephen F. Austin*, chap. 14; Stephen Austin, "The 'Prison Journal' of Stephen F. Austin," *Quarterly of the Texas State Historical Association* 2, no. 3 (1899). http://www.tshaonline.org/publications/journals/shq/online/v002/n3/issue.html.
6. Beals, *Stephen F. Austin*, v; Eugene C. Barker, *Mexico and Texas* (Dallas, Tex.: P. L. Turner, 1928), 1. Austin's most recent biography takes a more psychological approach but ends up challenging the role of slavery in the Texas revolution. Gregg Cantrell, *Stephen F. Austin, Empresario of Texas* (New Haven, Conn.: Yale University Press, 1999).
7. Resolution calling for the Convention of March 1, 1836, Washington, Texas, in Wallace, Vigness, and Ward, eds., *Documents of Texas History*, 94.
8. George William Featherstonhaugh, *Excursion Through the Slave States, from Washington on the Potomac, to the Frontier of Mexico; with Sketches of Popular Manners and Geological Notices* (New York: Harper, 1844), 124–25. According to my uncle Gordon Perkinson, an amateur genealogist, Featherstonhaugh is a distant forebear of mine.
9. Francis Lubbock, governor's message to the senators and representatives of the Ninth Legislature of the State of Texas, November 15, 1861 (Austin, Tex.: John Marshall & Company, 1861), 4; Alexis de Tocqueville, *Democracy in America* (London: Saunders and Otley, 1835), vol. 1, chap. 18.
10. Austin to Wily Martin, May 30, 1833; Austin to Rafael Llanos, January 14, 1834, in Barker, *Austin Papers*, 2:981, 1027–31; Cabeza de Vaca, *Cabeza De Vaca's Adventures in the Unknown Interior of America*, trans. Cyclone Covey (Albu-

querque: University of New Mexico Press, 1983); Frederic Gaillardet, *Sketches of Early Texas and Louisiana*, trans. James Shepherd, 3rd (Austin: University of Texas Press, 1839; reprint, 1966), 68.

11. Austin to Antonio Martínez, October 12, 1821, in Barker, *Austin Papers*, 2:417–19.

12. Austin to Antonio Martínez, October 13, 1821, in Barker, *Austin Papers*, 2:419–21; Eugene C. Barker, "The Influence of Slavery in the Colonization of Texas," *Southwestern Historical Quarterly* 28 (1924): 5; Benjamin Lundy, *The War in Texas; A Review of Facts and Circumstances, Showing That This Contest Is a Crusade Against Mexico, Set on Foot and Supported by Slaveholders, Land-Speculators, Etc. In Order to Re-Establish, Extend, and Perpetuate the System of Slavery and the Slave Trade*, 2nd ed. (Philadelphia: Merrihew and Gunn, 1837), 22–28.

13. John Durst to Austin, November 10, 1829, in Barker, *Austin Papers*, 2:285; Randolph B. Campbell, *An Empire for Slavery: The Peculiar Institution in Texas, 1821–1865* (Baton Rouge: Louisiana State University Press, 1989), 24.

14. Austin to Mary Austin Holley, December 29, 1831; Austin to Ramon Musquiz and Lorenzo de Zavala, Austin, June 23, 1829; Austin to Samuel M. Williams, Leona Vicario, April 16, 1831; Austin to Wily Martin, May 30, 1833 in Barker, *Austin Papers*, 2:730–31, 239, 645, 981.

15. Lundy, *War in Texas*, 3; Campbell, *An Empire for Slavery*, 42; Resolution calling for the Convention of March 1, 1836, Washington, Texas, in Wallace, Vigness, and Ward, *Documents of Texas History*, 94. See also Frederick Merk, *Slavery and the Annexation of Texas* (New York: Alfred A. Knopf, 1972).

16. Republic of Texas Constitution of 1836, Declaration of Rights, sec. 2; General Provisions, sec. 7.

17. Republic of Texas Constitution of 1836, General Provisions, secs. 9–10.

18. Friedman, *Crime and Punishment in American History*, chap. 3; David Montgomery, *Citizen Worker: The Experience of Workers in the United States with Democracy and the Free Market During the Nineteenth Century* (New York: Cambridge University Press, 1993), chap. 2; Richard Coke, Address to the Legislature, January 12, 1875, reprinted in *Governors' Messages, Coke to Ross, 1874–1891* (Austin: Texas State Library, 1916), 98–99, 102. See also Ayers, *Vengeance and Justice*, chap. 3; Christian Parenti, *The Soft Cage: Surveillance in America–From Slavery to the War on Terror* (New York: Basic Books, 2003).

19. "Apuntos relativos a la Colonia de Austin en Texas," June 1828, in Barker, *Austin Papers*, 2:64. By contrast, Austin's colonial legal code allowed severe penalties for nonwhites, fourteen to one hundred lashes for slaves and twenty-five for Indians. Paul Lucko, "Prison Farms, Walls, and Society: Punishment and Politics in Texas, 1848–1910" (PhD diss., University of Texas, 1999), 74. See also Charles S. Potts, "Early Criminal Law in Texas: From Civil Law to Common Law to Code," *Texas Law Review* 21 (1942): 394–98.

20. Frederick Law Olmsted, *A Journey Through Texas; or, A Saddle-Trip on the South-Western Frontier* (New York: Burt Franklin, 1860), 386, 314; Texas, Act to Provide for the Appointment of Patrols and to Prescribe Their Duties and Powers, May 9, 1846, in Hans Peter M. N. Gammel, ed. *The Laws of Texas, 1822–1904*, 58 vols. (Austin, Tex.: Gammel-Statesman Publishing Co., 1898–1904), 2:1497–501.

21. Wendell G. Addington, "Slave Insurrections in Texas," *Journal of Negro History* 35, no. 4 (1950): 412.

22. Austin to James F. Perry, May 10, 1834; Gary Clayton Anderson, *The Conquest of Texas: Ethnic Cleansing in the Promised Land, 1820–1875* (Norman: University of Oklahoma Press, 2005).

23. Stephen Austin, "Journal of Stephen F. Austin on His First Trip to Texas, 1821," *Southwestern Historical Quarterly* 7, no. 4 (1904), http://www.tsha.utexas.edu/publications/journals/shq/online/v007/n4/article_3.html; Kelly F. Himmel, *The*

*Conquest of the Karankawas and the Tonkawas, 1821–1859* (College Station: Texas A&M University Press, 1999), 48–51.

24. Anderson, *Conquest of Texas*, 7, 17.
25. Olmsted, *Journey Through Texas*, 300; Walter Prescott Webb, *The Texas Rangers: A Century of Frontier Defense* (Austin: University of Texas Press, 1935), 271, 214–15, xv.
26. Olmsted, *Journey Through Texas*, 327, 299–302.
27. Ranger hagiography remains popular. See Robert Utley, *Lone Star Justice: The First Century of the Texas Rangers* (New York: Oxford University Press, 2002); Charles M. Robinson, *The Men Who Wear the Star: The Story of the Texas Rangers* (New York: Random House, 2001); and "Texas Ranger Hall of Fame and Museum," http://www.texasranger.org/. But critical accounts of the conquest of Texas have increasingly gained prominence. See Benjamin H. Johnson, *Revolution in Texas: How a Forgotten Rebellion and Its Bloody Suppression Turned Mexicans into Americans* (New Haven, Conn.: Yale University Press, 2003); Julian Samora, Joe Bernal, and Albert Peña, *Gunpowder Justice: A Reassessment of the Texas Rangers* (Notre Dame, Ind.: University of Notre Dame Press, 1979); Rodolfo Acuña, *Occupied America: A History of Chicanos*, 3rd ed. (New York: Harper & Row, 1988); McEnteer, *Deep in the Heart.*
28. Anderson, *Conquest of Texas*, 10, 176, 178.
29. Olmsted, *Journey Through Texas*, 300, 163, 126.
30. David Montejano, *Anglos and Mexicans in the Making of Texas, 1836–1986* (Austin: University of Texas Press, 1987), 118, 133.
31. Randolph B. Campbell, *Gone to Texas: A History of the Lone Star State* (New York: Oxford University Press, 2003), 159, 207; Lawrence Goodwyn, *The Populist Moment: A Short History of the Agrarian Revolt in America* (New York: Oxford University Press, 1978), 25.
32. Featherstonhaugh, *Excursion Through the Slave States*, 124; Campbell, *Gone to Texas*, 210; Olmsted, *Journey Through Texas*, 360, 351.
33. Austin to Samuel M. Williams, Leona Vicario, April 16, 1831, in Barker, *Austin Papers*, 2:645. By mentioning San Domingo, Austin referenced the Haitian revolution, raising the specter of slave revolution and black rule. Campbell, *Gone to Texas*, 159, 207; Gaillardet, *Sketches of Early Texas and Louisiana*, 68.
34. Campbell, *An Empire for Slavery*, 2, 210.
35. Hallinan, *Going Up the River*, 82. The Gatesville area housed the first prisons outside East Texas, but it remained slave country, historically speaking. Not until the 1990s did TDCJ become an agency with a significant presence beyond East Texas.
36. Campbell, *An Empire for Slavery*, 209–10; Randolph B. Campbell and Richard G. Lowe, *Wealth and Power in Antebellum Texas* (College Station: Texas A&M University Press, 1977). See also Gavin Wright, *The Political Economy of the Cotton South: Households, Markets, and Wealth in the Nineteenth Century* (New York: W. W. Norton, 1978). On the differences between slave societies and societies with slaves, see Ira Berlin, *Many Thousands Gone: The First Two Centuries of Slavery in North America* (Cambridge, Mass.: Belknap Press of Harvard University Press, 1998); Philip D. Curtin, *The Rise and Fall of the Plantation Complex: Essays in Atlantic History*, 2nd ed. (Cambridge: Cambridge University Press, 1998).
37. "Allen V. Manning" interview, in T. Lindsay Baker and Julie P. Baker, eds., *Till Freedom Cried Out: Memories of Texas Slave Life* (College Station: Texas A&M University Press, 1997), 53. Although in practice masters had disciplinary sovereignty over their slaves except in the most egregious cases of abuse and murder, the letter of the law afforded some protections. Throughout the republic and

into statehood, masters were prohibited from killing their slaves except in the cases of insurrection or self-defense, and in some cases indicted slaves were promised trials before white juries. Texas, Act to Provide for the Punishment of Crimes and Misdemeanors Committed by Slaves and Free Persons of Color, December 14, 1837; Act Concerning Slaves, February 5, 1840, in Gammel, *Laws of Texas*, 1:1385, secs. 3–4; 2:345–46, secs. 3–4. See also Campbell, *An Empire for Slavery*, chap. 5; Paul Finkelman, *Slavery and the Law* (Madison, Wis.: Madison House, 1997).

38. Baker and Baker, *Till Freedom Cried Out*, 34, 36.

39. Millie Manuel interview, in George P. Rawick, ed. *The American Slave: A Composite Autobiography*, 41 vols. (Greenwood, Conn.: Greenwood Publishing, 1972), Supplement, 7:2568; Olmsted, *Journey Through Texas*, 66; John Williams interview, in Rawick, *American Slave*, pt. 7, 11A:172. On slave attitudes toward theft more generally, see Eugene D. Genovese, *Roll, Jordan, Roll: The World the Slaves Made* (New York: Pantheon Books, 1974), book 4; Lawrence Levine, *Black Culture and Black Consciousness: Afro-American Folk Thought from Slavery to Freedom* (New York: Oxford University Press, 1977).

40. W. E. B. DuBois, *The Souls of Black Folk: Essays and Sketches*, 1953 ed. (Greenwich, Conn: Fawcett Publications, 1961), 133. Sociologist Orlando Patterson argues that the cultural heritage of enslavement, in addition to the history of discrimination, partly explains black poverty and crime. Orlando Patterson, *Rituals of Blood: Consequences of Slavery in Two American Centuries* (Washington, D.C.: Basic/Civitas, 1998).

41. Austin to Mary Austin Holley, December 29, 1831, in Barker, *Austin Papers*, 2:730; Thomas Barrett, *The Great Hanging at Gainesville, Cooke County, Texas, October, A.D. 1862* (Austin: Texas State Historical Association, 1961); B. P. Gallaway, *The Dark Corner of the Confederacy: Accounts of Civil War Texas as Told by Contemporaries* (Dubuque, Iowa: W. C. Brown Book Co., 1968), 59–71; James Smallwood, "Disaffection in Confederate Texas: The Great Hanging at Gainesville," *Civil War History* 22 (1976): 349–60; Campbell, *An Empire for Slavery*, 219–20.

42. Olmsted, *Journey Through Texas*, 117–23, xvi; Martin Jackson interview, in Rawick, *American Slave*, series 1, vol. 4, pt. 2, p. 189; Martin Jackson, *American Slave*, supplement, series 2, vol. 5, pp. 1904–5.

43. Bertram Wyatt-Brown, *Honor and Violence in the Old South* (New York: Oxford University Press, 1986), vii–viii. See also David Hackett Fischer, *Albion's Seed: Four British Folkways in America* (New York: Oxford University Press, 1989).

44. John Hope Franklin, *The Militant South, 1800–1861* (Cambridge, Mass.: Belknap Press of Harvard University Press, 1956), 12–13; Ayers, *Vengeance and Justice*, 17; Lane, *Murder in America*, 350; Fox Butterfield, "Southern Curse: Why America's Murder Rate Is So High," *New York Times*, July 26, 1998, WK2. Southern homicides also tend to be more rural than their northern counterparts and to occur more often between people who know each other. As on its ancestral plantations, violence in the modern South remains an intimate affair.

45. Olmsted, *Journey Through Texas*, 124; Campbell, *Gone to Texas*, 231; Anderson, *Conquest of Texas*, 180.

46. Jeff Hamilton and Lenoir Hunt, *My Master: The Inside Story of Sam Houston and His Times* (Dallas: Manfred, Van Nort & Co., 1940), 111–12.

47. Texas, An Act Punishing Crimes and Misdemeanors, December 21, 1836, in Gammel, *Laws of Texas*, 1:1247–55, secs. 6, 13. See also Potts, "Early Criminal Law in Texas."

48. Lucko, "Prison Farms, Walls, and Society," 81–82; Paul Lucko, e-mail message to author, May 24, 2006.

49. Rush, "An Enquiry into the Effects of Public Punishments," Philadelphia, March 9, 1787, in Benjamin Rush, *Essays: Literary, Moral, and Philosophical* (Schenectady, N.Y.: Union College Press, 1988), 87.

50. David J. Rothman, *The Discovery of the Asylum: Social Order and Disorder in the New Republic* (Boston: Little, Brown, 1971); Beaumont and Tocqueville, *On the Penitentiary System*, 79. On the rise of the penitentiary in England and France, see Michael Ignatieff, *A Just Measure of Pain: The Penitentiary in the Industrial Revolution, 1750–1850* (London: Macmillan, 1978); Foucault, *Discipline and Punish*.

51. Peters, "Prison Before the Prison," in Morris and Rothman, *Oxford History of the Prison*, 19; Dario Melossi and Massimo Pavarini, *The Prison and the Factory: Origins of the Penitentiary System* (Totowa, N.J.: Barnes and Noble Books, 1981); Rusche and Kirchheimer, *Punishment and Social Structure*. This same demographic was forced into galley slavery along the Mediterranean.

52. Peters, "Prison Before the Prison," 41; Pieter Spierenburg, "The Body and the State: Early Modern Europe," in Morris and Rothman, *Oxford History of the Prison*, 53. See also Douglas Hay et al., *Albion's Fatal Tree: Crime and Society in Eighteenth-Century England* (New York: Pantheon Books, 1975); Edward Peters, *Torture*, expanded ed. (Philadelphia: University of Pennsylvania Press, 1996).

53. Petrus Cornelis Spierenburg, *The Spectacle of Suffering: Executions and the Evolution of Repression: From a Preindustrial Metropolis to the European Experience* (New York: Cambridge University Press, 1984); Peter Linebaugh, *The London Hanged: Crime and Civil Society in the Eighteenth Century* (Cambridge: Cambridge University Press, 1993). See also Karen Halttunen, "Humanitarianism and the Pornography of Pain in Anglo-American Culture," *American Historical Review* 100, no. 2 (April 1995): 303–34; Norbert Elias, *The Civilizing Process* (New York: Pantheon Books, 1982).

54. David Brion Davis, "Looking at Slavery from Broader Perspectives," *American Historical Review* 105, no. 2 (2000): 455 See A. Roger Ekirch, *Bound for America: The Transportation of British Convicts to the Colonies, 1718–1775* (New York: Oxford University Press, 1987); Don Jordan and Michael Walsh, *White Cargo: The Forgotten History of Britain's White Slaves in America* (New York: New York University Press, 2008).

55. Adam Jay Hirsch, *The Rise of the Penitentiary: Prisons and Punishment in Early America* (New Haven, Conn.: Yale University Press, 1992), 35. See also Michael Stephen Hindus, *Prison and Plantation: Crime, Justice, and Authority in Massachusetts and South Carolina, 1767–1878* (Chapel Hill: University of North Carolina Press, 1980).

56. Stuart Banner, *The Death Penalty: An American History* (Cambridge, Mass.: Harvard University Press, 2002), 8, 12, 25, 33.

57. Benjamin Rush, "An Enquiry into the Effects of Public Punishments upon Criminals, and upon Society," Philadelphia, March 9, 1787, in Rush, *Essays: Literary, Moral, and Philosophical*, 81, 86.

58. Louis P. Masur, *Rites of Execution: Capital Punishment and the Transformation of American Culture, 1776–1865* (New York: Oxford University Press, 1989), 59.

59. Morris and Rothman, *Oxford History of the Prison*, 114; Eric Foner, "Presidential Address: American Freedom in a Global Age," *American Historical Review* 106, no. 1 (2001): 7; Hirsch, *Rise of the Penitentiary*, 50–51.

60. Michael Meranze, *Laboratories of Virtue: Punishment, Revolution, and Authority in Philadelphia, 1760–1835* (Chapel Hill: University of North Carolina Press, 1996), chaps. 2–3; Hirsch, *Rise of the Penitentiary*, 50. Pennsylvania's curtailment of capital punishment represented a return to the philosophy of William Penn, whose Great Law of 1682 had put strict limitations on executions.

61. Benjamin Rush and George Washington Corner, *The Autobiography of Benjamin Rush; His "Travels Through Life" Together with His Commonplace Book for 1789–1813* (Philadelphia: American Philosophical Society, 1948); David Freeman Hawke, *Benjamin Rush, Revolutionary Gadfly* (Indianapolis, Ind.: Bobbs-Merrill, 1971); "Medicine and Health on the Lewis and Clark Expedition," University of Virginia Health System, online exhibits, http://www.healthsystem.virginia.edu/internet/library/historical/medical_history/lewis_clark/.

62. Christine Lehmann, "Roots of American Psychiatry Lie Deep in Philadelphia's Soil," *Psychiatric News* 37, no. 4 (February 15, 2002), http://pn.psychiatryonline.org/cgi/content/full/37/4/13; Hawke, *Benjamin Rush*, 389; Rush and Corner, *Autobiography of Benjamin Rush*, 369–71; Colvin, *Penitentiaries, Reformatories, and Chain Gangs*, 52.

63. Benjamin Rush, "Thoughts Upon the Mode of Education Proper in a Republic," in *Essays on Education in the Early Republic*, ed. Frederick Rudolph (Cambridge, Mass.: Belknap Press of Harvard University Press, 1965), 15–17.

64. Meranze, *Laboratories of Virtue*, 137–38, 179; Negley K. Teeters and John D. Shearer, *The Prison at Philadelphia, Cherry Hill: The Separate System of Penal Discipline, 1829–1913* (New York: Published for Temple University Publications by Columbia University Press, 1957), 5–8. On Shays's revolt and its significance, see David P. Szatmary, *Shays' Rebellion: The Making of an Agrarian Insurrection* (Amherst: University of Massachusetts Press, 1980).

65. Rush, "An Enquiry into the Effects of Public Punishments," 80, 85, 82.

66. Ibid., 94, 88, 87. See Cesare Beccaria, *Of Crimes and Punishments*, trans. Jane Grigson, 1964 ed. (New York: Marsilio Publishers, 1996); John Howard, *The State of the Prisons in England and Wales*, bicentennial ed. (Abingdon, UK: Professional Books, 1977).

67. Rush, "An Enquiry into the Effects of Public Punishments," 84, 91, 90.

68. Meranze, *Laboratories of Virtue*, chap. 5, 217–23; Colvin, *Penitentiaries, Reformatories, and Chain Gangs*, 54–71.

69. Teeters and Shearer, *Prison at Philadelphia*, chaps. 2–3; Hallinan, *Going Up the River*, 61–65.

70. Norman Bruce Johnston, Kenneth Finkel, and Jeffrey A. Cohen, *Eastern State Penitentiary: Crucible of Good Intentions* (Philadelphia: Philadelphia Museum of Art for the Eastern State Penitenciary Task Force of the Preservation Coalition of Greater Philadelphia, 1994), 36, chaps. 33, 35; Beaumont and Tocqueville, *On the Penitentiary System*, 57; Charles Dickens, *American Notes* (Greenwich, Conn.: Fawcett, 1961), 112–13.

71. Beaumont and Tocqueville, *On the Penitentiary System*, 65; W. David Lewis, *From Newgate to Dannemora: The Rise of the Penitentiary in New York, 1796–1848* (Ithaca, N.Y.: Cornell University Press, 1965), 88.

72. Beaumont and Tocqueville, *On the Penitentiary System*, 56, 78, 58; Rothman, *Discovery of the Asylum*, 87.

73. McKelvey, *American Prisons*, chap. 1; Colvin, *Penitentiaries, Reformatories, and Chain Gangs*, chap. 4.

74. Beaumont and Tocqueville, *On the Penitentiary System*, 73. See also Dorothea Lynde Dix, *Remarks on Prisons and Prison Discipline in the United States*, 2nd ed. (Philadelphia: Joseph Kite & Co., 1845), 16.

75. Nicole Hahn Rafter, *Partial Justice: Women in State Prisons, 1800–1935* (Boston: Northeastern University Press, 1985), 6; Estelle B. Freedman, *Their Sisters' Keepers: Women's Prison Reform in America, 1830–1930* (Ann Arbor: University of Michigan Press, 1984), 15; Colvin, *Penitentiaries, Reformatories, and Chain Gangs*, 138, 193.

76. Beaumont and Tocqueville, *On the Penitentiary System*, 73; Enoch C. Wines and Theodore W. Dwight, *Report on the Prisons and Reformatories of the United States*

*and Canada* (Albany, N.Y.: Van Benthuysen & Sons, 1867), 51; Meranze, *Laboratories of Virtue*, chap. 8; Hallinan, *Going Up the River*, 65; Colvin, *Penitentiaries, Reformatories, and Chain Gangs*, 102–3.

77. Dickens, *American Notes*, 111, 115.
78. Rothman, *Discovery of the Asylum*, 87. See Ricardo D. Salvatore and Carlos Aguirre, eds., *The Birth of the Penitentiary in Latin America: Essays on Criminology, Prison Reform, and Social Control, 1830–1940* (Austin: University of Texas Press, 1996). Michel Foucault observed, "For a century and a half the prison had always been offered as its own remedy: the reactivation of the penitentiary techniques as the only means of overcoming their perpetual failure." Foucault, *Discipline and Punish*, 268.
79. Beaumont and Tocqueville, *On the Penitentiary System*, 80.
80. Ayers, *Vengeance and Justice*, 18; Colvin, *Penitentiaries, Reformatories, and Chain Gangs*, chap. 9.
81. John C. Calhoun, "Speech on the Reception of Abolition Petitions," February 6, 1837, http://www.wfu.edu/~zulick/340/calhoun2.html. See Benjamin Rush, "Paradise of Negro Slaves—A Dream," in Rush, *Essays: Literary, Moral, and Philosophical*, 187–90. On slaveholder religion and republicanism generally, see David Brion Davis, *The Problem of Slavery in the Age of Revolution, 1770–1823* (Ithaca, N.Y.: Cornell University Press, 1975).
82. Elizabeth Fox-Genovese and Eugene D. Genovese, *The Mind of the Master Class: History and Faith in the Southern Slaveholders' Worldview* (New York: Cambridge University Press, 2005), 109; Ayers, *Vengeance and Justice*, 48.
83. Ayers, *Vengeance and Justice*, 47–52; Colvin, *Penitentiaries, Reformatories, and Chain Gangs*, 201–3; Hindus, *Prison and Plantation*.
84. Banner, *Death Penalty*, 95–96; Paul W. Keve, *The History of Corrections in Virginia* (Charlottesville: University of Virginia Press, 1986), 58–59; Ayers, *Vengeance and Justice*, 38. The architect who designed the actual penitentiary was Benajmin Latrobe.
85. Dix, *Remarks on Prisons and Prison Discipline in the United States*, 59, 26; Keve, *The History of Corrections in Virginia*, 51; Ayers, *Vengeance and Justice*, 61–62, 67. One of the penitentiary's first inmates was Gabriel Prosser, a slave accused of plotting a murderous revolt. Prosser was hanged, but by the 1840s, more than a third of Virginia's prisoners were black—a demographic reality that managers regarded as degrading to whites. Lawmakers therefore decided to sell free blacks convicted of crimes into slavery rather than confining them in the penitentiary. Criticized for being "incompatible with . . . morality and justice," the policy was soon abandoned. Nonetheless, it served as a precursor to the racialized convict lease system, which would develop across the South after emancipation.
86. Ayers, *Vengeance and Justice*, 60–69. On the antebellum penitentiary in Alabama and Mississippi, see Robert David Ward and William Warren Rogers, *Alabama's Response to the Penitentiary Movement, 1829–1865* (Gainesville: University Press of Florida, 2003); William Banks Taylor, *Brokered Justice: Race, Politics, and Mississippi Prisons, 1798–1992* (Columbus: Ohio State University Press, 1993).
87. Beaumont and Tocqueville, *On the Penitentiary System*, 90–91. The South's most prominent antebellum penal reformer was probably Beaumont and Tocqueville's translator Francis Lieber.
88. Coahuila and Texas, Decree No. 93, May 13, 1829, in Gammel, *Laws of Texas*, 1:240–41, 289. Because the penitentiary was never actually built, lawmakers later authorized "alcaldes [to] put delinquents in irons, manacles, and . . . stocks" in order to prevent escapes from local jails.
89. Reynolds, "The Administration of the Texas Prison System," 1–7. Texas's

lawmakers approved a penitentiary in 1842, 1845, and 1846, but never got beyond the initial construction stage.

90. Lucko, "Prison Farms, Walls, and Society," 83, 73; Crow, "Political History of the Texas Penal System," 30, 22.

91. Crow, "Political History of the Texas Penal System," 30; Texas, An Act Concerning Crimes and Punishments, March 20, 1848, in Gammel, *Laws of Texas*, 3:219–32.

92. Texas, An Act Concerning Crimes and Punishments, March 20, 1848, secs. 11, 36, 20, 10; Beaumont and Tocqueville, *On the Penitentiary System*, 52.

93. Lucko, "Prison Farms, Walls, and Society," 83; Texas, *Act to Provide for the Punishment of Crimes and Misdemeanors Committed by Slaves and Free Persons of Color*, December 14, 1837, secs. 6, 1. Ayers, *Vengeance and Justice*, 61 See also Gammel, *Laws of Texas*, 3:870–73, 911–12; Texas, Penal Code, February 12, 1858, in Williamson S. Oldham and George W. White, eds., *A Digest of the General Statute Laws of the State of Texas* (Austin, Tex.: J. Marshall & Co., 1859), Title 3, chaps. 1–2, pp. 562–63. According to an 1840 law, masters were prohibited from murdering or "unreasonably or cruelly treat[ing]" slaves, but prosecutions were exceedingly rare. In 1858, the legislature saw fit to clarify that "the right of the master to the obedience and submission of his slave, in all lawful things, is perfect, and the power belongs to the master to inflict any punishment upon the slave not affecting life or limb, and not coming within the definition of cruel treatment, or unreasonable abuse." Texas, An Act Concerning Slaves, February 5, 1840, in Gammel, *Laws of Texas*, 2:345–46; Texas, Penal Code, February 12, 1858, Title 2, pp. 560–61.

94. Texas, Penal Code, February 12, 1858, Title 3, chap. 1, p. 562; Crow, "Political History of the Texas Penal System," 42; Edmund T. Miller, *A Financial History of Texas* (Austin: University of Texas, 1916), 399. Before 1859, free blacks were occasionally sentenced to the penitentiary, but because the overall population was so small, there were never more than a handful at the Walls. Texas State Penitentiary, *Biennial Report* (1878), 34.

95. Directors, *Report of the Directors of the Texas Penitentiary*, October 1, 1849, RRP, box 022–4, file 11, p. 2.

96. Penitentiary Commissioners to Governor G. T. Wood, July 20, 1848, RRP, box 022–4, file 10; Directors, *Report of the Directors of the Texas Penitentiary*, October 1, 1849. See also D'Anne McAdams Crews, ed., *Huntsville and Walker County, Texas: A Bicentennial History* (Huntsville, Tex.: Sam Houston State University Press, 1976), 25.

97. Plan of the Texas Penitentiary, August 15, 1848, RRP, box 022–177, file 6. As architect and first superintendent, the state employed a contractor of wealthy homes, Abner Cook. Kenneth Hafertepe, *Abner Cook: Master Builder of the Texas Frontier* (Austin: Texas State Historical Association, 1992). Texas penitentiary advocates mentioned their admiration for the Auburn system, but they were more influenced by Mississippi's new prison, which directors visited in 1848. Taylor, *Brokered Justice: Race, Politics, and Mississippi Prisons, 1798–1992*.

98. *Report of the Directors of the Texas Penitentiary*, October 1, 1849; Lucko, "Prison Farms, Walls, and Society," 86.

99. "Early Days in Huntsville," in Crews, *Huntsville and Walker County, Texas: A Bicentennial History*, 25, pt. 1; Patricia Smith Prather and Jane Clements Monday, *From Slave to Statesman: The Legacy of Joshua Houston, Servant to Sam Houston* (Denton: University of North Texas Press, 1993), 22.

100. Walker County Historical Commission, "The Five Courthouses of Walker County," http://www.co.walker.tx.us/CourtHouses.htm; Hamilton and Hunt, *My Master*, 5; James Patton, Walker County Historical Commission, e-mail to author, May 16, 2005.

101. Crow, "Political History of the Texas Penal System," 84; Commissioners of the Texas State Penitentiary, *Biennial Report* (1878), 31.

102. Texas State Penitentiary, *Report* (1854), 35–36; Commissioners of the Texas State Penitentiary, *Biennial Report* (1878), 34. Out of 187 inmates at the penitentiary in 1856, 52 were categorized as Mexican, about 29 percent of the total.

103. Directors, State Penitentiary, to Governor Bell, November 10, 1850, RRP, box 022–1, file 1; Crow, "Political History of the Texas Penal System," 43–45, 54–57; B. W. Walker et al. to Sam Houston, [1860?], RRP, box 022–4, file 13.

104. Reynolds, "The Administration of the Texas Prison System," 12; Crow, "Political History of the Texas Penal System," 85–86; B. W. Walker et al. to Sam Houston, [1860?]. See also Gammel, *Laws of Texas*, 4:1029.

105. Texas State Penitentiary, *Report* (1855), 3, 15; Commissioners of the Texas State Penitentiary, *Biennial Report* (1878), 36.

106. Directors to Governor Bell, November 10, 1850. See also *Handbook of Texas Online*, s.v. "Besser, John," http://www.tsha.utexas.edu/handbook/online/arti cles/BB/fbe65.html; Edward A. Blackburn, *Wanted: Historic County Jails of Texas* (College Station: Texas A&M University Press, 2006), 340–41.

107. Texas State Penitentiary, *Report* (1855), 20, 30–34; Crow, "Political History of the Texas Penal System," 49. Texas had received $5 million in federal funds as part of a boundary settlement in 1851, which explains the legislature's uncharacteristic willingness to invest in infrastructure. In addition to the mill, much of the money went to courthouses, schools, and county jails. See Miller, *A Financial History of Texas*, 86–87. Present-day value calculated according to nominal GDP per capita. Economic History Services, "What Is the Relative Value," http://eh.net/hmit/compare/.

108. Texas State Penitentiary, *Report* (1855), 20, 31; Crow, "Political History of the Texas Penal System," 50.

109. William W. White, "The Texas Slave Insurrection of 1860," *Southwestern Historical Quarterly* 52, no. 3 (1949): 278–79, 273, 262–65, 275. Although Texas never experienced a true slave insurrection of the type fantasized in 1836 and 1860, there were regular acts of low-level and occasionally collective resistance. See Addington, "Slave Insurrections in Texas"; William D. Carrigan, *The Making of a Lynching Culture: Violence and Vigilantism in Central Texas, 1836–1916* (Urbana: University of Illinois Press, 2004), chap. 3; Vera Lea Dugas, "A Social and Economic History of Texas in the Civil War and Reconstruction Periods, 1861–1895" (PhD diss., University of Texas, 1963).

110. "Speech of Judge O. M. Roberts of the Supreme Court of Texas, at the Capitol, on the 1st of December 1860, Upon the 'Impending Crisis,'" in Governors' Messages and Public Documents, vol. 3, TSLAC, 32, 2–6; Lubbock, Governor's Message, November 15, 1861 (Austin: John Marshall & Company, 1861), 3–5; Campbell, *Gone to Texas*, 261, 264.

111. Lubbock, Governor's Message, November 15, 1861, 7; Francis Lubbock to John Winn, September 12, 1862, RRP, box 022–1, file 3. Prison directors signed their first Confederate contract, for roughly half of the mill's output, in October 1861, and the amounts increased steadily thereafter. For the fullest account of the Walls during the Civil War, see Lucko, "Prison Farms, Walls, and Society."

112. Major General Thomas Hindman to Governor of Texas, August 6, 1862, RRP, box 022–1, file 3; Major General Theophilus H. Holmes to Governor Lubbock, September 22, 1862, RRP, box 022–1, file 3. See Clayton E. Jewett, *Texas in the Confederacy: An Experiment in Nation Building* (Columbia: University of Missouri Press, 2002).

113. John Besser's report on Confederate cavalry incident, Huntsville, Texas,

December 8, 1863, RRP, box 022–1; S. B. Hendricks to Governor Murrah, December 6, 1863, box 022–1, file 5.

114. Texas State Penitentiary, *Biennial Report* (1863), 2; Lucko, "Prison Farms, Walls, and Society," 110; Miller, *A Financial History of Texas*, 140.

115. Texas State Penitentiary, *Biennial Report* (1863), 7–8.

116. Lucko, "Prison Farms, Walls, and Society," chap. 3, 119; Henry E. Portius to Texas State Legislature, February 13, 1863, RRP, box 022–1, file 4; Henry E. Perkins to Board of Directors, State Penitentiary, RRP, box 022–1, file 6.

117. Lubbock, Governor's Message, November 15, 1861, 3; Carter et al., *Historical Statistics of the United States*, 5:787; Campbell, *An Empire for Slavery*, chap 12; Alwyn Barr, "Texas Coastal Defense, 1861–1865," *Southwestern Historical Quarterly* 45, no. 1 (1961); "Speech of O. M. Roberts Upon the 'Impending Crisis,'" 6.

118. Message of Governor P. Murrah to the (Extra Session) of the Tenth Legislature, May 11, 1864 (Austin, Tex.: State Gazette Book and Job Office, 1864), 14.

119. Campbell, *An Empire for Slavery*, 244; "Speech of O. M. Roberts Upon the 'Impending Crisis,'" 7; Lubbock, Governor's Message, November 15, 1861, 13.

## 3: "WORSE THAN SLAVERY"

1. John Shotwell, *A Victim of Revenge, or Fourteen Years in Hell* (San Antonio, Tex.: E. T. Jackson Company, 1909), 16; R. M. Armstrong, *Sugar Land, Texas and the Imperial Sugar Company* (Sugarland, Tex.: R. M. Armstrong, 1991), 25; Mary Austin Holley, *Texas: Observations, Historical, Geographical and Descriptive: In a Series of Letters, Written During a Visit to Austin's Colony, with a View to a Permanent Settlement in That Country, in the Autumn of 1831* (Baltimore: Armstrong & Plaskitt, 1833), 6.

2. "Speech of O. M. Roberts Upon the 'Impending Crisis,'" 2.; Armstrong, *Sugar Land*, 28, 36.

3. Armstrong, *Sugar Land*, 30. On working conditions at Sugar Land, see Harold Melvin Hyman, *Oleander Odyssey: The Kempners of Galveston, Texas, 1854–1980s* (College Station: Texas A&M University Press, 1990). See also John Avery Lomax and Alan Lomax, eds., *Negro Folk Songs as Sung by Lead Belly, "King of the Twelve-String Guitar Players of the World," Long-Time Convict in the Penitentiaries of Texas and Louisiana* (New York: Macmillan, 1936), 87.

4. Webb, *Texas Rangers*, 217; Prather and Monday, *From Slave to Statesman*, 77; Campbell, *An Empire for Slavery*, 249, 244; Library of Congress, "Born in Slavery: Slave Narratives from the Federal Writers' Project, 1936–1938, Texas Narratives, Volume XVI, Part 2," s.v., Felix Haywood, http://memory.loc.gov/cgi-bin/ampage?collId=mesn&fileName=162/mesn162.db&recNum=137&itemLink=S?ammem/mesnbib:@field(AUTHOR+@od1(Haywood,+Felix)), p. 133.

5. Baker and Baker, *Till Freedom Cried Out*, 3, 79, 41, 32.

6. Campbell, *An Empire for Slavery*, 249; "Born in Slavery," s.v. Felix Haywood, 133–34. On the relative advantages of sharecropping, see Stephanie McCurry, *Masters of Small Worlds: Yeoman Households, Gender Relations, and the Political Culture of the Antebellum South Carolina Low Country* (New York: Oxford University Press, 1995); Jonathan M. Wiener, *Social Origins of the New South: Alabama, 1860–1885* (Baton Rouge: Louisiana State University Press, 1978).

7. Constitutional Convention of Texas, *Report of Special Committee on Lawlessness and Violence in Texas* (1868); Susan Merritt interview, in Rawick, *American Slave*, vol. 5, pt. 3, p. 78.

8. Barry A. Crouch, "A Spirit of Lawlessness: White Violence, Texas Blacks, 1865–1868," *Journal of Social History* 18, no. 2 (1984): 223, 226. There was a "war of the races" going on, acknowledged Republican investigators, but only "on the part of the whites against the blacks." Constitutional Convention of Texas,

*Report of Special Committee on Lawlessness and Violence in Texas.* Comparative homicide rates based on my calculations using historical census and modern FBI reports.

9. Eric Foner, *Reconstruction: America's Unfinished Revolution, 1863–1877* (New York: Harper & Row, 1988), 204–5. Between 1865 and 1868, there was only one court-ordered execution in Texas, of a freedman from Houston. See Marquart, Ekland-Olson, and Sorensen, *The Rope, the Chair, and the Needle.*

10. Crouch, "Spirit of Lawlessness," 217–18; Prather and Monday, *From Slave to Statesman,* 95, 80–81. See also Texas State Convention, Message of Governor A. J. Hamilton to the Texas State Convention (Austin, Texas, February 10, 1866), 11.

11. Campbell, *Gone to Texas,* 272. On Reconstruction politics in Texas generally, see Carl H. Moneyhon, *Texas After the Civil War: The Struggle of Reconstruction* (College Station: Texas A&M University Press, 2004).

12. Barry A. Crouch, "All the Vile Passions: The Texas Black Code of 1866," *Southwestern Historical Quarterly* 97 (July 1993): 21.

13. Eric Foner, *A Short History of Reconstruction, 1863–1877* (New York: Harper & Row, 1990), 93; Crouch, "All the Vile Passions," 23. See also Leon F. Litwack, *Been in the Storm So Long: The Aftermath of Slavery* (New York: Vintage Books, 1980).

14. Dugas, "A Social and Economic History of Texas in the Civil War and Reconstruction Periods, 1861–1895," 395, 375; Crouch, "All the Vile Passions," 27, 24, 26, 34.

15. Crouch, "All the Vile Passions," 28, 29; Campbell, *Gone to Texas,* 274.

16. Lucko, "Prison Farms, Walls, and Society," 162, 166; Clerk, Walker Country, to That McRae, governor's secretary, December 2, 1867, RRP, box 022–10, folder 13; District Clerk, Calhoun Country, to McRae, December 4, 1867, RRP, box 022–10, folder 8.

17. Thomas Carothers, superintendent, to Smith, Randall, and Gay, directors, [1865?], RRP, box 022–5, folder 18; Texas State Penitentiaries, *Biennial Report* (1904), 45; Superintendent to Governor Davis, October 11, 1870, RRP, box 022–1, folder 24.

18. Baker and Baker, *Till Freedom Cried Out,* 53–59; Thomas Goree, "Some Features of Prison Control in the South," *Proceedings of the Annual Congress of the National Prison Association,* Austin, Texas, 1897 (Pittsburg: Shaw Brothers, 1898), 132.

19. Barr, "Texas Coastal Defense, 1861–1865"; Campbell, *An Empire for Slavery,* 234–39; Texas, *Final Report of the Administration of Gov. Throckmorton When He Was Removed from Office* (Austin, Tex.: John Cardwell, State Printer, 1873), 19–23; Misc. Documents, December 19, 1866, BPL, 003–1, folder 4, 21; Gammel, *Laws of Texas,* 5:1110–13.

20. Foner, *Reconstruction,* 236.

21. Texas, *Final Report of the Administration of Gov. Throckmorton,* 101, 93–95; Crow, "Political History of the Texas Penal System," 73.

22. Foner, *Reconstruction,* 278; Moneyhon, *Texas After the Civil War,* 85, 115–16; Campbell, *Gone to Texas,* 280.

23. James Davidson, *Report of the Adjutant-General of the State of Texas, December 31, 1870* (Austin, Tex.: Tracy, Siemering & Co., 1870); Message of Governor Edmund J. Davis, January 10, 1871, Davis Records; Webb, *Texas Rangers,* 217. On the massacre in Brazos County, site of the present-day Hamilton Unit, see Moneyhon, *Texas After the Civil War,* 95. Davis also organized a frontier force to fight Indians and Mexicans, a measure that attracted less opposition from Democrats. On the other hand, his law-enforcement provisions imposed gun controls on white Texans for the first time.

24. Message of Governor E. J. Davis to Don Campbell, president of the Senate,

February 8, 1871, Davis Records, 4, 20; Crews, *Huntsville and Walker County, Texas*, 139; Prather and Monday, *From Slave to Statesman*, 141.

25. James Davidson, *Report of the Adjutant-General*, 11; *Proceedings of the Tax-Payers' Convention of the State of Texas*, September 22–25, 1871 (Galveston, Tex.: News Steam Book and Job Office, 1871), 16; Webb, *Texas Rangers*, 227.

26. Webb, *Texas Rangers*, 221; T. R. Fehrenbach, *Lone Star: A History of Texas and the Texans*, rev. ed. (New York: Macmillan, 2000), 424, 417–18. See also Christopher Waldrep and Donald G. Nieman, *Local Matters: Race, Crime, and Justice in the Nineteenth-Century South* (Athens: University of Georgia Press, 2001).

27. State Legislature, Special Committee on Penitentiary, *Report* (1871), 7; Texas, *Journal of the Reconstruction Convention* (1868), 771–73; Message of Governor Edmund J. Davis, January 10, 1871, Davis Records; Board of Directors, *Reports on the Condition of the Texas State Penitentiary* (1872), 4–5. Prison managers at Huntsville periodically proposed building a separate cell block for women, apparently unaware that the penitentiary's first plans included just such a structure.

28. N. A. M. Dudley, superintendent, Texas State Penitentiary, *Report on the Condition of the State Penitentiary* (1870), 8; Texas, *Journal of the Reconstruction Convention* (1868), 773, 805.

29. Texas, *Journal of the Reconstruction Convention* (1868), 805. See also State Legislature, Special Committee on Penitentiary, *Report* (1871). See *Report of the Commission Appointed by the Governor of Texas to Investigate the Alleged Mismanagement and Cruel Treatment of the Convicts* (Houston, Tex.: A. C. Gray, State Printer, April 10, 1875), 9–13; Board of Directors, *Reports on the Texas State Penitentiary* (1873), 3–4; Commissioners and Superintendent of the Texas State Penitentiary, *Biennial Report* (1878), 34.

30. Bond of the Lessees, July 5, 1871, in *Report of the Commission Appointed by the Governor* (1875), 14–15; Texas, Special Committee on the Penitentiary, *Report* (1876), 9.

31. Texas, Special Committee on the Penitentiary, *Report* (1876), 15–16.

32. J. K. P. Campbell to E. C. Dewey, February 19, 1875, RRP, box 022–2, folder 2, p. 2; Texas State Penitentiary, *Report* (1876), 20, 17, 13. On the Lake Jackson plantation history, see Abner J. Strobel, *The Old Plantations and Their Owners of Brazoria County, Texas*, rev. ed. (Houston, Tex.: Union National Bank, 1930).

33. Texas, Board of Directors, *Reports on the Texas State Penitentiary* (1873), 5; Commission Appointed by the Governor, *Report* (1875), 77–78, 102–3. On the origins of this contraption, see Cusac, *Cruel and Unusual*, 35. Prison records do not indicate what happened to the prisoner's baby, though in all likelihood she was allowed to care for her child at the Walls. This was common practice well into the twentieth century. See State Penitentiary Board, *Rules, Regulations, and By-Laws for the Government and Discipline of the Texas State Penitentiaries, at Huntsville and Rusk, Texas* (1883), RRP, box 032–178.

34. Texas, Special Committee on the Penitentiary, *Report* (1876), 8; Texas Attorney General, Testimony Re. Condition of Penitentiary (1875), RRP, box 022–11, 37. This testimony was omitted from the formal report but appears, crossed out by hand, in the draft report.

35. Texas, Special Committee on the Penitentiary, *Report* (1876), 2; Richard B. Hubbard, Initial message to the Sixteenth Legislature, n.d., in *Governors' Messages, Coke to Ross*, 727–33; "Texas State Prison," *Galveston News*, June 9, 1876. See also J. S. Duncan, "Richard Bennett Hubbard and State Resumption of the Penitentiary, 1876–1878," *Texana* 12, no. 1 (1974): 47–55.

36. Foner, *Reconstruction*, chap. 11.; W. E. B. DuBois, *Black Reconstruction in America* (New York: Harcourt, Brace, 1935), 30–31.

37. On the demographic dominance of Anglos and the comparative diminishment of other groups, see Terry G. Jordan, John L. Bean, and William M. Holmes, *Texas, A Geography* (Boulder, Colo.: Westview Press, 1984), chap. 4; Goodwyn, *Democratic Promise*, 31–33; Neil Foley, *The White Scourge: Mexicans, Blacks, and Poor Whites in Texas Cotton Culture* (Berkeley: University of California Press, 1997), 30–31; Nell Irvin Painter, *Exodusters: Black Migration to Kansas After Reconstruction* (New York: W. W. Norton, 1992), 200–201.

38. Moneyhon, *Texas After the Civil War*, 197; *Proceedings of the Tax-Payers' Convention of the State of Texas*, 14.

39. Texas Democratic Party, Platform (1871); Texas Democratic Party, Platform (1873), in Ernest William Winkler, ed., *Platforms of Political Parties in Texas* (Austin: University of Texas Bulletin no. 53, 1916), 125, 159–60.

40. Jordan, Bean, and Holmes, *Texas*, 81; Moneyhon, *Texas After the Civil War*, 176; Carrigan, *Making of a Lynching Culture*, 135; Strobel, *Old Plantations*, 31.

41. Citing violations of voting procedures, Davis refused to acknowledge his electoral defeat, but after President Grant indicated he would not intervene to protect Republican power in Texas, the defeated radical left the Governor's Mansion as an armed posse of Coke supporters were preparing to storm it by force. Rupert Norval Richardson, Adrian N. Anderson, and Ernest Wallace, *Texas, the Lone Star State*, 7th ed. (Upper Saddle River, N.J.: Prentice Hall, 1997), 233; Kenneth E. Hendrickson, *The Chief Executives of Texas: From Stephen F. Austin to John B. Connally, Jr.* (College Station: Texas A&M University Press, 1995), 97.

42. Richard Coke, inaugural address, January 15, 1874, in *Governors' Messages, Coke to Ross*, 10. On Coke's involvement in the 1860 slave hangings, see Carrigan, *Making of a Lynching Culture*, 77.

43. Richard Coke, Address to the Legislature, January 12, 1875, in *Governors' Messages, Coke to Ross*, 73; Texas, Constitution of 1876. For fear of reigniting northern outrage, some of the more reactionary proposals were shelved, including complete black disenfranchisement. Voting rights to all felons were denied.

44. Webb, *Texas Rangers*, 229; Samora, Bernal, and Peña, *Gunpowder Justice: A Reassessment of the Texas Rangers*; Montejano, *Anglos and Mexicans in the Making of Texas*; Johnson, *Revolution in Texas*, 12.

45. Author calculations based on census estimates and prison population reports. For additional demographic information, see Commissioners and Superintendent of the Texas State Penitentiary, *Biennial Report* (1878), 34; Paul M. Lucko, "Texas Prison Reform During the Oscar Branch Colquitt Administration, 1911–1914" (research paper, University of Texas, 1987), chap. 4; Donald R. Walker, *Penology for Profit: A History of the Texas Prison System, 1867–1912* (College Station: Texas A&M University Press, 1988), 114.

46. Texas, Special Committee on the Penitentiary, *Report* (1876), 8–9.

47. Texas State Penitentiary, Bond of Lessees (January 1, 1878). Governor Hubbard's initial message to the Sixteenth Legislature, in *Governors' Messages, Coke to Ross*, 727–33. See appended documents, in *Rules, Regulations, and By-Laws* (1883), 58.

48. Commissioners and Superintendent of the Texas State Penitentiary, *Biennial Report* (1878), 13.

49. George Waverly Briggs, ed. *The Texas Penitentiary* (San Antonio, Tex.: San Antonio Express, 1909), 12; Armstrong, *Sugar Land*, 30.

50. David Barboza, "Opening U.S. Sugar Program Is Free Trade's Final Frontier," *New York Times*, May 6, 2001, A1, A28; Armstrong, *Sugar Land*, 26.

51. Carothers to Smith, Randall, and Gay, [1865?], RRP, box 022–5, folder 18; Texas State Penitentiaries, *Biennial Report* (1904), 45.

52. Texas State Penitentiary, *Biennial Report* (1880), 12; Charles S. Potts, *Railroad Transportation in Texas* (Austin: University of Texas Bulletin no. 119, 1909); Campbell, *Gone to Texas*, 306; Dugas, "A Social and Economic History of Texas in the Civil War and Reconstruction Periods, 1861–1895."

53. Richardson, Anderson, and Wallace, *Texas*, 234; John Stricklin Spratt, *The Road to Spindletop: Economic Change in Texas, 1875–1901* (Austin, Tex.: Southern Methodist University Press, 1955), 32.

54. C. Vann Woodward, *Origins of the New South, 1877–1913*, rev. ed. (Baton Rouge: Louisiana State University Press, 1971), 424–25; Lichtenstein, *Twice the Work of Free Labor*, xix, 6–9; Wiener, *Social Origins of the New South*; Alex Lichtenstein, "Was the Emancipated Slave a Proletarian?" *Reviews in American History?* 26 (March 1998): 125–45; Robert Perkinson, "Between the Worst of the Past and the Worst of the Future: Reconsidering Convict Leasing in the South," *Radical History Review* 71 (1998): 207–16.

55. Texas State Penitentiaries, *Biennial Report* (1904), 45; Hubbard, initial message to the Sixteenth Legislature, 732; Penitentiary Investigating Committee, *Report and Findings* (1913).

56. Texas State Penitentiary, *Biennial Report* (1880), 21, 7; Governor Hubbard's Initial Message to the Sixteenth Legislature, 732–33; Commissioners of the Texas State Penitentiary, *Biennial Report* (1878), 5–6. Goree moved into the prisoner-built residence that had been used by A. J. Ward. The home was destroyed by fire just as the new lessees took charge and was rebuilt and refurbished for the superintendent.

57. See Spratt, *Road to Spindletop*, 33; Campbell, *Gone to Texas*, 306.

58. D. M. Short to Oran Roberts, July 19, 1879, Roberts Records, box 301–110; Texas Penitentiary Board, testimony taken before D. M. Short and Thomas J. Goree in regard to the treatment of convicts at wood camp near Mineola and at Lake Fork, [1879?], RRP, box 022–11, 49, 2, 13.

59. Texas, Committee to Investigate Mineola, *Testimony*, (1879), 5.

60. "Had the White Man and the Negro Common Parentage?" *Galveston News*, March 14, 1871; Texas State Penitentiary, *Biennial Report* (1880), 13, 21.

61. Texas State Penitentiary, *Biennial Report* (1880), 23; Commissioners of the Texas State Penitentiary, *Biennial Report* (1878), 7; Texas State Penitentiaries, *Biennial Report* (1904), 45. Escape and death totals are based on annual reports between 1878 and 1883.

62. George W. Cable, "The Convict Lease System in the Southern States," *Century Illustrated Magazine*, February 1884, 181; Matthew J. Mancini, *One Dies, Get Another: Convict Leasing in the American South, 1866–1928* (Columbia: University of South Carolina Press, 1996), chap. 12; J. C. Powell, *The American Siberia, or, Fourteen Years' Experience in a Southern Convict Camp* (Chicago: H. J. Smith & Co., 1891); Oshinsky, *"Worse Than Slavery,"* 58. Virginia embraced convict leasing less avidly than other southern states, pioneering the state plantation system that developed later in Texas, Arkansas, Louisiana, and Mississippi. See Keve, *The History of Corrections in Virginia*.

63. Oshinsky, *"Worse Than Slavery,"* 36; Taylor, *Brokered Justice*; Mancini, *One Dies, Get Another*, 133–34.; Lichtenstein, *Twice the Work of Free Labor*, 69.

64. Arlin Turner, ed., *Critical Essays on George Washington Cable* (Boston: G. K. Hall & Co., 1980), xv; John Cleman, *George Washington Cable Revisited* (New York: Twayne Publishers, 1996), 114.

65. Arlin Turner, *George W. Cable, A Biography* (Durham, N.C.: Duke University Press, 1956); "My Politics" in George Washington Cable, *The Negro Question: A Selection of Writings on Civil Rights in the South* (Garden City, N.Y.: Doubleday, 1958), 2–3.

66. "Silent South," in George Washington Cable, *The Silent South, Together with the Freedman's Case in Equity and the Convict Lease System* (New York: Scribner's, 1885), 105, 173.

67. "Our Mad-House Death Rate Explained," *Times-Democrat* (New Orleans), February 5, 1882; "Essays on Prison and Asylum Reform," in Cable, *Silent South*, 217–71.

68. Much to the chagrin of his publishers, he spent less and less time with his art and devoted himself almost entirely to social reform. An awkwardly didactic novel, *Dr. Sevier*, served as a vehicle for prison themes, but it disappointed critics. See "Mr. Cable's Dr. Sevier," *Times-Democrat* (New Orleans), October 5, 1884, in Turner, *Critical Essays on George Washington Cable*, 64–66.

69. "The Convict Lease System in the Southern States," in Cable, *Silent South*, 159, 181–82.

70. Mark T. Carleton, *Politics and Punishment: The History of the Louisiana State Penal System* (Baton Rouge: Louisiana State University Press, 1971), chap. 1, p. 37. In one investigation, lawmakers emphasized the case of Theophile Chevalier, an African American inmate whose feet had to be amputated after he was forced to work shoeless in the winter mud.

71. C. G. Ellis, the out-of-state bidder, was the son of Littleberry Ellis, Cunningham's original partner in the Texas lease. The younger Ellis leased convicts like his father and was shot to death by one of his guards in 1906. Armstrong, *Sugar Land*, 42.

72. Burk Foster, Wilbert Rideau, and Douglas Dennis, eds., *The Wall Is Strong: Corrections in Louisiana*, 3rd ed. (Lafayette: University of Southwestern Louisiana, 1991), 3; Carleton, *Politics and Punishment*, 45–46.

73. Cable, "The Convict Lease System in the Southern States," 173.

74. Cable, "Silent South," 107; Cable, "The Convict Lease System in the Southern States," 168.

75. Mancini, *One Dies, Get Another*, 105–6; Oshinsky, *"Worse Than Slavery,"* 76–80; Douglas A. Blackmon, "Hard Time: From Alabama's Past, Capitalism and Racism in a Cruel Partnership," *Wall Street Journal*, July 16, 2001, A10. See also Blackmon, *Slavery by Another Name*.

76. Mancini, *One Dies, Get Another*, 112, 109; Oshinsky, *"Worse Than Slavery,"* 81.

77. "History of U.S. Steel," U.S. Steel, http:// http://www.uss.com/corp/company/profile/history.asp; Blackmon, "Hard Time," A1, A10.

78. "The Freedman's Case in Equity," in Cable, *Silent South*, 1, 38.

79. Cable, *Silent South*, 66, 192.

80. Turner, *Critical Essays on George Washington Cable*, 163. W. J. Cash noted that any white critic of southern racism and the Democratic Party "stood in peril of being cast out for a damned nigger-loving scoundrel in league with the enemy." Wilbur Joseph Cash, *The Mind of the South* (New York: Alfred A. Knopf, 1941), 138.

81. Zebulon Brockway, "The Ideal of a True Prison System for a State," in Wines, *Transactions of the National Congress*, 42; Cable, "The Convict Lease System in the Southern States," 115–19.

82. Enoch Wines, "The Present Outlook of Prison Discipline in the United States," in Wines, *Transactions of the National Congress*, 18; Frederick H. Wines, "Punishment and Reformation" (1895), in Bacon, *Prison Reform*, 7; Christianson, *With Liberty for Some*, 183–88. In the North, most prisoners labored under the "contract system," in which inmates remained under state control and within prison walls but worked for private enterprise. A similar arrangement took hold inside of Texas's two penitentiaries after 1883.

83. David J. Rothman, *Conscience and Convenience: The Asylum and Its Alternatives in*

*Progressive America* (Boston: Little, Brown, 1980), 19–20. Years later, the "water cure" surfaced in America's counterinsurgency war in the Philippines; a century after that as an "approved interrogation technique" during the Bush administration's War on Terror. See Stuart Creighton Miller, *"Benevolent Assimilation": The American Conquest of the Philippines, 1899–1903* (New Haven, Conn.: Yale University Press, 1982); Alfred W. McCoy, *A Question of Torture: CIA Interrogation, from the Cold War to the War on Terror* (New York: Metropolitan Books, 2006).

84. Foner, *Reconstruction*, 25.
85. Wines and Dwight, *Report on Prisons and Reformatories*, 62; Larry E. Sullivan, *The Prison Reform Movement: Forlorn Hope* (Boston: Twyane, 1990), 17.
86. Enoch Wines, "The Present Outlook of Prison Discipline in the United States," in Wines, *Transactions of the National Congress*, 15, 14–12. For information about other prison congresses, see E. C. Wines, *The State of Prisons and of Child-Saving Institutions in the Civilized World* (Cambridge, Mass.: John Wilson and Son, 1880).
87. Zebulon Brockway to Enoch Wines, November 29, 1865, in Wines and Dwight, *Report on Prisons and Reformatories*, 344.
88. McKelvey, *American Prisons*, 90; Brockway, "The Ideal of a True Prison System for a State," 42, 40–41, 65.
89. "Declaration of Principles Adopted and Promulgated by the Congress," in Wines, *Transactions of the National Congress*, 541–47. Michel Foucault has written most elegantly on the philosophical consequences of this nineteenth-century redirection of state disciplinary power from the body to the soul. Foucault, *Discipline and Punish*.
90. "Declaration of Principles Adopted and Promulgated by the Congress"; Sullivan, *Prison Reform Movement*, 19. See also Brockway, "The Ideal of a True Prison System for a State," 62.
91. Brockway, "The Ideal of a True Prison System for a State," 52; Zebulon Brockway, *Fifty Years of Prison Service: An Autobiography* (New York: Charities Publication Committee, 1912), 105–6, 109; Rafter, *Partial Justice*, 26–27; Colvin, *Penitentiaries, Reformatories, and Chain Gangs*, 169–70. The House of Shelter held women of various types, not only those convicted of crimes but sometimes girls in trouble or women seeking refuge from abusive relationships.
92. McKelvey, *American Prisons*, 84; Rafter, *Partial Justice*, 25–26.
93. Brockway, *Fifty Years of Prison Service*, 110; Rafter, *Partial Justice*, 56, 34–37.
94. "Declaration of Principles Adopted and Promulgated by the Congress"; Alexander Pisciotta, *Benevolent Repression: Social Control and the American Reformatory-Prison Movement* (New York: New York University Press, 1994), 18–20; Brockway, *Fifty Years of Prison Service*, 163, 212.
95. Pisciotta, *Benevolent Repression*, 22, 26, 31.
96. Ibid., 63–64, 67–71, 36, 41, 46; Brockway, "The Ideal of a True Prison System for a State," 42.
97. Pisciotta, *Benevolent Repression*, 35, 31, 108; McKelvey, *American Prisons*, 169.
98. McKelvey, *American Prisons*, 138; Pisciotta, *Benevolent Repression*, 4.
99. Edgardo Rotman, "The Failure of Reform: United States, 1865–1965," in Morris and Rothman, *Oxford History of the Prison*; Foucault, *Discipline and Punish*.
100. Charles C. Campbell, *Hell Exploded: An Exposition of Barbarous Cruelty and Prison Horrors* (Austin, Tex.: privately published, 1900), 3; Oran Roberts, *The Political, Legislative, and Judicial History of Texas for Its Fifty Years of Statehood, 1845–1895*, in Dudley G. Wooten, ed., *A Comprehensive History of Texas, 1685–1897*, vol. 2 (Dallas, Tex.: William G. Scarff, 1898), 109, 191.
101. "Speech of Judge O. M. Roberts of the Supreme Court of Texas, at the Capitol,

on the 1st of December 1860, Upon the 'Impending Crisis'"; Roberts, *The Political, Legislative, and Judicial History of Texas*, 170, 108.

102. Roberts, *The Political, Legislative, and Judicial History of Texas*, 171; Alwyn Barr, *Reconstruction to Reform: Texas Politics, 1876–1906* (Austin: University of Texas Press, 1971), 43; Campbell, *Gone to Texas*, 317; Lelia Bailey, "The Life and Public Career of O. M. Roberts, 1815–1883" (PhD diss., University of Texas, 1932).

103. Oran Roberts, inaugural address, January 21, 1879, in *Governors' Messages, Coke to Ross*, 218; Oran Roberts to Thomas Goree, December 13, 1881, Roberts Records, Letterpress Book, 301–722.

104. Governor Roberts, general message to the Special Session, April 6, 1882, in *Governors' Messages, Coke to Ross*, 396; Roberts, "Penitentiaries," June 30, 1879, 332.

105. Texas, An Act to Provide for the Organization of the State Penitentiaries and for the More Efficient Management of the Same (1881), secs. 50–57, 80. The act replaced the board of directors with a new state penitentiary board, composed of Goree, the governor, and the state treasurer. Virginia and to a lesser extent North Carolina were the only other southern states to turn away from convict leasing in the 1870s and 1880s.

106. Texas State Penitentiary, *Biennial Report* (1884), 16; Thomas J. Goree, address on the penitentiary leases, February 14, 1883, Penitentiary Committees of the Senate and House, 18th Legislature (1883), 8; Penitentiary Board, *Biennial Report* (1882), 7. See also Roberts, General Message to the Special Session, April 6, 1882, 395–96.

107. Cable, *Silent South*, 115; Cahalan, "Historical Corrections Statistics," table 3–2. By 1890, Texas's prison population was almost twice the size of that of any other southern state. Only New York had a larger prison population, though lower in per capita terms.

108. See Andrew L. George, *The Texas Convict: Thrilling and Terrible Experience of a Texas Boy* (Austin, Tex.: Ben C. Jones & Co., 1893); Philip McIntyre, *Two Years in the Texas Hell at Huntsville* (Beeville, Tex.: Picayune Book Print, 1894); L. Rankin, *No. 6847, or the Horrors of Prison Life* (Author, 1897); Hardin, *The Life of John Wesley Hardin, as Written by Himself*; Campbell, *Hell Exploded*; J. S. Calvin, *Buried Alive, or a Term in the Texas State Prison, 1898–1902* (Paris, Tex.: Chester Printing House, 1905); O. J. Gillis, *To Hell and Back Again . . . Or, Life in the Penitentiaries of Arkansas and Texas* (Little Rock: Arkansas House, 1906); Henry Tomlin, *Life of Henry Tomlin: The Man Who Fought the Brutality and Oppression of the Ring in the State of Texas for Eighteen Years and Won—the Story of How Men Traffic in the Liberties and Lives of Their Fellow Men* (Dallas, Tex.: Johnston Printing & Adv. Co., 1906); Shotwell, *A Victim of Revenge*; Joe L. Wilkinson, *The Trans-Cedar Lynching and the Texas Penitentiary: Being a Plain Account of the Lynching and the Circumstances Leading Up to It, Also a Presentation of Conditions as They Exist in Our State Penitentiaries* (Dallas, Tex.: Johnston Printing & Advertising Co., 1912).

109. George, *The Texas Convict*, 5–7, 39, 37. There were earlier autobiographical tracts written by prisoners, of course. Texas history is littered with captivity narratives of various sources. Stephen Austin's prison musings certainly qualify; so might the extraordinary travel narrative written by Cabeza de Vaca, who spent a good deal of time in captivity of sorts. On the Civil War period, see A. J. H. Duganne, *Camps and Prisons: Twenty Months in the Department of the Gulf* (New York: J. P. Robens, 1865). George's memoir, however, is the first published memoir that deals with the convict leasing period.

110. George, *The Texas Convict*, 39, 72, 109.

111. "The Huntsville Prison Minstrels," *The Prison Bulletin* 1, no. 2 (December 15,

1897): 22. For a rosier report of conditions at the Walls in this period, see Texas State Penitentiary, *Biennial Report* (1882); John N. Henderson, "The Lease System in Texas," *Proceedings of the Annual Congress of the National Prison Association*, Austin, Texas, 1897, 305.

112. Texas State Penitentiary, *Biennial Report* (1884), 8; George, *The Texas Convict*, v–vi.

113. George, *The Texas Convict*, 139, 113–14, 134, 128–29. On the history of stripes and their symbology of subjection, see Michel Pastoureau, *The Devil's Cloth: A History of Stripes and Striped Fabric*, trans. Jody Gladding (New York: Columbia University Press, 2001).

114. George, *The Texas Convict*, 129–31.

115. Ibid., 131, 137–38.

116. Ibid., 113–15.

117. Ibid., 65, 76, 156, 204.

118. Texas Penitentiary Board, *Biennial Report* (1890), 11–12; George, *The Texas Convict*, 197, 199.

119. A prison ironworks had first been proposed by Governor Throckmorton shortly after the Civil War. James Throckmorton, Remarks, Texas State Legislature, *House Journal*, 11th Legislature (1866). On the subsequent planning and construction of the penitentiary, see Board of Directors, *Reports on the Texas State Penitentiary* (1873), 5; Directors, *Report of the State Penitentiary* (1876), 3. See also Sandra Fuller Allen, "The Iron Men: An Historical Review of the East Texas Penitentiary" (master's thesis, Sam Houston State University, 1982); Lucko, "Prison Farms, Walls, and Society," chap. 7; James Robertson Nowlin, "A Political History of the Texas Prison System, 1849–1957" (master's thesis, Trinity University, 1962), chap. 3; and Billy Martin Birmingham, "An Historical Account of the East Texas Prison at Rusk" (master's thesis, Sam Houston State University, 1979).

120. Roberts's predecessor, who presided over much of the work, declared the site "better in material and construction than any similar buildings in the Southern States." Richard Hubbard, initial message to the Legislature [January 1877?], in *Governors' Messages, Coke to Ross*, 733–34. Outside Rusk's walls stood the foundries, the blast furnace, a sawmill, and various other shops. Directors and Superintendent of the Texas State Penitentiary, *Biennial Reports* (1878–1880). The state built a 300-kilowatt power plant at Rusk in 1888, two years before electrifying the Walls in Huntsville. Lucko, "Prison Farms, Walls, and Society," chap. 7. Electricity did not arrive on most prison farms until the early twentieth century.

121. Nowlin, "Political History of the Texas Prison System," 90, 92.

122. Texas, Penitentiary Investigating Committee, *Report and Findings* (1913), 37. See also Ruth Allen, "The Capitol Boycott: A Study in Peaceful Labor Tactics," *Southwestern Historical Quarterly* 42 (1939); Ruth Allen, *Chapters in the History of Organized Labor in Texas* (Austin: University of Texas Publication no. 4143, 1941).

123. Penitentiary Board, *Biennial Report* (1884), 9–15, 45–50; Penitentiary Board, *Biennial Report* (1888), 12–14. For a survey of Rusk's financial failings and the Rusk-Palestine railroad, see Texas, Penitentiary Investigating Committee, *Report and Findings* (1913), 4–9, 20–21. Investigators attributed Rusk's economic failings to a variety of factors besides mismanagement and slack demand: Coke and limestone were in short supply. A private company controlled the only railway link and was thus able to charge exorbitant shipping rates. Manufacturing defects in the first furnace required expensive repairs and delays. Deforestation was another serious problem. Superintendent Goree estimated that full operations ate through charcoal equal to six acres of forest a day in

1889. Texas State Legislature, *House Journal*, 21st Legislature (1889), 502. On deforestation and the iron industry, see Michael Williams, *Americans and Their Forests: A Historical Geography* (Cambridge: Cambridge University Press, 1992).

Texas built its own railroad with convict labor to solve the transportation problem, but this resulted in even greater financial hemorrhaging. Texas, Penitentiary Investigating Committee, *Report* (1910), 20–21; Texas, Penitentiary Investigating Committee, *Exhibits and Testimony* (1910), 134–37; Miller, *A Financial History of Texas*, 261. For an early expression of doubts about Rusk's profitability, see Oran Roberts, *Supplemental Message*, June 16, 1879, in *Governors' Messages, Coke to Ross*, 317.

124. Texas, Penitentiary Investigating Committee, *Report and Findings* (1913), 5.
125. Campbell, *Hell Exploded*, 7, 8, 12, 13–14.
126. Ibid., 14.
127. Goffman, *Asylums*; Campbell, *Hell Exploded*, 16.
128. Campbell, *Hell Exploded*, 16–17.
129. Ibid., 24–25.
130. Ibid., 26.
131. Texas State Penitentiaries, *Reports* (1884), 18; Texas State Penitentiaries, *Biennial Report* (1904), 48.
132. Although Leadbelly helped narrate his biography, included in his 1936 songbook edited by John Lomax, no other African American or nonwhite prisoner I know of published memoirs until the 1960s. Lomax and Lomax, *Negro Folk Songs as Sung by Lead Belly*.
133. Texas State Penitentiaries, *Reports* (1884), 32–33, 36; Texas State Penitentiaries, *Biennial Report* (1904), 37, 30, 34–35; Walker, *Penology for Profit*, chap. 5. Horse theft gradually gave way to burglary as the prison system's most common conviction. Texas's median sentence length was longer than most other states by the turn of the century, though much shorter than today. See U.S. Census Bureau, *Prisoners and Juvenile Delinquents in Institutions 1904* (Washington, D.C.: U.S. Government Printing Office, 1907).
134. Tom Finty Jr., "Reform Suggested for Prison System," *Dallas News*, September 19, 1909, in Tom Finty Jr., ed., *Our Penal System and Its Purposes: Reprints of a Series of Articles Which Were Published in the Galveston and the Dallas News During the Summer of 1909* (Dallas, Tex.: Galveston-Dallas News, 1909), 58; Lawrence D. Rice, *The Negro in Texas, 1874–1900* (Baton Rouge: Louisiana State University Press, 1971), 98; DuBois, *The Souls of Black Folk*, 133. Remarkably, the 1886 pamphlet was circulated by the local Democratic Party, which hoped to invoke criminal justice bias to capture disaffected black voters away from the Republicans.
135. Superintendent of Texas State Penitentiaries, *Biennial Report* (1900), 8; Jordan, Bean, and Holmes, *Texas*, 48, 81. In 1900, Texas's rate of incarceration for African Americans was 350 per 100,000 compared to 48 per 100,000 for whites. A century later, Texas's incarceration rate for both whites and blacks has increased by more than 800 percent. The racial disparity between the two groups, however, remains the same.
136. Cahalan, "Historical Corrections Statistics," table 3–2; U.S. Census Bureau, *Prisoners and Juvenile Delinquents in Institutions 1904*, 17. New York had a significantly larger prison population than Texas in 1890 (8,190 vs. 3,319), but it was over 90 percent white.
137. Carrigan, *Making of a Lynching Culture*, 147; John N. Henderson, "The Lease System in Texas"; Benjamin A. Rodgers, Remarks, *Proceedings of the Annual Congress of the National Prison Association*, Austin, Texas, 1897, 314, 105. See also Texas State Penitentiary, *Biennial Report* (1880), 17; Blackmon, *Slavery by Another Name*.
138. Unsigned letter from Nacogdoches County Prisoner to Governor O. B.

Colquitt, June 8, 1912, Colquitt Records, box 301–332; Liberty County Prisoners to Governor O. B. Colquitt, May 17, 1912, Colquitt Records, box 301–332.

139. Goree, "Some Features of Prison Control in the South," 135.

140. Thomas J. Goree, address on the penitentiary leases, February 14, 1883, Penitentiary Committees of the Senate and House, 18th Legislature (1883), 13; *The Penitentiary Leases: Speeches Delivered in the House Favoring Their Ratification by Hon. J. Q. Chenoweth, Hon. H. J. Labatt, Hon. R. R. Hazlewood, Hon. A. K. Swan, Hon. W. F. Upton, and Hon. A. J. Chambers* (Austin, Tex.: Press of Deffenbaugh and Co., 1883), 5–6, 10.

141. "Hell on Earth," *Texas Siftings* 2, no. 46 (March 24, 1883): 12; *Texas Siftings* 2, no. 49 (April 14, 1883): back page.

142. Address of A. K. Swan, in *Penitentiary Leases*, 12; Texas State Penitentiaries, *Reports* (1884), 5.

143. *Texas Siftings* 2, no. 49 (April 14, 1883).

144. Texas State Penitentiaries, *Reports* (1884), 29; Teresa R. Jach, "Reform Versus Reality in the Progressive Era Texas Prison," *Journal of the Gilded Age and Progressive Era* 4, no. 1 (2005): 61; Texas State Penitentiaries, *Biennial Report* (1894), 11. Littleberry Ellis, Cunningham's former partner, generally received the second highest allocation of convicts in the 1890s.

145. Goree, "Some Features of Prison Control in the South," 134; Texas State Penitentiaries, *Reports* (1884), 50; Texas State Legislature, *Report of the Penitentiary Visiting Committee* (1887), 7.

146. Texas State Penitentiaries, *Reports* (1884), 7, 41–42; Texas State Penitentiaries, *Biennial Report* (1886), 68, 43–44. See also Texas State Penitentiaries, *Biennial Report* (1888), 34, 71.

147. Texas State Penitentiaries, *Biennial Report* (1886), 20–21; Texas State Penitentiaries, *Biennial Report* (1888), 71. See also Texas Penitentiary Board, *Biennial Report* (1890), 21; Texas State Legislature, *Report of the Penitentiary Visiting Committee* (1887), 4. The state purchased the farm from absentee owners in New York City, which may account for the plantation's ironic name.

148. Texas Penitentiary Board, *Biennial Report* (1890), 24–25; Charles K. Wolfe and Kip Lornell, *The Life and Legend of Leadbelly* (New York: HarperCollins, 1992), 79.

149. Texas State Penitentiaries, *Biennial Report* (1886), 80.

150. "Gatesville Triumph," *Dallas Morning News*, August 30, 1887, 6. "Reformatory for Vicious Boys," *Dallas Morning News*, April 4, 1887, 4.

151. Penitentiary Board, *Biennial Report* (1900), 12; Penitentiary Board, *Biennial Report* (1902), 21–22; Penitentiary Board, *Biennial Report* (1904), 19–20. The Clemens Farm was an especially important acquisition for the penitentiary board, signifying an emphasis on sugar development. The superintendent asserted that the purchase "marks the beginning of the end of the lease system."

152. Penitentiary Board, *Biennial Report* (1908), 15; Penitentiary Board, *Biennial Report* (1910), 17–18. In 1908, the penitentiary board added the 957-acre Riddick Farm, also in Fort Bend County, to the Harlem Farm, expanding it to 3,740 acres. The Imperial Farm had belonged to Littleberry Ellis and the Ramsey Farm to his joint venture with Cunningham, the Imperial Sugar Company. Both plantations started out as slave concerns. Strobel, *Old Plantations*.

153. Shotwell, *A Victim of Revenge*, 11. See also Wilkinson, *Trans-Cedar Lynching and the Texas Penitentiary*, 131.

154. Penitentiary Board, *Rules, Regulations, and By-Laws* (1883), 38, 40–41.

155. Clemens prisoners to Governor O. B. Colquitt, November 18, 1911, Colquitt Records, box 301–331; Testimony of Sam Tubb, in Texas, Penitentiary Investigating Committee, *Exhibits and Testimony* (1910), 276; Shotwell, *A Victim of Revenge*, 17.

156. Penitentiary Board, *Rules, Regulations, and By-Laws* (1883), 35; Henderson,

"The Lease System in Texas," 1897, 304–5; Wilkinson, *Trans-Cedar Lynching and the Texas Penitentiary*, 133–35.

157. A white prisoner at the Imperial Farm testified that convicts had to stay ahead of mounted guards, who headed to the lines at "a fast trot . . . to a lope." He complained, "I was brought in five miles once from the edge of . . . Cunningham Farm . . . [and] trotted all the way." Texas, Penitentiary Investigating Committee, *Exhibits and Testimony* (1910), 237.

158. On the transition from gang labor to sharecropping in the postbellum South, see Julie Saville, *The Work of Reconstruction: From Slave to Wage Laborer in South Carolina, 1860–1870* (New York: Cambridge University Press, 1994); Curtin, *The Rise and Fall of the Plantation Complex.*

159. Ben E. Cabell to J. T. Bowman, November 3, 1911, Colquitt Records, box 301–331, November 3–17, 1911 folder. Quotas were generally set according to race and perceived physical strength. On wood chopping squads, white prisoners were often expected to cut one cord of wood per day, while black prisoners were responsible for a 1.5 cords. Calvin, *Buried Alive*, 77.

160. Penitentiary Board, *Rules, Regulations, and By-Laws* (1883), art. 15, sec. 7; Testimony of Captain Flannigan, Texas, Penitentiary Investigating Committee, *Exhibits and Testimony* (1910), 900, 261; Posy L. Griffith to O. B. Colquitt, June 26, 1912; Shotwell, *A Victim of Revenge*, 17. Prison rules discouraged labor in inclement labor and on Sundays, and they prohibited nighttime work outright. Nevertheless, prisoners could be worked anytime if "absolutely necessary to prevent great loss." Camp bosses exploited this loophole liberally.

161. Calvin, *Buried Alive*, 80; "Go Down, Ol' Hannah" as recorded by Leadbelly. Lomax and Lomax, *Negro Folk Songs as Sung by Lead Belly*, 118–20. See also Alan Lomax, *The Land Where the Blues Began* (London: Methuen, 1993), 283–87; Bruce Jackson, *Wake Up Dead Man: Afro-American Worksongs from Texas Prisons* (Cambridge, Mass.: Harvard University Press, 1972), 111–18.

162. Texas State Legislature, Penitentiary Investigating Committee, *Report and Findings* (1913), 27, 22–23, 27; Frederick H. Wines, Remarks, *Proceedings of the Annual Congress of the National Prison Association*, Austin, Texas, 1897, 193.

163. Charles S. Potts, "The Convict Labor System in Texas," *Annals of the American Academy of Political and Social Science* 21 (1903): 88; Wilkinson, *Trans-Cedar Lynching and the Texas Penitentiary*, 132; Texas State Penitentiaries, *Biennial Report* (1904), 36. To Superintendent Goree's credit, prisoner deaths declined after the cancellation of the Ellis-Cunningham lease. In 1880, fully 7 percent of Texas's convicts had died, whereas fatalities rarely exceeded 4 percent in the state contract years. Still, considering that most prisoners entered the system as young men in fair health and that most served relatively short sentences, the death rate remained extraordinarily high. For an official defense of Texas's death rate, see Penitentiary Board, *Biennial Report* (1892), 6–7.

164. Texas State Penitentiaries, *Biennial Report* (1886), 37. There were 221 total prison deaths reported. "Proceedings of the State Convention of Colored Men of Texas, Held at the City of Austin, July 10–12, 1883," in Herbert Aptheker, ed., *A Documentary History of the Negro People in the United States*, 4th ed., vol. 2 (New York: Citadel Press, 1968), 689.

165. Texas State Penitentiaries, *Biennial Report* (1904), 36.

166. The years 1880, 1890, and 1900 used as a sample here. The population of prisoners on hand in those years was 1,972, 3,346, and 4,262, respectively. Texas State Penitentiaries, *Biennial Report* (1904), 45.

167. Prison Commission, *Annual Report* (1911), 36; Texas Prison System, *Biennial Statistics Ledger*, 1906–1920, TDCJ Records, 1998/038–269.

168. Cited in W. Fitzhugh Brundage, ed., *Under Sentence of Death: Lynching in the South* (Chapel Hill: University of North Carolina Press, 1997), 4.

169. Author's estimate of total prison deaths in southern states during the convict leasing period. Based on a 5 percent annual death rate and reported prison population figures.

170. Campbell, *Hell Exploded*, 14; Penitentiary Board, *Rules, Regulations, and By-Laws* (1883), art. 19, secs. 5–6; Comments by Lucius Whatley, *Proceedings of the Annual Congress of the National Prison Association*, Austin, Texas, 1897, 59–60; Testimony of Abraham Lincoln in Texas, Penitentiary Investigating Committee, *Exhibits and Testimony* (1910), 646.

171. Convict Record Ledgers, 1849–1954, TDCJ Records; Penitentiary Board, *Monthly Reports* (1900–1911), TDCJ Records; Ben E. Cabell to Governor O. B. Colquitt, December 16, 1911, Colquitt Records, box 301–331; George, *The Texas Convict*, 150.

172. Calvin, *Buried Alive*, 49.

173. Testimony of H. W. Johnson, R. W. Grace, Andrew Walker, W. J. P. Hill, and Will Westhall, in Texas, Penitentiary Investigating Committee, *Exhibits and Testimony* (1910), 243–57, 916–21.

174. Comments by Lucius Whatley, *Proceedings of the Annual Congress of the National Prison Association*, Austin, Texas, 1897, 61; George, *The Texas Convict*, 159. Since before the Civil War, Texas had banned convicts from testifying in court. See Texas, Penal Code, pt. 3, title 2, art. 802; Texas, *Code of Criminal Procedure* (Oldham and White 1859), art. 644; Jacob A. Herring to Governor Thomas M. Campbell, September 11, 1910.

175. "Torture in Texas," unidentified newspaper clippings, ca. 1912, Colquitt Records, box 301–332, August 19–23, 1912 folder; "Convict Camps," *Dallas Morning News*, November 2, 1909, 6. One lawmaker labeled the system an "organized hell." Hudspeth, Minority Report, in Texas, Penitentiary Investigating Committee, *Report* (1910), 21.

176. Wilkinson, *Trans-Cedar Lynching and the Texas Penitentiary*, 135.

177. George, *The Texas Convict*, 148; Campbell, *Hell Exploded*, 3, 25.

## 4: THE AGONIES OF REFORM

1. John N. Henderson, "The Lease System in Texas," in *Proceedings of the Annual Congress of the National Prison Association*, Austin, Texas, December 2–6, 1897 (Pittsburg: Shaw Brothers, 1898), 321.

2. Gregory, "Persistence and Irony," 45–46.

3. Lula Sanders to Thomas M. Campbell, October 2, 1907, Campbell Records, box 301–229.

4. State Penitentiary Board, *Biennial Report* (1906), 12, 42; Lula Sanders to Thomas Campbell, October 2, 1907.

5. Lula Sanders to Thomas Campbell, October 2, 1907.

6. Texas State Penitentiaries, *Biennial Report* (1908), 12–13. Eastham was operating as a share farm by 1907 with women confined at Camp 2. Share farms were privately owned but operated with prisoners by the state; profits were shared, as with tenant farming. Gregory, "Persistence and Irony," 49.

7. John Tardy to V. J. Douglas, September 16, 1907, Campbell Records, box 301–229.

8. Texas State Legislature, Penitentiary Investigating Committee, *Exhibits and Testimony* (1910), 218; Lula Sanders to Thomas Campbell, October 2, 1907; George Waverly Briggs, "Women's Farm a Disgrace," in Briggs, *Texas Penitentiary*, 15.

9. Penitentiary Investigating Committee, *Exhibits and Testimony* (1910), 215, 209; William F. Ramsey to A. M. Barton, September 30, 1907, Campbell Records, box 301–238. See also Jacob A. Herring to Thomas M. Campbell, September 26, 1907, Campbell Records, box 301–229.

10. Tom Finty, "The Texas Prison Investigation," *Survey*, December 18, 1909, 388; Briggs, *Texas Penitentiary*.
11. Texas State Legislature, Penitentiary Investigating Committee, *Report and Findings* (1913), 14. On the rival strains in Texas politics, see Key and Heard, *Southern Politics in State and Nation*; Davidson, *Race and Class in Texas Politics*; Lind, *Made in Texas*.
12. Texas State Penitentiaries, *Biennial Report* (1886), 14–15; Allen, "The Capitol Boycott: A Study in Peaceful Labor Tactics," 319; Mike Fowler and Jack Maguire, *The Capitol Story: Statehouse in Texas* (Austin, Tex.: Eakin Press, 1988). Although Texas remained a predominantly rural state until World War II, a surge of railroad and port construction led to an expansion of union activity in the 1880s. See Allen, *Chapters in the History of Organized Labor in Texas*; Nell Irvin Painter, *Standing at Armageddon: The United States, 1877–1919* (New York: W. W. Norton, 1987).
13. The Knights of Labor had won a serious strike against Jay Gould in 1885, but the railroad titan then precipitated another strike to crush the union a year later. See Ruth Allen, *The Great Southwest Strike* (Austin: University of Texas Publication No. 4214, 1942). See also Leon Fink, *Workingmen's Democracy: The Knights of Labor and American Politics* (Urbana: University of Illinois Press, 1983); Elizabeth Sanders, *Roots of Reform: Farmers, Workers, and the American State, 1877–1917* (Chicago: University of Chicago Press, 1999), chap. 3.
14. Finty, *Our Penal System and Its Purposes*, 4; Texas, An Act to Provide for the More Efficient Management of the Texas State Penitentiaries (1883), sec. 4.
15. Foley, *White Scourge*, 29–34, 80; *Texas Almanac* (Dallas, Tex.: A. H. Belo & Co., 1911), 179. See also Spratt, *Road to Spindletop*, chap. 4; Wright, *The Political Economy of the Cotton South*, 165–76. On the contrast between present-day heartland conservatism and nineteenth-century farmer radicalism, see Thomas Frank, *What's the Matter with Kansas? How Conservatives Won the Heart of America* (New York: Metropolitan Books, 2004).
16. Laurence Gronlund, *The Coöperative Commonwealth in Its Outlines: An Exposition of Modern Socialism* (Boston: Lee and Shepard, 1884); Goodwyn, *Democratic Promise*, 91, 279–80, 291–94; Woodward, *Origins of the New South*, 188–95; Painter, *Standing at Armageddon*, 61; Lawrence Goodwyn, "Populist Dreams and Negro Rights: East Texas as a Case Study," *American Historical Review* 76 (1971): 1435–56; Rice, *Negro in Texas*, chap. 4–5; People's Party of America, Platform (1892), in Richard D. Hefner, ed., *A Documentary History of the United States* (New York: Penguin Putnam, 1999), 236–37.
17. People's Party State Convention, Platform (Dallas, Texas, 1891); Greenback Labor State Convention, Platform (Waco, Texas, 1878); Independent Greenback Convention, Platform (1878), in Winkler, *Platforms of Political Parties in Texas*, 293, 188, 181.
18. People's Party of America, Platform (1892), 238, 236; People's Party State Convention, Platform (Dallas, Texas, 1891), 297.
19. See Winkler, *Platforms of Political Parties in Texas*; Barr, *Reconstruction to Reform*, chaps. 9–11.
20. F. E. Daniel, Evening address, *Proceedings of the National Prison Congress* (1897), 117; Potts, "The Convict Labor System in Texas," 89, 84. See also Samuel P. Benbrook, *First Annual Report* (Dallas, Tex.: Society of the Friendless, Texas Division, 1907).
21. Remarks by Major Whatley, Frederick Wines, Roeliff Brinkerhoff, *Proceedings of the National Prison Congress* (1897), 192, 61, 14, 297, 404.
22. Henderson, "The Lease System in Texas," *Proceedings of the National Prison Congress* (1897), 320, 300, 321.
23. *Proceedings of the National Prison Congress* (1897), 321–22, 136, 298.

24. See Richard Hofstadter, *Age of Reform: From Bryan to F.D.R.* (New York: Vintage Books, 1955).

25. *Proceedings of the National Prison Congress* (1897), 27, 289, 192–93. Although Wines endorsed the mainline tenants of reformatory penology, he emerged as a key apologist for racial segregation and plantation punishment in the South. See Wines, *Report Upon the Penal and Other State Institutions and Upon the Jails of Thirty-Nine Parishes* (Baton Rouge: Prison Reform Association of Louisiana, Board of Charities and Corrections, 1906), 7–8.

26. George T. Winston, "The Prevention of Crime," *Proceedings of the National Prison Congress* (1897), 288–89.

27. Ibid., 288–93.

28. Ibid., 292–93.

29. Joel Williamson, *The Crucible of Race: Black-White Relations in the American South Since Emancipation* (New York: Oxford University Press, 1984).

30. Bruce A. Glasrud, "Child or Beast?: White Texas' View of Blacks, 1900–1910," *East Texas Historical Journal* 15 (1977): 38–39. More generally, see Leon F. Litwack, *Trouble in Mind: Black Southerners in the Age of Jim Crow* (New York: Alfred A. Knopf, 1998).

31. Republican Convention, Platform (1892); "'Reform' Republican Convention, Platform" (Dallas, Texas, 1892), in Winkler, *Platforms of Political Parties in Texas*, 301–5; Rice, *Negro in Texas*, 134.

32. Pauline Yelderman, "The Jaybird Democratic Association of Fort Bend County" (master's thesis, University of Texas, 1938); Clarence Wharton, *History of Fort Bend County* (San Antonio, Tex.: Naylor Co., 1939), 196–97. Control of the court system proved vital in such vicious contests for power. In Fort Bend County, Jaybirds murdered a white opponent and then arranged for a grand jury to indict black community leaders. Threatened by mobs and arrest, many prominent African Americans, including the black sheriff, had to flee the county. Rice, *Negro in Texas*, 122.

33. Alwyn Barr, *Black Texans: A History of African Americans in Texas, 1528–1995*, 2nd ed. (Norman: University of Oklahoma Press, 1996), 79–80; Goodwyn, *Democratic Promise*, 304. Increasing numbers of Texas counties also adopted white-only political primaries from the 1890s forward, which, in the heavily Democratic state, effectively excluded nonwhite voters from influence. Subsequent "election reforms," namely the Terrell election laws of 1902, 1903, and 1907, exacerbated the segregationist impact of the poll tax. See Barr, *Reconstruction to Reform*, chap. 13; Robert V. Haynes, "Black Houstonians and the White Democratic Primary, 1920–1945," in Howard Beeth and Cary D. Wintz, eds., *Black Dixie: Afro-Texas History and Culture in Houston* (College Station: Texas A&M University Press, 1992). See also Montejano, *Anglos and Mexicans in the Making of Texas*, chap. 6; Charles Kincheloe Chamberlain, "Alexander Watkins Terrell, Citizen, Statesman" (PhD diss., University of Texas, 1956); Henry M. Laughlin, "The Election Laws of Texas, 1876–1928" (master's thesis, University of Texas, 1928); Rice, *Negro in Texas*, chap. 7.

34. Johnson, *Revolution in Texas*; James A. Sandos, *Rebellion in the Borderlands: Anarchism and the Plan of San Diego, 1904–1923* (Norman: University of Oklahoma Press, 1992).

35. Bruce A. Glasrud, "Enforcing White Supremacy in Texas, 1900–1910," *Red River Historical Review* 4, no. 4 (1979): 70. See also Carrigan, *Making of a Lynching Culture*, chaps. 6–7.

36. Winston, "The Prevention of Crime," 292; Glasrud, "Child or Beast?" 40–41.

37. Rice, *Negro in Texas*, 250; Glasrud, "Enforcing White Supremacy in Texas," 70. On lynching generally, see Brundage, *Under Sentence of Death*; Philip Dray, *At the Hands of Persons Unknown: The Lynching of Black America* (New York: Random

House, 2002); Joel Williamson, "Wounds Not Scars: Lynching, the National Conscience, and the American Historian," *Journal of American History* 83, no. 4 (March 1997): 1221–72. On the intersections of lynching and New South masculinity, see Glenda E. Gilmore, *Gender and Jim Crow: Women and the Politics of White Supremacy in North Carolina, 1896–1920* (Chapel Hill: University of North Carolina Press, 1996); Gail Bederman, *Manliness and Civilization: A Cultural History of Gender and Race in the United States, 1880–1917* (Chicago: University of Chicago Press, 1995).

38. Ida B. Wells, *A Red Record: Lynchings in the United States, 1892–1893–1894* (Chicago: Ida B. Wells, 1894), 92–95, reprinted in Jacqueline Jones Royster, ed., *Southern Horrors and Other Writings: The Anti-Lynching Campaign of Ida B. Wells, 1892–1900* (Boston: Bedford Books, 1997); "Lynching of Henry Smith in Paris, Texas, February 1, 1893. The Torture, Burning His Feet with a Red Hot Iron." Reprinted in R. W. Shufeldt, *The Negro, A Menace to American Civilization* (Boston: Richard G. Badger, The Gorham Press, 1907), 168b. See also Jacquelyn Dowd Hall, "The Mind That Burns in Each Body," *Southern-Exposure* 12, no. 6 (November/December 1984): 61–71.

39. Glasrud, "Child or Beast?" 41; Rice, *Negro in Texas*, chap. 12; Marquart, Ekland-Olson, and Sorensen, *The Rope, the Chair, and the Needle*, 1, 12.

40. Racial breakdown from Texas State Penitentiaries, *Biennial Report* (1890), 55; *Biennial Report* (1904), 11–12. See also Walker, *Penology for Profit*, 114; Texas Prison System, *Biennial Statistics Ledger*, 1906–1920, TDCJ Records, 1998/038–269. Imprisonment rates estimated from census data. See also *Prisoners and Juvenile Delinquents in the United States, 1910* (Washington, D.C.: U.S. Census Bureau, 1918), 98.

41. The pardon board began its work in 1893 and received expanded powers by 1896. Texas State Penitentiaries, *Biennial Report* (1894), 6–7; *Biennial Report* (1896), 6; S. A. MacCorkle, "The Pardoning Power in Texas," *Southwestern Social Science Quarterly* 15, no. 3 (1934): 222.

42. Glasrud, "Enforcing White Supremacy in Texas," 69–71; Glasrud, "Child or Beast?" 38, 41. See also Geoffrey C. Ward, *Unforgivable Blackness: The Rise and Fall of Jack Johnson* (New York: Alfred A. Knopf, 2004).

43. *Speech of Thomas M. Campbell Opening His Campaign for Governor of Texas, at Athens, Texas, April 21st, 1906 and Press Comments* (Palestine, Tex.: Palestine Printing Company, 1906), 14.

44. Ibid., 6, 1, 13–14. See also Janet Schmelzer, "Thomas M. Campbell: Progressive Governor of Texas," *Red River Valley Historical Review* 3 (1978): 52–64; Worth Robert Miller, "Building a Progressive Coalition in Texas: The Populist-Reform Democratic Rapprochement, 1900–1907," *Journal of Southern History* 52, no. 2 (1986): 163–82.

45. Thomas Campbell to Jacob A. Herring, March 8, 1907, Campbell Records, box 301–229. Jacob (Jake) Herring managed the Herring-Whatley share farm in Midway until he was appointed superintendent. Before that he served as a deputy sheriff and as warden at the Harlem state farm. Jacob A. Herring, Center for American History, Vertical File (hereafter CAH-VF).

In addition to ordering inspections, Campbell cooperated with an early prison reform advocacy group, the Society for the Friendless. He served on its advisory board and granted its leaders full access to punishment institutions. After a lobbying drive by the Texas Federation of Women's Clubs, he also signed a juvenile court bill into law during his first term. Benbrook, "First Annual Report"; Jacquelyn McElhaney, "Pauline Periwinkle: Prodding Dallas into the Progressive Era," in Fane Downs and Nancy Baker Jones, *Women and Texas History: Selected Essays* (Austin: Texas State Historical Association, 1993), 42–56.

46. PBM, August 14, 1907, box 1998/038–1, 1907–1909 folder.

47. Penitentiary Board, *Biennial Report* (1908), 15; Texas, Penitentiary Investigating

Committee, *Report and Findings* (1913), 21. On the antebellum history of Ramsey, see Strobel, *Old Plantations*.

48. The prison board added the Riddick Farm to the Harlem state farm in 1908. The board acquired L. A. Ellis's old lease property from his heirs' Imperial Sugar Company for $160,000. Rather than use cash, the state agreed to pay for the properties through crop proceeds, thus forcing convicts to generate the capital. Penitentiary Board, *Biennial Report* (1908), 15; Lucko, "Prison Farms, Walls, and Society," 424. For a more detailed history of the Imperial Farm, which became part of the Central Unit, see Don Hudson, "The Texas Department of Criminal Justice's Central Unit Main Building and Its Historical Significance" (Sugarland, Tex.: Texas Historic Commission, 2001).

49. Prison Commission, *Annual Report* (1911), 39; Penitentiary Board, *Biennial Report* (1910), 11. Campbell's administration also increased the portion of convicts working on share farms, from 10 percent to 23 percent between 1909 and 1910.

50. Finty, "The Texas Prison Investigation," 390; "Women's Farm a Disgrace," in Briggs, *Texas Penitentiary*, 16; Gregory, "Persistence and Irony," 41–43. Critics of leasing assailed Governor Campbell for not going far enough. See Benbrook, "First Annual Report," 2, 15; James R. Green, *Grass-Roots Socialism: Radical Movements in the Southwest, 1895–1943* (Baton Rouge: Louisiana State University Press, 1983), chaps. 1–2. In particular, opponents of the governor assailed his management of the state railway to Rusk, focusing particularly on his diversion of capital from the Texas School Fund. See Penitentiary Investigating Committee, *Report* (1910), 21; Penitentiary Investigating Committee, *Report and Findings* (1913), 20–21.

51. Finty, "The Texas Prison Investigation," 387; Rev. R. J. Briggs, Sermon, *Proceedings of the National Prison Congress* (1897), 280. *Handbook of Texas Online*, s.v. "George Waverly Briggs" http://www.tsha.utexas.edu/handbook/online/arti cles/BB/fbr48.html; "Is the Penal System Wrong?" and "Routine on Plantations," in Briggs, *Texas Penitentiary*, 4–5, 14.

52. "Woman's Farm a Disgrace" and "Brutalities Are Sanctioned" in Briggs, *Texas Penitentiary*, 14–15, 21.

53. "Outline of Road Plan" in Briggs, *Texas Penitentiary*, 58–61.

54. Finty, "The Texas Prison Investigation," 391, 388; Thomas M. Campbell, Message to the Legislature, January 14, 1909 (Austin: Texas State Legislature, 1909), 22.

55. Brinkerhoff, opening address, *Proceedings of the National Prison Congress* (1897), 27; Karen Shapiro, *A New South Rebellion: The Battle Against Convict Labor in the Tennessee Coalfields, 1871–1896* (Chapel Hill: University of North Carolina Press, 1998), 21–23. See also Clyde Ball, "The Public Career of Col. A. S. Colyar, 1870–1877," *Tennessee Historical Quarterly* 12 (1953): 106–28.

56. Cable, *Silent South*, 133; Clarissa Olds Keeler, *The Crime of Crimes, or the Convict System Unmasked* (Washington, D.C.: Pentecostal Era Company, 1907), 4–5; Shapiro, *A New South Rebellion*, 63–72.

57. Shapiro, *A New South Rebellion*, 35, 52, 63; Lichtenstein, *Twice the Work of Free Labor*, 96–97, 90.

58. Shapiro, *A New South Rebellion*, 81.

59. Lichtenstein, *Twice the Work of Free Labor*, 99; Shapiro, *A New South Rebellion*, 191, 243.

60. Lichtenstein, *Twice the Work of Free Labor*, 90–102; Shapiro, *A New South Rebellion*, chap. 9; T. J. Hill, "Experience in Mining Coal with Convicts," *Proceedings of the National Prison Congress* (1897), 388–97.

61. Reverend S. B. Wallace, "What the National Government Is Doing for Our Colored Boys: The New System of Slavery in the South" (Washington, D.C.: Israel C. M. E. Church, 1894), in the Daniel A. P. Murray Pamphlet Collection, Library of Congress, 35; Mary Church Terrell, "Peonage in the United States:

The Convict Lease System and the Chain Gangs," *Nineteenth Century* 62 (1907): 306. See also W. E. B. DuBois, *Some Notes on Negro Crime, Particularly in Georgia* (Atlanta, Ga.: Atlanta University Press, 1904); Milfred C. Fierce, *Slavery Revisited: Blacks and the Southern Convict Lease System, 1865–1933* (New York: Africana Studies Research Center, Brooklyn College, City University of New York, 1994).

62. Frederick H. Wines, *Punishment and Reformation: An Historical Sketch of the Rise of the Penitentiary System* (London: Swan Sonnenschein & Co., 1895), 313; James H. Kyle et al., "Report of the U.S. Industrial Commission on Prison Labor" (Washington, D.C.: U.S. Government Printing Office, 1900), 8.

63. Rebecca Latimer Felton, "The Convict System of Georgia," *The Forum* 2, no. 5 (1887): 486–87, 489–90; Williamson, *Crucible of Race*, 125; John Erwin Talmadge, *Rebecca Latimer Felton: Nine Stormy Decades* (Athens: University of Georgia Press, 1960), 98–99; Rebecca Latimer Felton, *"My Memoirs of Georgia Politics"* (Atlanta. Ga.: The Index Printing Company, 1911), 120. See also LeeAnn Whites, *Gender Matters: Civil War, Reconstruction, and the Making of the New South* (New York: Palgrave Macmillan, 2005).

64. Felton, "The Convict System of Georgia," 485–86; Williamson, *Crucible of Race*, 128–29; Talmadge, *Rebecca Latimer Felton*, 114.

65. Wilmington Race Riot Commission, *1898 Wilmington Race Riot Report* (Raleigh: North Carolina Department of Cultural Resources, Office of Archives and History, Research Branch, 2006), 177–80; Talmadge, *Rebecca Latimer Felton*, 116. See also Gilmore, *Gender and Jim Crow*.

66. Woodward, *Origins of the New South*, 369.

67. Robert E. Ireland, "Prison Reform, Road Building, and Southern Progressivism: Joseph Hyde Pratt and the Campaign for 'Good Roads and Good Men,'" *North Carolina Historical Review* 68, no. 2 (1991): 127; Lichtenstein, *Twice the Work of Free Labor*, 179–80. See also Jesse F. Steiner and Roy M. Brown, *The North Carolina Chain Gang: A Study of County Convict Road Work* (Chapel Hill: University of North Carolina Press, 1927).

68. Lichtenstein, *Twice the Work of Free Labor*, 176–77.

69. Like Texas, North and South Carolina, among other states, had purchased plantations for prisoners in the late nineteenth century. Louisiana, however, was the first state to transition entirely to a state plantation-based system. Mancini, *One Dies, Get Another*. Even after Angola became a state institution, however, large numbers of black prisoners continued laboring in state levee camps. Carleton, *Politics and Punishment*, 89.

70. Board of Control, Louisiana State Penitentiary, *Biennial Report* (1903); Mancini, *One Dies, Get Another*, 150. The old prison at Baton Rouge—once a "model" facility, one of the first penitentiaries built in the antebellum South—had become, observed the state's first annual report, "simply a relic of the past." Carleton, *Politics and Punishment*, 8, 91.

71. Mancini, *One Dies, Get Another*, 90; Robert Perkinson, "Angola and the Agony of Prison Reform," *Radical Philosophy Review* 3, no. 1 (2000): 9; Press, "Inside America's Toughest Prison."

72. Wilkinson, *Trans-Cedar Lynching and the Texas Penitentiary*, 35, 147.

73. Texas State Senate, Senate Investigating Committee, *Report and Proceedings*, 324.

74. Wilkinson, *Trans-Cedar Lynching and the Texas Penitentiary*, 148; Finty, "The Texas Prison Investigation," 387–88.

75. Finty, "The Texas Prison Investigation," 389; Texas State Legislature, Penitentiary Investigating Committee, *Report* (1910), 19.

76. Finty, *Our Penal System and Its Purposes*, 1; Penitentiary Investigating Committee, *Report* (1910), 15, 12; Claude Hudspeth, Penitentiary Investigating Committee, *Minority Report* (1910), 23. Senator Hudspeth agreed with most of the

majority's recommendations, but wrote with greater fury and added his own list of idiosyncratic policy fixes.

77. Penitentiary Investigating Committee, *Report* (1910), 20, 8; Penitentiary Investigating Committee, *Exhibits and Testimony* (1910), 609, 607, 616.

78. Gregory, "Persistence and Irony," chap. 4; Penitentiary Investigating Committee, *Exhibits and Testimony* (1910), 559, 572.

79. Penitentiary Investigating Committee, *Exhibits and Testimony* (1910), 560, 549, 551–53. Female relatives who came to visit imprisoned men also claimed they were sexually harassed or groped by prison officials. See Mamie Johnson to Ben E. Cabell, May 30, 1912, Colquitt Records, box 301–332, May 18–30, 1912 folder; K. F. Cunningham to the Board of Prison Commissioners, June 24, 1912, Colquitt Records, box 301–332, June 19–25, 1912 folder; H. W. Kelly to Board of Prison Commissioners, June 24, 1912, Colquitt Records, box 301–332, June 19–25, 1912 folder.

80. Penitentiary Investigating Committee, *Report* (1910), 14; Hudspeth, *Minority Report* (1910), 21; Penitentiary Investigating Committee, *Exhibits and Testimony* (1910), 252, 256.

81. Penitentiary Investigating Committee, *Exhibits and Testimony* (1910), 598, 917.

82. R. H. Underwood, "The Warden and His Work," in Finty, *Our Penal System and Its Purposes*, 19; Penitentiary Investigating Committee, *Exhibits and Testimony* (1910), 922–23, 917.

83. Penitentiary Investigating Committee, *Exhibits and Testimony* (1910), 896; Jacob A. Herring to Thomas M. Campbell, September 11, 1910, Campbell Records, box 301–244.

84. Underwood, "The Warden and His Work," 19.

85. Finty, "Our Penal System and Its Purposes," 1. See also J. A. Herring to Thomas M. Campbell, September 11, 1910, Campbell Records, box 301–244.

86. Finty, "The Texas Prison Investigation," 388; Penitentiary Investigating Committee, *Report* (1910), 16; "Reform Suggested for Prison System," in Finty, *Our Penal System and Its Purposes*, 61.

87. Penitentiary Investigating Committee, *Report* (1910), 7–19.

88. Finty, "The Texas Prison Investigation," 388; Lucko, "Prison Farms, Walls, and Society," 431.

89. With dubious command of the numbers, Campbell argued that "the financial showing for the past three years gave greater net results than that of the forty years preceding all put together." *Austin Statesman*, August 16, 1910, September 10, 1910, in Clippings file, CAH.

90. Texas, An Act Establishing a Prison System (1910), sec. 3.

91. Ibid., secs. 39–40, 45, 47–48, 55–57.

92. Ibid., secs. 30, 15; "Uncle Sam's Road to Reformation," in Finty, *Our Penal System and Its Purposes*, 24; Hudspeth, *Minority Report* (1910), 21.

93. Goree used to be a lumber camp annex of the Walls but was converted to a state farm by 1910. Women were moved to the farm from Eastham after the investigative committee issued its report. Texas State Penitentiaries, *Biennial Report* (1910), 16; Prison Commission, *Annual Report* (1911), 15–16; Gregory, "Persistence and Irony," 87.

94. Texas, An Act Establishing a Prison System (1910), secs. 34–38; Penitentiary Investigating Committee, *Exhibits and Testimony* (1910), 550; Penitentiary Investigating Committee, *Report* (1910), 14.

95. Texas, An Act Establishing a Prison System (1910), secs. 1, 26–27.

96. Ben E. Cabell, *Present Penitentiary Situation in Texas* (Waco, Tex.: State Conference of Charities and Corrections, 1912), 8; Texas, An Act Establishing a Prison System (1910), secs. 33, 42; Potts, "The Convict Labor System in Texas," 93. Potts quotes here from Alexander Maconochie, a famous critic of the British Transportation system in the early nineteenth century.

97. Lewis L. Gould, *Progressives and Prohibitionists: Texas Democrats in the Wilson Era* (Austin: University of Texas Press, 1973), 87; George P. Huckaby, *Oscar Branch Colquitt: A Political Biography* (PhD diss., University of Texas, 1946); Oscar B. Colquitt to *Waco Times Herald*, July 12, 1911, Colquitt Papers, box 2E110; "Will Make Prisons Pay," *New York Times*, October 6, 1912, X3.

98. Prison Commission, *Annual Report* (1911), 9, 32; Nowlin, "Political History of the Texas Prison System," 111. For a compelling account of the inaccessibility of many Texas prisons, see Rabbi David Rosenbaum to Henry Cohen, March 6, 1919, Cohen Papers, box 3M296; Letter to Thomas Campbell, January 29, 1910, Campbell Records, box 301–244, penitentiary correspondence.

99. Texas, An Act Establishing a Prison System (1910), secs. 4–11; PBM, January 27, 1911, box 1998/038–2; Tom Finty, "Troubles of the Texas State Prisons," *The Delinquent* 3, no. 12 (1913): 4; Ben E. Cabell to J. T. Bowman, July 17, 1912, Colquitt Records, box 301–332. On the commissioner form of government pioneered in Galveston after the hurricane, see Bradley Robert Rice, *Progressive Cities: The Commission Government Movement in America, 1901–1920* (Austin: University of Texas Press, 1977).

100. Cabell, *Present Penitentiary Situation in Texas*, 6–7; PBM, May 17, 1911, box 1998/038–2; Message of the Governor on Prison Affairs, January 30, 1913, *Messages of Gov. O. B. Colquitt to the 33rd. Legislature, Regular Session* (1913), 69; Robert W. Brahan to J. T. Bowman, December 29, 1911, Colquitt Records, box 301–331.

101. Cabell, *Present Penitentiary Situation in Texas*, 9, 2–3; *Message of the Governor on Prison Affairs*, January 30, 1913, 62; PBM, February 17, 1912, box 1998/038–2; Prison Commission, *Annual Report* (1911), 62–67, 93–94, 45; Robert W. Brahan to J. T. Bowman, December 29, 1911, Colquitt Records, box 301–331. See also Alexander Johnson, ed., *Proceedings of the National Conference of Charities and Correction, at the Thirty-Eighth Annual Session, Held in Boston, Mass., June 7–14, 1911* (Fort Wayne, Ind.: Fort Wayne Printing Company, 1911). Texas's all-white convict uniforms don't inspire much reverence among convicts today, but a century ago they were meant to signify hygiene and the promise of reclaimed innocence.

102. Wilkinson, *Trans-Cedar Lynching and the Texas Penitentiary*, 146; Prison Commission, *Annual Report* (1911), 7; Texas, An Act Establishing a Prison System (1910), secs. 44, 26, 58; PBM, September 25, 1911, box 1998/038–2. Whatever the intentions of the legislature, few prisoners ended up in single cells. The prison act encouraged the practice "as far as conditions and the welfare of the prisoners demand," but this loophole proved sufficiently wide for administrators to avoid the costs (*Act*, sec. 15). Instead, military-style barracks predominated, as they do today for minimum-security inmates.

103. PBM, March 20, 1911; June 10, 1911; September 25, 1911; February 9, 1912. Prison Commission, *Annual Report* (1911), 15–16. At Rusk prison, some convicts may have earned the informal right to receive conjugal visits, but this practice also ended once Cabell and the commissioners caught word of it (PBM, October 10, 1911).

104. Texas, An Act Establishing a Prison System (1910), secs. 42, 39. Commissioners also had the authority to confiscate money from prisoners' per diem accounts to punish rule violations.

105. "The Skeleton in the Closet," *Prison Bulletin* 1, no. 5 (February 1, 1898); Penitentiary Investigating Committee, *Report* (1910), 19.

106. Lucko, "Texas Prison Reform During the Oscar Branch Colquitt Administration," 16.

107. MacCorkle, "The Pardoning Power in Texas," 225; Prison Commission, *Annual Report* (1911), 37. One indicator that costs loomed large in pardon decisions

was that Governor Colquitt sometimes granted pardons but made them effective only after the fall harvest. See William Harmon [Ferris?] to Oscar B. Colquitt, December 17, 1911, Colquitt Records, box 301–331.

108. Peter Donnell to Oscar B. Colquitt and the Board of Pardon Advisors, [September 1914?], Colquitt Records, box 301–337; Pedro E. Rodriguez to Ben E. Cabell, July 16, 1912, Colquitt Records, box 301–332.

109. Louis Greenberg to Henry Cohen, August 26, 1916, Cohen Papers, box 3M296; Peter Donnell to Oscar B. Colquitt and the Board of Pardon Advisors, [September 1914?], Colquitt Records, box 301–337; Pedro E. Rodriguez to Ben E. Cabell, July 16, 1912, Colquitt Records, box 301–332, July 11–30, 1912 folder.

110. Hudspeth, *Minority Report*, 22; Peter Donnell to Oscar B. Colquitt and the Board of Pardon Advisors, [September 1914?], Colquitt Records, box 301–337.

111. John McGill to Oscar B. Colquitt, December 4, 1911, Colquitt Records, box 301–331; Samuel Kaufman to Henry Cohen, December 22, 1914, Cohen Papers, box 3M296. Despite his troubles, Kaufman eventually received his pardon, thanks perhaps to bribery. See Samuel Kaufman to Henry Cohen, March 28, 1915, Cohen Papers, box 3M296.

112. Unnamed prisoner to Governor O. B. Colquitt, November 24, 1911, Colquitt Records, box 301–331; Convict petition to Governor O. B. Colquitt, December 29, 1911, Colquitt Records, box 301–331; Clemens prisoners to Oscar B. Colquitt, November 18, 1911, Colquitt Records, box 301–331; Convict petition to Governor O. B. Colquitt, December 29, 1911, Colquitt Records, box 301–331.

113. Reynolds, "The Administration of the Texas Prison System," 94; Wilkinson, *Trans-Cedar Lynching and the Texas Penitentiary*, 148.

114. Prison Commission, *Annual Report* (1911), 32; Ben E. Cabell to Oscar B. Colquitt, November 6, 1911, Colquitt Records, box 301–331; Anonymous prisoner to Governor O. B. Colquitt, November 24, 1911, Colquitt Records, box 301–331.

115. Cabell, *Present Penitentiary Situation in Texas*, 16; Texas State Legislature, Penitentiary Investigating Committee, *Report* (1910), 17; Texas State Legislature, Penitentiary Investigating Committee, *Report and Findings* (1913), 8, 13. See also Robert W. Brahan to J. T. Bowman, December 29, 1911, Colquitt Records, box 301–331.

116. PBM, March 20, 1911; Tom Finty, "Troubles of the Texas State Prisons," *The Delinquent* 4, no. 1 (1914): 6; Anonymous prisoner to Governor O. B. Colquitt, November 24, 1911, Colquitt Records, box 301–331. In 1913, the attorney general finalized the board's suspension by declaring per diem pay unconstitutional. See "Payment of Wages to Prisoners," unpublished Prison Survey article, [1924?], "Prisons, Misc.," CAH-VF. Even the notorious Ward, Dewey, and Company had reportedly paid its convict field hands $2 a month. See "Our State Penitentiary," *Galveston Daily News*, May 4, 1873.

117. Texas, An act conferring upon the Board of Prison Commissioners authority to issue paroles to meritorious convicts (March 11, 1911), in Gammel, *Laws of Texas*, 15:64–67. The legislature also passed a suspended sentencing law in the same session (Gammel, *Laws of Texas*, 15:67), but it was soon overturned by the courts. Oscar Colquitt, *First Message of the Governor to the 33rd Legislature*, January 16, 1913 (Austin, Tex.: Von Boeckmann-Jones, 1913).

118. J. T. Campbell to E. O. Boggs, July 11, 1912, Colquitt Records, box 301–332; PBM, August 18, 1911. By comparison, lessees were required to pay $20 a month for healthy white field hands in 1911, up to $31 for blacks. PBM, August 18, 1911; Prison Commission, "Contract Farms," n.d., Colquitt Records, box 301–332, June 19–25, 1912 folder.

119. Ben E. Cabell to Oscar B. Colquitt, November 6, 1911, Colquitt Records, box 301–331; Prison Commission, *Annual Report* (1911), 8; Penitentiary Investigating Committee, *Report and Findings* (1913), 29.

120. Penitentiary Investigating Committee, *Report and Findings* (1913), 29; Walker, *Penology for Profit*, 113.

121. Escape record, TDCJ Records, box 1998/038–269; Prison Commission, "Escape Report," October 15, 1912, Colquitt Papers, box 301–332. There are some discrepancies in escape numbers. Some reports count only inmates who stay out more than twenty-four hours as escapees; others tally every run. In both cases, the numbers headed upward after abolition.

122. Posy L. Griffith to Governor O. B. Colquitt and the people of Texas, June 26, 1912, Colquitt Records, box 301–332. Griffith's taunting public letter inspired quick rejoinders from the prison commissioners and the Bonus farm management. See A. B. Kyle to *Houston Chronicle*, July 8, 1912, Colquitt Records, box 301–332; S. R. Vaughn to M. E. Foster, editor, *Houston Chronicle*, July 8, 1912, Colquitt Records, box 301–332.

123. Finty, "Troubles of the Texas State Prisons," 9.

124. PBM, February 2, 1911, February 4, 1911, box 1998/038–2.

125. PBM, February 14, 1911, March 13, 1911, March 16, 1911, March 29, 1911, July 21, 1911, May 7, 1911, May 11, 1911, October 7, 1911, and January 1, 1913. Prison Commission, *Annual Report* (1911), 62; Penitentiary Investigating Committee, *Report and Findings* (1913), 14.

126. Prison Commission, *Annual Report* (1911), 8; Penitentiary Investigating Committee, *Report and Findings* (1913), 29; Texas State Legislature, Joint Penitentiary Affairs Committee, *Testimony* (1921), vol. 3, 295.

127. "19 Escaped Convicts Retaken After Chase of 24 Hours Near Sugarland; Two Still Missing," *Houston Chronicle*, August 19, 1912; John H. Regan, "Addison Tells Convicts Repetition of Mutiny Will Mean Restoration of Bat," *Houston Chronicle*, August 20, 1912.

128. PBM, April 20, 1912; April 2, 1912. Hoping to calm tempers among employees, the commission also solicited farm managers' opinions on the best replacement punishments for the bat. Some replied curtly that only a "return to the strap" would restore order, but others offered a panoply of torments they thought would do the trick, from extended hours in the dark cell, to "hobble and ankle chain[s]," to "hanging by wrists with cuffs in chains." R. H. Cabiness, the manager at Goree, favored "depriving women of certain privileges, such as wearing citizen's clothes, playing ball, cards, dominoes, checkers." And "if this is ineffective," he favored "cutting hair close to scalp" (PBM, May 8, 1912).

129. Convict petition to Governor O. B. Colquitt, December 29, 1911, Colquitt Records, box 301–331; PBM, December 27, 1911. See also Clemens prisoners to Oscar B. Colquitt, November 18, 1911, Colquitt Records, box 301–331; Ben E. Cabell to Oscar B. Colquitt, November 25, 1911, Colquitt Records, box 301–331; Ben E. Cabell to J. T. Bowman, November 3, 1911, Colquitt Records, box 301–331.

130. Prison Commission, *Annual Report* (1911), 7.

131. See PBM, October 10, 1911; Robert Goodfellow to Ben E. Cabell, September 27, 1911, Colquitt Records, box 301–331; Fulsom, *Prison Stories: The Old Days*.

132. Finty, "Troubles of the Texas State Prisons," 9; Briggs, *Texas Penitentiary*, 20; Texas, Penitentiary Investigating Committee, *Report and Findings* (1913), 38; Prison Commission, *Annual Report* (1911), 8; PBM, September 6, 1912; September 7, 1912. See also Lucko, "Texas Prison Reform During the Oscar Branch Colquitt Administration," 19.

133. Ben E. Cabell's recommendations to the Board of Prison Commissioners, December 4, 1911, Colquitt Records, box 301–331.

134. Finty, "Troubles of the Texas State Prisons," 7; PBM, August 21, 1912; Gordon Lightfoot to K. F. Cunningham, June 17, 1912, Colquitt Records, box 301–332;

T. C. Blakely to Ben E. Cabell, March 15, 1913, Colquitt Records, box 301–334; Testimony of W. T. Eldridge and W. M. Brooks, in Texas, Penitentiary Investigating Committee, *Report and Findings* (1913), 225, 318; John H. Regan, "Addison Tells Convicts Repetition of Mutiny Will Mean Restoration of Bat," *Houston Chronicle*, August 20, 1912.

135. Robert W. Brahan to Oscar B. Colquitt, August 22, 1912, Colquitt Records, box 301–332. See also Texas, Penitentiary Investigating Committee, *Report and Findings* (1913), 225; Adelia A. Dunovant, *Who Is W. T. Eldridge?* (Houston, Tex.: n.p., 1913).

136. Nowlin, "Political History of the Texas Prison System," 112; Texas State Legislature, Penitentiary Investigating Committee, *Report and Findings* (1913), 6, 1. See also Miller, "Building a Progressive Coalition in Texas"; Ben E. Cabell's recommendations to the Board of Prison Commissioners, December 4, 1911, Colquitt Records, box 301–331.

137. Texas State Legislature, Penitentiary Investigating Committee, *Report and Findings* (1913), 1–2, 13, 15–16; Finty, "Troubles of the Texas State Prisons," 8.

138. Texas State Legislature, Penitentiary Investigating Committee, *Report and Findings* (1913), 5, 32, 25, 36.

139. Ibid., 27, 22–23, 27. Prison officers also defended the whipping of white prisoners. See testimony of Dr. S. B. Maxey in Texas State Legislature, Senate Committee Investigating the Affairs of the Prison System, *Testimony* (1915), file 4–2/1549c, TSLAC, 8.

140. Foley, *White Scourge*, 6. See also Edward Everett Davis, *The White Scourge* (San Antonio, Tex.: The Naylor Company, 1940), ix–x. On the stricter racialization of Mexican immigrants in the early twentieth century, see Montejano, *Anglos and Mexicans in the Making of Texas*.

141. Penitentiary Investigating Committee, *Report and Findings* (1913), 29.

142. Prison Commission, *Annual Report* (1911), 9; Texas, Senate Penitentiary Investigating Committee, *Complete Report* (1915), 17–19; Penitentiary Investigating Committee, *Report and Findings* (1913), 13. Rusk would close as a prison in 1917, only to be opened two years later as a hospital for the criminally insane. The state razed the ironworks in 1931. See Allen, "The Iron Men: An Historical Review of the East Texas Penitentiary"; Birmingham, "An Historical Account of the East Texas Prison at Rusk"; and Lucko, "Prison Farms, Walls, and Society," chap. 7.

143. Shortly after Colquitt vetoed the 1913 reorganization package, Texas's attorney general issued rulings that banned every sort of payment to prisoners, from per diem to overtime pay. Since many lessees had customarily paid token wages on Sundays, as had many slave owners before them, this meant that state convicts would now toil for less than they had under contract. Ben E. Cabell to Oscar B. Colquitt, November 6, 1911, Colquitt Records, box 301–331; PBM, October 7, 1911, August 25, 1913, September 30, 1913. On Sunday payments by lessees, see Texas State Legislature, Penitentiary Investigating Committee, *Report* (1910), 13–14. On antebellum restrictions on Sunday labor for slaves, see Campbell, *An Empire for Slavery*, 121. Washing his hands of prison matters, Governor Colquitt ordered all prisoner correspondence intercepted and scrutinized before it reached his desk. Lucko, "Texas Prison Reform During the Oscar Branch Colquitt Administration," 29.

144. PBM, June 27, 1913, February 9, 1912. Penitentiary Investigating Committee, *Report* (1910), 15; Cabell, *Present Penitentiary Situation in Texas*, 7.

145. PBM, January 27, 1911, box 1998/038–2; Finty, "Troubles of the Texas State Prisons," 4; Ben E. Cabell to J. T. Bowman, July 17, 1912, Colquitt Records, box 301–332.

146. PBM, August 21, 1912; March 16, 1912. Oscar B. Colquitt to Board of Prison

Commissioners, March 23, 1912, in PBM, March 25, 1912; Ben E. Cabell to J. T. Bowman, July 17, 1912, Colquitt Records, box 301–332. In order to build consensus on the Board, Colquitt and Cabell pushed for "suspending this mode of punishment" rather than banning it outright. "If it is found after trial that it cannot be dispensed with successfully by substituting other methods of discipline," the governor assured Tittle and Brahan, "then its use can be resumed." Whipping was subsequently reinstated, then banned again decades later. Texas Prison Board, *Annual Report* (1941), 7.

Besides dark celling, prison officials were authorized to use chaining, in which recalcitrant inmates were cuffed and hoisted up toward the ceiling—a time-tried technique that would make a comeback a century later in Afghanistan and Abu Ghraib. See Tim Golden, "In U.S. Report, Brutal Details of Two Afghan Inmates' Deaths," *New York Times*, May 20, 2005, www.nytimes.com/2005/05/20/international/asia/2; Mark Danner, *Torture and Truth: America, Abu Ghraib, and the War on Terror* (New York: New York Review Books, 2004).

147. PBM, August 21, 1912.
148. Penitentiary Investigating Committee, *Report and Findings* (1913), 37; PBM, July 13, 1911; May 8, 1912; September 6, 1912. See also Robert W. Brahan to Oscar B. Colquitt, August 22, 1912, Colquitt Records, box 301–332; "Torture in Texas," unidentified newspaper clippings, ca. 1912, Colquitt Records, box 301–332, August 9–23, 1912 folder.
149. Finty, "Troubles of the Texas State Prisons," 2; PBM, September 19, 1913. According to Finty, two guards were arrested and charged with negligent homicide for the mass suffocation but were later acquitted. No high-level officials lost their posts over the incident. See also Nowlin, "Political History of the Texas Prison System," 150.
150. Richard Barry, "Next Step in Prison Reform," *Century* 87 (March 1914): 746–51; Bill Mills, *Twenty-Five Years Behind Prison Bars* (Giddings, Tex.: Wilson's Selective Productions, 1938), 31; Texas, Senate Penitentiary Investigating Committee, *Testimony* (1915).
151. During a severe storm in 1899, for example, a building collapsed on the Clemens lease farm, killing nineteen convicts. Texas State Penitentiaries, *Biennial Report* (1900), 12.
152. W. O. Murray to Oscar B. Colquitt, September 8, 1914, Colquitt Records, box 301–337; Texas State Legislature, Senate Penitentiary Investigating Committee, *Complete Report* (1915), 11.
153. W. O. Murray to Oscar B. Colquitt, September 8, 1914, Colquitt Records, box 301–337.
154. Ben E. Cabell to Henry Cohen, September 5, 1913, Cohen Papers, box 3M296.

## 5: THE PENAL COLONY THAT WASN'T

1. Minnie Fisher Cunningham to Jane McCallum, November 1924, in Judith N. McArthur and Harold L. Smith, *Minnie Fisher Cunningham: A Suffragist's Life in Politics* (New York: Oxford University Press, 2003), 121.
2. Lomax and Lomax, *Negro Folk Songs as Sung by Lead Belly*, xi; Gordon Parks, "A Last Visit to Leadbelly," *New York*, May 10, 1976, 68; Wolfe and Lornell, *The Life and Legend of Leadbelly*, 75–76. Ledbetter started at the Shaw share farm in northeast Texas, then got transferred to Imperial.
3. Lomax and Lomax, *Negro Folk Songs as Sung by Lead Belly*, 15–16; Wolfe and Lornell, *The Life and Legend of Leadbelly*, 6, 8, 74–75. Lomax transcribed Leadbelly's remarks in dialect but made no such notations when recording his own Texas drawl or that of other professional-class whites.

4. Lomax and Lomax, *Negro Folk Songs as Sung by Lead Belly*, 16.
5. Ibid., 8, 16; Parks, "Last Visit to Leadbelly," 68.
6. Wolfe and Lornell, *The Life and Legend of Leadbelly*, 99, 120.
7. Parks, "Last Visit to Leadbelly," 66.
8. Minnie Fisher Cunningham to Mrs. T. A. Coleman, November 8, 1918, cited in Paul Lucko, "The Next Big Job: Women Prison Reformers in Texas, 1918–1930," in *Women and Texas History; Selected Essays*, eds. Fane Downs and Nancy Baker Jones (Austin: Texas State Historical Association, 1993), 72; Letter from the presidents of the Texas League of Women Voters, State Federation of Women's Clubs, and Texas Congress of Mothers to Fellow Citizens, [1921?], Ring Papers, box 2G445, form letters folder; Texas, Penitentiary Investigating Committee, *Report* (1921), 88.
9. Senate Penitentiary Investigating Committee, *Complete Report* (1915); Lomax and Lomax, *Negro Folk Songs as Sung by Lead Belly*, 17.
10. Prison Commission, *Annual Report* (1921), 8; Carrie Weaver Smith, "A Women's Reformatory for Women," unpublished speech, 1921, Ring Papers, box 2G445, Correspondence folder.
11. Smith, "A Women's Reformatory for Women"; Texas, An Act Establishing a Prison System (1910), sec. 36; Gregory, "Persistence and Irony," 86–89. Texas's first two matrons were hired with their husbands as well, but in their case the men came on as guards with a lower salary.
12. Smith, "A Women's Reformatory for Women."
13. Testimony of Ethel Dawson, Effie Polk, and Rosa Lee Greer, in Texas, Joint Penitentiary Affairs Committee, *Testimony* (1921), vol. 3, Goree.
14. Smith, "A Women's Reformatory for Women."
15. On the juvenile court campaign, see: Jacquelyn McElhaney, "Pauline Periwinkle: Prodding Dallas into the Progressive Era," in Downs and Jones, *Women and Texas History*, 42–56; Anthony M. Platt, *The Child Savers: The Invention of Delinquency*, 2nd ed. (Chicago: University of Chicago Press, 1977).

On the girls' school, see *Handbook of Texas Online*, s.v. "Gainesville State School for Girls," http://www.tsha.utexas.edu/handbook/online/articles/GG/jjg1.html. The facility was converted to a maximum-security juvenile prison for boys in 1988. Texas Youth Commission, "Gainesville State School," http://www.tyc.state.tx.us/programs/gainesville/index.html. On the effort by African American women to establish a separate institution for black girls, see Ruthe Winegarten, Janet G. Humphrey, and Frieda Werden, *Black Texas Women: 150 Years of Trial and Triumph* (Austin: University of Texas Press, 1995), chap. 9; Ruthe Winegarten, *Black Texas Women: A Sourcebook: Documents, Biographies, Timeline* (Austin: University of Texas Press, 1996), 141–44.
16. Suzanne Lebsock, "Women and American Politics, 1880–1920," in *Women, Politics, and Change*, eds. Louise A. Tilly and Patricia Gurin (New York: Russell Sage, 1990), 32.
17. Judith N. McArthur, *Creating the New Woman: The Rise of Southern Women's Progressive Culture in Texas, 1893–1918* (Urbana: University of Illinois Press, 1998), 140; Lucko, "Women and Texas History," 72; Mrs. R. C. Talbot Perkins to Elizabeth Ring, March 8, 1921, Ring Papers, box 2G445, Correspondence folder. See also Elizabeth Hayes Turner, *Women, Culture, and Community: Religion and Reform in Galveston, 1880–1920* (New York: Oxford University Press, 1997); Stella L. Christian, *The History of the Texas Federation of Women's Clubs* (Houston: Texas Federation of Women's Clubs, 1919).
18. Letter from the presidents of the Texas League of Women Voters, the Federation of Women's Clubs, and the Texas Congress of Mothers to Governor Hobby, May 25, 1920, Ring Papers, box 2G445, Form Letters; Letter from the presidents of the Texas League of Women Voters, State Federation of Women's Clubs, and Texas

Congress of Mothers to Fellow Citizens, [1921?]; "Chapter on Texas Prison Reform Is Organized Here," *Houston Post*, October 18, 1921, n.p., Ring Papers, box 2G447, clippings folder. See also E. Stagg Whitin, *Penal Servitude* (New York: National Committee on Prison Labor, 1912); Julia Kippen Jaffray and George Gordon Battle, *The Prison and the Prisoner: A Symposium* (Boston: Little, Brown & Co., 1917); *How Human Waste Is Being Saved*, Prison Leaflets, 65 (New York: National CPPL, 1922).

19. David B. Alpert, "Rabbi Henry Cohen of Galveston, A 1931 Account," *Western States Jewish History* 26, no. 4 (1994): 293; R. H. Baker to Lee Simmons, November 28, 1927, Moody Records, box 41; Executive Committee Minutes of the Texas Division of the CPPL, March 31, 1923, Cohen Papers, box 3M303, Prison Records, 1923 Labor folder; McArthur and Smith, *Minnie Fisher Cunningham*, 57; McArthur, *Creating the New Woman*, 131–32. See also Elizabeth Speer to Robert H. Baker, August 10, 1927, Cohen Papers, box 3M297; W. M. Odell to Senator McFarlane, February 12, 1929, Cohen Papers, box 3M299; Lucko, "Women and Texas History"; Paul M. Lucko, "A Missed Opportunity: Texas Prison Reform During the Dan Moody Administration, 1927–1931," *Southwestern Historical Quarterly* 96, no. 1 (1992): 27–52.

20. R. H. Baker, Walter Bremond, and Elizabeth Speer to potential CPPL donors, [1923?], Ring Papers, box 2G445, Correspondence folder; Appeal for survey funding from Texas Women's Organizations to the Legislature, [1923?], Ring Papers, box 2G445, Correspondence folder; J. E. Pearce, "History of Efforts at Reorganizing and Relocating the Penitentiary System of Texas" (Austin, Tex.: CPPL, 1924), Ring Papers, box 2G445, Correspondence folder.

21. CPPL, *A Summary of the Texas Prison Survey* (San Antonio, Tex.: Globe Publishing Co., 1924), 1:9, 11, 59–60; "Urge Re-Location of Texas Prisons Under Colony Plan," [1924?], unidentified newspaper clipping, "Prisons, pre-1975," CAH-VF.

22. CPPL, *Texas Prison Survey* (1924), 1:12, 30–40, 13, 61–63, 24–25, 27; "Payment of Wages to Prisoners," unpublished article, [1924?], 3, "Prisons, Misc.," CAH-VF.

23. Elizabeth Speer, CPPL press release, March 8, 1925, Ring Papers, box 2G445, Correspondence folder; CPPL, *Texas Prison Survey* (1924), 1:13–17. Moving the prison system away from Huntsville had first been proposed during Reconstruction. Message of Governor Edmund J. Davis, January 10, 1871. After the failures of the 1910–1913 reforms, Progressives returned to the idea. See Elmer Scott to Henry Cohen, October 28, 1918, Cohen Papers, box 3M296, Prison correspondence, 1916–1920.

24. Kate Friend to Elizabeth Ring, September 12, 1921, Ring Papers, box 2G445, Correspondence folder.

25. Pat M. Neff, *Battles of the Peace* (Fort Worth, Tex.: Pioneer Publishing Company, 1925), 38–39, 47, 40.

26. Neff, *Battles of the Peace*, 39, 169; "Our New Governor Abolishes the Pardon Board," *Home and State*, April 1, 1921, Pat Neff, CAH-VF; MacCorkle, "The Pardoning Power in Texas," 225. Texas's prison population increased by 40 percent during Neff's governorship, from 2,561 to 3,580. Prison Commission, *Annual Report* (1921), 48; Prison Commission, *Annual Report* (1924), 57.

27. Lomax and Lomax, *Negro Folk Songs as Sung by Lead Belly*, 20–22; Wolfe and Lornell, *The Life and Legend of Leadbelly*, 77–80.

28. Lomax and Lomax, *Negro Folk Songs as Sung by Lead Belly*, 21–22, 227; Neff, *Battles of the Peace*, 177. Leadbelly was not the first to broker art into a release ticket. In 1911, a Texas prisoner convicted of forgery managed to win over Oscar Colquitt with a poem. See "Poem Brings His Liberty," *Los Angeles Times*, November 26, 1911, 14.

29. Marquart, Ekland-Olson, and Sorensen, *The Rope, the Chair, and the Needle*, 197–201; Neff, *Battles of the Peace*, 43.

30. Marquart, Ekland-Olson, and Sorensen, *The Rope, the Chair, and the Needle*, 12, 200; Neff, *Battles of the Peace*, 37; "Texas Death Chair Snuffs Out Five Lives," *Austin Statesman*, February 8, 1924, 1.

31. Neff, *Battles of the Peace*, 176.

32. "Texas Death Chair Snuffs Out Five Lives." Neff approved a total of thirteen men for execution in 1924, twelve of them black, one Hispanic. Marquart, Ekland-Olson, and Sorensen, *The Rope, the Chair, and the Needle*, 201.

33. Neff, *Battles of the Peace*, 43.

34. William Joseph Simmons, "The Ku Klux Klan: Yesterday, Today, and Forever" (Atlanta, Ga.: KKK, 1924), KKK Papers, box 2–23/927, folder 1; Charles C. Alexander, *The Ku Klux Klan in the Southwest* (Norman: University of Oklahoma Press, 1995), 36–39, 79, 109; KKK membership card, Wallace Papers, box 2–23/1023, KKK clippings folder. On the War Department hangings after the Houston mutiny, see Robert Haynes, *A Night of Violence: The Houston Mutiny of 1917* (Baton Rouge: Louisiana State University Press, 1976).

35. "Evil-Doers Are Warned by Banners," *Austin American*, September 3, 1921; "Austin Ku Klux Klan in Big Parade: Thousands See White Robed Figures on Congress Ave.," *Austin American*, September 3, 1921, in Ku Klux Klan Scrapbook, CAH (hereafter KKK Scrapbook).

36. Simmons, "The Ku Klux Klan"; Campbell, *Gone to Texas*, 367. See also Nancy MacLean, *Behind the Mask of Chivalry: The Making of the Ku Klux Klan in a Georgia Town* (New York: Oxford University Press, 1994).

37. Alexander, *The Ku Klux Klan in the Southwest*, 127, 121.

38. Simmons, "The Ku Klux Klan"; W. C. Wright, "The Need of the Ku Klux Klan in America" (Department of Education, Knights of the KKK, Realm of Texas, March 31, 1924), Wallace Papers, box 2–23/1023, KKK clippings folder.

39. Norman D. Brown, *Hood, Bonnet, and Little Brown Jug: Texas Politics, 1921–1928* (College Station: Texas A&M University Press, 1984), 57; "Ku Klux Klan Speaker Heard by Audience of 5,000 Here; He Tells of Purposes of the Organization," *Temple Daily Telegram*, August 15, 1921, KKK Scrapbook.

40. Brown, *Hood, Bonnet, and Little Brown Jug*, 67–69; Campbell, *Gone to Texas*, 369–70.

41. Wright, "The Need of the Ku Klux Klan in America"; "The Klan in Texas," *The Survey*, April 1, 1922, in KKK Scrapbook; Alexander, *The Ku Klux Klan in the Southwest*, 77; "Evil-Doers Are Warned by Banners," *Austin American*, September 3, 1921.

42. Neff, *Battles of the Peace*, 44, 38.

43. Ibid., 40; Brown, *Hood, Bonnet, and Little Brown Jug*, 13, 70.

44. Elizabeth Speer to supporters, March 21, 1925, Cohen Papers, box 3M296; Statement of the Texas CPPL to Supporters, June 6, 1925, Ring Papers, box 2G445, Correspondence folder; Brown, *Hood, Bonnet, and Little Brown Jug*, 253; Hugh Nugent Fitzgerald, "Texas Discards Archaic System in Its Prisons," *Austin American*, March 19, 1925; Reynolds, "The Administration of the Texas Prison System," 119–22; "Private Parties Back Moody's $10,000,000 Penitentiary Law," *Ferguson Forum*, August 26, 1926.

45. McArthur and Smith, *Minnie Fisher Cunningham*, 121; Statement of the Texas Committee on Prisons and Prison Labor to Supporters, June 6, 1925, Ring Papers, box 2G445, Correspondence folder.

46. R. H. Baker and Elizabeth Speer to friends and co-workers, July 15, 1926; CPPL, *Annual Report* (1926) and *Annual Report* (1927), Ring Papers, box 2G448, folder 3, broadsides; Brown, *Hood, Bonnet, and Little Brown Jug*, 304, 302; Jacquelyn Dowd Hall, *Revolt Against Chivalry: Jessie Daniel Ames and the Women's Campaign Against Lynching*, rev. ed. (New York: Columbia University Press, 1993), 113–14.

47. CPPL, Legislative Program, June 1, 1926, Ring Papers, box 2G445, Correspon-

dence folder; R. H. Baker and Elizabeth Speer to friends and co-workers, July 15, 1926; CPPL, "Constitutional Amendment," brochure, 1926, Ring Papers, box 2G447, broadsides folder; Hall, *Revolt Against Chivalry*, 115; Brown, *Hood, Bonnet, and Little Brown Jug*, 307, 311–12, 304.

48. Moody clinched the Democratic nomination in an August runoff and marched unimpeded to the Governor's Mansion in the general election. Brown, *Hood, Bonnet, and Little Brown Jug*, 308, 316, 315, 326, 331, 337.

49. Brown, *Hood, Bonnet, and Little Brown Jug*, 327, 338.

50. Ibid., 340–41.

51. Thomas Mott Osborne, "New Methods at Sing Sing Prison," *Review of Reviews* 52 (October 1915): 449–56, excerpted in Bacon, *Prison Reform*, 129; Thomas Mott Osborne, "The Prison of the Future," in Bacon, *Prison Reform*, 305–9.

52. Ellen F. Fitzpatrick, *Endless Crusade: Women Social Scientists and Progressive Reform* (New York: Oxford University Press, 1990), 93–97; Freedman, *Their Sisters' Keepers*, 131–33.

53. Freedman, *Their Sisters' Keepers*, 110.

54. Rafter, *Partial Justice*, 70–71.

55. Freedman, *Their Sisters' Keepers*, 118. See Clara Jean Weldensall, *The Mentality of Criminal Women* (Baltimore: Warwick and York, 1916).

56. Freedman, *Their Sisters' Keepers*, 117; Rafter, *Partial Justice*, 69.

57. Thomas Mott Osborne, *Within Prison Walls; Being a Narrative of Personal Experiences During a Week of Voluntary Confinement in the State Prison at Auburn, New York* (Montclair, N.J.: Patterson Smith, 1914), 16. See also Frank Tannenbaum, *Osborne of Sing Sing* (Chapel Hill: University of North Carolina Press, 1933).

58. Osborne, *Within Prison Walls*, 12, 18–19.

59. Ibid., 27, 24, 35, 240.

60. Thomas Mott Osborne, *Society and Prisons* (New Haven, Conn.: Yale University Press, 1916), 126–27; Osborne, *Within Prison Walls*, 245, 241.

61. Osborne, dedication to *Within Prison Walls*; Denis Brian, *The Inside Story of a Notorious Prison: Sing Sing* (Amherst, N.Y.: Prometheus Books, 2005), 88; Osborne, "New Methods at Sing Sing Prison," 131. "We should relax the iron discipline and substitute a system that will be fair to all men," he argued, "a limited form of freedom" based on trust and opportunity rather than surveillance and repression (134).

62. Rebecca Mary McLennan, "Citizens and Criminals: The Rise of the American Carceral State, 1890–1935" (PhD diss., Columbia University, 1999), 301–3, 333–36, 277, 318–21, 328, 330, 307; Max Eastman, "Riot and Reform at Sing Sing," *Masses* 6 (June 1915): 5–6, reprinted in Bacon, *Prison Reform*. Osborne's plan for a self-governing prison was not entirely new. Katherine Bement Davis had set up a democratic council in the honor camp at Beford Hills, and during the 1913 prison investigation, Osborne and other commissioners had been impressed with self-government efforts at Great Meadow Prison for young first offenders. See Thomas Mott Osborne, George W. Kirchwey, and E. Stagg Whitin, "Preliminary Report" (Albany: Commission on Prison Reform of the State of New York, 1914), 18–20, 52. See also Rebecca M. McLennan, *The Crisis of Imprisonment: Protest, Politics, and the Making of the American Penal State, 1776–1941* (New York: Cambridge University Press, 2008).

63. Beaumont and Tocqueville, *On the Penitentiary System*, 162; "Sing Sing Prison," in Bacon, *Prison Reform*, 110; Osborne, Kirchwey, and Whitin, "Preliminary Report," 8–11; McLennan, "Citizens and Criminals," 353; Osborne, "New Methods at Sing Sing Prison," 134. Osborne opposed capital punishment and symbolically walked out of Sing Sing on electrocution nights. Banner, *Death Penalty*, 221.

64. Thomas Mott Osborne, "Prison Efficiency"; National CPPL, "Suggestions for Sermon Material," leaflet; F. M. White, "The True Sing Sing," *Outlook* 112 (January 5,

1916): 42–47, excerpted in Bacon, *Prison Reform*, 135, 144–45, 125; McLennan, "Citizens and Criminals," 360–65, 412–14, 307, 353–54.

65. McLennan, "Citizens and Criminals," 399–406. Osborne's most prominent successor, Lewis Lawes, became a noted penologist in his own right but never embraced Osborne's radicalism. Lewis E. Lawes, *Twenty Thousand Years in Sing Sing* (New York: Ray Long & Richard R. Smith, 1932).

66. Rafter, *Partial Justice*, 79–80; Freedman, *Their Sisters' Keepers*, 140–41; Fitzpatrick, *Endless Crusade*, 121, 128.

67. See Michael E. McGerr, *A Fierce Discontent: The Rise and Fall of the Progressive Movement in America, 1870–1920* (New York: Free Press, 2003).

68. Lane, *Murder in America*, 239–40; David E. Ruth, *Inventing the Public Enemy: The Gangster in American Culture, 1918–1934* (Chicago: University of Chicago Press, 1996), 11, 24, 35, 151.

69. Lane, *Murder in America*, 214; McKelvey, *American Prisons*, 267; Banner, *Death Penalty*, 223, 230; Rafter, *Partial Justice*, 56. New York's Mutual Welfare Leagues were abolished after the 1929 rioting.

70. Rothman, *Conscience and Convenience*, chap. 4; George Wickersham et al., "Report on Penal Institutions, Probation, and Parole" (Washington, D.C.: National Commission on Law Observance and Enforcement, 1931), 5, 16, 170. To a remarkable extent, the Wickersham Commission reached the same conclusion that Wines and Dwight had sixty years previously.

71. "Something New in Prison Life Here," *Echo*, November 1928, 2; Excerpts from Governor Moody's message to the 40th Legislature, February 16, 1927, Ring Papers, box 2G445, Correspondence folder; Prison Board, Minutes, June 15, 1927, Cohen Papers, box 3M303. As authorized by the 1926 constitutional amendment, the legislature voted to disband the Board of Prison Commissioners and replace it with the Prison Board in spring 1927. In 1909, the legislature had devised the tripartite commissioner structure to remedy the faults of the previous system, only to return to the old model (an unpaid board supervising a single general manager) eighteen years later. Moody appointed CPPL officers to four of the board's six seats. He also made two conservative appointments, Lee Simmons and A. H. Carrigan, both of whom opposed the most ambitious CPPL reforms.

72. "R. H. Baker Appointed to Board of Prison Commissioners," *Dallas Morning News*, January 27, 1927, n.p., CAH-VF, Dan Moody; R. H. Baker to Dan Moody, May 28, 1927, Moody Records, box 41. Prison records suggest that Baker had once leased convicts. See PBM, October 14, 1903, box 1998/038–1. On Speer's work as executive secretary, see W. M. Odell to Senator McFarlane, February 12, 1929, Cohen Papers, box 3M299; PBM, May 7, 1928, box 1998/038–8. Conservative legislators and farm managers regularly complained that Speer had too much power in the prison system and that Baker served as her proxy. That she had her own secretary and regular access to a state car with a trusty driver suggests her role was more executive than secretarial.

73. Elizabeth Speer to supporters, June 23, 1927, Cohen Papers, box 3M296; Texas CPPL, *Annual Report* (1927), Ring Papers, box 2G448, folder 3, broadsides; W. M. Odell to George B. Dealey, June 22, 1928, Moody Records, box 41; Texas Prison Board, Rules and Regulations (1927), Ring Papers, box 2G448, folder 2, broadsides; W. M. Odell to Senator McFarlane, February 12, 1929, Cohen Papers, box 3M299; "Far-Reaching Prison Reform Program Planned for Texas," *Galveston Tribune*, December 31, 1927, n.p., Cohen Papers, box 3M313, 1925–1927 file.

74. W. M. Odell to George B. Dealey, June 22, 1928, Moody Records, box 41; Texas Prison Board, *Annual Report* (1928).

75. Eugene Simons to Henry Cohen, September 16, 1928, Cohen Papers, box 3M298; "Inmates Organize Prison Welfare League," *Echo*, November 1928, 1–2; "What

the Welfare League Is Doing," *Echo*, December 1928, 1, 12; "Texas Prison Welfare League," *Echo*, April 1929, 2–3; "League One Year Old," *Echo*, September 1929, 1, 8; John Stratford to Dan Moody, October 4, 1928, Moody Records, box 41; "Inmates Organize Prison Welfare League," *Echo*, November 1928, 1–2. See also Charlotte A. Teagle, *History of Welfare Activities of the Texas Prison Board, 1927–1940* (Huntsville: Texas Prison Board, Welfare Committee, 1941), 155–57.

76. "Condemned Men See Show Thanksgiving," *Echo*, December 1928, 1; "Thanksgiving Day Celebrated at Huntsville Prison," [1928?], Cohen Papers, box 3M299; Inmate to Editor, *Houston Post-Dispatch*, November 30, 1928, Cohen Papers, box 3M299; "Something New in Prison Life Here," *Echo*, November 1928, 2. Simons is not listed as the author of this article, but its contents coincide with letters he wrote to Henry Cohen.

77. "Prison Paper Published by Welfare League," *Echo*, November 1928, 1–2; "Ye Editor of Ye *Echo* in Ye Gaol," *Echo*, November 1928, 4.

78. "Plain Hokum," *Echo*, November 1928, 3; "Aprovechad El Tiempo," *Echo*, December 1928, 3. Poetry published in the *Echo* also put forward more critical points of view. See "Please Forget," *Echo*, December 1928, 5.

79. Eugene Simons to Henry Cohen, September 16, 1928, Cohen Papers, box 3M298; "Inmates Organize Prison Welfare League," *Echo*, November 1928, 1–2. Simons first wrote Cohen to request a book of Jewish prayers in June 1928, and the two carried on a regular correspondence for several years. Eugene Simons to Henry Cohen, June 26, 1928, Cohen Papers, box 3M298.

80. Eugene Simons to Henry Cohen, November 15, 1928, Cohen Papers, box 3M299; Eugene Simons to Henry Cohen, May 25, 1929, Cohen Papers, box 3M300; Eugene Simons to Henry Cohen, March 20, 1929, Cohen Papers, box 3M300; Eugene Simons to Henry Cohen, May 17, 1929, Cohen Papers, box 3M300.

81. Eugene Simons to Henry Cohen, October 2, 1928, Cohen Papers, box 3M299; Eugene Simons to Henry Cohen, October 22, 1928, Cohen Papers, box 3M299; Elizabeth Speer to Henry Cohen, November 8, 1928, Cohen Papers, box 3M299.

82. Eugene Simons to Henry Cohen, June 2, 1929, Cohen Papers, box 3M300; Eugene Simons to W. H. Mead, June 5, 1929, Cohen Papers, box 3M300; Eugene V. Simons, "Proposed Welfare State Farm," June 5, 1929, Cohen Papers, box 3M300; Eugene Simons to Henry Cohen, July 11, 1929, Cohen Papers, box 3M300.

Not long after Cabell left the Prison Commission, Texas had set up an honor camp for road work. See Texas State Legislature, Penitentiary Investigating Committee, *Report and Findings* (1913), 30; W. O. Murray to J. T. Bowman, July 25, 1914, Colquitt Records, box 301–337; W. O. Murray to O. B. Colquitt, July 31, 1914, Colquitt Records, box 301–337; "Prisoners Building Roads, Photographs and Brief Essay," [1914?], unpublished photo essay, Colquitt Papers, Photo box 3Y17. See also PBM, September 22, 1924, box 1998/038–7.

83. Robert Baker to Henry Cohen, October 8, 1928, Cohen Papers, box 3M299; Robert Baker to Lee Simmons, November 28, 1927, Moody Records, box 41.

84. W. M. Odell to Senator McFarlane, February 12, 1929, Cohen Papers, box 3M299; W. H. Mead to Prison Board, May 10, 1929, Moody Records, box 44; B. M. Jameson to Dan Moody, May 10, 1929, Moody Records, box 43. See also PBM, May 29, 1929; Old Henry to governor, May 31, 1927, Moody Records, box 43; S. H. McLeod to Dan Moody, February 9, 1927, Moody Records, box 43.

85. W. F. Andrews to Dan Moody, April 15, 1929, Moody Records, box 43; "Letters on Prison System Sent to Senate Score Way Convict Farms Are Handled," *Dallas Morning News*, February 12, 1929, in Moody Records, box 44; F. K. Stevens to W. H. Mead, June 21, 1929, Moody Records, box 44; P. H. Singeltary to Dan Moody, June 22, 1927, Moody Records, box 43.

86. See W. F. Andrews to Dan Moody, April 15, 1929, Moody Records, box 43; John

Stratford to Dan Moody, October 4, 1928, Moody Records, box 41; Elizabeth Speer to Henry Cohen, January 25, 1928, Cohen Papers, box 3M297.

87. Goree prisoners to Dan Moody, September 19, 1928, Moody Records, box 41; "Camp Complaint," September 26, 1928, Cohen Papers, box 3M299.

88. W. H. Mead, Escape Analysis, July 1928, Ring Papers, box 2G446, clippings file; Texas Prison System, Escape Analysis, January 1929, Cohen Papers, box 3M304; Texas Prison Board, *Annual Report* (1928), 91–92. Of the 760 escapees, 527 were recaptured.

89. W. H. Mead, "Convict 'Bucks' in Camp," July 4, 1928, Ring Papers, box 2G446, clippings file; General Manager, Texas Prison System, *Annual Report* (1928), 5; W. H. Mead to Dan Moody, September 10, 1928, Moody Records, box 41; W. H. Mead to farm managers, September 15, 1928, Cohen Papers, box 3M298. On the deplorable and discriminatory conditions at Blue Ridge, see A. C. Scott, "Report on Health and Sanitation in the Texas Prison System" (College Station: Texas Prison Board, Sanitation Committee, September 23, 1929), Cohen Papers, box 3M303, "Health Survey" file; Teagle, *History of Welfare Activities of the Texas Prison Board*, 43, 60.

90. General Manager, Bi-Monthly Report, May 8, 1929, Cohen Papers, box 3M305; E. F. Harrell to Dan Moody, telegram, June 21, 1929, Moody Records, box 44; Ed Jones, "Four Convicts Shot in Chase," June 21, 1929, *Houston Post-Dispatch*, 1–2; "14 Fugitives from Prison Farm Sought," *Houston Post-Dispatch*, June 22, 1929, 1–2.

91. W. A. Mead to W. A. Paddock, September 28, 1929, Moody Records, box 44; H. R. Grobe, "Wide Search Is Made for 18 Convicts," *Houston Post-Dispatch*, September 29, 1929, 1, 15; "90 Convicts Marched from Danger as Fire Sweeps Wynne Prison," *Houston Post-Dispatch*, October 26, 1929, 1. On previous Wynne fires, see "Prisoners Set Fire to Structure," *Los Angeles Times*, October 3, 1928, 4; General Manager, Report, November 5, 1928, Ring Papers, box 2G446, clippings file.

92. Eugene Simons to Henry Cohen, September 14, 1928, Cohen Papers, box 3M298; Eugene Simons to Henry Cohen, November 10, 1928, Cohen Papers, box 3M299; Eugene Simons to Henry Cohen, November 15, 1928, Cohen Papers, box 3M299; Eugene Simons to Henry Cohen, July 12, 1929, Cohen Papers, box 3M300.

93. Henry Cohen to Eugene Simons, October 15, 1929, Cohen Papers, box 3M300; Eddie Stark to Henry Cohen, August 19, 1929, Cohen Papers, box 3M300; E. F. Harrell to Henry Cohen, September 28, 1929, Cohen Papers, box 3M300. Simons was expelled from the Prisoner Welfare League, outfitted in stripes, and sent to a work farm.

94. Paul M. Lucko, "A Resounding Echo of Prison Life, 1928–1992: Origins of a Prison Newspaper" (paper presented at the Texas State Historical Association, annual meeting, Austin, Texas, 1992), 9.

95. Robert Baker to Dan Moody, May 28, 1927, Moody Records, box 41; Texas Prison Board, *Annual Report* (1927); General Manager, Texas Prison System, *Annual Report* (1928), 10, 8; PBM, August 1, 1928.

96. Texas Prison Board, *Annual Report* (1930), 2; PBM, September 7, 1929; PBM, September 21, 1929.

97. "Jail Gates Will Shut, 'Ma' to End Her Pardon Orgy," *Los Angeles Times*, January 15, 1927, 2; MacCorkle, "The Pardoning Power in Texas"; Texas Prison Board, *Annual Report* (1928), 94, 2; Texas Prison Board, *Annual Report* (1929), E15; Texas Prison Board, *Annual Report* (1930), 2D.

98. W. A. Paddock et al., *Report of the Texas Prison Centralization Commission*, 12, 4–5, 8, 21, 27, 31; Robert Baker to Dan Moody, March 25, 1929, Moody Records, box 44; W. A. Paddock to George Gordon Battle, July 24, 1931, Sterling Records, box 301–467; "Prison Centralization Plan Suffers Severe Defeat in House Vote,"

*Houston Post*, February 7, 1930, Ring Papers, box 2G447, clippings folder. See also W. D. McFarlane, "The Penitentiary System of Texas" (Austin: Von Boeckmann-Jones, Co., 1930); Ed Kilman, "Prison Plagued Counties Demand Change to Moody Centralization System," *Houston Post-Dispatch*, August 16, 1928, Ring Papers, box 2G447, clippings folder.

99. Robert Baker to Dan Moody, March 25, 1929, Moody Records, box 44; Dan Moody to Robert Baker, March 26, 1929, Moody Records, box 44; W. H. Mead to W. A. Paddock, November 13, 1929, Cohen Papers, box 3M300; PBM, November 4, 1929. The warden at the Walls, E. F. Herrell, who had supervised the formation of the Prisoner Welfare League, was soon ousted as well. "Prison Post Is Resigned by Harrell," press clipping, Moody Records, box 45.

100. Henry Cohen to Dan Moody, September 18, 1929, Moody Records, box 44; Henry Cohen to Dan Moody, December 9, 1929, Moody Records, box 44; Henry Cohen to Robert Baker, July 12, 1929, Cohen Papers, box 3M300.

101. Robert Baker to Dan Moody, March 25, 1929, Moody Records, box 44; Lee Simmons, *Assignment Huntsville: Memoirs of a Texas Prison Official* (Austin: University of Texas Press, 1957), 189.

102. "Biggest Prison Show on Earth: Texas Prison Rodeo" (1948), Rodeo Records, box 1998/038–404, Texas Prison Rodeo Programs, clippings; Ed Kilman, "Simmons to Take Job as Prison Head," *Houston Post-Dispatch*, March 25, 1930, 1, 2; Dan Moody to C. C. Selecman, January 15, 1930, Moody Records, box 44; Simmons, *Assignment Huntsville*, 3, 52–55

103. Lee Simmons to H. W. Sayle, December 16, 1927, Moody Records, box 41; Lee Simmons to Robert Baker, January 3, 1928, Cohen Papers, box 3M297; PBM, May 7, 1928, box 1998/038–8; W. M. Odell to Senator McFarlane, February 12, 1929, Cohen Papers, box 3M299. Simmons's differences with Cohen, the most aggressively reform-minded member of the board, burst into the open after the rabbi was interviewed for an article in the *Galveston Tribune*. "Far-Reaching Prison Reform Program Planned for Texas," *Galveston Tribune*, December 31, 1927, n.p., Cohen Papers, box 3M313, 1925–1927 file.

104. Robert Baker to Joseph Wearden, November 14, 1929, Moody Records, box 44; Lee Simmons to Robert Baker, November 19, 1929, Moody Records, box 44.

105. Texas Prison Board, *Annual Report* (1930), 1, 1A; Simmons, *Assignment Huntsville*, 54, 52; Kilman, "Simmons to Take Job as Prison Head"; "Address of Lee Simmons, General Manager, to Inmates of Huntsville Prison," April 15, 1930, Moody Records, box 45.

106. Simmons, *Assignment Huntsville*, x, 75; Alonzo Wasson, "Texas Prison Inmates Held Well in Hand," *Houston Chronicle*, October 12, 1930, Ring Papers, box 2G447, clippings folder; Simmons, *Assignment Huntsville*, 80. Simmons was contemptuous of female prison management. He said that he initially declined his appointment to the 1923 investigative committee because he had to serve alongside a woman. However, once he met the woman, W. C. Martin, he was relieved to find that she was a "business woman of good sense and experience." He remarked, "She is all right. She wears flat-heeled shoes!" (Simmons, 52).

107. D. V. Wright to Lee Simmons, July 4, 1930, Moody Records, box 45; A. H. Carrigan to Ross Sterling, [1932?], Sterling Records, box 301–467, general folder; East Texas Chamber of Commerce, "Resolution Commending Lee Simmons," September 14, 1931, Sterling Records, box 301–467; Wasson, "Texas Prison Inmates Held Well in Hand."

108. Texas Prison Board, *Annual Report* (1933), 17–18; "Parole Bill Passes," *Echo*, May 1929, 1–2; "Governor Favors Liberal Parole Policy," *Echo*, July 1931, 1–2. Texas's escape tally fell precipitously under Simmons's watch, in part because of a

change in reporting procedures ordered by his predecessor. W. H. Mead to J. R. Jordan, April 25, 1929, Moody Records, box 44. The number of white prisoners officially enrolled in schools continued to increase during Simmons tenure. Teagle, *History of Welfare Activities of the Texas Prison Board*, 74–75.

109. W. A. Paddock to Ross Sterling, March 3, 1931, Sterling Records, box 301–467; Texas Prison Board, *Annual Report* (1930), 2–3; PBM, May 19, 1930; Texas Prison Board, *Annual Report* (1931), 2; Texas Prison Board, *Annual Report* (1932), 15. Governor Neff had proposed the same Brazos centralization scheme years earlier. See Reynolds, "The Administration of the Texas Prison System," chap. 5

110. W. A. Paddock, *Report of the Texas Prison Centralization Commission*, 21; "Official Program and Souvenir of the 8th Annual Prison Rodeo" (1939), Rodeo Records, box 1998/038–404, 34; Roscoe White, "Prisoner's Progress: Can This Be Texas?" *Houston Gargoyle*, Sterling Records, box 301–468, clippings.

111. Texas Prison Board, *Annual Report* (1932); Lee Simmons to Dan Moody, April 25, 1930, Moody Records, box 45; "Fire Dept. Banquet," *Echo*, February 1931, 1; Wasson, "Texas Prison Inmates Held Well in Hand." See also Roland Marchand, *Advertising the American Dream: Making Way for Modernity, 1920–1940* (Berkeley: University of California Press, 1985).

112. Teagle, *History of Welfare Activities of the Texas Prison Board*, 15, chap. 6; Simmons, *Assignment Huntsville*, 82, chap. 89; "Third Annual Christmas Smoker Held," *Echo*, January 1933, 2. Censorship of the *Echo* had started in 1929 after Eugene Simons's escape. PBM, September 7, 1929.

113. Simmons, *Assignment Huntsville*, 91; "Eastham Rodeo Thrills," *Echo*, August 1929, 9; "Prison to Start Rodeo," *Huntsville Humdinger*, September 7, 1931, 1; "Biggest Prison Show on Earth" (1948).

114. "Prison Rodeo Attracts 15,000," *Echo*, November 1933; Teagle, *History of Welfare Activities of the Texas Prison Board*, 159–60; Simmons, *Assignment Huntsville*, 94; "Stars Behind Bars," *Time*, October 21, 1940, www.time.com/time/magazine/article/0,9171,777456,00.html; William Rives, "Rogues' Rodeo," *Collier's*, November 22, 1947, 8, 14–16; "Texas Bad Men Ride Again," *Reader's Digest*, November 1941, 52.

115. "Prison Rodeo Attracts 15,000," *Echo*, November 1933; O. J. S. Ellingson to J. D. Hall, October 8, 1938, State Agency Files, Texas Prison System, 1931–1932 folder, box 2002/035–7, TSLAC; "Huntsville Prison Rodeo Draws Record Crowd First Sunday," *Echo*, October 1931, 1, 4; "Official Program and Souvenir of the 8th Annual Prison Rodeo" (1939), Rodeo Records, box 1998/038–404; Teagle, *History of Welfare Activities of the Texas Prison Board*, 5. See also Elizabeth Atwood Lawrence, *Rodeo: An Anthropologist Looks at the Wild and the Tame* (Knoxville: University of Tennessee Press, 1982).

116. Texas Prison Rodeo Programs, Rodeo Records, box 1998/038–404.

117. Simmons, *Assignment Huntsville*, 108–9; Teagle, *History of Welfare Activities of the Texas Prison Board*, 154.

118. Simmons, *Assignment Huntsville*, 109, 111.

119. John A. Lomax, *Adventures of a Ballad Hunter* (New York: Macmillan, 1947), ix, 103, 106. Lomax was one of the professors removed by Ferguson over the objections of UT's Board of Regents, a precipitating factor in the governor's impeachment.

120. Lomax, *Adventures of a Ballad Hunter*, 108, 130, 132, 111; John A. Lomax and Alan Lomax, *American Ballads and Folk Songs* (New York: Macmillan, 1934), xxvi; Wolfe and Lornell, *The Life and Legend of Leadbelly*, 125–26, 183–84. See also Nolan Porterfield, *Last Cavalier: The Life and Times of John A. Lomax, 1867–1948* (Urbana: University of Illinois Press, 1996); Benjamin Filene, *Romancing

the Folk: Public Memory and American Roots Music (Chapel Hill: University of North Carolina Press, 2000).

121. Lomax, Adventures of a Ballad Hunter, 129, 117, 115; Alan Lomax, "'Sinful' Songs of the Southern Negro: Experiences Collecting Secular Folk-Music," Southwest Review 18, no. 2 (1934): 120; Lomax and Lomax, Negro Folk Songs as Sung by Lead Belly, ix.

122. Lee Simons to John Lomax, February 17, 1934, Lomax Papers, box 3D171; Lomax, Adventures of a Ballad Hunter, 119, 166; Lomax, "'Sinful' Songs of the Southern Negro," 120; Lomax and Lomax, American Ballads and Folk Songs, xxx, xxxii; Lomax and Lomax, Negro Folk Songs as Sung by Lead Belly, ix.

123. "Ain' No Mo' Cane on de Brazis," in Lomax and Lomax, American Ballads and Folk Songs, 58–59.

124. Lomax, Adventures of a Ballad Hunter, 160; "Great God-A'Mighty," in Lomax and Lomax, American Ballads and Folk Songs, 79–82, 161.

125. Lomax and Lomax, Negro Folk Songs as Sung by Lead Belly, xii–xiii; Lomax, Adventures of a Ballad Hunter, 119, 121.

126. Lomax, Adventures of a Ballad Hunter, 29–33; Wolfe and Lornell, The Life and Legend of Leadbelly, chap. 14; "Murderous Minstrel," Time, January 14, 1935, in Lomax Papers, box 3D200, Leadbelly clippings. Lomax petitioned Louisiana's governor for Ledbetter's release but apparently to no avail.

127. Lomax and Lomax, Negro Folk Songs as Sung by Lead Belly, 36, 41. See also Hazel V. Carby, Race Men (Cambridge, Mass.: Harvard University Press, 1998), chap. 3.

128. Lomax, "'Sinful' Songs of the Southern Negro," 106; Lomax and Lomax, Negro Folk Songs as Sung by Lead Belly, 44, 38.

129. See Jackson, Wake Up Dead Man: Afro-American Worksongs from Texas Prisons.

130. On "pre-political" resistance generally, see Eric J. Hobsbawm, Primitive Rebels: Studies in Archaic Forms of Social Movement in the Nineteenth and Twentieth Centuries (New York: W. W. Norton & Company, 1959); James C. Scott, Domination and the Arts of Resistance: Hidden Transcripts (New Haven, Conn.: Yale University Press, 1990); Edward Palmer Thompson, Whigs and Hunters: The Origin of the Black Act (London: Allen Lane, 1975); Robin D. G. Kelley, Race Rebels: Culture, Politics, and the Black Working Class (New York: Free Press, 1994). On the politics of African American folk music, see Levine, Black Culture and Black Consciousness.

131. "Ol' Rattler," in Lomax and Lomax, Negro Folk Songs as Sung by Lead Belly, 105–8.

132. Texas Prison Board, Annual Report (1938), 139; Texas Prison Board, Annual Report (1932), 14. "Upper Texas Coast Tropical Cyclones in the 1930s," National Weather Service Forecast Office, http://www.srh.noaa.gov/hgx/hurricanes/1930s.htm.

133. "Clyde Barrow, in Desperate Raid, Frees 5 from Prison Farm," Dallas Morning News, January 17, 1934, 1, 12; "Prison Officials, Warned of Hamilton's Escape Plan, Ridiculed It, Dallas Men Say," Dallas Morning News, January 18, 1934, 1, 12; "Killer Frees Five Felons," Los Angeles Times, January 17, 1934, 4; Simmons, Assignment Huntsville, 114–17, 124–25.

134. PBM, December 19, 1932; "Salary List," TDCJ Records, box 1998/038–8. On the controversy surrounding Simmons's salary, see Editorial, "Lee Simmons' Salary," Dallas Morning News, February 25, 1933, VF-Prisons to 1975, CAH; William M. Thornton, "Prison Head's Job Held Bigger Than High Court Judge," Dallas Morning News, February 28, 1933, VF-Prisons to 1975, CAH.

135. "When Convicts Must Make the System Profits," Houston Press, March 28, 1932, Sterling Records, box 301–468, clippings. New Deal technocrats also

began looking critically at Texas's prison system. See Louis N. Robinson, chairman, et al., "The Prison Labor Problem in Texas" (Washington: U.S. Prison Industries Reorganization Administration, 1937).

136. Darrington State Farm prisoners to Attorney General, May 27, 1930, Moody Records, box 43; Jan Hanby to Henry Cohen, June 17, 1932, Cohen Papers, box 3M301.

137. John Neal Phillips, *Running with Bonnie and Clyde: The Ten Fast Years of Ralph Fults* (Norman: University of Oklahoma Press, 1996), 51; "Simmons Offers Convicts 'More Axes' to Chop Selves," [1935?], newspaper clipping, Cohen Papers, box 3M314; Texas Prison Board, *Annual Report* (1932), 56; Texas, Report of the House Committee to Investigate Retrieve State Prison Farm, May 6, 1935, Joint Legislative Documents, RG 100.72, box 1998/70, TSLAC.

138. Report of the House Committee to Investigate Retrieve State Prison Farm, May 6, 1935. See also Henry Cohen to Lee Simmons, June 19, 1933, Cohen Papers, box 3M301.

139. "Simmons Offers Convicts 'More Axes' to Chop Selves," [1935?], newspaper clipping, Cohen Papers, box 3M314; "Simmons and His Axes," *Houston Press*, April 10, 1935, Cohen Papers, box 3M314; Simmons, *Assignment Huntsville*, x–xi.

## 6: "BEST IN THE NATION"

1. Max Skelton, "Long-Range Program Planned to Make Prison System Best," *Austin Statesman*, December 12, 1947, 17; *Novak v. Beto*, 320 F.Supp. 1206, 1209 (1970).

2. Simmons, *Assignment Huntsville*, xi; R. C. Koeninger, "What About Self-Mutilation?" *Prison World*, March–April 1951, 3; Fulsom, *Prison Stories: The Old Days*, 37; Perkinson, "Angola and the Agony of Prison Reform"; Governor's Office, Meeting with the Texas Prison Board, transcript, March 3, 1947, Jester Records, box 4–14/113, p. 3.

3. Koeninger, "What About Self-Mutilation?" 3; C. V. Compton, *Flood Lights Behind the Gray Walls: An Exposé of Activities* (Dallas, Tex.: C. V. Compton, 1942), 9.

4. Compton, *Flood Lights Behind the Gray Walls*, 21, 31–32; Fulsom, *Prison Stories: The Old Days*, 41.

5. "Mutilation of Convicts Is Revealed," *Port Arthur News*, March 13, 1940, 1; Governor's Office, Meeting with the Texas Prison Board, transcript, March 3, 1947; Koeninger, "What About Self-Mutilation?" 30; "Epidemic of Self-Mutilation by Prisoners Breaks Out on Farm; Two Legs Chopped Off," *Galveston Daily News*, March 13, 1940, 1.

6. Paul Van Dyke, "An Investigation of Self-Mutilation at the Texas Prison System in Terms of the Minnesota Multiphasic Personality Inventory and Other Measures" (master's thesis, University of Texas, 1953), 99; Dan Richard Beto and James L. Claghorn, "Factors Associated with Self-Mutilation Within the Texas Department of Corrections," *American Journal of Correction* 30, no. 1 (1968); Texas State Legislature, *Committee Report on Investigation of Penitentiaries* (1947); Austin MacCormick to O. B. Ellis, June 14, 1949, Jester Papers, box 4–14/113.

7. ". . . Is It Nothing to You, All Ye Who Pass By?" *Prison World*, 12, no. 4 (July–August 1950): 22. See also Paul Terry to Governor Jester, October 7, 1947, Jester Papers, box 4–14/113, prison system 1948 folder; Louise Lawrence to Governor Jester, March 25, 1948, Jester Papers, box 4–14/113.

8. "Legislators Chased from Prison Room," unidentified newspaper clipping, February 1944, Pope Collection, box 4C801; Texas State Legislature, *Committee Report on Investigation of Penitentiaries* (1947). Some fifty thousand German

POWs were housed in Texas during the war, their benign conditions of confinement offering another contrast with the state's domestic penal farms. Campbell, *Gone to Texas*, 402.

9. Cahalan, "Historical Corrections Statistics," 29. Howard B. Gill, "The Prison Labor Problem," in Edwin H. Sutherland and Thorstein Sellin, eds., *Prisons of Tomorrow*, vol. 157 (Philadelphia: American Academy of Political and Social Science, 1931), 83–101. In Texas, the inmate population fell from 6,831 to 3,272 between 1939 and 1945. Texas Prison Board, *Annual Report* (1940), 138; Texas Prison Board, *Annual Report* (1945), 61.

10. "Prisoners at Work," *BusinessWeek*, September 11, 1943, 38; "Prison War Work," *Life*, December 7, 1942, 49–56; "Prisons at Work," *BusinessWeek*, February 19, 1944, 51. Texas's prisons contributed mainly canned goods and textiles. Texas Prison Board, *Annual Report* (1943), 13.

11. "Prisoners' Blood Bank for Defense," *Journal of the American Institute of Criminal Law and Criminology* 32, no. 6 (1942): 655; Harry Lee, "Prison Flag Shows Men Aiding in War," *Atlanta Constitution*, October 3, 1943, 10B; "They Know What Freedom Means," *Time*, November 23, 1942, 25.

12. Clemens J. France, "Shall There Be a 'New Prison World,' " *Prison World*, January–February 1944, 10–11, 22–24; Paul E. Lockwood, "Progressive Legislation in New York State," *Prison World*, May–June 1954, 4, 13; "Georgia's New Peach," *Saturday Evening Post*, August 28, 1943.

13. McKelvey, *American Prisons*, 319; John P. Conrad, "Foreword," in Richard A. McGee, *Prisons and Politics* (Lexington, Mass.: Lexington Books, 1981), ix.

14. Shelley Bookspan, *A Germ of Goodness: The California State Prison System, 1851–1944* (Lincoln: University of Nebraska Press, 1991); Hallinan, *Going Up the River*, 74–77; Clinton T. Duffy and Dean Jennings, *The San Quentin Story* (Garden City, N.Y.: Doubleday & Co., 1968), 252, 258–59.

15. Governor Warren gave a vital boost to California's postwar penal reforms, but several initiatives were under way by the time he took office, particularly at Chino and in the juvenile system. See Austin H. MacCormick, ed., *Handbook of American Prisons and Reformatories: Pacific Coast States*, 5th ed., vol. 2 (New York: Osborne Association, 1942).

16. In no small part thanks to Warren's urgings, 120,000 Japanese Americans were interned during World War II. California's state prison population was 5,960 in 1943. Roger Daniels, *Prisoners Without Trial: Japanese Americans in World War II* (New York: Hill and Wang, 1993); California Department of Corrections, "Prisoners Received Each Year and Annual Population of Institutions, 1851–1945," http://www.corr.ca.gov/ReportsResearch/OffenderInfoServices/Annual/CalPrisArchive.html.

17. Ed Cray, *Chief Justice: A Biography of Earl Warren* (New York: Simon & Schuster, 1997), 145.

18. Earl Warren, inaugural address, January 4, 1943, Governors of California, http://governor.ca.gov/govsite/govsgallery/h/documents/inaugural_30.html; "Warren Calls for Cleanup at Folsom," *Fresno Bee*, November 28, 1943, 1; Herbert L. Phillips, "Politics in Review," *Fresno Bee*, December 5, 1943.

19. John Irwin, *The Felon* (Englewood Cliffs, N.J.: Prentice Hall, 1970), 43; Earl Warren and Berdette J. Daniels, "California's New Penal and Correctional Law," *California Law Review* 32, no. 3 (1944): 229–41; Richard A. McGee, "California's New Penal and Correctional Program," *Prison World*, May–June 1945, 5, 14–17.

20. Earl Warren, "Community Responsibility for the Prevention of Delinquency and Crime," in *Proceedings of the 77th Annual Congress of Correction*, Long Beach, California, September 12–16, 1947 (New York: American Prison Association, 1947), 14. See Cray, *Chief Justice*; Jim Newton, *Justice for All: Earl Warren and the Nation He Made* (New York: Riverhead Books, 2006).

21. Warren, "Community Responsibility for the Prevention of Delinquency and Crime," 14; Joseph W. Eaton, *Stone Walls Not a Prison Make: The Anatomy of Planned Administrative Change* (Springfield, Ill.: Charles C. Thomas, 1962), 86, 93; John Bartlow Martin, *Break Down the Walls: American Prisons: Present, Past, and Future* (New York: Ballantine Books, 1954), 153; McGee, *Prisons and Politics*, 28.

22. McGee, *Prisons and Politics*, 137, 163–66; Richard A. McGee, ed., *A Manual of Correctional Standards* (New York: American Prison Association, 1954); John P. Conrad, "Foreword," in McGee, *Prisons and Politics*, xi.

23. Irwin, *The Felon*, 43–44; Malcolm Braly, *False Starts: A Memoir of San Quentin and Other Prisons* (Boston: Little, Brown, 1976), 156, 166.

24. Braly, *False Starts*, 157–58; Sheldon Messinger, "Strategies of Control" (PhD diss., UCLA, 1969), 285; Irwin, *Prisons in Turmoil*, 61.

25. Messinger, "Strategies of Control," 283; Clemmer, *The Prison Community*, xiii, 298, 313; McGee, *Prisons and Politics*, 84.

26. Irwin, *Prisons in Turmoil*, 41.

27. Eaton, *Stone Walls Not a Prison Make*, chap. 9, 53, 55–56; Messinger, "Strategies of Control," 27.

28. Caryl Chessman, *Cell 2455, Death Row* (New York: Prentice Hall, 1954), 230; Bookspan, *Germ of Goodness*, 109; Cummins, *The Rise and Fall of California's Radical Prison Movement*, 11.

29. Messinger, "Strategies of Control," 10; Eaton, *Stone Walls Not a Prison Make*, 55–56, 101; Braly, *False Starts*, 162; McGee, *Prisons and Politics*, 26; Irwin, *Prisons in Turmoil*, 49; Chessman, *Cell 2455, Death Row*, 221.

30. Irwin, *Prisons in Turmoil*, 60, 56; Messinger, "Strategies of Control," 16.

31. Braly, *False Starts*, 190; Irwin, *Prisons in Turmoil*, 43.

32. McGee, *Prisons and Politics*, 83; Martin, *Break Down the Walls*, 210; Cummins, *The Rise and Fall of California's Radical Prison Movement*, 1–2, 20. See also Sykes, *The Society of Captives*; Charles Bright, *The Powers That Punish: Prison and Politics in the Era of the "Big House," 1920–1955* (Ann Arbor: University of Michigan Press, 1996).

33. Cummins, *The Rise and Fall of California's Radical Prison Movement*, 26, 28; Irwin, *Prisons in Turmoil*, 60, 63–64.

34. Cummins, *The Rise and Fall of California's Radical Prison Movement*, 28, 25.

35. Braly, *False Starts*, 187; McGee, *Prisons and Politics*, 52–53; Theodore Hamm, *Rebel and a Cause: Caryl Chessman and the Politics of the Death Penalty in Postwar California, 1948–1974* (Berkeley: University of California Press, 2001); Cummins, *The Rise and Fall of California's Radical Prison Movement*, chap. 3.

36. McGee, *Prisons and Politics*, 53; Cummins, *The Rise and Fall of California's Radical Prison Movement*, 54–62; "The Chessman Affair," *Time*, March 21, 1960, http://www.time.com/time/magazine/article/0,9171,894774,00.html.

37. Governor's Office, Meeting with the Texas Prison Board, transcript, March 3, 1947.

38. Mac Roy Rasor, "Governor Promises Inquiry into 'Brutality' in Texas Prison System," *Austin Statesman*, August 28, 1947, 1; Governor's Office, Meeting with the Texas Prison Board, transcript, March 3, 1947; Texas State Legislature, *Committee Report on Investigation of Penitentiaries* (1947). See also Allan Bérubé, "Marching to a Different Drummer: Lesbian and Gay GIs in World War II," in Ann Barr Snitow, Christine Stansell, and Sharon Thompson, eds., *Powers of Desire: The Politics of Sexuality* (New York: Monthly Review Press, 1983), 96–99.

39. Compton, *Flood Lights Behind the Gray Walls*, 42; Women's Society of Christian Service, Canton Methodist Church, to Governor Jester, February 2, 1948, Jester Papers, box 4–14/113; Mrs. W. E. Horton to Governor Jester, March 2, 1947, Jester Papers, box 4–14/113; Mayo Dazey, letter to editor, *Galveston News*, October 18, 1947, 4.

40. PBM, February 11, 1941; Texas Prison Board, "Report on the Bat," February 11, 1941, TDCJ Records, box 1998/038–8; PBM, May 7, 1945, November 5, 1945. On earlier efforts, see Carl Basland, "Classification in the Texas Prison System" (Austin: University of Texas, 1938); Teagle, *History of Welfare Activities of the Texas Prison Board*; Joseph Wearden, "Accomplishments and Needs of the Texas Prison System," *Sheriffs' Association of Texas Magazine* 7, no. 8 (August 1938): 3–4.

41. Rasor, "Governor Promises Inquiry into 'Brutality' in Texas Prison System," 1; Mac Roy Rasor, "Prison Board to Decide Policy Issue Saturday," *Austin Statesman*, August 29, 1947, 2; Campbell, *Gone to Texas*, 412.

42. *Shelby County Farm* (Memphis, Tenn.: Shelby County Commissioners, 1946); "O. B. Ellis, 1902–1961," *American Journal of Correction* 23, no. 6 (November–December 1961): 34; PBM, March 1, 1948, 742, 736.

43. Lewis Nordyke, "A Prison Boss 'As Good as His Word,'" *Reader's Digest*, January 1960, 142; PBM, November 25, 1947; PBM, January 5, 1948; Ben M. Crouch and James W. Marquart, *An Appeal to Justice: Litigated Reform of Texas Prisons* (Austin: University of Texas Press, 1989), 32.

44. PBM, November 3, 1947, March 1, 1948; Oscar Ellis to James Spencer, June 3, 1948, Jester Records, box 4–14/113.

45. Texas Prison Board, "A Program for the Improvement of the Texas Prison System" (1948), TDCJ Records, box 1998/038–127; Nordyke, "A Prison Boss 'As Good as His Word,'" 144; "Prison Fund Hike Sought," *Austin Statesman*, July 26, 1948, 1; "Prison Program Finally Enacted by Legislature," *Valley Morning Star* (Harlingen, Tex.), March 4, 1949, 5; Hallinan, *Going Up the River*, 22.

46. "A Program for the Improvement of the Texas Prison System"; Allan Shivers, "The Texas Prison System: A Record of Progress," *State Government* 27, no. 6 (1954); TDC, "20 Years of Progress" (1967), 79, 100; "Ellis Spurs Prison Rule Revamping," *Austin Statesman*, March 9, 1949, 16; Fred Williams, "Prison System Cited as One of the Worst in U.S. by Experts," *Austin Statesman*, January 16, 1949, 1.

47. "A Program for the Improvement of the Texas Prison System," 5, 9. Although Ellis is widely credited with leading Texas's prisons out of barbarism, his "Ellis Plan," proposed in March 1948, was considerably more conservative than the prison board's own proposal, based on Austin MacCormick's recommendations, approved in November 1947. See also O. B. Ellis, "Correctional Growth Through Co-operative Effort," Presidential Address, 1959, *American Journal of Correction* 21, no. 5 (1959): 6–8, 30–33.

48. A. B. J. Hammett, *Miracle Within the Walls* (Corpus Christi: South Texas Publishing Company, 1963), 58, 40; James Harvey DeHay, "Recreation in the Texas Prison System" (master's thesis, University of Texas, 1952); O. B. Ellis, "The President's Page," *American Journal of Correction* 21, no. 2 (March–April 1959): 30; David M. Horton and George R. Nielsen, *Walking George: The Life of George John Beto and the Rise of the Modern Texas Prison System* (Denton: University of North Texas Press, 2005), 68.

49. "A Program for the Improvement of the Texas Prison System," 25, 12; Robert Crichton, *The Great Imposter* (New York: Random House, 1959), 189–90.

50. "A Program for the Improvement of the Texas Prison System," 25; Hammett, *Miracle Within the Walls*, 58, 40; Redbird McCarter, interview by author, August 7, 2003; Albert Race Sample, *Race Hoss: Big Emma's Boy* (Austin, Tex.: Eakin Press, 1984), 259; Steve J. Martin and Sheldon Ekland-Olson, *Texas Prisons: The Walls Came Tumbling Down* (Austin: Texas Monthly Press, 1987), 23; Gene Barnwell, "TPS Climbs Ladder of Efficiency," *The Texas Public Employee*, June 1954, 6.

51. PBM, January 5, 1948; Van Dyke, "An Investigation of Self-Mutilation at the Texas Prison System in Terms of the Minnesota Multiphasic Personality Inventory and Other Measures," chap. 4; Beto and Claghorn, "Factors Associated with

Self-Mutilation Within the Texas Department of Corrections"; Texas Prison Board, *Annual Reports* (1940–1960); PBM, March 1, 1948.

52. TDC, "20 Years of Progress," 35; TDC, *Annual Report* (1965); Barnwell, "TPS Climbs Ladder of Efficiency"; *Report on Agricultural Enterprises: An Economic Survey of the Texas Prison System* (College Station: Texas A&M, December 18, 1940); Hammett, *Miracle Within the Walls;* Crouch and Marquart, *Appeal to Justice,* 35; George J. Beto, "The Texas Prison System: Assets and Liabilities" (Huntsville: Texas Department of Corrections, 1962), 1–2.

53. Shivers, "Texas Prison System"; Jack Kyle, interview by author, July 20, 2002; Horton and Nielsen, *Walking George,* 109–10.

54. Hammett, *Miracle Within the Walls;* Margarit Davis, "The Texas Prison System After Three and a Half Years," *Prison World* 14, no. 1 (January–February 1952): 4–9; Nordyke, "A Prison Boss 'As Good as His Word,'" 144; Don Reid Jr., "A Newsman's Look at the Texas Department of Corrections," *American Journal of Correction* 21, no. 3 (May–June 1959): 12–17; Horton and Nielsen, *Walking George,* 103–4.

55. Jack Kyle, interview by author, July 20, 2002; Crichton, *The Great Imposter,* 181; Crouch and Marquart, *Appeal to Justice,* 38; Horton and Nielsen, *Walking George,* 104–8.

56. Horton and Nielsen, *Walking George,* 75, 120, 142.

57. TDC, *Thirty Years of Progress* (1967), 31–35; TDC, *Twenty Years of Progress,* 69–77. Horton and Nielsen, *Walking George,* 134–35; TDC, *Annual Report* (1971), 50; Dave Shanks, "Of Prison Industries: A Rehabilitation Boon," *Austin American,* May 31, 1963, 4.

58. George B. Mears, "The Texas Diagnostic Center," *American Journal of Correction* 27, no. 6 (November–December 1965): 26–29; TDC, *Twenty Years of Progress,* 27, 73; TDC, *Annual Report* (1966); TDC, "The Point Incentive Program" (1963); Jesse E. Clark, "The Texas Pre-Release Program," *American Journal of Correction* 29, no. 2 (1967).

59. TDC, *Annual Report* (1965), director's letter; Rachel Conrad Wahlberg, "Texas Prison Boss," *The Lutheran* 1, no. 6 (March 13, 1963): 19.

60. Horton and Nielsen, *Walking George,* 122; Crouch and Marquart, *Appeal to Justice,* 41; George Beto, "Texas Establishes Younger Offender Unit," *American Journal of Correction* 25, no. 4 (July–August 1963): 28–29; Riley Kennedy, *Prison in Texas: Facts, Features, Fotos* (Tyler, Tex.: Riley Kennedy, 1972), 22–23; TDC, *Annual Report* (1966), Ferguson profile.

61. TDC, *Annual Report* (1966), Goree profile; Helen Thompson, "From Prison to Freedom—The Perilous Gap: Behind the Walls at Goree," *Amarillo Globe Times,* October 18, 1967, 29–30; Babe Schwartz, interview by author, August 2, 2003.

62. Steve Martin, interview by author, March 28, 1999; Captain Cherry, interview by author, July 23, 2002. See also Douglas Freelander, "Probe of Nepotism, Military Hiring Practices in TDC Under Way," *Houston Post,* October 17, 1986.

63. TDC, *Annual Report* (1966); Dave Shanks, "Of Prison Industries: A Rehabilitation Boon," *Austin American,* May 31, 1963, 4. At the peak of iron and textile operations at Rusk and the Walls in the nineteenth century, a considerably higher portion of the convict population worked in industry.

64. As the housemaster at a Christian boys' school, Beto had first dabbled in the arts of what he called "benevolent discipline," but in his prison career he made order and obedience a creed. Horton and Nielsen, *Walking George,* 28. Beto developed his ideas on prison discipline under Ellis's tutelage when he served on Texas's Board of Corrections between 1953 and 1959. Later, when he moved to Illinois to head up the Concordia Theological Seminary, he continued working in corrections, serving on the Illinois parole board and developing a close relationship with Joseph E. Ragen, another famous advocate of hard-nosed "con-

trol" penology. See James B. Jacobs, *Stateville: The Penitentiary in Mass Society* (Chicago: University of Chicago Press, 1977).

65. TDC, *Rules and Regulations* (1964), 3; George Beto, "A Philosophy of Corrections," in *Readings in Prison Education*, ed. Albert R. Roberts (Springfield, Ill.: Charles C Thomas, 1973), 394.

66. Willett and Rozelle, *Warden*, 75; Lon Bennett Glenn, *Texas Prisons: The Largest Hotel Chain in Texas* (Austin, Tex.: Eakin Publications, 2001), 17.

67. John J. DiIulio, *Governing Prisons: A Comparative Study of Correctional Management* (New York: Free Press, 1987), 65. See also TDC, *Employee Manual of Rules and Regulations* (1964).

68. Crouch and Marquart, *Appeal to Justice*, 60–62, 76; Martin and Ekland-Olson, *Texas Prisons*, 23–25; DiIulio, *Governing Prisons*, 65.

69. Steve Martin, interview by author, June 28, 2002; Martin and Ekland-Olson, *Texas Prisons*, 23, 33; Thomas Thompson, "Huntsville's Cost Factor: $2.37 Per Day Per Man," *Amarillo Globe-Times*, October 11, 1967, 1; *Novak v. Beto*, 320 F.Supp. 1206, 1209 (1970).

70. Gary Taylor, "Dr. Beto Honored at Banquet by 9 State, Federal Agencies," *Houston Post*, n.d., Beto Papers, clipping, box 1-1-19; Jim Willett, interview by author, July 19, 2002; Bruce Jackson, "Our Prisons Are Criminal," *New York Times Magazine*, September 22, 1968, 45–47, 54–60.

71. Ray Hill, interview by author, July 20, 2002; Willett and Rozelle, *Warden*, 63; Rachel Conrad Wahlberg, "Texas Prison Boss," *The Lutheran* 1, no. 6 (March 13, 1963): 16–19; Esso "Woody" Woods, interview by author, August 6, 2003; Charles Brown, letter to author, July 3, 2004; Crouch and Marquart, *Appeal to Justice*, 39; Keith Elliott, "This Preacher Is No Pushover," *Lutheran Standard*, March 21, 1967, 10–11.

72. Esso "Woody" Woods, interview by author, August 6, 2003; Jack Kyle, interview by author, July 20, 2002; Babe Schwartz, interview by author, August 2, 2003.

73. Mary Bounds, "Millionaire's World Remains a Mystery," *Houston Chronicle*, May 8, 1988; Horton and Nielsen, *Walking George*, 62–63. For a summary of Beto's construction projects, see TDC, *Thirty Years of Progress* (1977); Kennedy, *Prison in Texas*; TDC, *Annual Report* (1966).

74. Keith Elliott, "This Preacher Is No Pushover," *Lutheran Standard*, March 21, 1967, 10–11; Jack Waugh, "A Strict Prison Is Either the Worst in the Nation or the Best, Inmates Believe," *Courier Times* (Levitown, Penn.), January 6, 1972, p. 7; Paul Harvey, "Tough 'Sheep' Following Shepherd with Know How," *Panama City News*, December 29, 1969, 4A; John DiIulio to George Beto, April 20, 1988, Beto Papers, box 4-1-2.

75. O. B. Ellis, "The President's Page," *American Journal of Correction* 20, no. 5 (September–October 1958): 3; George Beto, "From the President," *Corrections Today* 31, no. 5 (September–October 1969): 5; TDC, *Twenty Years of Progress* (1967), 23.

76. Cahalan, "Historical Corrections Statistics," 30.

77. George J. Beto, "Presidential Address: Continue Work, So Much to Be Done," *American Journal of Correction* 32, no. 6 (1970): 6–7; George Beto, "From the President," *American Journal of Correction* 32, no. 3 (May–June 1970): 5.

78. Beto, "Presidential Address: Continue Work, So Much to Be Done," 4; "Declaration of Principles Adopted and Promulgated by the Congress" (1870), arts. 2, 10, 13, 15, 10; "Declaration of Principles of the American Correctional Association, as Adopted by the American Congress of Correction, Cincinnati, Ohio, 1970," *American Journal of Correction* 32, no. 6 (November–December 1970): 32–34, arts. 3, 7, 23–25.

79. Michael Vines, "A View from Inside, Part One: TDC—Cracks in the Myth," *Texas Observer*, May 31, 1985, 7; DiIulio, *Governing Prisons*, chap. 2; Joan Petersilia, Paul

K. Honig, and Charles Hubay, "The Prison Experience of Career Criminals" (Santa Monica, Calif.: Rand Corporation, 1980); Ron Waldron and Bob Bozzelli, *State Corrections: Inmates, Expenditures, and Employees, 1973–1975* (Huntsville, Tex.: TDC Research and Development Division, 1975).

80. Martin and Ekland-Olson, *Texas Prisons*, xx; Willett and Rozelle, *Warden*, 36, 39; Crichton, *The Great Imposter*, 184.

81. Crouch and Marquart, *Appeal to Justice*, 47, 55; Glenn, *Texas Prisons*, 27; Esso "Woody" Woods, interview by author, August 6, 2003; Ben Crouch, "A Profile of the Typical Correctional Officer in the Eastham, Ellis, Ferguson, and Huntsville Units" (PhD diss., Texas A&M University, 1973); Jim Willett, interview by author, July 19, 2002.

82. Cody D. Ward, "The Texas Prison Hazard: Concerns for Public and Staff Safety," *Huntsville Item*, December 20, 2004; Crouch and Marquart, *Appeal to Justice*, 47; Jim Willett, interview by author, July 19, 2002; Steve Martin, interview by author, June 28, 2002; Jack Kyle, interview by author, July 20, 2002.

83. TDC, *Twenty Years of Progress* (1967), 1, 31; Texas Prison Board, "A Program for the Improvement of the Texas Prison System" (1948), 11; Glenn, *Texas Prisons*, 9. Inflation figures adjusted for 2005. MeasuringWorth.com, http://measuring worth.com/calculators/uscompare/.

84. Willett and Rozelle, *Warden*, 156, 169; TDC Director, Memorandum re. Houseboys, no. 14–65, October 14, 1965, TDCJ Records, box 1998/038–61.

85. Texas Prison Board, "A Program for the Improvement of the Texas Prison System" (1948), 10; Crouch and Marquart, *Appeal to Justice*, 49; Crouch, "A Profile of the Typical Correctional Officer in the Eastham, Ellis, Ferguson, and Huntsville Units"; Michael C. Murdock, "The Texas Correctional Officer: Factors Influencing Occupational Personality" (master's thesis, Sam Houston State University, 1973); Willett and Rozelle, *Warden*, 119.

86. Glenn, *Texas Prisons*, 29.

87. TDC, *Employee Manual of Rules and Regulations* (1964), 5; Crouch and Marquart, *Appeal to Justice*, 48.

88. TDC, *Employee Manual of Rules and Regulations* (1964), 30; Crouch and Marquart, *Appeal to Justice*, 78, 57.

89. Crouch and Marquart, *Appeal to Justice*, 52, 56; Crichton, *The Great Imposter*, 185; Glenn, *Texas Prisons*, 28; Willett and Rozelle, *Warden*, 87–89; Steve Martin, interview by author, June 28, 2002.

90. Elmas Mallo, "Chillin' in the Blazin' Texas Sun: A Return to the Horrific (TDC to TDCJ, 1978–2005)," *CounterPunch*, November 11–13, 2005, www.counter punch.org; Jackson, *Wake Up Dead Man: Afro-American Worksongs from Texas Prisons*, 43–44; Ray Hill, interview by author, July 20, 2002; Glenn, *Texas Prisons*, 8–9, 46, 81–86, 99–101.

91. TDC, *Employee Manual of Rules and Regulations* (1964), 30–31; Robert Lee Mudd, letter to author, July 19, 2005; Sample, *Race Hoss*, 336–37; Bruce Jackson, "Prison Nicknames," *Western Folklore* 26, no. 1 (1967).

92. TDC, *Employee Manual of Rules and Regulations* (1964), 31. Instructively, the TDC employee manual specifically prohibited the use of ethnic slang directed at European immigrant groups (e.g., "Dago," "Dutch"), but made no mention of racial slurs directed against African Americans or Mexicans. Lon Glenn maintains that guards rarely used racial epithets, but the other officers and convicts I have interviewed say otherwise. Glenn, *Texas Prisons*, 96.

93. James Yeager, letter to author, April 23, 2004; Steve Martin, interview by author, March 28, 1999, June 28, 2002; Captain Cherry, interview by author, July 23, 2002; Al Slaton, interview by author, July 6, 2002. See also *Lamar v. Coffield*, 951 F.Supp. 629 (1996).

94. TDC, *Rules and Regulations* (1964), 4–10; TDC, "The Point Incentive Program"

(1963); Crouch and Marquart, *Appeal to Justice*, 68; Sample, *Race Hoss*, 250, 224–25.

95. Sample, *Race Hoss*, 271–72; Willett and Rozelle, *Warden*, 163, 171–72, 194.

96. Jewell, letter to author, [fall 2004?]; James Yeager, letter to author, August 5, 2003; Redbird McCarter, interview by author, August 7, 2003; Glenn, *Texas Prisons*, 34.

97. Larry Casey, letter to author, June 27, 2004; Ray Hill, "Prison Years Show," public performance, Houston Media Source, July 20, 2002; Crouch and Marquart, *Appeal to Justice*, 78–81; Sample, *Race Hoss*, 233, 205. On possible homicides by guards, see "Inmate Deaths Since 1970," 1983, Pope Collection, box 4C937, numbered letters, folder 3; "Prison Brutality Charged by Rep. Graves," *Houston Chronicle*, February 7, 1968; Chris DeGrate, letter to author, November 18, 2004; "Trial Raises Questions on Texas Prison Conditions," *New York Times*, February 15, 1982, A13.

98. *Report of the Commission Appointed by the Governor* (1875), 8; Commissioners of the Texas State Penitentiary, *Biennial Report* (1878), 8. On the carryover of trusty guards from leasing, see Prison Commission, *Annual Report* (Austin, Tex.: unpublished, 1914), printed in Senate Penitentiary Investigating Committee, supplementary documents (1915), TSLAC, box 4–2/1549b, vol. 2, book 2.

99. Oscar Ellis to James Spencer, June 3, 1948, Jester Records, box 4–14/113; TDC director, memorandum to wardens, no. 27–63, November 8, 1963, TDCJ Records, box 1998/038–63; David Arnold, First Monitor's Report, October 16, 1981; Walter Siros, interview by author, July 24, 2002.

100. Esso "Woody" Woods, interview by author, August 6, 2003; Jack Kyle, interview by author, July 20, 2002.

101. Esso "Woody" Woods, interview by author, August 6, 2003; James Yeager, letter to author, August 5, 2003; David Arnold, First Monitor's Report, October 16, 1981.

102. Glenn, *Texas Prisons*, 12; Siros, interview by author, July 24, 2002.

103. Siros, interview by author, July 24, 2002; David Ruíz, interview by author, July 6, 2003; Al Slaton, interview by author, June 30, 2002; Brett Massey, letter to author, March 25, 2004.

104. John J. DiIulio, ed., *Courts, Corrections, and the Constitution: The Impact of Judicial Intervention on Prisons and Jails* (New York: Oxford University Press, 1990), 56; Horton and Nielsen, *Walking George*, 139.

105. Odus Rogers, letter to author, November 28, 2002; Willie Redis, interview by author, August 8, 2003.

106. Willie Redis, interview by author, August 8, 2003; Sample, *Race Hoss*, 162–63.

107. Sample, *Race Hoss*, 163–70.

108. Campbell, *Gone to Texas*, 325–26, 361, 404–9; Larry McMurtry, *In a Narrow Grave: Essays on Texas* (Austin, Tex.: Encino Press, 1968), 44.

109. TDC, *Thirty Years of Progress* (1977); Norris Trevenio, interview by author, August 7, 2003; Vines, "A View from Inside, Part One," 7–11.

110. David R. Roediger, *The Wages of Whiteness: Race and the Making of the American Working Class* (New York: Verso, 1991); Foley, *White Scourge*.

111. Siros, interview by author, July 24, 2002; Larry Casey, letter to author, June 27, 2004; Jewell, letter to author, [fall 2004].

112. Norris Trevenio, interview by author, August 7, 2003; Crouch and Marquart, *Appeal to Justice*, 101; Arturo Aranda, letter to author, October 1, 2003; Willie Redis, interview by author, August 8, 2003.

113. Strobel, *Old Plantations*, 28–31; Texas State Penitentiary, *Report* (1876), 13–19; *Report of the Commission Appointed by the Governor* (1875); Glenn, *Texas Prisons*, chap. 3; Sample, *Race Hoss*, 208–9, 184.

114. Sample, *Race Hoss*, 217, 236.
115. Norris Trevenio, interview by author, August 7, 2003; Jonathan Reed, letter to author, October 21, 2003; Michael Jewell, letter to author, [fall 2004]; Robert Lee Mudd, letter to author, September 12, 2004.
116. Harrison and Beck, *Prison and Jail Inmates at Midyear 2005*, 9; Campbell, *An Empire for Slavery*, 244.
117. *Boulware v. Hendricks*, 23 Tex. 667 (1859).
118. On total institutions generally, see Goffman, *Asylums*. Prisoners may have formed what sociologist Gresham Sykes called a "society of captives," but it was not as stable or cohesive as what historian John Blassingame termed "the slave community." Sykes, *The Society of Captives*; John W. Blassingame, *The Slave Community: Plantation Life in the Antebellum South*, rev. ed. (New York: Oxford University Press, 1979).
119. James Yeager, interview by author, August 5, 2003; Haneef Bilal, interview by author, November 18, 2004.
120. Orlando Patterson, *Slavery and Social Death: A Comparative Study* (Cambridge, Mass.: Harvard University Press, 1982), 13; *Ruffin v. Commonwealth*, 21 Gratt. 790 (1871).

## 7: APPEAL TO JUSTICE

1. William Wayne Justice, speech, May 31, 1986, quoted in Crouch and Marquart, *Appeal to Justice*, 117.
2. David Ruíz, interview by author, July 18, 2002.
3. Ken Jones, Pamela Baggett, interview by author, July 18, 2002; Jim Willett, interview by author, July 19, 2002.
4. Helen Thompson, "From Prison to Freedom—The Perilous Gap: Behind the Walls at Goree," *Amarillo Globe Times*, October 18, 1967, 29–30; Martin Dreyer and Ted Rozumalski, "Women Behind Bars," *Houston Chronicle*, March 10, 1963, 5–11; Martin and Ekland-Olson, *Texas Prisons*, 45. For a less sanguine perspective on Goree, see Joyce Ann Brown and Jay Gaines, *Joyce Ann Brown: Justice Denied* (Chicago: Noble Press, 1990).
5. David Ruíz, interview by author, July 6, 2003.
6. Ruíz, letter to author, artwork, August 3, 2004.
7. Al Slaton, interview by author, July 7, 2002; Ruíz, interview by author, July 6, 2003. On postwar Austin, see Raúlsalinas, *East of the Freeway* (Austin, Tex.: Red Salmon Press, 1995); Billy Lee Brammer, *The Gay Place* (New York: Houghton Mifflin, 1961).
8. Mary Mae Hartley, "David Ruíz: Chicano Hero or Tex-Mex Bandit?" (unpublished manuscript, 1997).
9. "Reformatory for Vicious Boys," *Dallas Morning News*, April 4, 1887, 4; "The State Reformatory Experiment," *Dallas Morning News*, May 6, 1889, 4; Texas State Penitentiaries, *Biennial Report* (1900), 113–14.
10. Ruíz, interview by author, July 6, 2003. Ruíz's grim memories of Gatesville in the 1950s correspond with those of his contemporaries. Don Weaver, e-mail to author, November 17, 2004; Richard Glimes, e-mail to author, September 24, 2004; Michael Jewell, letter to author, July 1, 2005. Federal district judge William Wayne Justice, the same judge who would preside over *Ruiz v. Estelle*, ruled Gatesville unconstitutional in *Morales v. Turman*, 383 F. Supp. 53 (E.D. Tex. 1974).
11. Ruíz, interview by author, July 6, 2003; Al Slaton, interview by author, July 7, 2002.
12. Ruíz, interview by author, July 6, 2003.

13. Mike Ward, "After 30 Years, Ruiz Is Ready for Case's Close," *Austin American Statesman*, June 12, 2002, A1, A4; Ruíz, interview by author, July 6, 2003.

14. David Ruíz, interview by author, July 6, 2003. David and Rose Marie divorced but subsequently remarried and remained together through the rest of his imprisonment.

15. David Ruíz, interview by author, July 6, 2003. According to Ruíz, the other two men in the car were Carl "Beartracks" McAdams and Jack Heard. Both would figure prominently in his federal lawsuit.

16. David Ruíz, interview by author, July 6, 2003; Carlton Carl, interview by author, December 14, 2004; Charles Sullivan, interview by author, February 25, 2003.

17. Horton and Nielsen, *Walking George*, 145; Walter LaFeber, *The Deadly Bet: LBJ, Vietnam, and the 1968 Election* (Lanham, Md.: Rowman & Littlefield, 2005), 132–33. On 1968, see Elena Poniatowska, *Massacre in Mexico* (New York: Viking Press, 1975); Tariq Ali and Susan Watkins, *1968: Marching in the Streets* (New York: Free Press, 1998); Mark Kurlansky, *1968: The Year That Rocked the World* (New York: Ballantine Books, 2004).

18. *Smith v. Allwright*, 321 U.S. 649 (1944); Darlene Clark Hine, *Black Victory: The Rise and Fall of the White Primary in Texas* (Millwood, N.Y.: KTO Press, 1979); *Sweatt v. Painter*, 339 U.S. 629 (1950); *Brown v. Board of Education*, 347 U.S. 483 (1954). See also Merline Pitre, *In Struggle Against Jim Crow: Lulu B. White and the NAACP, 1900–1957* (College Station: Texas A&M University Press, 1999); Michael J. Klarman, *From Jim Crow to Civil Rights: The Supreme Court and the Struggle for Racial Equality* (New York: Oxford University Press, 2004).

19. Campbell, *Gone to Texas*, 425–27; Robyn Duff Ladino, *Desegregating Texas Schools: Eisenhower, Shivers, and the Crisis at Mansfield High* (Austin: University of Texas Press, 1996); Ben F. Barnes, *Barn Burning, Barn Building: Tales of a Political Life, from LBJ Through George W. Bush and Beyond* (Albany, Tex.: Bright Sky Press, 2006), 170; Barr, *Black Texans*, 187.

20. Rubén Salazar, "Stranger in One's Land" (Washington, D.C.: U.S. Commission on Civil Rights, 1970), 2–3, 9; Montejano, *Anglos and Mexicans in the Making of Texas*, 282–85; Acuña, *Occupied America: A History of Chicanos*, 328–29; Barnes, *Barn Burning, Barn Building*, chap. 5; David Richards, *Once Upon a Time in Texas: A Liberal in the Lone Star State* (Austin: University of Texas Press, 2002).

21. On the repression of Black Muslim convicts in TDC, see "Prison Hits at Muslim Recruiting," *Austin American*, July 11, 1963, 8; Frances Jalet, "Ellis Report," November 6, 1968, William Bennet Turner Files, personal collection (hereafter Turner Files); Thomas Thompson, "Huntsville's Cost Factor: $2.37 Per Day Per Man," *Amarillo Globe-Times*, October 11, 1967, 1.

22. On the modern "code of the streets," see Philippe I. Bourgois, *In Search of Respect: Selling Crack in El Barrio*, 2nd ed. (New York: Cambridge University Press, 2003); Elijah Anderson, *Code of the Street: Decency, Violence, and the Moral Life of the Inner City* (New York: W. W. Norton, 1999).

23. David Ruíz, interview by author, July 6, 2003; David Ruíz, Original Complaint, Civil Action No. 5523, June 26, 1972, David Ruíz Files, personal collection (hereafter Ruíz Personal Files).

24. Steve Martin, interview by author, March 28, 1999; Charles Sullivan, interview by author, November 4, 2005; Redbird McCarter, interview by author, August 7, 2003. For background on Cruz, see *Novak v. Beto*, 320 F. Supp. 1206 (S.D.Tex. October 15, 1970); Susanne Mason, dir., *Writ Writer* (Independent Lens, 2008).

25. Harry H. Walsh, "Jailhouse Lawyers: The Texas Department of Corrections Revokes Their License," *Capitol University Law Review* 1, no. 1 (1972): 44, 55. Walsh was originally hired to represent inmates but later became TDC's chief counsel, defending the agency against inmates.

26. McCarter, interview by author, August 7, 2003. On TDC's treatment of Cruz, see *Cruz v. Beto*, 603 F.2d 1178 (5th Cir. [Tex] 1979).

27. *Lamar v. Coffield*, 951 F. Supp. 629 (S.D.Tex. 1996); Patricia Gail Littlefield, interview by author, July 8, 2004; *Cruz v. Beto*, 415 F.2d 325, 5th Cir. (Tex) (1969); William Bennett Turner, interview by author, September 15, 2003. Cruz was a prolific litigator, but he only began winning cases in the late 1960s. For one of his earliest setbacks, see *Cruz v. Beto*, 371 U.S. 916 (November 19, 1962).

28. *Novak v. Beto*, 453 F.2d 661 (1971); *Cruz v. Beto*, 603 F.2d 1178 (5th Cir. [Tex] 1979), 1180–81; Al Slaton, interview by author, July 7, 2002; Larry Casey, letter to author, March 28, 2004; Pete Wittenberg, "Inmates Allege Self Harm," *Houston Post*, October 4, 1978, 1A.

29. William B. Turner, interview by author, September 15, 2003; William Wayne Justice, "The Origins of the *Ruiz v. Estelle* Case," *Stanford Law Review* 43 (1990): 6.

30. David Ruíz, interview by author, July 6, 2003; William Bennett Turner, "Establishing the Rule of Law in Prisons: A Manual for Prisoner's Rights Litigation," *Stanford Law Review* 23 (1970): 473–518, in Jalet-Cruz Papers, box 94–042/9; Joe Morgenstern, "The Banker Who Robbed Banks," *New York Times Magazine*, November 12, 1989, 55–56, 73–75; Vanessa Jalet, interview by author, July 2, 2004; Al Slaton, interview by author, July 7, 2002.

31. Jalet, interview by author, July 2, 2004. For biographical information, see also Wolfgang Saxon, "Frances Jalet-Cruz, 84, Prison Rights Advocate," *New York Times*, December 2, 1994, D20; Misc. Jalet-Cruz clippings, Pope Collection, box 4C786; Mason, dir., *Writ Writer* (2008).

32. *Gideon v. Wainwright*, 372 U.S. 335 (1963); Jalet, interview by author, July 2, 2004; Chris Whitcraft, "Lawyer to Be Provided," *Austin American-Statesman*, June 24, 1967, 2.

33. "Legal Aid Action Summary," *Austin American-Statesman*, October 21, 1967, 32; Martin and Ekland-Olson, *Texas Prisons*, 29; Jalet, interview by author, July 2, 2004.

34. Frances T. Freeman (Jalet/Cruz), "How It All Began," *Alternatives to Imprisonment Communique*, August–September 1982; Jalet, interview by author, July 2, 2004.

35. Horton and Nielsen, *Walking George*, 36; Martin and Ekland-Olson, *Texas Prisons*, 30–31; Jalet, "Ellis Report," November 6, 1968; Jalet, interview by author, July 2, 2004; Freeman, "How It All Began."

36. Fred Cruz, diary entry, October 26, 1967, Jalet-Cruz Papers, box 94–042/2; Jalet, interview by author, July 2, 2004; Charles Sullivan, interview by author, February 25, 2003.

37. Beto counted among his admirers Princeton's John Dilulio and Harvard's Bruce Jackson. See Bruce Jackson, "Our Prisons Are Criminal," *New York Times Magazine*, September 22, 1968, 45–47, 54–60; Bruce Jackson, "Hard Time," *Texas Monthly*, December 1978, 138–43, 255–63; Dilulio, *Governing Prisons*.

38. *Dreyer v. Jalet*, 349 F. Supp. 452 (1972), 471; Freeman, "How It All Began"; Jalet, "Ellis Report"; "Frances Cruz vs. the State of Texas," misc. clipping, n.d., Pope Collection, 4C786; Jalet, interview by author, July 2, 2004.

39. *Cruz v. Beto*, 603 F.2d 1178 (1979); *Dreyer v. Jalet*; Horton and Nielsen, *Walking George*, 144–51; Jack Kyle, interview by author, July 20, 2002. At one point, a federal judge warned Beto that if he did not comply faithfully with court orders, he could face up to ten years in prison. Carl O. Bue Jr., U.S. District Judge, to George Beto, June 16, 1972, TDCJ Records, box 1998/038–63, *Dreyer v. Jalet* folder.

40. *Dreyer v. Jalet*, 472; Jalet, interview by author, July 2, 2004; Sullivan, interview by author, February 25, 2003.

41. Ruíz, interview, July 6, 2003; Linda Rocawich, "Texas Prisons on Trial," *Texas Observer*, September 22, 1978, 2–7; William Bennett Turner, interview by au-

thor, September 15, 2003; Patricia Gail Littlefield, interview by author, July 8, 2004; Al Slaton, interview by author, June 30, 2002.

42. David Ruíz, Original Complaint, Civil Action No. 5523, June 26, 1972, Ruíz Personal Files.

43. On the hands-off doctrine, see *Ruffin v. Commonwealth*, 62 Va. 790 (1871); *Banning v. Looney*, 213 F.2d 771 (1954); *U.S. v. Ragen*, 237 F.2d 953 (1956); *Graham v. Willingham*, 384 F.2d 367 (1967); *Bethea v. Crouse*, 417 F.2d 504 (1969). On the federalist retreat from Reconstruction, see *Slaughterhouse Cases*, 83 U.S. 36 (1872); *Civil Rights Cases*, 109 U.S. 3 (1883). See also Note, "Beyond the Critique of the Courts: A Critique of Judicial Refusal to Review the Complaints of Convicts," *Yale Law Journal* 72 (1963): 506–58; Malcolm Feeley and Edward L. Rubin, *Judicial Policy Making and the Modern State: How the Courts Reformed America's Prisons* (New York: Cambridge University Press, 1998), 31.

44. *Ex Parte Hull*, 312 U.S. 546 (1941); *Johnson v. Dye*, 175 F. 2d 250 (1949); *Dye v. Johnson*, 338 U.S. 864 (1949); *Atterbury v. Ragen*, 237 F.2d 953 (1956), *cert. denied*, 353 U.S. 964 (1957).

45. Morton J. Horwitz, *The Warren Court and the Pursuit of Justice* (New York: Hill and Wang, 1998); John Morton Blum, *Years of Discord: American Politics and Society, 1961–1974* (New York: W. W. Norton & Co., 1991), 214.

46. Michael J. Klarman, "Is the Supreme Court Sometimes Irrelevant? Race and the Southern Criminal Justice System in the 1940s," *Journal of American History* 89, no. 1 (2002): 119–53; *Green v. County School Board of New Kent County, Virginia*, 391 U.S. 430 (1968); Horwitz, *The Warren Court and the Pursuit of Justice*, xii.

47. Derrick A. Bell, *Silent Covenants: Brown v. Board of Education and the Unfulfilled Hopes for Racial Reform* (New York: Oxford University Press, 2004); Charles J. Ogletree, *All Deliberate Speed: Reflections on the First Half Century of Brown v. Board of Education* (New York: W. W. Norton & Co., 2004); *Hernandez v. Texas*, 347 U.S. 475 (1954); *Monroe v. Pape*, 365 U.S. 167 (1961). *Monroe* is a landmark case in prisoner rights law as it extended federal jurisdiction to state institutions. On persistent jury bias, see Randall Kennedy, *Race, Crime, and the Law* (New York: Pantheon Books, 1997); Cole, *No Equal Justice*.

48. *Mapp v. Ohio*, 367 U.S. 643 (1961); *Gideon v. Wainwright*, 372 U.S. 335 (1963); *Miranda v. Arizona*, 384 U.S. 436 (1966). Other important criminal justice cases include: *Griffin v. California*, 380 U.S. 609 (1965) and *Robinson v. California*, 370 U.S. 660 (1962). On the right to privacy, see *Griswold v. Connecticut*, 381 U.S. 479 (1965), which laid the groundwork for the most controversial decision of the Burger Court, the Texas-based abortion rights case, *Roe v. Wade*, 410 U.S. 113 (1973).

49. On the constitutional question of "incorporation," in which the Warren Court gradually ruled that almost all of the amendments in the Bill of Rights had been incorporated into the Fourteenth Amendment and thus applied to the states, see Horwitz, *The Warren Court and the Pursuit of Justice*, 91–98; Klarman, *From Jim Crow to Civil Rights*.

50. Horton and Nielsen, *Walking George*, 93–99; *Cooper v. Pate*, 378 U.S. 546 (1964); *Cooper v. Pate*, 382 F.2d 518 (1967); Jacobs, *Stateville*, 65; *Wolff v. McDonnell*, 418 U.S. 539 (1974), 555–56.

51. Feeley and Rubin, *Judicial Policy Making and the Modern State*, 31, 399, chap. 2; Clarke Forsythe, "The Historical Origins of Broad Federal Habeas Review Reconsidered," *Notre Dame Law Review* 70 (1995): 1075–171; William Wayne Justice, "Prisoners' Litigation in the Federal Courts," *Texas Law Review* 51, no. 4 (1973): 707–20. Section 1983 also appealed to prison litigants because its civil procedure rules allowed class-action status, extensive discovery, and creative solutions to systemic problems.

52. William Bennett Turner, "When Prisoners Sue: A Study of Prisoner Section

1983 Suits in the Federal Courts," *Harvard Law Review* 92, no. 3 (1979): 610–63; John Scalia, *Prisoner Petitions Filed in U.S. District Courts, 2000, with Trends 1980–2000*, NCJ 189430 (Washington, D.C.: BJS, January 2002). See also James Thomas, D. Keeler, and K. Harris, "Issues and Misconceptions in Prisoner Litigation: A Critical View," *Criminology* 24, no. 4 (November 1987): 901–19; John A. Filter, *Prisoners' Rights: The Supreme Court and Evolving Standards of Decency* (Wesport, Conn.: Greenwood Press, 2001). Federal prisoner litigation continued to expand through the 1980s and 1990s but was sharply curtailed by the 1996 Prison Litigation Reform Act, which set up legal barriers to prisoner suits that most plaintiffs have found insurmountable. See Margo Schlanger, "Inmate Litigation," *Harvard Law Review* 116, no. 6 (2003): 1555–706.

53. Malcolm Feeley and Van Swearingen, "The Prison Conditions Cases and the Bureaucratization of American Corrections: Influences, Impacts and Implications," *Pace University Law Review* 24, no. 2 (2004): 447; *Holt v. Sarver*, 309 F.Supp. 362 (1970), 368, 382. See also Feeley and Rubin, *Judicial Policy Making and the Modern State*, chap. 3; Bruce Jackson, *Killing Time: Life in the Arkansas Penitentiary* (Ithaca, N.Y.: Cornell University Press, 1977).

54. See Margo Schlanger, "Beyond the Hero Judge: Institutional Reform Litigation as Litigation," *Michigan Law Review* 97 (1999): 1994–2035; DiIulio, *Courts, Corrections, and the Constitution*; "Prison Reform Revisited: The Unfinished Agenda," special issue, *Pace Law Review* 24, no. 2 (2004).

55. *Holt v. Sarver*, 309 F.Supp. 362 (1970), 377; "Wilkinson Describes Texas Prisons as the 'Best in the World,'" *Houston Chronicle*, September 4, 1978; *Novak v. Beto*, 320 F.Supp. 1206 (1970), 1213.

56. Lynne E. Blais, "William Wayne Justice: The Life of the Law," *Texas Law Review* 77 (November 1998): 6; Martin and Ekland-Olson, *Texas Prisons*, 87; Frank R. Kemerer, *William Wayne Justice: A Judicial Biography* (Austin: University of Texas Press, 1991), 94; John Steinbeck, *Travels with Charley, in Search of America* (New York: Viking Press, 1962), 231.

57. Kemerer, *William Wayne Justice*, 357–58; Justice, "The Origins of the *Ruiz v. Estelle* Case," 3–5; Justice, interview by author, August 13, 2003. On the NAACP's Legal Defense Fund, see Jack Greenberg, *Crusaders in the Courts: How a Dedicated Band of Lawyers Fought for the Civil Rights Revolution* (New York: Basic Books, 1994).

58. *Novak v. Beto*, 453 F.2d 661 (1971); David Ruíz, interview by author, July 6, 2003.

59. Ruíz, Original Complaint; Ruíz, interview by author, July 6, 2003.

60. Ruíz, Original Complaint; Kemerer, *William Wayne Justice*, 76; Justice, interview by author, August 13, 2003; Justice, "The Origins of the *Ruiz v. Estelle* Case." Justice's docket was busier than most due to the practice known as "forum shopping," whereby plaintiffs attempted to place their cases before sympathetic judges. See Richards, *Once Upon a Time in Texas*, 89.

61. Turner, interview by author, September 15, 2003; Carey Adina Karmel, "Breaking Out of Prisoners' Rights," *American Lawyer* (March 1983): 50–51; Greenberg, *Crusaders in the Courts*, 457–59.

62. Turner to Frances Jalet, December 9, 1968, Turner Files; Michael Meltsner to Turner, December 5, 1968, Turner Files; Turner, interview by author, September 15, 2003; Karmel, "Breaking Out of Prisoners' Rights," 50–51; Feeley and Rubin, *Judicial Policy Making and the Modern State*, 51–79; Schlanger, "Beyond the Hero Judge," 2023. Turner had previously worked on *Novak v. Beto*, 453 F.2d 661 (1971) and *Cruz v. Beto*, 603 F.2d 1178 (1979).

63. Justice, "The Origins of the *Ruiz v. Estelle* Case."

64. Gail Littlefield, interview by author, July 8, 2004; *In re. Estelle*, 516 F.2d 480 (1975); Crouch and Marquart, *Appeal to Justice*, 124. TDC contested the involvement of the Justice Department but lost at the appellate level. The power of district judges to invite the Justice Department to join civil rights lawsuits

against the states was granted by statute in 1980. Civil Rights of Institutionalized Persons Act, 42 U.S.C.A. sec. 1997.

65. Justice, "The Origins of the *Ruiz v. Estelle* Case," 7; Ward Jim Estelle, "Introduction to Corrections," in Estelle Papers, box 3, folder 23; Martin and Ekland-Olson, *Texas Prisons*, 60, 95, 160; Feeley and Swearingen, "Prison Conditions Cases and the Bureaucratization of American Corrections," 470; Bill Habern, interview by author, July 19, 2002.

66. W. J. Estelle, "Prisons—Power—Politics," lecture, Sam Houston State University, June 12, 1974, Estelle Papers, box 3, folder 14; Martin and Ekland-Olson, *Texas Prisons*, 52. Most TDC watchers believed that Beto was a superior administrator: Jack Kyle, interview by author, July 20, 2002; Babe Schwartz, interview by author, August 2, 2003; DiIulio, *Governing Prisons*. But not everyone: Esso "Woody" Woods, interview by author, August 6, 2003.

67. *Ruiz v. Estelle*, 503 F.Supp. 1265 (1980), 1301, 1321; Wittenberg, "Inmates Allege Self Harm"; Martin and Ekland-Olson, *Texas Prisons*, 99; "Man Seeking Prison System Changes Denied Parole," *Houston Post*, November 15, 1978, 14A; Nolan Lewis, "The Inmate Who May Cost Texas Millions," *Houston Post*, January 11, 1987, 1A.

68. Estelle, "Prisons—Power—Politics"; Kemerer, *William Wayne Justice*, 360, 366; *In re Estelle*, 516 F.2d 480 (1975); Martin and Ekland-Olson, *Texas Prisons*, 161; *Estelle v. Justice*, 426 U.S. 925 (1976).

69. Littlefield, interview by author, July 8, 2004.

70. Justice, "Prisoners' Litigation in the Federal Courts," 720.

71. Martin and Ekland-Olson, *Texas Prisons*, 106–7; Crouch and Marquart, *Appeal to Justice*, 125.

72. Gloria Rubac, interview by author, August 6, 2003; Ernest Bailey, "Inmates Open Legal Attack Against Prisons," *Houston Post*, October 3, 1978, 1A, 5A; "Prisoners Resist Texas Prison Slave System" (Houston, Tex.: Prisoner Solidarity Committee, September 1978); Kemerer, *William Wayne Justice*, 86; Justice, interview by author, August 13, 2003.

73. Rubac, interview by author, August 6, 2003; Martin and Ekland-Olson, *Texas Prisons*, 119. In addition to Ruíz, L. D. Hilliard and O. D. Johnson attended the trial as representatives of the plaintiffs. This caused considerable tension, as Hilliard was a former building tender who didn't get along with the main group of writ writers involved in the case. Lawrence Pope to Stanley Bass, August 29, 1977, Pope Collection, box 4C922, *Ruiz v. Estelle* folder 1.

74. "U.S. Should Build Its Own Jail Here; Lindsay Protests," *Houston Post*, October 17, 1978; Gail Littlefield, interview by author, July 8, 2004.

75. Robert Lee Mudd, letter to author, June 18, 2004, March 2, 2004; "14 LULAC Councils Back Inmate Strike," *Houston Post*, October 8, 1978; "Inmates Hit 7 TDC Units with Strikes," *Houston Post*, October 11, 1978; Ernest Bailey, "TDC Director Lifts Blackout, Tells of Unrest," *Houston Post*, October 18, 1978, 1A, 27A. LULAC's support for TDC inmates was a bitter pill for Ed Idar to swallow, as he had previously worked with the group on Mexican American voting rights cases. For more on prisoner protests surrounding the case, see Rob Chase, *Civil Rights on the Cell Block: Race, Reform, and Violence in Texas Prisons and the Nation, 1945–1990* (PhD diss., University of Maryland, 2009).

76. Donna Brorby, interviews by author, September 14, 2003, September 15, 2003; William Bennett Turner, interviews by author, September 15, 2003; Karmel, "Breaking Out of Prisoners' Rights"; David Vanderhoof, e-mail to author; Gail Littlefield, interview by author, July 8, 2004. On Littlefield's previous prison case, see Larry W. Yackle, *Reform and Regret: The Story of Federal Judicial Involvement in the Alabama Prison System* (New York: Oxford University Press, 1989).

77. Martin and Ekland-Olson, *Texas Prisons*, 95–96; Kemerer, *William Wayne Justice*,

365; Richards, *Once Upon a Time in Texas*, chap. 10; Justice, interview by author, August 13, 2003.

78. Donna Brorby, interview by author, September 15, 2003; "Year of Testimony on Texas Prisons End with No Decision in Sight," *New York Times*, September 23, 1979, 52; Littlefield, interview by author, July 8, 2004; Justice, interview by author, August 13, 2003.

79. Justice, "The Origins of the *Ruiz v. Estelle* Case," 7. Justice argues that he had no alternative but to initiate the case. To do otherwise, he says, would have been to privilege formalism over reality, judicial deference over the law.

80. William Wayne Justice, interview by author, August 13, 2003; Donna Brorby, interview by author, September 15, 2003; William Bennett Turner, interview by author, September 15, 2003; Ernest Bailey, "Inmates Open Legal Attack Against Prisons," *Houston Post*, October 3, 1978, 1A, 5A; Martin and Ekland-Olson, *Texas Prisons*, 116–17.

81. Bruce Nichols, "Texas Prison System Goes to Trial," *Newport Daily News*, October 2, 1978, 12; Bailey, "Inmates Open Legal Attack Against Prisons"; Martin and Ekland-Olson, *Texas Prisons*, 117; Gail Littlefield, interview by author, July 8, 2004.

82. Martin and Ekland-Olson, *Texas Prisons*, 119; Ernest Bailey, "Inmates Open Legal Attack Against Prisons"; Justice, "Prisoners' Litigation in the Federal Courts," 712; Gail Littlefield, interview by author, July 8, 2004; William Bennett Turner, interview by author, September 15, 2003.

83. Richard Vara, "TDC Doctor Calls Hospital 'Very Unclean,'" *Houston Post*, November 2, 1978, 24A; John M. Crewdson, "Inmates Tell of Texas Prison Brutality," *New York Times*, November 11, 1978, 8.

84. *Ruiz v. Estelle*, 503 F.Supp. 1265 (1980), 1296, 1298; Al Slaton, interview by author, July 7, 2002; Ray Hill, interview by author, August 15, 2003; Martin and Ekland-Olson, *Texas Prisons*, 143–44; Willie Redis, interview by author, August 8, 2003; R. G. White, interview by author, August 14, 2003.

85. Texas was also involved in a precedent-setting case regarding the constitutional right of inmates to decent medical care; it was settled before the *Ruiz* case went to trial. *Estelle v. Gamble*, 429 U.S. 97 (1976). The plaintiff was later stabbed to death by another inmate in what one of the most prolific writ writers, Lawrence Pope, described as suspicious circumstances. "Inmate Deaths Since 1970," [1983?], Lawrence Pope Papers, box 4C937, numbered letters, folder 3.

86. Martin and Ekland-Olson, *Texas Prisons*, 153, 131–35, 157; Ernest Bailey, "Judge Dusts Off Rule Book in Halting TDC Questioning," *Houston Post*, October 20, 1978, 5A; Richard Vara, "Doctor Alleges Negligence in Prison," *Houston Post*, November 1, 1978, 6A; *Ruiz v. Estelle*, 503 F.Supp. 1265 (1980), 1341–44; Richard Vara, "TDC Inmate-Abuse Trial: Paraplegic Testifies to 3-Hour Pull Along Ground," *Houston Post*, October 18, 1978, 3A.

87. John M. Crewdson, "Inmates Tell of Texas Prison Brutality," *New York Times*, November 11, 1978, 8.

88. William Wayne Justice, interview by author, August 13, 2003; Donnis Baggett and Don Mason, "Ruiz Plays Down His Legal Expertise," *Dallas Morning News*, January 8, 1981, 5A; Donna Brorby, interview by author, September 14, 2003; Martin and Ekland-Olson, *Texas Prisons*, 147–48.

89. Gail Littlefield, interview by author, July 8, 2004; William Bennett Turner, interview by author, September 15, 2003; Donna Brorby, interview by author, September 14, 2003; Martin and Ekland-Olson, *Texas Prisons*, 140; William Wayne Justice, interview by author, July 31, 2002.

90. *Ruiz v. Estelle*, 503 F.Supp. 1265 (1980), 1341; Martin and Ekland-Olson, *Texas*

*Prisons*, 168; Donna Brorby, interview by author, September 14, 2003; William Wayne Justice, interview by author, August 13, 2003.

91. *Ruiz v. Estelle*, 503 F.Supp. 1265 (1980), 1391, 1289, 1384–85.
92. *Ruiz v. Estelle*, 503 F.Supp. 1265 (1980), 1391.
93. Wendell Rawls Jr., "Prisoner Conditions: Texas Officials Accept a Critical Decision as a Victory," *New York Times*, June 26, 1982, 9; *Ruiz v. Estelle*, 503 F.Supp. 1265 (1980), 1388. Justice's complete remedial decree is printed in *Ruiz v. Estelle*, 666 F.2d 854 (1982), 863–73. See also *Ruiz v. Estelle*, 679 F.2d 1115 (1982), 1146.
94. Filter, *Prisoners' Rights*; *Ruiz v. Estelle*, 666 F.2d 854 (1982), 873.
95. William Bennett Turner, interview by author, September 15, 2003; Robert Lee Mudd, letter to author, June 18, 2004.
96. Martin and Ekland-Olson, *Texas Prisons*, 185, 176; Kemerer, *William Wayne Justice*, 378.
97. *Ruiz v. Estelle*, 679 F.2d 1115 (1982), 1129; Martin and Ekland-Olson, *Texas Prisons*, 186.
98. Wendell Rawls Jr., "U.S. and Texas Seek Settlement," *New York Times*, December 19, 1981, 10; Andy Louis, "The Huntsville Hilton," *Texas Tribune*, December 10, 1981, 8; Gail Littlefield, interview by author, July 8, 2004. For more on Reynolds's controversial tenure at the Justice Department, see Anthony Lewis, "Is There No Respect?" *New York Times*, September 22, 1986, http://select.ny times.com/search/restricted/article?res=F50714FD3A550C718EDDA00 894DE484D81; Raymond Wolters, *Right Turn: William Bradford Reynolds, the Reagan Administration, and Black Civil Rights* (New Brunswick, N.J.: Transaction Publishers, 1996).
99. Crouch and Marquart, *Appeal to Justice*, 139; Glenn, *Texas Prisons*, 119.
100. TDC, *Annual Report* (1972), 9; TDC, *Annual Report* (1983), vi; *Ruiz v. Estelle*, 503 F.Supp. 1265 (1980), 1277–89; Rawls Jr., "U.S. and Texas Seek Settlement"; Texas, House Committee on Security and Sanctions, "Reference Information for Interim Meeting," report prepared by TDC, February 2, 1982; Betty Anne Duke, "Overcrowding in Texas Prisons" (Austin, Tex.: House of Representatives, April 18, 1979). Five new prisons went up in the decade after Ruíz filed his case, but there were never enough beds for bodies.
101. William T. Harper, *Eleven Days in Hell: The 1974 Carrasco Prison Siege in Huntsville, Texas* (Denton: University of North Texas Press, 2004); *A Time to Forget* (Huntsville, Tex.: TDC, 1975); Chet Brooks, interview by author, August 17, 2003.
102. Texas, House Committee on Security and Sanctions, "Reference Information for Interim Meeting," report prepared by TDC, February 2, 1982; Dwayne Komurke to Aubrey Komurke, November 23, 1981, Pope Collection, box 4C922, *Ruiz v. Estelle* folder 2.
103. Bill Habern, interview by author, July 19, 2002; "Trial Raises Questions on Texas Prison Conditions," *New York Times*, February 15, 1982, A13; Frank Klimko, "Inmate Witnesses in Eroy Brown Case Allege Harassment," *Houston Chronicle*, August 27, 1982, 27; DiIulio, *Governing Prisons*, 205–6.
104. Kemerer, *William Wayne Justice*, chap. 8; Richards, *Once Upon a Time in Texas*, chap. 10, p. 100; Mary Beth Rogers, *Barbara Jordan: American Hero* (New York: Bantam Books, 1998); Davidson, *Race and Class in Texas Politics*, chap. 8; Sam Kinch and Ben H. Procter, *Texas Under a Cloud* (Austin, Tex.: Jenkins, 1972); Barnes, *Barn Burning, Barn Building*, chaps. 11–12; Dave McNeely, "A Press Corps on the Lege," *Texas Observer*, May 27, 2005, 8–11.
105. Carlton Carl, interview by author, December 14, 2004; Campbell, *Gone to Texas*, 443; Babe Schwartz, interview by author, August 2, 2003.

106. Babe Schwartz, interview by author, August 2, 2003; Charles Sullivan, interview by author, February 25, 2003; Steve Martin, interview by author, June 28, 2002; Carlton Carl, interview by author, December 14, 2004; Martin and Ekland-Olson, *Texas Prisons*, 75–80; Chet Brooks et al., *Excerpts from the Final Report of the Joint Committee on Prison Reform* (Austin: Texas State Legislature, Joint Committee on Prison Reform, 1974), 11; Paul Keeper to Stephanie Malmros, January 20, 2003, Charles and Pauline Sullivan, private papers.

107. Charles Sullivan, interview by author, February 25, 2003; Charles Sullivan, e-mail to author, June 19, 2007; "Heroes of the People," *Texas Observer*, January 10, 1986, 16.

108. Brooks et al., *Excerpts from the Final Report of the Joint Committee on Prison Reform*, 11; Charles Sullivan, interview by author, February 27, 2003; Pauline and Charles Sullivan, "30 Years of CURE: The Struggle Is Its Own Reward," unpublished article (2002).

109. George N. Green, *The Establishment in Texas Politics: The Primitive Years, 1938–1957* (Westport, Conn.: Greenwood Press, 1979), chap. 10; John R. Knaggs, *Two-Party Texas: The John Tower Era, 1961–1984* (Austin, Tex.: Eakin Press, 1986); Roger M. Olien, *From Token to Triumph: The Texas Republicans, since 1920* (Dallas, Tex.: SMU Press, 1982); Davidson, *Race and Class in Texas Politics*, chap. 10; Carolyn Barta, *Bill Clements: Texian to His Toenails* (Austin, Tex.: Eakin Press, 1996).

110. *Ruiz v. Estelle* settlement conference notes, January 9, 1987, Ruiz SM Records, box 93–458/25, *Ruiz v. McCotter* file; Saralee Tiede, "He Stirs Up Prison Board," *Fort Worth Star Telegram*, February 8, 1983; Charles Sullivan, interview by author, February 25, 2003; Mary C. Bounds, "Locks Sprung on Prison Board," *Dallas Morning News*, December 11, 1984.

111. Karen Hastings, "Whittington Says Winning Is Worth the Price," *Fort Worth Star Telegram*, n.d., [1985], Ruiz Files, box 93–458/8, clippings folder; Tiede, "He Stirs Up Prison Board"; Simon Romero, "Profile of Harry Whittington," *International Herald Tribune*, February 15, 2006; Leslie Whitaker, "Prison Reform for the Mentally Handicapped," *Texas Observer*, September 16, 1983, 7–11; Bounds, "Locks Sprung on Prison Board."

112. Tiede, "He Stirs Up Prison Board"; Patti Kilday, "Maverick Sparks Controversies on Prison Board," *Dallas Times Herald*, May 29, 1983, 39, 42; Charles Sullivan, interview by author, February 27, 2003; Harry Whittington, Speech to Rotary Club, May 3, 1983, Estelle Papers, box 3, folder 15. Some Democrats accused Whittington of stirring up trouble for partisan gain. Crouch and Marquart, *Appeal to Justice*, 141.

113. DiIulio, *Governing Prisons*, 218; Rawls Jr., "U.S. and Texas Seek Settlement"; Gail Littlefield, interview by author, July 7, 2004; *Ruiz v. Estelle*, 679 F.2d 1115 (1982), 1146, 1164; Wendell Rawls Jr., "Prisoner Conditions: Texas Officials Accept a Critical Decision as a Victory," *New York Times*, June 26, 1982, 9.

114. Crouch and Marquart, *Appeal to Justice*, 137, 139; Charles Sullivan, "Prison Reform Finally Arrives," *Texas Observer*, July 8, 1983, 6–8; Saralee Tiede, "Legislator Says TDC Has Money for More Guards," *Fort Worth Star Telegram*, September 23, 1983; Martin and Ekland-Olson, *Texas Prisons*, 203–9; Steve Martin, interview by author, June 28, 2002; Ray Keller, "Reform Package Designed to Control Growth of State Prisons," *Dallas Morning News*, May 8, 1983, 3G; Anne Marie Kilday, "Prison Work Furloughs Urged to End Crowding," *Houston Post*, February 17, 1981, 2.

115. Ward Jim Estelle, statement on corruption allegations, February 2, 1984, Estelle Papers, box 3, folder 15; Estelle, resignation speech, September 1983, Estelle Papers, box 3, folder 15.

116. Jay Rosser, "Estelle Forced to Resign Early," *Corpus Christi Caller*, October 8,

1983, 23; Estelle, statement on corruption allegations; W. J. Estelle brochure for 1980 ACA Presidential Campaign, Estelle Papers, 1980, box 3, folder 1; Kevin Krajick et al., "Profile Texas," *Corrections Magazine*, March 1978, 16.

## 8: RETRIBUTIVE REVOLUTION

1. Quoted in Crouch and Marquart, *Appeal to Justice*, 195.
2. Campbell, *Gone to Texas*, 446; Michael Vines, "Looking at Prison Reform from the Inside," *Texas Observer*, September 16, 1983, 12–13; Robert Reinhold, "Texas Prison Reformer Sees Incompetence Behind Walls," *New York Times*, July 8, 1984, E5; Patti Kilday, "Prison Option Legislation Gains Support," *Dallas Times Herald*, February 26, 1983.
3. "Governor Signs Prisons Legislation," *Houston Post*, May 26, 1983; Vines, "Looking at Prison Reform from the Inside," 12–13; Charles Sullivan, "Prison Reform Finally Arrives," *Texas Observer*, July 8, 1983, 6–8.
4. "New Blood: Reformers Want Prison Director from Outside System," *Austin American-Statesman*, December 20, 1983, B4. Procunier was appointed in May 1984, taking over from Red McKaskle, the interim director. Although Procunier was regarded as a reform-minded outsider, he was a conservative in the California context. Bill Turner had previously been involved in a lawsuit against him, though the attorney welcomed Procunier's appointment in Texas. See *Procunier v. Martinez*, 416 U.S. 396 (1974). See also William Richard Wilkinson, John C. Burnham, and Joseph F. Spillane, *Prison Work: A Tale of Thirty Years in the California Department of Corrections* (Columbus: Ohio State University, 2005).
5. Crouch and Marquart, *Appeal to Justice*, 145–46; Virginia Ellis, "Legislature Faces Prison Reform Fight," *Dallas Times Herald*, November 25, 1984; DiIulio, *Governing Prisons*, 117, 296; Michael Vines, "A View from the Inside, Part II: TDC—The Procunier Era," *Texas Observer*, June 28, 1985, 5–9.
6. Crouch and Marquart, *Appeal to Justice*, 146–47; Martin and Ekland-Olson, *Texas Prisons*, 242–43; Charles Sullivan, "The Backlash That Failed," *Texas Observer*, July 12, 1985, 6–8. See also Glenn, *Texas Prisons*, 181; Harry Whittington, speech to Rotary Club, May 3, 1983.
7. Sullivan, "The Backlash That Failed," 8; Sullivan, e-mail to author, June 20, 2007; Vera Titunik, "Toward Nationwide Prison Reform," *Texas Observer*, January 10, 1986, 16–17.
8. Kemerer, *William Wayne Justice*; Sullivan, interview by author, February 25, 2003; Campbell, *Gone to Texas*, 440; Richards, *Once Upon a Time in Texas*, 100.
9. Ramsey Clark, "Prisons: Factories of Crime," in David M. Petersen and Charles Wellington Thomas, *Corrections: Problems and Prospects* (Englewood Cliffs, N.J.: Prentice Hall, 1975), 33, 50; Sullivan, "The Backlash That Failed," 8; Daniel Glaser, "The Prison of the Future," in Petersen and Thomas, *Corrections: Problems and Prospects*, 299–301. Glaser's piece recalled the deinstitutionalizing idealism of Thomas Mott Osborne.
10. Mauer, *Race to Incarcerate*, 15–16; Calvert R. Dodge, *A Nation Without Prisons: Alternatives to Incarceration* (Lexington, Mass.: Lexington Books, 1975); Robert Sommer, *The End of Imprisonment* (New York: Oxford University Press, 1976), 8–9; Horton and Nielsen, *Walking George*, 144. On the understudied connections between deinstitutionalization of the mentally ill and the incarceration boom, see Bernard E. Harcourt, "From the Asylum to the Prison: Rethinking the Incarceration Revolution," *Texas Law Review* 84 (2006): 1751–86.
11. Norval Morris, "Prison in Evolution," in Eldefonso, *Issues in Corrections: A Book of Readings*, 250; Morris, *The Future of Imprisonment*.
12. Robert Dallek, *Flawed Giant: Lyndon Johnson and His Times, 1961–1973* (New York: Oxford University Press, 1998), 112, 120.

13. Barnes, *Barn Burning, Barn Building*, 68; J. Evetts Haley, *A Texan Looks at Lyndon* (Canyon, Tex.: Palo Duro Press, 1964), 173, 229.

14. Thomas Byrne Edsall and Mary D. Edsall, *Chain Reaction: The Impact of Race, Rights, and Taxes on American Politics* (New York: W. W. Norton, 1991), 36, 47–48; Murakawa, "The Origins of the Carceral Crisis"; Simon, *Governing Through Crime.*

15. Lyndon Johnson, *The Choices We Face* (New York: Bantam Books, 1969), 125.

16. Dan T. Carter, *The Politics of Rage: George Wallace, the Origins of the New Conservatism, and the Transformation of American Politics* (Baton Rouge: Louisiana State University Press, 2000), 11; Beckett, *Making Crime Pay*, 34.

17. Beckett, *Making Crime Pay*, 31–32; Carter, *Politics of Rage*, 6.

18. *Crime and Justice Atlas* (Washington, D.C.: National Institute of Justice, June 2000), 38–39; "United States Crime Rates, 1960–2005," http://www.disaster center.com/crime/uscrime.htm; Thomas E. Cronin, Tania Z. Cronin, and Michael E. Milakovich, *U.S. v. Crime in the Streets* (Bloomington: Indiana University Press, 1981), 17. On the problems with longitudinal crime data, see Michael Maltz, *Bridging Gaps in Police Crime Data*, Discussion Paper, NCJ 176365 (Washington, D.C.: BJS, September 1999).

19. Ramsey Clark, *Crime in America: Observations on Its Nature, Causes, Prevention and Control*, 2nd ed. (New York: Pocket Books, 1971); Nicholas Katzenbach et al., *The Challenge of Crime in a Free Society* (Washington, D.C.: President's Commission on Law Enforcement and Administration of Justice, February 1967); George Jackson, *Soledad Brother: The Prison Letters of George Jackson* (New York: Bantam Books, 1970); Evans and Moore, *The Lawbreakers*; Cronin, Cronin, and Milakovich, *U.S. v. Crime in the Streets*, 5–10; Wilson, *Thinking About Crime*, 20–23; Zimring, *Great American Crime Decline*, chap. 3; Parenti, *Lockdown America*, chap. 2; Elliot Currie, *Crime and Punishment in America* (New York: Metropolitan Books, 1999), chap. 4.

20. Cronin, Cronin, and Milakovich, *U.S. v. Crime in the Streets*, 35; Beckett, *Making Crime Pay*, 4, 26; Stuart A. Scheingold, *The Politics of Street Crime: Criminal Process and Cultural Obsession* (Philadelphia: Temple University Press, 1991).

21. Philip A. Klinkner and Rogers M. Smith, *The Unsteady March: The Rise and Decline of Racial Equality in America* (Chicago: University of Chicago Press, 1999), 262; Beckett, *Making Crime Pay*, 31.

22. Cronin, Cronin, and Milakovich, *U.S. v. Crime in the Streets*, 18; Beckett, *Making Crime Pay*, 35.

23. Bart Barnes, "Barry Goldwater, GOP Hero, Dies," *Washington Post*, May 30, 1998, A1; "President Elect 1964," http://www.presidentelect.org/e1964.html; Edsall and Edsall, *Chain Reaction*, 36, 43. See Rick Perlstein, *Before the Storm: Barry Goldwater and the Unmaking of the American Consensus* (New York: Hill and Wang, 2001).

24. Cronin, Cronin, and Milakovich, *U.S. v. Crime in the Streets*, 27, 29.

25. Parenti, *Lockdown America*, chap. 1; Dan Baum, *Smoke and Mirrors: The War on Drugs and the Politics of Failure* (Boston: Little, Brown, 1996), 9; Cronin, Cronin, and Milakovich, *U.S. v. Crime in the Streets*, 30–33, 29; Malcolm Feeley and Austin Sarat, *The Policy Dilemma: Federal Crime Policy and the Law Enforcement Assistance Administration* (Minneapolis: University of Minnesota Press, 1980).

26. Richard Harris, *The Fear of Crime* (New York: Praeger, 1969), 10, 16; Cronin, Cronin, and Milakovich, *U.S. v. Crime in the Streets*, 39–40.

27. Katzenbach et al., *The Challenge of Crime in a Free Society*; Cronin, Cronin, and Milakovich, *U.S. v. Crime in the Streets*, 40, 38; Jonathan Simon, "Governing Through Crime," in *The Crime Conundrum: Essays on Criminal Justice*, eds. Lawrence M. Friedman and George Fisher (Boulder, Colo.: Westview Press, 1997), 94–97; Simon, *Governing Through Crime*, 90; Harris, *The Fear of Crime*, 14–15.

28. "The Work That Faces Us," *Time*, November 13, 1964, http://www.time.com/time/magazine/article/0,9171,898215,00.html; Dennis Simon, "The War in Vietnam, 1965–1968," http://faculty.smu.edu/dsimon/Change-Viet2.html.

29. Otto Kerner, chair, *Report of the National Advisory Commission on Civil Disorders* (New York: Bantam Books, 1968), 31; Cronin, Cronin, and Milakovich, *U.S. v. Crime in the Streets*, 60, 69, 75; Dan T. Carter, *From George Wallace to Newt Gingrich: Race in the Conservative Counterrevolution, 1963–1994* (Baton Rouge: Louisiana State University Press, 1996), 30.

30. Kerner, *Report of the National Advisory Commission on Civil Disorders*, 1–2; Jules Witcover, *The Year the Dream Died: Revisiting 1968 in America* (New York: Warner Books, 1997).

31. Richard Nixon, "What Has Happened to America?" *Reader's Digest*, October 1967, 3; Beckett, *Making Crime Pay*, 38; Parenti, *Lockdown America*, 8.

32. Baum, *Smoke and Mirrors*, 12–13; Beckett, *Making Crime Pay*, 31, 42; "Nixon's Acceptance of the Republican Party Nomination for President," August 8, 1968, http://www.watergate.info/nixon/acceptance-speech-1968.shtml; "Haldeman Diaries Reveal Nixon Fed Up with Blacks During His White House Tenure," *Jet*, June 13, 1994, 12.

33. "Nixon's Hard-Won Chance to Lead," *Time*, November 15, 1968, http://www.time.com/time/magazine/article/0,9171,723848,00.html; Jeremy D. Mayer, *Running on Race: Racial Politics in Presidential Campaigns, 1960–2000* (New York: Random House, 2002), 94; Rick Perlstein, *Nixonland: The Rise of a President and the Fracturing of America* (New York: Scribner, 2008), 354.

34. Tom Wicker, *A Time to Die: The Attica Prison Revolt*, 1994 ed. (Lincoln: University of Nebraska Press, 1975); Beckett, *Making Crime Pay*, 38–40; Cronin, Cronin, and Milakovich, *U.S. v. Crime in the Streets*, 76.

35. Parenti, *Lockdown America*, 10–12; Cronin, Cronin, and Milakovich, *U.S. v. Crime in the Streets*, 96, 84, 93; Baum, *Smoke and Mirrors*, 16–17; Simon, *Governing Through Crime*, 100.

36. Although Nixon aimed to shift the judiciary rightward, the Burger Court carried forward Warren's legacy to a substantial extent, handing down decisions like *Holt v. Sarver*, *Roe v. Wade*, and *Furman v. Georgia* (1972). The court also refused to aid Texas in the *Ruiz* case, thus ensuring that Judge Justice could continue riding herd on TDC. See Bernard Schwartz, *The Burger Court: Counter-Revolution or Confirmation?* (New York: Oxford University Press, 1998); James MacGregor Burns, *Packing the Court: The Rise of Judicial Power and the Coming Crisis of the Supreme Court* (New York: Penguin Press, 2009).

37. Parenti, *Lockdown America*, 9; Baum, *Smoke and Mirrors*, 61.

38. Baum, *Smoke and Mirrors*, 61, 42–44, 55–56, 24–25, 36, 66, 75; Parenti, *Lockdown America*, 13, 19.

39. Cronin, Cronin, and Milakovich, *U.S. v. Crime in the Streets*, 75, 68.

40. AFSC Working Party, *Struggle for Justice: A Report on Crime and Punishment in America* (New York: Hill & Wang, 1971), 97, v.

41. Malcolm X, *Malcolm X Speaks: Selected Speeches and Statements* (New York: Grove Weidenfeld, 1990), 8.

42. Ronald Reagan, inaugural address, January 5, 1967, http://www.reagan.utexas.edu/archives/speeches/govspeech/01051967a.htm; Jackson, *Soledad Brother*, 24–25; Cummins, *The Rise and Fall of California's Radical Prison Movement*, 209–10.

43. Charles Sullivan, e-mail to author, July 5, 2007; Jackson, *Soledad Brother*, 27.

44. McKelvey, *American Prisons*, 352; New York, *Attica: The Official Report of the New York State Special Commission on Attica* (New York: Praeger, 1972), 3–4.

45. New York, *Attica*, 2, 194, appendix. See also Wicker, *A Time to Die: The Attica Prison Revolt*.

46. "Prisons: The Way to Reform," *Time*, September 27, 1971, http://www.time

.com/time/magazine/article/0,9171,910033,00.html; "War at Attica: Was There No Other Way?" *Time*, September 27, 1971, http://www.time.com/time/magazine/article/0,9171,910027,00.html.

47. Cahalan, "Historical Corrections Statistics," 30; Kathleen Maguire and Ann L. Patore, eds., *Sourcebook of Criminal Justice Statistics 2002*, NCJ 203301 (Washington, D.C.: BJS, 2004), 495.

48. Cahalan, "Historical Corrections Statistics," 30; Texas, House Study Group, *Overcrowding in Texas Prisons* (Austin, Texas, April 18, 1979).

49. Davidson, *Race and Class in Texas Politics*, 17; Perlstein, *Before the Storm*, 469.

50. Davidson, *Race and Class in Texas Politics*, 234, 228, 238, 235; Richards, *Once Upon a Time in Texas*, 98.

51. Haley, *A Texan Looks at Lyndon*, 218; Elna C. Green, "From Antisuffragism to Anti-Communism: The Conservative Career of Ida M. Darden," *Journal of Southern History* 65, no. 2 (1999): 27.

52. Carlton Carl, interview by author, December 14, 2004; Crouch and Marquart, *Appeal to Justice*, 121; Barnes, *Barn Burning, Barn Building*, 104; James Reston, *The Lone Star: The Life of John Connally* (New York: Harper & Row, 1989), 130, 121, 106; Carlton Carl, interview by author, December 14, 2004; Dick Reavis, "Why I Turned in Lee Otis Johnson," *Texas Monthly*, July 1980, 107, 110.

53. Griffin, Smith, Jr. "How the New Drug Law Was Made," *Texas Monthly*, September 1973, 73, 67; G. Alan Robison, e-mail to author, September 24, 2004.

54. Smith, "How the New Drug Law Was Made," 68. Two years after Attica, New York would follow suit, passing its own draconian anti-narcotics statutes.

55. Smith, "How the New Drug Law Was Made"; House Study Group, *Overcrowding in Texas Prisons*, 5–8; Linda Rocawich, "Building Cells for 10,000 More Prisoners," *Texas Observer*, April 13, 1979, 10; Ray Hill, interview by author, July 21, 2002.

56. "Hill Edges Ahead of Clements," *Galveston Daily News*, October 22, 1978, 2A; Richards, *Once Upon a Time in Texas*, 201–3; "McCotter Should Be Fired, Clements Says," *Huntsville Item*, October 24, 1986, 1A, 10A; Dale Rice, "Board Rebuts Clements on Furloughs," *Dallas Times Herald*, October 22, 1988.

57. "McLoed Praises Clements' Last Veto," *Galveston Daily News*, June 15, 1979, 2A; Babe Schwartz, interview by author, August 2, 2003; Barta, *Bill Clements*, 232, 253, xi, 276; "Gov. Bill: Jail Them Kids!" *Texas Observer*, June 18, 1982; Bruce A. Lipshy et al., "Preliminary Report to the Governor" (Austin, Tex.: Blue Ribbon Commission for the Comprehensive Review of the Criminal Justice Corrections System, 1982); Linda Rocawich, "Building Cells for 10,000 More Prisoners," *Texas Observer*, April 13, 1979; Cahalan, "Historical Corrections Statistics," 29.

58. Baum, *Smoke and Mirrors*, 128–29, 131; Marsha Manatt, "Parents, Peers, and Pot II: Parents in Action" (Rockville, Md.: National Institute on Drug Abuse, 1983), 116–17, 119, 124; Barta, *Bill Clements*, 251.

59. Manatt, "Parents, Peers, and Pot II," 123, 125, 128; Baum, *Smoke and Mirrors*, 141, 146.

60. Dick Reavis, "Charlie Brooks' Last Words," *Texas Monthly*, February 1983, 101–5, 170–82; Marquart, Ekland-Olson, and Sorensen, *The Rope, the Chair, and the Needle*, chap. 8, 148.

61. Pickett, *Within These Walls*, 67.

62. Ibid., 63, 67; Willett and Rozelle, *Warden*, 136; Marquart, Ekland-Olson, and Sorensen, *The Rope, the Chair, and the Needle*, 143.

63. Kurt Anderson, "A 'More Palatable' Way of Killing," *Time*, December 20, 1982, http://www.time.com/time/printout/0,8816,923178,00.html; Pickett, *Within These Walls*, 75; Marquart, Ekland-Olson, and Sorensen, *The Rope, the Chair, and the Needle*, 128.

64. Willett and Rozelle, *Warden*, 139, 175.

65. Doug Cosper, "Mr. Fix-It: The Man Who Salvaged Four Prison Systems Working

His Magic on Texas' Penitentiaries," *Tyler Morning Telegraph*, September 9, 1984; Dale Rice, "Procunier Accepts Job's Challenges, Wins Confidence," *Dallas Times Herald*, November 25, 1984, 26A; DiIulio, *Governing Prisons*, 220; Sullivan, interview by author, February 25, 2003; "Governor Signs Prisons Legislation," *Houston Post*, May 26, 1983.

66. Banning Lary and John Sullivan, "Initial Interview: Director Raymond Procunier Reveals . . . ," *Echo*, August/September 1984, 1–2; "TDC Names New Director," *Joint Endeavor* 9, no. 2 (Summer 1984): 11; Cosper, "Mr. Fix-It"; Paul Reyes, "TDC Director Vows Get-Tough Policy to Re-establish Order," *Houston Chronicle*, August 25, 1984; Fred King, "TDC Woes Surprised Chief," *Houston Post*, November 18, 1984.

67. Paul Taylor, "When Inmates Quit Running Texas Prisons, Anarchy Came," *Washington Post*, September 9, 1984, A1; Press, "Inside America's Toughest Prison," 53; Vincent Nathan, "Reflections on Two Decades of Court-Ordered Prison Reform," 1988, Beto Papers, box 4-1-2; George Kuempel, "Power Struggle: Texas Prison Gangs Fighting for Control in Vacuum Left By Reforms, Officials Say," *Dallas Morning News*, October 1, 1984; Cosper, "Mr. Fix-It."

68. Crouch and Marquart, *Appeal to Justice*, 155, 158, 156. The expansion of the guard force required extensive recruitment and training, as the turnover remained high throughout the period. DiIulio, *Governing Prisons*, 221, 117.

69. Sergeant Meduna, interview by author, July 22, 2002.

70. Mary C. Bounds, "Texas Prison Costs Lowest in U.S., Study Shows," *Dallas Morning News*, September 2, 1984.

71. Crouch and Marquart, *Appeal to Justice*, 152–53.

72. Ibid., 175; DiIulio, *Governing Prisons*, 220.

73. Vines, "A View from Inside, Part One," 7; John Sharp, Texas Comptroller of Public Accounts, "Behind the Walls: The Price and Performance of the Texas Department of Criminal Justice" (Austin: Texas Performance Review, 1994); Press, "Inside America's Toughest Prison," 61; Crouch and Marquart, *Appeal to Justice*, 170, 174.

74. Taylor, "When Inmates Quit Running Texas Prisons, Anarchy Came."

75. Brett Massey, letter to author, March 25, 2004; J. W. Campbell, interview by author, August 5, 2002; Glenn, *Texas Prisons*, 162.

76. Frank Klimko, "2 Are Questioned in Inmate Torching," *Houston Chronicle*, September 20, 1984; Don Yaeger, "Gangs at Root of Attacks in Texas' Prison System," newspaper clipping, September 23, 1984, Pope Papers, box 4C936; Dick Reavis, "How They Ruined Our Prisons," *Texas Monthly*, May 1985, 244; Jewell, letter to author, January 8, 2006; Crouch and Marquart, *Appeal to Justice*, 190.

77. Captain Cherry, interview by author, July 23, 2002; George Kuempel, "Power Struggle: Texas Prison Gangs Fighting for Control in Vacuum Left by Reforms, Officials Say," *Dallas Morning News*, October 1, 1984; Don Yaeger, "Gangs at Root of Attacks in Texas' Prison System," newspaper clipping, September 23, 1984, Pope Papers, box 4C936; Crouch and Marquart, *Appeal to Justice*, 205–6. On the rise of prison gangs in Texas more generally, see Robert S. Fong, "The Organizational Structure of Prison Gangs: A Texas Case Study," *Federal Probation* 54, no. 1 (1990): 36–43; Robert S. Fong, "A Comparative Study of the Organizational Aspects of Two Texas Prison Gangs: Texas Syndicate and Mexican Mafia" (PhD diss., Sam Houston State University, 1987); Salvador Buentello, "Combating Gangs in Texas," *Corrections Today*, July 1992, 58–60.

78. Crouch and Marquart, *Appeal to Justice*, 165, 195; Fred King, "6 Units to House Unruly Inmates," *Houston Post*, August 30, 1984; Reavis, "How They Ruined Our Prisons," 159, 232; Glenn, *Texas Prisons*; Fred King, "TDC Guards Not in 'Control,'" *Houston Post*, August 2, 1984; DiIulio, *Governing Prisons*, 56.

79. Reyes, "TDC Director Vows Get-Tough Policy to Re-establish Order"; Paul Reyes

and Frank Klimko, "End the Violence or Else, White Warns TDC Brass," *Houston Chronicle*, August 4, 1984; Wayne King, "Governor Intervenes in Texas Prison Violence," *New York Times*, August 12, 1984, 27; Fred King, "McCotter Named TDC Director," *Houston Post*, June 18, 1985, 1A.

80. King, "McCotter Named TDC Director"; Doug Casper, "Lockdown: New TDC Director Brings 'Ultimate Control' to State's Violence-Plagued Prison System," *Tyler Morning Telegraph*, August 26, 1984; King, "6 Units to House Unruly Inmates"; Crouch and Marquart, *Appeal to Justice*, 212, 217.

81. Frank Klimko, "Death Row Riot Quelled by Guards," *Houston Chronicle*, January 23, 1985; Press, "Inside America's Toughest Prison," 56, 58; Crouch and Marquart, *Appeal to Justice*, 166; Robert Lee Mudd, "A View from an Isolation Chamber," unpublished essay (1987); Reavis, "How They Ruined Our Prisons," 245.

82. Mark Toohey, "Clements Tours New Prison, Says Texas Needs More Like It," *Houston Chronicle*, October 6, 1987; Kenneth Broussard, letter to author, January 17, 2006.

83. David A. Ward and Thomas G. Werlich, "Alcatraz and Marion: Evaluating Super-Maximum Custody," *Punishment and Society* 5, no. 1 (2003); Roy D. King, "The Rise and Rise of Supermax: An American Solution in Search of a Problem," *Punishment and Society* 1, no. 2 (1999); Casper, "Lockdown."

84. Frank Klimko, "Lewis Says Judge's Prison Decrees Serve Criminals," *Houston Chronicle*, January 5, 1985; Press, "Inside America's Toughest Prison," 56; Reavis, "How They Ruined Our Prisons"; Anonymous letter to William Wayne Justice, [1991?], Ruiz-SM Records, box 93–548/9; Candice Hughes, "At 65, Judge Considers Image in State He Has Changed," *Lufkin Daily News*, July 14, 1985, 4A.

85. "Texas Crime Rates 1960–2007," http://www.disastercenter.com/crime/txcrime .htm.

86. Sheldon Ekland-Olson and W. R. Kelly, *Justice Under Pressure: A Comparison of Recidivism Patterns Among Four Successive Parolee Cohorts* (New York: Springer-Verlag, 1993), 54, 37–38, 50; "Lapse of Sanity," *Waco-Tribune Herald*, August 27, 1984; Major Garrett, "Officials Decry Early Release of Convicts," *Amarillo Daily News*, February 24, 1985.

87. Gary Cartwright, "Free to Kill," *Texas Monthly*, August 1992; Glenn, *Texas Prisons*, 227–31; Lavergne, *Bad Boy from Rosebud*.

88. Willett and Rozelle, *Warden*, 174–75.

89. Jim Phillips, "Mired in Contradiction: Prison Expansion Can't Keep Pace with Population," *Austin American-Statesman*, August 25, 1987, A1, A10; Joe Vargo, "Tougher Prison Laws Requested," *Austin American-Statesman*, October 15, 1986.

90. Sam Johnson and Richard H. Collins, "Protecting the Rights of Victims," *Dallas Morning News*, May 12, 1988. On the victims' rights movement more generally, see Simon, *Governing Through Crime*.

91. "Texans Want Felons Locked Up," *Waco Tribune Herald*, February 24, 1985. In the 1982 campaign, a Clements mailing had dredged up an old drunk-driving citation. In the rematch, Rove accused White of bugging his office, the very crime that had snared his first political idol, Richard Nixon (the FBI later dropped the investigation but not before the press ran with it). James Moore and Wayne Slater, *Bush's Brain: How Karl Rove Made George W. Bush Presidential* (New York: Wiley, 2003), chap. 2.

92. Stuart Hall et al., *Policing the Crisis: Mugging, the State, and Law and Order* (New York: Holmes & Meier, 1978); Jamie Watson et al., *A Portrait of Prisoner Reentry in Texas* (Washington, D.C.: Urban Institute, March 2004), 11; Editor, "Crime-Fighting Bill Worthwhile Effort," *Brazosport Facts*, April 19, 1987, 4A; Nate Blakeslee, *Tulia: Race, Cocaine, and Corruption in a Small Texas Town* (New York: PublicAffairs, 2005), 202, 207; Scott Henson, *Too Far Off Task* (Austin, Tex.: ACLU, 2002).

93. Ekland-Olson and Kelly, *Justice Under Pressure*, 14, 17; Babe Schwartz, interview by author, August 2, 2003.

94. Ekland-Olson and Kelly, *Justice Under Pressure*, 15–17, 24; Jim Phillips, "Mired in Contradiction: Prison Expansion Can't Keep Pace with Population," *Austin American-Statesman*, August 25, 1987, A1, A10.

95. TDC, *Annual Report* (1980), 15, 54; TDC, *Annual Report* (1981), 25, 56–57; TDC, *Annual Report* (1982), 12–13, 38–43; TDC, *Annual Report* (1988), 69.

96. Jorjanna Price, "Put Inmates in K-Marts, Storage Lockers: Clements," *Houston Post*, January 8, 1988; Dave Denison, "Boom Times," *Texas Observer*, January 29, 1988, 3; Tony Fabelo, "Implementing the Most Far-Reaching Criminal Justice Reforms in the Nation: Can Texas Do It Right?" (Austin, Tex.: Criminal Justice Policy Counsel [hereafter CJPC], September 1993); "Officials Doubt Planned Prisons Will Fill Needs," *Austin American-Statesman*, April 4, 1988; Ekland-Olson and Kelly, *Justice Under Pressure*, 14; Martin and Ekland-Olson, *Texas Prisons*, xiv; Barta, *Bill Clements*, 369; Dave Denison, "Scholz Garden Debate: On Prison Construction—Is Gov. Clements Going Overboard in Expanding the Prison System?" *Texas Observer*, September 2, 1988, 6.

97. Denison, "Boom Times," 3; TDCJ, *Annual Report*, 1990, ii.

98. TDC, *Annual Report* (1980), 36; TDCJ, *Annual Report* (1991), 32; Reavis, "How They Ruined Our Prisons," 245–46; TDCJ, "Unit Directory"; Chuck Hurt, interview by author, July 17, 2002; Patsy Sims, "From Chain Gangs to Chain Stores: Sugar Land's storied prison farm gives way to suburban sprawl," *Texas Observer*, June 13, 2008, http://www.texasobserver.org/article.php?aid=2786.

99. Todd Vogel, "Jails Could Be Texas' Next Ten-Gallon Business," *BusinessWeek*, April 20, 1987, 33; TDCJ, *Annual Report* (1990); Ekland-Olson and Kelly, *Justice Under Pressure*, 22; Fabelo, "Implementing the Most Far-Reaching Criminal Justice Reforms in the Nation"; Dave Denison, "The Makings of a Prison Industry," *Texas Observer*, April 17, 1987, 2–4; Philip A. Ethridge and James W. Marquart, "Private Prisons in Texas: The New Penology for Profit," *Justice Quarterly* 10, no. 1 (1993): 37–41.

100. Ethridge and Marquart, "Private Prisons in Texas," 42–43.

101. Sharp, "Behind the Walls," 5–6; Walker, *Penology for Profit*.

102. TDCJ, *Annual Report* (1990), i–ii; TDCJ, *Annual Report* (1991), 2.

103. Molly Ivins, "Remembering Ann Richards," *AlterNet*, September 15, 2006, http://www.alternet.org/columnists/story/41688/; Rick Lyman, "Ann Richards, Former Texas Governor, Dies at 73," *New York Times*, September 14, 2006, http://www.nytimes.com/2006/09/14/us/14richards.html?hp&ex=1158292800&en=22b04a312a2fd14f&ei=5094&partner=homepage; Roberto Suro, "In Texas, Governor's Race Becomes a Horse Race," *New York Times*, October 29, 1990, http://select.nytimes.com/search/restricted/article?res=F3061FFF355F0C7A8EDDA90994D8494D81.

104. Gail Collins, "The Unsinkable Meets the Unthinkable," *Working Woman*, March 1995, 86; Richards, *Once Upon a Time in Texas*, 128; Ivins, "Remembering Ann Richards."

105. Collins, "The Unsinkable Meets the Unthinkable"; Tony Fabelo, "Testing the Case for More Incarceration in Texas: What to Expect in 2004" (Austin, Tex.: CJPC, 1994): 2–3; Glenn, *Texas Prisons*, 232; Ekland-Olson and Kelly, *Justice Under Pressure*, 24; Tony Fabelo, interview by author, September 7, 2004.

106. Ekland-Olson and Kelly, *Justice Under Pressure* ; Jack Kyle, interview by author, July 20, 2002; Fabelo, "Implementing the Most Far-Reaching Criminal Justice Reforms in the Nation," 2; Fabelo, "Shifting Punishment Philosophy in Texas: An Overview of the Recent Sentencing Reforms" (Austin, Tex.: CJPC, October 1993), 2; Christopher Palmeri, "The Texas Lockup," *Forbes*, September 12, 1994.

107. Sharp, "Behind the Walls"; Fabelo, "Implementing the Most Far-Reaching Criminal Justice Reforms in the Nation," 2.

108. Molly Ivins and Lou Dubose, *Shrub: The Short but Happy Political Life of George W. Bush* (New York: Random House, 2000), 46.

109. "Texas Crime Rates 1960–2007"; R. G. Ratcliffe, "Richards: Pull Plug on Bush Ad," *Houston Chronicle*, August 23, 1994, A13; Ivins and Dubose, *Shrub*, 48.

110. Sam Howe Verhovek, "Rock-Star Appeal or Not, Governor Faces Tough Race in Lone Star State," *New York Times*, September 25, 1994, http://select.nytimes.com/search/restricted/article?res=F30912FA395E0C768EDDA00894DC494D81; R. W. Apple Jr., "In Texas Race, a Bush Avoids Father's Errors," *New York Times*, November 7, 1994, http://select.nytimes.com/search/restricted/article?res=F30814FD385A0C748CDDA80994DC494D81; Maureen Dowd, "Playing 'Good Ol' Girl' Card Against Son of Ex-President," *New York Times*, November 2, 1994, http://select.nytimes.com/search/restricted/article?res=FB0813F7345B0C718CDDA80994DC494D81.

## 9: THE TRIUMPH OF TEXAS TOUGH

1. Clay Robison, "Campaign '94: On the Issues—Crime, Education in Texas," *Houston Chronicle*, October 30, 1994, 1.

2. Robert Suro, "Settlement Ends Federal Control of Texas Prisons," *New York Times*, December 13, 1994, 42; John Culberson, "Help Restore Our Sovereignty," *Houston Chronicle*, September 8, 1994, A27; Cindy Chen, "The Prison Litigation Reform Act of 1995: Doing Away with More Than Just Crunchy Peanut Butter," *St. John's Law Review* 78 (2004): 203–31; Margo Schlanger, "Inmate Litigation," *Harvard Law Review* 116, no. 6 (2003): 1555–706; Christy Hoppe, "AG Cornyn Pleased with Ruling Limiting Federal Judges' Control of Prisons," *Dallas Morning News*, June 29, 1999.

3. Brorby, interview by author, September 15, 2003; Bill Hensel, "Justice Department Seeks End to Ruiz Suit," *Houston Post*, July 8, 1992, A9.

4. Brorby, interview by author, September 15, 2003.

5. Ibid.; *Ruiz v. Johnson*, 37 F.Supp.2d 855 (S.D. Texas, 1999), 866–67.

6. *Ruiz v. Johnson*, 37 F.Supp.2d 855 (S.D. Texas, 1999), 864, 888, 929, 907–8.

7. David Maraniss, "Justice, Texas Style: A Populist Judge, Shaking Up the State from His Courtroom in Tyler," *Washington Post*, February 28, 1987, G1; William Wayne Justice, interview by author, July 31, 2002.

8. Mauer, *Race to Incarcerate*; Harrison and Beck, *Prison and Jail Inmates at Midyear 2005*, 3; "Wyoming Crime Rates, 1960–2007," http://www.disastercenter.com/crime/wycrime.htm; Cahalan, "Historical Corrections Statistics," 29–30; Martin Luther King, "I Have a Dream," August 28, 1963, http://www.mlkonline.net/dream.html.

9. Robert E. Tomasson, "Changes Pledged for State Prisons," *New York Times*, September 6, 1971, http://select.nytimes.com/mem/archive/pdf?res=F10613FE-345B1A7493C4A91782D85F458785F9; Frank Lombardi and Michael Finnegan, "Gov. Plans a Tough New State Prison," *Daily News*, December 12, 1995, 2; Michael J. Hindelang et al., *Sourcebook of Criminal Justice Statistics, 1973* (Washington, D.C.: U.S. Department of Justice, August 1973), 351; "United States Resident Population by State: 1930–1990," http://www.wnjpin.net/OneStopCareerCenter/LaborMarketInformation/lmi01/poptrd1.htm; Harrison and Allen J. Beck, *Prisoners in 2005*, 4.

10. Eric Schlosser, "The Prison Industrial Complex," *Atlantic Monthly*, December 1998, 56–63; Madison Gray, "A Brief History of New York's Rockefeller Drug Laws," *Time*, April 2, 2009, http://www.time.com/time/nation/article/0,8599,1888864,00.html.

11. *State of the Prisons* (New York: Prison Visiting Committee of the Correctional Association of New York, June 2002), 9; Schlosser, "The Prison Industrial Complex," 56–63.

12. Correctional Association of New York, "Trends in New York State Prison Commitments," February 4, 2004.

13. Hallinan, *Going Up the River*, 83–84; Schlosser, "The Prison Industrial Complex," 56–63; Prison Policy Initiative, "Three Trends in New York That Require a Changed Census," http://www.prisonersofthecensus.org/threetrends.pdf; Peter Wagner et al., *Phantom Constituents in the Empire State: How Outdated Census Bureau Methodology Burdens New York Counties* (Northhampton, Mass.: Prison Policy Initiative, July 18, 2007).

14. Cummins, *The Rise and Fall of California's Radical Prison Movement*, chap. 10; Sullivan, *Prison Reform Movement*, 123–24.

15. Sasha Abramsky, *Hard Time Blues: How Politics Built a Prison Nation* (New York: St. Martin's Press/Thomas Dunne Books, 2002), 48–50; George Hill and Paige Harrison, "Prisoners Under State or Federal Jurisdiction, 1977–1998," National Prisoner Statistics Data Series, NPS-1, electronic file, BJS, August 1, 2000.

16. Abramsky, *Hard Time Blues*, 49–50, 113.

17. Ibid., 52–59.

18. Vlae Kershner and Carolyn Lochhead, "Politicians React with Calls for Stiffer Sentences," *San Francisco Chronicle*, December 7, 1993, A4; "The Criminal Life of Richard Allen Davis," http://www.justicejunction.com/judicial_injustice_rich ard_allen_dean.htm; Michael Taylor, "The Polly Klaas Case: 2 Months of Crossed Paths and Missed Opportunities," *San Francisco Chronicle*, December 6, 1993, A6.

19. Susan Yoachum, "A Senseless Death, a Call to Action: Politicians at Polly's Memorial Urge Overhaul of Justice System," *San Francisco Chronicle*, December 10, 1993, A23; Greg Lucas, "Wilson Turns Up Heat on Crime: He Urges Legislature Session to Adopt Law-and-Order Measures," *San Francisco Chronicle*, December 30, 1993, A14; Abramsky, *Hard Time Blues*, 60–62.

20. Abramsky, *Hard Time Blues*, 116, 125–30; Scott Thurm and Mitchel Benson, "Election Arms Wilson with New Clout," *San Jose Mercury News*, November 10, 1994, 19A.

21. Donna Alvarado, "'Three Strikes' Is In, But Other Propositions Out," *San Jose Mercury News*, November 9, 1994, 8EL; Abramsky, *Hard Time Blues*, 217; *Ewing v. California*, 538 U.S. 11 (2003); Eric Salter, "Pizza Thief Receives Sentence of 25 Years to Life in Prison," *Los Angeles Times*, March 3, 1995, 9B. Three strikes was approved separately by the legislature. Richard Davis was sentenced to death.

22. Allen J. Beck and Paige M. Harrison, *Prisoners in 2000*, NCJ 188207 (Washington, D.C.: BJS, August 2001), 3. On California's ongoing prison crisis, see Jennifer Steinhauer, "Troubled Prisons Push California to Seek a New Approach," *New York Times*, December 11, 2006, http://www.nytimes.com/2006/12/11/us/11prison.html?ref=us; *Solving California's Corrections Crisis: Time Is Running Out* (Sacramento, Calif.: Little Hoover Commission, 2007); *Coleman v. Schwarzenegger*, Opinion and Order, August 4, 2009, http://www.ca9.uscourts.gov/datas tore/general/2009/08/04/Opinion%20&%20Order%20FINAL.pdf.

23. George Beto, "From the President," *Corrections Today* 32, no. 1 (January–February 1970): 5; Beto, "Presidential Address: Continue Work, So Much to Be Done," 7.

24. Wilson, *Thinking About Crime*, 14, chaps. 8–9; Wilson, "If Every Criminal Knew He Would Be Punished If Caught," *New York Times Magazine*, 53.

25. Robert Martinson, "What Works?—Questions and Answers About Prison Reform," *Public Interest*, Spring 1974, 22–23; Wilson, *Thinking About Crime*, 163; Hallinan, *Going Up the River*, 34–36. See also Martinson's retreat: Robert

Martinson, "New Findings, New Views: A Note of Caution Regarding Sentencing Reform," *Hofstra Law Review* (Winter 1979): 243–58.

26. Dilulio, *Governing Prisons*, 230, 236; John J. Dilulio Jr., "Arresting Ideas: Tougher Law Enforcement Is Driving Down Urban Crime," *Policy Review*, no. 74 (Fall 1995): 15; John J. Dilulio Jr., "Prisons Are a Bargain, by Any Measure," *New York Times*, January 16, 1996, A17.

27. Wilson, "If Every Criminal Knew He Would Be Punished If Caught"; Baum, *Smoke and Mirrors*, 77–78; Pepperdine University, "John Q. Wilson," http://pub licpolicy.pepperdine.edu/academics/faculty/default.htm?faculty=james_wil son; Bert Unseem, "A Prison Reformist Indicts Management," *Chicago Tribune*, April 7, 1988, n.p., Beto Papers, box 4-1-2.

28. Matthew Dallek, *The Right Moment: Ronald Reagan's First Victory and the Decisive Turning Point in American Politics* (New York: Free Press, 2000); Carter, *From George Wallace to Newt Gingrich*, 56; Peter Schrag, *Paradise Lost: California's Experience, America's Future* (New York: New Press, 1998), 48.

29. Paul Krugman, "Republicans and Race," *New York Times*, November 19, 2007, http://www.nytimes.com/2007/11/19/opinion/19krugman.html?scp=2&sq= reagan%20"strapping%20young%20buck"&st=cse; Carter, *From George Wallace to Newt Gingrich*, 64; William Raspberry, "Reagan's Race Legacy," *Washington Post*, June 14, 2004, A17; Mayer, *Running on Race*, 150.

30. Beckett, *Making Crime Pay*, 49–50.

31. Marilyn Berger, "Ronald Reagan Dies at 93: Fostered Cold-War Might and Curbs on Government," *New York Times*, June 6, 2004, http://select.nytimes.com/search/restricted/article?res=F50E11FB3A550C758CDDAF0894DC404482; Garry Wills, *Reagan's America: Innocents at Home* (Garden City, N.Y.: Doubleday, 1987); Richard Reeves, *President Reagan: The Triumph of Imagination* (New York: Simon & Schuster, 2005), 31.

32. Berger, "Ronald Reagan Dies at 93"; Wolters, *Right Turn: William Bradford Reynolds, the Reagan Administration, and Black Civil Rights*; Pamela A. MacLean, "In a Midterm Election Year, President May Face an Uphill Battle to Fill the Bench," *National Law Journal*, November 6, 2006, http://www.law.com/jsp/article.jsp ?id = 1162548322839; Beckett, *Making Crime Pay*, 47–48.

33. Mauer, *Race to Incarcerate*, 62; Eric Sterling, interview by author, August 5, 2006.

34. Beckett, *Making Crime Pay*, 54; Mauer, *Race to Incarcerate*, 61; Parenti, *Lockdown America*, 47–60; Baum, *Smoke and Mirrors*, 141, 199–200.

35. Mauer, *Race to Incarcerate*, 61, 155–56; Hallinan, *Going Up the River*, 45; Abramsky, *American Furies*, 54.

36. Western, *Punishment and Inequality in America*, 60; Mayer, *Running on Race*, chap. 9; Kenneth L. Karst, *Law's Promise, Law's Expression: Visions of Power in the Politics of Race, Gender, and Religion* (New Haven, Conn.: Yale University Press, 1993), 73–74; Beckett, *Making Crime Pay*, 6.

37. Beckett, *Making Crime Pay*, 24, 95, 58; Parenti, *Lockdown America*, 63.

38. Hill and Harrison, "Prisoners Under State or Federal Jurisdiction, 1977–1998"; Kathleen Maguire and Ann L. Pastore, eds., *Sourcebook of Criminal Justice Statistics, 2002* (Washington, D.C.: BJS, 2004), table 6.54; Maguire and Pastore, eds., *Sourcebook of Criminal Justice Statistics, 1994* (Washington, D.C.: BJS, 1995), table 6.36.

39. Parenti, *Lockdown America*, 63; Hallinan, *Going Up the River*, 45; Census Bureau, "Black Americans: A Profile," SB/93–2, March 1993, 1; Allen J. Beck and Darrell K. Gilliard, *Prisoners in 1994*, NCJ-151654 (Washington, D.C.: BJS, August 1995), 1, 9.

40. Sharon LaFraniere, "Governor's Camp Feels His Record on Crime Can Stand the Heat," *Washington Post*, October 5, 1992, A6; Michael Kramer, "The Political Interest Frying Them Isn't the Answer," *Time*, March 14, 1994, http://www.time .com/time/magazine/article/0,9171,980318,00.html.

41. Gwen Ifill, "Clinton's Tightrope: Presidency Takes on Shifting Politics of U.S. Role in Curbing Violent Crime," *New York Times*, November 15, 1993, http://www.nytimes.com/1993/11/15/us/clinton-s-tightrope-presidency-takes-shifting -politics-us-role-curbing-violent.html?pagewanted=all; Marc Mauer, "The Fragility of Criminal Justice Reform," *Social Justice* 21, no. 3 (Fall 1994): 14.

42. Parenti, *Lockdown America*, 65–66; Robert Perkinson, "Clinton's Politics of Punishment," *Z Magazine*, October 1994: 12–14; *Violent Crime Control and Law Enforcement Act*, 108 Stat. 1796 (1994).

43. Robert Perkinson, "Oklahoma Fallout," *Z Magazine*, July/August 1995, 11; Beckett, *Making Crime Pay*, 61.

44. Beckett, *Making Crime Pay*, 61, 105; Perkinson, "Oklahoma Fallout," 10; Mauer, *Race to Incarcerate*, 75; William Wayne Justice, interview by author, July 31, 2002; Chen, "The Prison Litigation Reform Act of 1995."

45. Beckett, *Making Crime Pay*, 60; Maguire and Pastore, eds. *Sourcebook of Criminal Justice Statistics, 2002*, table 6.1; Census Bureau, State and County QuickFacts, Washington, D.C. (2008), http://quickfacts.census.gov/qfd/states/11000.html; Allen J. Beck, Jennifer C. Karberg, and Paige M. Harrison, *Prison and Jail Inmates at Midyear 2001*, NCJ 191702 (Washington, D.C.: BJS, April 2002), 9, 12.

46. Hindelang et al., *Sourcebook of Criminal Justice Statistics, 1973*, table 6.18; Hill and Harrison, "Prisoners Under State or Federal Jurisdiction, 1977–1998"; Kathleen Maguire and Ann L. Pastore, eds., *Sourcebook of Criminal Justice Statistics, 2000* (Washington, D.C.: BJS, 2001), table 6.27.

47. Lind, *Made in Texas*, 3.

48. Sam Howe Verhovek, "Warehouse of Addiction: A Change in Governors Stalls Model Drug Program in Texas," *New York Times*, July 4, 1995, http://query.ny times.com/gst/fullpage.html?res=990CE2DE1438F937A35754C0A963958260& sec=health&spon=&pagewanted=print; Tony Fabelo, interview by author, September 7, 2004.

49. Dana Kaplan, Vincent Schiraldi, and Jason Ziedenberg, *Texas Tough?: An Analysis of Incarceration and Crime Trends in the Lone Star State* (Washington, D.C.: Justice Policy Institute, October 2000), 2; Jonathan Alter and Gregory Beals, "The Buzz on Drugs," *Newsweek*, September 6, 1999, 24.

50. Ivins and Dubose, *Shrub*, 154; Clay Robison, "Bush Signs 'Tough Love' Juvenile Crime Bill: Punishment Boosted for Young Offenders," *Houston Chronicle*, June 1, 1995, A29; Tony Fabelo, "Measuring the Initial Impact of Progressive Sanction Guidelines" (Austin, Tex.: CJPC, 1999); Texas, *Trends in Texas Government Finance, 1984–2009* (Austin, Tex.: Legislative Budget Board, 2001), 69.

51. Nate Blakeslee, "Hidden in Plain Sight: How Did Alleged Abuse at a Youth Facility in West Texas Evade Detection for So Long?" *Texas Observer*, February 23, 2007, http://www.texasobserver.org/article.php?aid=2428; Solomon Moore, "Troubles Mount Within Texas Youth Detention Agency," *New York Times*, October 16, 2007, http://www.nytimes.com/2007/10/16/us/16juvenile.html?scp=1 &sq=&st=nyt.

52. James Austin, Kelly Dedel Johnson, and Maria Gregoriou, *Juveniles in Adult Prisons and Jails: A National Assessment*, NCJ 182503 (Washington, D.C.: Bureau of Justice Assistance, October 2000), 38; Michele Deitch et al., *From Time Out to Hard Time: Young Children in the Adult Criminal Justice System* (Austin, Tex.: LBJ School of Public Affairs, 2009); Michele Deitch, interview by author, July 13, 2009; anonymous prisoner, interview by author, July 22, 2002.

53. Texas, *Trends in Texas Government Finance, 1984–2009*, 48, 64; David McNutt and Brad Livingston, *Closing of a Millennium: Reviewing the Past Decade* (Austin, Tex.: TDCJ, 2000), 1; TDCJ, *Annual Report* (2000), 6; U.S. Department of Justice, "State and Federal Prisons Report Record Growth During Last 12 Months" (Washington, D.C.: BJS, December 3, 1995), 5; Paige M. Harrison and Allen J.

Beck, *Prisoners in 2001*, NCJ 195189 (Washington, D.C.: BJS, July 2002), 3; James Marquart, interview by author, July 18, 2002.

54. Maria L. La Ganga, "Bush Defends Streamlined Texas Death Penalty System," *Los Angeles Times*, June 14, 2000, http://articles.latimes.com/2000/jun/14/news/mn-40858; Helen Prejean, "Death in Texas," *New York Review of Books*, January 13, 2005, http://www.nybooks.com/articles/17670; Alan Berlow, "Lethal Injustice," *American Prospect*, March 27–April 10, 2000, 54. Rick Perry has since surpassed Bush's execution record.

55. Sara Rimer and Raymond Bonner, "Capital Punishment in Texas: Bush Candidacy Puts Focus on Executions," *New York Times*, May 14, 2000, http://www.nytimes.com/2000/05/14/us/record-capital-punishment-texas-bush-candidacy-puts-focus-executions.html; Paul Duggan, "In Texas, Defense Lapses Fail to Halt Executions," *Washington Post*, May 12, 2000, A1; Dick Burr et al., *Lethal Indifference: The Fatal Combination of Incompetent Attorneys and Unaccountable Courts in Texas Death Penalty Appeals* (Austin: Texas Defender Service, 2002), xi; Dick Burr et al., *A State of Denial: Texas Justice and the Death Penalty* (Austin: Texas Defender Service, 2000), chap. 6.

56. Berlow, "Lethal Injustice"; Meredith Rountree, interview by author, August 16, 2002; Erika Casriel, "Bush and the Texas Death Machine," *Rolling Stone*, July 6, 2000, http://www.rollingstone.com/artists/georgewbush/articles/story/5924840/bush__the_texas_death_machine.

57. Fox Butterfield, "Governor Bush on Crime: Bush's Law and Order Adds Up to Tough and Popular," *New York Times*, August 18, 1999, http://www.nytimes.com/1999/08/18/us/record-governor-bush-crime-bush-s-law-order-adds-up-tough-popular.html?pagewanted=4; Bruce Shapiro, "What About Retarded Criminals?" *Salon*, June 13, 2001, http://dir.salon.com/story/news/feature/2001/06/13/death_penalty/index.html; Ivins and Dubose, *Shrub*, 145.

58. Alan Berlow, "The Texas Clemency Memos," *Atlantic Monthly*, July–August 2003: 91–96.

59. BJS, "National Correctional Population Reaches New High," August 26, 2001, table 2, http://www.ojp.usdoj.gov/bjs/pub/pdf/ppus00.pdf; Allen J. Beck, Jennifer C. Karberg, and Paige M. Harrison, *Prison and Jail Inmates at Midyear 2001*, NCJ 191702 (Washington, D.C.: BJS, April 2002), table 2.

60. Ashley Nellis and Ryan S. King, *No Exit: The Expanding Use of Life Sentences in America* (Washington, D.C.: Sentencing Project, July 2009), 8; Johnson, "From Extreme Isolation: Waves of Felons Are Freed," *USA Today*, December 11, 2002; Melissa Sickmund, *Juvenile Residential Facility Census, 2000*, NCJ 196595 (Washington, D.C.: U.S. Department of Justice, Office of Juvenile Justice and Delinquency Prevention [hereafter OJJDP], December 2002), 2; Maguire and Pastore, *Sourcebook of Criminal Justice Statistics, 2000*, table 6.31.

61. Census Bureau, "Census 2000 Data for the State of Texas," http://www.census.gov/census2000/states/tx.html; Allen J. Beck and Jennifer C. Karberg, *Prison and Jail Inmates at Midyear 2000*, NCJ 185989 (Washington, D.C.: BJS, March 2001), table 2; Hallinan, *Going Up the River*, 5; Death Penalty Information Center, "2000 Year End Report: A Watershed Year of Change," http://www.deathpenaltyinfo.org/2000-year-end-report-watershed-year-change.

62. Sasha Abramsky, *Conned: How Millions Went to Prison, Lost the Vote, and Helped Send George W. Bush to the White House* (New York: New Press, 2006).

63. Judith Greene and Vincent Schiraldi, *Cutting Correctly: New Prison Policies for Times of Fiscal Crisis* (Washington, D.C.: Justice Policy Institute, February 7, 2002), 1–3; Scott Ehlers and Jason Ziedenberg, *Proposition 36: Five Years Later* (Washington, D.C.: Justice Policy Institute, April 2006); Fox Butterfield, "States Easing Stringent Laws on Prison Time," *New York Times*, September 2, 2001, A1.

64. Vincent Schiraldi, "Finally, States Release the Pressure on Prisons," *Washington*

*Post*, November 30, 2003, B3; Fox Butterfield, "With Cash Tight, States Reassess Long Jail Terms," *New York Times*, November 10, 2003, http://www.nytimes.com/2003/11/10/national/10PRIS.html; Jon Wool and Don Stemen, *Changing Fortunes or Changing Attitudes? Sentencing and Corrections Reforms in 2003* (New York: Vera Institute, March 2004).

65. Beck and Karberg, *Prison and Jail Inmates at Midyear 2000*, 1; Harrison and Beck, *Prison and Jail Inmates at Midyear 2004*, 1; John M. Broder, "No Hard Time for Prison Budgets," *New York Times*, January 19, 2003, http://www.nytimes.com/2003/01/19/weekinreview/19BROD.html; Anne Gearan, "Prison Terms Too Long, High Court Justice Says," *Houston Chronicle*, August 10, 2003, 3A.

66. Schiraldi and Ziedenberg, *Texas Tough: Three Years Later*, 7; Schiraldi, "Finally, States Release the Pressure on Prisons"; Greene and Schiraldi, *Cutting Correctly*, 3.

67. Jim Vertuno, "TDCJ Says Cuts Could Hurt Inmate Programs," Associated Press, February 7, 2003; Connie Mabin, "Senate Passes $117.7 Billion Budget," Associated Press, April 29, 2003; Scott Nowell, "Lite Sentences: TDCJ Cuts Calories for Convicts, Leaving Them and Guards Grumbling," *Houston Press*, October 23, 2003, 2; Fabelo, interview by author, September 7, 2004.

68. Esso "Woody" Woods, interview by author, August 6, 2003; E. C. Dixon, interview by author, August 19, 2003; Nowell, "Lite Sentences"; Jonathan Reed, interview by author, August 7, 2003; Jonathan Reed, letter to author, December 5, 2004.

69. Chuck Hurt, interview by author, November 27, 2005; Anonymous guard, Ellis Unit, August 7, 2003; Jonathan Reed, letter to author, October 21, 2003; Robert Lee Mudd, letter to author, June 18, 2004; Gene Hathorn, "Trashcan Food and a Concrete Shithouse," unpublished manuscript (2003).

70. Grits for Breakfast, "Parole Board Counts 2,324 Separate Texas Felonies; Where Will It End?" http://gritsforbreakfast.blogspot.com/2007/07/bpp-counts-2324-separate-felonies-where.html; Jonathan York, "Prosecutors Get Pounded: The District Attorneys Meet Their Own Personal Alamo in the 79th Legislature," *Texas Observer*, June 24, 2005, http://www.texasobserver.org/article.php?aid=1982; Grits for Breakfast, "New Prison Beds Approved by the 80th Texas Lege," *Texas Observer*, June 12, 2007, http://gritsforbreakfast.blogspot.com/2007/06/new-prison-beds-approved-by-80th-texas.html; Michele Deitch, interview by author, July 13, 2009.

71. West and Sabol, *Prison Inmates at Midyear 2008*, 3; *One in 31*, p. 42; Sarah Livsey, Melissa Sickmund, and Anthony Sladky, *Juvenile Residential Facility Census, 2004: Selected Findings* (Washington, D.C.: OJJDP, January 2009), 2.

72. "Texas Gov. Vetoes Execution Bill," CBS News, June 17, 2001, http://www.cbsnews.com/stories/2001/06/17/deathpenalty/main297026.shtml?tag=contentMain;contentBody; Human Rights Watch, "The Death Penalty and Juvenile Offenders," Briefing to the 59th Session of the UN Commission on Human Rights, February 27, 2003, http://www.hrw.org/legacy/un/chr59/deathpenalty.htm#3; Michels, "Politically Correct: New Prisons, Tougher Sentences, with a Little Love Thrown In," 20.

73. *Atkins v. Virginia*, 536 U.S. 304 (2002); *Roper v. Simmons*, 543 U.S. 551 (2005); Adam Liptak and Ralph Blumenthal, "Death Sentences in Texas Cases Try Supreme Court's Patience," *New York Times*, December 5, 2004, http://www.nytimes.com/2004/12/05/national/05texas.html?pagewanted=print&position=; Michael Hall, "And Justice for Some," *Texas Monthly*, November 2004, http://www.texasmonthly.com/mag/issues/2004-11-01/feature4.php.

74. Bill Minutaglio, *The President's Counselor: The Rise to Power of Alberto Gonzales* (New York: Rayo, 2006); Editorial, "Filibustering Priscilla Owen," *New York Times*, April 17, 200; White House, "President Bush Signs Unborn Victims of Violence Act of 2004," April 1, 2004, http://georgewbush-whitehouse.archives.gov/news/releases/2004/04/20040401-3.html.

75. "Republican Senator Loses to Dead Rival in Missouri," CNN, November 8, 2000, http://edition.cnn.com/2000/ALLPOLITICS/stories/11/07/senate.missouri/; Paul von Zielbauer, "Rethinking the Key Thrown Away: As Ashcroft Cracks Down, States Cut Prison Terms," *New York Times*, September 28, 2003, 26.

76. Terry M. Neal, "Bush Assails Administration's Anti-Drug Record," *Washington Post*, October 7, 2000, A14; "John Ashcroft Discusses His New Job as Attorney General," Larry King Live transcript, CNN, February 7, 2001, http://transcripts .cnn.com/TRANSCRIPTS/0102/07/lkl.00.html.

77. Drug Policy Alliance, "Election 2004—President George Bush," October 14, 2004, http://www.drugpolicy.org/statebystate/elect_2004/profiles/bush/; Robert Dreyfuss, "Bush's War on Pot," *Rolling Stone*, July 28, 2005, http://www.roll ingstone.com/politics/story/_id/7504250?pageid=rs.Home&pageregion=single7 &rnd=1122625808807&has-player=unknown. The Clinton administration, too, had pursued hard-line anti-marijuana policies, as had many states. See Ryan S. King and Marc Mauer, *The War on Marijuana: The Transformation of the War on Drugs in the 1990s* (Washington, D.C.: Sentencing Project, May 2005).

78. Lisa Haugaard, Adam Isacson, and Joy Olson, *Erasing the Lines: Trends in U.S. Military Programs with Latin America* (Washington, D.C.: Center for International Policy, December 2005), 18; Drug Enforcement Administration, "DEA Staffing and Appropriations FY 1972–2005," http://www.usdoj.gov/dea/agency/staffing .htm; Office of National Drug Control Policy, *National Drug Control Strategy FY 2005 Budget Summary* (Washington, D.C.: White House, March 2004), table 3.

79. Dan Eggen, "Ashcroft Aggressively Pursues Death Penalty," *Washington Post*, July 1, 2002, A1; Julian Borger, "Ashcroft Pushes for More Death Sentences: US Attorney General Overrules Prosecution Deals," *Guardian*, February 7, 2003, 15.

80. "The Federal Death Penalty System: Supplementary Data, Analysis and Revised Protocols for Capital Case Review" (Washington, D.C.: Justice Department, June 6, 2001); Karen Gullo, "Justice Study Finds No Racial Bias," *Washington Post*, June 6, 2001, http://www.washingtonpost.com/wp-srv/aponline/20010606/apon line142749_001.htm; Joseph Rosenbloom, "No Death-Penalty Doubts at Justice," *American Prospect*, March 1, 2003, http://www.prospect.org/cs/articles?article= no_deathpenalty_doubts_at_justice.

81. Andrew Kohut, "The Declining Support for Executions," *New York Times*, May 10, 2001, 33; Turow, *Ultimate Punishment*; Eggen, "Ashcroft Aggressively Pursues Death Penalty."

82. Edward Walsh and Dan Eggen, "Ashcroft Orders Tally of Lighter Sentences; Critics Say He Wants 'Blacklist' of Judges," *Washington Post*, August 7, 2003, A1; Susan Schmidt, "Ashcroft Issues Tougher Prosecutorial Guidelines," *Washington Post*, September 23, 2003, A3; Von Zielbauer, "Rethinking the Key Thrown Away." Ashcroft also pressed prosecutors to ramp up gun-related prosecutions, even as he committed the Justice Department to an expansive view of the Second Amendment. See Eric Lichtblau, "Justice Dept. Plans to Step Up Gun-Crime Prosecutions," *New York Times*, May 14, 2003, 18.

83. "Data Collections for the Prison Rape Elimination Act of 2003," BJS, June 30, 2004; Allen J. Beck, Paige M. Harrison, and Devon B. Adams, *Sexual Violence Reported by Correctional Authorities, 2006*, NCJ 218914 (Washington, D.C.: BJS, August 2007); Joanne Mariner, *No Escape: Male Rape in U.S. Prisons* (New York: Human Rights Watch, 2001).

84. George W. Bush, State of the Union Address, January 28, 2003, http://www .washingtonpost.com/wp-srv/onpolitics/transcripts/bushtext_012803.html; George W. Bush, State of the Union Address, January 20, 2004, http://www .washingtonpost.com/wp-srv/politics/transcripts/bushtext_012004.html; Dan Eggen, "Bush Signs into Law a Program That Gives Grants to Former Convicts," *Washington Post*, April 10, 2008, A4; Darryl Fears, "Crack-Sentencing Reduc-

tions Decried; Mukasey: Gang Members Would Be Let Go," *Washington Post*, February 7, 2008, A2.

85. Von Zielbauer, "Rethinking the Key Thrown Away"; West and Sabol, *Prison Inmates at Midyear 2008*, 3; Paige M. Harrison and Allen J. Beck, *Prisoners in 2002*, NCJ 200248 (Washington, D.C.: BJS, July 2003), 1. Federal prison growth slowed down in Bush's second term, as it did nationally.

86. George W. Bush, Remarks by the President upon Arrival at Barksdale AFB, September 11, 2001, http://georgewbush-whitehouse.archives.gov/news/releases/2001/09/20010911–1.html; George W. Bush, Statement by the President in His Address to the Nation, September 11, 2001, http://georgewbush-whitehouse.archives.gov/news/releases/2001/09/20010911–16.html; George W. Bush, Address to a Joint Session of Congress and the American People, September 20, 2001, http://georgewbush-whitehouse.archives.gov/news/releases/2001/09/2001 0920–8.html; Bush, "Statement by the President in His Address to the Nation," September 11, 2001.

87. Department of Justice, FY 2005 budget overview, http://www.whitehouse.gov/omb/rewrite/budget/fy2005/justice.html; Veronique De Rugy, "Facts and Figures About Homeland Security Spending," American Enterprise Institute, December 14, 2006, http://www.aei.org/docLib/20061214_FactsandFigures.pdf; Department of Homeland Security, "Budget in Brief, Fiscal Year 2005," http://www.dhs.gov/xlibrary/assets/FY_2005_BIB_4.pdf/.

88. *Homeland Security: DHS' Efforts to Enhance First Responders' All-Hazards Capabilities Continue to Evolve*, GAO-05–652 (Washington, D.C.: Government Accountability Office, July 2005), figure 7.

89. George W. Bush, Remarks by the President at Signing of the Patriot Act, Anti-Terrorism Legislation, October 26, 2001, http://georgewbush-whitehouse.archives.gov/news/releases/2001/10/20011026–5.html; Jennifer C. Evans, "Hijacking Civil Liberties: The USA PATRIOT Act of 2001," *Loyola University Chicago Law Journal* 33 (Summer 2002): 933–90; Heather Hillary and Nancy Kubasek, "The Remaining Perils of the PATRIOT Act: A Primer," *Journal of Law and Society* 8 (Summer 2007): 1–74.

90. *Reclaiming Patriotism: A Call to Reconsider the Patriot Act* (Washington, D.C.: American Civil Liberties Union, March 2009); David Johnston and Eric Lipton, "Justice Department Says F.B.I. Misused Patriot Act," *New York Times*, March 9, 2007, http://www.nytimes.com/2007/03/09/washington/09cnd-fbi.html; Eric Lichtblau, "U.S. Uses Terror Law to Pursue Crimes from Drugs to Swindling," *New York Times*, September 28 2003, A1, A24. See also Nat Hentoff, *The War on the Bill of Rights* (New York: Seven Stories Press, 2004).

91. Rachel Clarke, "Ashcroft Trumpets Anti-Terror Laws," *BBC News*, August 20, 2003, http://news.bbc.co.uk/2/hi/americas/3164785.stm; David Cole, "We've Aimed, Detained and Missed Before," *Washington Post*, June 8, 2003, B1; Dan Eggen, "Report Scolds Terrorism Prosecutors; U.S. to Drop Convictions Against Trio in Detroit," *Washington Post*, September 2, 2004, A3; Danny Hakim, "Defendant Is Released in Detroit Terror Case," *New York Times*, October 13, 2004, 16; David Cole, *Enemy Aliens: Double Standards and Constitutional Freedoms in the War on Terrorism* (New York: New Press, 2004).

92. U.S. Immigration and Customs Enforcement (ICE), "Detention Management," http://www.ice.gov/pi/news/factsheets/detention_mgmt.htm; ICE, "Immigration Detention Facilities," http://www.ice.gov/pi/dro/facilities.htm.

93. "The September 11 Detainees: A Review of the Treatment of Aliens Held on Immigration Charges in Connection with the Investigation of the September 11 Attacks" (Washington, D.C.: Department of Justice, Office of the Inspector General, June 2003); Dan Eggen, "Justice Dept. Finds Evidence of Abuse of Sept. 11 Detainees," *Washington Post*, December 18, 2003; Aida Edemariam, "If They'd

Wanted One of My Eyes, I'd Have Said OK," *Guardian*, May 2, 2006, http://www.guardian.co.uk/world/2006/may/02/egypt.september11; Michelle Goldberg, "The Prisoner Abuse Scandal at Home," *Salon*, May 19, 2004, http://dir.salon.com/story/news/feature/2004/05/19/maddy/index.html.

94. George W. Bush, Remarks by the President to Employees at the Pentagon, September 17, 2001, http://georgewbush-whitehouse.archives.gov/news/releases/2001/09/20010917-3.html; George W. Bush, Address to a Joint Session of Congress and the American People, September 20, 2001, http://georgewbush-whitehouse.archives.gov/news/releases/2001/09/20010920-8.html.

95. Richard A. Clarke, *Against All Enemies: Inside America's War on Terror* (New York: Free Press, 2004); Ron Suskind, *The One Percent Doctrine: Deep Inside America's Pursuit of Its Enemies Since 9/11* (New York: Simon & Schuster, 2006); Charlie Savage, *Takeover: The Return of the Imperial Presidency and the Subversion of American Democracy* (New York: Little, Brown, 2007); David Cole, *Justice at War: The Men and Ideas That Shaped America's War on Terror* (New York: New York Review Books, 2008).

96. Tim Golden, "After Terror, a Secret Rewriting of Military Law," *New York Times*, October 24, 2004, 8; Alberto R. Gonzales, memorandum for the president, January 25, 2002; Colin Powell, memorandum to the White House, January 26, 2002, in Danner, *Torture and Truth*, 83–91; Neil A. Lewis, "Justice Memos Explained How to Skip Prisoner Rights," *New York Times*, May 21, 2004, http://www.nytimes.com/2004/05/21/politics/21MEMO.html.

97. George W. Bush, Military order of November 13, 2001, in Danner, *Torture and Truth*, 78–82; Matthew Purdy, "Bush's New Rules to Fight Terror Transform the Legal Landscape," *New York Times*, November 25, 2001, 1A.

98. Golden, "After Terror, a Secret Rewriting of Military Law"; Dick Cheney, remarks by Vice President Dick Cheney to the U.S. Chamber of Commerce, November 14, 2001, http://georgewbush-whitehouse.archives.gov/vicepresident/news-speeches/speeches/vp20011114-1.html.

99. Jane Mayer, *The Dark Side: The Inside Story of How the War on Terror Turned into a War on American Ideals* (New York: Doubleday, 2008); Clive Stafford Smith, *The Eight O'clock Ferry to the Windward Side: Fighting the Lawless World of Guantanamo Bay* (New York: Nation Books, 2007).

100. Sue Anne Pressley, "Detainees Arrive in Cuba Amid Very Tight Security," *Washington Post*, January 12, 2002, A12; Karen J. Greenberg, *The Least Worst Place: Guantanamo's First 100 Days* (New York: Oxford University Press, 2009); Tim Golden, "Administration Officials Split over Stalled Military Tribunals," *New York Times*, October 25, 2004, http://www.nytimes.com/2004/10/25/international/worldspecial2/25gitmo.html; Dana Priest and Scott Higham, "At Guantanamo, a Prison Within a Prison: CIA Has Run a Secret Facility for Some Al Qaeda Detainees, Officials Say," *Washington Post*, December 17, 2004, A1; Neil A. Lewis, "Gauntánamo Detention Site Is Being Transformed, U.S. Says," *New York Times*, August 6, 2005, http://query.nytimes.com/gst/fullpage.html?res=9E06E7DB163EF935A3575BC0A9639C8B63.

101. Ted Conover, "In the Land of Guantánamo," *New York Times Magazine*, June 29, 2003, 40–45; Tim Golden and Don Van Natta Jr., "U.S. Said to Overstate Value of Guantánamo Detainees," *New York Times*, June 21, 2004, http://www.nytimes.com/2004/06/21/world/the-reach-of-war-us-said-to-overstate-value-of-guantanamo-detainees.html.

102. Golden and Van Natta Jr., "U.S. Said to Overstate Value of Guantánamo Detainees"; Jo Becker, "The War on Teen Terror," *Salon*, June 24, 2008, http://www.salon.com/news/feature/2008/06/24/juveniles_at_gitmo/; James Yee and Aimee Molloy, *For God and Country: Faith and Patriotism Under Fire* (New York: Public Affairs, 2005); Tim Golden, "The Battle for Guantánamo," *New York*

*Times Magazine*, September 17, 2006, http://www.nytimes.com/2006/09/17/
magazine/17guantanamo.html; Tim Golden, "Military Taking a Tougher Line
with Detainees," *New York Times*, December 16, 2006, http://www.nytimes
.com/2006/12/16/washington/16gitmo.html.

103. Alan Cowell, "U.S. 'Thumbs Its Nose' at Rights, Amnesty Says," *New York Times*,
May 26, 2005, http://www.nytimes.com/2005/05/26/international/europe/
26amnesty.html?pagewanted=print; "Shut Guantanamo, Ex-Diplomats Say,"
*Los Angeles Times*, March 28, 2008, http://articles.latimes.com/2008/mar/28/
nation/na-advice28; Damien Pearse, "Obama to Revive Guantánamo Military
Tribunals," *Guardian*, May 15, 2009, http://www.guardian.co.uk/world/2009/
may/15/barack-obama-revives-guantanamo-tribunals.

104. John Hendren, "Officials Say Rumsfeld OKd Harsh Interrogation Methods,"
*Los Angeles Times*, May 21, 2004, http://articles.latimes.com/2004/may/21/
world/fg-rumsfeld21; Neil A. Lewis and David Johnston, "New F.B.I. Files Describe Abuse of Iraq Inmates," *New York Times*, December 21, 2004, http://www
.nytimes.com/2004/12/21/politics/21abuse.html; Ewen MacAskill, "Obama
Releases Bush Torture Memos," *Guardian*, April 16, 2009, http://www.guardian
.co.uk/world/2009/apr/16/torture-memos-bush-administration; International
Committee of the Red Cross, "ICRC Report on the Treatment of Fourteen 'High
Value Detainees' in CIA Custody," February 2007, http://www.nybooks.com/
icrc-report.pdf.

105. Mark Danner, "U.S. Torture: Voices from the Black Sites," *New York Review of
Books*, April 9, 2009, http://www.nybooks.com/articles/22530; David Johnston
and James Risen, "Aides Say Memo Backed Coercion Already in Use," *New York
Times*, June 27, 2004, http://www.nytimes.com/2004/06/27/world/reach-war
-interrogations-aides-say-memo-backed-coercion-already-use.html; "A Guide
to the Memos on Torture," *New York Times*, http://www.nytimes.com/ref/inter
national/24MEMO-GUIDE.html; Jay S. Bybee to Alberto Gonzales, August 1,
2002, in Danner, *Torture and Truth*, 109.

106. Walter Pincus and Steven Mufson, "Prisoners' Fate, Treatment Not in U.S. Hands,
Officials Say," *Washington Post*, November 30, 2001, A1; Irene Khan, Secretary
General, Amnesty International, to Donald Rumsfeld, January 10, 2002, http://
www.amnesty.org/en/library/asset/AMR51/005/2002/en/5c702580-fb03–11dd
-9fca-0d1f97c98a21/amr510052002en.pdf.

107. James Risen, "G.I.'s Are Accused of Abusing Iraqi Captives," *New York Times*,
April 29, 2004, A15; Seymour M. Hersh, "Torture at Abu Ghraib: American
Soldiers Brutalized Iraqis. How Far Up Does the Responsibility Go?" *New Yorker*,
May 10, 2004, http://www.newyorker.com/archive/2004/05/10/040510fa_fact;
Susan Sontag, "Regarding the Torture of Others," *New York Times Magazine*, May
23, 2004, http://www.nytimes.com/2004/05/23/magazine/23PRISONS.html.

108. Seymour M. Hersh, *Chain of Command: The Road from 9/11 to Abu Ghraib* (New
York: HarperCollins, 2004); Robert Perkinson, "Some U.S. Prisons as Bad as
Abu Ghraib," *Straits Times*, May 28, 2004, 34; Major General Antonio M.
Taguba, "Article 15–6 Investigation of the 800th Military Police Brigade,"
http://www.npr.org/iraq/2004/prison_abuse_report.pdf, p. 50.

## CONCLUSION

1. Reinhold Niebuhr, *Children of Light and the Children of Darkness: A Vindication
of Democracy and a Critique of Its Traditional Defence* (New York: Charles Scribner's Sons, 1944), xi.

2. David Ruíz, interview by author, July 6, 2003. See also Mark Ward, "After 30
Years, Ruiz Is Ready for Case's Close," *Austin American-Statesman*, June 12,
2002, A1, A4.

3. David Ruíz, "Steel on Steel," *Texas Observer*, December 2, 2005, 21; Ruíz, interview by author, July 6, 2003; "I Asked to Be Treated as a Human Being," *Echo*, December 2005–January 2006, 5; Mike Ward, "Shiney New Prisons Conceal Same Old Poison, Ruiz Says," *Austin American-Statesman*, February 6, 1999, A1, A8.

4. Ruíz, interview, July 6, 2003.

5. Mary Mae Hartley, letter to author, January 28, 2006; Gloria Rubac, e-mail to author, August 3, 2007; Clyde Cain, letter to author, December 18, 2005; Al Slaton, interview by author, July 7, 2002.

6. Mike Ward, "Austin Inmate's Lawsuit Brought Sweeping Reforms to State Prisons," *Austin American-Statesman*, November 15, 2005, A1, A6.

7. Meredith Martin Rountree, e-mail to author, July 31, 2007; Gloria Rubac, e-mail to author, August 1, 2007; Michele Deitch, e-mail to author, July 31, 2007.

8. "Guest Book for David Ruiz," www.legacy.com; Charlie Sullivan, e-mail to CURE, November 15, 2005.

9. Gardner Selby, "Texas Will Get Keys to Prison; Oversight Nears End," *San Antonio Express*, June 8, 2002, A1; Donna Brorby, interview by author, September 15, 2003; William Bennett Turner, interview by author, September 15, 2003; William Wayne Justice, interview by author, July 31, 2002.

10. Esso "Woody" Woods, interview by author, August 6, 2003; Jim Willett, interview by author, July 19, 2002, August 12, 2003.

11. TDCJ, *Statistical Report* (FY2006), 6; James Yeager, letter to author, August 5, 2003; Walter Siros, interview by author, July 24, 2002; Jewell, letter to author, August 2, 2003.

12. Lucko, "Prison Farms, Walls, and Society," 83; "Our State Penitentiary," *Galveston Daily News*, May 4, 1873; Selby, "Texas Will Get Keys to Prison; Oversight Nears End," A1.

13. On the problems associated with TDCJ's present-day medical system, see Mike Ward, "Sick in Secret: 'Deadly Inadequacies' Plague Inmate Wards," *Austin American-Statesman*, December 16, 2001; John E. Dannenberg, "$40.1 Million Verdict Against CSC in Texas Prisoner's Medical Neglect Death," *Prison Legal News* (February 2004): 9.

14. Christopher J. Mumola, *Suicide and Homicide in State Prisons and Local Jails*, NCJ 210036 (Washington, D.C.: BJS, August 2005), 3; Prison Commission, *Annual Report* (1911), 36.

15. Gene Hathorn, letter to author, August 23, 2004; Gene Hathorn, "Trashcan Food and a Concrete Shithouse."

16. Christopher Lasch, *The True and Only Heaven: Progress and Its Critics* (New York: W. W. Norton, 1991), 93; Seán McConville, "The Victorian Prison, England, 1865–1965," in Morris and Rothman, *Oxford History of the Prison*, 131.

17. Rush, "An Enquiry into the Effects of Public Punishments upon Criminals, and upon Society," 88, 90; Reverend Benjamin A. Rogers, quoted in Wines, *State of Prisons*, 189; Lucko, "Prison Farms, Walls, and Society," 84; "Reformatory for Vicious Boys," *Dallas Morning News*, April 4, 1887, 4; CPPL, *Prison Survey*; Charles Sullivan, "Prison Reform Finally Arrives," *Texas Observer*, July 8, 1983, 6–8; Clark, *Crime in America*, 211.

18. Wacquant, "Deadly Symbiosis," 96; Adam Liptak, "Serving Life, with No Chance of Redemption," *New York Times*, October 5, 2005, http://www.nytimes.com/2005/10/05/national/05lifer.html?pagewanted=print; Nellis and King, *No Exit*; Deitch et al., *From Time Out to Hard Time*; Adam Liptak, "Jailed for Life After Crimes as Teenagers," *New York Times*, October 3, 2005, http://www.nytimes.com/2005/10/03/national/03lifers.html; Sentencing Project, "Felony Disenfranchisement," http://www.sentencingproject.org/template/page.cfm?id=133; Darren Wheelock, "Collateral Consequences and Racial

Inequality: Felon Status Restrictions as a System of Disadvantage," *Journal of Contemporary Criminal Justice* 21, no. 1 (2005): 82–90; Monica Davey and Abby Goodnough, "Doubts Rise as States Hold Sex Offenders After Prison," *New York Times*, March 4, 2007, http://www.nytimes.com/2007/03/04/us/04civil.html; Damien Cave, "Roadside Camp for Míami Sex Offenders Leads to Lawsuit," *New York Times*, July 9, 2009, http://www.nytimes.com/2009/07/10/us/10of fender.html?_r=1&scp=1&sq=florida%20bridge%20lawsuit%20sex%20of fender&st=cse.

19. Dickens, *American Notes*, 111; Rush, "An Enquiry into the Effects of Public Punishments upon Criminals, and upon Society," 88; Rhodes, *Total Confinement*.

20. Applebome, *Dixie Rising*; Dedrick Muhammad et al., "The State of the Dream: Enduring Disparities in Black and White" (Boston: United for a Fair Economy, 2004), 10. See also Lee Daniels, ed., *The State of Black America: The Complexity of Black Progress* (Washington, D.C.: Urban League, 2004); Patterson, *Rituals of Blood*; David R. Roediger, *How Race Survived U.S. History: From Settlement and Slavery to the Obama Phenomenon* (New York: Verso, 2008).

21. Frederick Douglass, "The Color Line," *North American Review* (June 1881): 567–77; DuBois, *The Souls of Black Folk*, forethought.

22. Glasrud, "Child or Beast?" 39.

23. Hindelang et al., *Sourcebook of Criminal Justice Statistics, 1973*, 351; TSLAC, "United States and Texas Populations, 1850–2008," http://www.tsl.state.tx.us/ref/abouttx/census.html; Harrison and Allen J. Beck, *Prisoners in 2005*, 3; TDC, *Annual Report* (1965); TDCJ, *Statistical Report* (FY2005), 56.

24. Simon Beardsley, "TDCJ Statistical Report Historical Breakdown, 1967–1997," (Huntsville, Tex.: TDCJ, 1999); TDCJ, *Statistical Report* (FY2008), 1; West and Sabol, *Prison Inmates at Midyear 2008*, 3.

25. Western, *Punishment and Inequality in America*, 20–28; Bonczar, *Prevalence of Imprisonment in the U.S. Population, 1974–2001*, 1.

26. TDCJ, *Statistical Report* (FY2005), 1; Harrison and Beck, *Prison and Jail Inmates at Midyear 2005*, 11; Census Bureau, "Texas Becomes Nation's Newest 'Majority-Minority' State," press advisory, CB05–118, August 11, 2005, table 1, http://www.census.gov/Press-Release/www/releases/archives/population/005514.html. Historical imprisonment disparities calculated by author based on TDCJ data and census estimates.

27. Austin to Wily Martin, May 30, 1833; Census Bureau, "Metropolitan and Micropolitan Statistical Area Estimates," July 1, 2008, table 7, http://www.census.gov/popest/metro/CBSA-est2008-pop-chg.html.

28. Texas State Penitentiary, *Report* (1855), 15; Texas State Penitentiary, *Biennial Report* (1880), 2, 8; "White Says TDC Best in Nation," *Huntsville Item*, March 3, 1983, clipping in Pope Papers, box 4C842.

29. Reynolds, "The Administration of the Texas Prison System," 12; "Hell on Earth," *Texas Siftings*, March 24, 1883.

30. Nathaniel Hawthorne, *The Scarlet Letter* (New York: Doubleday and McClure, 1898), 60.

31. James Burton Campbell, "The Prison Experience: Beginnings" (master's thesis, University of Texas, 1983), 2.

32. Sergeant Meduna, interview by author, July 22, 2002.

33. Hathorn, "Trashcan Food and a Concrete Shithouse." The American Psychiatric Association's *Diagnostic and Statistical Manual of Mental Disorders-IV* now uses the term "anti-social personality disorder."

34. Clemmer, *The Prison Community*, xiii.

35. DiIulio, *Governing Prisons*, 2, 6–7.

36. Cahalan, "Historical Corrections Statistics," 29; Campbell Gibson, "Population of the 100 Largest Cities and Other Urban Places in the United States, 1790–1900,"

Population Division Working Paper, no. 27 (Washington, D.C.: Census Bureau, June 1998), table 14, http://www.census.gov/population/documentation/twps-0027/tab14.txt.

37. West and Sabol, *Prison Inmates at Midyear 2008*, 3; Minton and Sabol, *Jail Inmates at Midyear 2008*, 3; "Census Bureau Announces Most Populous Cities," press advisory, CB07–91, June 28, 2007, table 1, http://www.census.gov/Press-Release/www/releases/archives/population/010315.html; *One in 31*, p. 42; Census Bureau, State and County QuickFacts, Texas (2008), http://quickfacts.census.gov/qfd/states/48000.html; Harrison and Beck, *Prison and Jail Inmates at Midyear 2005*, 10; Warren, *One in 100*, 3.

38. William Spelman, "The Limited Importance of Prison Expansion," in Blumstein and Wallman, *The Crime Drop in America*, 97–129; TDCJ, "Mission Statement," http://www.tdcj.state.tx.us/. See also Levitt, "Understanding Why Crime Fell in the 1990s"; Zimring, *Great American Crime Decline*; Western, *Punishment and Inequality in America*, chap. 7.

39. BJS, "Justice Expenditure and Employment Extracts" (2006), http://www.ojp.usdoj.gov/bjs/eande.htm#selected; *One in 31*, p. 5; *Public Safety, Public Spending*.

40. Bureau of Labor Department, *News* (Washington, D.C.: Department of Labor, August 3, 2007), 1; Maguire and Pastore, *Sourcebook of Criminal Justice Statistics, 2002*, table 6.1, 478.

41. Sykes, *The Society of Captives*, xiii; Robert Perkinson, "The Prison Dilemma," *Nation*, July 6, 2009, 35–36; Bruce Western, "Reentry: Reversing Mass Imprisonment," *Boston Review*, July–August 2008, 7–11; Jim Webb, "Why We Must Fix Our Prisons," *Parade Magazine*, March 29, 2009, http://www.parade.com/news/2009/03/why-we-must-fix-our-prisons.html; Ryan S. King, *The State of Sentencing 2007: Developments in Policy and Practice* (Washington, D.C.: Sentencing Project, January 2008); Grits for Breakfast, "TCJC Issues Legislative Wrap-up," July 14, 2009, http://gritsforbreakfast.blogspot.com/2009/07/tcjc-issues-legislative-wrapup.html; Deitch, interview by author, July 13, 2009.

42. Katzenbach et al., *The Challenge of Crime in a Free Society*, 6.

# ACKNOWLEDGMENTS

The many debts I have incurred in crafting this book stretch from the Atlantic to the Pacific and across many years. In graduate school at Yale, I benefited from an attentive and inspiring dissertation committee, Hazel V. Carby, Glenda Gilmore, and Jean-Christophe Agnew, who modeled engaged, eloquent scholarship and supported me at every turn. Other mentors asked trenchant questions and offered fresh ideas at various stages, among them Ward Churchill, Nancy Cott, Angela Y. Davis, John Demos, Michael Denning, John Mack Faragher, Ruthie Gilmore, Robert Gordon, Evelyn Hu-DeHart, Alex Lichtenstein, David Montgomery, James C. Scott, Jonathan Simon, and Stanton Wheeler.

Librarians from Huntsville to Honolulu have gone above and beyond the call of duty to help me locate primary materials. A bow to the staff of the Beinecke, Sterling, Mudd, and law libraries at Yale; the Schomburg Center for Research in Black Culture; the Library of Congress and National Archives; the State Library of Louisiana and the Louisiana State Archives; the Georgia Archives; the Newton Gresham Library at Sam Houston State University; the Cushing and Evans libraries at Texas A&M; the Hamilton, Sinclair, and William S. Richardson libraries at the University of Hawai'i at Mānoa; and the Perry-Castañeda, Tarleton Law, and Benson Latin American Collection at the University of Texas. I am especially indebted to the archivists at the Center for American History at the University of Texas and the Texas State Library and Archives, where I spent many months. In addition, numerous scholars opened their personal archives to me, among them Anne Butler, Marianne Fisher-Giorlando, Burk Foster, Mary Mae Hartley, Paul M. Lucko, Steve Martin, Susanne Mason, Robert Pierce, and William Bennett Turner.

Most of America's prison history was available to me only through written records, but as my story approached the present I relied increasingly on first-person interviews. Scores of wardens, correctional officers, attorneys, officers of the court, legislators, journalists, and community activists answered my questions. I especially want to thank Donna Brorby, Carlton Carl, Helga Dill, Sheldon Ekland-Olson, Bill Habern, William Wayne Justice, Jack Kyle, Gail Littlefield, James Marquart, Gloria Rubac, A. R. "Babe" Schwartz, Charlie and Pauline Sullivan, Richard Watkins, Jim Willett, and Esso "Woody" Woods for submitting to lengthy interviews and assisting me in countless other ways.

Oral histories revealed the humanity of a dehumanizing bureaucracy—and none so much as the conversations I had with current and former prisoners. In visiting booths, dayrooms, and hospital wings, in the fields, and through meal slots in solitary, dozens of incarcerated people shared with me their thoughts and memories, often following up with lengthy written letters. For their smart, searing observations, willingness to challenge my preconceptions, editorial advice, and patience with my chronically overdue correspondence, I am extremely grateful to Big Black, Ken Broussard, Charles Brown, Clyde Cain, Larry Casey, Glenn Cecil, Don Conyers, Chris De'Grate, Douglas "Swede" Dennis, Leo Freeman, Rylee Gilstrap, Richard Glimes, Gene Hathorn, Ray Hill, Chuck Hurt, Michael Jewell, Donna Mae Jones, Alan Wade Johnson, Daniel Johnson, William Kershner, Kim Leavelle, Herb Lewis III, Ricky Long, Brett Massey, Redbird McCarter, Robert Lee Mudd, Scott Nowell, Roger Pirkle, Jon Reed, Willie Redis, Wilbert Rideau, Odus Rogers, David Ruíz, Walter Siros, Al Slaton, R. G. White, Cameron Todd Willingham, and James "Yogi" Yeager. My gratitude to the Research, Evaluation, and Development Group of the Texas Department of Criminal Justice for giving me access to prisoners, staff, and facilities and for assisting me with statistics and photographs.

Numerous and extended research trips to Texas, Washington, New York, and elsewhere required institutional support, and I am honored to have received awards and fellowships from the American Council of Learned Societies, American Historical Association, East Texas Historical Association, Southern Historical Association, University of Hawai'i, and Yale University. A Soros Justice Fellowship from the Open Society Institute was particularly vital as it allowed me to take a full year off from teaching and introduced me to a network of talented fellows; special thanks to Raquiba LaBrie, Kate Black, Adam Culbreath, Steve Hubbell, and Christina Voight. Teaching leave required the cooperation of the cash-strapped University of Hawai'i, and I am grateful to my dean, Tom Bingham, associate dean, Krystyna Aune, and a succession of department chairs, Paul Hooper, Dennis Ogawa, and especially David E. Stannard, for advancing my cause. The office staff in American Studies, led expertly by Sandy Enoki and Gerry Uyeunten, helped keep me on track in myriad ways, as did capable student assistants, including Roselena Adams, Judy Chan, Elizabeth Galang, Courtney Miyashiro, Erika Motohashi, Mizuho Murakami, Rebecca Schoch, Kalanikiekie Sherry, Nicole Shibata, Scott Thomas, and Sherisse Wong.

Material assistance poured in from noninstitutional sources as well. Mark Lawrence and Sarah Bird provided good company and accommodations in Austin, Ben Scott Luna gave me recording equipment, A. J. Halagao instructed me in legal research, Peter Wagoner and Stephanie Saephan lent technical expertise, and my Virginia cousins hosted me when I did research in Washington. Extra thanks to the Texas branch of the Fly family, especially to my great-great aunt Pete, who migrated to the Lone Star State in a covered wagon and, almost a century later, introduced me to San Antonio, as well as to Kittie Hall, who opened her home to me in Houston.

Of the many friends who provided the moral support, insights, and levity necessary to see this project through, I am especially thankful to those who read and commented upon various sections of the manuscript: Michael Berryhill, Rob Chase, Meg Daly, Marcus Daniel, Greg Grandin, Gordon Lafer, Shafali Lal, Michael Mullins, Diana Paton, Corey Robin, Leigh Raiford, Scott Saul, Anita Seth, Naoko Shibusawa, Heather Thompson, and Mari Yoshihara. I joined with many of these comrades to fight for a graduate student union at Yale, set up a prison reform organization in New Haven, and defend the rights of state workers in Hawai'i. In the process, I developed a deeper understanding of the challenges and opportunities facing three generations of Texas penal reformers than I could have gained in the archives alone.

My agent, Susan Rabiner, a fireball of wit and reason, helped not only package the manuscript but structure and sharpen it. Best of all she delivered me into the care of Metropolitan Books, under the leadership of Sara Bershtel, where Riva Hocherman provided the kind of sharp-minded, exacting yet kind editing that scarcely exists anymore in the trade.

My first and last thanks belong to my family: to my grandparents who first taught me about racism and justice; to my parents who tolerated lawyerly debate on every household rule and encouraged me to dream; and to Kieko Matteson, my loving partner and intellectual co-conspirator, who has torn apart a thousand sentences to make this book better and has held me together in the process. Authors often thank their young children for tolerating neglect, but I am grateful to my daughter, Amika, for every distraction; she is my life's joy. My hope is that she will live to inhabit a more forgiving society than the one into which she was born.

# INDEX